Paul and the Legacies of Paul

PAUL
and the
LEGACIES
of
PAUL

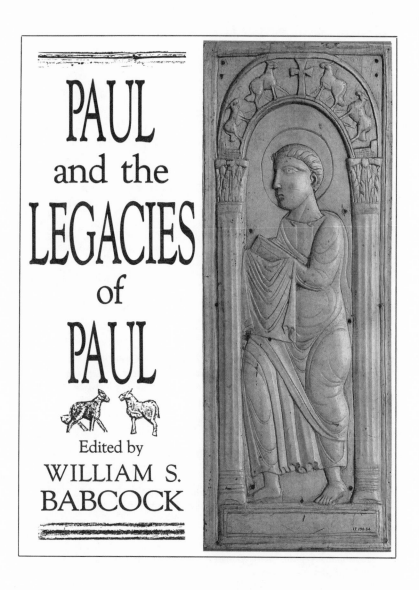

Edited by
WILLIAM S.
BABCOCK

SOUTHERN METHODIST UNIVERSITY PRESS
DALLAS

First edition, 1990
Requests for permission to reproduce material from
this work should be sent to:

Permissions
Southern Methodist University Press
Box 415
Dallas, Texas 75275

Cover photograph: Leaf of a diptych, St. Paul; ivory, early Christian,
probably Gallic, V–VI Century. The Metropolitan Museum of Art, Gift
of J. Pierpont Morgan, 1917. (17.190.54) All rights reserved, The Metropolitan
Museum of Art.

Library of Congress Cataloging-in-Publication Data

Paul and the legacies of Paul / edited by William S. Babcock. — 1st
  ed.
     p.   cm.
  Revised papers presented at the conference entitled "Paul and the
legacies of Paul," held at Southern Methodist University in March
1987.
  Includes bibliographical references.
  ISBN 0-87074-305-8. — ISBN 0-87074-306-6 (pbk.)
  1. Paul, the Apostle, Saint—Congresses. 2. Paul, the Apostle,
Saint—Influence—Congresses. 3. Theology—Early church, ca.
30-600—Congresses. I. Babcock, William S., 1939–
BS2506.P37 1990
225.9'2—dc20   89-78490

Contributors

William S. Babcock
  Associate Professor of Church History, Perkins School of Theology, Southern Methodist University

Elizabeth A. Clark
  Professor of Religion, Duke University

Ernst Dassmann
  Professor of Ancient Church History, Bonn University

Martinus C. de Boer
  Assistant Professor of New Testament, Princeton Theological Seminary

Paula Fredriksen
  William Goodwin Aurelio Professor of Biblical Appreciation, Boston University

Harry Y. Gamble
  Associate Professor, Department of Religious Studies, University of Virginia

Peter J. Gorday
  Canon for Education, Cathedral of St. Philip, Atlanta, Georgia

Rowan A. Greer
  Professor of Anglican Studies, Yale University Divinity School

Andreas Lindemann
  Professor of New Testament, Kirchliche Hochschule, Bethel (bei Bielefeld)

Dennis R. MacDonald
  Associate Professor of New Testament and Christian Origins, The Iliff School of Theology

R. A. Markus, F.B.A.
  Professor Emeritus of Medieval History, Nottingham
  University

Richard A. Norris, Jr.
  Professor of Church History, Union Theological Seminary,
  New York

Adolf Martin Ritter
  Professor of Church History, Heidelberg University

Daniel R. Schwartz
  Senior Lecturer in Jewish History, Hebrew University,
  Jerusalem

Robert D. Sider
  Charles A. Dana Professor of Classical Languages,
  Dickinson College

Stanley K. Stowers
  Associate Professor, Department of Religious Studies,
  Brown University

Basil Studer, O.S.B.
  Professor of Patristics, Pontificio Ateneo di Anselmo and
  the Patristic Institute (Augustinianum), Rome

Robert L. Wilken
  William R. Kenan, Jr. Professor of the History of
  Christianity, University of Virginia

Contents

Preface

The question of Paul's place and influence in the early history of Christianity seems ripe for reexamination. The more or less traditional—and perhaps still prevailing—view has been that Paul's most characteristic theological themes were taken up by marginal or heretical Christian groups, but were repressed or diminished by the groups that would turn out to be central to the emerging Christian tradition. Recently, however, this view has come under question. The present volume is the outgrowth of a conference on "Paul and the Legacies of Paul," held on the campus of Southern Methodist University in March 1987, which met to address just this issue. It includes all but two of the major papers presented at the conference (and now revised for publication). Those two are readily available elsewhere: Elaine Pagels' under the title "Exegesis and Exposition of the Genesis Creation Accounts in Selected Texts from Nag Hammadi" in *Nag Hammadi, Gnosticism, and Early Christianity*, ed. Charles W. Hedrick and Robert Hodgson, Jr. (Peabody, Mass., 1986), 257–85, and Albrecht Dihle's under the title "Philosophische Lehren von Schicksal und Freiheit in der frühchristlichen Theologie" in the *Jahrbuch für Antike und Christentum* 30 (1987): 14–28. This volume also includes several of the responses to the papers (limitations of space prevented the inclusion of all the responses), each presented as a "comment" on the essay to which it responds. To these papers and responses, I have added an introduction designed to serve both as a brief guide to the topics taken up in these studies and as one reading of their cumulative import. It is obviously no substitute for the essays themselves, but rather an effort to chart the direction in which they might lead.

There is a sense, of course, in which an edited volume might be said to belong to its editor. But there are other and far more important senses in which it belongs to its contributors and to the people who created the circumstances in which the volume came to be. Here I have many debts to acknowledge. The conference was held under the auspices of the Center for the Study of

Religion in the Greco-Roman World, itself jointly sponsored by Southern Methodist University and the University of Dallas; the Planning Committee appointed by the Center was responsible for conceiving the conference, applying for funding, and overseeing all the arrangements. Its members, in addition to myself, were Professor David L. Balás, O. Cist., of the University of Dallas; Professor Joseph B. Tyson of Southern Methodist University, Director of the Center; and Professor Victor Paul Furnish, also of Southern Methodist University, who served as Project Director (an unenviable position if ever there was one). It would be a good deal less than gracious if I did not also acknowledge the invaluable and indefatigable assistance of Eugene H. Lovering, then Assistant to the Director of the Center and a student in the Graduate Program of Religious Studies at SMU; he did everything from translating papers into English to supervising transportation. In addition, Hans Hillerbrand, then Provost of SMU, and John E. Paynter, Provost of the University of Dallas, supported both the Center and the conference with the backing that was needed from their respective universities.

Funding for the conference came from a grant from the National Endowment for the Humanities. In addition, the Foundation for the Carolinas, Texas Christian University, Temple Emanu-El in Dallas, and two anonymous donors provided funds that enabled us to meet the terms of the matching-funds portion of the NEH grant. Without the support of these institutions and individuals, neither the conference nor this volume would ever have come to pass. In this connection, there are further acknowledgments to be made: Professor Furnish authored the application to the NEH; Professor Tyson was instrumental in acquiring the added funding; Judith Pitney, then of the Provost's Office, and Mildred Haenel, then of the office of Research Administration at SMU, supplied essential help and guidance as the NEH application was being put together; and Mrs. Margot Goodwin of New York City offered a helpful suggestion during the application process. Southern Methodist University bore the not inconsiderable indirect costs of the conference.

In my role as editor, I have also incurred several debts in my own right. I am especially grateful to the contributors: their graciousness has made my work far easier than I had any reason to expect. Here also I must once again record my indebtedness to Gene Lovering. He provided the initial translations of the papers by Dom Basil Studer and by Ernst Dassmann, and he and I together produced the finished versions. We also worked together on the translation of Adolf Martin Ritter's essay. In all cases, the final responsibility for the translations rests with me; but without Gene, they would neither have been done nor have been done well. Also on this score, I want to acknowledge the generous help of my colleagues at Perkins School of Theology, Professors Klaus Penzel and Charles M. Wood. Time after time, they were both willing and able to resolve my puzzlements about rendering German into English. They are not responsible for my errors, of course, but they are responsible for greatly reducing the number of my errors. Finally I must indicate, if inadequately, my deep gratitude to Professor Furnish for his help and encouragement throughout the editorial process, to Ms. Laura Randall of the Bridwell Library at SMU for her unfailing and uncanny expertise in matters bibliographical, and to Ms. Mary Ann Marshall for the uncompromising standards according to which she does all her work, not least the word processing required by this volume.

Last of all, I should make one comment about a peculiarity in the editing of this work. Since it is intended for two groups of scholars—New Testament specialists and specialists in patristics—neither of which can be expected to know all the abbreviations that are commonplace to the other, I have tried to avoid abbreviations altogether in citing journals, monograph series, and editions of ancient works. The abbreviated titles of biblical books will, of course, be self-evident; and so, I think, will be the abbreviated Latin titles of ancient writings, both Christian and non-Christian. The abbreviations for ancient and modern translations of the Bible—LXX, RSV, NEB—are so widely known as to require no explanation. Apart from these, I have allowed only two abbreviations to stand:

PG *Patrologiae cursus completus. Series Graeca,* ed. J. P. Migne (Paris, 1857–66).

PL *Patrologiae cursus completus. Series Latina,* ed. J. P. Migne (Paris, 1844–55).

Introduction

Over the past century and a half, especially among Protestant scholars, assessments of Paul's place and legacy in the early history of Christianity have tended to fall into a distressingly stereotyped pattern. That pattern includes at least four elements. It holds, first, that Paul's theology exercised its greatest appeal—and came closest to being rightly understood—among versions of Christianity that would turn out to be marginal or heretical by the standards of what would become the dominant tradition. Second, and as the inevitable corollary, the pattern finds that the traditions that did ultimately give Christianity its enduring shape either ignored or misconstrued Paul, failing to grasp the most characteristic features of his theology or radically subordinating them to very different forms of faith and thought. Third, it maintains that only with Augustine, in the Latin West and at the turn from the fourth to the fifth century, did there emerge something like a recovery of the genuinely central motifs in Pauline thought and, in particular, a true sense for the great Pauline theme of justification by grace and faith apart from works. Fourth, it judges that the Greek Christian tradition never did—before or after Augustine—achieve an apt appreciation of Paul and thus, whatever its other theological attainments, remained fundamentally deficient in its understanding of human salvation. Taken as a whole, then, the pattern presents us with a picture of Christianity's early history in which Paul and Pauline thought, because either ignored or misconstrued, are most conspicuous for their absence. Neither the Christian sensibilities nor the Christian theology of the patristic era was significantly touched by Paul; and the legacies of Paul are largely to be sought elsewhere: in Augustine (the exception to the general rule), in the great figures of the Protestant Reformation, and in Paul's modern interpreters.

This stereotypical pattern rests, obviously enough, on the twin convictions that the true center of Paul's theology lies in his understanding of grace, interpreted in predominantly Protestant fashion, and that the evidence for the use of Paul in the first several centuries of Christian history represents a virtually unrelieved record of failure to recognize and appropriate that center. The two points are plainly mutually dependent and mutually reinforcing; it is clear that each has a major stake in the other. It is in the light of just this view of what is genuinely and centrally Pauline that patristic Christianity seems so dismally to have missed or to have misrepresented the crucial elements in Paul; and it is in the light of just this reading of the patristic evidence that the theme of justification by grace appears so distinctly to constitute the heart of Pauline faith. If we are to break with the pattern, therefore, we must be willing to hold both points open to question. We must be willing to acknowledge both that there may be other ways to construe Paul and that there may be other ways to interpret the patristic evidence. We cannot assume, in either case, that the issue has already been settled. The two points have become so intertwined that there is no other way to reopen the question.

And one thing at least is clear: there is good reason to take the matter up again. For Paul was not, in fact, a merely marginal figure in the early history of Christianity; nor was his influence a merely negligible factor in giving shape to what would become Christianity's dominant tradition. His letters (and others that had his name attached) were circulated, collected, and finally canonized as one element in Christianity's authoritative scripture. His person was represented and his actions, real or imagined, were recounted in narratives both within—the Acts of the Apostles—and beyond—*The Acts of Paul*—the canonical New Testament. Both his person and his writings were appealed to as authorities for the determination of questions having to do with the faith and life of Christian communities; and in fact, Paul came to be reckoned "the apostle" *tout court*, the only one to whom the title applied absolutely and without need for further specification. Pauline texts were cited regularly and frequently in the surviving writings of early Christianity, and by no means only on the side of themes or groups that would ultimately be judged heretical. Paul could be and was deployed against the "heretics" quite as much as by the "heretics"; and it is not unfair to suggest that on the "orthodox" side, the Pauline texts were woven into a theology that would not have had the character that it did if Paul had not written what he wrote or been accorded the authority he was accorded. None of this proves or even implies, of course, that Paul was rightly construed by the dominant tradition; but it does invite an investigation of the legacies of Paul that appear in this tradition and perhaps also of the Paul from whom these legacies derive.

It will not do, then, to think or speak as if Paul left little or no legacy in the Christianity of the patristic era (thus preserving him unscathed, as it were, for later legatees). He was simply too vast a presence in the early history of Christianity to permit such a notion. What is needed, rather, is an effort to trace the legacies he did leave: the ways in which he was represented in the early period, the uses to which he was put, the effects that he had in shaping Christian sensibilities and Christian theologies. The essays gathered in this volume undertake, each in its own way, aspects of precisely this task. Collectively they represent a distinct break with the stereotyped assessment of Paul's place in and significance for Christianity's early history. In this respect, they follow and develop a lead opened by such works as Maurice Wiles' *The Divine Apostle*, published in 1967, and, more recently, Andreas Lindemann's *Paulus im ältesten Christentum* and Ernst Dassmann's *Der Stachel im Fleisch*, both published in 1979. But the essays carry their approach to the question significantly beyond the earlier works, considering a wider range of evidence than did Wiles, who limited himself largely to commentaries on the Pauline writings, and pursuing the investigation further than did Lindemann and Dassmann, both of whom stopped at points in the second century. These essays do not, of course, provide exhaustive coverage; they neither address every pertinent question that might be raised nor examine all the relevant material that might be cited. They constitute, in this regard, far more a series of linked probes into an area of inquiry than a continuous mapping of the whole. But when these studies are taken together, their combined effect is to delineate a set of Pauline legacies that belong not on the margins but at the center of the Christianity that took form in late antiquity—and to intimate a Paul to whom these legacies may legitimately be ascribed.

The essays seem naturally to arrange themselves in three groupings. The first, "Early Delineations of Paul," contains studies dealing with the period that runs from the Acts of the Apostles to the writings of Tertullian in the early third century. From the very start, the ambiguities and uncertainties emerge. The author of Luke-Acts, according to Daniel Schwartz, presents us with a Paul in whom the great transition from a Jewish to a non-Jewish Christianity is finally and decisively realized, so finally and so decisively that even Jesus himself is reduced to the status of only one stage in the process that culminated in this outcome. At the same time, however, Schwartz argues that Luke has little interest in Paul as a figure in his own right and therefore can drop him in midstory, so to speak, once the great transition has been achieved. Thus Acts ends not with Paul's martyrdom but with a Christianity set free of its Jewish moorings, located in Rome rather than Jerusalem. On the other hand Lindemann, in his work on Paul in the apostolic fathers, finds that even at this early stage Paul was clearly being cited as a figure of authority to whom it was both appropriate and effective to appeal in cases of ecclesiastical dispute. There is no hint here that Paul was either ignored or regarded with suspicion as an alien and disruptive force; and there are at least some hints that Paul's distinctive theology, as known from his letters, was a modest influence in the thinking of the apostolic fathers who come under review: 1 Clement, Ignatius, and Polycarp.

Yet there are questions to be put to Lindemann, and Martinus de Boer, in his comments, brings some of them sharply into focus. De Boer usefully distinguishes between Paul as a figure of authority and Paul as an author of letters, labelling the latter the "epistolary Paul." Now the epistolary Paul will vary according to which of the Pauline letters, whether written by Paul himself or ascribed to him, were known in any given case; and even when the epistolary Paul can be specified in this case or that, it will still be far from clear that an appeal to Paul, the figure of authority, is also an appeal to the relevant epistolary Paul or to his theology. All sorts of difficulties and complexities beset the attempt to identify the Paul to whom our sources may refer; and always we must ask, which

Paul is at issue and how is this Paul deployed? Ultimately too, we will have to ask how well any of these Pauls, the Pauls we encounter in early Christian sources, correlate with the Paul of our own scholarship, the Paul of the seven letters that we now take as certainly genuine. In this sense also the key question becomes, which Paul? Which is the Paul whose impact and influence we are attempting to chart? We cannot simply presume that either the authoritative Paul or the epistolary Paul of the early Christian sources corresponds to what de Boer is willing to call "the historical Paul."

At the same time, however, a very similar set of questions can be pressed in exactly the opposite direction, as becomes clear in Stanley Stowers' comments on Dennis MacDonald's study, "Apocryphal and Canonical Narratives about Paul." Working primarily with the narrative representations of Paul in *The Acts of Paul* and in the canonical Acts of the Apostles, MacDonald finds that these representations are largely determined by literary considerations, that is, by the requirements of the acts genre itself. Although it is clear that a variety of influences was at work in giving literary shape to the acts literature of early Christianity, the dominant force was the "pull" of the form taken by the Christian gospels and their narrative renderings of Jesus. For MacDonald, then, the acts genre has the effect of transforming Paul into a kind of deutero-Jesus, investing him with miracles and visions and emphasizing his sufferings and death (even though, for reasons of political apologetic, the canonical Acts omits any account of Paul's martyrdom in Rome). Such a portrayal of Paul, however, ignores the Pauline letters and represents a fundamental distortion of the Paul whom we know from those letters. Presentations of Paul in narratives of this literary form almost inevitably give us an unpauline Paul.

Again there are questions to be asked. The most basic of these, Stowers suggests, are precisely the questions of what is to count as genuinely Pauline and of how that determination is to be made. MacDonald's own conclusions indicate that there are at least some significant respects in which the Paul of the acts literature is continuous rather than discontinuous with the Paul of the letters; and we need also to consider both how the letters might have been read in the light of subsequent circumstances and situations that may have been quite different from those in which Paul himself wrote and how the various themes and elements in the letters are to be weighted even if we do not take such changes of circumstance into account. Would our weightings be the same as those of the first recipients of the epistles or those of later readers in the first, second, or third century? And on what grounds, if at all, do we or should we disqualify one weighting or another as unpauline? There is no simple, uncomplicated way to discriminate between what is and what is not to be reckoned genuinely Pauline; and the issue is made all the more difficult because some Christian traditions have a heavy stake in a particular version of Paul or of Pauline theology, a version whose force may continue even when scholars believe that they have freed themselves from its grip. As Stowers remarks, we have no "Archimedean point" from which to make our discriminations.

Even if these difficult issues remain unresolved, it is clear enough that by the time Irenaeus produced his massive *Adversus haereses* toward the end of the second century, there was a Paul who was exercising a major and critically important influence on the shape and content of the theological scheme that would come to dominate the early Christian tradition. This Paul was the Paul of the Pauline epistles, including several that many current scholars would consider deutero-Pauline rather than from Paul's own hand. It is noteworthy, however, that most of the Pauline texts that Richard Norris finds to be central for Irenaeus, not only in the marshaling of his specific counterarguments against the Gnostics but also in the elaboration of his own positive theological vision, do in fact come from the letters that are today regarded as unquestionably genuine.

These texts do not function entirely on their own, of course, as if Irenaeus was concerned only to delineate a "theology of Paul" in its own right and in sharp distinction from the theologies of other portions of Christian scripture. Rather they are interwoven with other texts from other areas of scripture, including the Old Testament as well as the New; and since one of Irenaeus' aims is precisely to sustain the view that scripture, taken as a whole, is a continuous record of the creative and redemptive action of the one God, he reads all of these texts together, each in the light of the others. Nevertheless it is evident that the Pauline texts are not simply subordinated to or overridden by the others. They have their own distinctive role to play; and the theology that Irenaeus lays out, it is safe to say, would not have taken the shape that it did if they had not played that role. Rather than justification by grace and faith, the great and central themes for Irenaeus, in the setting of late second-century Christianity, were the oneness of God as creator and redeemer, the oneness of Christ as the divine-human agent of salvation, and perhaps above all the oneness of the complex dispensation of salvation enacted in the history that leads from Adam to Christ and from Christ's incarnation to his return at the end of time. But none of these themes are foreign to Paul, and none represent a fundamental displacement or distortion of what was central also to Pauline thought. The "Paul" of the Protestant reformers is not all there is to Paul; nor will justification by grace seem the most crucial Pauline theme in all settings and under all circumstances.

Finally, in this first group of essays, Robert Sider traces the representation of Paul—both Paul's person and Paul's theology—in the writings of Tertullian. Nowhere, of course, does Tertullian specifically draw a literary portrait of Paul in its own right and for its own sake. But from the allusions that he makes to Paul and from the purposes that those allusions serve, one can reconstruct something of Tertullian's sense for the apostle and for the decisive and paradigmatic episodes of his life. Furthermore, one can detect hints of difference between those aspects of Tertullian's Paul that have frozen, as it were, into the iconic visage of the saint and those aspects in which his Paul displays the more ordinary shifts and turns of human beings undergoing change and development. These aspects are not, in Tertullian, fully separate or fully separable, but they do show that for Tertullian, Paul is in both senses, both as icon and as changeable human being, a person as well as a set of authoritative texts and theological positions. Furthermore, although the theology that Tertullian draws from Paul centers on questions of the Spirit and the eschaton rather than of grace and justification, it is recognizably a Pauline theology and suggests, once again, that there is more than one gen-

uinely Pauline way to read Paul's thought, more than one appropriate way of weighting the various themes and elements of his
theology. There is, one might say, a Paul (perhaps more than one
Paul) who belongs neither to the heretics nor to the Protestant
Reformation and yet does play a distinct and by no means negligible role in Christianity's early history.

The essays in the second grouping, "Paul in the Theological
and Exegetical Tradition," take up aspects of the later patristic
period, the third through the fifth century. Once again, unexpected points emerge. In particular, it comes as something of a
surprise to discover just how central Paul was to the theological
developments of this era and just how important he was for the
definition of Christianity's distinctive identity over against its
cultural and intellectual environment in late antiquity. Nor was
the Paul who had this import for patristic Christianity a Paul
whose theology of divine grace and divine election was deliberately factored out or quietly ignored. Instead that theology had a
decisive impact. Its impact did not come, however, in the arena of
justification by grace and faith—at least as this theme is ordinarily
understood by Protestant theologians and exegetes—but rather
in the arena of theology proper, the understanding of God and
of the divine direction of the cosmos and of human affairs. It
is important, first of all, to get some sense for how the problem
emerged and what shape it took in the patristic era.

As Robert Wilken observes, Christian theologians early
aligned themselves with the philosophical defenders of free will
against the sometimes powerful currents of determinism and
fatalism in the culture of late antiquity. At issue were the responsibility of moral agents for their acts and, beyond that, the very
meaning of virtue, which seemed to be eviscerated of all moral
sense and significance if it was credited not to virtuous persons
themselves but to factors quite outside their own control. The
Christian defenders of free will, however, faced the problem in a
special sense. For them, the threat to human freedom seemed
to come not only from an unbroken chain of causes or from
blind fate but from their own God—the God, for instance, of
Romans 9—who could deliberately harden Pharaoh's heart or
could select Jacob and reject Esau before either had been born. For

the Greek Christian commentators on Paul's epistles, therefore, the problem that the letters posed was not the problem of justification apart from works; it was the problem of such a God, a God whose relation to human affairs is a function of the divine will and even—cutting still more deeply against the grain of the philosophic inclinations of the era—of emotive disposition. Wilken suggests some of the ways in which, in the works of the commentators, the language of Paul's letters interpenetrated and transformed the language that late-antique philosophy made available for speaking of the divine. It carried resonances that the philosophical vocabulary did not have, and it evoked a God who could not simply be contained by or equated with the god of the philosophers.

Peter Gorday's study of Paul in the theologies of Origen and Gregory of Nyssa, although it takes a very different tack, leads to not dissimilar results. Gorday identifies a cluster of Pauline texts that were central to Origen's understanding of Paul—and to the basic patterns of his own theology as well. Once again Romans 9 is critical and formative. Origen did not shirk the electing God whom he encountered in Paul. But he neither interprets election in terms of the interplay of law and grace, whether in the life of the person or in the history of humanity as a whole, nor conjures from it a dark, predestinarian God. Rather he spreads election out in a vast, cosmic economy of salvation in which God provides the evil as well as the good that will ultimately conduce to the redemption of all. In this sense God is, for Origen, an accomplice in evil, the hardener of Pharaoh's heart (although not, of course, the author of Pharaoh's—or anyone's—specific evil acts). God is the designer of the setting and the director of the events in which the economy of salvation is realized; and this means that God, without overriding free will, orchestrates the evil as well as the good intermixed in that setting and in those events. Gregory of Nyssa, writing at a later stage in Christianity's development, was no longer willing to retain the notion of divine complicity in evil and thus lost something of the mystery of Origen's God. But he did retain Origen's sense, derived from Paul, for the sovereignty of the divine will. Neither Origen nor Gregory may be said to have dissolved Paul—or Paul's theology of election—into the categories of middle or late Platonic philosophy.

There are, of course, other points at which Paul's import for patristic Christianity can be tracked. Rowan Greer takes a single passage from 1 Corinthians and uses it to explore, on a somewhat smaller scale, the divergent ways in which Apollinaris of Laodicea and Gregory of Nyssa construed the text in constructing their opposed christologies. Each interprets Paul within and in keeping with a broader theological context, Apollinaris veering toward a treatment of the incarnation as a timeless reality, Gregory locating it firmly in the temporal sequence of narrative. But no simple conclusions follow. It cannot be said that one interpreted the passage rightly, the other wrongly; there are points for and against each side. Nor can it be said that Apollinaris and Gregory merely impose their respective theologies on a text that is not allowed to speak for itself. Such clear-cut contrasts simply do not apply, and falling into them will tend to distort rather than to clarify our estimates of how Paul—or scripture generally—was understood among the patristic theologians. For the patristic interpreters, exegesis is not distinct from but rather is interwoven with theology; and we must learn to make the more complex, if perhaps less immediately satisfying, historical judgments that the intertwining of the two requires. In doing so, we may also learn—Greer suggests—to see Paul himself with new eyes, in this case discerning a tension between the timeless and the temporal in Paul that may run deeper than the more usual contrasts between a "justification by faith" Paul and a "two ages" Paul, a Protestant Paul and a Catholic Paul.

Adolf Martin Ritter's essay on John Chrysostom extends the discussion of Paul's significance for the patristic period into the realm of Christian social ethics. Ritter finds it inadequate to reduce Chrysostom's preaching to a mere moralism in the tradition of the Cynic-Stoic diatribe. His sermons urge more than individual progress toward moral wisdom, more than individual liberation from the false values of social convention; they display a more basic drive toward the transformation of the communal conditions in which human beings live and according to which their social and economic standing is determined. In this sense, Chrysostom preaches a Christian utopianism that reflects Paul's own sense that the dynamic of the gospel both elicits and commands communal transformation—within the church itself, first of all, but also beyond its borders. Elizabeth Clark's comment shows, however, just how ambiguous a figure Chrysostom is on this score. His social utopianism appears to be limited, if not compromised, by other strains in his thought that endorse the stratified social order of the late Roman Empire; and in any case, his utopian views seem to rest far more on the opening chapters of Genesis than on Paul, far more on the implications of creation than on the implications of redemption. This question is not closed.

Even with respect to Augustine, who is usually considered the one truly Pauline figure from the patristic period, there are unexpected things to be said. Dom Basil Studer shows just how deeply the Pauline theme of hope—especially in its linkage with the coordinated notions of faith and love as in 1 Corinthians 13—entered and shaped Augustine's thought. It is already present at the very earliest stage of Augustine's postconversion theological career, although mingled with a Plotinian or, more likely, a Porphyrian reckoning of the stages of the soul's ascent to the divine. Even when deployed in this Platonic key, however, the theme represents an Augustinian appropriation of Paul that was to have enduring and deepening significance for his subsequent theological development, especially as it came to be centered in Christ as the Christian hope and in the hope of the resurrection. It is clear, then, that we cannot adequately or accurately gauge Augustine's use of Paul—or the Pauline legacy in Augustinian theology—if we concentrate only on the themes of grace and justification or pay attention only to the passages in Romans and Galatians where those themes stand most clearly to the fore. Augustine's Paul was too richly and widely elaborated to be reduced to a single strand, no matter how important that strand might be. Yet, as R. A. Markus suggests in his comment on Studer's essay, it may have been precisely the new reading of Paul on grace, which Augustine discovered in the mid-390s, that led ultimately to the deepening of his view of hope and to the heightening of the sense for carnal beauty that he associated with hope for the bodily resurrection. It may be important to distinguish between various versions of Paul, and to map discontinuities as

well as continuities between them, in assessing the legacies of Paul
in Augustine.

Markus' comment provides a natural point of transition to
Paula Fredriksen's study of Paul's significance for a profound shift
in Augustine's thought and sensibility, a shift that would lead
him—in sharp contrast to the classical philosophical and cultural
tradition—from a broadly cosmological to a broadly historical
reading of humanity and the human condition. In her view, the
new interpretation of Paul achieved in the 390s sparked the developments that eventuated in Augustine's integration of the body
and its sexuality into his reckoning of the human person. For
Augustine, as against his Pelagian opponents and especially Julian
of Eclanum, the body and its sexuality are not "detachable"
features of human existence. The human self cannot be identified
with the separable soul alone but must include the unruly,
unmanageable complications of bodily and sexual life. Here
Augustine leaves behind the anthropological dualism and the
moral perfectionism of the classical tradition and its Pelagian representatives. Under the influence of Paul, he conceives another,
more psychologically complicated self. My own comment on
Fredriksen's essay does not question her conclusions but offers a
suggestion as to what might have made Augustine susceptible to
such a nonclassical Paul. In this sense, it reinforces a point that, in
one way or another, seems common to all the essays in this grouping: far from being submerged or subordinated in the patristic
period, Paul may have been one of the critical factors in giving
Christianity a distinctive shape over against the classical tradition
with respect both to things human and to things divine.

The final grouping of essays, "Other Aspects of Pauline Influence," carries the inquiry into two areas that are less commonly included under the heading of the legacies of Paul in
Christianity's early history. Harry Gamble's study addresses a
long-standing puzzle: why is it that the Christians were the first
group in late antiquity to make widespread use of the codex—as
opposed to the almost universal scroll—as the format in which
their writings were transcribed and circulated? No argument
based on the codex's supposed advantages of convenience for
Christians has so far produced a satisfactory solution, and the

answer may well lie elsewhere. Gamble points to evidence that an early, if not the original, edition of Paul's letters may have combined two features. By grouping letters to the same community, it may have presented them as "letters to seven churches"; and it may have arranged the letters by decreasing length, with the longest coming first and the shortest last. But the only bibliographic format in which both of these characteristics could have been preserved was the codex. It is possible, therefore, that such an edition of Paul's letters was what elicited and what authorized the use of the codex among Christians. If sustained, Gamble's proposal would mean that one of Paul's strongest, most enduring, and most pervasive legacies was the form in which we now, virtually without thought, expect written material to be produced, to be read, and to be stored: the leaf-book. It is difficult to imagine a more basic influence on human culture.

In contrast, Ernst Dassmann's essay traces what turns out to be the surprisingly thin archeological and iconographic evidence for veneration of Paul in those areas of the eastern Mediterranean that were, after all, the centers of Paul's activity. Outside of Rome and western areas dependent on Rome, Paul seems never to have become one of the saints who served as foci of Christian devotion or as patrons of the believer's approach to the divine. Thecla, his companion and disciple in *The Acts of Paul and Thecla*, had a major shrine at Seleucia which, in the patristic era, attracted pilgrims from throughout the Roman Empire. But there is no Pauline equivalent in the Empire's eastern regions. Thus the human figure of Paul, despite the narrative traditions about him that gained currency in the second century, remains somehow vague and ill-defined. The episodes from his life that are recounted in his letters or reported in Acts receive neither architectural delineation through buildings at the sites nor iconographic definition through the imagery of Christian art. His impact on Christian religion and culture belongs largely, then, to the less personal areas of theology and doctrine; but in these areas he emerges as "the apostle" and exercises a formative influence on the character of Christian sensibility and the content of Christian belief.

It is to be hoped that this volume will help to put the study of the legacies of Paul in early Christianity on a new footing, both by contributing to the breakdown of the stereotyped view that had come to prevail in this regard and by marking out new possibilities to be investigated and new conclusions to be drawn. Such an outcome would not be without ecumenical significance. It might permit us to see a Paul whose influence is not primarily to be registered in the Gnostics' antipathy to the creator God of the Old Testament, the Jewish God; and it might also permit us to see a Paul who is not exclusively the property of the Western or, even more narrowly, of the Protestant tradition. In these senses, this volume might help to dissolve ancient lines of religious division.

The immediate import of these studies lies, however, in the historical arena. Here, it seems to me, they suggest three particularly important points. First, they show just how critical it is to be clear about the meaning of *Paul* and the application of *Pauline* in discussions of this sort. *Paul* can mean a figure of authority to whom appeal can be made in cases of ecclesiastical or theological dispute; *Paul* can mean the author of letters (some of which—the deutero-Paulines—may not actually have been written by Paul) that may have been known in varying combinations and permutations prior to the fixing and the widespread circulation of the Pauline canon; and *Paul* can mean the holder of theological views expressed in these letters. In this last instance, of course, there are yet further complications. Paul's theology will vary not only according to the number and combination of letters known but also according to the ways in which the letters' various themes and elements are weighted in relation to each other. It is important too to remember that Pauline texts could be associated with and construed in the light of other texts from other portions of Christian scripture, creating still further variations of *Paul*. None of this means, of course, that *Paul* should be used as if the name were indefinitely elastic and could be assigned to just anything at all. But it does mean that we need to be particularly careful in applying the labels *Pauline* and *unpauline*. We need to be sure that we are using them in a sense that is in fact relevant to the materials under study and appropriate to the questions at issue. We cannot simply disqualify one version of *Paul* because it fails to conform to another that we happen to prefer.

Despite these complexities in designating *Paul*, or perhaps because of them, the studies presented here constitute a major break with the notion that the legacies of Paul are to be found only in marginal or ultimately "heretical" versions of early Christianity. The Paul of the acts literature, whether canonical or apocryphal, may not look, to our eyes, like the Paul of the genuine epistles; but there are significant questions to be raised about the vantage point from which we take our view. And in any case, this Paul at least shows that Paul had not simply been ceded to groups that the dominant tradition would finally reject. Furthermore, as Lindemann's essay indicates, there is no reason to suppose that Paul's authority was ignored or rejected by communities that seem to us to have represented streams of Christianity that would flow into that dominant tradition. There were also, of course, heretical versions of Paul, the Paul of the Marcionites and the Paul of the Christian Gnostics; but that fact does not mean that there was no nonheretical Paul or that the orthodox tradition could accommodate only a denatured Paul, domesticated and confined within a theology that would keep Paulinism under rigid and relentless control. Certainly Norris' study shows that Irenaeus, in weaving Paul into his theology and weaving his theology around Paul, was not engaged in a merely defensive effort. Perhaps it is time to acknowledge that there was an anti-Marcionite as well as a Marcionite Paul, an anti-Gnostic as well as a Gnostic Paul—a Paul, that is, who supports the identity of the one God of the Old Testament and the New Testament and who sustains the continuity of the one divine dispensation of creation and redemption. That Christian theology took just this shape—anticipated prior to Irenaeus, realized in Irenaeus, and preserved after him—may itself be, in large measure, a legacy of Paul.

Finally, these studies indicate, at least, that Paul may have been one of the critical factors giving Christianity its distinctive identity within and over against its late-antique cultural environment. Paul, in his understanding of the God of grace and election and in his reckoning of the human condition under sin, seems consistently to have represented an alternative to the classical tradition. It is not, of course, that we will find a representation of

Paul or of Pauline thought that has not been mingled with and influenced by the terminology and conceptuality of Greco-Roman, and especially of late Platonic, intellectual and religious culture. It is rather that the continuing Christian appropriation of Paul tended to disturb the settled patterns of that culture, to shift the meanings of its terms, and to alter the contours of its concepts. As Wilken urges, we must learn to pay attention to the subtle ways in which the vocabulary of scripture in general and Paul in particular penetrated the philosophic discourse of late antiquity. The results, if never pure or unadulterated, could still be monumental: a God whose relations to human beings are a function of will and whose purposes cannot be safely correlated with the rational order of nature; a hope that comes to be centered in the resurrection of the body and that eventuates in an unexpected praise of carnal beauty; a humanity that is intricately and inextricably implicated in its bodily and sexual existence so that the ancient dichotomy of soul and body must be translated into a clash of dispositions in the self. Not least among the legacies of Paul may have been a series of slippages that ended by making the Christian—and therefore the modern(?)—vision of deity and humanity something quite different from its classical counterpart. At the least it is true that we can no longer speak as if Paul were not a pervasive and formative influence on the sensibilities and theologies of patristic Christianity.

Paul and the Legacies of Paul

PART ONE:
EARLY DELINEATIONS OF PAUL

The End of the Line:
Paul in the Canonical
Book of Acts

DANIEL R. SCHWARTZ

There are two ways to approach the topic of Acts' portrayal of Paul: from the side of Paul and from the side of Luke-Acts. The first—from the side of Paul and his epistles—is the approach with which the modern debate on the subject began.[1] Philip Vielhauer's article "On the 'Paulinism' of Acts," published in 1950, initiated a tradition that Werner Georg Kümmel was to call "Luke as Accused by Contemporary Theologians."[2] This tradition, as Kümmel notes, was primarily theological in character, represented by theologians who took their point of departure from the New Testament theologian par excellence, Paul, and found Luke's rendition of him wanting. For everyone—or almost everyone—agrees that Luke's Paul does not sound like Paul's Paul. On this score, the only arguments that usually come into play concern just how irreconcilable the two versions of Paul are.[3]

The second approach is from the side of Luke-Acts: one can study Luke-Acts as a whole and then attempt to discover the meaning and function, within this context, of the material relating to Paul. This approach, it seems, has come more and more to be preferred in recent years.[4] This shift in orientation reflects not only the fact that Pauline scholars are again relegating Acts to the sidelines of their discussions,[5] but also the effect of certain other works that appeared at about the same time as Vielhauer's article and set in motion an opposing tradition dedicated to clarifying Lucan theology in its own right (something that many previous scholars, taken up with form-critical and source-critical studies, did not admit existed).[6] The pioneers of this other approach, usually termed *redaction criticism* or *composition criticism*, were Hans

Conzelmann, whose *Die Mitte der Zeit* appeared in 1954 (it was based on his 1952 dissertation and *Habilitationsschrift*), and Martin Dibelius, whose *Aufsätze zur Apostelgeschichte* appeared in 1951 (and included a previously unpublished essay, "Paulus in der Apostelgeschichte").[7] If pre-World War II scholarship had tended either to neglect Acts or to treat it only as history,[8] the work of these two scholars—and of their many followers—served to focus attention on the Lucan work as a whole, raising questions about the meaning that Luke attached to the events he reported—or distorted or failed to report—and the methods he used in doing so. This point of view became dominant with the publication of Ernst Haenchen's and Hans Conzelmann's commentaries on Acts, both of which show only relatively minor interest in history per se and are devoted rather to such topics as apologetics and kerygma.[9]

Now it is true that this approach can go much too far.[10] One occasionally has the feeling that some German scholars would be quite pleased if it were established beyond doubt that everything in Acts is historically false, for then it would be clear that Luke wrote his work only for kerygmatic or apologetic reasons. And although it is true that viewing the study of Acts only as a preface to the historical study of early Christianity—as in the case of the largest pre-World War II collaborative effort on Acts—leaves out much of importance, it is no less troubling to note that the largest postwar collaborative effort on Acts, published in 1979, leaves history entirely out of its purview.[11] Nevertheless it is in this direction—from Luke-Acts to Paul—that we must proceed here, for our concern lies not in deciding whether Acts may be used to amplify our knowledge of Paul but rather in clarifying Luke's understanding of Paul and his legacy and in tracing the use to which he put Paul.

Luke-Acts and the Lucan Paul

Acts tells the story of the transformation of Christianity from a community that is (a) Palestinian, (b) Jewish, and (c) Torah-observing into a movement that is, for the most part, (a) diasporan, (b) gentile, and (c) nonobservant of the Torah. In short, whether one regards "being Jewish" as a matter of territory, of race, of religion, or of some combination of these factors, Acts describes how Christianity came to be something non-Jewish. The adjectives *schematic, pragmatic,* and *apologetic* seem to me to capture the most salient aspects of this narrative and therefore provide useful headings for characterizing Acts' account of Paul (the Pauline material takes up roughly two-thirds of the book, chiefly chapters 9 and 13–28). After seeing just how well Luke's portrayal of Paul corresponds with (Luke)-Acts in general, we will turn to Luke's presentation of Paul's kerygmatic teachings in particular.

SCHEMATIC

Acts is *schematic* in that it organizes events not, or not always, according to their historical order but rather according to their meaning for the story as the author wishes to present it. Perhaps this is what Luke meant in promising to tell his story *kathēxes* (Lk. 1:3).[12] Already in his gospel, for example, Luke had moved the Nazareth pericope forward to the very beginning of Jesus' mission, thus giving the impression of a linear progression from Nazareth to Jerusalem.[13] Similarly, in Acts 11:19ff., we are told that those who were scattered by the persecution that arose in connection with Stephen reached Antioch and began to preach there to non-Jews. These happenings are obviously more or less contemporary with the events recorded in Acts 8 regarding other such refugees, but Luke postponed the story so as to locate it after the account of God's and the church's decision, in Jerusalem, to accept gentile converts (Acts 10–11).[14] If in the gospel everything must progress neatly toward Jerusalem, in Acts things must progress just as neatly in the other direction, outward from Jerusalem.[15]

In a more encompassing way too, Acts exhibits a quite schematic structure with regard to the departures of Christianity from Jewish land, race, and law. In the first six chapters, Christianity is limited to Jerusalem alone; those from outside who would associate themselves with it must come "centripetally" to the capital.[16] It is only after a speech (Acts 7) focusing on God's transcendence and lack of specific interest in Palestine or the temple (along with some other themes) that the movement begins to expand geographically (Acts 8).[17] Having thus broken with the territorial criterion, Luke next takes up the ethnic one, which he had left untouched in the earlier chapters.[18] After telling of some missionizing in what has been called a *Zwischenbereich* of those whose Jewish descent is unclear (the Samaritans and the Ethiopian eunuch of Acts 8)[19] and after Christianizing Paul (Acts 9)—the man who will be the main apostle to the Gentiles, as Luke's readers may already have known and would read a few chapters later— Luke fully and formally recounts how God opened the church to the Gentiles (Acts 10-11). At this point, Luke proceeds to show how the church came to be composed of increasing numbers of Gentiles, due both to the activities of missionaries and to rejection by Jews (Acts 11:19-14:28), thus making it necessary for the next topic to emerge: what obligations of the Torah, if any, devolve upon gentile Christians? And this is, in fact, the next topic addressed head on in Acts, just as programmatically as were Stephen's speech regarding territory and the Cornelius episode regarding race. The consequent discussion (Acts 15)—in which all participants, apart from the original troublemakers, are said to have agreed—results in the emancipation of Christianity from the last specific mark distinguishing Jews from non-Jews.[20] And just as the postponement of the missionizing to Gentiles (to Acts 11:19ff.) was, as we noted, the result of such Lucan schematization, so too the postponement of the question of "the Gentiles and the law" (to Acts 15) reflects a similar concern. The question should have been raised immediately upon the baptism of Cornelius in chapter 10, but Luke postponed it so that it would follow the successful missionizing of the man who was known to be the great missionary to the Gentiles and the great anti-legalist.

Having moved from Lucan schematization in general to Lucan schematization in relation to Paul in particular and having intimated that here too Luke has arranged his materials other than chronologically, I want now to explain why I believe that most of the Pauline material prior to chapter 15 is in fact out of place and that its placement is therefore a legitimate—and in fact an imperative—object for exegesis. The situation with regard to chapters 13-14 is rather simple. Since Galatians 1-2 indicate that Paul visited Jerusalem only once between his call and the so-called apostolic conference, whereas Acts reports two such visits

(9:25–30; 11:27–30 [with 12:25]),[21] it is clear that something must be done to account for the discrepancy. I shall do what is usually done; that is, I shall assume that 11:27–30 (with 12:25) and chapter 15 refer to one and the same visit but report different aspects of it.[22] Note, for example, that "both" visits begin with Judaean Christians coming to Antioch and Paul and Barnabas being sent back to Jerusalem in response.

The next question, however, is more difficult: once we have decided to equate the two visits reported separately in chapters 11 and 15, should we then move 11:27–30 forward in time or Acts 15 back in time to combine them into one? That is, did Paul's journeys of chapters 13–14 come before the famine visit and apostolic conference or after? The latter seems far more likely to me. Placing the events of Acts 15 prior to the journeys would bring the question of the Gentiles' obligations into immediate juxtaposition with that of their acceptance into the church—which, as noted above, is where it belongs. Furthermore, this placing eliminates another problem raised by the current order of Acts and left unresolved by the other option (i.e., moving 11:27–30 forward in time): why does the apostolic decree (Acts 15:23) address the Christians of Antioch, Syria, and Cilicia alone—all of whom are mentioned in Acts 11[23]—but ignore the many places Paul is said to have visited and successfully evangelized in chapters 13–14? Instead of supposing that Paul, as the narrative of Acts would have it, interrupted his journey of Acts 13–14 to return to Jerusalem and then went back to the same places to give them a decree not addressed to them at all (16:4), would it not be simpler to assume that the decree was in fact issued before Paul began his major missionary work in Asia Minor?[24] Then it would seem that Luke, assuming that the squabble arose and the decision was made with regard to Paul's work, postponed his account of the conference until after Paul had begun his missionizing in Asia Minor and taken his "turn to the Gentiles" and thus had Paul interrupt his journey to come back for the conference.

The situation is quite similar with regard to Acts 9, the other main block of Pauline material prior to chapter 15. We note first that in the material preceding chapter 9, Paul is mentioned only in reference to the persecution following Stephen's speech; but as has often been recognized, these references are redactional: the *Wiederaufnahme* at the beginning of 7:59 clearly marks the brief allusion to Saul the persecutor in 7:58 as a secondary insertion; and the redundance of 8:1 and 8:3 just as clearly does the same for the former of these two verses.[25] Furthermore, the only other New Testament reference to Paul's participation in the persecution at the time of Stephen comes in a Lucan addition to one of his versions of Paul's call (22:20).[26] Thus, on the one hand, we have no solid reason to assume that Paul was still unconverted at the time of Stephen's martyrdom and the subsequent persecution.[27] On the other hand, we have good reason to believe that Paul was in fact a Christian by the time of that persecution. As several scholars have argued, the Jewish initiative and the complete lack of Roman presence in the story of Stephen apparently indicate that the episode occurred during a break in Roman administration in Judaea following the removal of Pilate and the death of Tiberius. Tiberius died in March of 37, and Pilate was removed from office only shortly before.[28] Given the data of Galatians 1:18 and 2:1, where Paul dates his conversion fourteen (plus three?) years before the apostolic conference, and given the common dating of the latter (and of the famine as well) to around 48 C.E., it follows that Paul was already a Christian by the time of the death of Stephen and the attendant persecution.[29]

It is difficult to determine whether Luke knew that his chronology was wrong. As a fellow historian, I would prefer to give him the benefit of the doubt; and in fact, in at least one case, we are in a good position to see how Luke may have been misled. According to all scholars, the death of Agrippa I is out of place in Luke's narrative, for Josephus locates the famine of Acts 11:27–30 not under Agrippa but during the term of Tiberius Julius Alexander, the second governor of Judaea after Agrippa's death (*Ant.* 20.101). When we note that Acts calls Agrippa "Herod," a name that is never used of him elsewhere in ancient literature, we may suspect, however, that Luke thought the reference was to Herod of Chalcis, Agrippa's brother. And this Herod, according to Josephus (*Ant.* 20.104), did in fact die right after the famine. Thus, if Luke's source termed Agrippa "Herod"—perhaps because of the negative associations of that name for Christians—Luke may diligently have searched for a ruler of that name and found the only possible candidate in the relevant time frame.[30] Similarly, if Luke had a tradition that Paul participated in the persecution of Christians and if the only persecution known to him was the one related to Stephen, he could have inserted Paul there in complete good conscience. And if he had two sources reporting a trip by Saul and Barnabas to Jerusalem and what they did there, he might well have been hard put—as modern scholars frequently are in similar cases[31]—to decide whether the two sources referred to different trips or to the same one.

Nevertheless, whether intentionally misplaced or not, these episodes function eminently well in the structure of Luke's narrative. We have already noted that Paul's call in chapter 9 serves, along with the reports in chapter 8 about the Samaritans and the Ethiopian eunuch, to help prepare the way for the admission of the Gentiles in chapters 10–11. Now we are in a position to note that the persecution of chapter 12 is supported by the whole Jewish people (Acts 12:3, 4, 11). Such a generalization is possible only after the decision has been taken to open the church to others; otherwise the universal hostility of the Jewish people would simply spell failure on the church's part. Again, although we have already noted that chapters 13–14 prepare us for the urgency with which the question of Gentiles' legal obligations is raised in chapter 15, we may now add that it is only in chapter 13, in all of Acts, that Paul criticizes the law (13:38–39) and only here that he (or anyone else in Acts) speaks of "justification," and that by "faith."[32] In other words, when we note that it is not only the placement of this chapter but also the specific contents of its sermon that help to prepare us for chapter 15, we realize that we are not dealing with a simple cut-and-paste job but rather with a carefully considered scheme in which Paul has his role to play.

PRAGMATIC

Having thus arrived at a point of Pauline theology, we shall now turn to the second adjective that we applied to Acts: *pragmatic*. In Acts, history moves because things happen or fail to happen, not because of ideas alone. The many unfinished or shrugged-off speeches in Acts testify that Luke realized that most

people share Gallio's attitude toward "words and names" (18:15).[33]
In contrast, miracles, including Paul's miracles, are very efficacious; and it is thus no surprise that this aspect of Paul is very
prominent in Acts, far beyond anything that his epistles would
have led us to expect.[34] Again, in Paul's criticism of the law (13:38–
39), the point seems to be less theoretical or theological (works or
law and justification are inherently incompatible) than empirical:
the law did not grant you justification because you could not fulfill
it. The same point is made much more clearly by Peter and James
and their colleagues in 15:10, 21, 28.[35] It is therefore not surprising—however disconcerting or contemptible it may be for some
readers of Paul's epistles—that a sharp distinction between faith
and works is unknown to Luke's Paul, who rather demands
"works worthy of repentance" (26:20), just as Luke's John the Baptist had done (Lk. 3:8).[36]

The most important pragmatic aspect of the Lucan portrayal
of Paul, however, is that it was only pragmatic considerations that
led Luke's Paul, against his wishes, to break with Judaea and the
Jews. It was only Jewish misunderstanding and hostility that
forced Paul out of the temple and out of Jerusalem (9:28–30;
21ff.); it was only as a prisoner and to save his life that Paul was
sent away from Jerusalem to Caesarea (Rome's local representative);[37] and it was only to vindicate himself in the face of hostile
Jewish accusations that Paul was eventually transferred to Rome.
Thus, as Paul is made to tell us three times in Acts (13:46; 18:6;
28:28 [cf. 19:9]), it was only because the Jews rejected him that he
turned away. What then of the promise to Abraham that figures
so prominently in Romans and Galatians? And what, for that
matter, of Romans 9–11 and the theologically attractive, if un-
pragmatic, notion that Israel retains its primacy and that God will
eventually return to it? Nothing of this sort is to be found in Acts
as I read it.[38] Instead we have the simple notion that the gospel is
to be preached to those who will accept it. Although the gospel
indeed began with the Jews, they rejected it—and there is no
reason to bang one's head interminably against a stone wall.[39]
Note especially in this regard that of the three versions of Paul's
call in Acts, only the last two, which come after Paul has twice
announced his break with the Jews (13:46; 18:6), report that Jesus

charged Paul to evangelize Gentiles (22:15, 21; 26:17). In the first version, which comes before the Jewish rejection of the gospel, Gentiles figure only among those before whom Paul (like Jesus before him) will have to suffer (9:15–16; cf. 4:25–28 regarding Jesus).[40] Indeed, whereas it is almost universally held that Acts portrays Paul as fulfilling Jesus' mandate to the apostles to be his witnesses to the end of the earth (1:8)—including to the Gentiles[41]—it seems instead to be the case, as I have argued elsewhere, that the mandate refers to the end of the *land* (of Israel)—to Jews alone—and that Luke depicts Paul, in the wake of Jewish rejection of his message, as having reinterpreted *land* as *earth* with the aid of Isaiah 49:6 (Acts 13:47).[42] Below, in our review of Luke's version of Paul's kerygma, we will return to this matter.

APOLOGETIC

This last aspect of Luke's pragmatism with regard to Paul—that is, his claim that Paul left Judaea and the Jews only because they forced him away—leads us to our final adjective for Acts: *apologetic.* The claim that the Jews drove Paul away is the first of the two major features of Luke's apologetics in Acts. It puts the blame for the schism on the hostility and misunderstanding of others.[43] Specifically, in the first eleven chapters of Acts the opponents of the gospel are only certain segments of the Jewish people, mainly the high-priestly aristocracy.[44] Given the association of that aristocracy with the Sadducees (which Luke emphasizes in Acts 5:17), who denied resurrection (as stressed in Lk. 20:27 and Acts 23:8), this identification of the gospel's enemies coheres well with Luke's focus, in Acts, on the resurrection as the heart of the gospel (to which we will return below).[45] The "people," in contrast, are generally said to be favorably disposed toward the church; and it was, of course, from their ranks that new converts came in great numbers (who else was there?).[46] But after the events of chapters 10–11 made it possible to turn away from the Jewish people, Acts suddenly begins to claim in chapter 12, as we have noted, that the whole Jewish people was hostile to the church.[47] And in the account of Paul that follows, this claim is often repeated, even when the details of Acts itself reveal that the matter was not so clear-cut. Thus Acts 13:43 informs us that many Jews were among those who received Paul's message favorably, but 13:45 reports that "the Jews" jealously attacked Paul (so also 14:1–4; 17:4–5).[48] Paul, for his part, is time and again forced to suffer due to Jewish hostility; and his wanderings are to a certain extent simply a matter of perpetual flight. Nevertheless he continually returns to the synagogues to preach to the Jews; and as we have noted, he even twice overlooks his formal decision to give up the Jewish mission and preach to Gentiles alone.

It is in this context that Paul's strict adherence to the law, according to Acts' repeated testimony, is to be understood.[49] For this portrayal of Paul is just as efficient apologetically as it is difficult for readers of the epistles to accept.[50] Whether or not Acts was also intended for Roman eyes, as an appeal for recognition of Christianity as true Judaism and thus as a licit religion,[51] it is certain that the work was intended to be read by Christians. For such readers, the claim that the Jews rejected the gospel and Paul, and not vice versa, would serve to explain the need for God's intervention and for charting a new course. Luke makes this point very artistically in chapter 22, in the second account of Paul's calling, where—as is appropriate for a speech made in response to being arrested in the temple—a temple scene is included, which is not to be found in the other two versions of the call (Acts 9; 26).[52] Here Paul is said to have been praying in the temple, as the apostles were wont to do (Acts 3:1; 5:12, 42), when Jesus appeared to him and told him to flee Jerusalem immediately, since the Jews would not accept his testimony. Paul did not want to go and remonstrated, pointing out that the Jews knew that he used to persecute the Christians energetically. This reply is either a response to the admonition to flee (Paul means that the Jews, out of consideration for his former "merit," will overlook his current heresy) or a response to the prediction that the Jews will not accept his message (Paul means that his message will be especially convincing, coming as it does from a former persecutor).[53] But Jesus ends the debate with a sovereign command: "Go, for I am sending you far away to the Gentiles" (22:21, NEB). But—and this point is unmistakable—Luke here has Paul telling the story after he had again returned to worship in the temple and demonstrate his loyalty to it (Acts 21:26ff.). In other words, just as Paul twice ignored his own decision to give up on the Jews, so too he first disputed and later ignored Jesus' command to leave Jerusalem. It was only that exasperating Jewish hostility, combining misunderstanding and calumny into an attempt on Paul's life (Acts 21:27ff.), that compelled his departure. And although Paul is said to have been willing to die rather than stay away from Jerusalem (21:11–14), the Romans tear him away from the city to save his life (23:12–35) and also, as Luke reminds us just before the Romans take action (23:11), to fulfill Jesus' command that Paul leave Jerusalem to testify about him to the distant Gentiles (22:21). Despite all this, when Paul gets to Rome he again begins with the Jews; it is only when here too they reject him that he finally reaches the end of the line and, for the third and final time, turns away from them to the Gentiles. This is the Q.E.D. of the entire work, which is the reason the narrative may end here.[54] But Luke took his time in coming to this point; and he took his time in order to make it quite clear that there was ample justification for the transformation of Christianity into something non-Jewish: no one could demand more patience or persistence, but the time had now come to move on.

This theme brings us to the other main focus of Luke's apologetics: Rome. Acts is concerned to show its readers that the Christian religion posed no threat to Rome and that Christians had, on the contrary, always honored Rome and been respected and protected by it.[55] It has been debated whether this apologetic is addressed to Roman officialdom (as is usually assumed) to win toleration for the church or rather to Christian readers to conciliate them with the Empire or even to bring them to ascribe to it a positive role in the fulfillment of God's plans or perhaps to supply them with a model for self-defense in times of persecution.[56] I doubt, however, that it is necessary or justified to settle on any one such alternative. The case is much the same as that regarding the "apologetic" literature of hellenistic Judaism: when one side in a potential conflict portrays the other favorably, readers on both sides will, if convinced, be less disposed to hostility.[57] And indeed once a book is written—especially if, as in the case of Acts, it is written in the vernacular and in a familiar genre[58]— there is no telling who might read it. Authors must bear both internal and external readerships in mind. Thus, when Paul is portrayed as a Roman citizen (Acts 16:37; 22:25-29) who depends on the Roman legal system and is repeatedly found by that system to be innocent of all wrongdoing (25:25; 26:30-32; 28:18),[59] and when Paul's gospel is found to be of no concern to the Roman Empire (18:12-17; 25:19-20; 28:31)[60] and is even accepted by some Roman officials (13:12; cf. 16:25-34; 24:24; 26:28[?]), Luke is quite obviously being apologetic—just as he was in his similar claims about Jesus and the charges (phrased much more politically than in the other gospels)[61] brought against him (Lk. 23, especially 23:2).

In summary, then, we may conclude that Luke fits Paul into his schematic account of "the events that have happened among us" (Lk. 1:1) just as freely and deftly as he usually handles his material; that as a historian he focuses on events, not ideas; and that his depiction of Paul is just as apologetic vis-à-vis the Jews and Rome as is the rest of his work. We will be less than surprised, therefore, to find that the message Luke's Paul teaches is also a very Lucan message.

The Lucan Paul's Kerygma

Paul's preaching, according to Acts, has two foci: resurrection and the kingdom of God. Resurrection, on the one hand, is quite to be expected, for Paul was a Christian preacher whose only direct experience of Jesus Christ is said to have come after Christ's resurrection. Thus, in Acts 13:32-33, Paul summarizes his gospel as being the good news that God has fulfilled his promise to raise up his son;[62] and in 17:18, his teaching in Athens is summarized as "proclaiming Jesus and the resurrection" (not, it should be noted, "his resurrection"; see below). His speech in Athens ends with the claim that there will be a judgment: "of this He [God] has given assurance to all by raising him [Jesus, the judge] from the dead" (17:31, NEB). In 23:6, in his trial before the Sanhedrin, Paul claims that the true issue is his belief in resurrection, and he repeats that claim in 24:21 as well. In 24:15, he underlines his belief in the resurrection of the just and the wicked alike. Festus therefore quite appropriately summarizes the matter for Agrippa as an argument about "Jesus, some dead man whom Paul alleges to be alive" (25:19); and Paul punctuates his speech with a rhetorical question about the resurrection of the dead (26:8) and concludes with a summary assertion about the messiah as the first to be resurrected (26:22-23).

On the other hand, Paul's teaching is frequently represented as being about the kingdom of God. Thus the only specific content of Paul's (and Barnabas') "encouragement" to several Christian communities was that "to enter the kingdom of God we must pass through many hardships" (14:21-23). In 19:8, the whole of Paul's teaching in Corinth is characterized as being "about the kingdom of God"; and in his farewell speech in Miletus (20:25), Paul similarly summarizes the burden of his teaching as proclaiming the kingdom (of God).[63]

Thus, when the closing lines of Acts twice summarize Paul's teaching in Rome as being about the kingdom of God and about Jesus (28:23, 31), it seems clear—especially given the conclusive nature of these final verses[64]—that Luke is here summarizing the two foci of Paul's preaching in general, and not only in Rome. The teaching "about Jesus," here undefined, is most probably to be taken—as we have intimated with regard to 17:18 and as we shall discuss more fully below—as a reference to his having evidenced the reality of resurrection. This way of construing the matter is indicated especially by the fact that 28:23 reports that Paul tried to prove what he said "about Jesus" from the law and the prophets, to which he appeals in 24:14-15 and 26:22-23 (cf. 17:2-3) as proof texts for resurrection.[65]

Regarding these two points of the Lucan Paul's message, a few observations are in order. First, they are both very Lucan. The teachings of the apostles are summarized in Acts 4:2 as "proclaiming in Jesus [i.e., through the example of Jesus][66] the resurrection of the dead"; and Acts begins with a redundant account of Jesus' resurrection now amplified, in comparison with that in Luke 24, with a summary of his teachings as being "about the kingdom of God" (Acts 1:3). So too Philip's teaching (but not that of the apostles!—see below) is represented as being about the kingdom of God (and the name of Jesus Christ; Acts 8:12); and, of course, Luke's Jesus is at the very outset made to characterize his entire mission as "giving the good news of the kingdom of God

. . . for that is what I was sent to do" (Lk. 4:43).[67] Finally, Luke is
the only evangelist to bring John the Baptist into connection with
the kingdom of God (Lk. 16:16).[68]

Second, we note that Luke 4:43 differs from its parallel
(source?) in Mark 1:38 not only in that it refers to the kingdom of
God but also, and for us especially, in that Luke has a passive verb
where Mark has an active one. Mark's Jesus "came," while Luke's
Jesus "was sent."[69] This passive goes well with the term "kingdom
of God." It is *God's* kingdom, not Jesus', that Luke's Jesus is
proclaiming; and it is, correspondingly, God who is pulling the
strings.

Third, however, Luke knows that it was indeed *Jesus'* kingdom that was expected by his followers, who saw him as the
messiah, the restorer of the Davidic kingdom. It was this perception of Jesus that got him into trouble with the Romans.[70] But
Luke claims that this was a mistaken perception. Thus when
Jesus' accusers, according to Luke 23:2, told Pilate that Jesus
claimed to be "the messiah, a king" (Χριστὸν βασιλέα εἶναι),
Jesus' reply—however difficult it may be for us to construe[71]—
obviously amounts to a denial, for Pilate immediately concluded
that he found no guilt in (or grounds for a case against) Jesus
(23:3–4).[72] Nevertheless Luke knew that not only hostile Jews and
Romans might misconstrue Jesus as a messianic king; many of his
followers did as well. Thus, when the apostles hear from the risen
Christ about the kingdom of God (Acts 1:3), they eagerly infer
that Jesus will soon restore the kingdom of *Israel* (1:6). Jesus
immediately rebukes them, telling them—in a way very reminiscent of the passive verb in Luke 4:43—that it is the Father, not
Jesus, who decides such things and that it is not for them to know
the dates and times that the Father has set (1:7). But Jesus does not
correct their notion that the expected kingdom is the kingdom of
Israel.[73] And it is as such (see Lk. 24:21) that the apostles proclaim
it (and not, as noted above, as the kingdom of God): from Peter's
Pentecost sermon, where the point is laboriously made that Jesus
is the Davidic messiah to whom the throne is promised (2:30),
through the restoration language of 3:21 and the application of
the messianic Psalm 2 to Jesus in 4:25–26, and up to the summary
in 5:42 where the apostolic preaching is simply "proclaiming the

good news of the messiah, Jesus." Thus it is not surprising that just before the end of this apostolic section of the work, we find a Jewish defender of the Christians comparing the claims made regarding Jesus to those made previously by Judas the Galilean and Theudas (5:35–39), who had led revolts against Rome.[74] For it was as the messianic king of Israel that Jesus was then being preached, according to this part of Luke's narrative. Paul too, according to Luke, *began* by preaching Jesus similarly, proving that Jesus was the messiah (9:22) and even, in his first speech, giving a lengthy argument (reminiscent of Peter's in chapter 2) for Jesus' being the Davidic messiah (13:21–38).

Fourth—and most important with regard to the Lucan Paul—it is noteworthy that Paul only *began* preaching Jesus as the Davidic messiah. When, in the immediate sequel to his speech, the Jews reject and attack Paul, he rejects them in turn (i.e., proclaims that God has rejected them; 13:46–47). Just as he is now made to substitute Isaiah's "end of the earth" for Jesus' "end of the land,"[75] so too he now turns from the "kingdom of Israel" to the "kingdom of God." As a glance at a concordance will indicate, *basileia tou theou* is a favorite term of Luke's, but after using it more than a score of times in his gospel and again in Acts 1:3, he avoided the phrase in all the apostolic preaching until the rejected Philip and Paul had, so to speak, learned their lessons. After the occurrence in 1:3, the term appears again in Acts only in 8:12 (Stephen) and then several times in connection with Paul (14:22; 19:8; 20:25 [see n.63]; 28:23, 31). Correspondingly, whereas David's name appears ten times in Acts through 13:36–47, he is mentioned only once again (15:16, in a quotation from Amos that is given a very universalizing application).[76] And the only time Acts associates Jesus with the term *basileus*, the word is spoken by hostile Jews whom the magistrates in Thessalonica, like Pilate in Jerusalem, find no reason to take seriously (Acts 17:7–9; cf. Lk. 23).

Moreover, although the data are not as clear-cut as in the cases of "kingdom of God," "David," and *basileus*, it seems that Luke's usage of *christos*, which literally means "messiah," indicates a similar development with regard to the Lucan Paul. Whereas *christos* was used with great frequency in Luke and the early portions of Acts, after Acts 11:17—the decision to admit Gentiles—it all but drops from sight. It occurs only ten more times, of which two explicitly reflect the christology of a more primitive Jewish Christianity (15:26; 18:28) and two are textually uncertain (17:3b and especially 20:21). Moreover, in one of these last cases (20:21) and in three other instances (16:18; 24:24; 28:31), *Christ* is part of Jesus' name (as usual in Paul) and does not mean "messiah." Thus only three passages are left in which Paul identifies Jesus as the messiah (17:3; 18:5; 26:23).[77] The explanation for this infrequency would seem to be threefold: (1) the term *messiah* was meaningless for non-Jews, with whom this part of Acts is increasingly concerned,[78] and in fact Paul avoids *Christ* entirely in his preaching to Gentiles (Acts 25, 17); (2) the term was dangerous in the courtroom situation in which Paul found himself (beginning in Acts 21);[79] and (3) after Paul's break with the Jews in 13:46–47, as we have noted, he was not supposed to be interested in a Jewish national redeemer. We are now in a position, then, to note that all three of Paul's references to Jesus as the messiah, after chapter 13, cohere with the scheme I have been developing. In 17:3, Paul calls Jesus the messiah but is rejected by the Jews, who ascribe a political import to his teaching (17:5–9); and in the following story (17:10–32), which has to do with Jews in Beroea and Greeks in Athens, no such messianism appears. Similarly in 18:5, Paul's preaching of Jesus as the messiah simply elicits Jewish rejection, which Paul answers in kind (18:6); and in 26:23, Paul preaches Jesus as the messiah only in a denationalized and depoliticized form: "to proclaim light to the people"—not "his people"[80]—"and the nations." In passing, we may also note here that the downplaying of *christos*, which is an unambivalent epithet for Jesus, is reflected in—and hence attested by—two further phenomena in Acts: frequent confusion regarding the identity of *kyrios* (God or Jesus?);[81] and the sudden appearance of the title "Lord Jesus" (*Kyrios Iesous*), which occurs once at most in Luke (24:3) but twelve times or more in Acts, where it helps to take up some of the slack left by the departure of *christos.*[82]

The question of what the Lucan Paul is interested in, if not a Jewish national redeemer, leads to our fifth and final observation, which takes us back from the kingdom of God to Paul's other main theme in Acts, resurrection. Paul repeatedly refers to some "hope" (*elpis*) as the content of his belief, but it is not easy to determine precisely what this hope is. Thus, in 23:6, Paul claims that he is being judged because of "the hope and the resurrection of the dead" (*peri elpidos kai anastaseōs nekrōn*), a position that he claims to share with the Pharisees. The fact that *peri* is not repeated in Paul's phrase and the absence of definite articles lead us to suppose that both terms depend on *nekrōn*, so that Paul here, in a hendiadys, is referring to resurrection as the dead's hope.[83] The same is indicated by Acts 24:14–15, where Paul's hope, which is similarly said to be shared by his accusers, is defined as the expectation of the resurrection of the just and the unjust. It is also indicated by 24:21, where although the verse is otherwise strikingly parallel to 23:6, there is no reference to hope, and the reference to resurrection suffices. There are, however, counter-instances. In 28:20, Paul refers to the "hope of Israel"; and in 26:6–7, the "hope" is specifically the fulfilment of God's promises to "our fathers . . . our twelve tribes," something national and not individual and reminiscent too of 13:32–37, where (although *hope* is not used) God's promise to the fathers was fulfilled not in the resurrection of "the dead" in general but rather in the resurrection of the Davidic Jesus. How shall we account for this fluctuation?[84]

The use of *hope* as a pregnant term leads us to suspect an underlying biblical allusion, especially since Acts 24:14–15 appears to mean that the hope is grounded in the law and the prophets (and where else could God's promises be documented?). But although the reference to the resurrection of the just and the unjust in 24:15 points a steady finger toward Daniel 2:2, there is nothing in that context to suggest the term *hope*; and Daniel is strikingly individual and universal here, not national.[85] More to the point would be Ezekiel 37. Here, despite those who say that their *hope* (LXX: *elpis*) is gone (37:11), God revives the dry bones of Israel and restores the Davidic kingdom as well; and indeed we know that Ezekiel 37 served ancient Jewish and Christian writers and liturgists frequently in their meditations and preaching about resurrection, including the resurrection of Jesus.[86]

What is important for us is that Luke's Paul has denationalized this hope, leaving it individual and universal (as in Daniel 12). As in his preference for *kingdom of God* and his minimization of

Christ, king, and *David,* so also in his *hope* Luke's Paul has removed the national focus: he has made it equivalent to resurrection alone. Above we noted that certain passages (Acts 13:32-37;
26:6-7; 28:20) made us hesitate to accept the equation of hope and
resurrection that is indicated in other passages (23:6; 24:14-15,
21); and we took that apparent inconsistency as an opportunity to
consider the source of the term. Now, however, we must indicate
that these passages are not in fact obstacles to equating the hope
of the Lucan Paul with resurrection—quite the contrary! The
national focus of 13:32-37 is shortly thereafter turned into the
non-national matter of eternal life: the Jews who rejected Paul's
message are said not to have considered themselves worthy of
eternal life (13:46-47); and when Paul turns to the Gentiles with
the same message, "those who were appointed for eternal life
believed" (13:48). Similarly, after Paul's "hope" is represented in
26:6-7 as looking forward to what God promised "our fathers
. . . our twelve tribes," Paul immediately characterizes his opponents' position as simple doubt that God can (or will) revive the
dead (in the plural; see below). And Acts 28:20, the final instance
of "national" hope ("the hope of Israel") turns out to be very
similar to the case of chapter 13: since the Jews, or most of them,
reject Paul's message, an exasperated Paul tells them that "this
salvation of God has now been sent to the Gentiles, and they will
listen" (28:28; cf. especially ἀκούοντα δὲ τά ἔθνη in 13:48).[87] If this
same salvation can be offered to Gentiles, as it was to Jews, it must
be that there is nothing specifically Jewish about it.

    Now Acts 28:28, as we have just seen, says that salvation is
something to which one may "listen"; it is, therefore, a message.
But the message is that there is resurrection of the dead. How is
that a saving message? The answer is, quite simply, that the fact
that there is resurrection—a fact to which Paul can bear witness
because, as Acts tells us repeatedly and at length, he has met a
resurrected person—means that none can escape judgment.
Those who believe Paul and take resurrection seriously will
therefore repent and be saved. It is this repentance, this turning
to God before death and resurrection to judgment, that Paul
preaches (14:15; 17:30-31; 26:18, 20; 28:27; see also 15:19
of Paul's converts and 24:16 of his own behavior: *because* he

believes in the resurrection of the just and the unjust, *therefore* [ἐν τούτῳ] he strives always to keep his conscience clear). This is what it means to say that forgiveness of sins and justification are proclaimed through the resurrected Jesus and that all who believe therein will be saved (13:38–39).[88] The Lucan Paul's message is that of Jonah, of John the Baptist, and of Jesus, except that Paul is not thinking of the coming judgment of a single city or nation but rather of every individual.[89]

Conclusion: Luke on Paul and Jesus

This call for repentance before the coming judgment corresponds exactly, as we have just hinted, with the way in which Luke's story begins, with the preaching of John the Baptist. Indeed there is a noteworthy correlation between Paul's call for works worthy of repentance (26:20) and John's (Lk. 3:8); and in much the same way, it seems that the perplexing demonstrative pronoun *this* in Paul's final conclusion that "this salvation from God has been sent to the Gentiles" (Acts 28:28) refers back to the only other occurrences of the word *sōterion* in Luke-Acts, both of which come at the very beginning of the gospel. In the "Nunc dimittis," Simeon, holding the baby Jesus, praises God for letting him see "your deliverance which you made ready in full view of all the nations, a light that will be a revelation to the heathen and glory to your people Israel" (Lk. 2:30–32).[90] And at the outset of John's mission, Luke, alone among the gospels, not only cites Isaiah 40:3 but continues the quotation to 40:5: "and all flesh shall see God's deliverance" (Lk. 3:6; contrast Mt. 3:3; Mk. 1:3; Jn. 1:34).[91]

There are, however, two important differences between Simeon and John the Baptist at the beginning of Luke-Acts and Paul at its end, and both differences point to the thrust of Paul's function in Acts. In the first place, both Simeon and John remain within the framework of the Jewish people. Simeon speaks of a deliverance that brings glory to Israel alone, revealing its special status in God's eyes (cf. Dt. 28:10; Is. 52:10). John too, whatever criticism he may have for those who depend on their Israelite descent alone (Lk. 3:8), still considers the Gentiles as only an audience that will view God's deliverance.[92] But Paul claims God's salvation has been sent to the Gentiles.

The other difference between Simeon and John, on the one hand, and Paul, on the other, concerns not the beneficiaries of salvation but its timing. According to Paul, this salvation has been sent to the Gentiles. Nothing else need happen; they must only listen. Paul, it seems from the end of Acts, is not waiting for any further divine intervention in history.[93] Why not? The answer, I believe, goes hand in hand with our preceding observation. Paul, like John and Jesus, looks forward to a coming judgment and urges his listeners to repent so as to survive this judgment and be deemed worthy of eternal life. But whereas Simeon and John and even Jesus can only believe and hope that it will happen, Paul knows it will. The former, Luke says, were looking forward to a restoration of the people of Israel. They had promises but no empirical proof that it would happen. By the time Luke wrote, after more than a century of Herodian-Roman rule and after the destruction of the temple, it was clear that it would not happen; and Luke's apologetic point with respect to Rome is, as we have seen, the surrender of this hope.[94] This surrender, however, leaves only the resurrection of the dead (as in Daniel 12) as the context of judgment; and of resurrection Luke's Paul has ample empirical experience, as the thrice-repeated story of his call laboriously demonstrates.[95]

In other words, by the end of Acts, Jesus is important for Luke's Paul not for anything special he was (son of God or man or David or the like), nor for anything he taught (as in the gospel), nor for anything salvific accomplished by his death (as in Paul's epistles), but rather for what happened to him after he died: he was resurrected. That fact means that resurrection is real and judgment inescapable. As already in Acts 4:2 ("proclaiming in Jesus the resurrection"), so also in 17:31 and 26:23 ("first to rise from the dead") the resurrection of Christ is proof of the reality of resurrection.[96] In these three verses—and in 17:18, 32; 23:6; 24:14, 21; 26:8, 22–23 as well—the issue is not the resurrection of Jesus but rather the resurrection of the dead in general. The resurrection of Jesus is only a case in evidence. In Athens, Paul's teaching of "Jesus and resurrection" is misunderstood as referring to two things (17:18) but in fact means "resurrection as evidenced by Jesus" (see 17:31).[97] By the same token, when in the very last verse of Acts, Paul's activity is summarized as *proclaiming* the kingdom of God and *teaching* about Jesus, the denationalized and depoliticized kingdom of God means no more than resurrection to judgment, and Jesus is simply the concrete example that Paul may confidently adduce.[98]

We come, then, to our final point. The topic most frequently discussed regarding Luke's "Paulusbild" is the question of Luke's view of Paul's relation to the apostles. Does Luke try to "domesticate" Paul and subordinate him to the twelve apostles, as Günter Klein argued in *Die zwölf Apostel*? Or does he rather put Paul on a par with the apostles, as maintained especially by Christoph Burchard in *Der dreizehnte Zeuge*? Or does he make Paul the disciple of the apostles, as claimed, for example, by Eckhard Plümacher? Or should we agree, on the contrary, with Jacob Jervell, who in his most recent work on the subject argued that Luke portrayed Paul as an "Überapostel"?[99] This argument is perennial, fueled as it is not only by historical and philological considerations but also by debates over spiritualism, apostolic succession, and "early Catholicism" in the canonical New Testament, which may have implications for churches today.[100]

For my part, I would say that the inability to achieve clarity on this point, which is so important for exegetes today, probably indicates that it was not so important for Luke. If he gave three accounts of Paul's call and yet did not raise or settle the question of Paul's relation to the twelve apostles, the point must have been either clear or uninteresting to him. In fact, the manifold and frequently noted parallels in Luke-Acts between Paul and Jesus, between Peter and Paul, or between Jesus and Stephen and Paul seem to indicate rather that Luke was interested in telling a story and that the articulation of the different personalities in the story was not a dominant preoccupation for him.[101] The characters in the story each have a role to play; when that role is completed, Luke's interest in them ceases: if they do not die (John, Jesus, Stephen), they simply disappear (Philip, Peter) or are left hanging in the midst of their own stories, which hold no further interest for Luke (Paul).[102]

Consequently, instead of saying that Luke sees Paul as fulfilling Jesus' mandate to the apostles—and therefore worrying about

whether he considered Paul an apostle, or more or less than an
apostle—we should leave Jesus out and say that Luke sees Paul as
bringing to perfection the transformation of salvation history that
began with John the Baptist.[103] John, who saw himself as a forerunner; Jesus, whose apostles saw him as a messiah and who
preached repentance and comforted the poor but nevertheless
saw himself only as God's agent for Israel;[104] Stephen and Philip,
who, as might be expected of diasporan Jews, undercut the territorial and ethnic limits of Judaism; Peter, whom God directed to
overstep the ethnic limits altogether: these represent the preceding steps and stages of that transformation. Now it is Paul's turn
to continue this line and to take it to its consistent end: if Stephen
and Philip were anti-territorialists in Palestine and if Peter baptized a non-Jew there, then Paul would preach to Jews and non-
Jews abroad and would eventually concentrate on non-Jews alone.
If this transformation required viewing Jesus' messiahship as a
primitive conception discarded along the way—together with the
bounds of the Jewish land and nation—and required treating him
as one of the links in the chain of history rather than its focus (his
body a proof of God's miraculous powers, just as other miracles
gave similar testimony at other points of the story), then so be it.
We must remember, after all, that unlike Mark and Matthew and
even John in his own way, Luke never claimed that his gospel was
the story of Jesus Christ.[105]

Paul in the Writings of the Apostolic Fathers

ANDREAS LINDEMANN

In speaking of "Paul in the writings of the apostolic fathers," we need first of all to specify exactly what we will mean by the two terms *Paul* and *apostolic fathers*. In the context of this inquiry, the name Paul cannot refer to the "historical Paul," known to us as the author of seven authentic epistles written to various early Christian churches and to one individual. We must rather think of Paul as he was understood by the early church at the end of the first century and the beginning of the second. This Paul was the author of the letter to the Ephesians as well as of the letter to the Romans; and he was the writer not only of a letter to Philemon but also of letters to Timothy and to Titus. It is not true, of course, that the complete "canonical Paul" was known to every Christian who mentioned his name or quoted one or two of his letters. But neither is it true that when Ephesians or Colossians or the pastorals were cited, they were cited as "deutero-Pauline" rather than genuinely Pauline texts. These letters were considered as fully genuine as Romans or 1 and 2 Corinthians. As a final point, it should also be noted that for the second-century church, the Paul of Acts was naturally taken to be the "real" Paul.[1]

The term apostolic fathers is applied to several Christian texts written late in the first or early in the second century. Some of these texts were anonymous (e.g., the letter of "Barnabas") or received secondary titles or superscriptions (e.g., the "Didache of the Apostles"). Some were written and circulated under the names of their real authors.[2] None were written pseudonymously (see below). The designation apostolic fathers is actually an anachronism. The idea that any of these authors had direct contact with the apostles is certainly not correct (and perhaps, one might suggest,

25

the name would better fit the writers of the pseudo-Pauline letters in the New Testament).[3]

The writings of the apostolic fathers differ from most of the late New Testament texts in one particularly significant way: the fathers appear openly in their writings; they do not hide their identities behind a famous pseudonym. This fact is important for our study. Unlike the author of Ephesians or of 2 Thessalonians, the apostolic fathers try to convince their readers on the strength of their own theological, ethical, or ecclesiastical argumentation, not by using the name of a widely recognized authority. To say, "I, Paul, write this to you," is to take one approach to the reader; to say, "I, Ignatius, write this, and there are statements from Paul that support my view," is to take a very different approach. And in the case of a pseudonymous letter, it should be added, not only is the name of the author fictitious but so also is the name of the addressee.[4]

Our investigation will center on three authors in particular: the writer of the so-called *First Letter of Clement*, Ignatius of Antioch, and Polycarp of Smyrna. Their works can be dated between about 96 and perhaps 130 C.E. Both Ignatius and Polycarp make their official ecclesiastical position known; they were *episkopoi*.[5] The *First Letter of Clement* is a bit more difficult in this regard. The letter itself states that the sender is the *ekklēsia tou theou hē paroikousa Rōmen*, but the real author—and I think there must have been one author—makes no personal appearance in his work. None of the authors claim any formal authority in relation to the addressees. They did write to churches outside their own jurisdictions, but not in such a way as to suggest that they could or did exercise any kind of controlling authority. In each case, the readers knew perfectly well that the writer was not their own bishop but was the bishop of another, distant congregation. The fact that the authors had no formal authority over their readers[6]—and made no demand for such authority—is of great importance for our interpretation of their writings and especially of their use of Paul and the Pauline letters.

The remaining writings of the apostolic fathers are more difficult to classify. The *Didache*, of course, includes very early traditions, but in my view the redaction of this work belongs to a

more developed stage in the church's history and must have occurred somewhat later in the second century. At any rate, and
whatever the reason,[7] this work shows no contact with Paul or
with Pauline theology. The *Letter of Barnabas* appears to have
been written in the years 130–32. It is not, however, a true letter
written to some specific group of readers. Klaus Wengst describes
it as "ein in Briefform gekleidetes Propagandaschreiben" written
for "ein ideales christliches Publikum."[8] Once again, its author
claims no formal authority, and especially no fictitious authority
drawn from the past (the apostolic name Barnabas does not appear in the text itself). The real authority employed in this writing
is the Bible, the Old Testament, always interpreted in an allegorical manner. The author probably did make use of traditions in
which Pauline ideas were reflected,[9] but it seems to me that he
does not himself show any interest in Pauline theology or in
Pauline texts, whether he knew them or not. The so-called *Second Letter of Clement* is actually a homily addressed to a specific
community of Christian listeners. This community, of course,
was known to the "preacher," and vice versa; but they are both
quite unknown to us. The *Second Letter of Clement* shows no
connection to Paul; and the same is true of the last of the writings
included in the apostolic fathers, the apocalyptic (and parenetic)
Pastor Hermae.

Of the apostolic fathers, only *1 Clement*, Ignatius, and Polycarp mention Paul by name, cite Pauline epistles, and make allusions to Pauline texts or Pauline theological ideas; and only these
three wrote true letters to readers outside their own jurisdictions.
They are the authors, therefore, on whom we will concentrate
our inquiry. The fact that Paul's name is not mentioned and that
the Pauline letters are not used in the other texts of the apostolic
fathers should not be understood, however, as an indication of
open (or hidden) hostility toward Paul. Nor would it be right to
interpret this fact as a reaction of the church against the use of
Pauline texts by (Gnostic or other) heretics. All that we can say is
this: in the first half of the second century, some Christian authors did make explicit use of the Pauline letters and of Pauline
theological themes, and others did not. But of course we do not
even know all the Christian texts written in the early part of the

second century. Thus we are simply singling out those extant writings in which references to Paul do actually occur.

Surprisingly, no other person from Christianity's beginnings is mentioned as often in the writings of the apostolic fathers as the apostle Paul. Peter is named four times. Twice he is mentioned in conjunction with Paul (*1 Clem.* 5.4; Ignatius *Rom.* 4.3). Once he is said to have been among the disciples to whom the risen Christ appeared in the flesh (Ignatius *Smyrn.* 3.2). Only *2 Clement* 5.3–4 hands on a tradition (otherwise unknown) about Peter alone, namely, a little dialogue with the Lord about lambs among wolves.[10] The apostolic fathers, it would seem, knew nothing of Peter as "the prince of the apostles" or as "the rock on which the church is built" (cf. Mt. 16:18). Other than Paul and Peter, no woman or man from the first century—with the exception of Jesus' mother, Mary—is mentioned in the writings of the apostolic fathers, not even James, the brother of Jesus.

More important, the apostolic fathers do not make use of any other New Testament traditions or texts more often (relatively) than they do of the letters of Paul. Sometimes the Gospel of Matthew is said to have been used more often than the Pauline letters, but this is a somewhat misleading impression. It was neither the evangelist Matthew himself nor his book as such that played a special role in the early church, but rather the First Gospel as the supposedly reliable source of the Lord's words.[11] In contrast, when the Pauline epistles were cited or when events from Paul's life and work were recounted in the literature of the first half of the second century, the writers and readers may have known very well that Paul was an eminent man; but they also knew that Paul's letters did not have the same rank as the traditions about Jesus, traditions that supposedly came from the Lord himself. Nevertheless it is clear that Paul's letters were widely recognized in the church, as shown by the distribution of the letters, copies of which also existed in churches to which they had not originally been addressed. And yet, on the other hand, there was still no kind of formal canonization of the Pauline letters.[12] This means that the apostolic fathers were not citing Paul to prove or to secure their "orthodoxy" but rather were quoting Paul's letters "voluntarily." By quoting Paul, they apparently hoped to "impress" their addressees; and they seem to have believed that they could achieve their theological purposes more effectively with such quotations than without them.

The so-called *First Letter of Clement*, a letter from the church of Rome to the church of Corinth probably written in the last years of the first century,[13] mentions Paul twice (in 5.5-7 and 47.1-4). The first passage is of particular importance for our study. After the letter's prescript—which seems to be deliberately "Pauline"—the author begins to discuss the *stasis* in the Corinthian church. Then, interrupting himself, he describes the glorious past of the church of Corinth. The description includes the somewhat strange statement that "every sedition and every schism was abominable to you" (2.6).[14] In 3.1, the turning point is marked by the quotation of Deuteronomy 32:15: "My beloved ate and drank, and he was enlarged and waxed fat and kicked." From this came "jealousy and envy" (3.2), and the author's aim is to demonstrate how "jealousy and envy" give rise to every strife and every dissension. In chapter 4, he gives examples drawn from scripture; and in chapter 5, he turns to the most recent past. "By reason of jealousy and envy the greatest and most righteous pillars of the church were persecuted and contended even unto death" (5.1-2). In 5.3-7, the writer recounts the fates of the "good apostles" Peter and Paul. I believe the author here employs the rhetorical device of *Achtergewicht*—which means that the decisive person in this instance is not Peter but rather Paul, who is called *hypomonēs . . . megistos hypogrammos* (5.7). Paul is not put in Peter's shadow, as Karlmann Beyschlag has argued.[15] In fact, the very opposite seems to be true. Of Peter, the author says only that he "endured not one or two but many labors" (5.4). In contrast, the description of Paul's life and work, although written in a traditional manner, is far more impressive: "seven times he was in bonds, he was exiled, he was stoned." Furthermore, Paul "preached in the East and in the West" and "taught righteousness unto the whole world." Finally, "having reached the farthest bounds of the West," having borne testimony before the rulers, "he departed from the world," that is, he was put to death in

Rome. There is no need to try to specify exactly what kinds of historical detail "Clement" might have known or which oral or written sources he might have used. One point, however, seems clear: Paul is presented to the readers in Corinth as a truly unique pattern of patient endurance. He is the antitype of the Corinthian Christians, who had fallen into *stasis* instead of standing firm in *hypomonē*.[16]

In the following sections and chapters of the letter, the author mentions women persecuted through jealousy (6.2) and enumerates famous persons from biblical history (6.3–12.8), stressing again and again the need for "obedience and submission." Later, in support of this point, he draws examples from nearly every sphere of contemporary life, including even the relation between workers and their employers (34.1) and the structure of military authority in the Roman army (37.1–4).

This principle of "right order" (41.1) is carried over, in 42.1–4, into the idea of "apostolic succession." The "bishops and deacons," appointed by the apostles through country and town, serve according to an order that has its origins in God himself. "Clement" does not claim that the presbyters in Corinth, who had since been deposed from office by a majority (?) of the church, had been invested by the Apostle Paul himself. But he does want to leave with them the impression that this had indeed been the case. The idea of due succession receives additional stress in 44.1–4, in which "our apostles" provided that the *episkopoi* should have successors after their death. These successors were to be chosen with the consent of the whole church, but once appointed, they were to minister for the rest of their lives. In support of this rule, the writer cites biblical evidence (45.1–46.3) and quotes a specific statement of the Lord (46.7–8).[17]

It is in this context that the second reference to Paul occurs, in chapter 47 ("In truth he charged you in the Spirit"). The Corinthians are urged to "take up the epistle of the blessed Paul the apostle" (47.1). Paul had written of the "parties"—the author uses the term *proskliseis* rather than the Pauline key word *schisma*—"founded" by the Corinthian Christians in former times. In effect, the author presumes that the "charge" in the letter of the "blessed Paul" is still valid, and he applies it to the present sedition against the presbyters, an event that has just recently occurred. In this way, he reminds the Corinthians of the recognized and undiminished value of Paul's apostolic authority: from "the beginning of the gospel" (47.2), that is, from the opening chapters of Paul's (first) letter, they are to take instruction for their present situation. And once this reminder is given, it seems that no further argumentation is needed. What comes next (48.1) is the writer's call to repentance.

"Clement" seems, then, to take it as self-evident that he should make use of Paul's letter in support of his own argumentation. Furthermore, he seems to assume that the letter, sent to Corinth some forty years earlier, is still extant in the Corinthian community. Finally, he does not seem to consider it necessary to comment on the fact that a copy of 1 Corinthians also existed in Rome. Presumably he believed that this fact would be well known in Corinth or, at least, that the Corinthian Christians would not find it surprising that there was a copy of the letter in Rome.

Although *1 Clement* takes up a number of theological and ecclesiological themes and discusses them more or less exhaustively, the author seems to have assumed that there were no significant theological differences between the Roman and the Corinthian communities.[18] The one point at issue between them was the question of the ousting of the Corinthian presbyters from their ministry. In this light, it is clear that the references to Paul come at two of the most important points in the letter: first, the writer uses the example of Paul to show the high value of *hypomonē*; second, and even more important, he declares that the apostle, in his own letter to the Corinthians, had already provided the solution to the very problem they now faced. Why is Paul not also mentioned by name in the important passage on "apostolic succession" (42.1–4)? Perhaps the author did not count Paul as one of those who had received the gospel from the Lord Jesus Christ. If that was the case, however, we would not expect Paul to be called an "apostle" at all in *1 Clement*. It seems more likely, therefore, that "Clement" simply included Paul without question among the apostles authorized for the gospel by Christ. What the argument of 42.1–4 apparently shows is simply that the apostolic succession in Corinth, started by Paul's missionary activity, was not a special case but rather followed the general pattern. Thus, as a first result of our inquiry, we can say that "Clement" refers to Paul just where he seems to require the support of apostolic authority in relation to the strife in Corinth.

To what extent did "Clement" know Paul? He obviously used 1 Corinthians (47.1). However, it seems to be impossible to determine whether he also knew of a second letter of Paul to Corinth.[19] The expression "take up *the epistle* of . . . Paul" (emphasis added) yields no answer to the question. It may only presume that everyone in Corinth would understand at once which of the Pauline letters was intended; 1 Corinthians is, after all, the only one of Paul's letters to discuss (and to decide!) the problem of "parties" in the church. It is quite likely, in my opinion, that "Clement" also made use of Paul's letter to the Romans.[20] But a survey of every possible allusion to Romans would be of only limited value. It is more interesting to ask to what degree the author of 1 Clement, in developing his own theological views, shows himself acquainted with Paul's letters and Pauline theology in general. In this regard, four passages are of special interest: (1) the chapters on the doctrine of resurrection (23–27); (2) those on the doctrine of justification (30–34); (3) the instances in which the ecclesiological image of the "body" (*sōma*) is used (37.5–38.2 and 46.6–7); and (4) the prayer on behalf of rulers that appears, within a much longer prayer, near the end of the letter (61.1–2).

(1) The "eschatological section" (23–27) is framed by the idea of God's mercy at the beginning (23.1) and the idea of God's omnipotence at the end (27.4–7). Within this frame, the author, using arguments much like those in 2 Peter 3,[21] warns his readers not to become skeptical in view of the delay of the parousia (23.2–5). Then (in 24.1–5) he sets out to underscore the certainty of the future resurrection, following a train of thought that is—at least in part—distinctly in accord with 1 Corinthians 15.[22] "Clement" does not allude explicitly to Paul here, but it is quite possible that he did not consider it necessary to do so: there is no evidence that the doctrine of resurrection was in dispute in the Corinthian church or that it was a matter of controversy between Corinth and Rome. To us, the story of the phoenix, related in chapter 25, seems strange; but the author uses the myth only to illustrate the magnificence of God's promise (26.1).

(2) The passage on justification (or righteousness) begins with an expression of Paul's idea of what we now call the *indicative* and the *imperative*. The writer formulates the theme in almost classic fashion. "Seeing then that we are the special portion of a holy God, let us do all things that pertain unto holiness" (30.1). The point is obvious: in the writer's view, there is a deficiency of "holiness" in the Corinthian church.[23] The following statement—that Christians are justified "by works and not by words" (30.3)—is no contradiction of Paul (or of *1 Clem.* 32.3–4; see below). It does, however, have to be understood in its actual context, where it is clearly a parenetical expression. Christians, of course, must realize their status of "holiness" by doing works, not merely by speaking words. We should keep Paul's own statement in mind: neither circumcision nor uncircumcision has importance, "what matters is to keep God's commands" (1 Cor. 7:19). The dogmatic aspect of the doctrine of justification is asserted in *1 Clement* 32.4. "We, having been called through His will in Jesus Christ, are not justified through ourselves or through our own wisdom or understanding or piety or works which we wrought in holiness of heart, but through faith, whereby the almighty God justified all men that have been from the beginning."[24] One might again see Pauline influence in the text's opening reference to the "call to faith in Christ Jesus"; and such influence may also be present in the author's tacit definition of the relation between "righteousness by faith" on the one hand (32.4) and "every good work" (or "love") on the other (33.1). Here "Clement" uses the style typical of the diatribe, just as Paul did in the transition from Romans 5 to Romans 6. Unlike Paul, he does not put his argument in *christological* terms but rather, like Hellenistic Judaism, in *theological* terms: it is God—here called *ho despotēs tōn hapantōn* or *ho demiourgos* or *ho kyrios*—who is said to "rejoice in His works," that is, in the creation. But by comparing God and the righteous human being in this way, "Clement" shows quite clearly that he is not a teacher of "justification by works." The righteous produce good works, that is, works according to righteousness (cf. 33.8: "let us work the work of righteousness"), not the other way round.

(3) The great theme of *1 Clement* is the order of the church or, with respect to the Christian individual, submission under

God's will, under "his faultless ordinances" (37.1). The examples used at this point in the letter are the command structure of the Roman army (37.1-4) and the famous image of "the body and its members" (37.5-38.1). The key word *charisma* (38.1) and the allusion to the problem of "the weak and the strong" suggest dependence on 1 Corinthians 12, although the formula ὅλον τὸ σῶμα ἐν Χριστῷ Ἰησοῦ (38.1) seems more reminiscent of Romans 12:4. It is surprising that "Clement" does not employ (in 37.5) the deutero-Pauline image of Christ as the head of the body (since this figure would have suited his ecclesiology very well); and this fact makes it virtually certain that the author was not acquainted with Ephesians. For "Clement," the image of body and members has a specific and concrete meaning. Unlike the author of Ephesians, he is not interested in an ecclesiological theory but rather in the practical consequences of the image for the life of the church—which, in his eyes, the Corinthian Christians had overlooked or ignored. He seems to assume that the Corinthian readers are familiar with the image and that he can thus use it without having to remind them that they had already met it in Paul's Corinthian letter.

When he reverts to the image in 46.6-7, he does not appear to have any one particular Pauline text in mind. After the reference to body and members, he quotes a saying of the Lord—"woe unto that man" who offends or perverts "one of my elect" (46.8)[25]—and applies it to his addressees: "Your division has perverted many, has brought them to despair, to doubt . . . and still your sedition continues" (46.9). *Schisma* and *stasis* are the key words that then prompt the explicit reference to Paul and finally the quotation of his (first) letter to the Corinthians, in 47.1-3. It is not impossible that in chapters 46 and 47, "Clement" is deliberately appealing both to Jesus and to Paul, the two authorities on which the New Testament canon would shortly be based ("the Lord" and "the apostle"). I would not presume, of course, that "Clement" had reflected on this matter at the theoretical level; his chief interest in citing both Christ's word and Paul's letter—as in his use of the body-members image—was practical: he wanted to draw from them concrete instruction for a specific issue.

(4) Near the end of 1 *Clement* we find a long prayer (59.3-61.3), which includes, at 61.1-2, prayer for "our rulers and governors

upon the earth" (60.4). The theological basis for this kind of prayer can be found in the Judaism of the hellenistic diaspora; and the prayer shows the same sort of understanding of the (Roman) state as Paul presents in Romans 13.[26] Nevertheless "Clement" apparently did not make use of Romans 13:1-7 here. One may ask, however, whether his prayer does not perhaps stand close to 1 Timothy 2:1-3. There is probably no literary connection or mutual dependence, but there may be enough similarity to support the supposition that the pastoral epistles were written in Rome (whether earlier or later than 1 *Clement*) and that both texts represent the theology (or, more correctly, the ecclesiology) of the Roman Christian community at the turn from the first to the second century.

What role, then, did Pauline texts and Pauline themes play in the development of the theology of 1 *Clement?* In my judgment, a phrase in 1 *Clement* 12.7 can be read as a typical expression of the theological position of "Clement" himself. In the context of the story of Rahab (Jos. 2)—used as an example of faith and hospitality (12.1)—"Clement" interprets the "scarlet thread" as a prophetic sign "that through the blood of the Lord there shall be redemption [*lytrōsis*] unto all those who believe and hope on God" (12.7). Here, one can see, 1 *Clement* is very close to the traditions of Jewish-Christian soteriology; and it has been said that passages such as this indicate the theological distance between "Clement" and Paul.[27] But in fact, "Clement" could have read such statements about "redemption by the blood of the Lord" in Pauline texts (e.g., Rom. 3:25).[28] And more important, we should remember that 1 *Clement* is not at all a primarily theological or dogmatic text. The writer was not interested in theological reflection in its own right. Rather he was concerned to set out his view (or better, the view of the Roman church) regarding a major error on the part of the majority (?) of the Corinthian church. For "Clement," Pauline positions were of interest only so far as they served the purpose of refuting this error and putting matters to rights. Thus 1 *Clement* actually tells us very little about the strength of Pauline *theology* in the Roman church in the last years of the first century. On the other hand, 1 *Clement* does show that Paul carried great weight in the church of Rome as an apostle and as a teacher of the church in the context of actual conflicts of *ecclesiology*. One might want to deplore the fact that, at the time, such problems—rather than deep theological questions—obviously held the field. But we should not suppose that the theological concerns of Roman Christians around 96 C.E. were dominated *exclusively* by problems of this kind. What, after all, would we think of the theology of Paul himself, if we knew only 1 Corinthians and nothing else that he wrote?

The epistles of Ignatius require a somewhat different approach. They were written under extremely difficult circumstances in a situation very different from that of *1 Clement*: the bishop of Antioch is a prisoner, in the hands of Roman soldiers, on his way to martyrdom in Rome. Furthermore, Ignatius is not writing to address a specific conflict or controversy in the churches to which he sends his letters but rather to respond to churches whose representatives had come to meet him as he was being taken to Rome (the exception is his letter to the Romans). His letters can be understood, perhaps, as the "last words" of a bishop in the face of death. Consequently we cannot expect extensive reference to biblical (Old Testament) texts or to Christian literature.[29]

Ignatius mentions Paul's name in two passages, neither of which has much theological weight. In *Ephesians* 12.2, he praises the church of Ephesus as "the highroad [*parodos*] of those who are on their way to die unto God." A witness is Paul, who, Ignatius states, "was sanctified, who obtained a good report [sc., from God], who was worthy of the highest blessing." The epithets that Ignatius uses are without parallel in the Christian literature of this period, but they do not indicate that he had any special knowledge of Paul. And, of course, Ignatius is wrong when he tells his readers that Paul mentioned the Ephesians "in every letter." But it should be obvious that Ignatius' point is not to give precise information on the frequency of the word *Ephesus* in the Pauline corpus. Ignatius is simply trying to link the Apostle Paul and the church of Ephesus as intimately as possible. Apparently he knew some facts from 1 Corinthians and probably from Ephesians (which, of course, he thought to be authentic). Ignatius also mentions Paul, this time in conjunction with Peter, in a more incidental remark in *Romans* 4.3. "I do not enjoin you, as did Peter and Paul; they were apostles, I am a convict." This conjoining of Peter and Paul is reminiscent of *1 Clement* 5 (see above). Did Ignatius know of such a tradition about Peter and Paul in Rome?[30]

Is any substantial influence of Pauline theology to be discerned in Ignatius' letters? Four Ignatian texts are important in this regard: *Ephesians* 18-20; *Magnesians* 8-9; *Trallians* 9-10; and *Philadelphians* 8. In discussing these passages, my aim will not be to elaborate the literary details but rather to estimate the weight of Pauline tradition and Pauline thought for Ignatius generally.[31]

(1) In *Ephesians* 18-20, Ignatius develops the idea of the paradox of revelation, here understood as "the knowledge of God [*theou gnōsis*], which is Jesus Christ" (17.2). The opening sentence—the cross as a "*skandalon* to unbelievers, but to us salvation" (18.1)—seems to have been composed in distinct dependence on 1 Corinthians 1:18ff., although we have to remember that Ignatius would not have had a copy of 1 Corinthians with him in prison. The incarnational christology of *Ephesians* 18.2 is reminiscent of the early christological formula quoted by Paul in Romans 1:3-4.[32] In calling Jesus "our God," however, Ignatius goes far beyond any Pauline christology. *Ephesians* 19, which is highly mythological in character, contains (19.1) the so-called *Revelationsschema* ("hidden were the mysteries . . . then made manifest to the ages") to which Paul alludes in 1 Corinthians 2:6-9. But what follows—a christology of epiphany—is quite different from Paul's own thought.[33] At the beginning of chapter 20, Ignatius interrupts his line of thought to announce a "second tract" (which was never written) on his christological theme. The remainder of the chapter makes extensive use of Pauline terminology and, in particular, of the "in Christ" formula (including the idea of life "in Jesus Christ"). Thus *Ephesians* 18-20 certainly indicates that Ignatius was influenced by Paul. The Pauline theological categories seem, however, to be presumed rather than made explicit to the epistle's readers.

(2) The passage in *Magnesians* 8-9 is of great interest. It warns against the movement on the part of (at least an element in) the church of Magnesia to live *kata Ioudaismon*; and although it is

highly unlikely, in my judgment, that Ignatius was acquainted with Paul's epistle to the Galatians, he uses surprisingly similar arguments. The first of these ("be not seduced by strange doctrines or by antiquated fables, which are profitless" [*Magn.* 8.1]) actually resembles arguments used by the author of the pastoral epistles.[34] But the next is strongly christological and is Pauline not in the wording of the text but in the theological thought itself: "there is one God who manifested Himself through Jesus Christ His Son, who is His Word" (8.2). Earlier, Ignatius had said explicitly that "if we live after the manner of Judaism, we confess that we have not received grace" (8.1); and "the manner of Judaism" here means walking in ancient practices and observing sabbaths (9.1). The problem addressed in *Magnesians* 8 is not, for Ignatius, what we might call an *adiaphoron*, although the formal distinction between sabbath and Lord's day might resemble one. From Ignatius' point of view, the real problem is the content of the Christian confession (*homologein*). The expression "we confess that we have not received grace" probably means considerably more than merely failing to acknowledge the reception of grace. Ignatius' point seems rather to be that if a person, as a Christian, lives "after the manner of Judaism," that person has made the nonreception of grace the content of his or her confession. That, of course, is a highly polemical position. But Ignatius' theological point seems clear: what he calls "Judaism" is incompatible with the confession of God's revelation in Jesus Christ. The phrase *charin . . . eilēphenai* of 8.1 is reflected in the unique expression *elabomen to pisteuein* in 9.1; and, in this way, grace and faith are closely linked. It is true enough that the details of Ignatius' argumentation in *Magnesians* 8–9 differ from those of Paul's letters. But the theological structure of the Ignatian thinking in this passage does seem to recall Paul, in whose theology it may have originated.

(3) Much the same can be said of *Trallians* 9–10. In this case, Ignatius is combating a form of Docetic christology. He first quotes a creedal formula (*Trall.* 9.1–2): "Jesus Christ, who was of the race of David, who was the son of Mary, who was truly born and ate and drank, was truly persecuted under Pontius Pilate, was truly crucified and died in the sight of those in heaven and on earth . . . who moreover was truly raised from the dead. . . ." Ignatius then goes on to say that God himself "in like fashion

will also raise us who believe in Him" (9.2). His sentence, in my view, shows structural similarities to 1 Thessalonians 4:13–18 and 1 Corinthians 15, two passages in which Paul also moves from the Christian creed to its anthropological and ecclesiological consequences, particularly regarding the question of the resurrection.[35] Furthermore, Ignatius' allusions to his own fate in *Trallians* 10 recall Paul's similar comments in 1 Corinthians 15, especially at verses 32 and 15. Ignatius does not explicitly mention Paul here, for Paul had written nothing directed specifically against Docetism. Once again it is not so much the content of Ignatius' polemic as it is the structure of his theological thought and argumentation that obviously drew its orientation from Paul. But that was not something Ignatius could have made explicit in a brief letter—not to mention the possibility that perhaps he was not himself aware of the similarity with Pauline thought.

(4) In *Philadelphians* 8, Ignatius responds to adversaries who say, "If I find it not in the charters (*en tois archeiois*), I believe it not in the Gospel" (8.2). And again his struggle reminds us of Paul. The opponents declare that they believe in the Christian gospel only so far as it coincides with "the charters," that is, with the Bible (the Old Testament).[36] Ignatius' first reply is to claim that "it is written" (*gegraptai*), apparently an appeal to the Bible as Christianly interpreted. But when this claim is called into question, he changes and strengthens his response. "My charter is Jesus Christ, His cross, His death, and His resurrection, and faith through Him" (8.2). This line of thought, it seems to me, again strikes a Pauline chord and is reminiscent of Paul's own style of theological argumentation (note also the Pauline key word *dikaiousthai* at the very end of *Phld.* 8).

Allusions to Pauline texts or to Pauline themes in the Ignatian letters do not function as did such allusions in 1 *Clement*. The reasons are evident. Unlike "Clement," the bishop of Antioch is not addressing a specific problem of ecclesiology (or, more properly, of church order) in the life of a Christian community. Rather, facing addressees whom he does not know, he is setting forth the core of his theological views and doctrines. His dominant theme is the "unity" or "union" (*henōsis*) of the church; and he can turn to no specific texts of Paul—the pastoral epistles were probably unknown to him—in support of this idea. Furthermore, the people against whose views Ignatius was arguing obviously did not refer to Paul, whether positively or negatively. Thus there was nothing in the situation to compel reference to Paul or use of the Pauline epistles or of Pauline theology. Ignatius, we might say, was making an entirely unforced use of Paul, implicit rather than explicit, without rather than with any special thought or attention. If this view is correct, however, the allusions to Paul are all the more remarkable; they demonstrate just how far-reaching the Pauline influence on Ignatius apparently was.

The study of "Ignatius and Paul" has a long tradition.[37] Comparison of the bishop of Antioch and the apostle to the Gentiles might have been sparked by the bare fact that both wrote letters to several Christian communities and to one individual. Furthermore, as far as we know, Ignatius was the first author after Paul to write to churches under his own name, not pseudonymously. In comparisons with Paul, however, Ignatius usually comes out the loser. Of course, there are reasons for this view. In this regard, however, we should take note of two points. The first is that Paul and Ignatius wrote in quite different external situations. Paul was an apostle organizing an extensive mission. In his letters, he counseled churches that he himself had founded; he had to address their specific problems (theological or pastoral or social), answering questions or responding to information he had received from the churches themselves (the exception, naturally, is the letter to the Romans). He was able to develop a comprehensive theological scheme; or rather, his letters show that he had such a scheme to which he could refer and on which he could draw in particular situations. Of course, Ignatius also had a comprehensive theology. But he did not write in response to specific, concrete problems; as a result his theology appears more theoretical, more abstract.

The second, and perhaps more important, point is that Paul had an authority that was recognized, at least in principle, in the churches to which he wrote. Even in churches in which his authority was doubted or even denied by some Christians (e.g., in Galatia or in the Corinth of 2 Corinthians 10–13),[38] it was still, I believe, a factor of considerable weight. At the very least, it would have been impossible for the addressees to ignore a letter coming from Paul. In contrast, Ignatius probably carried no personal authority for his readers. In his letters, he writes of his own person and of his roles as a bishop, as a prisoner "in Christ," and as a martyr. This forms the basis for his admonitions to preserve unity in the community and to safeguard submission under the bishop. For the special aspects of ecclesiology (or church order) with which Ignatius was concerned, the Pauline letters could not have had great significance. The situation had changed, and Paul— we have to remember that Ignatius apparently did not know the pastorals—did not seem to fit the new conditions on this score. Nevertheless, as we have seen, Paul did influence Ignatian theology, at the implicit if not at the explicit level, in several areas: in christology; in the emphasis given to the idea of grace, especially in the context of ethics; and last but not least, in Ignatius' stress on the meaning of faith for the life of a Christian.

For our question Polycarp, the bishop of Smyrna, is in some respects the most remarkable of our three authors, and perhaps of the authors of the period generally. He was well aware that Paul had close connections with the church of Philippi; and in his letter to the Philippians—whether originally two letters or, as in its present form, only one[39]—he mentions Paul three times.

In the first case, Polycarp explains that he is not writing to the Philippians "concerning righteousness" (*dikaiosynē*, which is, of course, a Pauline key word) on his own initiative, but at their invitation (*Phil.* 3.1). Comparing himself adversely with Paul—a comparison prompted, perhaps, by the term *dikaiosynē*—he affirms that unlike himself, Paul wrote his epistles on the strength of his own apostolic authority. The "blessed and glorious Paul," whose wisdom is incomparable, had visited Philippi. While he was there, he taught the people of that time face-to-face; and when he was absent, he wrote "letters to you, and if you pay close attention to them, you can be built up into the faith given to you" (3.2). The reference to letters (in the plural) obviously poses a question. In my judgment, the plural *epistolas* does not indicate that Polycarp knew of several Pauline letters to the church in Philippi or that he knew that our Philippians originally consisted of two or three separate letters (which, I am convinced, is not the case).[40] What Polycarp means is that Paul's letters, no matter to which community they were originally written,[41] can strengthen all Christians and every Christian community in the present. In this light, he can speak of all of the letters as "written to you," that is, to the Philippians of his own day.

Paul is named again in 9.1, this time only in passing and without any distinguishing epithet. In the context, it is not surprising that Paul is mentioned so briefly. What is surprising is that he is mentioned at all. In a list of present-day examples of endurance, Paul is the only figure from the past.

Finally Paul appears in 11.2-3, part of a section (cc. 10-12) of the letter that exists only in Latin translation.[42] Here, quoting 1 Corinthians 6:2, Polycarp asks, "do we 'not know that the saints shall judge the world' as Paul teaches?" This is the only instance in which a formula of quotation—"sicut Paulus docet"—is connected with a citation from the Pauline epistles; and it is not impossible that the formula was inserted by the Latin translator. The introductory phrase ("aut nescimus quia"), on the other hand, seems to indicate Polycarp's supposition that his readers are acquainted with the quoted sentence, just as he is himself (cf. the Pauline *ē ouk oidate*). Polycarp apparently presumes that 1 Corinthians is well known to the church of Philippi. The general subject of chapters 11 and 12 is Polycarp's warning against *avaritia* and *idolatria* (11.1-2). But he hastens to add that he has not "discerned or heard of any such thing among you" (11.3). The reason that no such problem has arisen in Philippi is apparently that "the blessed Paul labored among you *qui estis in principio epistulae eius.*" Whatever the correct translation of this Latin phrase or the correct reconstruction of the underlying Greek—scholars have offered various conjectures[43]—it is at least clear that Polycarp ascribes the soundness of the Philippian church to the work of Paul, who had spent time in Philippi and had written a letter to its church.[44] Polycarp exaggerates when he says that Paul boasts of the Philippian Christians "in all churches" (11.3).[45] In fact, Paul mentions the church of Philippi only once, in 1 Thessalonians 2:2, and without any boasting. But this "error" does not mean that Polycarp was unacquainted with the Pauline epistles (or with Pauline tradition); it seems rather to be a kind of *captatio benevolentiae* that should not be interpreted too literally (nor, as we have seen, should the analogous "error" in Ignatius *Eph.* 12.2).

Polycarp's letter not only names Paul in these three passages; it is also full of allusions to New Testament writings and especially to Paul's epistles. I will give only a few examples.[46] In 1.3, there appears to be a quotation of Ephesians 2:8-9 ("you know that it is by grace you are saved, not by works"); it is possible, however, that Polycarp is not citing the "Pauline" text directly but rather is making use of a tradition that we may suppose to have been of Pauline origin. In addition, the transition from 1.3 to 2.1 is again reminiscent of the Pauline movement from indicative to imperative.[47] At 3:2-3, one of the passages where Paul is mentioned by name, we find the well-known triad of *pistis*, *elpis*, and *agapē*; and in this case, it is possible that Polycarp had 1 Corinthians 13:13 specifically in mind. There are allusions to the pastoral epistles in 4.1,[48] and the *Haustafel* in 4.2-6.2 alludes to the corresponding deutero-Pauline texts, with a quotation of Galatians 6:7 inserted at 5.1. The warning that "neither whoremongers nor the effeminate nor defilers of themselves with men shall inherit the kingdom of God" (5.3) comes, of course, from 1 Corinthians 6:9-10; and when, at the end of 6.1, Polycarp writes that "we are all debtors of sin," we should note that *hamartia* is in the singular. This linguistic usage, rarely found outside the Pauline literature, is the mark of a substantial Pauline theological influence. Finally, in the next sentence (6.2), we find a quotation of 2 Corinthians 5:10: "we must all stand at the judgment seat of Christ."

It would not be difficult to add examples of the use of Pauline texts or of Pauline theological ideas in Polycarp's letter. Of course, there are also examples of the use of the gospels, and probably of 1 John as well.[49] One might well conclude that Polycarp was not very independent as a theological author but took most of what he had to say from his sources. But the character of his letter may be a function of its purpose. If it was originally a literary unit, then Polycarp wrote only a cover letter for the corpus of the Ignatian epistles that he was sending to the church of Philippi; and if chapters 13 and 14 originally constituted a separate letter (as many scholars, since P. N. Harrison, have suggested), then Polycarp's "Second Philippians" (chapters 1-12) is simply his response to the Philippians' question concerning the problem of *dikaiosynē*. In either case, Polycarp did not set out to write an important theological work, whether he was capable of one or not. We can conclude that Polycarp was probably acquainted with 1 and 2 Corinthians, with Galatians and Ephesians (which, of course, he considered to be Pauline), and with the pastoral epistles or, at least, with 1 Timothy.[50] In addition, he knew that Paul had written a letter to the Philippians, but since he never quotes from this epistle, he may not have known the letter itself.

Did Pauline theology have any substantial influence on Polycarp's thinking? Some expressions in his letter do have a classically Pauline sound, for example, the "in the Lord" formula in 1.1 or the citation of the tradition on the doctrine of grace, which we noted in 1.3. The terminology of the Pauline doctrine of justification, however, does not occur. The Pauline key word *righteousness* is chiefly used in its moral or ethical sense, although there is one significant exception: Christ is once called *ho arrabōn tēs dikaiosynēs*, "the earnest of our righteousness" (8.1). In this case, at least, Polycarp obviously has in mind the eschatological sense of righteousness as the goal of our salvation. Pauline influence can also be discerned in Polycarp's understanding of faith: the content of the creed is christological (2.1-2); Christian faith is a gift given (3.2; 4.2); and faith is the condition of our eschatological salvation, "the inheritance of the kingdom of God" (5.2). Moreover, Polycarp makes deliberate—and not merely incidental—use of the triad of "faith, hope, and love" (3.2-3). When he writes that the person who is "occupied with these" (*toutōn entos*) has "fulfilled the commandment of righteousness" (3.3), he seems to take up—not verbally, of course, but in meaning—the idea that all the commandments are summed up in one rule (Rom. 13:8-10). There is no indication, however, that Polycarp used the Pauline letters or Pauline theology in a highly reflective way. He makes explicit use of Paul only where, for one reason or another, he finds Paul to be needed or to be useful. In this respect, his practice is no different from that of "Clement" or Ignatius. It is just that Polycarp seems to have found Paul useful more often than did the other two writers.

Perhaps we should draw a double conclusion from this review of the early Christian authors traditionally labeled the apostolic fathers. On the one hand, it is clear that they show no signs of interest in extended use of Paul—his letters or his theology—

"in his own right"; nor do they have any interest in what we would call "critical discussion" of Pauline theology (e.g., the writing of commentaries or the drawing of systematic conclusions from Pauline themes). Pauline texts and Pauline ideas were simply employed as needed (so to speak) or where the writer thought it important to call on an apostolic authority in support of his own argumentation. On the other hand, however, it is clear that in the last years of the first century and in the first decades of the second, Paul often was needed, not only in Rome and in Corinth (1 Clement) but also in Asia (Ignatius and Polycarp) and perhaps in Antioch (Ignatius) as well. Furthermore, it is of considerable significance that we could discern—in addition to the explicit references and citations in "Clement," Ignatius, and Polycarp—a far-reaching implicit use of Pauline thought and tradition.[51] There is certainly no basis for the notion that Paul was forgotten or unimportant in the (wing of the) church in which "Clement," Ignatius, and Polycarp did their work.[52]

Comment: Which Paul?

✠————————————✠

MARTINUS C. DE BOER

The Contribution of Andreas Lindemann

Andreas Lindemann's *Paulus im ältesten Christentum*, published in 1979, provides the background for the views he propounds in his essay "Paul in the Writings of the Apostolic Fathers." The earlier study programmatically seeks to call into question the common and prevailing view (based on the work of Adolf Harnack and Walter Bauer in particular) that Paul and his theological legacy became the exclusive domain of the enthusiastic-Gnostic stream of Christianity and that Paul was misunderstood, forgotten, or even consciously rejected by the "orthodox" or "catholic" church, which then only belatedly "rescued" him when Marcion forced the issue in the mid-second century. On the one side, according to Lindemann, Paul (wherever he was known) was from the beginning a constituent element of developing ecclesiastical tradition, and on the other side, he was not the sole authority, apostolic or otherwise, for Gnostic forms of Christianity.[1]

In tracing the image of Paul from the epistle to the Colossians to the *Epistula apostolorum*, for example, Lindemann concludes, "Dass das Paulusbild der Kirche durch den Widerstand gegen den 'Paulus der Gnostiker' bestimmt worden wäre, lässt sich nicht belegen." Similarly, according to Lindemann, the very early redaction of at least three of Paul's genuine letters, the collection of his letters by the turn of the century, and the existence of deutero-Pauline works suggest that Paul's legacy was not lost immediately after his death, at least not in certain geographical areas.[2]

For these reasons, argues Lindemann, the rise of the notion of a canon was tied from the beginning to the assumption that "zu einem solchen Kanon müssten auch die paulinischen Briefe gehören." Marcion apparently forced the church to undertake a reworking, or a reappropriation, of the theological legacy of the apostle, but "für die Annahme, die Kirche sei der Paulus-Tradition in Reaktion auf Marcion mit Zurückhaltung oder gar Ablehnung begegnet, gibt es kein quellenmässig zu belegenden Indizien."[3]

Of particular importance for Lindemann's thesis is the original Pauline mission field of Greece (Macedonia and Achaia) and Asia Minor, where, he argues, there was "eine nahezu geschlossene Paulus-Tradition."[4] A similar claim is made for Rome, the imperial capital, the city where Paul died and to whose Christians he wrote what we know to be his major letter.

Apart from the deutero-Pauline epistles and the book of Acts in the New Testament, the works that provide the primary substantiation of these important theses are the epistles of the three apostolic fathers discussed in Lindemann's essay: *1 Clement*, a letter written on behalf of the church in Rome to the church in Corinth in Achaia; a letter from Polycarp, bishop of the Smyrneans in Asia, to the Philippians in Macedonia; and seven letters of Ignatius, the bishop of Antioch in Syria, five of them to churches in Asia, one to the church in Rome, and one to Polycarp. All three writers explicitly mention Paul (1 *Clem.* 5.5-7; 47.1-4; Ignatius *Eph.* 12.2; *Rom.* 4.3; Polycarp *Phil.* 3.2; 9.1; 11.2-3); and they do so in an extremely positive manner. According to Lindemann, they also make a "far-reaching implicit use of Pauline thought and tradition." Early in his essay, Lindemann points out that the silence of the other apostolic fathers with respect to Paul is not necessarily to be construed as hostility toward the apostle or as deliberate rejection of his theological legacy. The final sentence of Lindemann's essay thus echoes the thesis of his book: "There is certainly no basis for the notion that Paul was forgotten or unimportant in the (wing of the) church in which 'Clement,' Ignatius, and Polycarp did their work."

In light of this basic thesis, Lindemann's primary concern in his essay is to highlight points of contact and continuity between the theological views of the three apostolic fathers and those of Paul, partly as a corrective of those scholars who overplay the points of discontinuity and thereby misconstrue the nature and extent of Paul's influence in ecclesiastical ("orthodox" or "catholic") Christianity between A.D. 70 and the mid-second century. Even so, he does acknowledge, in passing, the discontinuities that have been much more fully discussed elsewhere.

There is, I think, much to be said for an approach that attempts to read the apostolic fathers sympathetically in terms of their own limited intentions and concerns and that takes seriously the particular situations and circumstances in which and for which they were writing. After all, like Paul, these apostolic fathers wrote letters, that is, occasional works addressed to particular audiences at particular times under particular circumstances. The nature of their appeal to Paul cannot be grasped apart from a recognition and investigation of such matters.

A key concern of Lindemann's essay is the "authority" of these writers for their addressees and the way in which they use

Paul (his name and his letters) to establish it. According to Lindemann, none of the three apostolic fathers exercise any formal
authority over their addressees. They write to churches outside of
their own jurisdictions. "The fact that the authors had no formal
authority over their readers—and made no demand for such authority—is of great importance for our interpretation of their
writings and especially of their use of Paul and the Pauline letters."[5] Unlike the authors of the deutero-Pauline epistles, furthermore, these authors do not give themselves authority by hiding
their identities behind Paul's name. The nature of their appeal to
Paul is quite different. According to Lindemann, "Paul's letters
were widely recognized in the church" by the end of the first
century; and the three apostolic fathers quote these letters "to
'impress' their addressees," believing "that they could achieve
their theological purposes more effectively with such quotations
than without them." In short, these writers attempt to give their
letters authority by appealing to the continuing authority of
Paul's letters in the churches of Greece, Asia Minor, and Rome.

What is fundamentally at issue, then, in Lindemann's work
is the nature and extent of Paul's influence on these three apostolic writers. Lindemann's essay indirectly demonstrates that the
matter of "Paul in the Writings of the Apostolic Fathers" is much
more complex than first appears. A key question for me is, which
Paul is being appealed to by these apostolic fathers?

Which Paul?

In his essay, as in his book, Lindemann helpfully distinguishes
between an appeal to the person or name of Paul—a Paulusbild —
and the appropriation of his theological legacy as we know this
legacy from his letters—what we may label the "epistolary Paul."
All three apostolic fathers speak of Paul as (1) an apostle (1 Clem.
5.3; 47.1, 4; Ignatius Rom. 4.3; Polycarp Phil. 9.1); (2) a writer of
letters to churches (1 Clem. 47.1; Ignatius Eph. 12.2; Polycarp Phil.
6.2; 11.3); and (3) a martyr (1 Clem. 5.5-7; Ignatius Eph. 12.2;
Polycarp Phil. 9.1-2).[6] They appeal to Paul, as an "authority," partly
on these very grounds. Indeed they themselves have written letters
to churches, thereby modeling their work on the letters of the
apostle to whom they appeal. Paul is present in the very form that

these works take. But this Paul is not necessarily the epistolary
Paul. We know that the person of Paul, the controversial apostle
to the Gentiles and writer of letters, almost immediately became
(cf. Gal. 1:23; 2 Cor. 10:10) the stuff of legend and seems to
have had an impact on Christian life and thought independent of
(the theology of) his letters per se (cf. Acts). In short, if it may be
said that Paul's theology (the epistolary Paul) exerted little or no
influence on certain writers in sub- and post-apostolic Christianity, a certain image or picture of Paul, with legendary embellish-
ments, may well have.

Furthermore, the epistolary Paul may be defined in various
ways. Lindemann himself begins his essay by pointing out that for
the purposes of his inquiry, the term *Paul* refers to Paul "as he was
understood by the early church at the end of the first century and
the beginning of the second." This Paul is not the "historical
Paul," who, we know, wrote only seven extant letters, but the
"canonical Paul," to whom the New Testament ascribes thirteen
letters. The apostolic fathers did not consider letters such as
Ephesians or the pastorals to be deutero-Pauline. Lindemann acknowledges, however, that at the time the three apostolic fathers
were writing, the complete "canonical Paul" may not have been
"known to every Christian who mentioned his name or quoted
one or two of his letters."

This point seems to me to be of some importance. According
to Lindemann, 1 Clement knows only 1 Corinthians and, quite
probably, Romans. Lindemann specifically denies that the author
knew Ephesians. Ignatius, on the other hand, knew Ephesians, as
well as 1 Corinthians and Romans, but not the pastoral epistles.
And Polycarp knew even more letters of Paul, including the pastoral epistles. Hence, where the Paul of Polycarp may well be the
canonical Paul, the Paul of 1 Clement is the Paul of 1 Corinthians
and, perhaps, Romans, whereas the Paul of Ignatius comprises 1
Corinthians, Romans, and Ephesians. In short, each apostolic
father has a *different* espistolary Paul. Thus, when Lindemann in-
quires about the "influence" of "Pauline theology" on 1 Clement,
Ignatius, and Polycarp, he begs the question: *which* epistolary Paul
is at issue here? Is it the historical Paul, who wrote 1 Corinthians
and Romans (and five additional letters), or is it some other Paul,

the pseudonymous Paul of Ephesians or of the pastoral epistles? Or some combination of these?

Moreover, even where there is evidence of direct access to one or more of the Pauline letters (whether genuine or spurious), it still remains to be seen whether (the theology of) such letters had any discernible influence on the theology of the writers. Lindemann seems to say as much in his concluding remarks about 1 Clement. "The writer was not interested in theological reflection in its own right. . . . 1 Clement actually tells us very little about the strength of Pauline theology in the Roman church in the last years of the first century. On the other hand, 1 Clement does show that Paul carried great weight in the church of Rome as an apostle and as a teacher of the church in the context of actual conflicts of ecclesiology." It seems, then, that it is not the epistolary Paul of 1 Corinthians or Romans who is controlling in 1 Clement's appeal to Paul, but some other Paul, a Paulusbild, a picture of the great apostle whose work and missionary achievements provided the basis for the worldwide ordering of the churches under the leadership of presbyters or bishops (as well as deacons).[7]

It is this Paul who functions alongside another figure, Peter, who is also called an apostle. Paul is first mentioned alongside Peter in 1 Clement 5, where the two are introduced as "the good apostles" (5.3). It seems to me probable that whenever 1 Clement refers to "apostles" elsewhere, even in chapter 42, the author has only these two figures in view. When, in chapter 47, Clement exhorts his readers to take up the epistle of "the blessed Paul the apostle" and refers them to the discussion of the factions around Paul, Cephas, and Apollos in 1 Corinthians 1:10ff., he designates Peter and Paul as apostoloi memarturemenoi, "apostles who have been testified to or approved."[8] The two together "tested" (dokimazein) another man, Apollos, who is not an apostle (47.4). The same verb (dokimazein) occurs in connection with bishops (and deacons) appointed by the apostles in 42.4 and again in connection with those who succeeded these apostolic appointees in 44.2. It thus seems to me that Peter and Paul are the two figures 1 Clement refers to as "our apostles" in 44.1 or simply as "the apostles" in 42.1 who appointed bishops or presbyters and deacons (42.1-4; 44.2-6; cf. 47.6). In any event, there is little

indication that the author wants his readers to think he has
anyone besides Peter and Paul in view in these texts. We thus
have what amounts to an ecclesiastical image of Paul, an image
that is no different from Peter's.

As Lindemann points out, however, chapter 5 appeals to Paul
in a distinctive way. "Paul is presented to the readers in Corinth as
a truly unique pattern of patient endurance. He is the antitype
of the Corinthian Christians, who had fallen into *stasis* instead of
standing firm in *hypomonē*." I wonder only if this needs to be
stated more sharply: Paul is introduced as the supreme example of
patient endurance precisely in the face of "jealousy (*zelos*) and strife
(*eris*)," two words that occur in connection with "envy" (*phthonos*),
"schism" (*schisma*), and "sedition" (*stasis*) throughout 1 *Clement*,
most notably in chapters 42–49. Paul is thus the pattern of patient
endurance for the presbyters who have been removed from office;
and that means that the troublemakers in Corinth, those responsible for causing "sedition," etc., in the contemporary situation, are
cast in the role of *opponents* to Paul (and *mutatis mutandis* to Peter
as well).[9] Since the presbyters were appointed by "the apostles" and
the latter are "from Christ" as Christ is "from God" (42.2), the
troublemakers are by implication destroyers of God's own work.
In short, Paul is used as a weapon in ecclesiastical controversy to
support the author's position and to oppose the troublemakers.[10]
However that may be, it is not the epistolary Paul, that is, the
theology of 1 Corinthians or Romans, that controls or moves
the argument, but is instead some image of Paul, an ecclesiastical
image of Paul, the Paul who along with Peter provided the foundation for church order.

What then about the "far-reaching implicit use of Pauline
thought and tradition" that Lindemann discerns in 1 *Clement*,
Ignatius, and Polycarp? Lindemann will agree that an answer must
take into account the possibility that the *Paulusbild* found in the
writings of these three apostolic fathers encompasses certain theological conceptions or catchwords associated with the name of
the apostle, conceptions or catchwords that may in fact bear only
an indirect relationship to the possible influence of his (genuine
or disputed) letters. For example, Lindemann maintains that Ignatius does not seem to know Paul's letter to the Galatians when,

in *Magnesians* 8-9, he combats those Christians who want to live *kata Ioudaismon*, even though, as Lindemann writes, "the theological structure of the Ignatian thinking," with its appeal to grace and faith, "does seem to recall Paul, in whose theology it may have originated."

More notably, in *1 Clement* 5, Paul is characterized as the one who "taught righteousness to the whole world" (5.7). The previous line speaks of Paul's "faith." When the author discusses justification in chapters 30-33, there is no evident citation from Paul's epistle to the Romans. The author has learned a basic element of Paul's preaching and develops it in his own way, as Lindemann demonstrates. The argument in chapters 30-33 thus does not necessarily indicate familiarity with Paul's letter to the Romans.

We find a similar confluence of motifs in Polycarp's letter, where Paul is first introduced in connection with the theme of "righteousness" (*Phil.* 3.1, 3). Here we are told that Paul "taught accurately and steadfastly the word concerning the truth" (3.2). Righteousness is probably meant here, particularly in view of the context and in view also of 9.1, where Paul is mentioned a second time and Polycarp writes of "the word of righteousness." Polycarp tells his readers that Paul wrote them letters about "the faith given to you" (3.2); and he writes of Paul running (like other martyrs) "in faith and righteousness" (9.2). I suspect that Polycarp could have written these words even if he had known none of Paul's letters, particularly since, as Lindemann points out, Polycarp's notion of righteousness (with the possible exception of *Phil.* 8.1) is quite different from that of the Paul of the seven undisputed letters.[11] It seems to me, in fact, that the whole notion of "*teaching (didaskein)* righteousness," found in *1 Clement* and Polycarp, is a post-Pauline understanding of the work of the apostle, an understanding that has more to do with an image of Paul than with any direct knowledge of his epistolary legacy.[12]

The influence of Pauline theology—as *we* know and understand this theology from Paul's (genuine and spurious) epistles—on these apostolic fathers (and others!) is thus difficult to assess. We have to distinguish between the influence of the theology of the letters and the influence of certain theological traditions associated with Paul's name.[13] As Lindemann points out in connection with

Polycarp's statement in *Philippians* 1.3 ("by grace you are saved, not by works"), it is not always clear what is being cited: a tradition suspected of being Pauline or one of the extant Pauline letters. The fact that in this case the letter being cited (Eph. 2:8–9) may actually be deutero-Pauline complicates the issue further, for the author of Ephesians may himself be quoting a received Pauline slogan.

In sum, the key question raised in my mind by Lindemann's study, as earlier by his book, is *which* Paul? It seems to me there are various ways to speak of Pauline influence, depending at least in part on the way *we* may define or understand Paul (e.g., the Paul of the critical scholars, the one who wrote only seven of the letters attributed to him) or the way the *early writers themselves* define or understand Paul (e.g., an image of Paul that may have nothing directly to do with his epistles, genuine or otherwise, or an epistolary Paul encompassing letters not actually written by him).

For my part, I would like to see a discussion of the influence of the historical Paul (i.e., the epistolary Paul of the seven undisputed letters) carried out in a way that Lindemann only hints at in his essay.[14] In his discussion of Ignatius, Lindemann writes that (the historical) Paul "was able to develop a comprehensive theological scheme; or rather, his letters show that he had such a scheme to which he could refer and on which he could draw in particular situations"; and Lindemann attributes "a comprehensive theology" to Ignatius as well, though "his theology appears more theoretical, abstract," since he, unlike Paul, was not responding to concrete problems. It seems to me that the question of the influence of Paul's theology on these writers, a question that concerns the matter of continuity and discontinuity referred to earlier, entails an attempt to give an account of the controlling theological conceptions of Paul (the historical epistolary Paul)[15] and those of each of the apostolic fathers.[16]

Such an attempt is of course no easy task. Bauer rightly pointed out the "elasticity" of the historical Paul's own views. "In the long run," Bauer observed, "almost any gentile Christian could attach himself to the Apostle to the Gentiles so as to receive legitimation from him."[17] Among the reasons for this phenomenon, we may suppose, is the apostle's propensity for polemically incorporating into his theological argument the catchwords and slogans of

those with whom he is in sharp disagreement (witness 1 Corinthians or Galatians). Complicating matters further are Paul's frequent
use of already existing liturgical, hymnic, confessional, and parenetic traditions, derived from Jewish Christianity and from a gentile Christianity that had begun and would develop independently
of his missionary efforts, and Paul's evident indebtedness to various conceptions and traditions from both the Jewish and the non-
Jewish worlds (e.g., Jewish apocalypticism, Stoicism). Furthermore,
the "particularity" of his letters means, among other things, that
reading them is analogous to listening to only one side of a tele-
phone conversation. Such is not only the case today, but was already the case in the late first century, when Paul's genuine letters
(or some of them) became accessible to our three apostolic fathers,
making the Pauline letters difficult to understand (cf. 2 Pet. 3:15–
16). For us, of course, the letters of these apostolic fathers present
the same problem of particularity as do the letters of Paul, albeit to
a somewhat lesser degree. These factors, and others discussed previously, make the question of Paul's "influence" a very difficult one
to answer. Lindemann's careful and limited study of the pertinent
texts provides a solid foundation for further thinking and research
into the question.

Apocryphal and Canonical Narratives about Paul

DENNIS R. MacDONALD

arly Christian narratives about Paul display little interest in his epistles. Most, if not all, of the narrators seem to have known—or, at least, to have known of—Paul's letters and simply to have ignored them. The burden of this study is to discover why the Pauline epistles influenced the narrative accounts so weakly. The principle genres of Pauline narrative are two, the apocalypse and the *praxeis*, or acts. I shall discuss them in that order, briefly reviewing the apocalypses and then focusing primarily on the Pauline *praxeis*. My contention will be that, in each case, the very genre itself kept the narrative at a distance from the epistles.

Pauline Apocalypses

Stung by the claims of opponents who were apparently seeking to supersede him in Corinth, Paul momentarily gave in to the temptation to boast of his own "visions and revelations."

> I must boast; there is nothing to be gained by it, but I will go on to visions and revelations of the Lord. I know a man in Christ who fourteen years ago was caught up to the third heaven—whether in the body or out of the body I do not know, God knows. And I know that this man was caught up into Paradise—whether in the body or out of the body I do not know, God knows—and he heard things that cannot be told, which a mortal may not utter. (2 Cor. 12:1-4)

Paul's reason for boasting of his visions was to show that he too, like the *hyperlian apostoloi* (2 Cor. 12:11), had experienced such ecstasies. At the same time, however, he insisted that such boasting in revelations is illegitimate, since "power is made perfect in weakness"

(12:9). What Paul heard in this vision no mortal should disclose, for it consisted of *arrēta rēmata*, "unutterable utterances" (12:4).

The warning did not deter later authors. *The Ascension of Paul*, now lost, would seem to be the earliest attempt to narrate what Paul heard in the third heaven. According to heresiologists, it was used by second- and third-century Gnostics.[1] Likewise, the Gnostic *Apocalypse of Paul* from Nag Hammadi claims that the Holy Spirit "caught him [Paul] up on high to the third heaven" and then on to the fourth, the fifth, and finally to the tenth heaven, where Paul greets his "fellow spirits."[2] The author narrates what Paul saw and heard in each heaven. Paul does not descend.

The supreme example of this genre in Pauline apocrypha is a fourth-century Catholic *Apocalypse of Paul*, which was apparently known to Augustine.[3] Its popularity is evidenced by its rich manuscript legacy.[4] The book begins with a clear allusion to 2 Corinthians 12. "The revelation of the holy apostle Paul: the things which were revealed to him when he went up to the third heaven and was caught up into Paradise and heard unspeakable words." Unspeakable my eye! The translation of a reconstructed Latin version of the text extends for some forty pages. It ends like this: "I, Paul, came to myself and I knew and understood what I had seen and I wrote it in a scroll. And while I lived I did not have the time to reveal this mystery, but I wrote it (down) and deposited it under the wall of a house of that believer with whom I was in Tarsus, a city of Cilicia." We are told it was found there intact, along with the apostle's sandals, in an inscribed marble box during the reign of Theodosius the First (*Apoc. Paul.* 1–2).

The author has "the Saviour Christ" greet Paul as "honored letter writer,"[5] but the document contains little evidence of material Pauline influence apart from an ingenious spin given to Paul's discussion of the resurrection body. Paul sees the soul of someone recently deceased who is warned to remember what his old body looked like, for he would have to find it and enter it again in order to be raised at the resurrection (*Apoc. Paul.* 14).

Why do Pauline apocalypses display so little regard for Paul's letters? I suggest that the genre of the apocalypse itself dictated to a large degree that the content be unpauline. Even though Paul himself was profoundly influenced by Jewish apocalypticism, he never wrote an apocalypse. What Paul refused to disclose, Pauline apocalypses did. Quite apart from the particular content of these later apocalypses, once the authors decided to narrate Paul's ecstatic audition, the unpauline move had already been made. The conventions of the journey through the heavens and initiation into the secrets of the "other world" foreclosed the possibility that the letters would have a significant role to play. The apocalypse not only revealed what Paul had chosen to conceal; it also defined a literary context into which the material of the letters did not naturally fit.

Pauline Acts

Without question the most common genre of Pauline narrative is the *praxeis*. In addition to playing a central role in the canonical Acts, Paul is also the protagonist in *The Acts of Paul*,[6] in the first three chapters of *The Acts of Peter*,[7] and in *The Acts of Andrew and Paul*. By the fourth century, *The Acts of Paul and Thecla* had broken off from *The Acts of Paul* and was circulating separately; it was expanded in the fifth century into *The Life and Miracles of St. Thecla*.[8] The account of Paul's martyrdom in *The Acts of Paul* likewise circulated independently and inspired two further recensions.[9] *The Acts of Paul* also inspired *The Acts of Peter and Paul*[10] and *The Acts of Xanthippe and Polyxena*, in which Paul again plays a major part. From the little we know of *The Preaching of Paul* — which is mentioned by pseudo-Cyprian and which is quite possibly the untitled work, to which Lactantius once refers, containing a discourse of Peter and Paul in Rome—it too could perhaps be classified as a *praxeis*.[11] One of the striking features of this library of Pauline fabulosity is, once again, that Paul's own epistles and perspectives are virtually absent. The issue is not merely a disregard of the epistles; the Pauline *praxeis* communicate a theology largely alien to Paul.

Nowhere, perhaps, is the departure from the epistles clearer than in the theological weight attached to miracles. Paul himself, even though he did claim to have performed "signs and wonders and mighty works" (2 Cor. 12:12; cf. Rom. 15:19), as well as to have received visions, was reluctant to trade on supernatural powers as

evidence of divine approval or of apostolic authority.[12] Dieter
Georgi and others have shown that Paul's opponents in 2 Corinthians 10-13—the *hyperlian apostoloi*—claimed special divine status
by virtue of their ability to perform extraordinary signs and to
receive revelations.[13] On the other hand, the Corinthians found
Paul's own presence weak and his teaching unrevealing.

In contrast, Paul's presence in the Pauline acts is anything
but weak. In *The Acts of Paul*, he frequently receives visions; he
reduces a temple of Apollo to rubble; he escapes the jaws of a
lion; and five times he raises the dead to life. In *The Acts of
Andrew and Paul*, he plunges into the sea to visit the nether-
world and returns with a piece of its broken gate. In *The Acts of
Peter*, he paralyzes an adulteress who tries to receive the Eu-
charist; and in *The Acts of Peter and Paul*, he orders the entire
city of Puteoli to sink into the sea.[14] In the canonical Acts, moreover, the story is much the same. Paul blinds Elymas (13:8-13),
performs "signs and wonders" at Iconium (14:3), heals a cripple at
Lystra (14:8-18), survives a stoning (14:19-20), and exorcises a
slave girl (16:18). He is granted a convenient earthquake when in
jail (16:26). Handkerchiefs and aprons that have touched him
heal and exorcise (19:11-12). He exorcises a notoriously stubborn
evil spirit (19:13-16), raises Eutychus from death (20:10-12), heals
a man with fever and dysentery (28:8-9), and survives a deadly
snakebite (28:3-6).[15] The legendary Paul did many other signs
which are not written in this catalogue, but these are written that
you may believe that Pauline *praxeis* are no mere narrative reflections of his epistles. So far as the value assigned to miracle working is concerned, Pauline acts would seem to represent a victory
not for Paul but for his Corinthian opponents.

Various factors, no doubt, contributed to this divergence
from the epistles and to the creation of the legendary Paul. In the
most seminal period for the writing of Pauline acts—between 80
and 180, to which I would date the composition of the canonical
Acts, *The Acts of Paul*, and *The Acts of Peter*—there seems to
have been no established and widespread collection of Pauline
epistles available to Pauline storytellers or guiding what they told.
Furthermore, even if such a collection had been widely available,
it would have provided only a weak narrative impulse in a period

when the controversies so hotly engaged in Paul's own time had lost their fire and become passé. It is possible too that the authors of the Pauline *praxeis* were drawing on a quite different source: orally transmitted stories of Paul performing miracles as did other *theioi andres*, or "divine men," who demonstrated divine status through supernatural signs. In addition to such factors, however, there is also the question of the narrative genre itself. I want to discover what happened to Paul and to Pauline lore when they were poured into the literary mold of the *praxeis*. As in the case of the Pauline apocalypses, I suggest that the distortion of Paul results in large part—although by no means entirely—from the constraints of the genre.

Unfortunately, there is little consensus concerning what a *praxeis* is. In the case of the canonical Acts, scholars have suggested that Luke modeled the work after philosophical biographies,[16] didactic biographies,[17] hellenistic Jewish *antiquitates biblicae*,[18] or hellenistic historiography more generally.[19] Others claim that Luke had no intention of writing a history; instead he adopted the form of a novel[20] or created the first *hagiographon*.[21] Still others argue that Luke wrote with an eye to aretalogies of divine men which recounted their remarkable exploits.[22] The proposals advanced for the genre of apocryphal *praxeis* are equally diverse: the works are apostolic novels modeled after hellenistic romances;[23] they are popular religious aretalogies;[24] they are tales of the romances and exploits of popular heroes.[25] At the end of his excellent discussion of these hypotheses, Jean-Daniel Kaestli concludes, "Our texts [the apocryphal acts] do not correspond exactly to any literary genre of ancient literature [but are] an original creation of Christianity, born from a combination of diverse literary influences."[26]

I entirely agree. Each *praxeis* combines apostolic traditions and various literary influences into its own original and eclectic composition.[27] Nevertheless, I shall argue that in the case of Pauline *praxeis*, at least, the most important literary model is the gospel. Gospels and acts betray unmistakable affinities, most especially in their basic architectures. Both typically begin with a demonstration of divine empowerment: Jesus' baptism in the gospels, the baptism of the Holy Spirit in the canonical Acts and the apostle's commissioning in apocryphal acts. Gospels and acts

conclude with the deaths of their heroes; and the acts characteristically relate the death of the apostle to the death of Jesus.[28]
Between the poles of divine empowerment and death we find
episodic narratives—linked by itinerary—about preaching, controversies, healings, and exorcisms.

To be sure, the acts and the gospels also differ in some
significant respects; and when they do, the acts often betray the
influence of other genres of hellenistic composition. I would
nonetheless insist that the gospels and the (Pauline) acts are more
similar to each other than either is to other contemporary genres.
This hypothesis has been proposed for the apocryphal acts by
François Bovon and for the canonical Acts by Hans-Theo Wrege
(who argues that Luke patterned Acts after the Gospel of Mark).[29]
Both claim that perceived correlations between the death of Jesus
and the sufferings of the apostles, especially Paul, were what
prompted the imitation of the gospels in the composition of the
acts. To develop this proposal, I shall look first at the apocryphal
Pauline *praxeis*; then I shall suggest what the study of these apocryphal acts might imply for the canonical Acts, attributed to Luke
and resident in the New Testament.

EXTRA-CANONICAL PAULINE ACTS

The earliest, most extensive, and most influential of the apocryphal acts that shaped the subsequent Pauline legacy is *The Acts of
Paul*. Three features of this document suggest that it has been influenced by the gospel genre: (1) its narrative architecture; (2) its associations between Jesus and Paul; and (3) its allusions to the gospels.

(1) Assessing the narrative architecture of *The Acts of Paul* is
impeded by the lamentable fragmentation of the text. The Sti-
chometry of Nicephorus reports that the work originally filled
thirty-six hundred lines, eight hundred more than the canonical
Acts. If so, much of the work is still missing. Even so, we know a
good deal about its narrative sequence. After his conversion near
Damascus, Paul receives a command to go to Jerusalem (on the
journey he baptizes a ferocious lion). From Jerusalem he sets
out for Antioch, where he raises a dead boy. He then goes to
Iconium, where he converts Thecla. At this point attention
shifts to Thecla's ordeals and escapes. Then Paul travels to Myra,

where he heals two men and raises another from death. In Sidon he destroys a temple of Apollo; in Tyre exorcises a demon; in Ephesus reunites with the baptized lion; and in Philippi writes 3 Corinthians, escapes execution, and raises a dead girl. Paul leaves Philippi for Corinth and Rome, where he dies. After his death he appears to Nero in a vision.

Even from such an abbreviated précis one can detect structural and thematic affinities with the gospels: a divine, legitimating vision at the beginning; episodic narratives including discourses, travels, and miracle working; and at the end trial, execution, and even a vision of the risen Paul. Of course, gospels do not contain letters like 3 Corinthians, or *Märchen* like the story of the baptized lion, or romantic themes like those in the Thecla sequence; but the basic literary architectures of the two genres are clearly similar.

(2) In addition to the parallel literary depictions of Jesus and Paul, there are direct associations between the two. While Paul is on the ship carrying him to Rome, Jesus comes to him, walking across the sea. Paul asks why the Lord is downcast and gloomy, and Jesus replies, "Paul, I am about to be crucified afresh."[30] The implication is clear: it is in Paul's own death that Jesus will again be crucified; the author as good as tells the reader to see in the death of Paul the death of deutero-Jesus.[31]

This story is similar to the *quo vadis* episode in *The Acts of Peter*, where we read that as Peter was leaving Rome to avoid persecution, he saw Jesus entering the city. Peter asked, "'Lord, where are you going?' The Lord said, 'I am entering Rome to be crucified.' Peter said, 'Will you again be crucified, Lord?' 'Yes Peter,' said he, 'I will be crucified again'" (*Act. Petr.* 35). Peter, recognizing Jesus' meaning, returns to the city and is indeed crucified. After his death he appears to one of his followers.

It is unlikely that the similarities between these two stories derive from oral tradition. The relationship is literary, but it is not clear which version came first.[32] In either case, both *The Acts of Paul* and *The Acts of Peter* indicate that the deaths of their heroes were modeled after that of Jesus. Likewise, in *The Acts of Andrew*, which borrowed from both of these earlier *praxeis*, the apostle is crucified in imitation of Jesus.

(3) The literature cited in a work often indicates the work's compositional pretensions. In the case of *The Acts of Paul*, the author clearly knew some of Paul's letters and the canonical Acts.[33] Most prominent, however, are the gospels, especially the Gospel of Matthew. This influence is visible in the affinities between the beatitudes given in Paul's sermon in "The Acts of Paul and Thecla" and those in Matthew 5, and again in the gospel-like narrative, embedded in discourse, that recounts Jesus' life from birth to death.[34] Other allusions to the gospels are strewn throughout *The Acts of Paul*.

Why might the author have chosen the gospel genre for narrating the life of Paul? It is possible that he simply inherited the genre from the canonical Acts or perhaps from *The Acts of Peter*; it seems to me, however, that this genre was also a natural vehicle for and extension of earlier oral Pauline narratives. In *The Legend and the Apostle*, I argued that at least three stories now included in *The Acts of Paul* once circulated orally, especially among celibate women: the Thecla sequence, the story of Paul and the baptized lion, and that of the martyrdom. To these I would now add the story of Frontina in the Philippi section, preserved only in fragments, in which Paul and Frontina are condemned to die but miraculously escape.[35] All four stories peak in the near-death or death of one of the protagonists—Thecla, Frontina, or Paul. Thecla miraculously escapes the pyre and later a host of beasts. Paul escapes executions in Ephesus with the lion and in Philippi with Frontina, but finally succumbs to the sword in Rome.

There can be little doubt that stories of Paul's execution did, in fact, circulate orally. Papias (in Eusebius *Historia Ecclesiastica* 3.39.8-10) heard from the daughters of Philip that a certain Barsabas Justus, who was forced to drink poison, did not die. This Barsabas Justus also appears in *The Acts of Paul*, in the account of Paul's martyrdom; and what is said of him there squares with the tale Papias earlier recorded. The author of the pastoral epistles was obviously aware of Paul's death when he or she wrote 2 Timothy, since the letter presents itself as Paul's last will and testament.[36] 1 Clement reports that "seven times [Paul] was in bonds, he was exiled, he was stoned," and presents him as "the greatest example of *hypomonē*" by virtue of his exemplary death (5.5–7). Ignatius claims in *Ephesians* that "those who are being slain for the sake of God" are *Paulou symmystai*, "fellow-initiates with Paul" (12.2). Knowledge of Paul's death is also evident in *The Acts of Peter*, which begins with Paul imprisoned in Rome. He is soon released and sails off for Spain, even though it is revealed to him that he must ultimately return to Rome to be "perfected" at the hands of Nero; and again, at the very end of the *Acts*, we are reminded that Paul would soon return to Rome to die (*Act. Petr.* 1, 40).

If stories of Thecla's ordeals and of Paul's tribulations and death were indeed the primary types of Pauline lore available to the author of *The Acts of Paul*, the book as we can now reconstruct it is a linear development of these Pauline legends: it is a Pauline passion narrative with a long introduction.[37] The fascination with Paul's final days in Rome confirms the thesis that Pauline *praxeis* issue from perceived similarities between the careers and, especially, the deaths of Jesus and Paul. These similarities found expression in that literary genre most congenial for narrating the deaths of such Christian heroes: the gospel.

THE CANONICAL ACTS

As in the case of the extra-canonical *praxeis*, I shall argue that the apparent distortions of Paul in the Lucan Acts derive largely from the conventions and constraints of the gospel genre. This thesis faces, of course, an immediate and obvious problem: the absence of a passion narrative in Acts. Since Paul's death is not recorded, the very element that made the apocryphal acts most like the gospels is missing. Before turning to this problem, however, I want to call attention to three features of the canonical Acts that suggest—even without an account of Paul's death—that the gospels exercised a narrative impulse on this work: (1) its allusions to the gospels; (2) its parallelisms between Paul and Jesus; and (3) its narrative architecture.

(1) An author may, of course, cite literature without imitating its genre. When one text displays a dense literary interplay with other texts, however, it is reasonable to suspect that those texts have influenced the composition. The author of Acts obviously

knew the gospels: he or she had already written a gospel modeled after Mark, and it seems clear not only that the Gospel of Luke influenced the writing of Acts as its companion piece but also that Mark's gospel informed Acts directly.[38]

(2) Many scholars have identified parallels in Acts between Paul and Jesus.[39] Nowhere are those parallels clearer than with respect to the deaths of Paul and Jesus. "Jesus' journey to Jerusalem [in Luke] is his movement toward his martyr's death, but it is also . . . a lesson in the realities of discipleship. The journey of Paul in Acts first to Jerusalem and then to Rome analogously occupies a major part of the book (effectively 19:21–28:31) and represents the working out in the life of the model disciple the same journey toward suffering and death that was Jesus'."[40]

(3) These similarities between Paul and Jesus correspond to similarities in literary architecture between Luke and Acts. In this case too, scholars have demonstrated the parallels so frequently that it seems superfluous to delineate them all over again.[41] A partial listing, including Mark along with Luke and Acts, should suffice to show the degree to which these three works share a common structure (see chart on p. 65).

In spite of these contacts between the gospels and the canonical Acts, few scholars have gone so far as to suggest that the closest generic relatives to Acts are the gospels.[42] The major reason for this reluctance, obviously enough, is the absence in Acts of a passion narrative, generally considered the sine qua non of the gospel genre. I shall argue that Luke intentionally suppressed a story of Paul's death in order to avoid the implication of political antagonism to Rome and in order to make the book open-ended. He intended the reader to look for a story of Paul's death and to be surprised at not finding one.[43]

It is certain that the author of Acts knew of Paul's execution in Rome. He has Paul forecast his imprisonment and death to the elders of Ephesus at Miletus (20:23) and claim that he is willing to die at Jerusalem (21:11–14); and the last chapter clearly anticipates Paul's death after his two years of teaching in his rented quarters in Rome (28:30–31). In fact, I would maintain that the author anticipates Paul's death throughout the work by keeping Paul under constant threat of death from the beginning.[44] The

	Mark	Luke	Acts
Preface	1:1	1:1–4	1:1–5
Preparation of actor(s) and baptism	1:2–15	1:5–4:15	1:6–2:13
Call of disciples	1:16–20	(5:1–11)	(1:12–26)
Sermon at beginning of ministry	(6:1–6)	4:16–30	2:14–40
Ministry	1:21–9:50	4:31–9:50	3:1–19:20
[Compare:]	2:1–12	5:17–26	3:1–10
[Compare:]	—	7:1–10	10:1–48
Journey to Jerusalem	(8:27–9:50)	9:51–19:27	19:21–21:15
Resolves to go to Jer. to suffer	—	9:51–53	19:21 (cf.21:13)
At Jerusalem	10:1–16:8	19:28–21:38	21:16–26:31
Positive reception	11:1–10	19:37	21:17–20
Conflict in temple	11:11–19	19:45–48	21:26–22:29
Legal proceedings	14:53–15:20	22:1–23:49	22:30–26:32
1. Sanhedrin	14:53–68	22:63–71	23:1–35
hero slapped	14:67	22:63–64	23:2
2. Pilate/Felix	15:1–5	23:1–5	24:1–27
3. Herod/Festus	—	23:6–12	25:1–27
4. Pilate/Herod Agrippa	15:6–15	23:13–25	26:1–32
willing to release hero	—	23:16, 22	26:32
Death of hero	15:21–41	23:50–24:53	Paul leaves for Rome; death anticipated
Burial and resurrection	15:42–16:8	23:50–24:53	—

reader is never allowed to forget that Paul's career, even more than Jesus', was played out in the shadow of death.

Why, then, is there no narration of the death itself? I am convinced that Luke deliberately attempted to avoid or suppress the political radicalism, the antagonism to Rome, that could attach itself to Paul's execution. That stories of Paul's death could communicate this message is apparent from *The Acts of Paul*. According to this account, Paul hires a barn outside Rome in which to preach. Nero's cupbearer, Patroclus, arrives late at the barn and, unable to find a place inside, sits at a high window to hear Paul's teaching; but he falls from the window and dies, and the news is immediately carried to Nero. When he is raised back to life, he tells the emperor that "Christ Jesus, the king of the ages" who will destroy all kingdoms under heaven, raised him. Patroclus, Barsabas Justus, Urion, and Festus, all of whom are in the emperor's service, confess to Nero that they are soldiers of this "king." Nero orders them to be executed and asks Paul how he dared "to come secretly into the empire of the Romans and enlist soldiers." Paul answers that he enlists soldiers for his king from the whole world. If Nero does not repent, he too will perish when Christ destroys the world with fire. Paul is then beheaded, and his ghost returns to haunt Nero. The political volatility of the story is plain to see. The church is presented as the empire's counterpart and competitor; it has its own emperor and its own soldiers and is assured of its eschatological victory. No one can serve Christ and Caesar.[45]

We have no way of knowing whether Luke knew of stories of Paul's martyrdom that scored against Rome.[46] My guess is that he did, a guess informed not only by the actual circulation of such stories somewhat later but also by Luke's obvious embarrassment at the political dimensions of the Markan passion narrative. Luke obviously could not avoid recounting the death of Jesus, as he could the death of Paul; instead, he repeatedly chipped away at Mark's account to blunt its political edge. His goal was to shift responsibility for Jesus' death away from the Romans and exclusively onto the Jews. Many of Luke's alterations in Mark's passion narrative correspond with his depictions of Paul in Acts; they also suggest why he failed to record Paul's death: it was too politically potent.[47]

For example, Luke places the beating of Jesus by the Jewish authorities prior to the trial, not after it, as in Mark (Lk. 22:63–65). Likewise in Acts, Jews in the temple assaulted Paul without giving him the right of trial (21:27–36). Again Luke adds to Mark three specific Jewish charges against Jesus, all of them political: (1) that he stirred up the people, (2) that he forbade tribute to Caesar, and (3) that he called himself a king (Lk. 23:2). The reader knows these charges are false: it is the Jews themselves who caused the disturbances; Jesus spoke ambiguously about tribute (cf. Lk. 20:25); his kingship is not political. The first and third of these charges are also lodged against Paul in Acts, and once again the reader is to assume they are without foundation (17:6–7). Twice in Luke, without parallels in Mark, Pilate pronounces Jesus innocent (Lk. 23:4 and 22). In Acts, Paul too is declared innocent by Roman functionaries (25:28, 25a; 26:30–32). Luke has Pilate send Jesus to Herod, a half-Jew; and Herod's soldiers, not Pilate's, are the ones who torture Jesus. Notice also that they do not dress Jesus up as a mock king in the way that Pilate's soldiers do in Mark. Likewise in Acts, Roman authorities never beat Paul; in fact, they repeatedly rescue him from Jewish violence (18:12–17; 21:31–32; 23:12–35). In Luke, the final verdict on Jesus pronounced by a Roman is the word of the centurion, altered from Mark: "truly this man is innocent" (Lk. 23:47). The last verdict spoken on Paul by political authorities in Acts is the same: "They said to one another, 'This man is doing nothing to deserve death or imprisonment.' And Agrippa said to Festus, 'This man could have been set free if he had not appealed to Caesar'" (26:31a–32).[48] As Henry Cadbury noted, Paul's "journey to Rome is recorded not as the commitment of a criminal, but as the appeal to the supreme court of an innocent man enjoying from Roman officials all the privileges of citizenship."[49]

There are two telling stories in Acts, almost certainly dependent on personal observation or more likely on oral tradition, for which Paul's epistles provide a point of comparison and in which Luke again seems to have shifted the blame for Paul's persecutions from political authorities onto Jews. In 2 Corinthians 11:32–33 Paul claims to have escaped from Damascus by basket, thereby eluding "King Aretas," that is, the Nabatean Aretas IV. When

Luke tells the same story in Acts 9:19–25, he says nothing whatever about Aretas, claiming instead that those who "were watching
the gates day and night" were *hoi Ioudaioi*.[50] Again, in Acts 17:1–9,
Luke reports that Thessalonian Jews gathered a crowd against Paul
and Silas and accused them of sedition before city authorities.
From Paul's correspondence with the Thessalonians, however, it
would appear that the persecutions in Thessalonica had nothing
whatever to do with the Jews but instead involved gentile neigh-
bors (see 1 Thes. 2:14: "from your own countrymen"). External
evidence for Jews in Thessalonica is nonexistent prior to the
fourth century, rendering it all the more unlikely that Jews could
have instigated widespread turmoil in the first century.[51]

Thus Luke's alterations of tradition, whether with respect to
Jesus' passion or with respect to Paul's experience, demonstrate
his desire to erase earlier memories of conflicts between the
church and Rome.[52] "Throughout his writings Luke has carefully,
consistently, and consciously presented an *apologia pro imperio* to
his church. Where he found anti-Roman innuendos in his
sources he has done his best to neutralize such materials and to
emphasize the positive aspects of Roman involvement in the history of the church."[53] The silence on the execution of Paul at the
end of Acts is consistent with this political redaction in the rest of
the work; and it has the peculiar effect of making the Pauline
portion of the canonical Acts a long introduction without a concluding passion narrative. Instead of a passion narrative, we find
Paul "preaching the kingdom of God and teaching about the Lord
Jesus Christ" (28:31). The final words of Luke-Acts are, "with
all boldness, entirely unhindered." In other words, Rome found
nothing whatever objectionable about Paul's preaching of the
Kingdom of God. Even in Rome, Paul's troubles were due to unrepentant Jews (28:17–29). But this ending does not negate the
influence of the gospel genre on the canonical Acts. Rather, it
plays upon it; the ending derives its power precisely from the
reader's surprise not to read of Paul's death.[54]

Conclusion

In this study, I have argued that the distortions of Paul and
the apparent disregard of his epistles in early Christian narratives

about Paul derive in large part from literary considerations. Both primary genres of Pauline narrative, apocalypses and *praxeis*, dictate to a large degree that the content be unpauline. It is the business of an apocalypse to reveal hidden mysteries in writing, something Paul did not do. With respect to Pauline *praxeis*, it is clear that their authors borrowed tale-types, motifs, conceits, and themes from various genres of contemporary composition—most obviously romances and aretalogies of great historical personalities—but the primary genre informing them was the gospel. The powerful hold of the gospel genre on the early Christian imagination ineluctably reshaped Paul into a second Jesus and the acts into apostolic gospels. Since the gospels characteristically contain, *inter alia*, miracle stories and visions, Pauline acts likewise include them, even though Paul himself devalued such teratological logic. Much the same can be said for the acts of Peter, of John, of Andrew, and especially of Thomas, Jesus' twin.[55]

The impulse for the adaptation of the gospel genre may well have come from preliterary legends about Paul that told of his sufferings and martyrdom, such as those now contained in *The Acts of Paul*. The author of the canonical Acts knew such stories and sometimes altered them to express antagonism for Jews or, as in the case of Paul's execution, omitted them to avoid their political radicalism.[56] He preferred to depict Paul preaching the kingdom of God in Rome "entirely unhindered."

Although it is true that Pauline *praxeis* misrepresent Paul's theology, they also, by retelling stories of Paul's death, articulate a fundamental Pauline insight, namely that suffering is a consequence of following Jesus the Christ.[57] To the Thessalonians, Paul wrote, "you became imitators of us and of the Lord, for you received the word in much affliction" (1 Thes. 1:6). To the Corinthians: "we share abundantly in Christ's sufferings so through Christ we share abundantly in comfort also" (2 Cor. 1:5; cf. 4:8–12). To the Philippians: "That I may know him and the power of his resurrection, and may share his sufferings, becoming like him in his death, that if possible I may attain the resurrection from the dead" (Phil. 3:10–11).

Pauline tradition soon interpreted Paul's death as the fulfillment of this desire to become like Christ in death. For example,

the author of Colossians has Paul say, "I rejoice in my sufferings
. . . and in my flesh I complete what is lacking in Christ's afflictions" (1:24). Surely it is not accidental that pseudo-Pauline
epistles usually present themselves as prison letters and comment
on Paul's suffering.[58] Narrators of Paul's life underscored his
death as an emulation of the death of Jesus and encouraged their
readers to the *imitatio Christi* by way of the *imitatio Pauli*.[59] In
doing so, they molded the story of Paul to the gospel genre, and
thereby distorted his memory. His reluctance to boast in visions
and miracle working was overridden by the desire to make Paul
into a deutero-Jesus. The theological concerns of the epistles are
now missing, except as clichés. But we must not be too harsh on
these storytellers; in their *praxeis*, they echo Paul's own exhortation: "Be imitators of me as I am of Christ" (1 Cor. 11:1).

Comment:
What Does Unpauline *Mean?*

✠——————————————✠

STANLEY K. STOWERS

Early Christian narratives about Paul, Dennis MacDonald
argues, do not reflect or reproduce the Paul of the letters.
Instead, the narratives highlight Paul as miracle worker and
martyr, producing portraits of Paul that distort the genuine Paul
and his theology. The major cause of this distortion is to be found
in the constraints of the acts genre, a kind of apostolic gospel that
has the effect of forcing Paul into the mold of the Jesus of the
gospels. These are interesting and challenging historical and literary theses.

Two questions are basic to the paper: what does and what does not count as genuinely Pauline? To what genre or genres do the gospels belong? Framed according to MacDonald's approach, the first question comes out like this: what makes the valorization of miracles and martyrdom a distortion of Paul? MacDonald writes:

> Nowhere, perhaps, is the departure from the epistles clearer than in the theological weight attached to miracles. Paul himself, even though he did claim to have performed "signs and wonders and mighty works" (2 Cor. 12:12; cf. Rom. 15:19), as well as to have received visions, was reluctant to trade on supernatural powers as evidence of divine approval or of apostolic authority. Dieter Georgi and others have shown that Paul's opponents in 2 Corinthians 10–13—the *hyperlian apostoloi*—claimed special divine status by virtue of their ability to perform extraordinary signs and to receive revelations. On the other hand, the Corinthians found Paul's own presence weak and his teaching unrevealing.

There is, however, other evidence about Paul's valuation of the miraculous. In Galatians 3:5, Paul appeals to the Galatians' experience of conversion and asks: "Does he who supplies the spirit to you and works miracles (*dynameis*) among you do so by works of the law, or by the message about faithfulness?" Again, speaking of his missionary work in 1 Corinthians 2:4, he writes: "my speech and my message were not in persuasive words of wisdom, but in demonstration of spirit and of power (*dynameōs*)." 1 Thessalonians 1:5 reads: "our gospel came to you not only in word but also in power (*en dynamei*) and the Holy Spirit." It is clear that Paul did place a high valuation on the miraculous and that he saw miracles as essential to his missionary task. "I will not venture to speak of anything except what Christ has wrought through me to win obedience from the Gentiles, by word and deed, by the power of signs and wonders (*en dynamei sēmeiōn kai teratōn*), by the power of the Holy Spirit, so that from Jerusalem and as far round as Illyricum I have fully preached the gospel of Christ" (Rom. 15:18–19).

As for 2 Corinthians 10–13, I find Georgi's interpretation unpersuasive. His exegesis is only possible with the most undisciplined mirror-reading of the text; and even then, it cannot reverse the plain sense of 2 Corinthians 12:12. Paul was not inferior to the superlative apostles: "The signs of a true apostle were performed among you in all patience, with signs and wonders and mighty works (sēmeiois te kai terasin kai dynamesin)." Morton Smith has shown that what he calls the magical—and most New Testament scholars would call the miraculous—is present in several generally unrecognized texts.[1] When one adds visions, prophecy, gifts of miracle working among the body's members, speaking in tongues, and miraculous endurance of sufferings, it becomes difficult to deny that the miraculous occupies a prominent place in Paul's letters. I see no reluctance in Paul to trade on the miraculous as long as the miracles are attributed to God's power and not to his own skills and abilities; and I doubt that the writers of the narratives about Paul would have claimed anything else.

With the exception of gadflys like Morton Smith, scholars generally relegate the miraculous to the background in New Testament studies. That is part of the unconscious heremeneutic of contemporizing the scriptures for the church. But we cannot expect ancients to employ our rationalistic ways of reading texts. What would a second-century Asian presbyter have imagined on reading Paul's statement that his missionary success was due to miracles that he performed through God's power? In all likelihood the presbyter would have imagined a pattern of missionary work very much like what we have in The Acts of Paul. Who more distorts the "genuine Paul," the ancient writer who tried to imagine what these remarkably persuasive miracles were like, or the modern scholar who systematically de-emphasizes something that is pervasive in Paul's thought and important to his self-understanding?

The weight that the narratives about Paul attach to his martyrdom and the way that they liken it to Jesus' passion are also, in MacDonald's view, distortions of the genuine Paul. This treatment of Paul's death, he argues, is the result of molding Paul to the gospel genre. There is no need, however, for an appeal to the gospels to explain the emphasis on Paul's martyrdom in The Acts of Paul. That emphasis can be accounted for, quite apart from the gospels, on the basis of Paul's own letters and wider Jewish and Greco-Roman traditions.

Paul's interpretation of his own sufferings and his theology of Jesus' martyrdom provide a base from which to start. The two are clearly linked, as 2 Corinthians 1:5 shows: "we share abundantly in Christ's sufferings." In 2 Corinthians 4:10–11, Paul writes of apostolic suffering: " . . . always carrying in the body the death of Jesus, so that the life of Jesus may also be manifested in our bodies. For while we live we are always being given up to death for Jesus' sake, so that the life of Jesus may be manifested in our mortal flesh." And in 1 Thessalonians, he describes the Thessalonian Christians as imitators of himself and of the Lord in the way that they received the word with great joy in affliction (1:6; cf. 2:14). In Philippians 1:20, he is sure that Christ will be honored in his body, whether he lives or dies.

There is, of course, much dispute about how to understand such passages and relate them to each other. Work done by several scholars in the last few years has, however, uncovered a tradition that seems to make Paul's thought highly comprehensible.[2] Paul understands the meaning of Jesus' death in conceptualities drawn from a martyrological tradition seen in a great number of Greek writings and in Jewish literature as well, most notably 4 Maccabees. According to this tradition, God regards the suffering and death of the heroically faithful and obedient martyr as a purification, ransom, and propitiation. For Paul, Jesus is the ultimate martyr; and those who display a faithful obedience like his share in the benefits of his death. Paul's language about his own sufferings and his reflections on his death also draw on this martyrological tradition.[3] Imitation of Christ's passion reflects, for Paul, what it means to participate in Christ's death.

Thus it is hardly a distortion of Paul's theology when, after Paul's actual martyrdom, the writers of Colossians, Ephesians, and the pastoral epistles focus on Paul's suffering and death. The martyrological tradition, to which Paul gave a unique shape in his letters, makes perfect sense of Colossians 1:24, "Now I rejoice in my sufferings for your sake, and in my flesh I complete what is lacking in Christ's afflictions for the sake of his body the church."

When one adds to this the extremely important place that
heroic death holds in Greek literature, it seems unnecessary to
suppose that the fascination with Paul's martyrdom derived from
forcing him into the mold of the canonical gospels. I can think of
nothing in Greek literature that is better documented than the
obsession with noble death revolving around the themes of sacrifice for the fatherland, heroic death for truth and piety, and
suffering on account of *philanthropia*. The figures of Socrates,
Antigone, Heracles, Iphigenia, Alcestis, and Menoeceus—a ran-
dom few—generated many dozens of dramas and narratives about
heroic death.

Here the genre question arises. Are the Pauline narratives
Pauline gospels, that is, passion narratives with long introductions? If "passion narrative with a long introduction" is construed
so broadly that about half of the tragedies of Euripides would fit,
then the answer is "yes." But if we look more narrowly for the
generic relations of a complex pattern of thematic, stylistic, and
rhetorical traits, then the gospels might be at best only one relative of the Pauline acts. MacDonald has pointed to genuine and
important similarities between gospels and acts, but determining
genre is a matter of locating a particular work in the whole field
of a culture's literary production. Work on generic description of
the gospels has been hindered by the gross romanticism of Franz
Overbeck, Karl Ludwig Schmidt, and much of the form-critical
tradition. We can no longer hold the fantasy that the gospels were
unique creations of the church (although in one sense, of course,
every piece of literature is unique). We cannot say how determina-
tive the gospels were for the various acts of Paul until we have
located the gospels themselves in the larger world of Greco-
Roman literature. Certainly there are similarities between the
gospels and the acts of Paul, but are they the closest generic
similarities we can find? And would they have been the most
culturally pervasive similarities?

MacDonald gives three arguments for his thesis that the
Pauline acts are most closely modeled on the gospels: narrative
architecture, the association of Jesus with Paul, and allusions to
the gospels. The last is, in itself, irrelevant to genre considerations; any kind of literature can contain allusions to any other

kind of literature. I have already suggested that the impulse to associate Paul with Jesus, especially in regard to suffering and death, probably stems from a reading of Paul's own letters and the letters of the Pauline school. The important consideration, then, is literary architecture.

MacDonald emphasizes that both gospels and acts begin with divine empowerment and end with the hero's death. Again, I would argue, this is a sound and useful observation; but it corresponds to a phenomenon so literarily pervasive that it may not be very helpful with regard to the determination of narrative genre. The empowerments—Jesus' baptism, Pentecost in the canonical Acts, and Paul's conversion in *The Acts of Paul* —are what literary theorists since the Russian formalists have called the contract: an arrangement between the hero and a superior power, which occurs near the beginning of the narrative. The death of the hero, of course, belongs to the narrative's ending. MacDonald is, I believe, correct in arguing that the canonical Acts deleted Paul's death for apologetic reasons. But that move in itself dramatically separates Acts from the main martyrological tradition, where boldly taking on any and all authorities is central (for example, *The Acts of Paul and Thecla*). I cannot imagine *The Acts of the Pagan Martyrs* or *Fourth Maccabees* deleting an incident for apologetic reasons. The canonical Acts is different.

Let me briefly suggest that a useful way to distinguish the synoptic gospels and the Pauline acts is to describe the gospels as encomiastic narrative and the acts as romantic narrative. The two are constructed differently. The encomiastic narrative of the gospels grows directly out of didactic, epideictic rhetoric. Except for the prologues of Matthew and Luke and the passion narratives, the gospels are composed of *chreiai* and *gnomai* elaborated in ways taught in the *progymnasmata*. Plot is minimal and its sequential element lacks dynamic qualities. This is why there is so much truth to the idea that the gospels are passion narratives with extended introductions. The plot lies almost entirely in the passion and its context of meaning (although Matthew and Luke do broaden the biographical aspect by adding birth narratives). The encomiastic narrative with its minimal plot and construction out of *chreiai* and *gnomai* is well known from

Greco-Roman literature. The acts are quite different. In them, plot is fundamental. Typically the subplots of their episodes are tied together in a narrative framework based on the hero's travels. Episodes do not have the form of elaborated *chreiai* where story is subordinated to didactic rhetoric; instead story is everything. Thus the similarities between gospels and acts may be less impressive—or, at least, no more impressive—than their differences. Both gospels and acts are narratives, but narratives of quite different sorts.

Finally, MacDonald's study raises for me the question of what it means to look for the genuine Paul. What does *unpauline* mean?

1. Does *unpauline* mean that Paul would not have done or said whatever is reckoned unpauline in his own time and circumstances? What about other times and circumstances? Would that Paul be the Paul we know or someone else? In asking these questions are we trading on romantic and essentialist conceptions of authorial intentionality? We cannot look into Paul's mind. Did everything he write have just one legitimate implication?

2. Does *unpauline* mean something that contradicts beliefs and practices that are explicitly valorized in his letters? How do we know that the valorizations are to be universalized beyond the immediate circumstances of their utterance?

3. Are secondary implications and deductions from Paul's statements unpauline? Paul may not have emphasized martyrdom in quite the same way as *The Acts of Paul*, but can one speak of logical implications? The romantic literary motifs and the fabulous elements in the later depiction of Paul's miracles are certainly fictional, but at what point does such material become illegitimate literary and theological fictionalization? I am convinced that if Paul himself had written an autobiographical narrative, it would almost certainly have been considered unpauline by New Testament scholars. In all likelihood it would show little interest in his letters.

4. Does *unpauline* mean a "theology" alien to Paul? But Paul did not write a theology. What would be its organizing

principle? Its center? Imagining Paul's theology is always a highly constructive secondary activity.

5. Is saying that something is *unpauline* a normative theological statement which means: in my tradition's appropriation of Paul, "x" is unpauline? This may be one of the most realistic perspectives. There is no Archimedean point. In reality the modern historian's account of Paul's career and theology is, like those of the writers of Pauline acts, based on imaginative narrative constructions. There are, of course, better and worse imaginative reconstructions, but all are constructions. I am convinced that the post-Reformation construction of Paul in terms of theological controversy is highly anachronistic; and I would argue that to highlight theological controversy is not so very Pauline and that to emphasize miracles and martyrdom in Paul is not unpauline.

Above all, I believe that determining what is Pauline and what unpauline is an extremely difficult task that most of us do without much critical reflection. MacDonald's work is commendable for balancing scholarly imagination with critical reflection.

Irenaeus' Use of Paul in His Polemic Against the Gnostics

RICHARD A. NORRIS, JR.

Not a great deal has been written, of a systematic sort, about Irenaeus' use or interpretation of Paul since the influential 1889 monograph of Dr. Johannes Werner.[1] Such work as has appeared, moreover, has most often touched on Irenaeus' part in the reception of the Pauline corpus as an element in the emerging New Testament canon; and in this connection a great deal of stress has been laid on his role as a legitimizer or domesticator of the Pauline and deutero-Pauline letters at a time when, as it has seemed, their principal advocates and exponents were followers of Marcion or of Valentinus.[2] By contrast, less attention has been directed to the question of what sense Irenaeus himself made of the apostle's writings. Even when this task has been undertaken, moreover, the method adopted has as often as not been, in effect, that of testing Irenaeus' understanding of Paul by reference to Luther's, or Calvin's, or even F. C. Baur's.[3]

It seems apparent, however, even from a cursory reading of the treatise *Adversus haereses*, that Irenaeus, as he cites, alludes to, and muses over Paul's writings, is not merely engaged, as Werner thought, in an unwelcome apologetic task that circumstance had more or less forced on him. To be sure, he is committed to establishing the thesis that the Apostle Paul was neither an explicit Marcionite nor a concealed Valentinian. If, however, one surveys Irenaeus' references to the Pauline corpus, it quickly becomes apparent that the majority of them serve no merely defensive purpose. No doubt they function—at least as we encounter them— in the setting of a polemical enterprise; and the agenda of that enterprise must be expected to provide the framework within which we see Irenaeus reading Paul. For this reason if for no other, it is useless to inquire whether Irenaeus' Paul conforms to the image of the apostle that was later unveiled by the interests and perceptions of evangelical Protestantism. His concerns and questions—and those of his opponents—were of a different order. To say this, however, does not entail the conclusion that Irenaeus cared nothing for, and made nothing of, the Pauline corpus. Hence it is reasonable to ask how Irenaeus himself reads the letters associated with the name of Paul—or, in other words, to ask whether, and how, they contribute positively to his own theological vision.

The aim of this study, then, will be a simple one: to trace or indicate the outlines of what I shall call Irenaeus' "reading" of Paul. To this end it is important to distinguish the different purposes for which Irenaeus appeals to Paul in the course of his polemic against his opponents—and in particular to distinguish the cases in which he is controverting his opponents' exegesis of Paul from those in which he is using Paul either to refute their general position or to build and support his own. On the basis of such an analysis, it should be possible to identify Pauline texts or passages—or combinations of them—that feed Irenaeus' own theological vision, and so to suggest what Paul "meant" to a bishop of Lyons around the end of the second century. In pursuing this general aim, I shall be much less interested in questions about Irenaeus' exegetical methods, or about the "correctness" of his interpretation of Paul, than simply in the sort of thing he discovers in Paul's letters. And since Irenaeus was unaware of any distinction between "Pauline" and "deutero-Pauline" works, I shall, for the purposes of this investigation, mean by the expression "Paul's letters" just what Irenaeus would have meant by it: the entire Pauline corpus with the exception of Hebrews and (probably) Philemon.

The first—and no doubt most obvious—manner in which Irenaeus treats of Pauline texts is in the narrowest sense controversial. I refer to those cases in which he seeks directly to controvert what he regards as a wrongheaded reading of some particular verse or passage.

On several occasions in Book 1 of the *Adversus haereses*, Irenaeus indicates the drift of Valentinian exegeses of particular Pauline texts. His opponents saw, for example, a reference to the pleromatic savior in Colossians 3:11 and 2:9, where the apostle states that Christ is "all things" and that "in him the whole fulness of deity dwells"; and they saw a similar confirmation of their teaching that the Savior is the "All" in Ephesians 1:10 with its reference to the "summing up" of all things "in Christ" (*AH* 1.3.4). In Paul's references to the cross at 1 Corinthians 1:18 and Galatians 6:4, the disciples of Ptolemy found an allusion to the eon "Limit," to which they also gave the name "Cross." The Valentinians further took the assertion of Colossians 1:16—"in him all things were created"—to mean that the Savior is responsible for the chain of events that led to the formation of the visible cosmos (*AH* 1.4.5). Later on (*AH* 1.8.3), Irenaeus also notes that his adversaries supported or derived their distinction between hylic, psychic, and pneumatic persons out of various texts in the Pauline letters. They appeal not only to statements in which Paul opposes "pneumatic" to "psychic" (1 Cor. 2:14) and "earthy" to "heavenly" (1 Cor. 15:48), but also to Romans 11:16, asserting that the sanctification of the "whole lump" by the "firstfruits" signifies the relation between pneumatics and psychics (i.e., between themselves and the ordinary Christians) in the church. Above all, they characterize their own status by citing Paul's assertion that "the pneumatic person judges all things, but is himself judged by no one" (1 Cor. 2:15). Finally, Irenaeus notes that the Marcosians apply the words of Psalm 14:2,[4] as quoted by Paul in the third chapter of Romans, to ignorance of the ultimate Depth (*AH* 1.19.1), and that one group of heretics—traditionally identified as the "Ophites"—quote the words "Flesh and blood do not grasp the kingdom of God" (cf. 1 Cor. 15:50) to show that the disciples of Jesus were deceived in thinking that he was raised up *in corpore mundiali*. Later in his treatise, however, Irenaeus says that "all the heretics" appeal to this text, not with reference to Jesus' resurrection but to prove that the *plasmatio* of God is not saved (*AH* 5.9.1).

In Book 1—Irenaeus' *narratio*—none of these exegeses are controverted, save perhaps by a rhetorical lifting of the eyebrow.

Clearly, they are submitted principally by way of illustration; and in some cases at least, one suspects that Irenaeus does not regard them as worthy of attention. Some of them, however, recur for extended discussion in later books of *Adversus haereses*. In Book 4, Irenaeus offers his own lengthy account of the identity of the *pneumatikos* who "judges all things" (AH 4.33.1–15), and he devotes a significant section of Book 5 to developing his own understanding of the difference between "psychics" and "pneumatics."[5] In these cases, however, his attention is focused less on a particular text than on the general outlook that informs Valentinian exegesis of the Pauline statements in question. The same appears to be true in the case of Ephesians 1:10. Irenaeus has—as I need hardly observe—his own way of understanding what it means that "all things" are "summed up" in Christ, and in articulating it he is clearly aware of his opponents' way of handling this text,[6] but he does not address the text, or their exegesis of it, directly, perhaps because his difference with them in fact lies at the deeper level of the assumptions with which the text is approached. The expression "all things," he says significantly (AH 3.16.6), includes in its denotation the visible and tangible *plasmatio Dei* that is humanity. Hence he concludes that "things visible and corporeal" too are necessarily incorporated in what the Christ "sums up."

But if, in these cases, Irenaeus in effect replies to his opponents simply by employing a controversial Pauline text in the exposition of his own beliefs, there are also a number of instances in which he addresses their exegesis of a text directly. The most notorious of these, perhaps, is the case of 2 Corinthians 4:4, which contains the phrase *Deus saeculi huius* ("the god of this world"). Plainly Irenaeus' opponents—or some particular group of them—appealed to this expression to justify their belief in a second, cosmic deity hostile to, or ignorant of, the supreme Father. Irenaeus' reply takes the form of a verbal quibble that serves to display his rhetorical learning, in which he no doubt took great pride. Paul, he says, *propter velocitatem sermonum suorum* (AH 3.7.2), was in the habit of using the rhetorical device of *hyperbaton*, inversion of words. To understand the text properly, therefore, one must take the phrase "of this world" not with "God" but with "unbelievers." In that way one obtains the true sense: "God blinded the minds of the unbelievers of this world" (AH 3.7.1).[7] Irenaeus takes a less high-handed way with his adversaries when, in dealing with the same range of issues, he urges that the phrase "every so-called god" at 2 Thessalonians 2:4 cannot be referred to the creator, on the ground that "the Father of all things" can scarcely be regarded as a member of a class of "so-called gods" (AH 3.6.5); and again when he argues that 1 Corinthians 8:5, in referring to "so-called gods whether in heaven or on earth," does not mean *mundi fabricatores* but "the moon and the stars" to which Moses referred in Deuteronomy.[8]

But the instance of heretical exegesis that he takes the greatest pains to refute is the Gnostic handling of 1 Corinthians 15:50 ("Flesh and blood cannot inherit the kingdom of God"). His adversaries of course saw in this text a denial that the material shell of the human person can share in salvation, that is, in the resurrection. Irenaeus devotes, in all, six chapters of Book 5 to an exposition of these words. His objections to the interpretation proposed by his adversaries are carefully summarized in *Adversus haereses* 5.13.2–3. His fundamental negative point is that they take the expression "flesh and blood" *nude*—which means, presumably, "in its most obvious and ordinary sense"—and hence fail to grasp the true force of the words or the intent of the apostle (AH 5.13.2). Irenaeus thinks (AH 5.13.3) that 1 Corinthians 15:53–55, where among other things it is said that "this mortal thing must put on immortality" and that "death is swallowed up in victory," provides a clear indication that Paul did not mean what the Valentinians had taken him to mean—as, for that matter, does Philippians 3:20–21.[9] Their exegesis, he asserts, makes Paul appear to contradict himself. As to the correct exegesis, he wants to insist on two points. In the first place, he concludes that "flesh and blood" refers here primarily to "the works of the flesh" and not to materiality as such; but then, in the second place, he wants to argue that flesh—taken now to mean precisely the physical dimension of the human constitution— *does* "inherit the kingdom of God" in the sense that "death is swallowed up in victory" and that flesh *is inherited* by the Spirit. These two contentions he has already defended at greater length.[10] They depend, as we shall see, on Irenaeus' assessment of the general "drift" of Pauline theology.

From this brief and summary examination—no doubt incomplete—of heretical exegeses that Irenaeus sets out to controvert, two tentative conclusions seem to emerge. First, it is only on occasion that he directly and deliberately notes and seeks to refute a Valentinian—or possibly, in some cases, a Marcionite—interpretation of Paul. In many instances he simply "re-handles" the text in question; that is, he "exhibits" what he takes to be its meaning by letting it speak within the frame of his own theological understanding or argument.[11] Second, all of the exegeses that he *does* attack in a direct way concern one or the other of two broad sets of issues: the distinction between an ultimate God and a cosmic demiurge, or the Valentinian understanding of human nature and its redemption. If, as I suspect, this circumstance provides a clue to the themes that dominated his opponents' interpretation of the Pauline letters,[12] it may also, in the end, provide a useful backdrop against which to measure Irenaeus' own way of reading Paul.

There is, however, a second manner in which Irenaeus uses the Pauline letters in his polemic, one that defines a much more numerous class of citations and allusions. I refer to those passages in which Irenaeus appeals to a Pauline text in order to refute not a contrary exegesis of the text itself but some teaching that he takes to be an integral part of his opponents' *hypothesis,* whether or not that teaching has any relation to their interpretation of Paul.

The first issue concerning which Irenaeus appeals to Paul is—inevitably—that constituted by the Valentinian and Marcionite distinction between the cosmic creator and the supreme Father. Irenaeus, as one need hardly say, is determined to show that Paul affirmed *one* God—God the creator. We have already seen how, in *Adversus haereses* 3.6.5 and 3.7.1, he contradicts the Valentinian (?) exegesis of certain Pauline texts that had been taken to support this distinction. His primary appeal, however, is to texts in which Paul deprecates pagan polytheism. In particular, he cites Galatians 4:8–9 (with its contrast between "God" and "beings that by nature are no gods") and, of course, 1 Corinthians 8:4–6, with its assertion of "one God, the Father, from whom are all things"—a passage that, taken in its full extent, seems to have dictated, among other things, the basic outline of Book 3 from the sixth chapter on. In this connection—and, interestingly enough, in this connection alone—Irenaeus also appeals to two speeches attributed to Paul in the Acts of the Apostles (although only in a section of his argument that is devoted exclusively to the evidence of that work).[13] He does not raise the issue of whether these denials of polytheism are in fact relevant to the sort of question with which both he and his opponents were concerned; he simply assumes that they are.

A second issue on which Irenaeus appeals to the authority of Paul against the teaching of his heretics is, of course, that of the person of Christ. In accordance with the language of 1 Corinthians 8:6, Irenaeus wants to maintain that there is "one Lord Jesus Christ" just as there is "one God the Father"; and this against views which separated the pleromatic "Christ" from the cosmic "Jesus" in such wise as to deny that the former suffered or was born—or, indeed, shared in any way in the human condition as Irenaeus understood the human condition. In opposition to such views, he wanted to assert that Jesus and the Christ are *unus et idem*, a phrase that echoes back and forth through three chapters (16–18) of Book 3. Needless to say, this precise issue was, again, not one to which Paul had ever bent his mind, but Irenaeus' invocation of the two texts in which the apostle happens to attach the epithet "one" to the style "Jesus Christ"[14] may be less contrived than it appears at first sight to a modern reader. His point seems to be merely that in Paul's habitual usage, "Jesus" and "Christ" denote the same person and not two separate beings.

Closely related to this is Irenaeus' citation of Pauline texts to show that the apostle ascribed death to the one he referred to as "Christ" or "Jesus Christ" or "Son of God"—and not only death but also birth and resurrection from the dead.[15] Here the issue is not so much the unity of the person of Christ as it is whether that unity encompasses what Irenaeus understands humanity to be— that is, flesh, the *plasmatio* of God that is subject to birth, suffering, and death. The fact that he does not distinguish these two questions very clearly in his mind no doubt lends an air of imprecision to his argument, but the point is clear. He makes it positively at the very beginning of his christological disquisition, where, after submitting the teaching of the Fourth Gospel by title and passing on to Matthew, he arrives finally at Paul, quoting Romans 1:1–4 at length and then Galatians 4:4–5. Both texts speak of "the Son of God"—whom Irenaeus, following the lead of John 1:1–14 and Colossians 1:15,[16] understands to be that "Word" who is "the first-born of all creation"—and at the same time characterize him as human: he is "of the seed of David according to the flesh" and he is "born of a woman." This of course is what Irenaeus wants to argue: that Paul, unlike the Valentinians, speaks of Christ as one person who is God's "Son . . . born of a woman."

A third issue on which Irenaeus appeals to Paul against his opponents is the complex and difficult one of the continuities and discontinuities between the new covenant in Christ and the covenants with Abraham and Moses. In the first instance, this issue was one that concerned Christian use and interpretation of the Jewish scriptures; but it also touched, for Irenaeus, on two more general but not less central matters: the question of the unity of humanity's history with God and, underlying that, the fundamental question of the unity of God. Furthermore, this issue was rendered the more complex by the fact that Irenaeus saw himself confronted by two distinct groups of opponents: the followers of Marcion, who simply repudiated the Jewish scriptures, and the Valentinians, who, if Ptolemy's *Letter to Flora* can be taken as representing their general outlook, saw themselves as occupying a middle ground, at least on the subject of the law.

By contrast both to Marcion and to the Valentinians, Irenaeus argues that the same God who "sent his Son" into the world is the author of the Mosaic law. To support this thesis, he cites (AH 4.2.7) Paul's statement that the law was *paedagogum nostrum in Christum Jesum* (Gal. 3:24). He appeals not only to Jesus' summary of the law but also (AH 4.12.2) to Paul's statement that "love is the fulfilling of the law" (Rom. 13:10). His aim here is to argue that it is not the legislation of Moses as such but the human "tradition" of the elders that the gospel repudiates.[17] The essential law—which Irenaeus, not unlike Ptolemy, clearly identifies with the *moral* injunctions of Moses—is fulfilled in Christ. Paul's assertion that Christ is the *telos* of the law (Rom. 10:4) thus means, for Irenaeus, not that Christ simply abolishes the law but that he is the goal toward which it points and moves. Hence, as he sees it, the apostle's assertion also entails the proposition that Christ is the *arche* of the law (*AH* 4.12.3)—presumably because that which functions as the end or goal of something must, in Irenaeus' mind, serve also as its ultimate and original explanation. He of course agrees with Ptolemy that the ceremonial laws of the Mosaic covenant are—for Christians if not for those who originally received them—simply "types"; and to this point he cites, one need hardly add, 1 Corinthians 10:11 (*AH* 4.14.3). He also agrees with Ptolemy that, as the Lord himself said, some laws were given to the Israelites by Moses in his own right "on account of the hardness of their heart" (Mk. 19:7f.); but Irenaeus is swift to note that such regulations exist even under the new covenant, since Paul too, in 1 Corinthians 7, gives instructions on his own authority by way of concession to human weakness (*AH* 4.15.2). Irenaeus further (*AH* 4.16.4) counters the suggestion that the Mosaic legislation was given by the demiurge out of self-regarding motives by repeating the commonplace that God stands in need of nothing; in fact, he argues, it was given out of love, as the apostle suggests, and for the benefit of human beings, because they "fall short of the glory of God" (Rom. 3:23). Thus the same God is the author of both covenants, and Irenaeus makes this point against Marcion by firmly quoting Romans 3:21: the righteousness of God is indeed manifested "apart from the law," but it is nevertheless attested by the law and the prophets (*AH* 4.34.3). The brightness of Moses' face, which because of its splendor the Israelites could not gaze upon (2 Cor. 3:7), was the glory of "the person who loves God" (*AH* 4.26.1). As such, it was a foreshadowing of the destiny that God wills for all human beings.

Irenaeus also makes great play with Paul's treatment of Abraham in Romans and Galatians. For him, however, the point is not primarily that the "father" of Israel was reckoned acceptable to God on the basis of faith rather than on the basis of observance of the Mosaic covenant. Instead it is that Abraham represents both a foreshadowing and a beginning of the life of the church.[18] The promise to Abraham was that his seed should be *quasi stellas caeli*. The fact that Paul refers to his congregation at Philippi as "lights in the

world" (Phil. 2:15) and to believers as "children of Abraham" (Rom.
4:12f.) indicates, on the one hand, that the community of believers
fulfills that promise (AH 4.5.3) and, on the other, that Abraham
himself was "a follower of the Word" (AH 4.5.4)—the same Word
who said, "Abraham rejoiced to see my day" (Jn. 8:56). It is John,
then, who teaches Irenaeus to envisage Abraham as a prophet who
saw what was coming in God's *oikonomia*; Paul's Abraham stands
rather as an attestation of the fact that God's way of dealing with
humanity has not changed in substance even if it has changed in
the manner of its administration. *Una et eadem illius et nostra sit
fides* (AH 4.21.1).

The fact is, of course, that Irenaeus is fairly sure that God's
way of dealing with humanity has not changed in every respect.
This attitude emerges in his treatment of arguments—quite probably Marcionite in origin[19]—that denigrated the Jewish scriptures by
dwelling either on the reprehensible deeds of ancient kings, judges,
and patriarchs or on the creator's unfortunate habit of imposing
peremptory demands and punishments. Irenaeus points out, referring to 1 Corinthians 10:1-12, that Paul himself does not bother to
condemn the sins of the Israelites but envisages the sins—and the
punishments they evoked—as warnings to us (AH 4.27.3). This
means, however, that the apostle saw Christian believers as standing in the presence of the same God, the same moral demand, and
the same judgment as had their forebears in faith (AH 4.27.4). Did
he not say that *all* "fall short of the glory of God" (Rom. 3:23)?
The situation in that respect has not changed. Nor is it true that the
God of the elder covenant was a God of judgment while the God
revealed by Christ is purely a God of grace. Following his nameless
presbyter, Irenaeus alludes to a whole catena of Pauline texts that
speak of the judgment or the wrath of God, leading off with the
question (1 Cor. 6:9), "Do you not know that the unrighteous will
not inherit the kingdom of God?" He concedes, indeed, that there
is, in at least one respect, a significant difference between the
Christian and the Mosaic dispensations. In the former the promise
is greater; hence its demand for righteousness of life is more thoroughgoing and the punishment it threatens more lasting (AH
4.28.2). But neither sin nor its judgment is a speciality of the old
covenant.

Here, then, we have Irenaeus using the Pauline corpus to attack his adversaries on central points of their teaching. The greatest mass of Pauline evidence is marshaled to contradict Valentinian and Marcionite estimates of the Jewish scriptures— estimates that subserved their contention that there is a difference between the creator God of the old covenant and the Father of Jesus Christ. By the same token, Paul's writings are used to criticize this latter contention directly and also to controvert Valentinian christology, both in its dualism and in its refusal to incorporate humanity as "flesh" in the person of Christ. If, as I suggested earlier, Irenaeus reflects the agenda of a "Gnostic" reading of Paul when he attacks Valentinian exegesis of particular texts, his agenda in these forays manifests rather his own notion of the issues on which his opponents' *hypothesis* went systematically wrong. His use of Paul, in other words, is governed by his determination to defend the three basic—and related—principles of one God, one Christ, and one providentially ordered history. And while this polemical agenda may, as I suspect, have been suggested to him in part by a Pauline text (i.e., 1 Corinthians 8:6), the issues are clearly not Paul's own; and Irenaeus' use of the apostle, whether apt or not, can therefore project no clear "picture," no "reading," as I have called it, of the thematic structures of Paul's teaching. For that, we must look further—not at Irenaeus' polemics but at the theological vision he articulates when he is suggesting how and why his three principles make coherent sense.

To see how—and to what extent—a reading of Paul contributes to this theological vision, one can do worse than begin with a Pauline text whose language is not only intermittently quoted by Irenaeus[20] but seems, as a matter of fact, to have become part and parcel of his own vocabulary. "But when the fulness of time arrived, God sent his Son, born from a woman, born under the law, to redeem those who were under the law, in order that we might receive the adoption of sons. And because you are sons, God sent the Spirit of his Son into our hearts" (Gal. 4:4-6). The phrases "fulness of time" and "adoption of sons"[21] (or simply "adoption") recur regularly in Irenaeus' writing, regularly enough to indicate that the thought—or better, perhaps, the picture—that he culled from these verses was, for him, a central and thematic one. Therefore, it is worth seeing not only how Irenaeus uses this text itself but also how he connects its language and the ideas he finds in it with other Pauline passages.

We can begin our inquiry by asking how Irenaeus understands the words "God sent his Son, born of a woman." As we have already seen, *Adversus haereses* 3.16.3 sets them alongside Romans 1:1-4 and Colossians 1:15ff., and together the three passages interpret one another for Irenaeus. The mention of "God" in Galatians is given precision by the passage from Romans: the "God" in question is the one who "promised" good news "beforehand through his prophets in the holy scriptures" (Rom. 1:2). This God is, in short, the creator God of the Jewish scriptures. In a similar way, the meaning of "Son" is specified by Colossians 1:15ff. The Son in question is "the first-born of all creation," whom Irenaeus, as we have seen, identifies, not imperceptively perhaps, with the *Logos* of John 1:1-14. Hence the words "born of a woman"—in effect reiterated and confirmed by the expression "of the seed of David according to the flesh" (Rom. 1:3)—represent a restatement of the Johannine "became flesh." Paul in Galatians, then, is locating the central redemptive event in the incarnation of the divine Son or Word. But more than that, he is presenting this event as the outcome of an initiative on the part of the God of the prophets—the God who spoke in the Jewish scriptures and who, indeed, *promised* this redemption *ahead of time* in those very scriptures. How, then, do Pauline texts and ideas figure in Irenaeus' development and expansion of these two themes that he sees adumbrated in Galatians, the themes of redemption as worked (a) by the creator God revealed in law and prophets, and (b) through the incarnation of God's Son?

Where the first of these themes is concerned, we do well to attend, at least initially, to another phrase from the text in Galatians: "in the fulness of time." What it conveys to Irenaeus in the first instance is nicely suggested in *Adversus haereses* 3.16.7. There he is, in effect, explaining what it means that there is a divine *oikonomia* that embraces everything (*universa dispositio*: *AH* 3.16.6) and culminates in the enfleshing of God's Son. It means that "all thing are foreknown by the Father and carried out by the Son . . . at the moment that is appropriate (*apto tempore*)." God, then, has a *history* with humanity, and humanity with God, and in that history different things happen at different times. The phrase "fulness of time" itself, of course, refers to one moment in that history, the time of the Word's being made flesh (*AH* 3.17.4), but it also implies for Irenaeus that there are other "times" that have their place in the same divine scheme. This conclusion is confirmed for him, moreover, by a variety of Pauline texts. He notes, no doubt recalling Galatians 4:21ff., that the one divine householder "who brings out of his treasure what is new and what is old" (Mt. 13:52) had one commandment for "slaves," the old covenant, and another for those who have been liberated by faith—the latter of which Irenaeus sums up in the words of Psalm 96:1: "Sing to the Lord a new song" (*AH* 4.9.1). By the same token, when Paul says (1 Cor. 13:9–10) "We know in part and we prophesy in part, but when that which is perfect comes, the imperfect will pass away," he testifies that the history of God with humanity is still not completed (*AH* 4.9.2).[22] Indeed Irenaeus thinks that the spelling-out of the story of humanity's creation and salvation in time is implied not only by Paul's insistence that the race moves from the "psychic" to the "spiritual" (1 Cor. 15:46) but also by his statement "I fed you with milk, not solid food; for you were not ready for it" (1 Cor. 3:2).[23] Irenaeus is very conscious, then, that Paul sees God's dealings with humanity to be susceptible of analysis in terms of "befores" and "afters"; and to him this means not only that humanity's history with God is a story of change and growth but also that at any "time" one can name—including the moment that he refers to as "the fulness of time"—there is always a "more" that God has to give and a "more" that humanity has to receive.[24]

It seems to be Paul, moreover, who supplies Irenaeus with a way of envisaging the unity of this history in all its variety.[25] The bishop's basic theme, of course, is simply that the one God is the single source of all things. This he seeks to establish, at the opening of his little treatise on the prophets, by referring not only to Paul[26] but also to Hermas' *Shepherd* and to the prophet Malachi. He further argues that since Christ said "All things are delivered to me by my Father" (Mt. 11:27), it is the one Son, the Word, in whom God must be understood to carry out the works of creation, revelation, and salvation (AH 4.20.2). But even when he has established these points to his satisfaction, Irenaeus remains grimly aware of his opponents' delight in exploiting whatever evidence the scriptures contain of discontinuity between the Mosaic and the Christian dispensations. Accordingly, he must somehow show that the presence of variety and change in the *oikonomiai* of God is not in itself inconsistent with the operation of a single divine initiative and purpose in all of them. To this end, he transfers—interestingly and oddly—Paul's image of one body with many members to the history of God's self-revelation. He speaks of the *integrum corpus operis Filii Dei* (AH 4.33.15), different aspects or traits of which the different prophets manifested by their words (or actions); and in another place he explains that the prophets were "members of Christ" and that their prophecies therefore make up a whole, even though each prophesied in accordance with his individual calling as a member (AH 4.33.10). In 4.20.6, he alludes directly to 1 Corinthians 12:4-7. The saying that there are "diversities of operations, but the same Lord" Irenaeus applies to the different ways in which the prophets were led to understand and express the truth that human beings should come to the vision of God and to immortality; but this leads him, in 4.20.7, to go further and to suggest that the different *oikonomiai* of the divine Word must be conceived on the analogy of the successive notes that constitute a single melody. Paul's image for the church thus becomes Irenaeus' image for the history of creation and salvation as a single organic whole constituted of a variety of differing "parts"; and the connection between the two uses of this image lies, one suspects, in Irenaeus' perception of the *history* of salvation as, so to speak, the variegated spectrum that articulates in the medium of time the *integrum corpus operis Filii Dei*. And with this idea Irenaeus brings us back to the theme of the "fulness of time" and to the fleshly advent of the Son of God that constitutes that fulness.

For, of course, it is notorious that Irenaeus envisages God's "Son . . . born of a woman" as being, in accordance with Ephesians 1:10, one in whom all things are "summed up." In the first instance, Irenaeus develops this notion, as we have seen, along lines suggested to him by Colossians 1:15ff. The Word who is "first-born of all creation" takes flesh, dies, and becomes "first-born from the dead." In thus recapitulating humanity in himself and raising it, Christ becomes the one in whom God and creation, invisible and visible, meet (*AH* 3.16.6). He is the "summing up," then, and the unification of what we may, in un-Irenaean language, call the orders of being. But there is yet another dimension, as Irenaeus sees it, to this "summing up" of things in Christ. When, at *Adversus haereses* 3.18.1, Irenaeus faces the objection of people who say that if Christ was born at a particular time, then "he did not exist beforehand," his reply is twofold. He of course refers back to his development of the idea that the Son of God is, as Galatians puts it, *sent*, and sent "in the fulness of time" (*AH* 3.17.4). This clearly implies (for Irenaeus) that "the Son of God did not begin to be at that point, since he always exists with the Father" and so has always dwelt with the human race. But then, if the occurrence of the incarnation at a particular time is thus part of a providential divine scheme whose executive, so to speak, is the Logos, what the sending of God's Son fulfills and so "sums up" is, as Irenaeus now argues, the *longam hominum expositionem,* the "narrative"[27] or history of the human race in its relation with God. And this idea, in turn, Irenaeus works out in terms of the Pauline contrast between the disobedient Adam and the obedient Christ (*AH* 3.18.2).[28] The incarnation of the Logos encompasses and embraces the disobedient Adam in the victory of the Son of God, who was—as the apostle explains in Philippians—obedient even to the point of death on the cross (Phil. 2:8). Thus it "fulfills the scheme (*oikonomia*) of our salvation." The source, then, of Irenaeus' notion of recapitulation as "reversal" or "inverse repetition" appears, in the end, to be Romans 5:12ff., which portrays the "logic" of humanity's *longa expositio* as one of an inclusive sin reversed by an equally inclusive righteousness. Naturally enough, therefore, it is Paul whom Irenaeus quotes to explain the "reason" (*ratio*) of this act: "For to this end Christ died and lived again, that he might be Lord both of the dead and of the living" (Rom. 14:9). The "summing up" that occurs in the incarnation of the Son whom God sent "in the fulness of time" embraces and joins not merely the visible and invisible orders, as Colossians suggests, but humanity's past, its present, and (one supposes) its future. The "summing up" exhibits humanity as created "after the image and likeness of God"—that is, it exhibits the finished, the "second" Adam, of whom the apostle speaks in 1 Corinthians 15.

So far, however, in this attempt to understand Irenaeus' Paul through the lens of Galatians 4:4–6, we have virtually ignored what, for Irenaeus, is the second central theme of this passage: its assertion that the purpose of God's sending his Son "in the fulness of time" was to confer on humanity the "adoption of sons." What Irenaeus understands by this phrase is evident from a number of texts. The adoption of sons, he tells us, depends on humanity's *koinonia* with the Son of God (*AH* 3.18.7)—on the fact that, as a result of the incarnation, humanity "bears and grasps and embraces the Son of God" (*AH* 3.16.3). This notion in its turn, however, is closely bound up with Irenaeus' reading of 1 Corinthians 15:53–54. There Paul speaks of the corruptible "putting on" incorruption and the mortal "putting on" immortality, and drives his point home by quoting a form of Isaiah 25:8: "Death is swallowed up in victory." Irenaeus seizes upon this image of "swallowing up," which Paul also uses at 2 Corinthians 5:4.[29] For him, the "putting on" of immortality and incorruption defines the *filiorum adoptio*, but it comes about because in Christ "that which was corruptible is swallowed up (*absorberetur*) by incorruption" (*AH* 3.19.1) and because humanity—which for him of course means "flesh," the *plasmatio* of God—is "swallowed up . . . in the victory and the patience . . . and the resurrection" of the Son of God (*AH* 3.19.3).[30]

Behind this picture, however—which is a picture of the humanity both of Christ and, by implication, of Adam—there lies yet another Irenaean excursion through Pauline thought. The fact that humanity's "adoption" comes about through a "putting on" of immortality and through a "swallowing up" of death in victory means for Irenaeus that it comes about through a gift of God, through the power of God. This is—and must be—the case, moreover, because the human being in itself is "flesh," as Paul among others suggests, and because flesh in itself is weak. Indeed the apostle says as much at Romans 7:18: "I know that no good dwells in my flesh" (*AH* 3.20.3). What Paul means, however, is not that flesh is beyond salvation but that "the good thing which is our salvation is not from us but from God." For what Paul teaches is that God's "power is made perfect in weakness" (2 Cor. 12:9)—a text on which Irenaeus dwells at *Adversus haereses* 3.20.1, and then again at 5.3.2–3, and which seems to define a thematic element in his anthropology. In both passages he connects this idea with 1 Corinthians 15:53: the perfecting of power in weakness *is* for him the conferring of incorruptibility on what is corruptible. The phrase "power . . . made perfect in weakness" therefore describes both the incarnation of the Son of God and the redemption of humanity through its *koinonia* with him, that is, the *filiorum adoptio* (cf. *AH* 3.20.2). It also leads Irenaeus to reflect on the meaning of Paul's statement that "God has consigned all to disobedience that he may have mercy upon all" (Rom. 11:23). As Irenaeus sees it, the point of this assertion is that God permits human beings to experience their own mortality and weakness so that they may the better appreciate the grace and power of God (*AH* 3.20.2).[31] The apostle makes the same point, Irenaeus notes, at 1 Corinthians 1:29, where he says that God chose what is "low and despised . . . lest any flesh should glory before the face of God." The truth is, Irenaeus insists a bit later on, that flesh has nothing of its own to glory in: "the glory of a human being is God."

But how does a human being participate in this glory—in the "adoption of sons," "the redemption of our bodies" (Rom. 8:23), incorruptibility? It is, we have said, through a sharing, a *koinonia* with Christ (*AH* 3.18.7). And in characterizing this sharing, Irenaeus draws on the whole array of Pauline language that describes believers' unity with Christ. He uses the language of membership in Christ (*AH* 5.2.3). He appeals to 1 Corinthians 15:20, where Christ is characterized as "the first fruits of those who have fallen asleep." His understanding of this text is manifest from the fact that he almost immediately turns to the head-and-body image in Ephesians 1:22 and Colossians 1:18 and then develops it by allusion to Ephesians 4:16: the resurrection of the head brings with it, in the end, that of "the rest of the body" as it is "strengthened by the growth that comes from God" (*AH* 3.19.3).

Believers are to be "conformed to the image of [God's] Son," as Paul says in Romans 8:29 (AH 5.6.1, cf. 4.37.7); that is yet another aspect of what is meant by "adoption of sons."

But if one asked Irenaeus *how* this sharing in Christ comes about, he would doubtless appeal, as he does in Book 5, to the work of God's other "hand," the Spirit. Irenaeus notes (AH 5.6.2) the passage in which Paul speaks of the body as the temple of God's Spirit (1 Cor. 3:16). He also notes (AH 5.7.1) Romans 8:11: "If the Spirit of him who raised Jesus from the dead dwells in you, he who raised Christ Jesus from the dead will give life to your mortal bodies also through his Spirit which dwells in you." In Book 5, this text is employed by Irenaeus primarily to argue that it is indeed "mortal bodies" that are raised; but it is also closely connected in his mind with his exegesis of 1 Thessalonians 5:23, where Paul speaks of "spirit and soul and body," apparently as constituents of the human person. Irenaeus' idea is that "spirit" in the text from Thessalonians in fact refers to that same *divine* Spirit which is mentioned not only in Romans 8:11 but also in Ephesians 1:13f., where the apostle says that believers are "sealed with the promised Holy Spirit"[32] and that this gift is "the guarantee of our inheritance" (AH 5.8.1). The complete or "perfected" human being therefore is, as Irenaeus sees it, one who has received the Holy Spirit—one who is not "unclothed, but . . . further clothed" (2 Cor. 5:4) with the "wedding garment" of the Holy Spirit (AH 4.36.6) or, in another image, "flesh possessed by Spirit" (AH 5.9.3) and inherited by Spirit. And this conclusion, he thinks, agrees with what Paul says in 1 Corinthians 15:42-50. There a distinction is made between body enlivened by soul, which corresponds to the "first Adam," the "earthy one," and body enlivened by Spirit, the "final Adam" and "the human being from heaven." And the perfection of humanity occurs as the transition is made from a state in which people bear "the image of the earthy one" to a state in which they bear "the image of the heavenly one." But this transition, Irenaeus thinks, is to be understood in the light of 1 Corinthians 6:9-11, with its reference to the washing of baptism in which the gift of the Spirit is conveyed and people put off "the works of the flesh" (AH 5.11.2). The adoption of sons, then, in which believers receive the gift of incorruption and are conformed to the image of God's Son, is the doing of the Spirit, in whose power "the works of the flesh" are put aside and humanity is "adjusted to God" (*aptare Deo*; cf. *AH* 3.17.2).

All this, furthermore, connects back with Irenaeus' understanding of the person and work of Christ, with which we started these explorations. It helps us, in fact, to understand why, in Book 3, Irenaeus takes time out to make a direct attack on the idea that it was the Christ from the pleroma who descended on Jesus at his baptism in the Jordan. The motive of this attack is not so much— as in the rest of this section of Book 3—to insist on the *unity* of the Christ. Rather it is to insist that *as a human being* the Christ was endowed with the Spirit—was indeed, as 1 Corinthians 15:45 suggests, a "lifegiving Spirit," a *sōma pneumatikon*—and this apparently for two reasons. In the first place, Irenaeus is eager to maintain the analogy—indeed the commonality of nature— between the Christ and believers that is presupposed by his understanding of the adoption of sons.[33] If only for this reason, Christ's humanity must be a Spirit-endowed humanity: in Christ, the Spirit becomes "accustomed . . . to dwell in the human race" (*AH* 3.17.1). But in the second place, Christ for Irenaeus is the *source* of the Holy Spirit for the rest of the human race. When Paul, at Romans 12:5, speaks of believers as "one body in Christ," what he says is strictly incomprehensible, Irenaeus thinks, apart from the gift of the Spirit in baptism; and this, in turn, "the Lord . . . gives to those who have a share in him (*qui ex ipso participantur*), sending the Holy Spirit into the whole earth."

But what are we to make of all this? There are at least two places in *Adversus haereses* where Irenaeus sums up what he takes the essential message of Paul to have been.[34] In both passages the summary follows the outline suggested by 1 Corinthians 8:6 but in each case with significant importations and additions. Paul is said first to have taught that there is one God—an element that, Irenaeus argues, was necessary in the preaching of one who brought the gospel to Gentiles uninstructed in the first principle of Jewish faith. Second, Paul is said to have taught the doctrine of the incarnation of the (preexistent) Son or Word of God. This is, no doubt, Irenaeus' interpretation of the phrase "one Lord Jesus

Christ"—an interpretation that is indebted, as we have seen, to Galatians 4:4–6 read in conjunction with John 1:1–14 and certain other Pauline passages. But to this Irenaeus adds, in each case, a statement of the aim or purpose of the incarnation, which turns out to be not only the conquest of Satan, the *inimicum hominis*, but also the re-formation of the human race (*AH* 4.24.1) or "the adoption of sons" (*AH* 3.16.3).

We have seen how Irenaeus develops these three themes and weaves them together. The first—the principle of monotheism—functions exclusively in Irenaeus' directly polemical use of Paul—as indeed does the second to the extent that "one Lord Jesus Christ" is taken by Irenaeus simply to register the fact that for Paul there are not different Christs at different levels of being. Insofar, however, as this second theme incorporates, in Irenaeus' mind, the picture of God's dealings with humanity that he sees focused in Galatians 4:4–6, it immediately spills over into the third—the theme of adoption and renovation—which, as we have seen, Irenaeus develops on the basis of a reading of 1 Corinthians 15, Romans 5, and a variety of other Pauline passages. And this, I would argue, is the area in which one must look to discern what it is that Irenaeus himself takes to be the burden of Paul's teaching in his letters. In the first instance, what he sees there is an account of human salvation that is centered in the work of God's "Son . . . born of a woman," who through the pouring out of the Spirit brings human persons to share in his divine sonship—which to Irenaeus means a sharing in the incorruption promised in Christ's resurrection. But he also finds in Paul intimations of a theology of history that turns not only, or even primarily, on controversial questions about the status of the law and the prophets in God's purposes, but more particularly on the movement from Adam to Christ, from the first to the ultimate humanity. And in the same assemblage of Pauline passages Irenaeus finds the outline of his anthropology, which appeals not only to Paul's language in 1 Corinthians 15 and 1 Thessalonians 5:23 but also to the thematic idea of power made perfect in weakness. Irenaeus' Paul is less interested in justification than in the transfiguration of humanity after the image of God's Son.

Literary Artifice
and the Figure of Paul
in the Writings of Tertullian

ROBERT D. SIDER

The question of the representation of Paul in Tertullian is by no means new to modern scholarship. Although the issue frequently arises in an incidental way, for example in the analysis of Tertullian's exposition of the Pauline letters,[1] it has been directly addressed by three signal studies, bridging almost a century, each of which endeavored to show how Tertullian misrepresents the apostle. The first of these, by Fritz Barth, argued that Tertullian had misrepresented the position of Paul in the early church, particularly in relation to the other apostles, transforming the strong independence of Paul evident in Galatians into amicable agreement with the other apostles, even dependence on them in matters of doctrine. Moreover, distorting the apostle's theology of grace, Tertullian looked for a doctrine of satisfaction and rewards, and for him the "New Covenant," far from freeing believers from the law, imposed a new law much more severe than the old. In 1937 Barth's position was reasserted with even greater rigor by Eva Aleith, who concluded that Tertullian's personality, his religious life and experience, were entirely foreign to that of the apostle, virtually eliminating the possibility of a sensitive interpretation of Paul. Finally, in a series of articles published in 1976-77, Claude Rambaux attributed Tertullian's deliberate misrepresentation of Paul on the subject of marriage to the basic character of his thought, which, Rambaux argued, was of a psychological rather than an intellective order.[2]

Two observations on these three studies will help to set the present essay in perspective. First, these studies were chiefly concerned with Tertullian's representation of the thought and doctrine of the apostle. But although one can hardly dispute the paramount importance in the history of Christianity of the legacy of Paul's teaching as derived from his epistles, it would be a mistake to measure the legacy of Paul in a writer such as Tertullian solely in terms of the representation of the apostle's thought. For Tertullian, the legacy of Paul also includes a lively image of the person of the apostle conveyed through the narrative of events in his life both in the Pauline epistles and in the Acts of the Apostles. Tertullian's method is not that of the systematic theologian but that of the literary artist and the master of rhetoric. He does not offer us a single sustained exposition of a well-reasoned theology in which Paul plays a precisely measurable role, but rather a varied corpus of artful compositions, individually self-contained for the most part, where both allusions to Paul the man and citations from the epistles as witness to Pauline thought play a part in the orchestration of an argument intended to be immediately persuasive. In the literary art and rhetorical design of Tertullian, the life of Paul can be as important as his thought.

Second, the charge made by Barth and reiterated by Aleith that Tertullian misrepresented the theology of Paul stems no doubt from these authors' own perceptions about the nature of Pauline theology. These perceptions, from our contemporary point of view, seem to define Pauline thought too exclusively in terms of a theology of grace as enunciated in Romans and Galatians. They fail to recognize the rich variety of the apostle's thought, which included, for example, a strong sense of the Spirit as wisdom and power and vivid images of the eschaton as anticipated in the present and expected in the near future—conceptualizations forcefully projected in Paul's letters to the Corinthians.

From these observations, it should be clear that if we are to appreciate the legacy of Paul in Tertullian, we must endeavor to trace the figure of the apostle as he is made to appear *both* in the events of his life *and* in the lines of his thought. Given the nature of Tertullian's art, we should not expect an architectonic biography to emerge, a consistent interpretation of a life where action and thought are seen to cohere. Instead we have kaleidoscopic allusions, phrases, sentences, and passages employed with a rhetorician's gifts for the telling *exemplum*, for making the evidence fit the case. Nevertheless, it will perhaps surprise to find how extensively the life of Paul is canvassed in Tertullian's compositions. We shall seek to discover where the nodal points of interest are, to what degree a human being capable of change and growth emerges, and to what extent we look on what amounts to the holy icon of a sainted apostle. Moreover, in spite of the special pleading so characteristic of rhetorical art, it will not be impossible, I shall argue, to see in Tertullian's compositions a representation of Pauline theology that coheres well with the evidence of the Pauline letters. We shall begin by searching for the figure of Paul reflected in allusions to the events of his life; we shall then consider the tension between the man and the icon in this representation; we shall conclude with an outline of his "theology" as represented by Tertullian.

Images from the Life of Paul

I have indicated that we should not expect to derive from the treatises of Tertullian a fully articulated biography of Paul; we have primarily allusions, frequently fleeting. These allusions appear to be motivated by two considerations. On the one hand, aspects of Paul's life have become the focus of debate, in most cases with "heretics" but sometimes in debates within the church. On the other hand, many allusions, perhaps the majority, belong to the literary artifice of the treatises and have an essentially literary motivation, above all to provide illustrations and *exempla*. The figure of Paul carried weight, and we may suppose that a passing allusion riveted attention, won *auctoritas*. Characteristically, moreover, it is to the highly dramatic episodes of the apostle's life that Tertullian appeals; and the inherent drama of the incidents themselves is enhanced by the brevity, the intensity, of Tertullian's style.

The sources of these allusions are the epistles and the Acts of the Apostles.[3] Tertullian gathers many details from the epistles—indeed, as we shall see, in the recollection of Paul's rebuke of Peter in Antioch, the epistle is primary. There is no reason to doubt, however, that the narrative in Acts provided the biographical outline for his conception of the apostle's life. Tertullian explicitly mentions the book with respect and deference, most sharply in his work against Marcion. "The Acts of the Apostles," he says, "has handed down to me this sequence (*ordo*) in the life of Paul" (*Adv. Marc.* 5.1.6). It is appropriate, therefore, to review Tertullian's allusions to Paul following the narrative order of Acts.

It is the struggle against heresy that evokes an interpretation of Paul's dramatic conversion. For Tertullian, Paul's transformation "from persecutor to preacher" was already anticipated in Old Testament figures who serve as a type of Paul. He is Benjamin, represented in Jacob's blessing (Gn. 49:27 LXX) as the ravening wolf who devours his prey in the morning but gives nourishment in the latter part of the day. He is King Saul (1 Sm. 19–26; see especially 1 Sm. 26:21–25) who persecuted David, the Lord's chosen, only to repent and make reparations (*Adv. Marc.* 5.6.5–6; cf. *Scorp.* 13.1). His pre-Christian life in Judaism interests Tertullian almost solely insofar as he is the persecutor of the Christians.[4] Addressing Marcion, Tertullian includes Paul among the "children of unbelief"; he had the devil as his *operator*[5] when he persecuted the church of God (*Adv. Marc.* 5.17.9). Tertullian concentrates his sense of Paul's radical and abrupt transformation in one sharply formulated antithesis that evidently relies on the apostle's own account as depicted in Acts (22:1–21; 26:4–23): *demutatus in praedicatorem de persecutore* (*De praescr.* 23.6). Antithesis, we know, was congenial to Tertullian's mode of thinking; but it is clear that he found Paul's transformation significant also as appropriate to a man in whom, as we shall presently observe, change, growth, and development were characteristic.[6]

Beyond the fact of transformation, the narratives of Paul's conversion in Acts contain vivid images that Tertullian did not fail to exploit. Paul's loss of sight in the light that shone on the Damascus road is a detail whose primary function in the *De baptismo* (13.4) would appear to be simply to rivet attention; but it exemplifies the main point of the argument in the *Adversus Praxean*, where the impossibility of seeing the Father is inferred from the fact that the light even of the Son blinds (15.7–8). The commanding voice that bade Paul find his further instructions within the city (Acts 9:6, 22:10) illustrates the universal precept that everyone must be baptized. Such must be the implication, argues Tertullian, since there was now nothing else Paul lacked and therefore no further instruction still to be given (*De bapt.* 13.4). Tertullian normally recalls these images of Paul with great accuracy, but not quite always. In *De baptismo* 18.3, for example, he confuses Paul's host, Judas (Acts 9:11), with Peter's host, Simon (Acts 9:43).

No event in Paul's life receives more insistent attention in Tertullian than Paul's rebuke of Peter at Antioch. Tertullian explains the episode in four contexts, which contain some substantial differences in his exposition of the events.[7] In three instances (*De praescr.* 23-24; *Adv. Marc.* 1.20; 4.3), he closely follows the narrative in Galatians (1:11-2:21). In the fourth (*Adv. Marc.* 5.2.7-3.7), the Galatians account is trimmed to fit the story of the council of Jerusalem in Acts 15. In all four cases there is a studied effort to obscure the framework of time and place in order to establish, it would seem, a narrative of convincing dramatic unity. Not once, for example, is it observed that the rebuke took place in Antioch. Moreover, the two visits to Jerusalem (as Galatians has it) appear to collapse into a single meeting with Peter and the apostles, which the rebuke evidently follows at once.[8] Thus in the *De praescriptione* (23-24), immediately on his conversion Paul is introduced to the brethren by brethren. He then goes to Jerusalem to see Peter, where all are amazed[9] and glorify God. Peter and the apostles accordingly extend the right hand of fellowship, thus witnessing to a faith they held in common while they exercised different ministries (Peter to the circumcision, Paul to the Gentiles). The rebuke therefore was not directed at differing doctrines, but at Peter's inconsistent behavior. In the first book against Marcion (*Adv. Marc.* 1.20), almost all details are sacrificed in an impressionistic picture of the zealous new convert challenging the wiser, more experienced apostles. Here Paul's conference with the apostles at Jerusalem and his confrontation of them at Antioch appear as a single meeting. "Then for the first time, inexperienced in grace, he conferred with those who, as apostles, had preceded him. It was therefore as a neophyte, still burning against Judaism, that he thought their conduct should be rebuked" (1.20.2-3). In the fourth book against Marcion little effort is made to establish a sequence; the conference and the confrontation form not so much a connected narrative as discrete *exempla* to demonstrate the derivative character of Paul's teaching and his concern, therefore, not with doctrine but with conduct (*Adv. Marc.* 4.2.4–3.4).

The fifth book against Marcion offers some rather striking differences in Tertullian's reconstruction of the narrative. There is an explicit attempt to associate the Galatians account with the events recorded in the Acts of the Apostles. The first years of Paul's conversion are dismissed with a mere allusion, and the council of Jerusalem of Acts 15 is evoked as the "very subject" (*ipsa materia*) of the epistle to the Galatians (*Adv. Marc.* 5.2.7). Hence Paul does not here confer with the apostles as a neophyte. Tertullian explicitly cites the "fourteen years" specified in Galatians 2:1, noting the length of time that had elapsed (*tot annis*; 5.3.1); the tender faith (*fides rudis*) now belongs not to the apostle but to those disturbed by the "false brethren" (Gal. 2:4).[10] To tender faith Paul himself made a concession in the circumcision of Timothy. No question of doctrine was concerned; therefore Paul received the right hand of fellowship from the apostles, and he censured Peter only on a question of behavior (*Adv. Marc.* 5.2.7–3.7).[11]

In these several accounts we should not overlook two important features in the representation of Paul. First, Tertullian invariably explains the rebuke by an appeal to the Pauline principle of "becoming all things to all" (1 Cor. 9:22). It was a principle the young neophyte of *Adversus Marcionem* 1 had still to learn, a principle on whose application, in the *De praescriptione*, the apostles did not always agree (so, similarly, in *Adv. Marc.* 4.3). Second, Tertullian attempts to reduce the stature of Paul as conceived by the heretics. In *De praescriptione* 24.3–4 he suggests that Peter might likewise have rebuked Paul when the latter circumcised Timothy and then concludes that the two apostles were made equal in martyrdom. In *Adversus Marcionem* 1, Paul is the neophyte who addresses the pillars of the apostolate (1.20.2); in the fourth book Marcion's Luke is said to be, as the follower of Paul, as much behind the apostle (*certe tanto posterior*) as Paul is behind the other apostles, his *antecessores* (4.2.4). Even in *Adversus Marcionem* 5, where Paul is represented as the mature apostle, it is nevertheless for the patronage (*ad patrocinium*) of Peter and the other apostles that he goes to Jerusalem (5.3.1).

The missionary journeys of Paul (as represented in Acts) provide for the most part a reservoir of illustration and *exempla* rendered the more effective by their sharply chiseled images and inherent dramatic power. Tertullian, however, makes surprisingly limited use of them. From the "first missionary journey," we have the story of the sorcerer Elymas smitten with blindness at the command of Paul (Acts 13:7-12), a vivid story to which Tertullian refers on several occasions.[12] From the second missionary journey Tertullian cites the stirring events in the Philippian jail, where Paul and Silas began to pray—publicly (for the prisoners heard them)—showing that the prohibition against public prayers (Mt. 6:5-6) must be qualified by the command to pray at all times and every place (*De orat.* 24; see Eph. 6:18; 1 Tm. 2:8). From the third missionary journey we find an allusion to the disciples at Ephesus baptized into John's baptism (Acts 19:1-6); their reception of the Holy Ghost from Paul's hands shows that the baptism of John was not from heaven (*De bapt.* 10.4-5; see Mt. 21:25). It is probable that Tertullian would also have located on this journey Paul's fight with beasts at Ephesus (1 Cor. 15:32), which he includes among the perils of the flesh (*pericula carnis*; *De res. mort.* 48.12).

This is not a long list of items from the missionary journeys of Paul. Moreover, as the above account will have shown, Tertullian's allusions are generally not focused on Paul in his own right but rather on the import of the events in which Paul was involved. I have yet to mention, however, two events from these journeys that are more germane to our portrait of Paul, for they reflect Tertullian's interest in growth or change in Paul's life.[13] First, Tertullian recalls (*De fug.* 6.5) the encounter of Paul and Barnabas with the Jews at Pisidian Antioch; here Paul determined that henceforth his ministry was to be to the Gentiles (Acts 13:46).[14] Second, if Pisidian Antioch constituted one major turning point in Paul's Christian life for Tertullian, Paul's association with pagans in Athens constituted another. It was when he had witnessed, at Athens, the philosophies warring against one another over the pretense of truth that he discovered the dangers of philosophy (*De praescr.* 7.7-9); it was after he had had a taste of all the "innkeepers of wisdom and eloquence" at Athens that he conceived his warning edict against philosophy (*De an.* 3.1; see

Col. 2:8); it was the incredulity of the pagans at Athens that forced him to enunciate the doctrine of the resurrection of the body (*De res. mort.* 39.7-8).[15] In each case, Tertullian calls attention to a dramatic shift in Paul's outlook and orientation.

From the final chapters of Acts, Tertullian chiefly pictures a Paul who serves as a model of dauntless courage in the face of persecution and martyrdom. Paul's resolute disregard of Agabus' prophecy, his cheerful determination to suffer for Christ (Acts 21:11-13), is described twice, once in *De fuga* 6[16] and again in *Scorpiace* 15.4-5; similarly, his refusal to pay Felix for his escape (Acts 24:26) reveals the ideal martyr (*De fug.* 12.6). The allusion to Paul's Roman citizenship in *Scorpiace* 15.3, where Paul is said to have gained Roman citizenship by birth when he was reborn in Rome through martyrdom, is also apparently derived from the last period of his life as reported in Acts (see Acts 22:24-29).[17]

Tertullian's allusions to the sufferings narrated in Acts are enriched by references to the epistles themselves.[18] In *Scorpiace* (13.5-8) he quotes at length from Paul's own account of his sufferings in 2 Corinthians to demonstrate that the apostle believed the Christian must bear suffering. In *De jejunio* (8.4) he notes that fasts are among the labors and perils and sufferings borne by the apostle. In the *Adversus Marcionem* (5.12.8) he mocks Marcion's god for permitting the creator's Satan to buffet his apostle; and in *De pudicitia* (13.16) he identifies the "thorn in the flesh" (2 Cor. 12:7-9) as a pain in the ear or head—"as they say." I have already mentioned the fight with beasts in Ephesus (1 Cor. 15:32), which Tertullian identifies (*De res. mort.* 48.12) with Paul's sufferings in Asia (2 Cor. 1:8). Thus it is primarily the sufferings of the apostle that Tertullian derives from the Pauline epistles and weaves into his mental picture of Paul.[19]

This survey of references to Paul in Tertullian does not by any means produce a "life of Paul." This is quite precisely the result, I have argued, of the nature of Tertullian's art. Even so, Tertullian's references do yield a picture of Paul that is not without interest. The references cluster around certain nodal points in Paul's life, and these are the points that dominate Tertullian's representation of Paul: the conversion portrayed as a dramatic transformation "from persecutor to preacher," typologically anticipated in the figures of Benjamin and Saul; the rebuke of Peter, depicted in a unified narrative given coherence by Tertullian's artistic sleight of hand and used to reduce the point of difference between the two apostles to behavior rather than doctrine; the encounters with the Jews at Pisidian Antioch and with the pagan philosophers at Athens, each construed as a turning point for Paul, the one determining his ministry to the Gentiles and the other determining his opposition to philosophy; and finally—a feature of Paul's life no longer concentrated in a single event— the courage and endurance that he demonstrated in the face of suffering and persecution, making him a model for the Christian life and for Christian martyrdom.

The Identity of Paul: Individual and Icon

The apostle who has thus far emerged from Tertullian's literary artifice is a figure identified, often rather superficially, by a selection of his deeds. Does Tertullian's Paul have, at the same time, a more "essential" identity that can be defined and portrayed in terms of his role and character? And if so, how does Tertullian draw this portrait? Does he show us an individualized Paul, marked by particularities and idiosyncrasies and present to us, so to speak, in flesh and blood? Or does he set before us the iconic figure of an apostle, vested with a holiness and an authority that leave the figure somewhat remote from us and yet addressed to us as an icon is addressed to the viewer?

THE APOSTLE'S ROLE

Barth was quite right to observe that Tertullian generally minimizes the distinction between Paul and the other members of the apostolic college, and indeed sometimes our apostle is made to appear the follower of the other apostles.[20] We have already seen that in Tertullian's anti-Gnostic works Paul is portrayed, at least once, as a neophyte among them and is made dependent on them for his doctrine. So the debate required, and Tertullian's artifice did not fail. Yet Tertullian does seem to distinguish Paul from the other apostles by representing him beyond the others as the apostle of peace and the teacher of the nations.

For Tertullian, Paul is first the apostle of peace. The title belongs to him by virtue of the transformation that took place in his life. In words that echo the prophecy of peace in Micah (4:3), Tertullian contrasts the persecutor, who first shed the blood of the church, with the convert, who exchanged the sword for the pen and turned the spear into the ploughshare (*Scorp.* 13.1). The title belongs to him also because he was called to proclaim the gospel of peace. It was Paul who understood the message of peace, enunciated in Ephesians (2:14), between Jew and Gentile (*Adv. Marc.* 5.17.14; cf. *Ad ux.* 2.2.2–3). Moreover, he changed the customary epistolary salutation from "greetings" to "grace and peace"; he did so because he was the preacher of peace, personally embodying the word of Isaiah (52:7): "How beautiful are the feet of those . . . who preach the gospel of peace." He knew that peace accompanied the gospel of grace (*Adv. Marc.* 5.5.1–2). Finally, the title belongs to him because he fulfilled the role of peacemaker in the church. This may be seen, signally, in the Corinthian church, where Paul generally refrained from baptizing so that, in a congregation torn by dissension, he would not appear to claim everything for himself (*De bapt.* 14.2).[21]

Paul is distinguished among the apostles, in the second place, as a teacher and specifically as the teacher of the nations. Tertullian assigns him the role of teacher in two sets of striking images. In the first of these, Tertullian plays on the images of *magister* and *discipulus*. In *De carne Christi* (22.3), Paul is described as *discipulus* and *magister* and *testis* of the gospel because an apostle of Christ. In a very different context he is said to be the *magister* of Luke, his *discipulus* (*Adv. Marc.* 4.2.4); and Tertullian recognizes him as the common *magister* alike of Marcion and the church (*Adv. Marc.* 3.14.4). In the *De pudicitia*, Tertullian concludes the debate over the identity of the forgiven offender of 2 Corinthians 2:5–11 with a summary appeal to the character of the apostle. "Those do not know the apostle who understand anything . . . contrary to the form and rule of his doctrines, as the *magister* of all sanctity even by his own example" (15.11). In the second set of images, Paul appears as the teacher of the Gentiles. In *De resurrectione mortuorum* (23.8), he is called the chosen vessel, the *doctor nationum* who knew *omnia sacramenta*. These images are repeated in *De pudicitia*

(14.27), where Paul is called the apostle of Christ, the *doctor nationum*, the chosen vessel.

Again, it is probable that Tertullian intends to suggest the apostle's role as teacher when, writing against Marcion, he equates the wise master builder of 1 Corinthians 3:10—the *architectus prudens*—with the cunning artificer of Isaiah 3:3—the *architectus sapiens* who will be taken away from Judaea. This signifies Paul, says Tertullian, the *depalator* of the divine *disciplina*, who was taken from Judaism for the upbuilding of Christianity; and the image finds clarification, although in an ironic aside, in the suggestion that *doctrina* is built on the one foundation, that is, Christ (*Adv. Marc.* 5.6.10–11).[22] The image of Paul as teacher acquires further detail if we observe some of the contexts in which the word *doceo* appears.[23] Most striking perhaps is the implication that the apostle as teacher is the interpreter of both testaments, which, in the *De monogamia* at least, refers to Paul's allegorical explanation of the Old Testament (*De mon.* 6.3). So in the third book against Marcion, the words *interpretor* and *doceo* are used of Paul's allegorical interpretation (*Adv. Marc.* 3.5.4). Moreover, it is possible that Tertullian intends to suggest Paul's skill as a master teacher in a passage such as *Adversus Marcionem* 5.7.10 where he points out that Paul teaches with the generous use of examples, or again in *De exhortatione castitatis* 4.2–3 where Paul the teacher invites his *discipuli* to draw conclusions from a series of exemplary considerations.

THE MAN AND THE ICON:
HISTORICAL IMAGINATION AND THE IDEAL APOSTLE

Although there can be little doubt that Tertullian shared the legacy common to early Christianity of a highly idealized conception of the first apostles, his writings are nevertheless marked both by the fullness with which they portray the character of the "divine apostle" and by the degree to which they were able, through their artful composition, to achieve a subtle fusion on the one hand of the historical Paul imaginatively remembered and on the other of the portrait of the saint already become an icon. Even though the iconic saint appears as the predominant element in this "fusion," the relationship of the images of historical person and Christian saint can hardly be quantified; it must rather be witnessed in the exposition of the text. In general, we may say that in descriptive-expository narrative the image of the idealized saint predominates, while in extended tracts of biblical exposition there are occasions where a tension between the man and the icon may be felt with at least limited force.

We have already seen how, in Tertullian's reckoning, the life of Paul is anticipated in Old Testament types, thus establishing a point of comparison with Christ. At other points, Paul appears as the "most holy apostle" (*sanctissimus apostolus; De bapt.* 17.2; cf. *De orat.* 20.1), who sanctifies a phrase from secular literature merely by using it (*Ad ux.* 1.8.4). In Paul's utterances, his identity with the Holy Spirit is all but complete (see, e.g., *De pat.* 7.7, 12.8; *De praescr.* 6.5.6; *Adv. Marc.* 5.7.1-2; *De virg. vel.* 4.2-3); one cannot therefore imagine inconsistencies and contradictions in the letters of the apostle (*De mon.* 5.11). His is a soul raised aloft *ex summa sanctitate et ex omni innocentia* (*De pud.* 13.16). As an apostle he possesses the Holy Spirit in full, not in part as others do (*De exhort. cast.* 4.5-6). He possesses also the moral virtues of the ideal man: what does Paul mean, asks Tertullian, when he says, "I please all"? That he himself joins the pagans in their festivities? Does he not rather please all by *modestia* and *patientia*, by *gravitas, humanitas, integritas* (*De idol.* 14.3-4)? Elsewhere, he is a man of *tanta constantia* (*Adv. Marc.* 5.7.2).[24] Moreover, the apostle, in his nature, bears comparison with the Lord. He does indeed share our nature, but his is a nature so purified that he can in his own person demonstrate the true qualities of human nature. Thus in the *De anima* when Tertullian demonstrates his view that the rational element of the soul, though it is from God, nevertheless has both an irascible and a concupiscible part, he points first to the Lord, who, as divine, was wholly rational yet knew both anger and desire, then to the apostle, who not only allows us desire but also himself experienced indignation (*De an.* 16.5-6).[25] Finally, in Tertullian's portrait, the apostle's gaze is fixed, like that of a saint in an icon, on the world beyond; his desire to depart and be with Christ (Phil. 1:23) is a model for us (cf., e.g., *De spect.* 28.5; *De pat.* 9.5; *Ad ux.* 1.5.1; *De exhort. cast.* 12.3).

In Tertullian's exposition of extended Pauline texts, on the other hand, the complementarity in the figure of Paul between the divine apostle writing with the lofty gaze of holy inspiration and the human agent responding with feeling to specific situations begins to come into view; we may even catch a glimpse of a somewhat irascible personality. In one rather striking case, the "symbiosis" of the human and divine voice becomes fairly explicit. In the second book *To His Wife*, Tertullian reviews the seventh chapter of 1 Corinthians until he comes to the crucial phrase "only in the Lord" (1 Cor. 7:39). At this point the human figure of the apostle himself (*ille sanctus*)[26] comes into full view as one who personally prefers widowhood, encourages us to follow his example, then permits marriage but with a weighty condition: "only in the Lord." In the words that follow there is perhaps a hint of a human personality, determined and severe: "He orders and persuades, he teaches and exhorts, he asks and threatens. The statement is bare and unencumbered, eloquent by its very brevity." But then, by the addition of a simple sentence, the human figure suddenly merges into the divine voice. Tertullian immediately continues: "Thus is the divine voice accustomed to speak so that you may at once understand, at once obey" (*Ad ux.* 2.2.4–5). The authority, the brevity, the clarity are characteristics at once of the voice of Paul and of the *vox divina*. Somewhat similarly, in the *De jejunio* (15.1), the apostle severely rebukes (*reprobat*) those who enjoin total abstinence from meat, but he does so, Tertullian asserts, from the *providentia* of the Holy Spirit.[27]

Perhaps nowhere has Tertullian shown such complete control over the Pauline corpus directed toward mastery in argumentation as in the *De resurrectione mortuorum*. The Pauline text is divided up, rearranged, each part summoned at precisely the right moment as a witness for the truth of the resurrection of the dead.[28] The exposition reveals also, particularly as Tertullian moves to the climax of his argument, an apostle who is, like any author, intent on his task as writer; at the same time, however, the authority and the clarity (associated as we have seen with the *vox divina*) of the text raise Paul's words, for Tertullian, to the level of inspired scripture. A brief review of salient passages from the central chapters (*De res. mort.* 40–54) must suffice. First, let us note the human author, keenly aware of human incredulity and choosing his language with care. When Paul says we have an eternal "house" in heaven (2 Cor. 5:1), he chooses the word *house* as a metaphor for *flesh* because he "wished to make an elegant comparison" with the word he had just previously used (*De res. mort.* 41.1-2). Similarly the metaphor of the *peregrinus* (2 Cor. 5:6-9) represents a deliberate choice by Paul. "Did words fail the apostle to describe the departure from the body or does he have reason to speak in a new way? Indeed he wished to signify a temporary absence from the body since whoever is temporarily absent (*peregrinatur*) returns home" (43.6). In chapter 49 Tertullian invites his reader to see the determination of the apostle reflected in his language. "So firmly does he direct this whole passage to moral behavior that . . . he speaks in the imperative mood (49.8)."[29] Finally Tertullian evokes a visual image of the historical Paul at his desk, so to speak: the apostle, with foresight, and struggling hard to help you to understand that the *mortale* that will put on immortality is the very flesh itself, actually touches his flesh as he speaks the words (51.9). At the same time, however, even where the historical figure seems to come most sharply into view, the divine source of the words has not fallen out of mind. The allusion to the apostle's "foresight" is itself a cue for the reader to recognize the divine *persona*.[30] But it is particularly in the clarity of the apostle's speech that Tertullian would have us recognize the authority of scripture. Not even the possibility of a hyperbaton, which perhaps may be found in 2 Corinthians 5:10, need obscure the bright light of apostolic speech (43.6-9).[31] And in chapter 47 the clarity of the apostle's speech becomes specifically the clarity of scripture. "Come now, how will those who flee the light of the scriptures understand that passage written to the Thessalonians, so clear that I should think it written by a ray from the sun itself" (47.17).

However clearly a human figure has emerged in Tertullian's discussion of 1 Corinthians 15, it is not, strictly speaking, a figure with a personality. The figure may be more "fleshy" than we would expect of an icon, but the context provides little opportunity to develop the idiosyncrasies of Paul's individuality. I turn finally, therefore, to a series of passages where Tertullian's exegesis may be thought to evoke an impression of at least an aspect of the character of Paul. In these passages, Paul appears as an intense, severe, and unyielding man. We meet this Paul most obviously in the *De pudicitia*, where Tertullian attempts to reconstruct the situation that led Paul, in his second letter, to pardon an erring Corinthian.[32] For Tertullian, the first Corinthian letter revealed a multitude of evils in Corinth, which elicited from Paul a response laden with the strongest personal emotions. "Let us observe that entire first epistle" says Tertullian, "written I should say not with ink, but with bile, swelling, indignant, disdainful, threatening, invidious" (*De pud.* 14.4). At one point the apostle afflicts the Corinthians with the "sting of humility" (14.6), at another with arrogance (14.8), elsewhere with sharp rebuke (14.9), and still again "he smites them on the face" (14.10). If such terms are found more extravagantly in the *De pudicitia* than elsewhere, they are still applied, somewhat mutedly, to Paul's manner in other writings as well. In the relatively early *De praescriptione*, Paul "marks" those Corinthians who deny the resurrection; he "inveighs" against the Galatians who defend the law; to Timothy he "reviles" those who forbid marriages (33.3–6). In the *De jejunio*, like the *De pudicitia* a late treatise, Paul "thrusts the knife" into the detractors of xerophagies (15.3) and "thunders" against them (15.5).

Vivid as such language is, caution is in order. The appearance of similar terms in several treatises suggests that we have here something of a stereotype for Tertullian; the *De pudicitia* may not, therefore, reflect a very active interest in the character of the historical Paul. Furthermore, all of these passages portray the indignation of the apostle, and we may remember that we found indignation a characteristic of both the incarnate Christ and the sainted apostle. We have also seen that "rebuke" is associated with the Holy Spirit. Hence in these passages the indignation may belong as well to the icon as to an image recalled of the actual man.

Thus far, our investigation should have shown that whatever the degree to which the "iconic" and "historical" aspects of the image of Paul shade into one another, for Tertullian Paul does have an identity as an individual. He is an individual capable of dramatic change and development, distinguished from the other apostles in conversion and calling, given a special role as teacher of the nations and apostle of peace, exemplifying in his speech that union of human intellect with the divine spirit appropriate to the convincing *auctoritas* of a saint. Moreover, even where it becomes unsafe to distinguish between historical individual and Christian icon, Paul remains, in Tertullian, a colorful figure, a man of strong character and of irascible personality. Certainly, he emerges from the design of Tertullian's literary artistry with a much fuller identity than a mere name attached to a series of quotable texts.

The Mind and Message of Paul

We have seen that Tertullian's Paul received some individualization by the designations "preacher" and "teacher." Thus far, only a general content has been given to these terms: Paul is the preacher of peace, the teacher of the Gentiles, the interpreter of both testaments. Can we go further to describe what Tertullian viewed as the central aspects of Paul's message in his letters, the theological "wellspring" of his mind? The task is fraught with difficulties, which may forestall a completely satisfactory solution. Tertullian's literary artifice may provide some clues to the reconstruction of his own thought;[33] our task, however, is not to construe his own theology but rather to grasp his view of the dynamic center of *Paul's* theology. Here the literary art may hinder rather than help. Varied allusions, references, and quotations from the apostle mingled, sometimes anonymously, with those from the rest of scripture; the frequently tendentious rearrangement of the Pauline text; the ubiquitous shaping of materials on the basis of flagrant *parti pris*—these tend to defy our attempts to trace the image Tertullian might have drawn of Paul as *doctor* and *praedicator*. Nevertheless, it is possible to sketch a provisional outline of Pauline themes and images that assume vitality in Tertullian's argumentation and come into prominence through repetition.[34]

If we recall Tertullian's later Montanist sympathies, we shall not be surprised that he represents Paul as the proclaimer of the Spirit and the Spirit's gifts. In the *De anima* (9.4), the apostle is cited as the sufficient guarantor (*idoneus sponsor*) of the truth of the vision received by a Carthaginian sister as the gift of the Spirit; and in the *Adversus Marcionem* (5.8.9, 12), it is through his proclamation of the gifts of the Spirit that the apostle is identified as belonging to the God of the Old Testament. Two features are noteworthy in Tertullian's representation of the Pauline message of the Spirit: first, Tertullian's citations from Paul on the Spirit do not belong simply to his Montanist phase but can be seen in some of his earliest writings; and second, one observes a shift, as time elapses, from an emphasis on the tenderness of soul and tranquillity of mind requisite for the Spirit to an emphasis on the wisdom conveyed by the Spirit—a shift from moral to intellectual categories in the definition of the Spirit's nature and function.

In the early *Ad martyras*, after a brief introduction, Tertullian places in the forefront of his discussion the words of Ephesians 4:30, "Do not grieve the Holy Spirit" (*Ad mart.* 1.3), and suggests that it is first in dissension that the Spirit is grieved (1.5). A similar point is made more explicitly in *De spectaculis* 15.2, with a reference evidently to such Pauline texts as Ephesians 4:30 and Galatians 5:22: "God teaches us to treat the Holy Spirit with tranquillity, gentleness, quietness and peace, as it is tender and delicate, according to the goodness of its nature, and not with wrath, jealousy, anger, or grief."[35] Pauline allusions (Eph. 4:30; Rom. 14:17) are again apparent in *De oratione* 12, where we are bidden to be free from perturbation of mind in prayer, since a defiled spirit cannot be acknowledged by a Holy Spirit, nor a sad spirit by a joyful Spirit.[36] With the *De praescriptione*, we begin to see the importance of the Spirit as the source of wisdom. In 7.7 Tertullian adds, strikingly, to the apostle's words from Colossians 2:8 ("Let no one spoil you through philosophy and vain deceit, according to the tradition of men") what appears to be his own gloss, *praeter providentiam Spiritus sancti* ("contrary to the wisdom of the Holy Spirit"). Perhaps the most decisive statement on the Spirit as the essential companion of the mind that would truly know is to be found in the later work *Against Marcion* (2.2.4–6). The apostle has said that the ways of God are past finding out (Rom. 11:33) and that no one can know what is in God except the Spirit of God (1 Cor. 2:11). Those who have the spirit of the world do not know God for they do not receive the things of the Spirit (1 Cor. 2:14). The implication is clear that it is only the Christian who can truly know by virtue of possessing the Spirit.

I have already anticipated a second prominent theme that Tertullian associates with Pauline texts—the knowledge of God through natural and divine revelation.[37] It was a theme appropriate to Tertullian's designation of Paul, as we have already seen, as *magister ecclesiae* and *doctor nationum*.[38] Though Tertullian is himself somewhat ambiguous about the value of natural revelation, the possibility is repeatedly affirmed in his work and is on occasion so firmly attached to Paul's teaching that we may confidently assume the source everywhere to be Pauline, whether the thought emerges specifically from Romans 1 and 2, 1 Corinthians 11:14, Acts 17:22–31, or more generally from all of these. It is in *De corona* 6 that the Pauline background for Tertullian's expression of the idea is most explicit. He challenges his opponents to consider the law of God written on "the tables of nature," "to which even the apostle is accustomed to appeal." Here he reviews Romans 1:20–26, Romans 2:14, and 1 Corinthians 11:14, then offers a summary conclusion: "We know God himself first according to nature, calling upon him as God of gods, assuming that he is good, invoking him as judge (*De cor.* 6.1–2). We may recognize in this conclusion an abbreviated statement of the theme adroitly developed around a forensic image in the much earlier *De testimonio animae*, where, however, the language appears to be deliberately secular, drawing on neither the Pauline corpus nor any other part of scripture. Again, the doctrine forms a brief preface to the discussion of the creation and fall in the second book against Marcion; and, in this case, Romans 1:20 or possibly Paul's speech on the Areopagus may be the point of reference. "But now the almighty God, the Lord and creator of the universe, is the subject of criticism (*negotium patitur*), for this reason, I suppose, because he was known from the beginning, because he never lay hidden, because he always shone brightly" (*Adv. Marc.* 2.2.1).[39]

But if Tertullian saw in Paul the preacher of natural revelation, it appears that he was more intimate with the Paul who proclaimed the necessity of divine revelation, above all in such passages as 1 Corinthians 1:20, 27 and 3:19. Indeed, Tertullian frequently sets in contrast natural and divine revelation. In the *De resurrectione mortuorum*, he acknowledges the possibility of natural revelation, recalling images from the *De testimonio animae*. "It is possible to be wise in the things of God even from the *communis sensus* . . . some things are known by nature . . . I shall accept the common conscience which attests the God of gods. . . . But when they say, 'Death is the end,' then I shall remember . . . that the very wisdom of the world has been pronounced folly" (*De res. mort.* 3.1–3). The contrast also appears in the first chapter of the *De paenitentia*, with a less positive evaluation of natural revelation; and already in the *De spectaculis*, those who know God *naturali iure*, from "far off," are contrasted with those who know God as members of his family, *de proximo.* [40] It was, of course, in the discussion of "heresies" that Tertullian had to insist on the indispensability of the divine revelation and the insufficiency of human knowledge, and here the Pauline texts could be effectively cited. The effect of baptism is beyond our human understanding, but then we have the divine declaration that God has chosen the foolish things of the world to confound its wisdom (*De bapt.* 2.3). Tertullian again quotes the appropriate phrases from the Pauline texts as a prelude to his famous formula in *De praescriptione* 7: "What has Athens to do with Jerusalem" (see *De praescr.* 7.1–2 and 7.8–9). In the *De carne Christi*, arguing against Marcion, he recalls 1 Corinthians 1:27 in order to contrast purely human judgments with the divine wisdom; and in the *Adversus Marcionem*, he summons the same text to contrast the simplicity of the truth with the clever arguments (*ingenia*) of the heretic (5.19.8). [41]

Paul would appear then to have been, for Tertullian, a figure deeply concerned with the problem of knowledge, and especially Christian knowledge. Tertullian was also keenly aware that Paul sensed he was living in the end of time; and he understood the apostle's message as strongly eschatological in its orientation. I shall not discuss here the *De resurrectione mortuorum*, since the very question addressed in that work made extensive discussion of Pauline eschatological texts virtually inevitable. But Pauline eschatology supports a variety of arguments elsewhere. The Pauline dictum from 1 Corinthians 7:29—"the time is short" (in Tertullian, *in collectum* [or, *in collecto*] *tempus est*)—is central in Tertullian's discussion of marriage and becomes a veritable refrain in the *De monogamia.* [42] It is also summoned in *Adversus Marcionem* 5.8.7 to demonstrate that the last days to which the prophet Joel refers (Joel 2:28) are the same last days in which the apostle lives. Other "eschatological" phrases from the Pauline letters are closely woven into Tertullian's text and show the Pauline background of Tertullian's eschatological thought. Job preferred to have his children restored "in that day," meaning evidently in the life beyond (*De pat.* 14.7).[43] This phrase, presumably from 2 Timothy 4:8, appears again in *De cultu feminarum*, where Tertullian attempts, with splendid irony, to place the ornamentation of women in the light of eschatology. "Would that I might 'in that day' of Christian exultation raise my head, even if below your heels" (2.7.3). In the previous chapter (2.6.4), Tertullian speaks of the "incorruptibility" we are to put on (see 1 Cor. 15:54). Again, 1 Corinthians 15 plays its part in laying the ground for the trinitarian definitions of the *Adversus Praxean*.[44]

Of all the eschatological terms and images in Paul, however, none seems to have fascinated Tertullian so much as that from 1 Corinthians 6:2 and 3: "Do you not know that the saints will judge the world . . . that we shall judge angels?" In Tertullian, the image is used to console the martyrs: "They may expect this world's judge; let them remember that they will judge their judges" (*Ad mart.* 2.4). It also consoles those who must give up magistracies here on earth which are tainted with idolatry, for it assures them that they will be magistrates in the heavens (*De idol.* 18.9). In *De fuga* 10.2 the image is again used to instill courage: "Should the Christian fear men, when he who is to judge angels should be feared by angels, when he who is to judge the world should be feared by the world?" Tertullian traces the origin of female ornamentation to the "angels" who desired the daughters of men (Gn. 6:2, 4). "These," he says, "are the angels we are to judge. . . . With what consistency will we ascend that tribunal to judge those whose gifts we have sought? For to you [women], too, . . . is promised . . . the same honor of judging as is promised to men" (*De cultu fem.* 1.2.4–5).

I have by no means exhausted the account of Pauline themes and images prominent in Tertullian's work. In particular, we might add to the list those Pauline images that accommodate Tertullian's fondness for paradox and antithesis: images of conflict and warfare, of light and dark, of Christ and Belial. Yet the themes I have traced enable us to construct, however cautiously, the image Tertullian could have entertained of the mind of Paul, an image whose coherence suggests that the clues provided have not been misleading. Tertullian appears to have understood Paul as the preacher of a new age, the last age, which was the age of the Spirit. In the view of Tertullian's Paul, the Spirit furnished those who entered the new age with gifts, above all the gift of knowledge, a knowledge that was not, however, in conflict with ordinary human knowledge insofar as normal human knowledge had not been distorted by the prejudices of the former age. Meanwhile the present age of the Spirit was moving to its glorious *telos* when the sanctified would ascend the great tribunal to pronounce judgment on the enemies of God, and so God would become all in all.[45]

The picture I have drawn suggests that the "Pauline" contrast between grace and law plays a less significant part in Tertullian's image of Paul than Barth wanted to find. The gospel as a new law does indeed find expression in Tertullian, an expression, however, in which on occasion the Sermon on the Mount provides the point of reference.[46] It has in any case been argued that in Tertullian, the word "grace" (*gratia*) has the prevailing sense of "gift," or "endowment."[47] As suggested earlier in this essay, Tertullian's Paul, it would seem, emerges more from the Epistles to the Corinthians than from the Epistles to the Romans and the Galatians.[48]

In this essay, I have argued that the special nature of Tertullian's writings—highly artful compositions motivated by powerful ecclesiastical and theological concerns—demands that we do not constrict our view, in the search for the legacy of Paul, merely to an interpretation of "Pauline theology" in Tertullian. Tertullian does indeed have an understanding of Paul as theologian; as I have shown, however, it is an understanding that does not take its point of departure from an antithesis between law and grace but from a vivid sense of the significance of the age in which we live and of the presence of the Spirit as the sign of that age. Nevertheless, for Tertullian, the record of Paul's life was also an important legacy bequeathed to the church—capital, as it were, for astute investment in literary art. Tertullian's experiment in a Christian literary art whose ends the apostle was made to serve should in itself command our attention. But out of his rhetorical art a figure of the apostle emerges worthy also of our interest, a figure capable of change and growth, rendered present to the reader in the sound of his voice and the touch of his flesh, but at the same time a figure with the power and authority appropriate to a haloed saint.

PART TWO:
PAUL IN THE THEOLOGICAL AND EXEGETICAL TRADITION

Free Choice and the Divine Will in Greek Christian Commentaries on Paul

ROBERT L. WILKEN

"There is," wrote Theodoret of Cyrus, "a certain kind of rock, called magnetic, which leaves all other materials unmoved and attracts only iron." The holy scriptures can be compared to this rock, for they too draw only some human beings to themselves while leaving the others quite untouched. Magnetic rock, however, draws iron by necessity, whereas the grace of the divine oracles does not force anyone to approach. Rather, the scriptures gush out streams of living water, and by free choice (*authaireton*) those who are thirsty come to drink and those who have no desire turn away. The physician of souls does not coerce the will of those who do not wish to savor his goodness. He has created human nature independent and free; by his exhortations and laws he turns us from evil and points us in the direction of what is better; he does not compel us against our will to partake of better things.[1]

If one eliminated from this passage the mention of the holy scriptures and put in their place laws and precepts and examples, it could have been written by Plato, by Carneades, by Plutarch, by Alexander of Aphrodisias, or by any number of other defenders of free will in the ancient world. This is, of course, Theodoret's point; for the passage I have cited comes from his apology called, immodestly and ironically, "the curing of Greek maladies." Book Five, from which the text is taken, is a discussion of human nature, and one of the aims of that book is to offer a philosophical and scriptural defense of freedom of choice (*autexousion* or *authaireton*). Against the determinists, chiefly the Stoics, Theodoret deploys citations from Plato and the scriptures to show that human beings are subject neither to "necessity (*anagkēs*) nor to fate (*heimarmenēs*) nor to the threads of *moira*; their deeds and activities are not dependent on the revolution of the heavens nor on the conjunction of the stars." The human soul is free, and human beings are responsible for the things that happen to them. We do not sin by necessity or by constraint, says Theodoret, but because of our free choice.[2]

In the ancient world the philosophical problem of freedom and determinism was felt most acutely in the moral realm. Virtue was a fragile plant whose growth was frustrated by forces beyond its control; yet its growth could only take place in dependence on external factors like sun and rain and cultivation. "Human excellence (*aretē*)," wrote Pindar, "grows like a vine tree, fed by the green dew, raised up, among wise men and just, to the liquid sky." A large measure of the intellectual effort of antiquity was given over to discovering a sure and certain path of virtue, to achieving self-sufficiency by rational means in a world that seemed to work against one's best efforts. "This splendid and equivocal hope," as Martha Nussbaum writes in *The Fragility of Goodness*, "is a central preoccupation of ancient Greek thought about the human good. A raw sense of the passivity of human beings and their humanity in the world of nature, and a response of both horror and anger at that passivity, lived side by side with and nourished the belief that reason's activity could make safe, and thereby save, our human lives—indeed, must save them, if they were to be humanly worth living."[3]

By the time Christianity had begun to set its roots down in the Mediterranean world, there had been a long tradition of reflection on these issues.[4] One of the legacies of this discussion was a doctrine of free choice, adumbrated centuries earlier, for example in Aristotle's *Nichomachean Ethics*.[5] With the rise of Stoicism, especially as its teaching became identified with the determinism of Chrysippus in the late third century B.C.E., and later as astrology gained popularity and articulate spokesmen, determinism became an attractive philosophical option. Its most articulate critic was Carneades, the founder of the new Academy in the second century B.C.E., whose work was directed explicitly at Chrysippus. However, Carneades also addressed the new problems posed by astrology, arguing that the empirical and rational grounds for believing that the stars determined human behavior were fragile and unscientific. People born, for example, under the same sign of the zodiac have different fortunes in life.[6]

In philosophical works dealing with fate and determinism during the early imperial period—for example, Alexander of Aphrodisias' De fato or Maximus of Tyre's If Divination Exists, What Is Left to Free Choice? (Oratio 13)—Carneades' arguments, as well as those of Plato and Aristotle, are repeated again and again.[7] The one argument that appears most consistently is the appeal to "rewards and punishments," that is, to the social and legal fact of praise and blame. If everything is determined by fate or by the conjunction of the stars, responsibility, and hence virtue, is rendered otiose. Alexander of Aphrodisias makes the point this way:

> But if long beforehand, and even before that, and before any of them ever came to be in the first place, it was true to predict of each of them that thing which they are censured for having done, how could they still themselves be blamed for the actual things that came to be? And how will anyone explain how virtues and vices, too, depend on us? For if it is because we are in such a state, how will it still be reasonable for some to be praised and others blamed?[8]

The life of a virtuous person is evidence for free choice. Virtue lies within our own power.

When we first turn to Christian discussions of free will, it is evident that they stand within the philosophical tradition that opposed determinism and fate, and hence asserted both freedom of choice and responsibility for one's actions. Like other philosophers, Christians appeal to "rewards and punishments" as well as to other arguments that were commonplace in the antecedent tradition (e.g., the different destinies of twins as discrediting astrology). How much Christian thinkers are dependent on the philosophical criticism of determinism can be seen in the discussion of free choice in the third book of Origen's De principiis.[9]

Yet there is a difference, one that is noteworthy and important. In contrast to the philosophers, Christian thinkers enter the discussion on the defensive. On the basis of their knowledge of the new movement, outsiders thought Christians expounded a new form of determinism. In the *Octavius*, Minucius Felix allows us to catch a glimpse of the impression that Christian teaching made on outsiders. "Others say that all our actions are due to fate; you [Christians] say, similarly, that they are due to god. This entails that it is not of their own free will that human beings desire to join your school; they have been chosen (*electos*). Therefore the judge that you fashion is unjust; he punishes human beings not for their intentions (*voluntatem*) but for their lot in life."[10]

The first mention of "free choice" in Christian writings occurs in Justin Martyr's *First Apology*; and it would seem, from his description of the problem, that he is replying to precisely the kind of charge mentioned by Minucius, namely, that Christians are deterministic. Justin writes: "So that none may infer from what we have said that the events we speak of, because they were foreknown and predicted, took place according to inevitable destiny—I can explain this too" (Justin had a ready answer for all difficulties). Prophecy seems to imply necessity because the Spirit knows beforehand what things are to happen and "speaks of them as if they had already occurred." However, that is not our view, Justin counters, because we have also "learned from the prophets . . . that penalties and punishments and good rewards are given according to the quality of each person's actions. If this were not so, and all things happened according to destiny, nothing would be dependent on ourselves (*to eph hēmin*)."[11]

To support his defense of free will, Justin cites several passages from the Septuagint (e.g., "Behold I have set before you good and evil, choose the good" [Dt. 30:15]) and a line from Plato's *Republic*.[12] Justin's argument is, of course, commonplace. What is not traditional is the claim that he learned the doctrine of free choice from the scriptures. Although the arguments are well worn, the claim that free choice is a Christian teaching appears here explicitly for the first time.

Justin, of course, does not concede that there is any basis in Christian teaching for the charge of determinism. He cites only those texts from the scripture that support free choice, ignoring those that intimate the reverse. It is not until Origen that the problem is faced forthrightly. "There are in the scriptures,"

Origen writes, "ten thousand passages that prove the existence of free choice with utmost clarity." But, he continues, "certain sayings from both the Old and the New Testaments incline us to the opposite conclusion." Among the texts in the latter category are the story of the hardening of Pharaoh's heart in Exodus 4, Ezekiel 11:19–20 ("I will take away their stony hearts and will put in them hearts of flesh that they may walk in my statutes"), and Romans 9:16 and 18 ("So it depends not upon man's will or exertion, but upon God's mercy," and "So then he has mercy upon whomever he wills, and he hardens the heart of whomever he wills").[13]

And so we come to Paul. At the outset it is well to state the obvious: early Christian interpreters of Paul brought to the interpretation of his writings an agenda derived in large measure from the classical intellectual tradition.[14] There was no other way for them to read Paul's letters than with ears attuned to the accents of the culture that formed them. Nevertheless, there is a subtle shift of emphasis even in the earliest sources. For in classical antiquity, the discussion of freedom of choice was an ethical and moral issue, as Nussbaum's book illustrates, whereas in Christian writers, as pagan observers noted, it is first and foremost a theological problem: "the judge you fashion is unjust." Recall the words at the beginning of Origen's discussion of free choice in *De principiis*: "Since the teaching of the church includes the doctrine of the righteous judgment of God," it is of the utmost urgency to discuss "free choice."[15] The doctrine of free choice has to do, first of all, with the question of God's relation to humankind.

One of the texts that formed the exegetical basis for the discussion of these issues was, of course, Romans 9; so we should first review what is said there.[16] Romans 9 takes up the topic of the place of Israel in the divine economy. At the end of chapter 8, Paul had asserted that nothing could separate us from the love of God in Christ. But now he acknowledges that, for some, the coming of the Christ seems to have done just that. Those who were the objects of God's love, the Jews, to whom belong the "giving of the law, the worship, and the promises" (Rom. 9:4), appear now to be cut off from God's love. Does this mean that the "word of God" has failed?

This question leads Paul to a discussion of the story of Jacob and Esau, which he sees as an analogy to the present dilemma. For the story seems to overturn any idea of God's fairness and justice. Jacob and Esau were born of one mother, Rebecca, by the same father, Isaac, yet the one was chosen and the other rejected—as it was written, "Jacob I loved, but Esau I hated." Is God then unjust? In response, Paul cites Exodus 33:19: "I will have mercy on whom I have mercy, and I will have compassion on whom I have compassion." He concludes: "So it depends not upon man's will or exertion, but upon God's mercy" (Rom. 9:15–16). As further support he mentions the story of Pharaoh, whom it is said that God used to "show forth his power." God has mercy on whomever he wills, and he hardens the heart of whomever he wills (Rom. 9:17–18). Finally, Paul introduces the metaphor of the potter who makes from the same lump of clay a vessel for beauty and another for menial use. What right has the clay to speak back to the potter (Rom. 9:19–21)?

On first reading, this passage must have startled Christians and pagans alike. It is as though hemlines had moved from the ankle to the knee without warning or hats had become de rigueur for fashionable male dress. Paul's language shatters conventional assumptions, and its examples offend common sensibilities. Romans 9 early acquired unwanted notoriety and was surely known to pagan critics of Christianity. Origen speaks of the "famous problem concerning Jacob and Esau."[17] Paul not only seems to deny human responsibility but also locates the cause of human blessings or bane in the arbitrary will of God. This text, among others, says Origen, "disturb[s] the many with the belief that human beings do not possess free will (*autexousion*), but that God saves and destroys whomever he himself wills."[18]

For early Christian commentators, Romans 9 presented almost insurmountable obstacles. One way of overcoming the obstacles was to read it as a debate between two conflicting points of view, assigning the more extreme statements not to Paul but to a fictive opponent. Origen, in his commentary on Romans, was the first to suggest this reading of the text. He takes the phrase "it depends not upon man's will or exertion, but upon God's mercy" (Rom. 9:16) not as Paul's own statement but as an inference drawn by Paul's opponents from the passage in Exodus: "I will have mercy on whom I have mercy" (Ex. 33:19; cf. Rom. 9:15). Theodore of Mopsuestia adopts a similar strategy for the same reasons, as do a number of other commentators.[19]

The text had to be read in light of recognized and accepted teachings, namely, the justice of God and free choice. If one abandoned these teachings, there could be no rational understanding of Christian faith. "It is agreed," Theodore writes, "that the power of choosing good or worse things lies within ourselves, and it is also . . . proved decisively that we are the *cause* of the things that happen to us."[20] In their efforts to defend human responsibility, patristic commentators employ familiar arguments in defense of free will; and the parallels with non-Christian thinkers are close. Compare, for example, the words of Alexander of Aphrodisias: "Only the actions of human beings among all living creatures depend on themselves, because only human beings have the power of not doing the same thing."[21] Defense of free choice is a recurring theme in the commentaries on Romans 9.[22]

John Chrysostom also saw the difficulties in the text and, like Theodore, wished to avoid the implication that the text subverted human freedom. To establish his interpretation, he argues that Paul is using an analogy; and in any analogy, the interpreter must focus only on the "point of comparison," not the individual details. The text "does not abolish free choice," he writes, "but shows to what extent it is necessary to obey God." When, for example, scripture speaks of God as a lion, we must note the "indomitable and awesome part," not the brutality of the lion. In the case of Romans 9, we must center on God's sovereignty and economy, for if we take the passage to mean that we are not responsible for our actions, Paul will be at odds with himself.[23]

Christian expositors of Paul were reluctant to relinquish the acquired wisdom of Greek antiquity and, by the fourth century, of Christian tradition. In this they were surely correct. Without human responsibility and hence, in their terms, without free choice, there is no moral personality (as Paul himself taught: "Do you suppose . . . that those who do such things . . . will escape the judgment of God. . . . For he will render to every man according to his works" [Rom. 2:2]). Modern interpreters of early

Christian thought, many of whom approach the fathers with the cadences of Luther's *De servo arbitrio* in mind, make much out of the adherence to free will. Valentin Weber's study of the interpretation of Romans 9:14–23, for example, argues that early Christian exegetes were so completely captive to the doctrine of free will that they failed to grasp the implications of the text.[24] As Maurice Wiles writes in *The Divine Apostle*: "Those who regard the Greek tradition in theology as combining admiration for Paul's person with a serious failure to understand his teaching point especially to the subject of divine grace and human freedom. Thus A. Puech is surprised to find an obvious affection for Paul on the part of Chrysostom, when he is such an emphatic exponent of free will and, so Puech claims, consistently misinterprets the predestinatory texts in Paul's writings."[25]

Such a reading of the commentaries is tendentious and misleading. It overlooks the way in which the very language of the scriptures affected the early commentators' thinking, subtly altering their approach to philosophical problems and creating for them a new context in which to address long-debated issues. If we look closely at the concrete discussion of terms and phrases in the commentaries, we can observe surprising shifts that are not easily reconciled with the commentators' professed views. In the actual practice of exegesis, the language of scripture did not easily contract to fit cultural expectations. The words came coded with a different history. Problems that had earlier taken one form acquired a new appearance when they were set in the new context. Let me offer a few examples.

I begin with Apollinaris of Laodicea on Romans 9, and specifically with his comments on the phrase "it depends not upon man's will . . . but upon God's mercy." Do not think, he says, that these words do not conform to the "logic of justice," as though God is unjust because the economy has to do with mercy. Justice has to do with "human measurements," whereas mercy is dispensed according to the wisdom of God. "Therefore being shown mercy is not a result of our deeds, but of God who has it within his power to show mercy." Then he adds: "Showing mercy must be distinguished from judging." In the one case, a person is seen as a "cause to himself reaping what he sows," but in the other case, "the one who shows mercy is the cause."[26]

Apollinaris' use of the term *cause (aitia)* in this connection is striking because it is a term used in discussions about free choice, as can be seen in the passage from Theodore cited above and in Alexander of Aphrodisias: "The things that come about in this way do not come about without a cause, having their cause from us. For a human being is the beginning and cause of the actions that come about through him."[27] Apollinaris seems almost deliberately to flaunt the conventional language, and for a very good reason. His point is that mercy and judging are incommensurate, for they imply different kinds of relations.

Origen makes a similar observation in commenting on Romans 3:9 ("there is no one righteous, no not one"). Justice (*dikaiosunē*), he says, is a relative term. There is no such thing as justice in the abstract. A person is just in relation to another person, one who is inferior. Do not think, he argues, that the scriptures are contradictory if in one place they say someone is just and in another the opposite. Paul knows that there have been just people, even though he says, "no not one." "For the same man is just when compared to so and so, but when compared to God, he is not just." Elsewhere Origen says that there are "two types of righteousness, one which justifies before God, which is by faith, the other before the rest of the *logikoi*, which is by works."[28]

Apollinaris' argument can, I think, be read in this same way. Romans 9 is not about justice in the conventional sense because justice requires measurement; Paul is speaking about actions of God, and these do not conform to the standards of human measurement. Indeed, in the light of Apollinaris' comments on the opening chapter of the epistle, it appears that he regards Romans 9 as the fullest statement of the argument of the letter as a whole. Romans is a book not about justice but about mercy. In his summary of the argument of the book, at Romans 1:16–17, he explains: "In place of justification through works which is neither pure nor lifegiving," Paul speaks about "life as a gift of grace through faith."[29]

Another parallel to Apollinaris' distinction between justice and mercy can be found in Origen's discussion of Romans 4. In that chapter, Paul distinguished (Rom. 4:4) between that which is received by gift (*kata charin*) and that which is rendered as due (*kata opheilēma*). "No one," writes Origen,

> by the nature of human beings or of any of the creatures, is so capable of doing what is right that the reward given by God to those who do rightly is not by grace but by due. For I would even say that nothing of what God gives to the created nature does he give as being due; rather, he bestows all things as grace; and all who are shown kindness receive kindness not from a kindness owed them, but rather God wills by his own grace to show kindness on whomever he shows kindness.

Origen then proceeds to interpret the Pauline text by reference to the parable of the laborers in the vineyard who worked different lengths of time yet all received the same pay (Mt. 20:1-16). They received their money not by due, or by recompense, but by grace. Even those who were hired early in the morning and thought that they had earned what they received, received it by grace.[30] Origen's language here ("show kindness on whomever he shows kindness") is obviously similar to the language of Romans 9; and his observations on Romans 4 suggest that he was reading that chapter in the light of what was to come in chapter 9.

My first point, then, is that the text of Romans forced inter- preters to address questions that could not be fitted easily into received categories of understanding. Exegesis required a reorder- ing of familiar concepts. Old words acquired new vitality as they were given new referents, and new words entered the traditional lexicon. In the issue before us, as the intellectual and spiritual horizons of the interpreter expanded, the question of free choice came to be seen as part of the theological problem of divine intervention.

This shift from what had been an exclusively moral issue to what now became also a theological problem is evident in other ways. Paul's letters presented the interpreter with a problem un- familiar to classical thought: the nature of divine intentionality. Romans 9, for example, makes it clear that what happened to

Jacob and Esau happened for a purpose. Similarly, Pharaoh's heart was hardened not simply to punish him but to show forth God's power in the world; and the vessels made by the potter are designed for beauty or for menial use. Anyone who is familiar with the scriptures is at home with this language, but it is offensive to Greek thinking. On this point the cleavage between the scriptures and classical thought is deep and unbridgeable, as Galen was the first to note. Speaking of the biblical account of creation, he wrote, "It was certainly not sufficient merely to *will* things coming into being."[31]

In the philosophical tradition, freedom was set over against necessity and fate, external causes that work ineluctably and inexorably to determine one's place in the world. "Fate is some cause that is unalterable and inescapable," wrote Alexander of Aphrodisias. Fate and destiny are closely linked to nature. Fate, wrote Chrysippus, is a "natural ordering (*phusikē suntaxis*) of all things from on high, one thing following another and being rolled out according to an inviolable arrangement."[32] In the scriptures, however, nature is always subject to God's will. Hence Romans 9, which seemed to require a determinist explanation of events, was seen as proof that God did not "follow" the demands of nature but acted on the basis of inscrutable purposes. Theodoret of Cyrus wrote, "This text [Rom. 9:14] is able to show and to teach clearly that it is not customary for the God of all to give heed to nature, but that he seeks after a higher purpose (*gnōmē*)." Other commentators make a similar point. Theodore of Mopsuestia writes, "These things have been said . . . to show that God does not conform to the endowment of nature, but that out of grace and munificence he considers some to be worthy of his election."[33]

While proclaiming a Greek doctrine of free choice, Greek commentators on Paul embrace Paul's voluntaristic language for God even though it weakens their defense of free choice. Indeed, in places they seem to exaggerate rather than to temper its implications. Now it hardly needs saying that the idea of divine will is foreign to classical thinking. This point has been demonstrated with judicious learning in Albrecht Dihle's recent work, *The Theory of Will in Classical Antiquity*. For the Greco-Roman philosophical tradition, Dihle notes: "Everything that goes on in the universe has been arranged and initiated by the same reason that man has been given, so that he may understand his own position in the universe and act accordingly. There is no need for assuming behind or apart from the entirely rational program-ming of reality a will of which the impulse or manifestation is unpredictable."[34] Occasionally the term *will* was used, but its meaning was always carefully circumscribed so that will could not be set over against nature, against the order and regularity that governed the cosmos.

To illustrate the impact of the Pauline language on this problem, let me turn to another passage from Paul's letters, Eph-esians 1. "Blessed be the God and Father of our Lord Jesus Christ, who has blessed us in Christ with every spiritual blessing . . . even as he chose us in him before the foundation of the world . . . He destined us in love to be his sons through Jesus Christ, according to the purpose of his will" (Eph. 1:3–5). And later in the chapter Paul writes, "In him, according to the pur-pose of him who accomplishes all things according to the coun-sel of his will, we who first hoped in Christ have been destined and appointed to live for the praise of his glory" (Eph. 1:11–12).

Ephesians lacks the concreteness of Romans 9; it makes no mention of Jacob and Esau, nor of Pharaoh, nor of any other historical figure. But its terminology is close to that of Romans 9 (note, for example, the terms *prothesis, thelēma,* and *thelō*), and it clearly draws on a similar store of ideas. What is of particular interest, however, and what struck Greek-speaking readers of the text, is the unusual term that occurs here: *eudokia,* "good pleas-ure," a word that also occurs in the well-known passage in Theodore of Mopsuestia's *De incarnatione* on the nature of the union between God the Word and the man Jesus.

Eudokia is not used in good Greek prose. Its use is almost entirely confined to the Septuagint, to Jewish literature, to the New Testament, and, of course, to ecclesiastical Greek. Origen was the first to observe this point; and in his commentary on Ephesians 1, he suggests that the word was coined by the transla-tors of the LXX. To explain its meaning, he refers to its use in the Psalms ("You were favorable [*eudokēsas*], Lord, to your Land" [Ps. 84:1; LXX]; "Remember us, Lord, in your good pleasure [*eudokia*] toward your people" [Ps. 105:4; LXX]) and in a passage in Habakkuk (2:4).[35] Origen dutifully explains that the term is derived from *eu* and *dokeō*, to think well or to seem good, so there is no mystery about its meaning. Yet its very singularity suggests that it bore a distinctive sense, that it was used in the Bible to express aspects of God's activity that were otherwise vague and undefined. It was a kind of cognitive tool.

On the basis of the word's conjunction with *thelēma* in Ephesians 1:5, early Christian exegetes construed *eudokia* as another term for the divine will. Since *thelēsis* and *energeia* are similar ideas, wrote Severian of Gabala, instead of saying "the will of his will," Paul says "the good pleasure of his will."[36] Theodoret of Cyrus makes a similar point. *Eudokia thelēmatos autou* means "he willed this"; it refers to "the active will" (*tēn ep' euergesia boulēsin*). Hence in the first chapter of Ephesians Paul teaches that God "who does whatever he wills chose us for this life."[37]

Eudokia, however, implied more than will or intention. In its biblical use it carried overtones of feeling or emotion. Hence it came to be associated with the intensification of will through ardor and attachment, even through desire. Take, for example, John Chrysostom's homily on Ephesians 1:5: "he destined us in love to be his sons through Jesus Christ, according to the purpose [or good pleasure] of his will." John comments: Paul uses the term *eudokia* of God because he wishes to say that

> [God] willed it earnestly (*dia to sphodrōs thelēsai*). This is, one might say, his desire. The term *eudokia* everywhere refers to the primary will. There is also another will. Just as the first will is that sinners not perish, the second is that those who have become evil should perish. He does not punish them by necessity, but because he wills. This can be seen in Paul when he says, "I wish all men to be like me" (1 Cor. 7:7). And again, "I want young widows to marry and bear children" (1 Tm. 5:14). *Eudokia*, therefore, refers to the first will, the earnest will, the will with desire, the fixed intent (*to peisma*). I will not deprecate the use of a more common mode of speech for making the matter clear to the more simple. For we also, in showing the intensity (*epitasis*) of our will, say "according to our fixed

resolve" (*peisma*). What he says, then, is this. God earnestly
(*sphodra*) wishes, earnestly desires (*epithumei*) our salvation.[38]

In this passage the biblical language seems to sanction a description of God that would be quite unacceptable on philosophical or theological grounds.

One might doubt whether Theodore of Mopsuestia would have spoken so incautiously, and in general he did not. Yet he too thought *eudokia* in Ephesians 1:5 meant an intensification of divine purpose and hence "love." He punctuates verse four in such a way that "in love" goes not with the phrase "holy and blameless before him," but with "elected" or "destined." Hence he interprets Paul as follows: "elegit [God] nos non absolute sed in caritate." Then he adds, "it pleased him exceedingly (*sphodra*) that these things be done on our behalf," or in the Latin translation, "valde voluit in his nos participes fieri."[39]

Paul's letters thrust on Christian thinkers a new and discordant vocabulary with which to speak about God; and even though their commentaries show that they have to struggle to make his ideas intelligible, they do not shun that vocabulary. On the contrary, they begin to adopt the voluntarist language—which, of course, appeared deterministic within the older philosophical framework—as a way to break out of natural determinism or fatalism.

Recall the discussion of *eudokia* in Theodore's *De incarnatione*. There the topic is the nature of God's indwelling among human beings, whether it is a matter of essence or of activity. Theodore rejects both of these possibilities, the former because it would circumscribe God's essence and the latter because God's activity (*energeia*) is universal in scope and not limited to particular cases. Theodore says that a more appropriate way of speaking about indwelling would be in terms of *eudokia*, good pleasure. "Good pleasure is the name for that very good and excellent will of God which he exercises because pleased with those who are earnestly devoted to him; the word is derived from his 'good' and excellent 'pleasure' in them. Scripture frequently speaks of God being thus disposed." In support of his point, Theodore cites several passages from the Psalms (e.g., Ps. 146:11: "The Lord has good pleasure in those who fear him and in those who hope in his mercy").[40]

Now the important point for our discussion is that good pleasure is distinguished from necessity. To say that God is present in his good pleasure, and not by essence or activity, means that he "is not subject to any external necessity. If on the other hand he were universally present in his good pleasure, this again would make him in a different way subject to external necessity. In that case he would not be determining his presence by choice of will; it would be a matter of his uncircumscribed nature and his will would be simply consequent on that."[41]

Richard Norris interprets this passage in the light of Theodore's Neoplatonic metaphysics. An intelligible being cannot enter into relations with material entities. A relation is possible only through will or inclination. But then Norris notes, with some surprise, that Theodore identifies this intentional presence (expressed with terms such as *diathesis* or *schesis*) with grace. In commenting on the Psalms, Theodore uses words such as *love* or *desire* to express the same idea.[42] Of course, Theodore's thinking is shaped in part by the philosophical tradition in which he stands; and it would certainly overstate the case to make the term *eudokia* bear the entire weight of his argument in *De incarnatione*. Yet might not one ask whether it was not the voluntarism built into the term *eudokia* that made it so appropriate to express the relation between God and human beings and, in a more highly charged sense, between the divine Word and the assumed man in the incarnation?

This leads to my final point. It was only within the context of the scriptures that voluntaristic language for God was intelligible and could be appropriated for theological and philosophical purposes. Romans 9 (as well as Ephesians 1) could not be and was not read as a discussion of the philosophical problem of freedom and determinism *tout court*. The stories of Jacob and Esau and of the hardening of Pharaoh's heart fit within the framework of biblical narrative, a narrative that speaks of divine purpose, of promise and hope, of faithfulness and fulfillment. Isaac was born to Abraham and Sarah, wrote Origen on Romans 4, not by sexual ardor (*purōsis*) but by promise.[43]

The theological issue in Romans 9, according to Greek Christian commentators, is whether God's purpose follows nature—that is, blood, kinship, race—or whether it follows God's will or intention. But it must not be forgotten that the issue of freedom and determinism only arises because of the story of Jacob and Esau. Gennadius of Constantinople argues that Paul is responding to Jewish objections that God's promise is tied to race, that is, to nature. Did God mislead his people with his promises to them, ask the Jews, or is the gospel false? In relating the story of Jacob and Esau, Paul wishes to show that God does not follow "lineage according to nature." "God does not serve the necessity of nature." Rather God acts according to "his own purpose, not dependent on [human] deeds or natural kinship."[44]

The Jewish claim to have received the promises of God is made a matter not of divine intention, but of nature. Admittedly this seems to avoid the hard problem posed by Paul, namely, how can God forsake those to whom belong the "sonship, the glory, the covenants, the giving of the law" (Rom. 9:4)? But the opposition between nature and promise is rooted in the text: "not all are children of Abraham because they are his descendants" (Rom. 9:7). Only children of promise, not those who are Jews by birth, are reckoned as descendants. As Theodore of Mopsuestia's comment makes clear, the story of Jacob and Esau forces a sharp distinction between divine purpose and natural order at just this point. "What then would you say about Esau and Jacob, who had one father and one mother and the same conception. . . . And hence in every way they are united with their forefathers in kinship and in birth, likewise God before they were born and had done good or evil, anticipating what was to come not only distinguished them but also overturned . . . the order of nature."[45] In the Greek commentators of the fourth and fifth century, Romans did not become, as it did for Augustine, a treatise on the various stages in the life of an individual: prior to the law, under the law, under grace, and finally in peace.[46] Romans was first and foremost a book about God's purpose in the history of the Jews and in the life of the Christian community.[47] It was read in the context of Paul's mission to the Gentiles.

But that is not the point on which I wish to close. As I have already emphasized, one cannot but be impressed at the power of the scriptural language, in the context of the biblical narrative, to alter well-established ways of looking at the world. To be sure, arguments are trotted out in favor of free will, and Paul's words are bent to fit the requirements of that doctrine. Yet in the end the patristic exegetes adopt a position that seems not only to undermine free choice but to accentuate divine intervention and election. The problem of freedom can no longer be formulated in terms of necessary or accidental events but now has to be viewed in the light of the purposeful actions of a gracious God.

Paul's language, his metaphors and images, rearranges the conceptual world the commentators were accustomed to inhabit. Not completely, of course, because they do not follow Paul blindly. They read him critically, that is, in the light of ideas and beliefs they consider reasonable and true. But there was something new in Paul, and in the Bible; and the task of exegesis was to find out how the language of the Bible worked, to draw out its implications, to try out a new vocabulary in relation to received wisdom. And as we in the twentieth century know well, the vocabulary one uses fashions the world one knows and experiences.

In her suggestive book *Metaphor and Religious Language*, Janet Soskice observes that revelation is not a "body of free floating truths that can be picked up anywhere indifferently" or stated without reference to a distinctive language as formed by a tradition of use and application. "For this reason," she argues,

> it is dull and misguided to suggest [for example] that Shakespeare and the Old Testament might be considered as religious texts of equal value to Christianity, if this is to suggest that the value of a text consists wholly in the set of moral or spiritual dicta which may be extracted from it. . . . The [Bible's] importance is not principally as a set of propositions but as the milieu from which Christian belief arose and indeed still arises, for these books are the source of Christian descriptive language and particularly of metaphors which have embodied a people's understanding of God.[48]

The language of the scriptures was not the language of Homer or Plato or Chrysippus; and one way to see how much difference it made for Christianity that the Bible was the church's book is to read the early Christian commentaries, to look not at what they say about method or principles of exegesis, and certainly not to fret over the use of allegory or typology or historical exegesis, nor to argue over the conflict between Alexandria and Antioch, but to look closely and patiently at the way the early Christian commentators read the Bible, the way biblical language enters into their vocabulary, the way new words and images shape and mold their patterns of thought. The patristic commentaries have too often been read against what presumes to pass for exegesis today; they need to be read as genuine efforts to understand what the scriptures say, within, of course, the context of the ancient world and its assumptions and beliefs. Perhaps then they can lead us to look at the scriptures with fresh eyes.

Finally, what shall we say about Theodoret of Cyrus' analogy of magnetic rock, especially in the light of his interpretation of Romans and Ephesians? Let us be kind to him. He was a sophist, a rhetor, a man of letters; and for all who write, it is hard, so very hard, once one has found a good metaphor, to cast it to the winds even when it limps. He could have said more.

Paulus Origenianus: *The Economic Interpretation of Paul in Origen and Gregory of Nyssa*

PETER J. GORDAY

This study develops the thesis that Origen, in response to the interpretation of Pauline theology current among some Gnostics, constructed a way of understanding the epistles of the great apostle that was distinctive in (a) the selection made of key Pauline passages and themes, (b) the relating of these passages to one another and to the major themes of Origen's theology, and (c) the influence it exercised on the Paulinism of the Cappadocian theologians, particularly Gregory of Nyssa. A contrast is set up between Origen and Gregory in order to sharpen, as well as illustrate, a structural continuity that obtains in how these two patristic thinkers use Pauline texts. A subsidiary purpose of this essay is to suggest that the conventional view of Origen's interpretation of Paul—that he simply transposes the categories of biblical thought into those of middle Platonism, thereby hellenizing the gospel and completely distorting Paul—is a prejudice of the old history-of-dogma school that should be laid to rest.[1] In fact, Origen, in his own way, focused his view of Paul around a concern—the nature and implications of divine election in salvation—that very much concerns us in the present as a key to Pauline theology.

The specific argument is that Origen constructed his understanding of Paul around a number of key passages: parts of Romans 9:6-24, Romans 8:18-39, 1 Corinthians 15:20-28 and 35-58, Colossians 1:15-20, Philippians 2:5-11, with a multitude of scattered uses of verses from the Corinthian correspondence and Ephesians that underline points of spirituality or ecclesiology. These passages are the ones that appear most often in Origen's work when he is developing key points in his doctrines of God, the soul, the cosmos, Christ, and redemption. They often appear in combination with one another and are, in fact, among the most frequently used in the whole Origenian corpus, according both to my count and to that of *Biblia Patristica*.[2] Romans and 1 Corinthians are the Pauline epistles most used by Origen, initially in *De principiis* and then throughout his remaining work. The themes of these passages—cosmic, eschatological, christological, and hermeneutic, with all of these growing out of, and returning to, the simultaneous defense of divine oneness and goodness along with real human free will—are the ones that related most closely to the broad shape of Origen's thought and also, in a different way, to the thought of Gregory of Nyssa. It is the associating of these passages in various ways in order to construct a view of the "economy," of the entire universal process of creation, fall, christological intervention, and human redemption in the restoration of the cosmos, that gives Origenian Paulinism its flavor and identity in a distinctive blending of Pauline texts. Origen's understanding of Paul's theology derives its special note—as over against that of his successor Gregory—from the fact that, following the Gnostics, he was willing to acknowledge some measure of divine *connivance* with the presence and power of evil in the world. By Gregory's time, in contrast, this admission was no longer acceptable; and the Pauline texts which functioned in such a way as to require for Origen some way of including evil within the divine providence no longer served that purpose. Gregory in fact opened a deep abyss between the divine goodness and activity on the one hand and the reasons and predisposing conditions for human wrongdoing on the other. At that point a significant element in the complexity and subtlety of Paul's thought had been lost and the drama of redemption robbed of some of its characterological mystery.

My procedure will be as follows: first I shall sketch Origen's use of Pauline texts in *De principiis*, then I shall corroborate this picture and enrich it by tracking this usage through other of his writings, then I shall examine more briefly Gregory of Nyssa's appropriation of some of this same pattern of employing Pauline texts for a parallel theological agenda, and finally I shall draw some conclusions about this Origenian chapter in the great church's formulation of the theology of the Pauline corpus. The age of a speculative Paulinism derived from the study of the text of Paul had now begun, the age of commentary and exposition—a different thing from the age of *Paulusbild*, with its hagiographical and pseudepigraphical portraits of the apostle and his teaching.

Origen's Use of Paul

Without question Origen's exegesis of Paul takes its rise from a prior Gnostic interpretation of the epistles. Certainly there were "orthodox" interpreters of Paul prior to Origen's time (as his occasional references suggest), but when he specifically names other exegetes, he always refers to Marcion or Valentinus or Basilides or other Gnostics. These appear to have been the first to engage in commentary on Paul.[3] The development of a deutero-Pauline literature is evidence for the emergence of a kind of history of interpretation of Paul, as is the large use made of Pauline texts in second-century authors.[4] It seems safe to say, however, that there was no massive attempt to base careful theological thought on his writings apart from the work of Marcion and of the Valentinian Gnostics toward the end of the second century. For our purposes, it is important to note that some recent work on both Marcionite and Valentinian theology has argued that both systems, insofar as they made use of Pauline thought, contained an attempt to honor the priority of God in defining the causes of the human dilemma in a material and corruptible world. At stake here has been the classic Gnostic view of the *Dreimen-schenklassenlehre*, the doctrine that humankind is classed by God into the three divisions of hylic, psychic, and pneumatic, with only the last of these sure to attain salvation. According to Valentinian teaching, this division is a product of divine action and sets the boundaries within which any exercise of free will by enfleshed creatures can be meaningful, that is, only the freedom exercised by pneumatics will be efficacious in procuring their salvation. Similarly R. Joseph Hoffman argues, "Paul's libertarianism is clearly programmatic for Marcion's anthropology: the blame attaching to the exercise of free choice must be referred to the Creator, and not to the creature" (citing Tertullian *Adv. Marc.* 2.9.1).[5] Hoffman takes the view, then, that Marcion's ditheism is an attempt at a nonspeculative statement of the position that Marcion holds as a theologian of religious experience, that salvation comes as a free gift from God.[6] But just as salvation is a gift from God, so also is the situation of sin, which is likewise experienced as given in materiality. The solution is two gods, one a harsh creator, the other a loving redeemer. Freedom exists for Marcion only within the bounds of what God has given.

The specifically Valentinian perspective on this divine priority in determining the human situation is discussed by Elaine Pagels, who has suggested that the Valentinian appropriation of Paul took precisely the form of an emphasis on divine election. It is election that has classed human beings into their three groupings and thus made grace the means of salvation for all who will in fact be saved.[7] Pagels has, I think, polemicized too strongly against the view that determinism and free will define the central concern of Gnostic exegesis, but she is surely correct in insisting that the Gnostic interpreters of Paul made it a central task to derive from the apostle a view of the divine causation of both good and evil in the world, that both are the result of divine action. Whatever position one might take on the use of the term *election* to describe this Valentinian view that the dualism of conflicting forces in the universe arises from within the divine and manifests itself in the classes of humankind, it is clear that for the Valentinians, the destiny of human beings does in fact originate in the transcendent world of spirit that precedes this material world both ontologically and temporally. Finally, Marguerite Harl's work points us to an understanding of this divine election as the mainspring, so to speak, of a vast, cosmic scenario in which two "hypotheses," the Gnostic and the orthodox, are being pitted against one another in Origen's exegesis. The Gnostic scenario is absurd, a farce on the order of the theatre of mime, because in effect it makes God look foolish and immoral, whereas the orthodox version, in rightly construing the scriptures, follows the high drama of the "Creator God loving and wishing to save his people."[8] However one portrays the Gnostic exegesis at this point, it is still true, as Kurt Rudolph has argued, that Gnostic thought as a whole exhibited a clear notion of a cosmic history from creation to eschaton in which the myth of redemption was subjected to a linear and contingent history of unfolding dependent to some degree on real free will in humankind.[9] What Origen and the Gnostics share is this sense of the cosmic drama with God as a master-director and energizer of the whole process, shaping the drama and calling the shots.

One must keep this larger picture of Origen's anti-Gnostic polemic in mind when interpreting his explicit exegesis of Paul. In both *De principiis* and the commentary on Romans he suggested that what impelled him to take up the task of interpreting key Pauline texts was most especially the impiety of those who believed that Paul's teaching supported the notion of fixed natures, what he called the "diversity of nature." Such a notion stands in stark contradiction, he believed, with the clear biblical view that human beings are free in their pursuit of salvation.[10] It is evident, moreover, that Origen's aim here was to defend his whole salvation-historical picture of God, in which scripture (including an array of Pauline texts) is full of obscurities intended to point the pious reader to a true perception of divine mysteries. Scripture, for Origen, as Marguerite Harl has again emphasized, is a maze in which obstacles and contradictions point to deep truths that are accessible only through the polyvalence and multilayered significations of language as well as the ambiguities of specific terms and images.[11] Consequently, in the opening sentences of the preface to the commentary on Romans, he linked in one breath his outrage at the impieties of those who interpret Paul according to the concept of fixed natures with his dismay at the complexity and abstruseness of Paul's language.[12] The matter is complex; but it would be a fair generalization, based on the work of Harl and Patricia Cox Miller, to say that for Origen, Paul's terminology and the semantic range of his expression allow the interpreter to experience the scandal of salvation, a scandal in which the apparent contradiction or nonsensicality or ambiguity of words draws the exegete into the very center of the dynamic of creation and incarnation. In this scandal and in the response that it generates in the interpreter, the divine "economy" entices and enables the believer to bear the unbearable and to see the unseeable.[13]

The first Pauline text to receive extended treatment from Origen was Romans 9:16—"it does not depend on him who wills or him who runs, but on God who has mercy"—together with its immediate context, in which the question of Jacob and Esau precedes and the image of God as the potter who makes vessels for honor and dishonor out of the same lump follows. In this context Paul repeated the teaching from the book of Exodus that God used Pharaoh for divine purposes, purposes that were facilitated by the hardening of Pharaoh's heart. Origen never stopped coming back to this passage as a crux in his thinking precisely because it seemed to support so well the Gnostic line of argument.[14] In *De principiis* 3.1 he wrestled with it in a way that he still considered definitive when, in the much later commentary on Romans, he referred readers back to the earlier presentation.[15] Beginning with the traditional argument that human free will is derived from the essential rationality of the soul, itself reflective of the divine creator and his image, the Logos, Origen tackled a number of biblical texts that seem to belie this teaching: the account of the hardening of Pharaoh's heart (*De princ.* 3.1.7) is one of the foremost. Origen first appealed to the logic of the situation: how could God harden a heart that was not already free, since a heart that can be hardened is in fact changeable (3.1.8)? Origen takes the position that God *really did* harden Pharaoh and does not try to talk the text out of what it indeed says; that is, he does not suggest that the hardening is simply something that Pharaoh does to himself. Lest, however, such a point of view smack of too much impiety (3.1.10), Origen then launches into a careful argument, with the help of Hebrews 6:7f., to the effect that God causes both fruits and thorns to grow from the same earth and with the same watering. This line of thought leads Origen to the conclusion that he felt he must maintain: that God is indeed providentially good in supplying the resources from which both good and evil will come and that much will depend on the free response of the finite subject. At the same time, however, it is important to see that the Pauline text has required him to find a way of accommodating the view, learned from the Valentinians, that evil comes from the divine realm. The fully elaborated appeal to a paideutic providence will become, in due course, his rationalized response to Paul and to Paul's Valentinian and Marcionite interpreters—as if to say, "Yes, evil does originate with the divine activity, but not in the way that some might think; it does not come from an evil deity nor is it eternal, but instead it plays a part in the divine determination to create life and then to absorb its flaws into a comprehensive plan of restoration, a plan which could not operate without the existence of such evil."

Indeed, for the remainder of De principiis 3.1 Origen contended that the divine hardening of Pharaoh was for his salvation, that such hardening simply manifests the providential process by which hearts are purified through suffering and through the punishment that comes for moral flaws. The Gnostic postulate of two gods is avoided, and instead, the unity and goodness of the one God are upheld. Origen had no intention of suggesting that what appears to be evil really is not so in the long run; rather, he believed that in a rational universe, evil itself can be seen to have served some purpose consistent with the nature of God. Further, by emphasizing the divine foreknowledge of who will respond favorably to grace and who will not, Origen could advance the additional view that God's selection of who will be hardened is itself based on and justified by the prior knowledge of how he will be received by different souls (3.1.17). Finally Origen presented the case for a full synergy of divine and human collaboration in the working of salvation (3.1.21), incorporating into his argument a treatment of the imagery of God as the potter and human beings as the vessels from Romans 9:22 and 2 Timothy 2:20f. (the latter representing a reworking of the Pauline text to emphasize the human element in salvation). The result was the contention that God's action on the human heart is relative to the state in which he finds persons, a view that for Origen entailed the doctrine of the preexistence of souls and the premundane fall by which some souls have merited a less happy lot in earthly life. So it is that Jacob and Esau inherited unequal situations in the world, though neither had done anything while in the womb to deserve election or rejection (3.1.22; on Romans 9:12f.).

Origen often came back to this portion of Romans 9, always with the intention of commenting again on the mystery of divine doing and human doing, emphasizing sometimes divine initiative, sometimes the indispensability of human response.[16] To unravel the mystery entirely, were that possible, would be to open up "hidden veins of living water" (*Hom. in Gen.* 12.4), something he preferred not to do indiscriminately because of the controversial nature of the notion of the preexistence of souls. It is clear, however, that his interpretation of this passage from Romans implies, in effect, his whole scenario of creation and redemption: God is the perfectly good creator who makes all souls from one lump, loving them all equally and yet bound by the possibility that free will may lead them astray, until a fall occurs in which each soul (except that of Jesus!) is enfleshed, relative to the degree of its sin, in a divinely foreseen earthly state, there to struggle with good and evil in order to be purified for a return to the spiritual world at the restoration of all things. In this view the whole biblical story is a recital of a continuous divine activity rendered in accord with human need at every point in the story, activity performed with the intention of fitting souls for their eventual journey home and away from the bonds of corporeality. Origen was perfectly aware that the *actual* situation of any particular person is the product of a chain of causation, which at some point precedes his own willing—the willing of his earthly self, that is—and that there are antecedents which determine his lot, but—and *this is the catch that makes Origen akin to the Gnostics*—these antecedents are premundane, belonging to a transcendent realm where both evil and the form of enfleshment taken by any particular soul originate. The implication is that sin is rendered inevitable and necessary—not any particular sin (free will is responsible for *that*), but some kind of sin—since otherwise corporeality could not exact its price on the soul and providence could not proceed with its purification. Hal Koch rightly contended that Origen made the concept of a beneficent divine providence the cornerstone of his thought and the substance of his response to the Valentinians.[17] I would add that it may very well have been the debate over this portion of Romans that prompted, and even required, such a response on Origen's part, however Stoic or middle-Platonist his arguments may look.

Origen's use of a second Romans text, 8:18–39, allowed him to develop the same picture, though without such a strong emphasis on the argument about free will. He made generous use of this text in the process of setting out his views on the origin of this present world of corporeality. In *De principiis* 1.7.4-5 he argued that souls exist prior to the bodies in which they are placed by the creator, who has subjected this world (i.e., the world of souls) to vanity and to the sufferings of this present time (i.e., the moral travail of living in bodies) as a punishment (i.e., "not of its own will"), in order that healing can take place in the chastise- ment for premundane sin. In this way the creation has been subjected in hope for the good things yet to come. A link with Romans 9:14 in this context makes it clear that there is no un- righteousness with God and that, in fact, the subjection of the creation is done in such a way as to reflect the rational order of beings, in which the celestial bodies (higher souls in Origen's view) will minister to the earthbound bodies as part of the process of their mutual redemption. The groaning of the universe in Romans 8:22f. is, for Origen, a positive experience of the renewal taking place in this penal and therapeutic state of corporeality.[18] The work of prayer in 8:26f., as well as the statement about the conformity of Christians to the likeness of Christ in 8:28-30, and the witness in 8:31-39 to the indefectibility of God's love in Christ are all demonstrations, for Origen, of the ultimate will of the creator as revealed in a cosmic order that bespeaks, for the spiritual person, the presence of unconquerable love.[19] In the relatively late *Contra Celsum*, Romans 8:19-23 served the pur- pose of providing a warrant for the injunctions against idolatry,[20] since one implication of Paul's teaching for Origen is that the corporeal world is an inferior world in which nothing may take the place of the devotion owed to the creator alone. With this kind of statement, Origen showed how easily his cosmology could move to exhortation and to a particular understanding of the spiritual person precisely as the one who has refused to sub- stitute the world of appearance for that of reality.

We can now appreciate the massive use made by Origen of texts from 1 Corinthians 15 throughout the body of his writings, where passages from 1 Corinthians and Romans often function side by side. The themes of the body and of the relationship between flesh and spirit, which preoccupy Paul in 1 Corinthians, are a central concern for Origen also, but nowhere more so than when he comes to explain the resurrection and, especially, the way in which the resurrection fulfills the creation. As Joseph Trigg has pointed out, 1 Corinthians 15:19—"If it is for this life only that Christ has given us hope, we are most of all to be pitied"—was an important text for Origen in defending his view of spiritual resurrection as a view that affirms the seriousness of morality during earthly life.[21] Origen had to rebut the criticisms not only of speculative Gnostics but also of the simple faithful, the *simpliciores* within the church, for whom the resurrection of the flesh was understood in literal terms. By denying that the earthly body would participate in the resurrection, Origen seemed to take up a stance that was Gnostic, but he balanced the argument by insisting that life in this world of corporeality is essential to moral growth. This perspective comes to expression in his treatment of 1 Corinthians 15:23, where he agreed with Paul that in the resurrection each would be in his proper place, that is, each creature would be raised to a pureness of spirit consistent with his place in the hierarchy of rational souls formed at creation and with his moral progress while in the body.[22]

In 1 Corinthians 15:24-28, where Origen saw the completion of the entire process of cosmic change and transformation, a text lay ready to hand that he employed constantly for emphasizing not only the inclusiveness of the final consummation—"God will be all in all"[23]—but also the availability to God of whatever vast amount of time might be required for the dominion of Christ in heaven to be realized in every heart—"he is destined to reign until God has put all enemies under his feet."[24] The discussion of the resurrection body itself in 1 Corinthians 15:35ff. allowed him to develop these ideas further: each soul has during its earthly sojourn a body assigned by God according to merit ("God clothes it with the body of his choice, each seed with its own particular body"); there are different bodies for earthly and heavenly (i.e., for Origen, celestial) beings ("the sun has a splendour of its own, the moon another splendour," etc.); the contrast between the earthly body and the spiritual body, beginning at 15:45, is a final and definitive Pauline testimony to the superiority of the spiritual over the corporeal and yet at the same time to the presence of spirit within the corporeal as Christ, the last Adam, comes to redeem the first with whom he shares the kinship of spirit.[25] It is in

fact the purification of the natural body, the certainty of its continuing purification at the resurrection, that is in Origen's view
the great hope contained in the church's proclamation of the
resurrection of the dead. This is the mystery, the deep truth that
"we shall not all die, but we shall all be changed in a flash, in
the twinkling of an eye, at the last trumpet-call" (1 Cor. 15:51).
The christological material in 15:45-49, with Paul's comparison of
the earthly and the heavenly man in terms of the "form" of earth
and the "form" of heaven, then led into Origen's use of other
texts, which are again frequently combined with the Corinthians
and Romans material.

The Christ-hymn of Colossians 1:15-20 is virtually om-
nipresent in Origen's work, as it was to be later in the christological controversies of the fourth century.[26] Origen's view of the
Logos-Christ who alone is the true image of God found confirmation in the beginning of the passage, as did his view of the creative
role of the Logos in the origin of the cosmic orders of spirits. His
entire theology of God as perfect monad and perfect mind, supplying through an intermediary which is an extension of himself
the order—the ontological bonding—of the cosmos, is substanti-
ated by the Pauline assertion that "all things are held together in
him" (Col. 1:17). Origen often saw in this passage a strong statement of the majesty of Christ at the same time that an equal
emphasis was placed on his presence in the corporeal world by
virtue of his role in the creation. In Origen's trinitarianism,
Christ's redemptive function as the Holy Spirit is then ecclesial:
"He is . . . the head of the body, the church . . . He is its
origin, the first to return from the dead, to be in all things alone
supreme" (Col. 1:18). Redemption is in and through the church's
life of word and sacrament but with the proviso that, as always for
Origen, the church is a supramundane and cosmic reality that
cannot be confined to finite categories.

The Christ-hymn from the second chapter of Philippians
likewise functioned for Origen as a statement of the majesty of
Christ; but it also, in distinction from the Colossians text, helped
to explain the nature of redemption through the Logos' descent
into the world of corporeality.[27] The act of humility in the incarnation is, for Origen, the actual assumption of the physical nature

of human existence by a God whose very being is pure spirit. This is the point, as Robert Berchman has reminded us in a recent study, where Origen departed from the presuppositions contained in the middle-Platonist understanding of the divine.[28] For Origen, following Paul at this point, God comes down into, makes a movement toward, the enslaving conditions of human life. In *De principiis* 3.5.6, for instance, he linked Philippians 2:7f. with 1 Corinthians 15:27f. to argue that Christ has come into the world, the creator has actually submitted to mortality, in order to teach obedience and to restore the rightful structure of super- and subordination that makes the cosmos cohere, and all of this for the perfecting of all creatures. Origen's conviction that a real subjection of the Son[29] (so that human beings can learn what they must learn and so that the Son can himself be perfected) is essential to his eternal relationship to the Father (*De princ.* 3.5.7) drew sustenance from this complex association of texts from Colossians, Philippians, and 1 Corinthians, as well as from Paul's statement that Christ is the eldest among many brethren, the image to whom all are to be conformed (Rom. 8:29). It was the Pauline combination of majesty and humility in the Son, the dialectical relating of ruling and submitting in the first-born of all creation, that forced Origen to puzzle out a christology that can allow for the necessity of a divine descent that is at the same time consistent with the highest requirements of divine lordship and of unbroken, continuous ontological presence on the part of the Logos to all the universe.

The practical result of Origen's use of Pauline texts was that he elaborated a picture of the spiritual person and of the insight and vision that such a person will always possess. The very structure of *De principiis*, with its concluding treatment of biblical hermeneutics in the fourth book, points to such an ultimate concern on Origen's part.[30] It is the right handling of scripture and thus the discernment of the incorporeal within the corporeal world that provide the criterion for Origen of all spiritual maturity. Here it is clear that part of the purpose of Christ's coming was to prove by miracles the divine inspiration of the prophets and the spiritual nature of Moses' law (*De princ.* 4.1.6) so that those who are believers might be enabled to read the sacred text correctly. It is this spiritual reading that allows one to see that the God described in the Old Testament is the same God of providential care who is represented in Christ (4.2.1). The hermeneutical key is provided by the insight that the structure of scripture is exactly that of the nature of human beings and of the whole universe, a threefold hierarchy of body (or letter), soul, and spirit (4.2.4), so that biblical passages are to be viewed as open in principle to interpretation on all three levels.

A number of Pauline texts that refer to the figurative interpretation of scripture were pressed into service by Origen to underscore his basic contention that the surface meaning of a biblical passage is frequently insufficient to an adequate understanding. But it is the idea that both logical impossibilities in the narrative and certain "obscurities" in the way scripture describes God and his laws require spiritual interpretation that is most arresting.[31] At this point, beginning at *De principiis* 4.3.6, Origen again made use of Romans 9, in this case 9:6 and 9:8, to argue that the whole history of Israel reveals the necessity for a discerning reading of the prophecies, such a reading as can be accomplished only by those who have submitted to the spiritual discipline of Christ. In a final section (*De princ.* 4.3.11), Origen compared the surface of scripture to the field of the world, full of variety and rich with hidden truth that lies ready for the individual who is graced by God (the "spiritual Israel" implied in Romans 9:6) and is determined to reach the promised land. Here again, as in many other contexts, Origen employed favorite Pauline texts to make the point that correct reading of scripture is the expression of the whole dynamic of salvation crystallized into a single act. Karen Jo Torjesen's recent work on Origen's hermeneutics has made us aware of how central this right reading of biblical passages was for Origen: such a reading is *paideia*, an experience of being morally purified through intellectual attainment such that the divine, providential process of becoming finds its full realization. The lifting of the veil from Moses' face in 2 Corinthians 3, or the recognition that spiritual circumcision has superseded the physical rite of ancient Israel (Rom. 2:28f.), or the view that Hagar and Sarah are representative of two covenants (Gal. 4:21ff.), all functioned for Origen as warrants for this spiritual reading that uncovers his scenario of creation and redemption at the same time that it *presupposes* it as the dynamic process that makes such a reading possible in the first place.

Is it possible to say that Origen, in construing Paul in the way described above, sets one Gnostic scenario of redemption against another, his own in contrast to that of Marcion and Valentinus? My answer must be in the affirmative, particularly if we note that salvation, for Origen, is radically intellectual, radically a matter of spirit coming to know itself as mind. This contention is intended not so much in contradiction of the perspective of Marguerite Harl, mentioned earlier, as in modification of it: there is a basic contrast to be drawn between Origen's "hypothesis" and that of the Valentinians, but there is also a kinship between them, a kinship generated in part by the challenge offered to Origen by these Pauline texts. Indeed, the important Pauline passages for Origen are those that lend themselves to cosmic theorizing in the Gnostic way and that lend themselves to a view of the relationship between spirit and matter in which knowledge constitutes a higher or more complete version of faith in the appropriation of salvation.[32]

In such an ambiguous world as Origen described this physical universe to be, the origin of evil—that which clouds the vision of God—lies hidden in processes that precede any person's awareness and that qualify as ontic, as seemingly built into the structure of the world itself. What begins to set Origen apart from the other Gnostics is his conviction that the corporeal order of the universe has been made instrumental by God to a plan, willed and deliberate, in which a fully finite arena is required for spirit to work out its destiny. This view can do justice to Origen's absolute insistence on free will as that which can ultimately make sense of life-in-bodies, where everything is subject to decay but where everything is changeable and therefore perfectible. This statement then brings me to a briefer consideration of Origen's greatest and most capable admirer in antiquity, Gregory of Nyssa, who simultaneously retained and altered the shape of Origen's Paulinism.

Gregory of Nyssa

In the fourth-century Cappadocian circle in which Gregory of Nyssa moved, the first and most obvious appropriation of

Origen's use of the Pauline texts appears in the *Philocalia* of passages from Origen's work, compiled by Basil of Caesarea and Gregory of Nazianzus to preserve the memory of Origen during a time of growing hostility to his teaching. *Philocalia* 21-27, dealing with the subject of free will, contains all of *De principiis* 3.1 as well as a variety of other texts from *Contra Celsum* and the scholia and homilies on the Old Testament. Much of the material dealing with the theme of the hardening of Pharaoh's heart and the meaning of God's mercy within a providential order was reproduced here. Eric Junod has rightly suggested that the particular selection of texts assembled by the Cappadocians tends to emphasize Origen's concern with the medicinal nature of God's hardening of Pharaoh, rather than with the defense of free will as such, unlike much of the later patristic discussion of this theme which seems distant from Origen and much more concerned with free will per se.[33] This perspective is helpful, I think, in appreciating Origen's preoccupation with the divine source of evil, but it does not reflect as strongly as Junod implies the interests of the Cappadocians, interests sharply focused on the free-will issue and only marginally on a defense of divine goodness. One senses that for Gregory of Nyssa, the question raised by the Pauline texts is not so much about God and the nature of divine action as it is about the nature of human willing and growing—a focus that has become more anthropological and less fundamentally Pauline than Origen's theocentrism.

The difference can be seen when one turns to the *De vita Moysis* 2.73-88, where Gregory dealt with the hardening of Pharaoh in a manner strongly reminiscent of Origen and Origen's use of Pauline texts.[34] There is no direct citation of Romans 9, but other texts important to Origen—such as Romans 1:26, 28, where God is described as handing sinners over to the consequence of their sin—are used; and it is apparent that the issue of God's intent in the hardening is at stake. Like Origen, Gregory made his whole view of divine action and human response central to his exegesis; and as Origen did in *De principiis* and elsewhere, Gregory resorted to Romans 2:5f. to justify God's patience with sinners (*De vit. Mos.* 2.86). What is notable is that for Gregory, God's treatment of the Egyptians is entirely a matter of punishing their freely willed sin with a chastisement that, to be sure, is to their benefit, but that does not, as for Origen, proceed from a prior divine decision about the nature and means of providential goodness in the universe. For Origen, God has chosen to include the sin necessitated by corporeality within the actual mechanisms of providence; for Gregory, God's medicinal cleansing of sin is only after the fact and occurs only as a specific response to each individual sin. Gregory did carry over into his treatment of the theme the possibility of repentance on the part of the Egyptians (*De vit. Mos.* 2.82), as well as the idea of God as the divine physician (2.87). As a consequence, what one soon becomes aware of in pondering Gregory's use of these Origenian themes, which Origen derives in part from Paul, is the surprising fact that by rejecting Origen's notion of the preexistence and pre-mundane fall of souls, Gregory has also dispensed with the note of mystery attached to Paul's own concern with divine sovereignty in the hardening of Pharaoh's heart. For Paul, and for Origen, the hardening of Pharaoh comes from beyond, from transcendental sources; Gregory misses this note.

Gregory also did not subscribe to the view that corporeal existence is necessary to the purging of premundane sin so that souls can return to the heavenly realm in a cleansed and pure state.[35] In his short treatise on the premature death of infants, he used Romans 9 and, in particular, the hardening of Pharaoh's heart to show that the beneficence of God takes the form of allowing some sinners to grow to full stature in their sin only in order to use them as examples for the virtuous.[36] In this way, so to speak, God the artisan molds malleable Israel on the hard anvil of Pharaoh's sin. From Gregory's perspective, corporeal existence is not penal and therefore not morally necessary; and the goodness of God is actually witnessed in the death of infants in that they go to their heavenly place without having to acquire the stains of earthly life. In his discourse *In sanctum Pascha* and in the *Oratio catechetica*, he compared God to a potter who can mold raw material into any shape he wishes and retains the power to remold it when it has been smashed—a theme probably derived from Jeremiah 18 and Romans 9:22 and serving here to affirm that the creator of all can easily be the restorer of all when he so chooses (and *has* chosen in the resurrection of the dead).[37] Gregory then used Paul's presentation in 1 Corinthians 15:36f. to press the point that as the seed grows to the full ear of corn, so the power of God can restore humankind in the resurrection; moreover, as Paul says, the resurrection validates the moral strivings of individuals in a way that is absolutely required if God's justice is to be served. In a powerful passage of *De anima et resurrectione*, Gregory echoed the theme of Romans 9:21ff. when he described God as an artist who designs each feature of the world with regard to a universal economy in which human beings are vases ready to be filled, by their own choice, with whatever substance is poured into them. Each individual chooses his own poison, so to speak, in order then to pursue the hard road of learning to reject lesser pleasures for greater, the values of the earthbound body for the heavenly body.[38]

By contrast with Origen, then, the necessity that Gregory conceives for embodiment is not moral, not that of having to learn perfection in a hard school; rather, it is metaphysical, that of the divine musician who, as Gregory argued in *De hominis opificio*, must have an instrument on which to play—and of the rational soul that must have a body with which to exercise its power.[39] An implication of this perspective is that each soul must become enfleshed, *but not for long*, and resurrection can come none too soon. Thus for Gregory, corporeality is essential to the being of rational souls (notice the diminution of ambiguity in embodiment), but it is corporeal behavior from which souls must be rescued. One conclusion is that at the resurrection—here Gregory based himself on 1 Corinthians 15:35–38 and 42–44— persons will have bodies mysteriously compounded by God from the earthly elements that are dispersed at death. Though much of the structure of Origen's thought has been discarded here, I suggest that the Origenian cluster of Pauline texts is present and influential.

One is not surprised, then, to discover that Romans 8:19–23, along with portions of 8:24–39, plays a part in Gregory's depiction of the present world-situation. In several passages in the *Contra Eunomium*, where he struggled to make sense of the notion that Christ is the first-born of all creation but not himself a creature, he combined christological texts such as Colossians 1:15, 18, and

Philippians 2:7, 10, with Romans 8:29 (Christ as the first-born among many brethren) and Romans 8:19ff. to argue that the "creation" into which Christ enters is that of sinful human beings and that he enters it precisely in order to save them.[40] Here Gregory hit the note of the corporeal world as sinful and, further, indicated that the slavery to which Christ submits in the incarnation is that of being subject to the vanity of human lostness, the conditions of corporeal life. In this way, Gregory believed, Paul could use the language of creation to describe Christ and his entry into the world, while in other places he could describe Christ in the language of absolute preeminence, that is, of uncreatedness. In part, it was the blend of passages which I am calling the Origenian cluster that allowed him to develop these thoughts, even though he never analyzed them with the same close attention to detail that marked the work of Origen himself—this because, I think, Gregory's work and that of later thinkers is structured much more according to a set of sharply defined dogmatic questions than by general reflection on scripture with great speculative freedom (as in Origen's case). By Gregory's time, the need was to arbitrate terminology and phraseology for the sake of orthodoxy, not to defend general propositions by assembling large numbers of biblical texts. Thus Gregory's use of passages from 1 Corinthians is limited strictly to contexts in which the precise details of the resurrection are under consideration, such as in *De hominis opificio* 22.6 where he appealed to 1 Corinthians 15:51f. to show that the moment of the resurrection will come when the foreordained number of souls has been created—a point made in response to those who questioned the continuing delay in the coming of the final resurrection of the dead. Interestingly enough, Gregory of Nazianzus captured more of the Origenian use of this material when, in a hymnic passage in *Orationes theologicae* 2.30f., he used 1 Corinthians 15:41 and allusions to Colossians 1:16 and other Pauline descriptions of the heavenly powers to sing the praises of the creator, who has so coordinated the universe that the higher powers minister to the lower in a rational order. Finally Gregory of Nyssa, like Origen, found in 1 Corinthians 15:28 the definitive text for the universal consummation of all things, a consummation that appeared to be, for Gregory, all-comprehensive and, as for Origen, mental: in the awareness of redeemed individuals God will be the sole object of consciousness.[41]

In his *Oratio catechetica* Gregory outlined the whole cosmic scenario of salvation, from creation to consummation, in a manner that sets him in the Origenian camp. Divine providence engineers a beneficent process, which consists of the fashioning of human beings in the divine image, the implanting of souls with rationality and free will, the fall and then the suffering that sin necessitates, the incarnation of the redeemer, his victory over the devil, and the final restoration. All that is wrong in the world is directly attributable to the erroneous choices of finite spirits; the Pauline focus on life according to the flesh has become simply a matter of sins, individual deeds, and no longer a matter of mysterious alliance between the nature of the cosmos and the weakness of creatures.

What set Gregory off from Origen, even when he stood in the same tradition, was the loss of the insight derived by the latter from the Gnostic exegesis of Paul, even when he fought against it, that God as the electing one is mysteriously implicated in the fact of evil and that, therefore, human free will cannot carry the entire load.[42] Origen was aware of this when he made corporeality penal, but medicinal, in the suffering that it necessarily entails; he was aware of this when he tried to honor Paul's statements—because the Gnostics made him honor them—that God chose Jacob and rejected Esau, that God hardened Pharaoh's heart, that God made the vessels of honor and dishonor, that God subjected the world to vanity, that God created the different orders of embodied creatures, that God made Christ the head of all that is and a slave to redeem all that is. Although, for Gregory, God is enshrouded in thick darkness, as for Moses on Mount Horeb, this darkness is again an ontological barrier to human understanding, not a moral one, as for Origen.[43] Spiritual growth is for Gregory summed up in the *epektasis*, the unceasing journey of finite souls into the infinite, where there can only be greater *theoria*, greater insight in rational terms, whereas for Origen there is the promise of communion in the moment of hermeneutic rapture, where knowledge is constitutive of a moral sharing in divinity.[44] That instant is an event of marriage (compare Origen's commentary on Canticles with that of Gregory) in which body yields to spirit and all ambiguity is resolved wordlessly in the divine embrace. For example, when Gregory did advance the notion—so dear to Origen—of the true Israelite who reads scripture correctly (*De vita Moysis* 2.84ff.), it was to offer a correct list of exegeses of certain passages, not to invite the reader into an encounter with a multilayered divine text.[45] Something more akin to the sublimity of Origen's views on the sublimity of scriptural interpretation is found in later writings, such as those of Maximus Confessor who emphasizes the mystical approach to the presence of God the Word incarnate in the text, although he is very careful to avoid any occasion for creating an idolatry of the text. By Maximus' time, however, the use of the theme of the hardening of Pharaoh's heart had become a set piece for reaffirming the absoluteness of human free will, a characteristic that makes all persons equal in the sight of God.[46]

In the West, the young Augustine inherited the tradition of focusing on Pauline passages about the origin of the world and of evil—thus we find much commentary on the book of Genesis and on the theme of the bondage of the will. Perhaps influenced by Gnosticism from the Manichees, Augustine would deal with Paul in terms of the mystery of sin and finitude.[47] Augustine would also deal with evil in terms of *presbyterai aitiai*—prior causes—but unlike Origen, with his view of the premundane fall of souls, and unlike Gregory, with his focus on the instability of created being, Augustine chose to situate the origin of evil in the history of the race and its disordered willing. On the one hand, Augustine thus works out a psychology of sinning whose sophistication is unmatched by earlier theologians precisely because of its emphasis on the social and historical connectedness of all persons. On the other hand, by insisting more and more that saving grace is a pure gift from beyond the soul, Augustine sets the stage for the hard doctrine of double predestination. Whether I am saved or rejected by God finally rests in the mystery of divine decision, in a sovereign act, which is just toward all and forgiving only toward some, the elect. Salvation here is no longer, as for Origen and Gregory, a matter of cosmic process in which divine election is sovereign in its purpose—to save the entire created order—but variable and contingent in the finite mechanisms by which it works, that is, by "gathering up" and using evil for redemptive ends. The Augustinian tradition of the *felix culpa*, the fall by which human redemption is procured, strikes something of the same note—sin is required before grace can come—not, however, by means of a divine "drawing forth" of salvation from the evil itself but rather by a sovereign and in-scrutable act of God in which new grace is transmitted to those persons whose salvation in Christ is predestined.

Augustine wrestled with the same Pauline texts; and he too was deeply conscious of the way in which Paul labored to include Pharaoh's hardening, and the other elements we have underscored here, within the divine purpose for the creation. But he did not share the Origenian and Pauline conviction that because the "prior causes" of mortality, corruption, and sin are to be located in the forces present in the origin of the world (the world that we know and live in), evil itself (including corporeality) is a "given," and as such is revelatory of the good God, whose purpose for the world could not come to pass without it. As in a drama where there is no action, no life, without the presence of evil, so in the history of salvation there *must* be sin if the created potentiality of human beings is to come forth in the course of time. God does not create the sin, but enters into alliance with it for the sake of humankind. *This* kind of thinking and interpretation of Paul has, I believe, re-emerged only in modern thought of the revolutionary type where, as Eugene TeSelle has recently emphasized, theologians have strug-gled to include the open-endedness and contingency of human willing *within* the unfolding of divine purpose for the world.[48]

General Conclusions

My intention in this study has been to argue that Origen *in his own way*, and in a way that Gregory of Nyssa was to retain only in part, offered an interpretation of Paul that was faithful to the apostle and at the same time allowed for a genuinely Pauline influence on the shape of a contemporary theological presenta-tion. Origen saw Paul as a theologian of *election*, a theologian for whom the central problem in understanding the relationship be-tween God, the world, and humankind is that of trying to fathom the rationale by which God has apparently created and graced persons in an uneven, and perhaps unjust, way. This concern leads by degrees to the question of *unde malum* and of God's relation to evil, these questions in turn providing the context for the defense of free will in human beings. What can divine goodness mean for a world that is intractably corrupted and sinful? And what can salvation mean, and how does it come? Insofar as the world is the way it is because God wanted it so, how can we make sense of the divine purpose? I believe that this cluster of questions is implicit in Paul's discussion of the "Israel question" in Romans 9-11, but also in his entire theology of divine righteousness in Christ. When Origen developed his views on the preexistence of souls, the premundane fall into corporeality, the descent and purification of the redeemer, and the providential *apokatastasis*, it was God as the electing God that he wanted to understand. It is also clear that the Pauline texts themselves were—as the Gnostics had forced them to be—the problem to be solved, and to that extent they dictated the terms of the discussion for Origen. The result was a coherent theology of God and the divine *oikonomia*.

Indeed, as I have argued elsewhere, the best single term for understanding the kind of coherence that Origen and his successors found in Pauline theology is *oikonomia*.[49] As a comprehensive way of describing the divine activity in relation to world order and human well-being, it appears often enough in Origen's work at the same time that it functioned for him as a way of understanding the full mystery of an act of biblical interpretation. His use of the concept, for example, in the Greek commentary on Matthew— where it became simultaneously a means of making sense of Jesus' parabolic speech to his followers (by economy only some are prepared to hear correctly), of seeing the rationale behind the descent of the Logos into human flesh (by economy corporeality is necessary for salvation both for human beings and ultimately for Jesus), and of helping the exegete to be conscious of what must be done to get at the spirit contained in the biblical text (by economy the letter of the text hides the spirit within so that a special act of discernment is required)—is characteristic of the multi-faceted character of the *oikonomia* for Origen. The scriptural warrant for the use of the term, Ephesians 1:10, is Pauline and occurs in the context of a hymnic description of the divine providence in the history of salvation; it is no wonder that it also functioned to gather up Origen's views on beneficent providence at work in the cosmic process of embodiment, suffering and release. This is its valence in De principiis in particular, as well as in many places in the Old Testament homilies. Patristic and Byzantine writers made such abundant use of the term that it became synonymous with divine activity in general. Its essential function, as Ian Ramsey pointed out, was to help the interpreter find a meaningful and all-inclusive pattern in events, from the tiniest to the greatest, and to relate that pattern to the administrative activity of a purposeful governor.[50]

The need to find just such a pattern is what was at work in Origen's Paulinism. In other words, it was his concern for the rationality of the universe, where there must be an adequate representation of the work of the good God, that pushed him to the use of this term. All evil begins to find a place within such a structure, but it is a place circumscribed by the fact of free will (for Origen, the Valentinians went too far). In this way, to use the language of comparative religion, *mythos* had become *logos*, the inexplicable had somehow received a rational exposition. By this means Origen and later exegetes who walked in his path absorbed the Gnostic insights and the Pauline perception of the awful sovereignty of God's will while forcing these insights to yield to some measure of thoughtful elaboration, that is, to the demands of theology. Consequently, they could offer reasons as to why and how God has mercy on whom he will have mercy, why and how God hardens some hearts and makes some vessels for honor and dishonor, why and how he has subjected the creation to vanity, why and how the redeemer had to be a slave at the same time that he was in all and the head of all, why and how a certain kind of mental activity could function as the only way back to the world of spirit and, thus, to salvation. To use a remark of Ramsey's, the Origenians would have said, "Those who know the economy know God."[51]

The Man from Heaven:
Paul's Last Adam and
Apollinaris' Christ

ROWAN A. GREER

Thus it is written, "The first man Adam became a living being"; the last Adam became a life-giving spirit. But it is not the spiritual which is first but the physical, and then the spiritual. The first man was from the earth, a man of dust; the second man is from heaven. (1 Corinthians 15:45–47)

There can be little doubt that these words of Paul's were central to Apollinaris' understanding of Christ. A pillar of old Nicene orthodoxy, a friend of Athanasius', an expert counselor to the youthful Basil the Great, Apollinaris developed his christology in the midst of the Arian controversy between the councils of Nicea (325) and Constantinople (381). Of course, his theology represented a thinking through of the tradition he had inherited and a sharpening of that tradition in opposition to what he regarded as a "two sons" christology.[1] But it also represented an attempt to be faithful to scripture and in particular to the Pauline understanding of the new humanity already found in Christ and destined to belong fully to those who were Christ's in the age to come. Paul's use of the Adam typology in Romans 5 and 1 Corinthians 15 may be regarded as one point of departure for the theology of Christ's body in Ephesians and Colossians and for the notion of Christ as the new humanity, which also appears in as early a writer as Ignatius of Antioch and which finds full expression in the writings of Irenaeus toward the end of the second century.[2] Indeed, one can argue for a broad measure of agreement between Apollinaris and Irenaeus. Both read the same

165

texts; both saw Christ as the new Adam; both treated the new humanity as transcendent of the old. Paradise was not simply closed pending repairs; it had been abandoned for good.

Despite Apollinaris' concern to be true to scripture and to theological tradition, his clarification of Christ's new humanity was rejected as a betrayal of both. By no means of least importance was the charge that his christology rested on a misinterpretation of 1 Corinthians 15:45ff.[3] How are we to assess such a charge? Large issues are raised. May we speak of a "correct" interpretation of a biblical passage, or can there be a number of valid interpretations? Can the interpretation of one passage be judged incorrect without denying that in broad terms a given writer has provided a valid interpretation of scripture? For example, it could be argued that Augustine misunderstands Romans 5:12 when he interprets it to mean that in Adam's fall we all sinned, but that his theology does represent a fair understanding of Paul's emphasis on the gratuitous character of redemption.[4] How are we to construe the relationship of theology and exegesis? It would be a delusion to suppose that a study of Apollinaris' use of 1 Corinthians 15:45ff. will settle any of these questions. My claim is the more modest one that it will help us think more carefully about the questions themselves.

Apollinaris' Understanding of the Man from Heaven

We cannot rightly assess Apollinaris' account of Christ's person without emphasizing that it derives from his convictions about redemption. With a clear allusion to 1 Corinthians 15:45ff., Apollinaris puts the point this way: "For we say that the Word of God became man for our salvation, so that we might obtain the likeness of the heavenly one and be made divine after the likeness of him who is by nature the true Son of God and by the flesh the Son of man, our Lord Jesus Christ."[5] At first, there seems to be nothing peculiar about Apollinaris' formulation. God the Word became human that we might be divinized. The proposition was universally accepted by orthodox Christianity and is best known as stated by Irenaeus and Athanasius. Moreover, Apollinaris insists that the Word is consubstantial with the Father, since if he is the Saviour and only God can save, then he must be divine in the fullest possible sense. What is peculiar is that Apollinaris implies that "the heavenly man" explains not how the Word became human but how we are divinized. The more one puzzles over Apollinaris' language, the more one wonders whether the heavenly man is a man at all. "Humanity" becomes a way of talking about our becoming God, rather than about God's becoming human.

This impression is confirmed by the use Apollinaris makes of 1 Corinthians 15:45ff. in several of the syllogisms he constructs in the *Anacephalaiosis* to demonstrate the novelty of Christ's humanity. The fact that Christ is the man from heaven in contrast to the man of dust demonstrates that he is not human in the same sense we are, since we, like Adam, are of dust.[6] Christ's flesh is said to have come down from heaven, and he gives life.[7] Both statements sharply distinguish Christ's "humanity" from ours and supply Apollinaris with further reasons for the repeated refrain of the *Anacephalaiosis*: "thus Christ is not human." One final reference in this treatise clarifies the point Apollinaris wants to make: "If Christ's nature is the same as ours, then he is the old man, a living being (soul) and not a life-giving spirit (1 Cor. 15:47), and as such he will not give life. But Christ does give life and is a life-giving spirit. Thus, he is not of our nature."[8] Following 1 Corinthians 15:45ff., Apollinaris argues that Christ's humanity is a way of talking about human destiny and how we become divine. What is disturbing is not this point of departure, but two conclusions Apollinaris draws with strict logic. The new humanity so transcends the old that it begins to lose any continuity with it. From another perspective, problems arise when we think of the new humanity as Christ's. If his flesh came down from heaven, is that flesh eternal, preexisting the incarnation? Is the eternal Word a man from the beginning, before his birth from Mary? Apollinaris' use of 1 Corinthians 15:45ff. leads us into all these tangled questions, but we cannot understand them properly without trying to explain the view of Christ Apollinaris thinks required by his commitment to Nicea and to the proposition that the Word became human that we might be made divine.

The form of Apollinaris' account of the new humanity in Christ can best be described by saying that he defines it as a composition of spirit and flesh. "The confession is that in him the creature is in unity with the uncreated, while the uncreated is commingled with the creature, so that one nature is constituted out of the parts severally, and the Word contributes a special energy to the whole together with the divine perfection."[9] Apollinaris continues by arguing that this one nature is strictly analogous to the composition of an ordinary human being "made up . . . of two incomplete parts which together fill out one nature and are signified by one name." The whole may be called "flesh" or "soul" without in any way denying the reality of the two elements that are united into one living being. Similarly, in the case of Christ, the new Man, the whole may be called "flesh" as in John 1:14 ("the Word became flesh") or it may be called "spirit" as in 1 Corinthians 15:45 ("The last Adam became a life-giving spirit").[10] Consequently, the one "born of a woman, born under the law" (Gal. 4:4) is the composite Christ, and so we must speak not merely of a human birth but of the descent of the Son of man from heaven (Jn. 3:13). Three inferences may be drawn from Apollinaris' account of Christ. First, he is concerned to base that account on scripture, and "the man from heaven" is the one described in 1 Corinthians 15:45 and John 3:13. Second, although he does not forget points in time like the virgin birth, his concern is with a timeless account of Christ. Finally, the one nature he describes is related to the issue of salvation rather than to the incarnation alone.[11] That is, Apollinaris is answering the question of how a new humanity is established rather than how the Word became incarnate, however much those two questions may be involved with one another.

Let me elaborate this account of Apollinaris' christology by turning to his *Apodeixis*, where he presents Christ as the man from heaven of 1 Corinthians 15:45. The fragments of the treatise are preserved for us in Gregory of Nyssa's *Antirrheticus adversus Apolinarium*, probably written toward the end of his life and after the council of Constantinople in 381.[12] Although Nyssa does not cite for us the whole of Apollinaris' text and sometimes resorts to paraphrase, what he does cite enables us to discern the main line of Apollinaris' argument. An introduction argues that the faith must be carefully examined lest it be unthinkingly reduced to "the opinions of Greeks or Jews" (13).[13] What Apollinaris means immediately becomes clear. We must speak of a composition of God the Word and flesh rather than of a man inspired by God (*anthrōpos entheos*). Both the synod that condemned Paul of Samosata in 268 and the Nicene creed support this view (14-15). Apollinaris continues by defining "the man from heaven" (16-31), by drawing the conclusion that what later came to be called the *communicatio idiomatum* requires us to speak of the Word as human and the flesh as divine (32-65), and by opposing this view to the "two sons" or "adoptionist" christology he wishes to reject (66-107).

Let me begin by calling attention to Apollinaris' definition of Christ as "the man from heaven." Identifying "spirit" in 1 Corinthians 15:45 with "mind," Apollinaris concludes that the man from heaven has God (the Word) as the mind that governs the (irrational) soul and the body (25). The definition, though trichotomous, by no means argues against Apollinaris' early tendency to think in dichotomous terms.[14] To say that a human being is a rational soul (or mind) governing a body is no different from saying that a human being is a mind governing an ensouled or animated body. The animating soul in this perspective is simply an aspect of the body.[15] Consequently, the man from heaven is a mind, though an uncreated one, governing an animated body. Although it is clear enough to us that Apollinaris depends on conventional philosophical understandings of human nature, he claims that his analysis comes from Paul (23, 72, 88). Paul's contrast of spirit and flesh refers to the mind or rational soul in contrast to the body, and this dichotomous analysis conceals the trichotomous structure of 1 Thessalonians 5:23: "spirit, soul, and body." In other words, Apollinaris employs what he regards as Paul's definition of a human being to explain the man from heaven.

The main point of this definition, however, is to contrast the new humanity with the old. Appealing to 1 Corinthians 15:45ff., Apollinaris argues that the first Adam is a rational soul governing a body, even though Paul does not mention the body. Moreover, the reason Paul uses "soul" (RSV: "being," "physical") to define Adam is to contrast his human mind with the divine mind or spirit found in the last Adam (26, 28, 29). In other words, the contrast in the Pauline text between "living being" (*psychēn zōsan*) and "life-giving spirit" (*pneuma zōopoioun*) is the contrast between a rational soul governing an animate body and God the

Word governing an animate body. This is why there is a sharp contrast between the earthy man from dust and the man from heaven. Both are "human," but the contrast is more important than their resemblance. Nevertheless, Apollinaris does insist that despite the absolute distinction of the two governing principles, both Adams have the same structure. If the heavenly man consisted of a human mind, soul, and body and the divine spirit was added as a fourth element, then Christ would be "a receiver of the heavenly God" and not the heavenly man (90). In one sense, the Pauline text suggests this conclusion to Apollinaris by its contrast in parallel of the two Adams. In another sense, Apollinaris' explicit disavowal of a human mind in Christ explains his interpretation. Let me defer discussion of this point to a later stage of the argument.

Granted that the heavenly man is a composite single nature in which the divine Word has appropriated to himself an animated body, Apollinaris goes on to argue that what properly belongs to the body or flesh can be predicated of the Word, and divine attributes can be predicated of the body. That is, Apollinaris insists on the *communicatio idiomatum* and does so by appealing to the analogy of the body-soul relation in the case of an ordinary human being. This point, to which I have already referred, means that Christ "is God in virtue of the spirit which is enfleshed but human in virtue of the flesh assumed by God" (19). However much Apollinaris' philosophical assumptions may be involved, his argument for this view depends on noticing that scripture interchanges the two sorts of names for Christ, speaking of him as God where we should expect a human term and applying divine categories to his humanity. For example (18), it is the Son of *man* who came down from heaven (Jn. 3:13; cf. 1 Cor. 15:45), while it is the Son of *God* who was born of a woman (Gal. 4:4). It is, then, no surprise that Paul calls the incarnate Word the *man* from heaven.

A long section of the *Apodeixis* seeks to demonstrate the truth of this point of view from scripture. The fact that human attributes may be applied to the eternal Word of God means that "the man Christ preexists not on the grounds that the spirit, that is, God, is someone other than he, but on the grounds that the Lord, since he is the divine spirit, is in the nature of the God-man"

(32). Although Apollinaris puts the idea somewhat obscurely, it is plain enough what he means. He is trying to take account of the peculiarities of scripture. In John 8:58 it is Jesus who claims to be "before Abraham" (33, 34). John the Baptist (Jn. 1:15) testifies to Jesus' preexistence (33). Zechariah 13:7, which refers to the incarnation (the "awakening of the sword"), defines Christ as of the same clan (*symphylos*) as God (33, 37, 40, 41). Hebrews 1:1-3 equates "the man who spoke the Father's words to us" with the Word of God and makes no distinction between the one who "reflects the glory of God and bears the very stamp of his nature" and the one who "made purification for sins" (38). Scripture not only refers human terms and activities to the divine Word but also applies divine terms to Christ's human activities. John 10:18 ("No one takes my life from me") proves that God is not to be separated from the crucified one (61; cf. 54).

Apollinaris' argument lends itself to misunderstanding, even though it is clearly meant to support his vision of the new humanity and the one nature of the incarnate Lord. The misunderstanding revolves around the possible implications that Christ's humanity as such preexisted and that his flesh was some sort of eternal, divine flesh. Both Gregory of Nyssa and Gregory Nazianzen attack Apollinaris as though this is what he were saying.[16] That this is a misunderstanding is perfectly apparent, and Apollinaris himself repudiates it as such.[17] The flesh of Christ did not literally come down from heaven but was made his own from Mary's womb. The misunderstanding is just that, but it is not a surprising one for the simple reason that Apollinaris' discussion of Christ very rapidly moves away from the narrative of the incarnation and from any sense of time. To speak of Christ is to speak of a timeless reality. Apollinaris does not think through what this might mean. Instead, his concern in insisting so strongly on the *communicatio idiomatum* is with a unitive account of Christ. Let me conclude my discussion of Apollinaris first by explaining the alternative he fears and second by turning to the fundamental motive behind his deliberate omission of a human mind in Christ.

As I suggested earlier, the illegitimate alternative that Apollinaris sees to his own unitive christology is a definition of Christ as an inspired man (*entheos anthrōpos*). He certainly has in mind

the divisive christology of Diodore, but he also attacks Gregory of
Nyssa for teaching two persons (*prosōpa*) in Christ (67) and for
speaking of "the assumption of a man" rather than "the union of
flesh" (66).[18] Part of Apollinaris' fear is that Christ will be divided
into two sons (81) and that this will involve worshiping the flesh
(84–86) or adding a human being to make a quaternity instead of a
trinity (82). But his deeper concern is that Christ will be thought
no more than a glorified prophet. If Christ is not an enfleshed
mind, then the obvious alternative is to think of him as a man
enlightened by God's wisdom (70–71). The trouble with this view
is that we should then be obliged to speak of many gods because
many are capable of receiving God (83). Or, alternatively, if we
insist that only one man was united to God in this way, then
we destroy free will for angels and for other people by denying
that they have the freedom to welcome God into their lives (87).
Apollinaris refuses to believe that there can be a way of talking
about God's assumption of a full human being that will not be
adoptionist and that will enable one to speak of the incarnation as
something unique.

The deeper reason for this judgment, however, and the motive for Apollinaris' christology may be found in his pejorative
assessment of the human mind. In virtue of its created status, the
human mind is changeable (74–76). It can choose evil as well as
good and, indeed, is inevitably "captive to polluted reasonings."[19]
Consequently, the human mind as a principle of self-governed
willing must necessarily come into conflict with God the Word.
Any assumption or adoption of a complete human nature will
founder because of this, and redemption will be frustrated. This is
why there cannot be two spiritual principles in Christ. According
to Apollinaris, "If the flesh as warring against the mind has been
separated from the mind according to the apostle (Rom. 7:23),
then God who took the flesh has from it the movements that war
against the mind, but they are subject to him in a different
way than to the mind that must struggle against them."[20] What
Apollinaris means is that if human perfection requires that the
mind perfectly govern the body and its passions, then created
humanity can never attain perfection. Instead, what is needed is a
stronger spiritual principle to establish hegemony over the body

and its motions. Only in this way can humanity gain not only moral perfection but also the incorruption of the resurrection. The Word, of course, is the stronger spiritual principle; and the man from heaven represents the new humanity that gives us the possibility of escaping from the predicament of our created status.

Apollinaris clearly believes that his theology correctly interprets 1 Corinthians 15:45-47. Let me conclude this section by suggesting that a number of considerations support Apollinaris' claim. The context of the passage in Paul's letter is one in which he is arguing for the bodily character of the general resurrection. But Paul must show that by *body* he does not mean this corruptible body but the new incorruptible one. He contrasts the corruptible natural (*psychikon*) body we now know with the spiritual (*pneumatikon*) body of the resurrection and ties the contrast to that between Adam and Christ. Citing Genesis 2:7, Paul argues that the created Adam is a "living being" (*psychēn zōsan*) and "from the earth, a man of dust," whereas the last Adam is a "life-giving spirit" and "from heaven." Our destiny, then, is defined by the spiritual body of the man from heaven. In crucial respects Apollinaris follows Paul's logic. His emphasis is on the new humanity of the last Adam, which supplies for us a paradigm of redemption. And in defining more closely the man from heaven, he appeals explicitly or implicitly to his broader reading of Paul and of the whole of scripture. "Spirit" must be related to Paul's contrast of spirit and flesh and to the anthropology that contrast implies. Granted that philosophical conventions enter the picture at this point, it is arguable that they are not necessarily contradictory of Paul's usage. Next, Apollinaris reads "spirit" in verse 45 in the light of the "from heaven" in verse 47, and he concludes that the reference is to the divine redeemer. Although he understands this in the light of a developed trinitarian theology, the patristic development itself rests on what we now call the redeemer myth. And there can be no doubt that Paul thinks of Christ as the one who "in the form of God" has "equality with God" (Phil. 2:6ff.). Furthermore, Apollinaris is surely correct in arguing that Paul in particular and scripture in general indiscriminately mix the human and the divine terms for Christ. It is no surprise, then, that the divine redeemer should be called a man.

If Apollinaris, in understanding the man from heaven as the new humanity paradigmatic of redemption and in defining the new man as he does, may be reckoned as giving a persuasive interpretation of Paul, one final point is still more decisive. He rightly sees that Paul is contrasting Christ not to the fallen Adam, as in Romans 5:12ff., but to the created Adam. Paul's explicit citation of Genesis 2:7, which refers to God's creation of Adam, is decisive. It follows that here, at any rate, Paul associates the human predicament not with sin but with the old creation.[21] Redemption, then, represents an overcoming and a transcending of the created order. Apollinaris' exclamation "O new creation and divine mixture! God and flesh completed one and the same nature!" may well go beyond Paul, but it does depend on his logic.[22] In sum, let me conclude in a preliminary way that Apollinaris' christology can claim to be based on a careful reading of the passage from 1 Corinthians 15 that he regards as one of its chief scriptural warrants. The problem that remains is whether this preliminary conclusion can be challenged. Let me turn to Gregory of Nyssa's refutation of Apollinaris in order to explore the question.

Gregory of Nyssa's Refutation of Apollinaris

Gregory's *Antirrheticus*, like many ancient polemical works, follows the order of the treatise being attacked; and so one is left with the initial impression that we are dealing with a long list of specific objections that as often as not seize on small details rather than the larger, underlying issues. For example, at a number of points Nyssa seeks to show that Apollinaris cannot himself escape the objections he makes to the view of Christ he is opposing. For instance, if Apollinaris says that God is the mind of the new man, we may object that he too is speaking of Christ as an inspired man (*entheos anthrōpos*).[23] We can argue that Apollinaris' christology is a "two sons" christology (3.1:199). Moreover, if the Word could not be united to a changeable mind, then the same objection ought to attach to his union with changeable flesh (3.1:194–95). Sometimes the detailed objections Nyssa makes are more substantive. He faults Apollinaris for appearing to deny

Adam a human mind (3.1:144). Although he is clearly playing on the obscurity of Apollinaris' language and deliberately misunderstanding him, he may well be correct in that Apollinaris comes close to denying that the human mind can function positively; and this is not so very different from denying the mind altogether. More to the point, he sees Apollinaris' tendency to treat the human mind as evil, and he denies that this is true (3.1:141). And he argues that if death is the separation of mind and body, then Christ must have possessed a human mind (3.1:153–54).

Behind particular arguments like these, however, two fundamental lines of attack on Apollinaris can be discerned in Nyssa's work. First, he argues that Apollinaris' "entire aim has this in view—to say that the divinity of the only begotten Son is mortal, and that it did not receive passion by something human, but was altered to participation in passion, though it is an impassible and unalterable nature" (3.1:136). In other words, Apollinaris' christology, by uniting the Word with a human body, renders the Word changeable and mortal and so calls his divinity into question. Nyssa denies that Christ's human operations and sufferings can be predicated of God the Word (3.1:167–68). Of course, Apollinaris might reply that the Word as the vital principle in Christ is never affected by the body and its motions, but this involves him in redefining human passions as divine activities, a view Nyssa finds inadequate.[24] Second, Apollinaris' view may be faulted not only for theological reasons because it compromises the divinity of the Word but also for soteriological reasons. When the Word of God, the good shepherd, came to find the lost sheep of humanity, he did not rescue the skin and leave everything else behind (3.1:151–52). In other words, for salvation to have been effected, the Word must have identified himself with every aspect of human nature. The principle, of course, is that what the Word has not assumed he has not redeemed.[25] The union between humanity and divinity in Christ must be so full and complete that Nyssa can compare it to a drop of vinegar mixed into the ocean (3.1:201).

The two general points Nyssa makes do serve his purpose in refuting Apollinaris, but they become difficulties if we think of trying to write a coherent christology. Theologically, the Word must always be kept distinct from his humanity. But soteriologically, he must be fully united with it. Nyssa sees the problem, and he can speak of the christological union in a divisive way as a "fellowship" (koinōnia; e.g., 3.1:168) and in a unitive way as a "mingling" (anakrasis; 3.1:161). It would take me beyond the scope of my argument to pursue this puzzle in detail, but since my solution to it bears on one of Nyssa's arguments against Apollinaris' exegesis, let me summarize my conclusion and present it at least as an hypothesis. By recognizing the contradiction between his theological and his soteriological refutations of Apollinaris, Nyssa also recognizes the mystery of the incarnation (3.1:184). We cannot explain how the uncreated and the created are united, nor how the Word remains impassible when the man receives him.[26] But what we can see is how the incarnation expresses the character of God, who presides over the course of human history, and where it belongs in the process that completes creation and ushers in the age to come. In other words, Nyssa turns from a timeless analysis of Christ's person to the salvation history in which the incarnate Lord plays the focal role.

Let me turn from these general comments about Nyssa's polemic against Apollinaris to points that Nyssa makes that are more specifically related to the interpretation of 1 Corinthians 15:45ff. Nyssa by no means disagrees with Apollinaris' fundamental conviction that the man from heaven is in some sense the divine redeemer and that he supplies the paradigm of redemption for all. He is even willing to admit that the man from heaven is a life-giving spirit and consists of three elements (3.1:213). But his explanation of the sense in which this is so provides an alternative to Apollinaris' interpretation. "But he who is mingled with the heavenly one and who has transformed what is of earth by his mixture with what is better is no longer of dust, but may be called heavenly. And he who by the life-giving Spirit effected his operation on us is also a life-giving spirit" (3.1:213).

Nyssa has made two crucial changes in Apollinaris' exegesis. First, without meaning to deny the unity of the man from heaven, he insists that there must be a distinction between the heavenly one, that is, the eternal Word of God, and "he who is mingled with the heavenly one." Of course, Apollinaris would regard this move as a denial of scripture's insistence on a single subject in

Christ; but Nyssa's reply is that Apollinaris' own distinction between the divine Spirit and the flesh risks compromising the principle as much as his. This move is related to Nyssa's theological line of attack on Apollinaris by which he insists that God the Word must remain distinct in nature from the created aspect of Christ. Nevertheless, he qualifies the distinction by using the highly unitive terms *mingled* (*anakratheis*) and *mixture* (*epimixias*) to describe the relation of the two.

The second change Nyssa makes in Apollinaris' interpretation of 1 Corinthians 15:45ff. is indicated by the phrases "transformed what is of earth" and "no longer of dust." In other words, the one mingled with the heavenly one is, to begin with, of earth and dust like the old Adam. The new humanity, though contrasting sharply with the old, is a transformation and not an abolition of it. To make this point, Nyssa appeals to 1 Corinthians 15:48: "As was the man of dust, so are those who are of heaven." It seems obvious to Nyssa that Christians are in solidarity with both Adams and that Paul's point is that they have been transformed from their likeness to Adam to their new likeness to Christ and that their citizenship has been transferred from earth to heaven (Phil. 3:20; 3.1:145). It follows, then, that the comparison of believers with the heavenly man requires that "after the likeness of humans there also be a mind in him" (3.1:145). However much we must think of the last Adam as the divine redeemer, the Word of God, we must also recognize that in his created aspect his humanity is to be identified with ours. Redemption does not abolish our humanity; it simply abolishes its mortality. Here Nyssa can appeal to the Adam typology of Romans 5:12ff. (3.1:160). The obedience of the second man undoes the disobedience of the first, thereby changing us from earth to heaven, from death to resurrection. And, of course, Nyssa's insistence on our total solidarity with Christ reflects his soteriological line of attack on Apollinaris.

In all but one respect Nyssa's alternative interpretation of 1 Corinthians 15:45ff. is persuasive. What he seems to be saying is that we must read the passage in its full context. Verses 48 and 49 make it clear, first, that our humanity, including the mind, is capable of being identified with the new humanity and, second, that the new humanity is a transformation of, rather than a substitution for, the old. In appealing to Romans 5:12ff., Nyssa is able to show that this transformation represents the transition from death to resurrection, and he treats death as a consequence of the fall. The one aspect of Apollinaris' interpretation he fails to treat is Apollinaris' recognition that the Adam compared to Christ in 1 Corinthians 15 is the created rather than the fallen Adam. Nyssa would have to argue that the new humanity, far from rejecting creation, brings it to completion. The strength of Nyssa's exegesis lies in his appeal to the broader context of 1 Corinthians 15:45–47; Apollinaris ought to have read all of Paul. But its weakness lies in its failure to deal adequately with the peculiar fact that Paul here compares the created Adam to Christ.

Nyssa's refutation of Apollinaris' exegesis goes further by rejecting Apollinaris' understanding of Paul's anthropological terms. He refuses to agree that Paul in 1 Thessalonians 5:23 is using "spirit and soul and body" to refer to "three parts" of a human being (3.1:209ff.). His appeal is to 1 Corinthians 2 and 3, where Paul speaks of "spiritual men" (*pneumatikois*; 3:1), "men of the flesh" (*sarkinois, sarkikoi*; 3:1, 3), and "the natural man" (*psychikos*; 2:14; cf. 15:44ff.). The context shows that Paul is not talking about the structure of a human being but rather about human behavior and moral orientation. The anthropological terms are ways of talking about the orientation of human capacities for moral agency. The terms define differing exercises of freedom (*prohairesis*). Consequently, when Paul refers to spirit, soul, and body in 1 Thessalonians 5:23, all he means is to pray that God may "sanctify you wholly," that is in every human capacity (3.1:211; *pan to somatikon kai psychikon kai pneumatikon epitēdeuma*). If Apollinaris would have been happy with the New English Bible's translation of the Pauline term *flesh* as "lower nature," Nyssa would have agreed with Bultmann's insistence that Paul's anthropological terms refer to orientations of the human being as a whole. Nyssa does not strongly insist on his interpretation, since he is prepared to accept a philosophical definition of human nature. But he certainly hits on a weakness in Apollinaris' exegesis.

One final line of attack on Apollinaris' exegesis seems to me the most important of all. Nyssa begins by rejecting those statements of Apollinaris' that would seem to imply the eternal coexistence of Christ's humanity and of his flesh with the Word of God. It may be that Nyssa supposes Apollinaris is teaching some sort of eternal humanity of Christ, but I think that the main force of his objection lies in a slightly different direction.[27] At one point Nyssa argues that Apollinaris' view requires us to think of all the properties of the flesh coexisting with the Word before the ages—"toil, grief, tears, thirst, sleep, hunger" (3.1:149). Still more senseless, we must think eternal the birth in Bethlehem, the story of the shepherds coming to the manger, and Jesus' growth in stature, wisdom, and grace. In another context Nyssa replies to Apollinaris' objection that if Christ is a man receiving God, there would be many gods, "since many receive God" (3.1:202). Nyssa's answer is that the objection might hold if there were many virgin mothers, if Gabriel had made his announcement to many, if the prophets had proclaimed many children and many sons. Nyssa goes on to speak of Christ's miracles, his death on the cross, his resurrection and ascension, his being seated at God's right hand, and his return to judge the world.

The conclusion I should like to draw is that Nyssa appeals to the story of Christ (cf. also 3.1:139, 140, 222). That is, what bothers Nyssa most about Apollinaris' view is that it turns the incarnation into a timeless reality. Instead, the incarnation is to be treated as a narrative that begins with the virgin birth, finds its climax in the death and resurrection, and reaches its completion in the age to come. In terms of 1 Corinthians 15:45ff., Nyssa's view implies that Paul's account of the new humanity and of the last Adam should not be severed from the salvation history in which it belongs. In terms of his christology, as I suggested earlier, what Nyssa is saying is that we cannot give an adequate account of the union of uncreated and created in Christ; but we can describe the salvation history. We can know timeless truth only as it has been given us in the context of time and history. If I am correct in my assessment of Nyssa, it is clear that he would have been distressed by the tendency of the church from the fifth century onward to treat the incarnation as a timeless theological problem confined to giving an account of Christ's person. In a sense, even though Apollinaris' christology was rejected by the early church, the approach he took ended by prevailing.

Concluding Reflections

What have we learned? We have certainly found two differing interpretations of 1 Corinthians 15:45 and two differing theological perspectives. At the exegetical level, the identity of the man from heaven and his relation to created humanity are the chief issues. Apollinaris can justify his view of a single nature of the Word made flesh by appealing to Paul's failure to make any christological distinction in his description of the last Adam; and he can argue for the novelty of the new man by showing that Paul contrasts Christ with the created Adam, possibly implying that death and creation belong together and that our predicament is that we are created. Nyssa can argue for his view by appealing to the wider context of the verses—a context that implies that the new is a transformation of the old—and by using other passages in Paul that relate this transformation to the salvation history. It seems hard to draw absolute conclusions, and I hesitate to say that one interpretation is correct and the other incorrect. Both seem to me valid within limits, and both probably fall short of being complete interpretations. So far as theology is concerned, it is easy enough to see that Apollinaris is wrong by Chalcedonian standards. But though Nyssa clearly violates none of Chalcedon's rules, it is hard to see that his christology gets beyond appealing to the mystery. In other words, little light is shed on the true meaning of our text. And although we can see that two very different theological traditions are capable of assimilating it, we find no help in coming to terms with the relationship between theology and exegesis. The fathers assume that we are dealing with a two-way street and that scripture and theology belong together, mutually informing one another. They draw a circle around the problem we vainly seek to solve, a problem compounded for us by modern historiographical assumptions.

Nevertheless, as I suggested at the outset, the value of our study lies not in providing answers about exegesis or theology, but in sharpening our questions. Let me try to explain what I mean by trying to articulate what seems to me the most important thing I have learned. It has long occurred to me that two sorts of interpretations of Paul's thought are to be found in modern exegetes. The Paul of justification by faith has predominated, but there are some who would give the Paul of the two ages pride of place. Interpreting Paul the first way puts his own idiosyncratic ideas at center stage and focuses on the perennial issue of the individual's redemption by God's gratuitous forgiveness. Interpreting him the second way underlines the eschatological dimension of his thought, the themes that he has in common with other writers in the early church, and his sense of the new people of God as a corporate body. There would, of course, be other ways of making the contrast between the "justification by faith" Paul and the "two ages" Paul. What intrigues me, however, is that Nyssa's insistence on the salvation history suggests a deeper way of seeing the contrast. Justification by faith runs the risk of being treated as a timeless truth, divorced from the salvation history. The "two ages" Paul, however, can be more readily tied to the narrative of God's purposes from creation to the age to come.

At the same time, Nyssa's insight leads me to suppose that the tension between the timeless and the temporal runs deeper in Paul's thought than the contrast, as it were, between a Protestant and a Catholic Paul. As we have seen, the "two ages" Paul can be interpreted by giving a timeless account of the new humanity. Could we say that this is not unlike Tillich's account of the new being? None of the fathers before Augustine read Paul as though justification by faith were central to his thought, yet their differing readings of him reflect the tension between the timeless and the temporal. Other dimensions of Paul's thought can be added to the picture. Only once does Paul treat the Old Testament as predictive of Christ (Rom. 1:2), and even there he may be employing a traditional formulation to which he is not fully committed. Instead, there is much to be said for understanding his approach to the Old Testament as revolving around the conviction that Christ removes the veil from it to reveal the timeless truths of faith (2 Cor. 3).[28] On the other hand, it is equally clear that the content of his interpretation of scripture more often than not must be related to the salvation history. Again, Paul can say that "we look not to the things that are seen but to the things that are unseen; for the things that are seen are transient, but the things that are unseen are eternal" (2 Cor. 4:18). Yet this perspective, which rejoiced the hearts of the early Christian Platonists, must be balanced against Paul's usual tendency to think in eschatological terms.

Of course, I could argue that the debate between Apollinaris and Nyssa helps us see other problems in the text of Paul: his use of the created Adam in the typology of 1 Corinthians 15, his problematic use of anthropological terms. Nevertheless, the most important problem that seems to me revealed by the debate is what I have called the contrast between a timeless and a temporal perspective in Paul. Perhaps the problem is not one that can or should be solved, though as an unreconstructed new critic I should be reluctant to make the admission. More important, perhaps, is the observation that tensions like the one I have described are precisely what make interpretation possible as an ongoing task. That they can never be fully resolved prevents any interpretation from being final. That they are there at all, as the rabbis said, is to supply the grit capable of producing the pearls of exegesis.

John Chrysostom as an Interpreter of Pauline Social Ethics

ADOLF MARTIN RITTER

I f I am not mistaken, there is widespread agreement among
New Testament exegetes today—against the classical Marxist
theory of the proletarian origin and revolutionary character of
earliest Christianity—that neither Jesus' "gospel for the poor"
(still less the Pauline and Johannine preaching) nor even the
"piety of the poor" that characterizes the Lucan writings and
the Epistle of James (although in different ways and to varying
degrees) contains a social-revolutionary program. That possibility
is as good as excluded by the immediate expectation (intensified
by foreign rule, social grievances, and various forms of distress) of
an immanent parousia. This expectation, however, defines the
horizon and framework within which Jesus and earliest Christianity live and think. The measure is full; the "time is fulfilled, and
the kingdom of God is at hand" (Mk. 1:15).

Jesus propagates no program.[1] But he does encourage people,
among other things, to discover and to try out new possibilities
for common action appropriate to the situation (one need only
think of Mt. 5-7 and parallels). These seem impossible, indeed
absurd, only so long as one is unwilling to look away, even for
a moment, from one's previous experience of life. For just this
reason, however, these possibilities are—perhaps—adapted to
break up the mechanisms of hate and retaliation!

Jesus preaches the God who comes near; and he preaches
this God to the "poor," to the hungry, to the afflicted, to those
who seek justice in vain. In doing so, he seeks to make it believ-
able that this God does not give up in the face of human failing
but rather desires that such failing no longer be inevitable and

irremediable. Thus Jesus' trust in God's "forwardness" and tire-
lessness is no invitation to passivity. Its aim is rather to liberate the
person who takes up this attitude of trust in the face of incalcula-
ble oppositions, failures, and constraints; and one aspect of the
liberation is precisely to guard the person against a disastrous
overestimation of himself. God's kingdom comes; and, Jesus
says, it comes "of itself" (αὐτομάτη), inconspicuously and "wholly
otherwise" than one expects (Mk. 4:26–29). The person who acts
with this in mind is, in Jesus' view, protected against burdening
himself with the more-than-human task of trying to execute divine justice in an unjust world. Instead he can concentrate his
strength—which is limited, in any case—on giving practical-
"political" expression to the hope for God's coming kingdom.

The Pauline view is similarly unprogrammatic, similarly
"dialectical." Belief in creation is not, in the final analysis, constitutive for Paul's concept and understanding of the world. What is
fundamental is rather belief in the new epoch brought into effect
in the Christ-event, belief in the dawn of a "new creation" into
which the believer is already incorporated through baptism (2 Cor.
5:17). In other words, for Paul, κόσμος means first of all "unre-
deemed creation," the world that only "in Christ" has again
become recognizable as God's creation. It is not, so to speak, a
"neutral" system of order but an "epoch" and a realm of "world-
liness," a time and place of subjection to the "powers" and elements of the "world" or, at least, of assault on believers by these
powers and elements.[2]

This complex view has the result, among other things, that
the ethics of Paul (as of the New Testament generally) has a "primarily ecclesiological character." That is, its instructions regarding the conduct of the individual (in church and in world) "are
essentially designed for the believer."[3] In this regard, however, it
should be kept in mind that Paul does not conceive the church as
a *civitas Platonica*, beyond space and time, but rather as that
domain of the "world" in which the lordship of Christ is already
recognized, proclaimed, and attested in the obedience of faith.[4]
Thus, for both Jesus and Paul, "conservative" and "revolutionary" impulses become intertwined in a quite distinctive way.[5]
The "revolutionary" impulses also have the potential, however, to

break through the self-imposed limits of New Testament ethics and to go beyond the particular ethical judgments reached at that time, for example, with regard to slavery.[6]

We ought now to consider the relevant texts in detail. The limits of space, however, prevent that. Instead I will confine myself to a single text and will simply indicate how it offers support for the sketch I have given. The text is Romans 12:1–8, a particularly concise expression of "Christian ethics" in Paul's view and, at the same time, a *locus classicus* for his understanding of the gifts and operations of the Spirit, the charismata.

On what basis does Paul speak here? He makes his appeal "by [the evidences of] the mercy of God" διὰ τῶν οἰκτιρμῶν τοῦ θεοῦ).[7] That is the antecedent for everything else. There is no precondition in this regard. No prerequisite is stipulated that must first be met on the part of the addressees. Similarly, in the same letter Paul can say to the same addressees, to their face as it were, that they have received the Spirit as surely as they have received the gospel of Jesus Christ.

What does Paul appeal for? The text's exhortations can be summarized in three key words without doing violence to its sense: *sacrifice, transformation,* and *community.* "Therefore I appeal to you, brethren . . . to present yourselves unreservedly [bodily] as a sacrifice which is living, holy, pleasing to God. Let this be your reasonable worship." That the believer may learn to exist wholly for God *because* God exists wholly for him (διὰ τῶν οἰκτιρμῶν τοῦ θεοῦ) is certainly the meaning of the "living cult," the λογικὴ λατρεία, of which Paul speaks here (taking up a concept that had already been coined).[8]

Even where this process is only beginning, however, it has consequences. One of these consequences (the second key word: *transformation*), according to our text, is that one begins to distrust the rules and standards of this "age" and instead "proves" for oneself "what is God's will"; in other words, one allows oneself to be "transformed" and makes a beginning in the renewal of the mind (ἀνακαίνωσις τοῦ νοός). The other consequence (the third key word: *community*) could perhaps be paraphrased this way: one begins to attach less importance to oneself; or, to put it in Paul's own words, "let no one think more of himself than he

ought to think, but keep prudence in mind"—true to the principle of *suum cuique!* Then, in what follows, this is spelled out and
made concrete regarding membership in the "body of Christ,"
which for Paul is made up purely of charismata and charismatics.
But what is essential for our purposes has already come into view.
It is implied, at bottom, in the way in which—as is entirely typical
of Paul—the imperative is referred back to and is based on the
indicative of salvation already bestowed.[9]

When one turns from Paul to John Chrysostom, it is evident
that the impulses to transformation instead of to accommodation
to the σχῆμα of "this age" (in this case, to the living conditions
that obtained in late antique society with its sometimes striking
abuses and its mass distress) have become stronger rather than
weaker. It is certainly true of Chrysostom, at any rate, that all
through his years as presbyter in Antioch, the third largest city in
the *oikumene*, and later as bishop in Constantinople, the imperial
capital, he expressed his position on questions of social justice
with a constancy, an urgency, and a fearlessness that are hardly
matched by any other theologian of the early church, whether
"orthodox" or "heretical."[10] Many have wanted, on this account,
to see him as a forerunner of socialistic ideas.[11] And in fact, he
could express his views on questions of property, quite regularly,
as if he simply considered property equivalent to "theft."[12]

Yet that is only the more spectacular side of his social engagement, the side most often noted in the literature—or at any rate
in the older literature. The other side, and probably more characteristic for him, is that in his preaching, whenever the occasion
arose, he made himself an advocate and petitioner on behalf of
the "poor Christ" (Mt. 25:31–46). In this way, he tried to arouse
and to keep alive among his hearers a sense of responsibility for
the socially deprived.[13]

Nevertheless Chrysostom has often enough been seen only
as a "moralist" in the tradition of the Cynic-Stoic diatribe—and
this still happens, as Arnold Stötzel's work shows. Nor is this
surprising when "the public below his pulpit" is viewed as "not
essentially different" from that of the popular philosophers.[14]
And in fact, anyone who reads Chrysostom's sermons can easily

gain the impression that their chief business was to censure the vices and extol the virtues.[15] In just the same way, centuries before, Cynic-Stoic itinerant and mendicant philosophers (people, for example, such as Dio of Prusa [ca. 40–112 C.E.], who also was nicknamed "Chrysostom") tried to gather young and old to themselves "until they became wise and lovers of righteousness," until they had "learned to despise gold and silver" and hold "it of little account," as also "rich food, fragrant ointments and sexual love," and so came to live "as masters of themselves and finally as masters also of others" (ἄρχοντες μάλιστα καὶ πρῶτον αὐτῶν, ἔπειτα καὶ τῶν ἄλλων ἀνθρώπων).[16]

On closer examination, however, this impression proves too superficial in my judgment. It is important to note that Chrysostom also knows how to set limits—for example, with reference to the "social" character of Christianity—to this popular philosophy, if not to the ethics of Greco-Roman antiquity in general. For Chrysostom, whose competence in the ethical realm can hardly be questioned, the decisive "rule of the most perfect Christianity, its exact definition and highest summit," is this: "to seek what serves the welfare of the community" (τοῦτο κανὼν χριστιανισμοῦ τοῦ τελειοτάτου, τοῦτο ὅρος ἠκριβωμένος, αὕτε ἡ κορυφὴ ἡ ἀνωτάτω, τὸ τὰ κοινῇ συμφεροντα ζητεῖν). It is to know that one's own well-being is for better and for worse bound up with that of the neighbor.[17] Or, to speak (with Rudolf Bultmann) in the sense of Paul and of his way of resting the imperative on the indicative of salvation,[18] it is to know that the chief issue is no longer "individual progress to perfection" (προκοπή) but rather communal "edification" (οἰκοδομή)—and it is this precisely because the person who has been set on a new foundation by the οἰκτιρμοί of God, and is no longer burdened by care for himself in his action, can and should take the neighbor's cry as the decisive motive and measure of his action.

It should be no objection here that the πάντα πρὸς τὸ συμφέρον of 1 Corinthians 12:7 was not first discovered by Paul but is also quite common in Greek and Roman sources (and still more common, naturally, in Jewish sources). Every useful commentary on Corinthians confirms this point, if confirmation is needed. But this does not alter the fact that for the Greeks and Romans,

every social ethic, "no matter how far-reaching its demands," is derived "from an absolute valuation of the individual" and his "happiness." This was worked out most consistently in Stoicism with its
οἰκείωσις-doctrine, according to which all the moral postulates follow "step by step from the first instinct of all living beings, the
instinct of self-preservation and self-realization."[19] Furthermore,
given the wealth of social-ethical approaches to emerge on the
ground of the intense political life of the Greek πόλεις in classical
times, it is striking (and in need of some explanation) that so many
of these disappeared in the course of the imperial period.[20] One
reason may be that hellenistic philosophy—"which could appeal
to Socrates, and probably with good reason, in support of its
one-sidedly individual orientation in ethics"—had already "out-
distanced, as it were" this rich variety of approaches.[21]

If, as I am convinced, matters have a somewhat different cast
in Chrysostom's case, then it can no longer be enough for him
simply to free individuals from their greed, their bondage to things.
Something must also be said about how possessions are to be used.
And in fact, Chrysostom did repeatedly raise this point.[22] In my
judgment, a sharp eye for social realities and an understanding of
Christian "perfection"—according to which "perfection" also has
essentially to do with social justice—led him, in the end, to the
insight that the means of private almsgiving are hardly adequate,
even if the aim is to address only the most grinding poverty. On
the contrary, we must look in all earnestness for other possible
solutions. Thus Chrysostom often, and publicly, pushed toward a
comprehensive "social utopia," a utopia that would be based on the
principle that "God did not in the beginning create one person
rich and another poor . . . but left the same earth free to all."
Where there is no talk of "mine" and "yours," he insisted, "no
conflict or strife arises. Therefore community of goods is the more
fitting form of life"—because it is clearly God's intention for us—
"than private property; and it conforms to our nature." Furthermore, Chrysostom is convinced, this is the most effective form of
the utilization of goods (a point on which Aristotle, as is well
known, held precisely the opposite view).[23]

For Chrysostom, all this was obviously no *pium desiderium,*
no "favorite pet idea," "of whose impracticability" he had "at heart

become convinced."[24] It is also more than doubtful, to my mind, whether one can really say that, "in hindsight," his "solution to the social question" appears "naive."[25] This claim keeps in mind neither general economic perspectives—which in the compass of what was conceivable in Chrysostom's time is certainly wrong—nor the concrete conditions that then obtained. Its point can only be that Chrysostom seems never even to have imagined making demands on the "Christian state" for a social policy along the lines of his (if you will pardon the expression) "religio-socialistic utopia." The question is, however, whether such an attempt would have had even the slightest chance of success in the circumstances, circumstances about which we are also "in hindsight" fairly well informed. It may well be that the only "realistic" course, the only course in keeping with the conditions of the time, was to consider the church's powers and its possibilities for effective action.[26]

It is quite true, of course, that much of the scholarly literature takes a very different approach to the whole question of how slavery was regarded in antiquity, although not always in such glaring colors as the following:

> In pre-Christian and non-Christian antiquity (but not in the Old Testament!), doubts about the lawfulness of slavery were expressed from time to time. A slave-free humanity could even be imagined in certain Greek social utopias; and, under the influence of Stoicism, the Roman slave laws were humanized and liberalized. . . . [But] from the beginning, Christian preaching stabilized the practice of slavery.[27]

But what are the facts of the matter? So far as the Greek social utopias are concerned, such information as has come down to us is so fragmentary that there is no way to determine clearly how much "political" content they had.[28] And what the Stoics and Epicureans had to say about the slave problem—in the context of the Sophistic enlightenment—would, in any case, have been of greater consequence.[29] In contrast to Aristotle's teaching that human beings are by nature either slave or free and that it is both beneficial and just for the slaves that they are slaves,[30] the Stoics laid down the principle of the equality of all men (as rational beings) as a matter of natural law. From this principle, however, they drew no practical consequences at all regarding the social stratification that had become so pronounced in the imperial period. In their view, the human value of the individual remained the same in every situation. Thus they did not dispute the legitimacy of the institution of slavery as it was embodied in all ancient legal codes and, of course, in Roman law as well.[31] From the appeal to "natural law" they derived, in the first instance, "only" the call for more humane treatment of slaves.

Similarly the gradual humanization and liberalization of the Roman slave laws—above all, no doubt, a result of Stoic influence, but also a reaction to the increasingly difficult problem of the flight of slaves[32]—was limited to removing some of the worst brutalities. When he became emperor, Constantine—who was also the first to enact a law protecting against the break-up of slave families[33]—still had expressly to prohibit the punishment or torture of slaves by hanging, poisoning, slow incineration, deliberate dehydration, or allowing them to rot in the flesh.[34] Furthermore, the legal affairs of slaves continued to be regulated in the sphere of private law, and slaves were not considered "legal subjects" (*personae*) in the strict sense but were ranked with "things" (*res*). The state did not pass verdict in their affairs as it did for other "persons"; rather, as a rule, their masters were also their judges.[35] As objects of "international law" (*ius gentium*), despite their immense economic significance, slaves were never viewed as a state-supporting class. As a result, they never actively participated in the official state cult but instead followed a variety of unofficial cults (especially the mystery associations).[36]

Here, to our knowledge, the Christian world first introduced an overriding religious principle to which even the emperors themselves submitted in the end. "Apart from the manifold legislative measures [taken] for the mitigation of slavery," the emperors raised "the promotion of liberty, the *favor libertatis*, to the level of a general and widely accepted legal principle."[37] Here we have— to quote a witness who is above suspicion in this regard, given his highly critical stance toward the established Christianity of his own time—"the greatest upheaval which has ever occurred." The phrase comes from the great historian Jacob Burckhardt.[38]

To what extent was this principle already operative in the Christian communities at the beginning?[39] Let us put this question to Paul. He credited it to the dynamic of the gospel that, under its impulse, master and slave discovered themselves as brothers (cf. Phlm. 16–20). From the equality of all "in Christ" (cf. 2 Cor. 5:17; Gal. 3:26–28), however, he did not go on to draw any direct conclusions in favor of legal change in the everyday realm. Nevertheless he also did not "simply piously ignore" the legal conditions of his time or "accept and sanction" them "in faith."[40]

By and large, the church of subsequent centuries took a similar approach: "in Christ," that is, in the community, individual slaves were accorded full recognition, respect, and "freedom." But no program for the universal emancipation of slaves was set forth. And in this respect, as the example of Chrysostom shows, there was no fundamental change in the post-Constantinian period. Certainly Chrysostom was able repeatedly to denounce the "domination of man over men" (as we would say today) simply as sin, or rather as the consequence of sin, instead of glorifying it as an "order of creation."[41] But he could anticipate a "decisive change of the social institution of slavery" only through an "inner transformation of masters and slaves, in the community, into servants of God," inasmuch as slavery had itself arisen "through the inner alienation of man from God." In this regard, it is true, he was capable of talking about the relation between free and unfree—in the context of a new evaluation of work and servitude, for instance!—in a way that still sounds promising today and that makes it appear unthinkable that the *status quo* of the distribution of power and property could, in the long run, remain totally untouched by what it means to be "in Christ."[42] Paul too appears already to have reckoned it quite obvious that the Christian brotherhood would also strive to prove itself "in circumstances and conditions outside the church" (καὶ ἐν σαρκὶ, Phlm. 16).[43]

Here I must break off; I want only to make some concluding observations. In the first place, I must admit that I should also have discussed Chrysostom's concept of monasticism in relation to the church. In his case, as in Basil of Caesarea's, to my mind, a deeper insight into his life and work can be achieved only when one tries to do justice to the fact that he made the journey from monasticism to ministry without abandoning the monastic ideal or even calling the *raison d'être* of monasticism into question.[44] Only in this framework does what I have tried to show in this study take its rightful place with Chrysostom—and perhaps also its plausibility.

Even so, this study may still have shown that, so far as Chrysostom is concerned at any rate, the ethics and eschatology of Jesus and Paul—despite their pronounced expectation of an immediate parousia—have not lost their critical power or permitted a complete surrender of the "reasonable worship" (λογικὴ λατρεία) of Christians to the established system. Perhaps one can even go a step further and say that what I suggested at the start will prove true: that the revolutionary impulses of New Testament ethics and eschatology, arising from the distinction between the ultimate and the penultimate and even more from a radically interpreted "agape," tend to break through the self-imposed limits and to go beyond the particular ethical decisions and judgments made at Christianity's beginning.

Finally, as this suggests, there is in my view an important "Christian chapter" in the book of the history of utopia, a chapter to which belong not only all kinds of marginal figures (e.g., the Gnostic infant prodigy Epiphanes) but also a Paul and a John Chrysostom. Therefore, one of the things to which we ought now to be giving consideration is a Christian rehabilitation of the category of utopia. But that would lead us too far beyond the scope of this study—at least at the moment.[45]

Comment: Chrysostom and Pauline Social Ethics

✠————————————✠

ELIZABETH A. CLARK

R itter argues that Paul's "unprogrammatic" and "dialectical" position on social issues such as poverty and slavery was theologically grounded in his understanding of the gift of God's mercy, a mercy that should prompt Christians to "sacrifice, transformation, and community." Ritter interprets Romans 12:1–8 to mean that since God exists entirely for the believer, the believer may learn to exist entirely for God. Paul's "body of Christ" metaphor thus serves to remind his audience that they exist in community.

According to Ritter, in John Chrysostom's writings we find an impetus to social change intensified over that found in the teachings of Jesus and Paul. Some interpreters have even viewed Chrysostom as a proto-socialist.[1] Ritter argues that Chrysostom's concern for the poor stemmed not so much from the preaching of individual improvement that was characteristic of the Cynic-Stoic diatribe as from a Christian, specifically Pauline, focus on the edification of the neighbor, on the welfare of the whole community.

For Chrysostom, it would not suffice simply to free people from greed: even the Greek philosophers cast away their wealth.[2] Rather, the Christian must use his possessions to benefit the poor. According to Ritter, Chrysostom's views here point beyond mere voluntary and private "solutions" to social problems and can even be called "utopian," for example, his theory that private property was not God's intention for the human race. Although Chrysostom thought that slavery was a result of human sin, "the domination of man over men," his only recommendation was for an attitudinal change between master and slave. Ritter posits, however, that any Christian writer who so strongly believes that being "in Christ" will alter our values must expect that these changed values will manifest themselves in the wider social world.

Ritter concludes with the addendum that he should have set Chrysostom's ascetic views as the backdrop for his study, since Chrysostom never abandoned those monastic ideals even when he served as priest and bishop. According to Ritter, only by position-ing Chrysostom in this monastic framework do his teachings on the above-mentioned issues make sense.

My reading of Chrysostom differs *in emphasis* from Ritter's. My comments will be addressed to the following three points. First, although Chrysostom's corpus does indeed include a few utopian passages such as Ritter cites, the views Chrysostom cus-tomarily expresses do not tend in this direction. On some issues, Chrysostom adopts a *more* conservative stance than Paul: he sides with the "Paul" of the deutero-Pauline and pastoral Epistles rather than with the "Paul" we today accept. Moreover, Chrysostom all too often slides over the top of the Pauline verses—for example, Galatians 3:28—that might have stirred him to explore a more socially liberal position.

Second, Chrysostom's "utopian" vision, limited as it is, rarely emerges from his reflection on Paul. Rather, it stems from his reflection on Genesis 1 and 2, and this as linked to the ancient philosophical discussion of "the natural." Indeed, I remain uncer-tain whether any specifically New Testament passages contributed significantly to the utopian dimension of Chrysostom's thought as Ritter has sketched it.

Third, I agree with and shall press further Ritter's point that monasticism is central as the frame for Chrysostom's social think-ing. For Chrysostom, the hope for a "utopia" realizable on earth finds its locus in the monastic community.

On the first point, the conservative nature of Chrysostom's thought emerges frequently in his discussion of property and slavery—two issues raised by Ritter—and also in his discussion of women and marriage, a third topic about which I shall briefly comment. Ritter rightly insists that for Chrysostom, it is not a matter simply of despising wealth but of using wealth for the benefit of the community. This indeed is the whole point of

Chrysostom's exegesis of the gospel story of the rich young man. Moreover, Chrysostom argues, since it is not so much a matter of freeing the rich from their burden as it is of helping the impoverished, even people of the humble classes should be encouraged to give.[3] As is well known, Chrysostom interprets the "oil" that the foolish virgins lacked (in the parable of the wise and foolish virgins) as almsgiving.[4] Likewise, he gives a rigorous exegesis of Matthew 25:31–41 (the questions that will be asked us at the Last Judgment): although we do not have the ability to cure the sick or free the prisoners, we are obliged to do whatever is in our power to lend assistance to unfortunates.[5] Given this approach, Chrysostom's criticism of female adornment centers not so much on the sexual lure that fine clothes, jewelry, and makeup can constitute as on the help that could have been given to the poor if the money had been correctly used.[6] Charity, Chrysostom concludes, is one of the few virtues we can rightly say humans share with God.[7]

Despite these emphases, Chrysostom's practical solutions to poverty remain within the province of individual charity. Thus he complains that if *individuals* would give as they ought, priests would not have to spend time buying corn and wine for the poor relief—an activity that subjects them to ridicule—and could devote themselves more fully to their religious duties. If each of the approximately one hundred thousand Christians in Antioch gave one loaf to a poor person, all would have plenty to eat. Moreover, although Chrysostom admires the communal arrangements of the early Jerusalem church as described in Acts 4, he assures his readers, both rich and poor, that they should not "get excited" by his description of it: after all, he is neither demanding the renunciation of private property, on the one hand, nor inciting the poor to claim it as their own, on the other. Even when Chrysostom states that injustice is the original source of riches (as he does in *Homily 12 on 1 Timothy*, cited by Ritter), he softens his conclusion both by exonerating those with inherited wealth from the deeds of their forefathers and by claiming that wealth is not in itself evil, since it can be used to help the poor. Thus Chrysostom's advice for daily living is not seasoned with much utopian salt.[8]

On the topic of slavery, Chrysostom's most generally expressed views are also conservative, at least as conservative as

Paul's. One message he derives from Paul's letter to Philemon is that slaves should not withdraw their service from their masters. After all, Chrysostom argues, if the slave is excellent and serves his master's household well, why "hide the candle under a bushel"?[9] Significantly, Chrysostom reads 1 Corinthians 7:21 (usually now translated as "if you can gain your freedom, avail yourself of the opportunity") as "rather, continue as a slave."[10] Thus Paul, according to Chrysostom, has *not* given permission for the slave to seek his freedom even if he can lawfully gain it. According to Chrysostom, Paul wrote these words in 1 Corinthians 7 to inform the slave that he gains nothing by being freed, that it is even an *advantage* for him to remain a slave. Besides, Chrysostom claims, even slaves can exhibit a noble freedom when they disdain the passions, suppress anger, and do not envy riches.[11] Chrysostom's comments on the slaves mentioned in the household codes are similar: servants are "free" if their souls are free; their servitude is "only" of a "fleshly" kind. They even gain a benefit from their servitude, for their lack of possessions prompts them to be "philosophers." Chrysostom sharply reminds the slaves he addresses not to imagine that they are free in the legal and social sense.[12]

On the topic of women, Chrysostom again takes a more conservative stance than Paul. In part, this is because he reads the post-Pauline material as Pauline, thus crediting to Paul himself the injunctions that women be silent and submissive. To his credit, Chrysostom recognizes that the advice in what he thinks are Paul's letters is not self-consistent: why should women be told that they will be saved through childbearing (1 Timothy 2:15) when in 1 Corinthians 7, virginity is held to be the higher state? And in any case, shouldn't people be saved by their own virtue, not by that of their offspring?[13]

Chrysostom is likewise puzzled by Paul's allowance of the rather free activity enjoyed by women in the early Christian communities. Chrysostom's explanation for this allowance—something that he cannot imagine for his own day—rests on a theory of "decline" in moral virtue from the days of the early church. Women in the first decades of Christianity were "more spirited than lions"; they traveled with the male apostles and "also performed all other ministries."[14] In his own time,

Chrysostom sadly acknowledges, women are not of this virile cast: they can scarcely be restrained from wrongdoing by their watchful husbands and by being kept shut at home.[15] Certainly they cannot aspire to the priesthood.[16]

Moreover, any "utopian" thoughts Chrysostom may have entertained about God's original plan for the human race were severely compromised by his notion that a household is a minia-ture monarchy, of which there is only one king—or, if the wife may be called a "second king" to her husband, she cannot wear the diadem, as he does.[17] At times, Chrysostom imagines this hierarchy to have been present from the moment of creation: only the male was made in the image of God, since "image" connotes authority. When God made "male and female one," according to Chrysostom, he made one a ruler and the other a subject.[18] And if we look at Chrysostom's discussions of Galatians 3:28, we do not find him using that verse to urge the liberalization of women's position in his own day, except for women who adopt the ascetic life.[19]

On the second point, it is not Paul's writings that lead Chrysostom to posit an original equality of humans so much as it is reflection on Genesis 1. Ritter cites the central passage, in Chrysostom's *Homilies on 1 Timothy*, in which Chrysostom ar-gues that at creation God did not make one person rich and another poor; the earth was to be free to all; the sun, moon, air, and so forth were to be shared in common by all, just as everyone received eyes, hands, and feet.[20] Although this discussion occurs in a treatise devoted to a book that Chrysostom thought was Pauline, it is the moment of creation—that is, the Genesis ac-counts—that motivates him to posit a theory of an original equal-ity among humans.

The utopian strand in Chrysostom's thinking about slavery also seems not to be motivated so much by his reflection on Paul as by that on the Genesis stories. According to Chrysostom in *Homily 40 on 1 Corinthians*, there was no slavery at the time of creation: if Adam had needed a slave, God would have supplied him with one. Rather, slavery is the penalty for sin.[21] Chrysostom does not find any reference to slavery down through the genera-tions to Noah. He argues that slavery began with "rebellion against parents," which apparently refers to the penalty placed on Ham and his descendants in Genesis 9. Abraham's servants, according to Chrysostom, were not really slaves at all, so Abraham is exonerated from the charge of slaveholding. Although Chrysostom notes that Galatians 3:28 should be taken to mean that slavery is at an end, he immediately concedes that a man may have one or two slaves (not troops of them) if he needs assistance.[22] Once again, we see Chrysostom "adjusting" his more radical position to the mores of the world around him.

Likewise, Chrysostom's brief consideration of the equality of women comes not from reflection on the Pauline verse we might expect but from thinking about Genesis—and even here he posits only an "equality of honor."[23] Yet these references to an "equality of honor" between Adam and Eve are likewise compromised by Chrysostom's reflection on "female nature." Although Chrysostom does not have an explicit biological theory concerning woman's "nature" to back up his dominant subordinationist position (as, for example, Thomas Aquinas does),[24] he appears to think that woman's "nature" is inferior to man's. Thus he refers many times to women as "weaker," light-minded and easily led astray, and "naturally" more feeble and simple than men.[25] None of this sounds either like the "equality" of the sexes or like Paul.

On the third point, I would stress that the only "utopia" Chrysostom imagines for his own era lies in the monastery. Monasticism provides the closest parallels with both Eden before the Fall and the early Christian community in Jerusalem. Just as those early Christians lived without private property, distinctions between rich and poor, or slaves, so live the monks of Chrysostom's own day. They have plenty of everything to go around, just as did the Jerusalem Christians; their life replicates the exemplary practices of the first Jerusalem Christians as Chrysostom imagines them.[26]

Monks of his own time live in a bliss that reminds him of Eden prior to sin. Like Adam in Paradise, they converse with God and have no worldly cares; a minimum of effort provides for their physical needs. Just as, in Eden, there was nothing to give rise to envy, jealousy, passions, and "diseases of the soul," so nothing in monastic life should (theoretically) prompt such manifestations of vice. The monastic life can be called "angelic," an adjective Chrysostom uses to describe the monks' sharing of everything in common.[27]

In these ways, I think, Chrysostom's limited utopian vision was speedily compromised. Moreover, even that limited utopian vision was prompted by reflection on Genesis 1, not on Paul's writings. Galatians 3:28 is interpreted to promote not genuine social change but only changes in attitude that make one's servitude more "kingly." The verse holds out no hope to men and women of Chrysostom's day for any modification of legal or social structures. Thus Paul's phrase "for freedom Christ has set us free" (Gal. 5:1) receives from Chrysostom little commendation as an exhortation toward social reform.

Augustine and the Pauline Theme of Hope

BASIL STUDER, O.S.B.

In his article "Hoffnung," H.-G. Link asserts with regard to the patristic age: "While early in the patristic period the theme of hope did not generally play a central role, in Augustine it belongs among the themes to which particular attention is given."[1] If one considers that monographs on the theme of hope limit themselves almost exclusively to Augustine's theology, one can understand this claim to some extent. Nevertheless it must be judged to be quite one-sided. To persuade oneself of this, one need only realize that a Tertullian could define the Christian religion as *corpus de conscientia religionis [fides], disciplinae unitate et spei foedere.*[2] In the same way, one can set over against this one-sided judgment the fact that Gregory of Nyssa combined the theme with three basic principles of his theology: the temporality of human existence, the never-ending ascent to perfection, and his description of eternal bliss.[3] And this is entirely aside from the fact that Christian communities, from the earliest times, celebrated Easter as the feast of hope, sang the Psalms, or the Jewish songs of hope, and had Paul's letter to the Romans read and expounded to them long before Augustine.[4] Of course, the fact that hope really occupied a central place for Augustine himself should not be put in question by any of these points.

As in his theological thinking generally, Augustine was influenced in his ideas of Christian hope by the stamp of his own life. In the terrible sufferings of his conversion he had to learn the extent to which faith requires a humble and prayerful hope, an ardent orientation toward eternal life.[5] The pastoral concern to which he had dedicated himself at his ordination to the priesthood in the year 391 constantly pushed him to pass his own religious experience on to others in homilies, in catechesis, and especially in his letters of consolation. In theological polemic against the Manicheans, Donatists, pagans, and Pelagians, he had again and again to come back to the basic theme of expectation and fulfillment, to the tension between *spes* and *res.* Here he let himself be guided especially by the Psalms, which he had cherished from the time of his conversion. But above all, and most interesting for our purposes, he put himself under the guidance of the Apostle Paul in his reflections on and in his expositions of Christian hope.

It is not possible to treat the entire complex of the Augustinian theology of hope in this study. Instead, I shall limit myself to an examination of three texts: (1) a section of the *Soliloquia,* a work written at Cassiciacum; (2) the exposition of Psalm 91 from the year 412, and (3) the relevant passages in the *Enchiridion de fide, spe et charitate,* a late work. Precisely on the basis of these texts we can throw full light on Augustine's reception of Paul. In them it becomes fully clear how impressed he was by the apostle even at the start of his more intimate involvement with the Christian faith, what basic significance Paul had for him when he began the controversy with Caelestius and Pelagius over precisely the Pauline teaching on the grace of Christ, and also what place Paul's letters occupied in his theological thinking as it reached its final maturity.

Faith, Hope, and Love in the Soliloquia (1.6.12–7.14)

In the winter of 386–87, as Augustine prepared in Cassiciacum for his baptism, he occupied himself with the rational foundation of his faith.[6] In particular, he gave attention to the questions of God and of the immortality of the human soul.[7] He sought, not only in conversations with his friends but also in dialogue with himself, to reach clarity on these points.[8] The *Soliloquia,* that unique written witness to the dialogue of *Augustinus cum Augustino,*[9] reveals in an impressive manner how concerned he was at that time to grasp truth not only in belief but also in knowledge[10] and how he tried to achieve the intellectual confirmation of the faith of his childhood[11] above all through dialectic.[12] At the same time, he never doubted that one can attain full knowledge of the truth only by way of moral cleansing. The tension between knowledge and virtue quickly became his fundamental concern.[13]

In this connection, Augustine now developed a suggestive scheme of ascent.[14] Three, or really four, stages can be distinguished: the possession of the pure eyes of the Spirit, the turn to the divine light, the vision of the light in this corporeal existence, and the eternal vision of God in the consummation.[15] Faith, hope, and love likewise belong to this graded ascent. Whereas Augustine regarded these three virtues as absolutely indispensable to the first three stages, he holds that in the consummation only love remains. Faith convinces a person of the necessity of purification; it instills the belief that one can attain the state of bliss only by turning to God; and it protects one from the doubts that are always possible in this world of sense so long as one cannot fully see God.[16] Hope, for its part, keeps the person from despair of his salvation, difficult though that salvation may be; it lets one count on (*praesumere*) the vision and helps one to hold out amid the many troubles of the body.[17] Finally, out of love for the promised light, the person no longer clings to cherished habits and does not repulse his physician. Rather, in his turn toward God, love increases his desire for the unifying vision. In the full vision of God, however, only love remains, for then the soul is totally united with God.[18] In fact, in contemplation of unique and true beauty, love can only intensify all the more. Were the soul not to remain concentrated on God in unending love, it could not remain in that blissful vision.[19] By contrast, faith will no longer be necessary at that point: what need is there for faith when the soul has already acquired sight[20] and can no longer be threatened by error? Similarly, hope is no longer necessary, for now the soul is in possession of that for which it had hoped; indeed it possesses everything in complete certainty.[21]

Even though Augustine does not explicitly refer to the apostle in these remarks concerning the ascent to God, he has nevertheless taken the triad of faith, hope, and love from 1 Corinthians.[22] About that there can be no doubt. Not only the designations and the sequence of the three attitudes of the soul but also the stress on the permanence of love points quite clearly in that direction.[23]

The same Pauline terminology and sequence are also present in other passages from Augustine's early writings, and once in an unequivocally Christian context.[24] One may justifiably ask, however, whether it was not an outside influence that prompted Augustine to refer to the Pauline triad in this connection.[25] The stages *sanatio–aspectus–visio* obviously call to mind the three-tiered ascent in Plotinus' discussions of virtue. The allusion to the *molestia corporis*, which the soul hopes will no longer continue after this life, also sounds very Plotinian.[26]

Most noteworthy is the connection with the Plotinian doctrine of the hypostases, according to which subject and object are united in the vision that completes the return.[27] In the *Soliloquia*, moreover, Augustine himself points explicitly to Plotinus.[28] Whether on the basis of these Plotinian reminiscences one is really justified, as Ragnar Holte claims, in connecting the *fides* and the *caritas* of Augustine with *pistis* and *eros* in Plotinus is another question.[29] It is certainly possible to associate the faith under discussion here with a text in which Plotinus contrasts *pistis* based in *historia* with *apodeixis*. But Plotinus' distinction obviously corresponds to the antithesis universally current among the sophists and philosophers between *probationes atechnicae* and *probationes technicae*.[30] Naturally there is a connection between the Augustinian contrast of *auctoritas* and *ratio*, which stands behind the *credere* and *scire* of the *Soliloquia*, and this rhetorical distinction between "historical" and rational proofs.[31] But in the Cassiciacum dialogues, Augustine does not speak of any kind of "historical" proofs. Rather, it is already quite clear to him here that *fides*, in the sense of an uncomprehending or not yet comprehending assent, is based solely on the *auctoritas* of Christ or of the church.[32] It is precisely in this sense also that he uses the expression *credere Deo*.[33] Even though he does not employ the biblical formulation *credere in Deum* in the *Soliloquia*, or apparently at all prior to 391, but only the classical expressions *credere Deo* and *credere Deum adesse*,[34] the Christian note in the use of *credere* still cannot be overlooked. Aside from the fact that the term does not refer simply to a human being but to God,[35] it quite clearly includes the sense of trusting surrender to the blessings of God, even if it does so in a very Roman manner. Thus, one reads toward the end of the first book: "Quando placet sese ostendat; iam me totum eius clementiae curaeque committo. Semel de illo credidi quod sic erga se affectos sublevare non cesset."[36]

Holte does not speak of any possible connection between *spes* in the *Soliloquia* and Plotinian conceptions. And yet it is remarkable how, in his dialogue with himself, Augustine connects hope with the longing for beauty. "Nam quanto augetur spes videndae illius qua vehementer aestuo pulchritudinis, tanto ad illam totus amor voluptasque convertitur," he says in response to *Ratio*. At the very least this is in accordance with good Platonic tradition.[37] It appears that Plotinus himself does not connect *elpis* with *eros*. But the idea of longing anticipation of beauty can be found in his work as well.[38] Again, surely, one has to take note of how in the opening prayer of the *Soliloquia*, Augustine himself supports his turn to God with expectant hope: "Dic qua attendam, ut aspiciam te, et omnia me spero quae iusseris esse facturum. Recipe, oro, fugitivum tuum, Domine, clementissime Pater."[39] On the other hand, he not only presupposes a patient hopefulness but also, in his emphasis on certainty, takes up a hopeful confidence.[40] Above all, he finds the motivation for hope's firmness in the promises of God.[41] No one will dispute, finally, that there are good reasons to recall the Plotinian *eros* in the Augustinian *caritas*. Augustine does speak of *caritas*, as of *amor*, with reference both to the vision of divine beauty and to total unification with God in a way that undoubtedly calls Plotinian texts to mind. Yet even here the Christian note should not be overlooked.[42] Aside from the fact that he is speaking not of *eros* but of *agape* (*caritas*), he explicitly refers to the *restare* of *caritas*; and, in any case, the triad of faith, hope, and love cannot be demonstrated in Plotinus' works.[43]

One who wants to assume a non-Christian, philosophical influence in the linking of the ascent to God with the necessity of faith, hope, and love in the *Soliloquia* will be more inclined to point to Porphyry's letter to Marcella.[44] In his discussion of prayer, Porphyry wants to have four principles observed in regard to God: faith, truth, love (*eros*), and hope. Reference to Porphyry is all the more justified because in the turn to God, in his view, *pistis* alone can attain *soteria*. Surprisingly similar is the statement in the *Soliloquia*: "fides qua credat ita se rem habere, ad quam convertendus aspectus est, ut visa faciat beatam."[45] Furthermore, the enumeration of faith, love, and hope is not limited to Porphyry's work. Similar formulas can also be found in Iamblichus and above all in Proclus.[46] But aside from the fact that Porphyry, as is well known, was acquainted with the New Testament scriptures and could have been inspired either indirectly or directly by Paul,[47] he speaks of *eros* rather than *agape*, puts hope in the last place, and inserts truth between faith and love.

If it can be maintained that Augustine draws on Plotinian concepts and images whenever he has occasion to give expression to his own religious experiences,[48] then this is naturally true above all in the case of the philosophical dialogues and especially of the *Soliloquia*. But already here one must not underestimate the Christian element. For the text under discussion here, this means that one may see a genuine, if still not very extensive, reception of Paul. Augustine has done more than just take over the Pauline triad of faith, hope, and love in a superficial way, even if he was stimulated to do so by Porphyry. Such a claim is entirely consistent with the reports in the *Confessiones* of how Augustine became acquainted with the apostle.[49] It is confirmed by an explicit reference to the reading of Paul in *Contra Academicos*, as well as by other allusions to Pauline texts in the early writings.[50] Finally, the climate of prayer that appears everywhere in the *Soliloquia* must also be taken into account. It attests in an impressive manner how much Augustine already at that time relied on the grace of God. Precisely the words with which he concludes his dialogue with himself bear eloquent testimony to this: "Ratio: Bono animo esto; Deus aderit, ut iam sentimus, quaerentibus nobis, qui beatissimum quiddam post hoc corpus, et veritatis plenissimum sine ullo mendacio pollicetur. Augustinus: Fiat ut speramus."[51] It must certainly be admitted that the reception of Paul in the writings from Cassiciacum remains remarkably hesitant. What is missing above all is the theme of the *spes resurrectionis*, which would later become fundamental. The *omne corpus fugiendum* of the Neoplatonic tradition still plays too powerful a role here, as Augustine himself would lament in the *Retractationes.*[52] But that will be treated in what follows.

The New Song of Faith, Hope, and Love (Psalm 91)

During the Lenten season of 412 Augustine expounded a whole series of Psalms to the congregation of Hippo.[53] To these *enarrationes in Psalmos* belongs the sermon on Psalm 91: *Bonum est confiteri Domino.*[54] The title in his Latin psalter, *Psalmus cantici in diem sabbati*, supplied Augustine with the main theme of his interpretation. For all the multiplicity of the *mysteria* of scripture that a preacher has to make known to his faithful, there is always, at root, only one thing at stake. In scripture, God sets before us nothing other than the *canticum* of faith, hope, and love. As long as we, in our faith, cannot see God, our faith should be firmly rooted in him. Thus, we shall someday be able to enjoy the full light of vision. Hope, for its part, must be as stable as the God in whom it is anchored, never wavering. It must never allow itself to be disquieted by any fears or trials but must endure patiently to the very end (Rom. 8:24f.). Finally, love stands above faith, which exists only as long as a person still cannot see (*videre*), as well as above hope, which will give up its place as soon as the person comes to possess (*tenere*) the reality itself. Love itself can only grow. Its longing can only increase. We are Christians, in fact, for the sake of the future (*christiani non sumus nisi propter futurum saeculum*), not for the sake of any present happiness (*felicitas mundi*). No Christian looks forward to merely present goods (*nemo praesentia bona speret*), even if one may make use of them so far as one can. Whether God in his benevolence consoles us with present goods or, in his just care for us, withholds them, we ought always to sing praises to the Lord (*confiteri*) and to extol the name of the Most High (*En. in Ps. 91* 1). Inner calm of conscience and joyful hope (Rom. 12:12) constitute the Sabbath, the *sabbatum cordis* (*Ipsum autem gaudium in tranquillitate spei nostrae, sabbatum nostrum est*; *En. in Ps. 91* 2). In this basic attitude, the Christian ascribes his good deeds to God but his sins to himself (*En. in Ps. 91* 3). He praises God's goodness when things go well with him and makes no complaint about God's righteousness when he has to suffer (*En. in Ps. 91* 4). With joy he always fulfills God's commandments (_En. in Ps. 91_ 5). But he knows that it is only as permeated by God's warmth and illuminated by God's light that he can take the path of the commandments for which he was created (_En. in Ps. 91_ 6). Not even the prosperity of sinners embitters him against God (_En. in Ps. 91_ 7). In view of the Lord's suffering he submits himself to the inscrutable purposes of God (_En. in Ps. 91_ 8). How quickly, then, the evil ones will perish (_En. in Ps. 91_ 9). God, in contrast, endures forever (Ps. 91:9). Even more, Christ, who speaks this Psalm in our name, has already united us with God's eternity (_En. in Ps. 91_ 10). "What, then, is your hope," Augustine asks the church, the body of Christ, "when Christ himself already sits at the right hand of the Father, but to endure until the final exaltation?" (_En. in Ps. 91_ 11). The one who is just has nothing to fear at the judgment (_En. in Ps. 91_ 12). He will flourish like the palm trees and the cedars of Lebanon (_En. in Ps. 91_ 13). Such an attitude, such a calmness (_tranquillitas_), constitutes the true Sabbath. This is the fruit of a pure conscience, of honest recognition of one's own weaknesses, and of confident hope in the divine promises (_En. in Ps. 91_ 14).

In these comments about the _canticum fidei, spei et caritatis_ made in connection with Psalm 91, it immediately strikes us that Augustine does not draw his inspiration simply from the love hymn of 1 Corinthians. Rather, in this sermon, which is tuned above all to the theme of hope, he cites, almost always explicitly, a whole series of other Pauline texts. First among these is the fundamental passage in Romans 8: "But hope that is seen is not hope, for why should one still hope for what he already sees? But if we hope for what we do not yet see, we wait patiently for it" (Rom. 8:24f.). Also noteworthy is the brief reference to the twelfth chapter of the same letter: "Rejoice in hope" (Rom. 12:12).[55] This increasing affinity for Paul no longer comes as a surprise. From 394 on, Augustine occupied himself much more intensively than he had before with the letters of the apostle. He certainly did not comment on the whole _corpus paulinum_, as he had perhaps intended. But he did take up just those letters in which Paul gave us his deepest thoughts about Christian hope, namely, Romans and Galatians.[56] Whereas at an earlier time he had been most interested in the Pauline contrast between spirit and flesh, the inner and the outer person, he now became convinced, in his more thorough studies, of the absolute preeminence of divine grace over human freedom.[57] Thus he influenced the development of the Paulinism that had just recently started to emerge in the West in a way that made a confrontation with Pelagius, who took a different course, almost inevitable. This conflict was the less avoidable because the ascetic monk from Britain, in his own expositions of Paul, had openly taken up a position against Augustine himself.[58] But of course our *enarratio* on Psalm 91 was delivered at a time when the Pelagian controversy was only just beginning.[59]

Another fact is even more noteworthy than Augustine's obviously more extensive knowledge of Paul. No longer does Augustine present his ideas concerning the Pauline triad within the circle of a few trusted confidants with whom he struggles after the philosophical deepening of his faith. Rather, he is preaching to his congregation, the simple faithful of Hippo who, together with him, want to strengthen their Christian outlook in the *schola Christi*.[60] These common people of the African port city experienced their faith, their hope, and their love in singing the Psalms. Thus when, in connection with Psalm 91 as read by the lector at the pre-Easter celebration of the liturgy, Augustine reminded his congregation of the only true *canticum*, he no longer did so in the spirit of the time when, before and after his baptism, he had prayed the Psalms with his friends.[61] Since that time he had come to know the Psalter, this "Song of Songs" of hope, much better. Since that time he had commented on a whole series of Psalms, either in dictated notes or in preaching.[62] Still more important, he had acquired, primarily with the aid of the Donatist Tyconius, a particular method of expounding the Psalms.[63] Specifically, for quite some time he had been accustomed to reflecting with his community on the complaints, petitions, and expressions of joy in the Psalms. The extent to which he had acquainted himself during his twenty years of ministry with one of the main themes of the Psalms, namely hope, is likewise quite evident in the exposition of Psalm 91. This song of praise does not speak explicitly of hope except perhaps in the words *tranquilli erunt* (v. 15).[64] And yet the whole Psalm is filled with confidence in the power of God. In his joy the psalmist gives himself over entirely to his God, even though he does not understand the depths of God's thoughts. Thus Augustine was simply adopting the tone of this joyful song when in his exposition he explicitly treated the hope that is linked with faith and love. The same can also be said of the other *enarrationes* that Augustine delivered to his faithful during Lent in 412. All of them deal with similar themes—with the questions of divine justice, human suffering, the prosperity of sinners, in short with questions that have to do with trust in God's goodness and power. And several of them do explicitly develop the theme of hope, which is common to them all.[65]

Augustine's progressively deepening grasp of this unshakable trust in the promises of the just and merciful God, which underlies the psalmist's complaints and cries for help, certainly did not come only or even primarily from his continuing study of the Psalter or his activity as a busy preacher. His experiences in pastoral ministry were much more important in this regard. The question of the origin and role of evil, which had always concerned him, took on harsher outlines in the wider controversy with the Manicheans,[66] became perhaps still more acute under the burden of daily routine in the community,[67] and was made especially urgent by the fall of the eternal city.[68] In this context Augustine learned that to become purified and freed from error by accepting the authority of Christ in faith mattered very little. It was rather necessary, on the example of God's humility, to overcome the sin of pride and, above all, patiently to endure on the path of Christ's cross in the face of all the dispensations of the just and wise God.[69] In a similar fashion, the question of the tension between the inner and the outer person, which had driven Augustine into his religious crisis,[70] broadened out, in the internal conflict with the Donatists and in the argument with pagan and Christian accusations against divine providence, into the question of a rift in the one church and of a fissure running through humanity as a whole. Convinced that the *catholica* could exist in this age only as a *corpus mixtum*,[71] Augustine had for years admonished his faithful to bear with sinners and to await the final judgment. Even though, in 412, he had not yet fully developed his conception of the history of the *duae civitates* or the *duo amores*, he had already much earlier, along this line, urged Christians to trust solely in God and his righteous judgment.[72] Finally, the question of the provisional character of the present life, which recurred again and again in his early writings, especially in reflections on the ascent of the soul to blessedness, had likewise received a new meaning. The issue was no longer simply one of escaping from the world of sense in order to see God in the purity of spirit. Instead it had become clear to Augustine, certainly not least under the influence of the annual Easter celebration, that the baptized Christian would attain full happiness at the resurrection of the body.[73] The *spes resurrectionis*, which presupposes belief in the already accomplished resurrection of Christ, had become a foundation stone of his preaching and his theological reflection.[74] At the same time, interestingly, he also came to include the *bona temporalia* within the range of Christian hope. Thus in his letter to Proba (411) he not only stresses the Pauline exhortation to leave everything behind and reach out only to that which lies ahead (Phil. 3:13), but he points out too that a Christian may also hope for worldly things if he does this *propter Deum*.[75]

In this framework, then, which on the one hand was given by the text of Psalm 91 and on the other was determined by his personal and pastoral experiences, Augustine had, of necessity, to broaden and deepen his reception of the Pauline triad and in particular of the Pauline theology of hope. In view of the total context of his exposition of Psalm 91, we better understand, in fact, why he throws the special character of faith and hope into such strong relief. He does not simply adopt the antithesis of *non-videre*–*non-tenere*, which in any case he does not rigorously maintain, since for him, as for Paul, faith and hope are often virtual synonyms.[76] He also speaks of the joy of the future vision and even more explicitly of the joy of hope, which disperses all clouds of sadness.[77] To that end, he links the *certitudo* of hope with the immutability of God, on which it rests.[78] But above all he develops, in relation to Romans, the theme of a hopeful patience that has to prove itself not in prosperity but in adversity.[79] In this regard, he calls to mind not merely the healing activity of the divine physician but also the pedagogical regimen (*disciplina*) of the encouraging and admonishing Father.[80]

In what follows it becomes clearer to us why Augustine now distinguishes love from faith and hope more strongly than he had previously done. By inserting the Pauline triad into the apocalyptic tension of the "already" and the "not yet," itself taken over from Paul, he makes it clear that faith and hope belong only to this aeon, whereas love alone continues in the other aeon. This does not simply mean that there "it will no longer be said, 'Believe what you do not see,' but 'rejoice because you do see,'" but also that "spes enim modo vocatur, tunc non spes, sed res erit" and above all that, *adveniente re*, hope will no longer exist, whereas *caritas* can only increase.[81] This apocalyptic tension is, of course, brought expressly to bear in other texts as well, especially in the *enarratio* on Psalm 60.[82]

Above all, we now have a better grasp of how much more, at this point, Augustine stands under the influence of the apostle's christocentrism.[83] The Christian, he explains in our *enarratio*, should cling to Christ. Then he can confidently endure the tribulations of this life with patience. For then he also knows that the reason Christ did not delay his resurrection to the end of time was so that we could hope for our resurrection without doubting.[84] This also gives a clear meaning to a philosophical-sounding passage in which Augustine calls attention to the fact that Christ has already, in our name, joined himself in union with the *aeternitas Dei*.[85] In other sermons delivered during the same period, to be sure, the *spes resurrectionis* found even clearer expression. Thus in the exposition of Psalm 60, precisely in view of the mystery of Easter, Augustine calls Christ "our hope": "Unde factus est spes nostra? Ecce sic quomodo audistis quia tentatus est, quia passus est, quia resurrexit, factus est spes nostra."[86] With that, he goes right back to the beginning. In his death, Christ shows us the life that we now have; in his resurrection he shows us the other, the life we hope for. In giving us the Holy Spirit (Rom. 5:3ff.), he made it possible for us to move toward hope. For we would not move, if we did not have hope.[87] In a word, in a context such as this, bearing the imprint of a reception of Paul that is by now highly developed, it comes as no surprise that Augustine sees in hope a basic feature of the Christian life. "Christiani non sumus, nisi propter futurum saeculum; nemo praesentia bona speret, nemo

sibi promittat felicitatem mundi, quia christianus est."[88] Since this
hope presupposes belief in Christ's resurrection and no longer
belief simply in God's authority made visible, it stands far beyond
that hope which coincides with the knowledge rooted in faith and
the longing for eternal life that follows from it. Now, to hope
means rather to be an Easter-person: to bring to fulfillment, in
patient and joyful hope, with the grace of the Holy Spirit, that
participation in the *transitus Christi* for which the ground was laid
through baptism.[89]

The Little Handbook on Faith, Hope, and Love

When Augustine referred to the Pauline triad of faith, hope,
and love in the *Soliloquia* in relation to the question of the ascent
to God, he certainly did not yet discern the significance this
scheme would have for him later on. In fact, he will not be at all
content to speak of the one song of faith, hope, and love given us
by God. On the contrary, he will return again and again to this
theme. In the *De doctrina christiana*, a work that is fundamental
to his theological thought, he clearly asserts that one might well
be a Christian without the Holy Scriptures, as in the desert, but
not without faith, hope, and love.[90] In more than a few other
texts, he extends this basic requirement of the Christian life to
the church as a whole. In his view faith, hope, and love constitute
the foundation of the church's unity.[91] Only through them does
the church hold fast in persecution. In particular, the church
must show itself to be a community of hope.[92] It is nothing other
than the *civitas gloriosissima*, which lives by faith and patiently
awaits its final fulfillment. For this reason too, Enoch, who was
the first to put his hope in the invocation of God's name, was the
prototype for this *civitas*, which takes its origin from belief in
Christ's resurrection and lives in hope so long as it is on pilgrimage on this earth.[93] The church lives out its faith, hope, and love
above all in worship, as at Christmas.[94] These virtues, however,
belong even more to Easter, the sacrament of that *transitus Christi*
that in baptism becomes a *transitus christianorum* maintained in
hope.[95] On Easter night, Christians watch and pray in devout
faith, in firm hope, and in fervent love, and think about their own
resurrection.[96] Thus they are, at root, nothing other than people

of Easter hope.[97] For the rest, it is not surprising that the crisis of 410 drove Augustine to cast this basic feature of Christian life in a still brighter light.[98]

In these allusions and more or less extended explanations, one must be struck by how frequently, most often in connection with Galatians 5:6 and James 2:19, Augustine sets the bare faith that can make even the demons tremble in contrast to full faith working in love.[99] He even devoted a special treatise to this thesis, the *De fide et operibus*.[100] No less noteworthy are those passages in which he linked true faith as tightly as possible not only with love but also with hope.[101] He does not even hesitate to stress hope alone. Thus he explains that three things are necessary to the Christian life: *abstinentia a malo et operatio boni et spes praemii aeterni*.[102] Finally, it is not to be overlooked how Augustine brings 1 Corinthians 13:13 into connection with 1 Timothy 1:5 and thus equates hope with *bona conscientia*. "Ipsa enim caritas bene operantis dat ei spem bonae conscientiae. Spem enim gerit bona conscientia; quomodo mala conscientia tota in desperatione est, sic bona conscientia tota in spe."[103] Thus hope appears as the very heart of the person's religious stance, as what *parrēsia* signifies for the apostle.[104]

In the light of this pronounced interest in the triad of the apostle and in particular in his theology of hope, it is not surprising that when, in 421 or perhaps 423, Laurentius, an educated layman, inquired about the essence of Christianity, Augustine took the opportunity to summarize Christian teaching under the leitmotiv of faith, hope, and love and thereby to give to hope a special place.[105] The fact that in this late work, for which he was able to draw on the fullness of his theological thought, Augustine also brought his reception of Paul to a certain conclusion already hints at the interest that just this handbook found in Protestant histories of dogma, which readily place Augustine between Paul and Luther.[106] This high point of Augustinian Paulinism did not, of course, consist in the use of Pauline texts to which he had previously given little or no consideration. It is rather the theological method used in the *Enchiridion* and the antipelagian background that comes into play which inform us of the stage at which the assimilation of the triad of faith, hope, and love, and of the Pauline theology of hope connected with it, had arrived.

It is by no means uninteresting to begin the investigation of the *Enchiridion* with a glance at its *genus litterarium*. Laurentius had requested a summary of the Christian faith and, in doing so, had obviously insisted on a certain brevity. Augustine agreed to his request.[107] But the difficulty of composing such a sketch of Christian teaching was clear to him from the start.[108] Thus even at the close of his treatise he questions whether he has succeeded in writing a "handy little book" or has only produced another "voluminous thing" (*volumen*).[109] The literary distinctiveness of the *Enchiridion* does not, however, consist primarily in its intended, if perhaps not quite realized, handiness. It lies instead in the manner in which Augustine, even in his old age, acts the schoolmaster. Long since, to be sure, learning gained from experience had become more important to him than school knowledge.[110] But is it surprising that he "teaches" in this manual when he cannot even keep from teaching in his sermons before the ordinary faithful?[111] In any case, certain scholastic remarks are indicative.[112] The numerous quotations from Vergil are also worth noticing.[113] Above all, in his *sermo*, as he calls his presentation, Augustine sticks quite closely to the structure that was common for such "speeches."[114] He prefaces the *corpus* with a prologue and concludes the whole with a short, summarizing epilogue.[115] In the prologue he begins with a *captatio benevolentiae*. Here he praises the learning (*eruditio*) of his reader but at the same time expresses the wish that he may gain that true wisdom that can come only from God.[116] This wish leads to the first announcement of the theme. Since there can be no true wisdom without piety (*pietas*), the question arises of how God should be worshipped.[117] A first and immediate answer is that this can happen only in faith, in hope, and in love.[118] In a second start, which arises out of Laurentius' particular questions, Augustine first of all inserts a remark about his method, according to which he intends to rely on *ratio* as well as on *fides* grounded in the witness of Holy Scripture.[119] Then he summarizes once more the topic under discussion. The

question to be answered is how the soul (*mens*), with a faith realized in love, can attain the blissful vision of inexpressible beauty by
an upright life. "Inchoari fide, perfici specie" (see 1 Cor. 13:12).
"Haec etiam totius definitionis summa est."[120] Since, however,
Laurentius did not request a demarcation of the Christian religion
simply over against paganism but also over against heresies, Augustine immediately fills out his main theme with the assertion
that Christ alone is *certum propriumque fidei catholicae fundamen-
tum.*[121] In this whole formulation of the question, finally, the concept of *summa* should be noted. Certainly in the first instance
Augustine has in mind the summary that Laurentius had requested.[122] But if one also keeps in view the technical meaning of
this *locus communis* in a prologue, it is not at all unreasonable to
see in the *summa* the leitmotiv of the whole work—all the more
since Augustine undertook to carry out his presentation in a sort
of commentary on the baptismal symbol and the Lord's prayer.[123]

From these more literary observations it clearly follows that
Augustine wished to do nothing else in his *Enchiridion* than to
present the Christian philosophy as he had understood it since
Cassiciacum. The true wisdom that he wished for Laurentius at the
outset consists of not only the correct *cognitio Dei et hominis* but
also the genuine worship of God.[124] For just this reason it must be
grounded in faith, hope, and love. What is new, in relation to what
went before, is only the fact that now, with regard to the request
of his reader, Augustine defines the generic idea of true religion
more closely with the specific idea of the *fides catholicae* grounded
in Christ and, in that very process, allows Paul to be heard more
than before.[125]

The last part of the prologue still remains to be discussed.
There, as was also customary, Augustine announces the arrangement of his work. He intends to follow the creed and the *Pater
noster*. This methodological observation gives him the opportunity
to come back to the Pauline triad. For faith, hope, and love are
connected in the closest way to prayer, the invocation of the
Lord's name (Jl. 2:32; Rom. 10:14), as also to its basis as summed up
in the baptismal confession.[126] In this connection, interestingly,
Augustine gives special consideration to hope. First of all, with a
reference to Lucan and Vergil, he excludes the inaccurate notion

according to which *spes* has more the sense of fear.[127] Then, he distinguishes hope from faith in three respects.[128] Whereas hope refers solely to the future, faith embraces also the present and the past. Whereas hope is directed only toward the good, one can believe in both good and evil. Whereas faith can have other things and other persons as its object, hope pertains only to the one who hopes. It is not difficult to recognize behind the first two distinguishing characteristics, the *futura* and the *bona*, the classical distinction of the *exspectatio bonorum futurorum* to which Augustine frequently recurs.[129] Whether the entirely personal character of hope also appears prior to Augustine, I leave open. In any case, Augustine does not find the distinction between faith and hope here in the invisibility of their object. In that respect, they are instead in agreement, as Augustine must stipulate in connection with Hebrews 11:1 and Romans 8:24f. In concluding, he points out that there can be no faith either without love or without hope.[130]

The inclination to distinguish and define, which characterizes the prologue,[131] surfaces again in the section devoted particularly to hope.[132] There, after Augustine has briefly pointed out that a person, especially in prayer, may direct his hope to God alone,[133] he takes up the Lord's Prayer as it is transmitted by Matthew and Luke.[134] In the first version he distinguishes three petitions for eternal things and four petitions for temporal things. In Luke, on the other hand, the seven petitions of Matthew have been reduced to five, two for eternal and three for temporal things.[135] Meanwhile, in the distinction between the *aeterna* and the *temporalia*, two points are noteworthy. On the one hand, the *temporalia* are requested for the sake of the *aeterna*. And on the other hand, the Christian can already begin to possess the *aeterna* in this life and can possess them more and more, even if still not fully.[136] Augustine now applies this distinction between *aeterna* and *temporalia* to hope. Accordingly, the believing Christian hopes for the ever greater hallowing of God's name, for the ever more powerful coming of the kingdom of God, and for the ever more extensive fulfillment of the divine will. Similarly, but for the sake of eternal things, he hopes for daily bread, for the forgiveness of sins, for preservation from temptation, and for deliverance from evil.

The actual unfolding of the reception of Paul in the *Enchiridion*, meanwhile, has no relation to the scholastic mode of distinguishing and defining employed in it. Rather, it is occasioned by the theological background around 420. That is evident in a rather undramatic passage in which Augustine compares the four stages of the spiritual life with the four ages of humanity.[137] He had already given considerable attention to this theme earlier when, partly in opposition to the Manicheans, he had occupied himself with Romans.[138] Here he takes up this religious theme, developed from Paul, and gives it an anti-Pelagian thrust.[139] In fact, one can hear in this dense text the main themes of the polemic against Pelagius and Caelestius (brought to its dogmatic conclusion in 418), as well as the broader, still continuing, debates against Julian and others: infant baptism and universal human sinfulness, nature and grace, freedom and predestination.[140] These are the themes, moreover, in the treatment of which Augustine further developed his theology of hope. For in opposition to Pelagius and his followers, Augustine had again and again to make the point that righteousness has no more than its beginning in baptism and thus can achieve its perfection only in a life of faithful and patient hope.[141] In particular, these disputes led him to emphasize, even more than before, hope for the resurrection, the indispensable presupposition of the eternal vision of God.[142] Above all, he became concerned to make it clear that the ultimate and most fundamental thing that God expects from us—love of his righteousness, unbounded acceptance of his will—can be achieved here on earth only in hope.[143] In the doctrine of grace presupposed in the text in question, the only theme missing is that of the incarnation of Christ as the archetype of totally unmerited grace. In this theme of his later theology of grace—first fully developed in the *Enchiridion*, although in another passage—Augustine brings his Paulinism to its most radical expression.[144] The extent to which the other themes mentioned are to be taken into account for a full understanding of our text can already be estimated, however, from the bare fact that Augustine gave them so much space in the preceding sections.[145]

Our text is immediately preceded by a consideration of the preeminence of love over faith and hope.[146] Here, in an initial survey, Augustine distinguishes four stages: the stage of ignorance, in which a person simply gives way to his impulses,[147] the stage of law, which leads a person to knowledge of his sin,[148] the stage of struggle against the flesh, fought out in the power of love,[149] and finally the stage of peace, first in death and then finally in the resurrection.[150] These four stages of the religious life correspond, in turn, to the fourfold division—inspired by Paul—of the history of God's people: *ante legem, sub lege, sub gratia, in pace,* four distinct periods in all of which, however, the forgiveness of sins was and is possible.[151]

What interests us here is the third stage of the religious life, which Augustine defines as *tertia bonae spei hominis* and to which he gives the most attention here as elsewhere.[152] On closer scrutiny, this stage itself can likewise be divided into four steps: (1) belief in the necessity of the help of God's grace in fulfilling God's commandments, or the beginning of the work of the Holy Spirit in the soul; (2) life in faith, with its resistance to evil concupiscence, achieved through the power of love, and with the victory of delight in righteousness; (3) progress in devout perseverance; and (4) perfection in peace after death and finally in the resurrection of the flesh.[153] Is it so far off the track to recall in connection with these four stages the four in the *Soliloquia*? In any case, the first stage mentioned there, trust in the possibility of the soul's healing, recurs in our passage. Similarly, the *praecepta* are discussed again. Here, to be sure, Augustine no longer speaks only of healing the eyes of the soul but also of the work of the Holy Spirit.[154] Most important, he now makes it clear that the fulfilling of God's command is possible only through God's grace.[155] The longing that, in the power of love, opposes the flesh, recalls, for its part, the turn to the divine light. It is not a question of the former *aspectus*, however, but rather of the struggle against evil concupiscence, to which the believing Christian does not yield because delight in righteousness increasingly gains the upper hand.[156] The anticipatory *visio* on earth coincides with progress in devout perseverance.[157] The ultimate *visio*, finally, is not simply equated with *pax*. Rather, its full realization is made dependent on the resurrection.[158] Above all, Augustine no longer alludes to the role that faith, hope, and love have to play at the individual stages. Instead, he conceives the whole ascent as the one *bona spes*. From the more intellectual ascent to the vision of God, in which even the *disciplinae* had their place, there has emerged belief in grace, being grasped by the Holy Spirit, struggle against evil concupiscence, life in faith, delight in righteousness, and steadfastness in persever-ance. Even though the Pauline triad hardly appears in this text, Augustine's main concern is fully conveyed by the most important themes of the Pauline theology of hope. Furthermore, it is signifi-cant that in the preceding section on the preeminence of love, Augustine has already pointed out that one can long for eternal life, even if one perhaps does not yet love the righteousness neces-sary to it. Such a person can at least believe that he can obtain by prayer what he does not yet possess in love.[159] This is only a begin-ning of hope. But when this initial hope progresses to *bona spes*, to *bona conscientia*,[160] it becomes trusting and patient anticipation as the apostle understood it.

Concluding Reflections

It has not been possible within the scope of this study to represent even approximately the tremendously complex problem-atic of Augustine's reception of Paul. Nevertheless, the investiga-tion of three texts, perhaps somewhat arbitrarily chosen but at least differentiated by date and literary type, has allowed us, with respect to their single common theme of faith, hope, and love, to gain an insight into important aspects of Augustinian Paulinism. In the process, it has become apparent that Augustine was quite probably stimulated by Porphyry to reach back to the Pauline triad in 1 Corinthians 13:13. In any event, it is obvious that he speaks of faith, hope, and love in a Neoplatonic perspective, in relation, that is, to prayer and the ascent by stages to God. At the same time there is no doubt that from the beginning and increasingly thereafter he understood the three virtues in the same way as did Paul himself.

If I have given a greater place to hope in my discussion, that was not by accident. For it seems to me that it is precisely by means of the Augustinian theology of hope that one can best measure the extent to which Augustine followed the apostle. Insofar as *fides* is not understood as *assensio mentis*, as *cogitatio cum assensione*, it is actually broadly coincident with hope. On the other side, *cari-tas*, to the extent that it is practiced on earth, is tightly linked with hope. In any case, in the theology of hope as Augustine developed it in connection with his doctrine of grace, the fundamental Pauline postulate of the "already–not yet" clearly comes to bear.

Here also the antitheses that Paul draws in his major letters—law and gospel, the resurrection of Christ and the resurrection of the dead, justification in baptism and endurance in patience, faith and sight—become important. In particular, the core of the apocalyptic tension that governs the entire theology of the apostle is found again in Augustine.

In the line of Paul's letters, especially the letter to the Romans, Augustine sees in Christian hope a wholly personal assurance of salvation. Hope, for him, is no longer the classical expectation of the future, which suffers from an irrational uncertainty and, for that reason, signifies more fear than hope.[161] It is rather a trust—never without peril, but rooted in the work of the Holy Spirit—in the promises of the merciful and faithful God, the promises already fulfilled in Jesus Christ and in him still to be fulfilled. It is the confidence of salvation to which Paul testifies, for himself, in a text that Augustine repeatedly makes his own: "Brothers, I do not consider that I have attained it; but one thing I do, I forget what lies behind me, I stretch forward to what lies ahead, and I pursue, with the goal before my eyes, the prize of the upward call of God in Christ Jesus" (Phil. 3:13–14).[162]

Comment:
Augustine's Pauline Legacies
R. A. MARKUS

D om Studer's lucid and penetrating study combines two themes: Augustine's "Pauline legacy" and his thinking about hope. Studer's meticulous and perceptive commentary on three well-chosen texts, spread over Augustine's career as a thinker, serves to bring out both the significant development and the profound continuity crystallized around a Pauline core and arrayed within the conceptual framework of the Pauline triad. His work has set a task that is either very hard or very easy: very hard in the sense that it seems scarcely possible to find any point at which his carefully differentiated account of Augustine could be revised without destroying its delicate balance; too easy in that it offers a gold mine of points at which one might register assent and perhaps yield to the temptation, at the same time, of shifting the emphasis in one direction or another. I shall try to pick a path between the too easy and the too difficult.

To begin, perhaps I may underscore two of Studer's points: first, his insistence on the ecclesiological dimension of Augustine's understanding of hope. By 412, the date of the sermons on the Psalms that Studer discusses, Augustine had behind him some twenty years of sustained debate with the Donatists. The first news of Pelagius' teachings reached him at just about this time; and Augustine seized on the affinity he detected between them and Donatism: both, he thought, anachronistically demanded a pure church, without spot or wrinkle. With such a demand Augustine had long ago learnt how to deal, and Pelagius' perfectionism triggered a long-meditated response. It was formulated in terms well settled in his mind: what Pelagius failed to allow for, so Augustine wrote, was "the interim, the interval between the remission of sins which takes place in baptism and the permanently established sinless state in that kingdom which is to come . . . this middle time (*medium hoc tempus*) of prayer," and of hope.[1] Hope is simultaneously the sign of the gulf that divides the imperfect from the perfect, *via* from *patria*, the now from the then, and the link that unites them; and it is as fundamental to Augustine's conception of the Christian community as to his view of the Christian individual.

The second point I should like to underline is Studer's stress on the resurrection of the body as encompassed by hope, as Augustine conceived it, and on the way in which this allowed Augustine to "include the *bona temporalia* within the range of Christian hope." Indeed. I shall return in a moment to Henri Marrou's Augustine Lecture of 1964,[2] in which he undertook to set the score straight and to correct with light but magisterial sureness of touch the stereotype that fails to take seriously the lyrical praise that Augustine lavishes on corporeal beauty in the writings and the popular preaching of his old age. Here, however, I should like to set this reminder against the more somber backdrop of Augustine's views on *concupiscentia carnis*—another, and by no means negligible, part of his Pauline inheritance.

There can surely be no doubt about the Pauline roots of hope that Studer has unearthed in the rich soil of Augustine's thought. From the start, as he makes clear, the text of 1 Corinthians set the direction. At the same time Augustine saw Paul in the perspective of the "Platonists," whose acquaintance he had so recently made, and there were distinctively Plotinian overtones—to which Studer has pointed—audible in some of Augustine's expressions: notably his image of the soul's ascent through healing to *visio*, and its liberation from the "nuisance of the body." And again with Studer, we should note at least in passing the inner connection (although not directly Plotinian) between *elpis* and *eros*: that ardent longing for beauty which is intensified by the hope of its attainability.

And yet, we must give much weight to Studer's emphasis on the superficiality of Augustine's penetration into his Pauline legacy at this stage in his career. After those idyllic days in Cassiciacum, the problem Augustine was wrestling with was that of reclaiming Paul from his Manichean opponents. Their favorite proof text, 1 Corinthians 15:50 ("neither flesh nor blood . . ."), figured very largely in his attention at this time and continued to play an important part in the development of his thought. We shall not be able to come to grips with that development, however, without appreciating the tensions within it, which, in the mid-390s, produced that landslide in Augustine's understanding of Paul that no one has elucidated more powerfully than Paula Fredriksen, both in her translation of Augustine's attempts at commenting on Romans and in her subsequent study of the scriptural accounts of Paul's conversion and their subtle interplay in Augustine's rendering of his own conversion.[3] I wonder whether we ought not to distinguish the several Pauls whom Augustine encountered on the spiritual journey Fredriksen has traced; but for our present purpose, we must certainly distinguish sharply between the Paul he had met before 395, the Paul who had made it possible for him to deal with moral evil and had furnished him with concepts that could be wrested from the Manichees without bringing about a collapse of his Neoplatonic sense of a moral and rational cosmic order, and the Paul whom he met in his rereading of the Pauline letters, and now especially of Romans[4] and Galatians rather than the 1 Corinthians that had done so much to shape the context of his views on hope. This is the rediscovery that Augustine himself singled out as a literally catastrophic turning point in his Christian career. Fredriksen has described the Paul Augustine now encountered as "the sinner inexplicably redeemed from his former life by the unmerited gift of God's grace."[5] I should like to add all the emphasis I can to the word *inexplicably*.

Nothing would be more revealing for an understanding of Augustine's theology than a full study of what Paul meant for him. Fredriksen has made a valiant start, especially by drawing attention to Augustine's autobiographical exegesis of Paul and to the consequently changing role Paul plays in his thought. We need to come to grips with the Paul who brings about the intellectual earthquake that shook Augustine's mind out of the mold into which it had begun to settle before the mid-390s, as well as the Paul who somehow, miraculously, was the unbroken thread that endured through it. This brings me, finally, to the resurrection and to Augustine's praise of carnal beauty.

Perhaps here we can catch the shift. Studer has reminded us that for Augustine, nothing short of the risen body could count as a fulfillment of Christian hope, and he has drawn our attention to the growing importance given to the resurrection by Augustine in his preaching, to the extent even of making it a condition of the full attainment of *visio* in the *Enchiridion*. I should like to orchestrate these points by dwelling, for a moment, on that hymn of praise for carnal beauty into which Marrou saw Augustine pouring his finest artistry in Sermon 243: "If even in this infirmity of the flesh and even in the frailness of our members such a loveliness of the human body is apparent, a loveliness which entices the voluptuous and excites them to seek it . . . How much more [beauty will appear] there, where there will be no voluptuousness, no deformity, no depravity, no dire necessity . . . ?" (*Serm.* 243.8).[6] This could not have been written, any more than the thirteenth and fourteenth books of the *City of God* could have been, by an Augustine unshaken by the Paul he met in 394–95.

Such language reveals a theological density scarcely disguised by the simplicity of utterance; and it owes its density to several layers of Pauline legacies in Augustine's mind: the Paul whom he had had to retrieve from the Manichees and to repossess in order to vindicate the flesh and corporeal beauty; the Paul who had taught him to despair of the possibility of attaining the order and the beauty inscribed in the cosmos by its creator through his creatures' moral and rational resources; and the Paul who convinced him of man's need to depend on God's inscrutable ways for his salvation. If we are to attain a better mapping of Augustine's thought, perhaps we ought to attend to the discontinuities between these Pauline legacies, and especially to the discontinuity that Augustine himself saw as a watershed, his rereading of the Pauline corpus in the mid-390s. Those years between 395 and 400, which Fredriksen has shown to be as critical for Augustine's understanding of himself as for his understanding of Paul, are as obscure as they are crucial. It is here, in this brief spell, that we need to look for a Paul who engendered a despair in Augustine's mind on the other side of which Augustine would find another Paul, a new Paul who could give him a new hope.

For that investigation, Studer has given us a fine framework within which the question can, and indeed must, be pursued. Without raising the question itself, he has set the conditions for its further exploration.

Beyond the Body/Soul Dichotomy: Augustine's Answer to Mani, Plotinus, and Julian

PAULA FREDRIKSEN

A ugustine, said Julian, was still a Manichee. His views on sexuality and on the incarnation condemned him.

The unwary might think that simple ignorance of medical science had led Augustine to see human coitus as the means by which original sin was transmitted across generations. Augustine did not understand that his *concupiscentia carnalis* represented an unnecessary theologizing of the physiological sine qua non of conception, that heating through *voluptas* required for human procreation. Without this warming of human seed (both male and female), no conception could occur. And if the *calor genitalis* was required by Nature, it could not in and of itself be evil.[1]

Augustine could not think that the Creator had made human sexuality inherently sinful—that would be blatantly Manichean. Had it only *become* sinful as a result of Adam's fall? Then whenever married couples sought to fulfill God's command ("Be fruitful and multiply"), they would actually sin of necessity. But man can sin only if he has the option not to, or else God would not be just in condemning sinners. Augustine himself, defending Paul and free will, had long ago argued exactly this case against the Manichees.[2] Perhaps the root of his confused views on sexuality, then, really was ignorance, not heresy.

But Augustine's concept of sexually transmitted original sin was revealed for what it really was when he attempted to discuss the person of Christ. Augustine maintained that Jesus was sinless because, conceived of a virgin without concupiscence, he had avoided inheriting Adam's sin.[3] Is sin then, asked Julian, transmitted

227

through the flesh? If so, and if Jesus really did take on flesh through Mary, he would have contracted the sinfulness inhering there through the carnal concupiscence of her parents.[4] Does the soul transmit sin—is it somehow inherited? Then parents regenerated through baptism should give birth to already regenerate infants.[5] This could work neither way. If, for Augustine, either the human body or the human soul was inherently sinful, then his Christ, since sinless, could not have been truly human. Thus even if Augustine did not begin with Manicheism, he ended there, said Julian. Such a Christology is Docetic, and Docetism is Manicheism.[6]

We see in Julian's polemic a configuration of issues that had confronted Augustine at earlier, and equally crucial, points in his life: the problem of evil and the seductive resolution offered by dualism; Paul's letters and the questions they posed on free will and predestination, divine foreknowledge, grace, and faith; the construction of God, man, and the universe presupposed by classical culture and late Platonism. At Cassiciacum in the 380s and again, after many changes, reviewing his earlier life and especially his conversion once back in Africa, Augustine had wrestled with these issues. When Julian challenged him, he responded by pointing to the works that he had produced in those years, especially those that turned on questions arising from Paul.[7]

In part, Julian's polemic forced this retrospection. Julian claimed, justly, to be using against the old bishop his own earlier arguments against the Manichees; Augustine had to make the counterargument.[8] But once allowances are made for his rhetorical excesses, Augustine's claim to have settled long ago the questions Julian now raised, especially concerning his exegesis of Paul, is substantially legitimate—providing we go back only as far as 396. His stance against "Pelagianism" was indeed a coherent development from positions he had taken earlier, but not until he had written the *Ad Simplicianum* and the *Confessions*.

Augustine's views change more drastically between 394 and 396–98 than between 398 and 430. I will review his works on Paul in this earlier period in order, first, to see not only *how* Augustine came to understand especially Romans 7 and 9 in the ways he did but also *why*; and, second, to trace out the continuities between his position against the Manichees and, later, against the Pelagians, especially as these touch on concepts of person—body/soul, free will, sexuality, and so on. As Augustine moved beyond the various dualisms of his opponents and his sources—Fortunatus and Faustus, Pelagius and Julian, Plotinus and Porphyry, and even Paul himself—he left behind the views of man and the cosmos that late hellenism had bequeathed, variously, to them all.

Grace, Faith, and Will: The Early Works on Paul

Whatever his early familiarity with the Pauline epistles during his years as a Manichean "hearer" (373–85?) and whatever part these may have played in his conversion experience in Milan (386), Augustine concentrated his attention on the Pauline corpus only several years after his arrival back in Africa and his induction into the clergy. His earlier attacks against the Manichees had focused on their moral determinism: he had framed his answer to their position on the problem of evil in terms of the freedom of the will, the philosopher's defense of individual virtue.[9] But in 392 Fortunatus, before a watching crowd of both Catholics and Donatists, confronted Augustine publicly with the Manichean interpretation of scripture and, especially, of Paul.[10] Fortunatus lost the debate but apparently touched a nerve: from this point onward, Augustine proceeded against the Manichees by arguing exegetically.[11] In 394, then, after an interrupted attempt to interpret Genesis literally and a study of the Sermon on the Mount, Augustine turned directly to the Pauline epistles in order to show that the apostle "neither condemns the Law nor takes away man's free will."[12]

To this end—explicitly in his commentary, implicitly in the writings that follow—Augustine interpreted Romans through the rubric of four stages of salvation history: *ante legem, sub lege, sub gratia,* and *in pace.*[13] These four historical stages, which stretch from humanity before Israel to the second coming of Christ, are recapitulated in the spiritual development of the individual believer.

> Prior to the law, we pursue fleshly concupiscence; under the law, we are pulled by it; under grace, we neither pursue nor are pulled by it; in peace, there is no concupiscence of the flesh.

. . . Thus [under grace] we still have desires but, by not obey-
ing them, we do not allow sin to reign in us (Rom. 6:12). These
desires arise from the mortality of the flesh, which we bear
from the first sin of the first man, whence we are born fleshly
(*carnaliter*). Thus they will not cease save at the resurrection
of the body, when we will have merited that transformation
promised to us. Then there will be perfect peace, when we are
established in the fourth stage (*Prop. ad Rom.* 13–18).

Scriptural history and the individual's experience thus coin-
cide at their shared extremes: birth in Adam, eschatological resurrection in Christ. Augustine here expands on the one biblical
theme that he had sounded during his debate with Fortunatus,
the consequence of Adam's sin for all humanity (C. *Fort.* 22). As
punishment for the first sin of the primal parent, man's *body* is
mortal, which involves man in change and weakness, and man's
nature is *carnal*, because Adam's sin was a sin of humanity's
nature: *natura nostra peccavit.*[14] The body itself remains a good
created by God, but the Fall has affected the individual in such a
way that the soul is now susceptible to the concupiscences of the
flesh. Indeed, before the law intervenes, the soul gives way without any hesitation.[15] But, consistent with his earlier position that
sin is an active moral failing of the mind, Augustine carefully
distinguishes between *caro* and *qualitas carnalis*. The flesh is a
neutral material substratum. It is the *qualitas carnalis*, the result
of the first sin, that is a negative value, and descriptive primarily of
the soul.[16] Man thus inherits from Adam not only mortal flesh
but also his soul's carnal quality whence he, by indulging it, lapses
into sin. The agent in sinning is the soul.

Law at this point is introduced salubriously, so that the sinner might know how low he lies.[17] He can neither fulfill the law
nor cease sinning: the best he can do is struggle and fail. This
means, in fine, that man's will after Adam is not as free as Adam's
once had been. All man can do now is "groan" (Rom. 8:22) while
he awaits redemption.[18]

How then can he move from stage two to stage three, from
"under the law" to "under grace"? "One must take care," cautions
Augustine, "lest he think that by these words our free will is

taken away, for this is not so" (*Prop. ad Rom.* 44). On the contrary, free will is the key to this transition. The sinner, realizing the depths of his sin and helplessness, can turn in faith to Christ and beg divine assistance.[19] "Man by free will can believe in the liberator and receive grace so that, with Christ freeing and giving aid, he does not sin" (*Prop. ad Rom.* 44).[20] Christ's grace gives man the strength to resist the body's troubling appetites so that he can serve God *mente*—inwardly, with his mind. The soul, therefore, while still in this life, can die to sin, on the analogy of the widow whose husband's death frees her from his "law" (Rom. 7:1ff.).[21]

But the Epistle to the Romans relates two Old Testament episodes notoriously difficult to reconcile with a strong view of man's free will: 9:11–13, on Jacob and Esau,[22] and 9:17, on the hardening of Pharaoh's heart. The relatively simple picture that Augustine has sketched so far must accordingly grow more complicated in order to accommodate Paul's discussion of God's call, election, and predestination.

"Those whom he called, these also he justified" (Rom. 8:30). But clearly, says Augustine, not everyone is elected, called to justification. But God makes no preselection. Grace is offered freely to all: "Many are called" (Mt. 22:14; *Prop. ad Rom.* 55). But it is equally clear that "few are chosen." How are these relatively few chosen? By God's predestination and foreknowledge. God predestines individuals on the basis of his foreknowledge of their response to his *vocatio*. God's call is gracious: it goes out to sinners.[23] Man's belief depends on God's prior call, but once called, man can choose freely whether to respond with *bona voluntas*. If he does respond with good will, his faith will lead him to turn to Christ. This faith, in brief, is the free gift of God because it is necessarily preceded by his call; but the source of the receptive "good will," foreknown to God, is man himself.

Thus God foreknew that Jacob would respond in faith to his call and that Esau would spurn it. So also with Pharaoh: his heart was indeed hardened, but as the justly merited punishment for his infidelity, which God had foreknown. All three were called *secundum propositionem Dei* (*Prop. ad Rom.* 55), as determined by God's foreknowledge of their free response. Augustine goes on to say what his argument in any case implied: election is based on merit, the merit of faith. *Non opera sed fides inchoat meritum.* Through the merit of freely willed faith, man moves from *sub lege* to *sub gratia.*[24]

Memory, Love, and Will: The Works on Conversion

Augustine continued this discussion of sin, grace, and free will, begun in the Pauline commentaries and questions 66–68 of the *De diversis quaestionibus 83*, in Book III of *De libero arbitrio.* Perhaps his decision to resume work on this essay—begun in 388, in much different circumstances, when he was still in Rome[25]— was prompted specifically by these preceding writings: in the course of his exegesis of Romans, he had had to insist repeatedly that neither he nor Paul was denying the freedom of the will.[26] Having defended free choice in his commentaries only obliquely, Augustine could now apply himself directly to the task by returning to this unfinished work.[27]

Book I, a synopsis of views Augustine had held at Cassiciacum, had been unblushingly optimistic about the effectiveness of man's will. Man sins because he chooses to, otherwise God would not be just in punishing sinners; and man makes this bad choice because he turns from learning (*disciplina*). "Hence evil is nothing but to stray from education" (*De lib. arb.* 1.1.2). But when man wills rightly, in accordance with divine law, he accrues merit (*ut in voluntate meritum sit,* 1.14.30) and ultimately attains the happy life. "For whoever wishes to live rightly and honorably," says Augustine, "and prefers that to all transient goods, attains his object with perfect ease. To reach it, he has only to will it" (1.13.29, trans. Burleigh).

Books II and III were written much later, perhaps as late as 396.[28] There, toward the end of Book II, when Augustine attempts to consider the root cause of the will's uncoerced defection from the good, the tone of his discussion cools considerably. He draws a picture of man "on the road," *in via,* in this life, running the risk of wandering off the path, of becoming shrouded in darkness, because of his weakness.[29] This gloomy tone continues into Book III. Man sins because his loves are misordered; his desires and affections elude his conscious control because they are directed by carnal custom, *consuetudo.* The penal condition of ignorance and difficulty, merited by the sin of the primal parent, retards man's progress.[30] These punishments are "infections" from the flesh, not natural to the soul, and are not reckoned to the soul as guilt (*reatus*).[31] Guilt arises, rather, because the soul need not remain in this state, but *chooses* to. Man's pride prevents his supplicating Christ.[32]

Augustine had sounded these themes in his earlier Pauline commentaries, but there they had been woven into the essentially optimistic pattern of salvation history. Here, though Augustine again asserts that free will holds the key to man's redemption, he emphasizes the extremity of man's situation. Mortality and habit weigh man down; his own sins compound his ignorance and difficulty. He moves in a situation of acute danger, through an intense darkness, trying to keep his gaze riveted on the bright, distant light of Christ while the night presses in on all sides, and the devil hovers near to hand. And if love of light does not hold him to the path, says Augustine, then let man be held by fear. "And if any suggestion springing from a desire for the inferior should deflect our purpose, the eternal damnation and torments of the devil will recall us to the true path" (3.25.76, trans. Burleigh).

At some point shortly thereafter, in 396, Augustine received a request from Simplicianus, his old spiritual mentor in Milan. Simplicianus asked for a clarification of several scriptural passages, among them Romans 7:7-25 and 9:10-29. Though Augustine by this time had written on these passages several times, he admits that he still does not understand them.[33] Shortly thereafter the first book of Augustine's episcopacy appeared, his answer to Simplicianus' questions.

The basic argument of this work—namely, that election is entirely unmerited—and its importance in the Augustinian canon are well known. I want to review some of its particular details, however, in order to establish my explanation for its surprising and novel answers to the familiar Pauline questions. For in *Ad Simplicianum* 1.2, considering once again the problem of Jacob's election and Esau's rejection while both were still in the womb, Augustine repudiates the exegesis of Romans 9 that he had so painstakingly worked out such a short time earlier. Jacob cannot have received election because God foresaw his faith, Augustine now argues.

Paul had stressed that both Jacob and Esau were still in the womb precisely to avoid giving the impression that election was on the basis of foreknowledge of any sort.[34]

God showed mercy in Jacob's case by calling him, so that he believed. "But then the chief difficulty remains: why did God's mercy fail in Esau's case?" (_Ad Simpl._ 1.2.9). Departing from his earlier position, Augustine now says that Esau's rejection could not have been because he was (or was to be) unwilling to respond to God's call in faith.[35] If this had been so, Jacob would have had faith because he had willed it. But "then God did not give him faith as a free gift [cf. 1 Cor. 4:7], but Jacob gave it to himself" (_Ad Simpl._ 1.2.10, trans. Burleigh; cf. _Exp. ep. ad Rom. inch._ 9).

Paul points to the answer in Philippians, Augustine says. "God works in you both to will and to do of his good pleasure" (Phil. 2:13; _Ad Simpl._ 1.2.12). Paul thus clearly shows that the _bona voluntas_ itself is the work of God in man. Previously, Augustine had expressed a very similar idea, also with reference to Romans 9. "It depends not on man's willing or running, but on God who has mercy" (Rom. 9:15; _Prop. ad Rom._ 62). In the _Propositions from the Epistle to the Romans_, he had argued that man is unable to will unless called; and when after the call he has willed, this will is insufficient unless "God gives strength to our running and leads where he calls." But the "will" that Augustine intended in the _Propositions_ was man's ability to will to fulfill the law: _sub lege_, man could only long to fulfill the law; until his will was strengthened _sub gratia_, he could not. Man's _bona voluntas_, however, had preceded God's call. Good will was man's, by means of which he initiated the merit of faith. So too _De diversis quaestionibus 83_ 68.5: "parum est enim velle, nisi Deus miseretur; sed Deus non miseretur qui ad pacem vocat, nisi [bona] voluntas praecesserit. . . . "

But in the _Ad Simplicianum_, Augustine deliberately conflates the two wills: the will God aids is the good will itself. "But because the good will does not precede calling, but calling precedes the good will, the fact that we have a good will is rightly attributed to God who calls us. . . . So the sentence, 'It is not of him that willeth nor of him that runneth but of God that hath mercy' cannot be taken to mean simply that we cannot attain what we wish without the aid of God, but rather that without his calling we cannot even will" (1.1.12, trans. Burleigh).

Augustine had come to this conclusion through a reassessment of man's autonomy with respect to God's call. Puzzling over Matthew 22:14, "Many are called but few are chosen," he had earlier held that man was free to accept God's call or to reject it. God, foreseeing a rejection, would call such men so that they would not follow, according to his purpose of election.[36] Now Augustine sees such moral autonomy as compromising divine omnipotence. "If . . . not everyone who is called obeys the call, but has it in the power of his will not to obey, it could be said correctly that it is not of God who hath mercy, but of the man who willeth and runneth, because God's mercy would not be sufficient without the obedience of man who was called." But this is unacceptable: "The effectiveness of God's mercy cannot be in the power of man to frustrate" (1.2.13, trans. Burleigh, slightly altered). Having excluded faith as a grounds of merit, having attributed man's good will itself to God's action, having indeed excluded any form of merit whatsoever as the grounds for man's election, Augustine must redefine the only variable left in his equation—the nature of God's call.[37]

God does not call all men the same way. Those whom he elects he calls *congruenter*, "effectively" or "appropriately," so that they will follow. Those whom he rejects he does not so call, so that they will not follow. The proof is tautological: if God had chosen these people, he would have called them effectively, so that they would have followed; since they did not follow, although they must have been called, God must have called them but not *congruenter*. Thus divine omnipotence is preserved, because the initiative of salvation rests solely with God's will, not man's, and "God has mercy on no man in vain" (1.2.13, trans. Burleigh).

So then why does God call some *congruenter* and others not? Why was Esau rejected? Why was Pharaoh's heart hardened? One suspects, says Augustine, that such an aversion or hardening is the result of some divine penalty. God's unwillingness to be merciful is entirely his own decision, absolutely unaffected by any predisposition or merit on man's part. But there cannot be any unrighteousness with God. How, then, is his selectivity to be accounted for? At this point, Augustine invokes the *massa peccati*.

Augustine had used the word *massa* in the *Propositions* as a synonym for *conspersio*, the reading his text had for Romans 9:21. It described man's condition *sub lege*, when he could not avoid sin of his own will. Augustine had queried the description then. Is this too harsh? *O homo tu quis es?* Who is man to say? *Sub lege*, man is a lump of clay, a *conspersio* or *massa luti*, out of which the divine potter can mold different vessels as he pleases. Until man ceases to live "according to this lump" (*secundum hanc conspersionem*), he is carnal. Only when he puts away the *prudentia carnalis*, his carnal self, the "man of clay" (*homo luti*), can he investigate spiritual things. Until then, he should hold his tongue (*Prop. ad Rom.* 62). In *De diversis quaestionibus 83* (q.68), the metaphor of the *massa luti* gives way to a more literal *massa peccati*, a condition visited upon man specifically because of his origin in Adam, through whose sin *natura nostra peccavit*. Still, in these earlier writings man is morally autonomous to the degree that he can freely choose to greet God's call with good will.

Not so in the *Ad Simplicianum*. Here all mankind, born *de traduce peccati et de poena mortalitatis*,[38] is bound by the inherited mortal condition into one sinful mass. All men, in other words, share in Adam's offense against God because they share the mortal condition that arose because of Adam's sin. All, accordingly, must pay the debt of punishment owed to the supreme divine justice (*Ad Simpl.* 1.2.16–20). Man's penal state has changed from a condition imposed by God for man's correction to the sufficient grounds for his condemnation.[39] Therefore, argues Augustine, if man is condemned, there is no unrighteousness with God, since God, by leaving man condemned, simply exacts the payment of a penalty justly imposed. He does not thereby make man any worse; he simply declines to make him better (*Ad Simpl.* 1.2.15–18).

The question becomes, rather, why redeem any sinner? Why give Jacob grace? Turning to Paul's image of the potter and his lump of clay, Augustine says that God is free to shape some vessels of honor and some of dishonor: God is the potter. His decision is inscrutable; and if man does not like this, Augustine answers with

Paul: "*Tu quis es?* Who are you, O man, to answer back to God?"
All man can rightly do is commend God's discipline whereby
God graciously chooses to save some from the mass of the justly
condemned (*Ad Simpl.* 1.2.18).

What then of man's free will? "It exists, indeed," says
Augustine, "but of what value is it in those who are sold under
sin?" (*Ad Simpl.* 1.2.21, trans. Burleigh). Man's will, as Paul says in
Galatians 5:17, is beyond his control. He cannot even motivate it
unless something presents itself to delight and stir his mind. But
"that this should happen is not in any man's power" (*Ad Simpl.*
1.2.22, trans. Burleigh). Delight is not subject to conscious control; man cannot will to love.

> Who can believe unless he is reached by some calling, by
> some testimony borne to the truth? . . . Who can welcome
> in his mind something which does not give him delight? But
> who has it in his power to insure that something that delights
> him will turn up, or that he will delight in what turns up? If
> those things which delight us serve to turn us to God, this is
> not due to us but to him (*Ad Simpl.* 1.2.21, trans. Burleigh;
> last sentence altered).

So crucial is delight to man's motivation that God uses it as the
psychological mechanism of salvation: he redeems by enabling
his elect to love correctly.[40] Man cannot do this himself. *Restat
ergo voluntates eliguntur.* The wills themselves, Augustine concludes—to love rightly and, thus, to believe—are elected (*Ad
Simpl.* 1.2.22). All are justly bound into one sinful mass, and
God's selection of some from that mass, man must believe,
"belongs to a certain hidden equity," incomprehensible by any
human standard. "Inscrutable are his judgements, and his
ways past finding out" (*Ad Simpl.* 1.2.16, trans. Burleigh; citing
Rom. 11:33).

Once, says Augustine, he had thought that he understood
election by observing how some people were relatively free from
sin, or possessed great abilities, or uttered great and profitable
teachings. In such cases, the man would seem worthy of election
who had only the slightest sins, or a keen mind, or who was
cultivated in the liberal arts. Augustine had judged by such

standards at Cassiciacum.[41] Now all that has changed. "If I set up this standard, 'he will laugh me to scorn' who has chosen the weak and the foolish to confound the strong and the wise" (*Ad Simpl.* 1.2.22; a reference to 1 Cor. 1:27).

How can we account for this drastic shift in Augustine's assessment of the process of salvation? And how can we evaluate it? Scholars search, naturally, for sources, both literary and environmental. And some unanimity has been reached. All point, for example, to the wearing effects of Augustine's job on his general outlook. Within a very short time, he had moved from the quiet of lay piety as a *servus dei* to the rough-and-tumble world of North African ecclesiastical politics. No longer in a small community of like-minded scholarly ascetics, Augustine found himself confronted by the "compulsive force of habit" in the behavior of his own congregation, whose addiction to swearing, astrology, and raucous *laetitiae* he tried to reform.[42] And as he wrestled with these African Christians, he likewise reentered the spirit of African piety: the Platonist who had sought to be a friend of God now stressed the salubrious merit of anxiety, fear, guilt, humility, repentance, confession.[43]

Social environment sets the stage, but it provides context, not content. How can we account for specific aspects of Augustine's exegesis? Here scholars turn to literary sources, and we encounter, most commonly, the names of Ambrosiaster, Tyconius, and Paul.

By the time Augustine wrote his own commentaries, Ambrosiaster, an anonymous Christian in Rome, had used *massa* to describe the situation of humanity after, and as a result of, Adam's fall. Considering Romans 5:12, Ambrosiaster says: "In quo—id est in Adam—omnes peccaverunt. . . . Manifestum est itaque omnes in Adam peccasse quasi in *massa*. Ipse enim per peccatum corruptus quos genuit, omnes nati sunt sub peccato. Ex eo igitur cuncti peccatores, quia ex ipso sumus omnes" (*Comm. in Rom.* 5:12).

This notorious misunderstanding of Paul's *eph ho*, together with this particular interpretation of Romans 5:12, will later loom large in the Pelagian controversy. Augustine will then cite Ambrosiaster, who he thinks is Hilary.[44] In 394–95, however, Augustine does not support his new argument with an appeal to Romans 5:12

and Ambrosiaster's congenial interpretation of it. *Massa*, rather, comes into play through the *conspersio* of Romans 9:20, and Augustine's interpretation of it can easily be seen as a development internal to his new ideas on the nature of God's call.[45]

For these ideas we have a surer source: Tyconius. We know from a letter sent to Aurelius, Bishop of Carthage, that Augustine had read and appreciated the Donatist layman's handbook on exegesis, the *Liber regularum*, in the same year that he wrote the *Ad Simplicianum*.[46] But what, precisely, would his reading of Tyconius have suggested? The question of grace as it arose in Paul's letters had exercised Tyconius too; and in Rule 3, *De promissis et lege*, he had explored the problem. Man, says Tyconius, is justified only by faith; but he has faith only by grace, and he does not have grace unless he has been predestined.[47] Free will is preserved, however, because God predestines according to his divine foreknowledge of the will of his elect.[48] Nonetheless, Tyconius explains, man must keep in mind the meaning of 1 Corinthians 4:7: "What do you have that you did not first receive?" God is properly considered the source of faith and good works, so that boasting is prohibited.[49]

Augustine too, in the *Ad Simplicianum*, will emphasize 1 Corinthians 4:7. But I think, on the evidence of *Epistle* 41, that we must assume that Tyconius suggested to Augustine something more precise, and crucial, than simply some particular verses in Paul.[50] For Augustine to have been as excited about the *Liber* as he apparently was, he must have seen something in Tyconius' presentation that would have saved it from being identical to the argument that he himself had already presented in 394–95 in the *Propositions*, the *Inchoata Expositio*, and qq.66–68 of *De diversis quaestionibus 83*, and had subsequently, in the *Ad Simplicianum*, rejected. What might this have been?

Faith, says Tyconius, might be man's good work, but it is of God to the degree that it represents the measure of his influence. "Omne opus nostrum fides est quae quanta fuerit tantum Deus operatur nobiscum."[51] This divine influence on man, resulting in faith, acts directly on man's will. *Man does not have the option to reject God's call* because that would not be consonant with God's foreknowledge and, thus, omniscience. "Non ipsis dicitur Si me audieritis, cui dicitur Si me audieritis potest et non audire; numquid convenit in eum quem Deus ante mundum praevidit auditurum."[52] The wills of the elect are thus *conformed* by God's will so that, in faith, the elect fulfill the law.

Tyconius, in other words, may have suggested to Augustine an aspect of God's grace that, as Augustine reflected on it, became central to his new interpretation. God's grace is absolutely irresistible; man cannot have the option of spurning God's call. And thus as we have seen, for the Augustine of 396, that means that God does not call all men. It is better, apparently, that God's justice seem obscure than that his omnipotence seem compromised.[53]

And, lastly, there is Paul himself. Historians will point to Augustine's constant reading of the epistles in these years as an implicit explanation for Augustine's radical new theology of grace, as if Paul's augustinianism had been there all along, waiting for Augustine finally to perceive it.[54] We can do better than this, I think. Again, Augustine had read these back in Italy and probably before then as a Manichee; Christian theologians had been reading them for centuries; Latin commentators in particular and in this century in particular—Pelagius not least of all[55]—turned frequently to Paul. Yet no one had ever formulated an interpretation like the one Augustine offered in 396. Nor, until 396, did Augustine. So how are we to understand this factor?

I think our clue is to be found in the final paragraph of the *Ad Simplicianum*: we should have in mind not Paul, but Saul. The Paul with whom Augustine would have been most familiar back in Milan, both as an ex-Manichee and as a philosophically inclined Catholic, would have been the Paul of the Epistles. And Augustine presents his conversion, at this time, in a manner reminiscent of Justin's self-description in the *Dialogue with Trypho* (1–8), as progress made in philosophy, whose "shining face" the apostle's letters had revealed to him.[56] But as Augustine works through the Epistles in the mid-390s, the Paul of Catholic tradition, the blasphemer and persecutor (1 Tm. 1:13), the foolish, impious, and hateful man enslaved to various pleasures (Ti. 3:3), imposed himself (*Exp. ep. ad Rom. inch.* 21).[57] And Augustine has before him, of course, Luke's narrative in Acts.

Hence Augustine's conclusion to his exhausting exercise in scriptural exegesis and dialectical reasoning. Abruptly, dramatically, he closes his answers to Simplicianus by again invoking Paul—not his theology, but his biography.

> The only possible conclusion is that it is wills that are elected. But the will itself can have no motive unless something presents itself to delight and stir the mind. That this should happen is not in any man's power. What did Saul will but to attack, seize, bind and slay Christians? What a fierce, savage, blind will was that! Yet he was thrown prostrate by one word from on high, and a vision came to him whereby his mind and will were turned from their fierceness and set on the right way towards faith, so that suddenly out of a marvellous persecutor of the Gospel he was made a still more marvellous preacher of the Gospel. And yet what shall we say? . . . "Is there unrighteousness with God? God forbid!" (*Ad Simpl.* 1.2.22, trans. Burleigh; cf. Acts 8:3; 9:1-22; Rom. 9:14).

The essentially classical model of self-improvement and moral freedom, even in the extremely attenuated form in which it survives into Augustine's early Pauline commentaries, could not withstand Augustine's double encounter with Tyconius' emphasis on God's absolute omnipotence and his own growing sensitivity to Paul's past as a persecutor. No tender conscience had prompted Saul to call on Christ so that he might move from *sub lege* to *sub gratia*. He had been sinning with a high hand, and evidently enjoying himself. But God—mysteriously, ineluctably, even violently—had redeemed Saul from the errors of his past, without Saul's having done the least thing to deserve it (indeed, he deserved condemnation) and without Saul's having the option to refuse it (which, judging from his prior record, he would have). What could Paul do but humbly praise divine inscrutability? "For his judgments are unsearchable, and his ways past finding out" (Rom. 11:33, at the finale of the *Ad Simpl.*).

Thus, Augustine concludes, not man's will but solely the absolutely unmerited gift of God's grace can orient man's loves toward the divine. Having made this case exegetically in the *Ad Simplicianum*, Augustine restates it, autobiographically, in the *Confessions*.[58] From his new perspective on the dynamics of love, will, and grace, he reviews his own life. Nothing escapes his scrutiny; everything is seen in terms of the perversion of loves that marks every child of Adam. *Ante legem*, in childhood, he had spontaneously thrown himself into affective perversions: preferring fiction to grammar, weeping deliciously over Dido's death and various dramatic tragedies, and even once sinking so low that he had sinned for the sheer love of sinning, gratuitously pillaging a neighbor's fruit tree.[59] And when in adulthood, *sub lege*, he had realized which way salvation lay—within the church, which for Augustine meant celibacy as well[60]—he found himself paralyzed by the memory of his former delights, those things he had once loved that, though he wanted to love them no longer, had woven a chain of habit in his soul, binding his will yet further to its own disorder. The man who, shortly after his conversion, had held that one could obtain the goal of a righteous life with "perfect ease," since it required only an act of will,[61] now saw his conversion in quite different terms.

> Many years had flowed by—a dozen or more—since the time when I was nineteen and had read Cicero's *Hortensius* . . . and yet I was still postponing giving up this world's happiness. . . . I prayed in my great unworthiness, "O Lord, grant me chastity and continence, but not yet." . . . I turned to Alypius and cried out, "What is wrong with us? The unlearned take heaven by storm, while we with all our learning wallow in flesh and blood!" . . . I was frantic in mind, in a frenzy of indignation at myself for not going over to your law and your covenant, O my God, where all my bones cried out that I should be. . . . The way was not by ship or chariot or foot; it was not as far as I had gone when I went from the house to the place where we now sat. *For I had only but to will to go, in order not merely to go but to arrive; I had only to will to go*—but powerfully and whole-heartedly, not turning and twisting a half-wounded will this way and that. . . . Whence is this monstrousness? Where is its root? Might the answer not lie in the mysterious punishment that has come upon all men, the deep, hidden damage in the sons of Adam? (*Conf.* 8.7-9, emphasis added).

The *Confessions* is a tremendously complicated book, and the temptation to see it primarily as autobiography should be resisted. It is, rather, Augustine doing theology in a new key, using his own past experiences as privileged evidence for his new theological propositions. Its true autobiographical status, in fact, may lie less in the particulars of its historical narrative than in the biographical fact to which it attests: in denying man's ability to do anything toward his own salvation, Augustine had broken completely with the classical ideal of virtue by which he had been reintroduced to Catholicism back in Milan. Enmeshed in ecclesiastical responsibilities, struggling almost as much with his own congregation as with schismatics and heretics, aware—through his dream life— of the deeper struggles continually going on within himself,[62] Augustine now found such an ideal dangerous, ridiculous, and puerile. He ruthlessly renounces it in the *Confessions*.

Augustine had come to his new evaluation of Paul, himself, and all humankind in the process of exegetically extracting both Paul and the problem of evil from the moral determinism of the Manichees. Yet against Julian of Eclanum, Latin Christianity's last public spokesman for the traditional view of man's moral freedom, Augustine used many of these same arguments and indeed drew particular attention to these last two writings of his early episcopacy. How did he do this, and why?

Body, Soul, and Person: The Works against Julian

Julian challenged Augustine on a number of closely interrelated issues: God's justice; the nature of Adam's sin and the way its consequences were communicated to later generations; the freedom of the will; the theological status of sexuality, conception, and unbaptized babies; the origin of the soul. We may reduce these to one fundamental question: if sin is inherited, then how?

Classical anthropology, free of the constraints imposed by Genesis, inclined toward seeing the body, or more accurately the matter on which it depended, as the reason for moral evil. This tendency held dangers: taken too far, it might reduce to irrelevance the question of the soul's freedom. Plotinus, the great representative of the classical tradition in late Roman culture, had only with difficulty and mixed success avoided holding the body as somehow particularly responsible for human error.[63]

Nevertheless, this tug toward the sort of dualism condemned as "Gnostic" both by pagan Neoplatonists and their Catholic counterparts was the inevitable consequence of an anthropology that identified what was most truly human with the soul itself. The body served, essentially, as the soul's inconvenient vehicle while it sojourned in the realm below the moon. Indeed, by virtue of his soul's embodiment, man expressed in his own constitution those tensions—ontological and, therefore, moral—that existed between the divine and material reality in his mental picture of the cosmos.[64] His "true self," the soul, was drawn to reason, virtue, and the higher spiritual realities,[65] whereas the demeaning urges of his immediate material environment, the body, distracted the soul through its senses. Surely the body was not the soul's natural home. But man, the lonely sublunar outpost of the spirit, had to endure its importunings until, through mystical experience or finally death itself, the body could be shed as a first step in the soul's ascent back toward the One.

For the man who would lead the virtuous life, then, the body was clearly a liability. But according to classical tradition, the freedom of the will—that attribute unique to and indeed definitive of the rational soul—offset the inherent dangers of bodily existence. Through the exercise of his free will, man could train the eye of the soul toward the intelligible verities. The very difficulty of the soul's struggle was in fact the measure of its virtue.[66] And by practicing virtue, man could overcome and subdue the obstacles that the body put in his path—could indeed overcome the "obstacle" of the body itself.

The Pelagian reformers stood within this classical tradition of man's moral perfectibility—as indeed, prior to 396, did Augustine.[67] And though they naturally defined humanity scripturally—the good God, as Genesis related, had created man both body and soul—the Pelagians assumed much of the anthropology that the classical tradition implied. Thus things bodily, and in particular things sexual, were "detachable," were not essentially human in the way the soul was.[68] And the soul in its freedom could choose continence and live chastely, overcoming the disadvantages of physical existence, many of which were the consequence of the flesh's mortality—which *was* inherited, together with the flesh, from Adam. Failure to do so might be sin; but attribute such sin, Julian argued, to the justly punished failure of an individual's will, not to a universally inherited fatal disability.

Such a disability, further, was incoherent theologically, philosophically, and scientifically. Theologically, it insulted God's justice by claiming that he condemned innocents, such as unbaptized babies, for the sin of a distant ancestor. Philosophically, it meant that man sinned by necessity and thus that the will was not free. This too impugned God's justice, besides eviscerating the concept of virtue. Scientifically, it misinterpreted the value-neutral role that the *calor genitalis* plays in conception. And if Augustine, to avoid the charge of Manicheism, insisted that the seat of sin was in the soul, not the body—that is, that physical existence as such was not inherently evil—but likewise insisted that not just mortality *but Adam's sin itself* was passed from generation to generation, then he said that the soul itself was the *matrix peccati*. But how could the soul be inherited?

Catholic theology had hardly settled the question of the origin of the soul. The North African tradition, as represented by Tertullian and Cyprian, supported the *traducianist* answer: soul came from soul.[69] Julian, and the Pelagians generally, were *creationists*: the body was inherited, the soul created afresh in every child. The third option, the one everyone would have preferred and the one most natural to the Greek metaphysics that most of these theologies presupposed, was *preexistence*: souls lived before coming into the body. But the Origenist controversy had demolished this last as an option for orthodoxy; and theologians, when pushed on the issue, had either traducianism or creationism to choose from.[70]

Augustine, when the storm he did so much to bring on finally broke, had not taken a firm position on this question. His previous discussions on the soul had focused on what we would call "psychology" in the modern sense—what motivates the soul, how affect effects volition, and so on. And though his acuity in analyzing the quality of carnality drove him in the mid-390s to genuinely original conclusions with regard to the soul, his views on the body continued to express—albeit, surely, in a Christian key—the mistrust and devaluation of physical existence traditional to Greco-Roman learned culture. The body weighed on the soul; it was the source of the soul's miseries (*Prop. ad Rom.* 13-18; *De lib. arb.* 3.20.57); to love the body was to be estranged from the self (*De Trin.* 11.5.9).[71] Augustine closely considered the problem of the soul's origin—and came in turn to truly original opinions about the body—only during his controversy with Julian.

Against Pelagian creationism, Augustine counterposed a consideration of both scripture and church practice: the exegesis of Genesis 1 and 2 on the issue of Eve's soul, on the one hand, and the practice of infant baptism, on the other.[72] Together, these inclined him to affirm the essence of the traducianist view: all souls, even Eve's, originated in Adam; the damage wrought in Adam's soul by his sin of disobedience was thereafter transmitted, together with the flesh, to all his progeny.[73] The genetics or mechanics of this transmission—how a soul, on the analogy of some material thing like a body, might be inherited—did not concern Augustine; and he specifically denounced the materialist traducianism of Tertullian.[74] Rather, reasoning backward from the universal necessity of salvation in Christ to the condemnation of all men—*even infants*—except baptism intervene,[75] Augustine concluded that the reason for this condemnation proceeded from Adam, who passed it along not to *bodies* but to *persons* and, thus, to souls as well.[76]

He could, further, pinpoint the immediate agent of this damage: the carnal concupiscence necessarily present for human conception. This had entered human history at the moment of Adam's disobedience. Augustine was claiming neither that bodies in general nor that sexuality and procreation in particular were evil: indeed, in his commentary on the literal interpretation of Genesis, he could state that God had created Adam and Eve both body and soul specifically *for* the purpose of procreation and thus with the capacity for the *summa voluptas* of orgasm necessary to achieve conception.[77] What had changed with the Fall was not "man's great purpose, the begetting of children,"[78] but rather the psychological means by which this was accomplished. Prior to the Fall, man's capacity for pleasure was coordinated with his will;[79] after, the connection between the two was sundered. Thus, immediately after eating the fruit, Adam and Eve perceived that they were naked, and were ashamed: they had experienced, for the first time, the "stirrings of lust"—involuntary, and hence shame-producing, sexual appetite.[80]

As a result of the Fall, the relation of body and soul was doubly disjointed: lust, that great motivator which man could neither will to have nor will not to have, necessarily attended conception; and the soul, although created to embrace the body as marriage partners had been created to embrace each other, was inevitably wrenched, unwilling, from the body at death.[81] Both sexual activity and death thus bespoke the abiding effects of the Fall; neither, as now constituted, could be considered "natural," native to man as created. And sexuality in particular was only the most extreme instance of the disjuncture between will and affect that marked man's every erotic attachment. For this reason in Romans Paul had lamented: "Wretched man that I am! Who will deliver me from this body of death?" Even though the apostle delighted in the law of God in his inmost self, he nonetheless saw another law at work in his members, "making me captive to the law of sin" (Rom. 7:22-24).

Hence Augustine directs his enemies' attention to the *Ad Simplicianum* and the *Confessions*. Augustine recognized these two earlier works as a watershed in his understanding of grace—and, thus, of Paul.[82] But even in these, he now maintained, he had not gone far enough. For originally he had thought that Paul in Romans 7 spoke rhetorically, as the man *sub lege* who yearns to live *sub gratia*. But no man not yet under grace, Augustine now argues, could possibly rejoice in God's law, even if only *secundum interiorem hominem*. The man who so rejoices must already be *sub gratia*; in fact, Augustine now concludes, the "I" of Romans 7 could only be the great saint himself, lamenting the tensions that inescapably continued to torment him *despite* his reception of grace.[83] Even the apostles had "groaned" because of the concupiscence of the flesh, Augustine argues; even Peter and Paul had been afraid to die.[84] So much for Julian's uncomplicated ideas on human freedom and the relations of body to soul!

This brings us to Augustine's christology. He had argued that the nature of both body and soul, flesh and spirit, had been vitiated by the Fall because it was *one* nature, human nature. The sin in the garden had had psychosomatic effects. Adam and Eve's love both for God and for each other was deflected by the *amor sui* that rooted in their souls and compromised their wills while their bodies, subjected involuntarily to carnal concupiscence, rebelled against themselves. With the resurrection of the flesh, however, the tensions between soul and body, spirit and flesh, would be ended. The resurrection would reintegrate human love and human will, as both body and soul are made "spiritual," oriented toward God. Unlike the Manichees, for whom "spirit" and "flesh" were cosmic principles, and unlike the Pelagians, for whom these were the component parts of current human existence, Augustine took "spirit" and "flesh" as primarily moral categories.[85] The flesh, which is now subject to demeaning appetites and ultimately to death, and the soul, which cannot control its own divided will, are both carnal. Both will be made spiritual, for both must be redeemed (1 Cor. 15:44).

But one man loved God, and thus others, with perfect selflessness, and that man was Jesus Christ. Not just because Christ's flesh was sinless, as Julian claimed Augustine claimed: according to Augustine's anthropology, a human soul marked by Adam's sin would have sufficed to make Christ "carnal."[86] But since Christ did indeed have both a human body *and a human soul*—since, in other words, Christ was truly human—his nature could not have been as man's is now. Rather, Christ enjoyed a union of love and will unknown to humankind since Eden. Born of a virgin, Christ had been conceived without concupiscence and thus did not suffer the enervating effects of Adam's penalty. Free of original sin, Christ was likewise free to love and to act not *carnaliter*, but *spiritualiter*. Through his real incarnation, Christ revealed to man both how he should have been—but after the Fall no longer could be—and how, after the resurrection, he would be: redeemed body and soul.

Augustine's efforts against Julian led to his formulating a definition of what it meant to be human that went well beyond the ancient view of a soul occupying a body. And precisely by so focusing on sexuality, and insisting that as now constituted sexuality was the symptom of the Fall *par excellence*, Augustine, curiously, dignifies sexuality, making it an essential, not detachable, aspect of the human person, elevating it from the realm of the purely biological to the conflicted, compulsive, indeed uniquely human world of the psychological. Sex to Julian is reproductive biology; sex to Augustine is eroticism. This is a more complex (not to mention more interesting) phenomenon. And for Augustine, it is the measure of a theological problem more complex, and a human situation more desperate, than the Pelagians, with all their healthy-minded talk of medical science and philosophical freedom, could or would acknowledge.

Further, in Augustine's view, Julian's naive insistence that the will was free and therefore man morally perfectible, that the sexual drive was morally neutral and certainly—through the free exercise of the will—controllable, and that flesh alone was inherited tended too strongly toward that assumption common to Manichees and pagan philosophers alike: that what was most truly human was the soul. He saw in Julian's anthropology that physical/spiritual dualism that was implicit in the classically informed moral perfectionism the Pelagians championed and that he himself, in considering his own life, had come to reject. Their explanation of sin as the unhappy effect of the carnal body on the pure, newly created soul suggested, to Augustine, an anthropology as dangerously dualistic as that of the Manichees. Their argument called into question the unity of human nature, which, Augustine maintained—on the basis of creation as described in Genesis and redemption as described in Paul—had to consist of both body and soul together.

Augustine's insistence on the unity of human nature, however, was purchased at the price of man's moral freedom. The conflict between desire and will, whether in the sexual act or in the process of conversion, could be resolved in this life, and then only tenuously, solely by the unmerited grace of God. And by abandoning the traditional understanding of man's moral independence and the traditional anthropology that defined person primarily as soul, Augustine likewise abandons the educational ideology of classical paideia, the liberal arts. Education or lack of education matters not at all: God chooses whom he will. Perhaps for this reason, Augustine resumes and completes after his controversy with Julian another treatise that he had begun in the late 390s, *De doctrina christiana*. Only scripture, Augustine maintains, can reveal the face of God; only scripture, therefore, can serve as the basis of Christian culture. The *Ad Simplicianum*'s theological renunciation of the assumptions of classical paideia, continued into the autobiographical renunciation rendered in the *Confessions*, culminates in *De doctrina* with a cultural renunciation as well.[87]

But Augustine's anthropology takes him even further beyond classical dualism. As he leaves man's freedom, the soul's integrity, and traditional education behind, he also leaves behind the cosmic architecture of the late hellenistic universe and the resonances that culture had established between God's relation to the physical universe and the soul's relation to the body. No longer, for Augustine, is the human being a miniature map of the cosmos. That world, with its hairline fractures between orders of being and its twin fault lines dividing the universe just below the moon and dividing man, neatly, between soul and body, could not speak to the infinitely more complicated man of Augustinian anthropology—the man through whose soul ran the ancient fault line arising from the sin of Adam.

Augustine's coolness to Paul's vision of cosmic redemption (Rom. 8:19ff.), for which he has been chided by thoughtful critics from Fortunatus to Henri Marrou,[88] may thus be due to something more in character than simple prudence in the face of Manichean cosmogonic fantasy.[89] The cosmos did not motivate his interest because it did not speak to his construction of the problem of evil and the nature of man. The exterior world was irrelevant. What mattered—what was crucially, terrifyingly relevant—was the interior world: man's loves, man's will. Ideologically free of late antiquity's map of the cosmos, Augustine's concept of the person could survive Galileo's revolution and could endure, meaningfully, into the modern period.

Augustine explored this inner world with searching, scrupulous honesty in part because he understood Paul, whom he credited with the same searching introspection, to have compelled him there. And it is through this reading of Paul, finally, that the young Manichee grappling with the mystery of evil, the driven professor of rhetoric imbibing Plotinus, the churchman making his way in the jungle of North African ecclesiastical politics, and the old man affirming his God's justice in the face of the sufferings of tiny babies, come together to present, to the West, the first "modern" man: affirming embodied existence; psychologically complicated; turned toward history rather than eternity, and toward himself rather than the cosmos, for an answer to the question of the origin of evil.

Comment: Augustine, Paul, and the Question of Moral Evil

✠————————————✠

WILLIAM S. BABCOCK

Paula Fredriksen provides a marvelously rich and penetrating study of the path Augustine followed to the typically Western "modernity" that marks the final stages of his theological development—and of the role his successive interpretations of Paul played in moving him along that path. Within the frame of this account, the critical point lies in that "drastic shift" in Augustine's thought and sensibility that took place in the mid-390s, in intimate association with his concentrated study of Paul. That shift set in motion the developments that led to the outcome Fredriksen has charted. Augustine did integrate the body into his conception of the person, making both it and its sexuality "essential, not detachable," features of human being; and he can, in fact, be described as "the first 'modern' man" in terms such as those Fredriksen has used. My concern here, therefore, is not to challenge or to dispute her reckoning of the outcome but rather to register certain points with regard to her treatment of the shift itself.

In particular, I want first to intensify the question about the role of Paul in moving Augustine away from the classical philosophical tradition, and to do so by suggesting that Paul played this role not once but twice in Augustine's theological career. Second, I want to take issue with certain elements in Fredriksen's discussion of the "sources" of the new interpretation of Paul that emerges exegetically in Augustine's reply to Simplicianus in 396 and autobiographically in the *Confessions*.[1] And finally I want to make a proposal about what it was in Augustine's early—and later—thought that made him vulnerable to a Paul at odds rather than in harmony with the classical tradition. The proposal is that Augustine was never quite able to contrive an enduring way of understanding how it is that persons are morally responsible for—are the moral agents of—the evil that they will and do; but the proposal must come later.

Augustine, it would seem, could not long breathe the clean, clear air of the classical philosophical tradition, at least not in the setting of his native North Africa. He encountered that tradition twice, once in Carthage when he read Cicero's *Hortensius* and again in Milan when, by accident or divine direction, he came across the famous *libri Platonicorum*.[2] In each case, the classical tradition hit him with tremendous force, setting him on fire for philosophy (Cicero) and opening before his eyes a whole new vision of God, the cosmos, and the human condition (the Platonists); but in each case the result was more than passing strange.

After reading the *Hortensius*, Augustine turned to scripture and, reacting with a classically informed sensibility, found it both aesthetically and morally distasteful. As a result—and here is the oddity—he joined that most unclassical of late antique religious movements, the Manichees, attracted perhaps by the Manichean claim to rationality in the religious sphere.[3] The impact of the classical tradition was more enduring in the sequel to Augustine's reading of the books of the Platonists; and in this instance, it precipitated him into a version of Christianity more compatible with itself. After his return to Africa and especially after his ordination to the priesthood in 391, however, the classical influence seems to have wilted under the fierce pressures of ecclesiastical life in Hippo Regius, in Carthage, and in the neighboring cities and towns. Five years later, Augustine's views would have altered beyond recall, and the classical forms of the philosophic quest for the moral life and for the supreme good would have lost their hold on his thought and feeling.[4]

It is noteworthy that in each of these two cases, Paul belonged far more to the factors shaping Augustine's departure from the classical outlook on the cosmos and on the human condition than he did to the enticements attracting Augustine to it. It was, presumably, among the Manichees—"the most radical and self-confident of Paul's expositors" in the Latin Christianity of the late fourth century[5]—that Augustine first encountered Paul in any serious way; and it is certainly true that, although there are important traces of Paul in Augustine's first writings after his conversion and baptism, Paul does not come to the forefront of his concern until 391 or 392 and increasingly thereafter until 396 and the writing of the *Ad Simplicianum* and the *Confessions*. For Augustine, at least, Paul and the classical philosophical tradition seem largely to have run on different tracks. Whenever Paul attracted Augustine's full attention, the effect was to draw him ineluctably away from the traditions he had found in Cicero and among the Platonists.

It did not have to be so. No one accuses Clement of Alexandria of departing from the classical philosophical tradition. Yet his writings, according to Eric Osborn, are dotted with citations of the Pauline letters (some four hundred citations of 1 Corinthians, some three hundred of Romans), and his *morale chrétienne* is deeply shaped by Paul.[6] Origen, in the third book of the *De principiis*, had invented a Paul quite compatible with his version of the classical tradition; and Rufinus made Origen's Paul, the Paul of his commentary on Romans as well as of the *De principiis*, available in Latin at roughly the time when Augustine was enmeshed in his own study of Paul. Marius Victorinus, Jerome, Pelagius[7]—all of these knew and, in their commentaries, presented a Paul who neither evoked nor compelled any sudden breaks with the philosophical inheritance of late antiquity. Clearly, as Fredriksen notes, it is not the case that Paul's augustinianism was there all along, merely "waiting for Augustine finally to perceive it." The question is: why was Augustine's Paul, whether the Paul of the Manichees or the Paul of his own writings in the years from 392 to 396, so adamantly alternative to the classical philosophical tradition and outlook? The answer, presumably, will have something to do with Augustine's inability to breathe the air of that tradition for very long at a time.

We know relatively little about how the Manichees interpreted Paul and still less about how Augustine appropriated and deployed that interpretation either in understanding himself or in debating with Catholic Christians. The development of Augustine's interpretation of Paul in the years from 392 to 396, however, we can trace in intricate detail.[8] The decisive episode in the development is presented, clearly enough, in his reply to Simplicianus, written in 396; and its significance is registered briefly, but acutely, in Augustine's own later comment on this work: he "tried hard to maintain the free choice of the human will, but the grace of God prevailed."[9] What brought Augustine to this point? What defeated the free choice of the human will in his interpretation of Romans and especially of Romans 9?

Fredriksen is right, I think, to point out that the North African ecclesiastical scene defines context, not content—although one might observe that it is within context that some views appear plausible and others do not. She is also right, I believe, to discount "Ambrosiaster" and his famous misinterpretation of the *eph ho* in Romans 5:12. With regard to the real or imagined influence of Tyconius, however, I would be inclined to take a rather different tack than she does. I do not understand Tyconius to claim that we have faith only by grace—and neither did Augustine when he reviewed the *regula tertia* of the *Liber regularum*, years later, in *De doctrina christiana*.[10] Nor do I understand Tyconius to argue that man "*does not have the option to reject God's call* because that would not be consonant with God's foreknowledge and, thus, omniscience." Rather Tyconius argues that God already knows that some men will not exercise their option to reject the divine call and that, on this basis, God can make the unconditional promise to Abraham reported in

Genesis (that is what foreknowledge means, not the foreclosing of options but knowing ahead of time which option will be chosen); and this interpretation, I might add, is precisely the view Augustine rejects in *Ad Simplicianum* (even though he himself had once held it).[11] Furthermore, the whole drift of Tyconius' argument in the *regula tertia* (as I understand it) follows lines quite different from those that Augustine pursues in his reply to Simplicianus' questions.[12] In short, Tyconius, taken in himself, does not supply an immediate source of the new understanding of Romans that Augustine elaborated in 396.

Yet Augustine *was* excited by Tyconius. Fredriksen rightly asks why. It would be helpful if we knew when, in fact, Augustine read the *Liber regularum*. In 396 Augustine wrote to Aurelius seeking his opinion of the *Liber*, as he had often written before (*sicut saepe iam scripsi*).[13] How often? Over how long a period of time? Should we be correlating Augustine's reading of Tyconius with the *Ad Simplicianum* or perhaps with one of his earlier discussions of Romans or Galatians? I do not know the answer to these questions, but I do think we can say something about what Augustine found in Tyconius' *regula tertia*: he found a treatment of Paul that emphasized that no one can be justified by the law but only by faith and grace; he found an interpretation of Paul that insisted that no person can meet the demands of the law save through the action of grace and not at all through individual moral effort; he found a discussion of faith, grace, and the divine direction of human history and human redemption that put human freedom at risk (although Tyconius recognized the risk and thought he had counteracted it); and, perhaps most of all, he found an interpretation of Paul that linked the plight and salvation of the human individual to the plight and salvation of humanity at large, spread out across the full canvas of biblical history and, beyond that, to the question of the very reliability of God. Trying to reduce a complex matter to brevity, we might say that Augustine found in Tyconius a Paul and a problematic that were recognizably similar to the Paul and the problematic with which he himself was wrestling in the last years of his priesthood. He found, that is, a conversation partner who was considering the same problems he was considering (although Tyconius was not giving the same answers that

Augustine would give in 396); and neither the problems nor the mode in which they were considered was particularly marked by the classical philosophical tradition.

I am inclined, in the search for sources, to give rather more weight than Fredriksen does to Augustine's reading of Paul himself—not in the sense that Paul's augustinianism was there all along, simply waiting for Augustine to discover it, but rather in the sense that it was precisely in his repeated reading and interpretation of Paul in the years from 394 to 396, and not in some other forum, that Augustine invented, perhaps with some help from Tyconius, Paul's augustinianism. Nor am I convinced that we need to look for some new and previously untried image of Saul the persecutor suddenly wrenched into Paul the apostle to account for the startling interpretation of Romans 9 that Augustine produced in 396. Augustine had already encountered and commented on Paul's persecuting past in his *Commentary on Galatians*.[14] And the reference to Saul and to his "savage, blind will to attack . . . and slay the Christians" at the end of the first book of *Ad Simplicianum* seems to me, at least, more a product and an illustration of the discovery that "it is wills that are elected"[15] than a spark or a cause of that discovery. Even without the narrative in Acts, Augustine would, I think, have painted essentially the same picture of Paul's theology and, quite probably, of Paul's biography.

Simply to point to Augustine's repeated reading of Paul between 394 and 396, however, is not enough to explain the extraordinary shift in Augustine's views that took place during that period: the break with the classical model of self-improvement and moral freedom, the invention of a new Paul, and the willingness to entertain the dark vision of a God whose justice could be asserted but could not be understood. Something must be said in order to account, as best we can, for the facts that Augustine read Paul this way and that he developed a theology which obliterated human freedom and obscured divine justice. To account for Augustine's break with the classical tradition, it is not enough merely to observe that he read Paul. It was quite possible to read Paul carefully and well—as Origen and many others did—and still to draw him into the classical scheme of things human and divine. Why was Paul, for Augustine, a port of exit from rather than a port of entry into the classical tradition? Why was it that, in North Africa at least, Augustine could not sustain the classical outlook that he at the same time obviously found tremendously appealing?

By his own account, Augustine had been driven into the arms of the Manichees by a quite specific version of the more general problem of evil. His question—which he put into the mouth of Evodius in the opening sections of De libero arbitrio — was not unde malum (why is there evil?), but unde male faciamus (why do we do evil?). The difficulty, as Augustine went on to specify, is that "if sins originate with souls which God has created and which therefore have their origin with God," it would seem that sins must ultimately be ascribed to the God who made the souls that sin.[16] For this problem, the Manichees supplied an answer. There are in human beings two souls, one good and a very particle of the divine, the other evil and an expression of the very principle and power of darkness. What we would call the "self" is, of course, to be identified with the good soul; and since it does not sin, it does not implicate God in evil. Human evil arises instead from the intrusion of the evil soul, which neither stems from God nor is the self.

The Platonism that Augustine discovered and embraced in Milan permitted him to make a clean, sharp break with the Manichees on several fronts: his view of God, his view of the cosmic order and its graded levels of goodness, and his view of Christian scripture. In each of these areas Christian Platonism offered a distinct alternative, one to which Augustine could unambiguously adhere. But the problem of human moral agency and human moral evil lingered on. Augustine thought he could answer it by maintaining that what makes an act morally evil is not the outward act itself but the lust (libido) or cupidity (cupiditas) that motivates it.[17] Lust means loving or pursuing temporal things as if they had high and enduring value rather than eternal things which do in fact have high and enduring value;[18] and what makes human beings morally responsible for the evil they do is the fact that their lust is not and could not be compelled: "nothing makes the mind a companion of cupidity except its own will and free choice."[19]

This argument will hold, of course, only so long as it can be shown that human beings once were or now easily could be wise and so did once or do now "choose to descend and become a servant of lust."[20] In this context, Augustine was willing, in 388, to intimate the preexistence of souls and to imply that it was in their preexistent state that souls, then wise, chose to descend.[21] But he knew that this notion would hardly be satisfactory to all, and so he argued more explicitly that wisdom, the good and rightly ordered life, is immediately and easily available to all. To attain it we need only to will it, and that we can do "with perfect ease" since nothing is "so completely within the power of the will as the will itself."[22]

It is important, however, to recognize that these statements— which Augustine was later to regret[23]—were not deeply embedded in his thought. Their role was simply to compensate for an argu- ment he felt he could not fully use (the preexistence of souls); and their purpose was simply to show that human beings could be judged morally responsible for their descent into lust because they could, at any given moment, easily escape that lust merely by willing the good life. In Augustine's argument, these statements serve to support the claim that humans are morally responsible for the evil that they do. They do not indicate that human beings are equally capable of the evil and the good; nor do they belong to an indepen- dent argument that humans can attain the good entirely on their own resources. Unexpectedly, then, the very points at which Augustine seems most clearly and most vigorously to assert the will's unaided ability to will the good actually represent no more than a stage on the path that he was traveling—the path that led from his earlier Manichean identification of the "self" with the good soul, responsible only for the good, to his later declaration (in the *Confessions*) that the human "I," his own "I," is responsible only for its evil while God alone is responsible for its good: "bona mea insti- tuta tua sunt et dona tua, mala mea delicta mea sunt et iudicia tua."[24]

Augustine could imagine a soul, a "self," responsible only for its good or only for its evil. What he could not imagine—and could never fully grasp—was a soul, a "self," responsible equally for its good and for its evil. At this crucial point, he was never a full participant in the classical tradition (even if we grant, as we should, that the classical tradition itself had certain difficulties in this regard). And consequently he was open (as a Clement, an Origen, or a Pelagius was not) to a Paul who would insist that we cannot do the good we want—and ultimately, in Augustine's view, that we cannot even want the good—apart from an intervention from outside, the grace of God determined not by anything we do but only by the mysterious, hidden workings of the divine.[25]

But Augustine's slide from a self uniquely responsible for good to a self uniquely responsible for evil did not, in fact, resolve the problem that had first driven him to the Manichees. Rather it created new, more intricate, and more troublesome variations on the difficulty with which he had begun.

(1) In making God responsible only (and immediately) for the good that persons do, Augustine seemed to exempt God from responsibility, direct or indirect, for human moral evil. But so long as divine grace comes only to some and not to all and is given utterly without regard to human merit, God's exercise of that responsibility remains hopelessly obscured in mist. We can only claim, we cannot see or understand, that there is no unrighteousness with God.[26] Augustine found in Paul, especially in Romans 9, apostolic support for such a view. Obviously it is no accident that whereas a Pelagius (or other commentators) would assign the difficult verses of Romans 9 to a speaker other than Paul, an interlocutor breaking in with an objection to be answered and dismissed, Augustine would insist that these verses were spoken and asserted by Paul himself.[27] Augustine derived from Paul a God whose judgments truly are unsearchable and whose ways are past all human finding out.[28] The equity of this God is impenetrably hidden from human sight.[29]

(2) Already in the first book of De libero arbitrio, Augustine had recognized that there is a penal character to the self's subjection to lust.[30] Over the next eight years (388–96), his views on this point were to take firmer, harsher shape; and they were to be reinforced by his growing conviction that the self is not at its own

disposal, that the inertial force of habit not only puts up a stiff resistance to moral change but is, in fact, an obstacle that the self cannot overcome. By 392, he had drastically revised his earlier position. He no longer held that sin, to be sin, must be voluntary, an unforced exercise of will. Prompted at least in part by Manichean citations of Romans 7, he was ready to speak of involuntary sin, sin that persons cannot help but commit due to the very lust to which they have subjected themselves and whose grip—forged into the chain of habit and imposed as divine penalty—they cannot break.[31] These developments made it more difficult for Augustine to answer his initial question satisfactorily. *Unde male faciamus?* The answer could not be that we do evil because we have no alternative—not if, in any sense at all, we (and not God or some other external force) are responsible for our sin. The emerging shape of Augustine's thought was forcing him to place all the weight and urgency of his question on the first instance, the first evil choice or, rather, the first evil will making the first evil choice that plunges us all, individually and collectively, into involuntary subjection to sin. It was forcing him, that is, to locate the one genuine instance of moral agency in evil in the fall of the first human pair and, behind that, in the fall of the evil angels.

(3) And just here, Augustine was driven into a position he could neither avoid nor fully defend: the first evil will must be uncaused.[32] The stakes, in this regard, were high. To admit a cause would be either to implicate God or to ascribe responsibility to some other external force, that is, it would be to revert either to the initial question, still unresolved, or to the Manichean view to which that question had driven Augustine in the first place. The claim that the first evil will was uncaused was, then, Augustine's bulwark against Manicheanism in the arena of human moral agency—a fragile bulwark, however, and of uncertain value. For if the first evil will is uncaused in the sense that Augustine seems to have in mind, then it simply happens inexplicably and, as it were, by accident. But people are not responsible for what happens to them accidentally; such happenings cannot be construed as actions that agents have performed. Augustine still has not forged a link between the agent and the evil that the agent wills and does.

When Augustine relinquished his view (never very deeply held) that persons can attain the good "with perfect ease" simply by willing it,[33] he also lost his argument for the voluntary character of human sin and the moral responsibility of the human sinner. On this score (but only on this score!), he had in effect dropped himself back into the position he had occupied as a Manichee—although now without the mythological apparatus of cosmic principles of good and evil or the psychological apparatus of two souls in human beings. Despite his own best, most earnest efforts, he could not find an enduring way to connect persons to the evil that they will and do as the responsible moral agents of that evil. My proposal is, then, that it was just this inability that left Augustine vulnerable to a new (whether a Manichean or, perhaps, a Tyconian), nonclassical Paul who would draw him away from, rather than confirm his place in, the classical philosophical tradition.

PART THREE: OTHER ASPECTS OF PAULINE INFLUENCE

The Pauline Corpus and the Early Christian Book

HARRY Y. GAMBLE

The legacy of the Apostle Paul is enormously rich and varied. If it is cultivated chiefly in the history of Christian theological and ethical reflection, which has repeatedly found in Paul fresh stimulus and direction, it is hardly confined to Christianity, or even to the field of ideas, but can be discovered under other guises as well. One of these, as I will argue in what follows, is the form of the modern book.

The modern book, composed of leaves folded and stitched to form pages, is a direct descendant of the codex, or leaf-book, which was developed in Greco-Roman antiquity. The problem of the origin of the codex and of its popularization as a medium of literature in the Roman Empire remains obscure in many particulars, despite valuable modern studies.[1] One of the most intriguing questions is when and why the codex came into Christian usage. This is a question of importance not simply for an understanding of ancient Christianity but for the history of the codex generally, since to every appearance the codex found its earliest popular use as a format for literature within Christianity. The evidence for this can only be summarized here.[2]

By about the middle of the present century, manuscript discoveries in Egypt sufficed to prove two things. The first is that the codex was in use considerably earlier than had previously been supposed by scholars. Many examples can now be dated to the second century. The second is that Christianity, in a marked departure from the usages of its Greco-Roman and Jewish contexts, had an early, decided, and nearly exclusive predilection for the codex in the transcription of its literature, and especially for the transcription of those writings that were valued as "scripture."[3] Nearly all Christian manuscripts that can be dated to the second century—

and these are the earliest available Christian manuscripts—are parts of codices, and this early preference for the codex holds good for Christian manuscripts of the subsequent centuries as well.[4] Outside Christianity, however, the traditional roll-book maintained its hegemony. For Greek literature generally, the codex was virtually unknown in the second century and only gradually made headway against the roll until achieving a relative parity with the roll in the late third and early fourth centuries.[5] The Christian partiality toward the codex is thrown into relief not only by comparison with Greek manuscripts of the period but also by the fact that Christian copies of Jewish scriptures were regularly written in codices, whereas in Judaism the scriptures were traditionally and by regulation transcribed only in rolls. Thus the early Christian use of the codex as the vehicle of its literature constitutes a genuine and pronounced idiosyncrasy in its cultural milieux and as such begs for explanation.

Many efforts have been made to account for this state of affairs by referring to particular advantages that the codex is supposed to have had over the roll and that would have commended the codex to Christians in particular.[6] It has been claimed, for example, that the codex was preferred by early Christianity for reasons of economy. Because the leaves of a codex were inscribed on both sides, the codex could accommodate roughly twice as much text on the same amount of writing material as would be required for a roll inscribed only on one side. This undoubtedly resulted in some savings, but these should not be overestimated.[7] It is an assumption of this explanation that the early Christians were not affluent and that therefore economy was a powerful motive. But even if this were so—and modern sociological analyses of early Christianity do not provide strong support—it does not appear from the manuscripts themselves that their makers were unusually parsimonious, for we do not find among them any other space-saving measures, such as compressed hands or very narrow margins. Also there are no palimpsests and very few opisthographs. In short, the earliest manuscripts do not suggest that considerations of cost had any bearing on the Christian use of the codex.

Or again, it has been supposed that convenience constituted the primary value of the codex over the roll. Quite apart from the alleged difficulties of handling rolls, which, incidentally, are scarcely mentioned in antiquity but might have commended the codex to anyone,[8] two features of the codex have been thought to have particular appeal to Christians. One of these is the codex's relative compactness, gained through the reduction of writing material. This might have had a special value to those who traveled with books; and just this feature is noted as a special advantage of the codex by Martial, who happens to be our first witness to its innovative use for literature.[9] It is conceivable that in the Christian setting compactness may have popularized the codex with journeyman missionaries, who must have carried with them some books of Jewish scriptures and perhaps also of Christian writings. The value of this feature would not have become obvious, however, until an extensive text or group of texts was at hand, since otherwise a roll or group of rolls was not less portable; this would probably not have been the case as early as the beginning of the second century. Another aspect of the supposed superior convenience of the codex has been seen in ease of reference. This too may have been a matter of moment for Christians engaged in discussion and debate where points could be scored by the citation of texts. Arguments from scripture would presumably be helped by the possibility of turning quickly to a given page or of marking particular pages. But in fact it is not at all clear whether this was a real advantage of the codex over the roll, for on the one hand exact citation was not as necessary or desirable in antiquity as it later became, and on the other hand features that would have made for ease of reference were as scant in the codex as in the roll.[10]

A third characteristic of the codex sometimes thought to have promoted its early Christian use is its comprehensiveness. Unlike the roll, the codex could contain in one physical entity either a single text long enough to have required a series of rolls or a group of texts each of which would normally have occupied a separate roll. Comprehensiveness, however, is a relative term, and early single-quire codices, simply because of the method of construction, were not unusually capacious, rarely exceeding two hundred pages.[11] Really large codices constructed on the multiple-quire method and usually of parchment are not found before the fourth century. Therefore it seems unlikely that comprehensiveness alone would have been an inducement to the Christian usage of the codex as early as the second century. At that time not only was the capacity of codices limited, but the scope of Christian literature and the tendency toward its collective transcription were likewise limited.[12]

Although it cannot be denied that the codex had some small actual and some larger potential advantages over the traditional roll, none of these, or even all of them together, seem sufficient to explain why the codex found early and almost exclusive favor for the transcription of Christian literature but required centuries longer to gain a similar degree of use for non-Christian literature. Consequently, it has sometimes been suggested that there must have been a material reason for this phenomenon, beyond merely practical ones. In the words of C. H. Roberts, "So striking an effect must have had a cause of comparable weight."[13] In particular, it may be supposed that some early Christian document of high authority was originally made available in the form of a codex and that the authority of its content carried over to the type of book in which it was transcribed, and so decisively promoted the codex into general use in Christian circles. Two theories of this type have been proposed.

Roberts originally argued that it was the Gospel of Mark that had this far-reaching result.[14] Relying on the tradition (Papias in Eusebius H. E. 3.39.15–16) that Mark wrote down the reminiscences of Peter, on the frequent supposition that the Gospel of Mark had a Roman origin, and on the assumption that the parchment codex was developed in Rome (cf. Martial), Roberts conjectured that Mark's gospel was initially drawn up in a parchment codex. Small codices made of waxed wooden boards or parchment had been in use as notebooks for recording memoranda, school exercises, accounts, and other ephemera; and it may be imagined that the author of Mark's gospel "should use the same format for a work intended to be copied but not to be published as the ancient world understood publication." Since, however, it is necessary to account for early Christian *papyrus* codices in

Egypt, Roberts appealed to the tradition (Eusebius H. E. 2.24) associating Mark with the founding of the Alexandrian church, and more generally to the western associations of that church, and reasoned that Mark's gospel must have had some early significance for Egyptian Christianity. This made it possible for him to think that if the Gospel of Mark penetrated to Egypt as an authoritative document in a parchment codex, it would surely have been copied there onto papyrus, but the codex format would have been preserved because it had "a sentimental and symbolic value as well as a practical one."[15]

Ingenious as it is, the explanation is liable to objection at almost every point. That Mark's gospel consists of Peter's recollections or that it had any original connection with Rome has little to be said for it, and much to be said against it, by modern scholarship. Further, although there were early positive links between Alexandrian and Roman Christianity, the notion that Mark the evangelist was instrumental in the establishment of the Alexandrian church is merely legendary, and Eusebius' report to this effect is without corroboration.[16] It is also dubious whether the Gospel of Mark had any early or authoritative importance for Egyptian Christianity, not least because among the manuscripts recovered in Egypt, Mark is very poorly represented in comparison with other gospels.[17] Finally, even if the parchment codex was a Roman invention, which is unclear, it is far from certain that the papyrus codex was derived from it; and if it was not, Rome need not be drawn into consideration as the original locus of the Christian use of the codex.[18] A hypothesis depending on such a string of uncertainties and improbabilities has no explanatory force.

In recognition of such problems, Roberts and T. C. Skeat have now offered a different explanation. They observe that in Judaism, in spite of a general proscription against writing down the oral Torah, individual halakic decisions or rabbinical pronouncements could be and were noted down for private use, either on tablets (pinakes) composed of waxed boards, polished surfaces, or papyrus, or on small rolls.[19] Given this, they suppose that such tablets might have come into early use for transcribing "the Oral Law as pronounced by Jesus, and that these tablets might have developed into a primitive form of codex." And if such collections of dominical sayings then evolved into a full-blown gospel, that gospel might well itself have been written in a primitive papyrus codex. Since that gospel would have carried substantial authority, it would have promoted into general Christian usage the codex format in which it was available. On this view, the Christian use of the papyrus codex has no necessary connection either with the parchment codex or with Rome but could have emerged in a Christian community with a strong Jewish constituency and within the orbit of Jerusalem. Antioch is ventured as the likeliest setting.[20]

This theory too is open to various criticisms. It relies for its starting point on extremely sketchy information about the use of papyrus codices in Judaism. The relevant notices are rather late, none of them before the mid-second century, and they do not give much prominence to the papyrus notebook as compared to tablets of other material or to the roll. The theory depends equally on an analogy between the sayings of Jesus and oral Torah, yet the content and the forms of Jesus' teachings were not such as to encourage comparable treatment; and the idea that Jesus' sayings were first inscribed on tablets, let alone on papyrus codices, is entirely speculative. Roberts and Skeat admit as a possible objection that since the use of tablets for writing down oral Torah did not result within Judaism in the development of the codex, neither should the Christian use of the codex be explained on that basis. But they counter that such a development in Judaism was precluded by the fact that there the roll was "rooted in tradition and prescribed by the Law," while Christians felt no such scruples.[21] Yet it would be peculiar if Christians *did* feel bound by Jewish conventions as to how oral Torah might be written but at the same time were *not* constrained by the stronger Jewish convention of the roll-book. In the end, this theory too is unappealing. Because it is conceived so abstractly, without reference to any particular document, it has only speculative interest, and no argumentative value.

Neither of these theories, then, is persuasive. Nevertheless, the fundamental assumption seems sound, namely, that there was some decisive, precedent-setting development in the publication and circulation of early Christian literature which rapidly led to the dominance of the codex within Christianity, and that this effect was a function of the religious authority vested in a document or a group of documents that had been put into circulation in codex form. If we ask what document or group of documents this may have been, there are excellent grounds for the claim that it was an early edition of the letters of Paul.

Roberts and Skeat have tacitly assumed that only a gospel-type document, because it evoked dominical authority, would have been capable of establishing the codex as the characteristic form of the Christian book. But this is unwarranted. Although Jesus-traditions undoubtedly had a primitive and preeminent authority, that authority apparently did not accrue immediately to written gospels. The testimony of Papias (Eusebius *H. E.* 3.39.4) and the practice of the apostolic fathers generally indicate that oral tradition was often, and perhaps typically, preferred well into the second century.[22] The situation is quite different with the letters of Paul, which were from the outset—and indeed in accordance with Paul's intentions—documentary media of his teaching and authority. Not only were these probably the earliest Christian documents; they were also the earliest to be valued, circulated, and collected. An appreciative knowledge (if not an extensive use) of them is already evident very early in the second century. Clement, Ignatius, and Polycarp were each acquainted with a number of Pauline letters and hence with collections of some sort.

Theories about the agents, motives, shape, and provenance of the early collection(s) of Paul's letters are various, but there is broad agreement that such a collection must have come into being by about the end of the first century.[23] Unfortunately, there is no early or clear indication of the precise shape and substance of a presumably original collection of the Pauline letters. Yet it is possible to reason backward from later evidence and to draw some conclusions that are important for the issue at hand.[24]

There is solid and direct evidence for the currency during the second century of two distinct editions of the *corpus Paulinum*. One of these is the edition used by Marcion. It consisted of ten letters arranged in the following order: Galatians, Corinthians (1 and 2), Romans, Thessalonians (1 and 2), Laodiceans (= Ephesians), Colossians, Philippians, and Philemon.[25] A different edition lies behind most early Greek manuscripts, including the earliest extant manuscript of the Pauline letters, p^{46}, dated about 200. This edition provided the community letters in the order: Romans, 1 and 2 Corinthians, Ephesians, Galatians, Philippians, Colossians, 1 and 2 Thessalonians. Other manuscripts attesting this arrangement normally also include the "personal" letters, which are given in the order: 1 and 2 Timothy, Titus, Philemon.[26] This arrangement of the letters is dictated by the principle of decreasing length, and it eventually became the standard "canonical" order of the letters, but with Galatians preceding Ephesians (these two being of almost equal length).

There is also evidence, though somewhat less direct, for yet a third early edition of Paul's letters. This edition is not preserved in any manuscript but may be inferred from an old theory widely found in ancient sources and first attested in the Canon Muratori (ca. 200).[27] This theory held that Paul wrote to precisely seven churches and that therefore (i.e., because the number seven symbolizes wholeness or universality) Paul addressed the church at large. This theory very likely rests on an actual early edition of Paul's letters which presented them as "letters to seven churches." Although such an edition does not survive in manuscripts, it has left traces in some enumerations of Paul's letters which imply the following order: Corinthians, Romans, Ephesians, Thessalonians, Galatians, Philippians, Colossians (Philemon?).[28] This can be seen to be an order of decreasing length, with the two Corinthian letters comprising one length-unit, and likewise the two Thessalonian letters. But reckoning length in this particular way—that is, by taking together letters to the same community—can only be due to a special interest in the number of churches to which Paul wrote. This is a firm indication that there once was an edition of the letters containing all ten community letters and representing them as directed to seven churches. Such an edition must go back to a very early time and in fact has the best claim to be the most primitive edition of the *corpus Paulinum*.[29] The following observations support this conclusion.

First, an edition of Paul's letters as "letters to seven churches" is closely related to an early and persistent problem with Paul's correspondence, namely its particularity.[30] The fact that Paul had written to individual, local communities and had dealt almost exclusively with issues of local and immediate interest posed a standing inhibition to the acknowledgment of the general value and authority of his letters. How could such letters be relevant and useful to other churches, even if they were written by an apostle? Traces are still discernible in the textual tradition that at an early time, and certainly already in the first century, this problem was met by the expedient of deleting or generalizing the specific addresses of some letters, and sometimes also by the omission of other locally specific matter, thus mechanically conferring on particular letters the appearance of general letters.[31] This was not a workable solution, for the particularity of most of the letters was too pervasive to be countered by textual emendations.[32] An edition of Paul's collected letters as "letters to seven churches," however, served to solve exactly the same problem by a different and more effective means: Paul's catholic relevance was made to depend on the *number of communities* to which he wrote and was indicated by *the form of the collection itself*. In this way, the particularity of the letters could be at once admitted and overcome. An edition of this sort, then, is closely linked with a problem that had already arisen in the late first century in the context of the early circulation and use of Pauline letters among others than their original recipients.

Second, although there is no necessity to suppose that there must be a genetic relationship of some sort among all three of the editions of the corpus attested for the second century, there does appear to be a genetic relationship between two of them, namely between the seven-churches edition and the edition used by Marcion.[33] In the edition used by Marcion the letters are manifestly not arranged by decreasing length, for Galatians stands at the head, and Laodiceans (= Ephesians) follows the Thessalonian letters. But it is important to observe that, apart from these exceptions, the rest of this order *is* an order of decreasing length, if the two Corinthian letters and the two Thessalonian letters are counted together as length-units.[34] Since the principle of order by decreasing length is not consistently followed and has no constitutive importance for the edition used by Marcion, the presence of its clear vestiges shows the indebtedness of this edition to an earlier one that *did* follow this principle.[35] And since the Corinthian letters were taken together as one length-unit, and the Thessalonian letters as another, the earlier edition from which Marcion's was derived must have been one that gave emphasis to the number of communities addressed by Paul, that is, an edition of Paul's "letters to seven churches."[36] It is worth recalling here that the edition used by Marcion lacked the letters to Timothy and Titus and so consisted of community letters only, except for Philemon. But it is entirely possible that in Marcion's *Apostolikon*, Philemon did not stand at the end as a letter addressed to an individual but followed Colossians and preceded Philippians, so that Colossians and Philemon represented companion letters to the same community, like the Corinthian and Thessalonian letters.[37] In that case all Paul's letters, including Philemon, were regarded as church letters. There are, then, very good reasons to think that the edition used by Marcion was a modification of an older, seven-churches edition of the Pauline letters.[38] And if it was older than Marcion's time, it must have been very early indeed, going back at least to the beginning of the second century.

Third, although this is a consideration of much slighter importance than those preceding, it is noteworthy that in the last years of the first century and the early years of the second there appear two other collections of letters addressed to seven churches. These are the letters that stand at the beginning of the Apocalypse (2:1–3:22) and the letters of Ignatius. This may, of course, be the merest coincidence, but given the period and region of these collections, it is entirely possible that they reflect the influence of a primitive edition of Paul's letters in the format of letters to seven churches.[39]

In summary, a collection of ten Pauline letters, a collection that was arranged on the principle of decreasing length but that counted together letters to the same community and thus represented Paul as having written to seven churches, was available in the early second century and perhaps already in the late first century. By reason of its antiquity, its interest in promoting Paul's

catholic use, and its relationships to other second-century editions of the letters, this collection has every claim to represent the
most primitive edition of the *corpus Paulinum*.

This leads to the question of immediate interest: in what
type of book was this edition of the letters of Paul drawn up and
put into circulation? The publication of such an edition is not
really conceivable except in the form of a *single* codex or a *single*
roll. The two outstanding features of this edition were, first, its
emphasis on the number of communities addressed by Paul and,
second, its arrangement of the letters by decreasing length. Neither of these features, however, could be established or maintained unless the letters were contained in a single physical entity.
If the edition had consisted of a group of codices or rolls, even a
group so small as two, its fundamental intention of promoting
Paul's catholic relevance would have been put at risk from the
outset, since there would have been nothing to insure that individual codices or rolls would not be taken separately and the
sevenfold disposition of Paul's correspondence thereby obscured
or lost altogether. Further, the order of the letters from longest to
shortest would have been equally insecure, since there would
have been nothing to prevent a reordering of individual codices
or rolls. Thus the very nature of this primitive edition of Paul's
letters required its presentation as a physical unit. But was this
unit a codex or a roll?

Theoretically, it certainly could have been a roll. The manu-
facturer's and the retailer's unit of papyrus was not the individual
sheet but the made-up roll that was produced at the factory by
pasting together individual sheets.[40] From a technical point of
view, a papyrus roll of almost any length could be constructed.
According to Pliny, however, the length of manufactured papyrus
rolls was standardized at twenty sheets.[41] The actual length of a
twenty-sheet roll nevertheless varied, depending on the width of
the individual sheets and on the amount of overlap between
sheets at the joins. Calculations based on actual measurements of
individual sheets in extant rolls (and in codices cut from rolls)
indicate that the standard twenty-sheet roll would ordinarily have
been between 10½ and nearly 12 feet long.[42] Rolls longer than

this could be and apparently were manufactured, but the twenty-sheet roll appears to have been the common retail unit in the papyrus trade.[43] Even so, the papyrus retailer was perfectly capable of pasting together standard rolls in order to meet the length requirements of his customers. Thus nothing in papyrus manufacture or in papyrus trade necessarily limited the length of a roll.

It is far more important to ask about the lengths of inscribed rolls, that is, of actual books. It is true that some very long rolls are known, the longest being P. Harris 1, a chronicle of the reign of Ramses II, at 143 feet. Egyptian hieroglyphic rolls inscribed for burial with the dead were often quite long, extending to 50 feet or more. Greek rolls, however, were considerably shorter than these, commonly running between 20 and 30 feet, with the maximum length being about 35 feet.[44] The establishment of such normal and maximal lengths was, however, not due to technical factors but to purely utilitarian concerns. Given the method of reading a roll, whereby the roll was held in both hands, with the left hand rolling up what had been read and the right unrolling what was to be read, a roll in excess of about 35 feet was extremely inconvenient. The longer the roll, the more cumbersome it was to handle and the more difficult it was to discover any particular place of reference if the roll was not simply being read through.[45]

If a primitive edition of ten Pauline letters had been inscribed in a roll, what length roll would have been required? This question admits of no exact answer because of transcriptional variables such as size of script, height of upper and lower margins, width of intercolumniations, etc., but it is possible to make a reasonable estimate. Taking our oldest copy of the Pauline corpus, p[46], as a basis and assuming the same size hand, the same number of letters to a line, and the same number of lines to a column, we can readily calculate what length roll would have been required for the same text.[46] The columns of writing in p[46] (one per page) range from $5\frac{1}{4}$ to $3\frac{3}{4}$ inches wide, decreasing with page width toward the center of this single-quire codex. This yields an average column width of $4\frac{1}{2}$ inches, which is, incidentally, somewhat wider than the normal column in the extant evidence (two to three inches). The cumulative width of columns from 208 pages (assuming that all pages of the original codex were inscribed) would then be 936 inches ($4\frac{1}{2} \times 208$). To this must be added the space required by intercolumniations. Assuming for these a width of $\frac{3}{4}$ of an inch, which is representative, they would total 155 inches ($\frac{3}{4} \times 207$).[47] Thus columns and intercolumniations together would have required a roll of 1091 inches, or almost 91 feet. Of course, p[46] includes Hebrews, but if this is omitted we must still think of a roll roughly 80 feet in length. No estimate that attaches plausible values to the transcriptional variables will produce a figure very much smaller than this, and certainly not sufficiently smaller to make a difference for the point at issue. A roll of 80 feet, however, is more than double the *maximum* length known in Greek rolls and, indeed, is roughly three times what may be considered a normal length. Because the length of rolls was dictated by custom and convenience, a roll of such extent is highly unlikely on general grounds. But for a roll that was intended to be read and studied, and thus regularly handled, as an edition of Paul's letters assuredly was, such a length is virtually inconceivable, since its very bulk would have been a standing inhibition to its use.[48]

These considerations urge the conclusion that if Paul's letters were transcribed in a single book, as the fundamental features of the earliest recoverable edition required, that book must have been a codex rather than a roll.[49] In this particular case the codex had a special and indeed essential value, namely its comprehensiveness. It could contain in a manageable physical unit various texts by one author which could otherwise be made available only singly or in small groups on rolls. It is *only* in connection with such an edition of the Pauline letters that we can discover early in the history of Christian literature both a genuine occasion and a practical motive for the use of a codex as opposed to a roll, for in the late first or very early second century, by which time the codex must have been introduced into Christian usage, there simply were no other Christian texts for which there existed either the materials or the motives for collection and for presentation as a corpus.[50]

Furthermore, the adoption of the codex into routine Christian use as the fixed medium of "scriptural" texts, a development that must be located near the beginning of the second century at the latest, cannot be more plausibly explained than as a function of the early availability of an edition of the *corpus Paulinum* in codex form. Judging from our sources, the only Christian texts that were broadly known and valued at that time were the letters of Paul. They are respectfully mentioned, and customarily in the plural, by Clement of Rome, Ignatius of Antioch, Polycarp of Smyrna, and the author of 2 Peter (3:15–16); and they are the earliest Christian writings to be reckoned as apostolic in origin and to be designated as "scripture." Hence, if it is a question of what early Christian document(s) possessed the force of authoritative substance to establish its format, the codex, as *the* preferred format for other early Christian texts, then in the relevant period only Paul's letters come into serious consideration.[51] The codex, which was the necessary format for the early seven-churches edition of the Pauline letters, was commended by the authority of its contents as the format of other pieces of early Christian literature for which it was not necessary but was yet convenient and was symbolic of the status intended for their contents.

A particular merit of this hypothesis lies in its capacity to recognize that one of the peculiar features of the codex, namely its comprehensiveness, *was* a factor conducive to its adoption within Christianity, if only initially and only in conjunction with Paul's letters. It does not contradict this to admit at the same time that apart from the Pauline letters, comprehensiveness was apparently not a factor in the subsequent broad popularity of the codex in Christian circles. Most Christian codices of the second and early third centuries appear to have contained only one document, which, as regards length, might just as easily have been transcribed in a roll. For this reason it cannot be claimed that the use of the codex had any constitutive importance for the valuation and use of Christian literature generally in the second century. Nevertheless, Roberts and Skeat go too far when they say, "It may be doubted whether the existence of the codex had *any* effect upon the canon" (emphasis added).[52] Here only one point, though it is not the only one, will be adduced against this view.

It has often been assumed that the gospels of Matthew, Mark, Luke, and John had already been shaped into a four-member collection by the mid-second century, or perhaps even earlier.[53] But the evidence suggests, to the contrary, that virtually throughout the second century these gospels circulated separately, competing with persistent oral tradition, with a considerable number of other ("apocryphal") gospels, and with each other for esteem and use by individual Christian communities.[54] Manuscripts of the gospels datable to the second century contained as a rule single gospels.[55] The preeminence of our four gospels among all others emerged only toward the close of the second century. The strict insistence by Irenaeus (A. H. 3.11.8-9) and the Muratorian Fragment (lines 1-35) on the essential unity and exclusive value of these four does not presuppose a well-established view but instead marks an early stage in the formation of a fourfold gospel. Otherwise it cannot be understood how, in the same period, the Gospel of Peter was still being read in Syria (Eusebius H. E. 6.12.2), how Clement of Alexandria could grant a good measure of authority to the Gospel of the Egyptians and the Gospel of the Hebrews, and how, in Rome, the Gospel of John could still be liable to criticism and rejection. It may very well be that "the fact that Irenaeus and the Muratorian canon regard the fourfold gospel as a spiritual unity is a theological phenomenon and nothing to do with book production."[56] But it is important to notice that their theological conviction, though it need not have presupposed the codex, could find its appropriate concrete expression only in a codex that contained together these four gospels exclusively. And indeed it is first in the third century that we find a manuscript that actually comprises these four gospels (with Acts) in codex form, p[45]. The availability of the codex did not *cause* the collection of the four gospels any more than it caused the collection of Paul's letters. But in both cases the codex provided the medium by which a theological valuation could be given bibliographical form. As such, the codex served to promote and to standardize the four-gospel collection in Christian usage, even as it had earlier done for the letters of Paul. This alone must be judged an important influence of the codex on the history of the canon.

The ordinary reader of the modern leaf-book may not wonder about its origins as the bearer of the written word, but there is
much to indicate that it belongs to the legacy of Paul. Introduced
into Christian usage as the medium of an early edition of Paul's
letters, the codex thus set the precedent for the transcription of
other Christian literature in the same format. This may or may
not be the most important dimension of Paul's legacy, but it is
unarguably the most pervasive.

Archeological Traces of Early Christian Veneration of Paul

ERNST DASSMANN

I n the footsteps of Paul" is a program as popular for educational tours of Bible lands as it is for illustrated volumes devoted to the life and works of the apostle.[1] In content, the "footsteps" are landscapes through which Paul traveled and places in which he stayed. Bays, mountain ranges, and pictures of landscapes, along with the archeological remains of cities, temples, and buildings that Paul could have seen, are supposed to bring one into the closest possible touch with the world in which Paul lived and, in this way, to help in deepening one's understanding of his apostolic work.

But to follow "in the footsteps of Paul" can also mean to track down the actually surviving reminders and recollections of his stay and his activity in the corresponding places and communities, whether these are monumental or literary, historically verifiable or legendary, still visible for inspection or known only from tradition. That most of these "footsteps" are scattered to the winds is to be acknowledged from the outset. What can still be traced, however, will be considered here in varying degrees of comprehensiveness. First, in a rapid overview, the traditions attached to the most important Pauline locations and still alive today will be critically noted and described. The numerous publications of O. F. A. Meinardus, who has studied the learned travel literature from the seventeenth century on and who, in numerous travels of his own, has investigated the surviving reminders of Paul, provide a rich source in this regard.[2] Second, we shall examine more thoroughly the few cities where early Christian veneration of Paul can be established archeologically. Finally, our results will be discussed from the standpoint of whether—in comparison with apparently similar hagiographical instances—they match the significance of the apostle himself, whose literary effect on the theology and life of the church through his letters is beyond all exaggeration.

Historically assured traces left behind by Paul in the places where he lived and worked are always scarce and, in many cases, decidedly rare. In his birthplace, *Tarsus*, for example, there are no remains that demonstrably go back to the early Christian period. The *Apocalypse of Paul (Visio Sancti Pauli)*, to be sure, mentions the house in which Paul was born. There, through the appearance of an angel, a marble box is said to have been discovered, and in it, the "revelation of Paul" that is contained in the *Apocalypse*, along with the apostle's shoes "in which he used to go about when he was teaching the word of God."[3] But this report has no topographical value, since it is obviously designed to explain why the apostle's visions were so late in coming to light. Tourists today are shown a well that—without any sort of proof being offered—is supposed to have stood in Paul's childhood home.[4] A "gate of Paul" (Bab Bulus) dates from the time of the crusades, but it does not appear to reflect any early Christian traditions.[5] The church that, from personal devotion to the apostle, the emperor Maurice (582–602) had built in Tarsus in honor of Paul has been a mosque for centuries.[6]

Even more meager are the traces in *Jerusalem*. There are no early Christian recollections of any houses where Paul stayed (see, e.g., Acts 21:16, Mnason of Cyprus). The oldest historical tradition goes back to the Russian abbot Daniel, who, after the conquest by the crusaders, visited the holy city in the company of monks from the Mar Saba monastery (1106–8). In the vicinity of the Praetorium, he was shown a whole series of places of interest.

> Là se trouve aussi la Prison juive d'où un ange fit sortir le saint apôtre Pierre pendant la nuit. C'est là qu'était aussi l'Enclos de Judas qui trahit le Christ. . . . Non loin vers l'orient, est le lieu où le Christ guérit une femme d'une perte de sang. A côté se trouve la fosse où fut jeté le prophète Jérémie; c'est là qu'était sa maison, aussi que l'*Enclos de l'apôtre Paul, lorsqu'il professait encore le judaisme.* Un peu plus loin à l'orient, à un

détour près du chemin, se trouvait la maison des saints Joachim et Anne.[7]

Other reminders of Paul in Jerusalem are either undatable or very recent. In the church of the Flagellation on the Via Dolorosa there is a side altar dedicated to Paul; the modern church of the Schmidt-School has a window with Pauline motifs.

Far more lively, by contrast, is the Pauline tradition in *Damascus*. Here are preserved recollections of all the places mentioned in Acts in connection with Paul's conversion and the ensuing events in the city—although the recollections are of varying age and historical value. Thus the house of Judas (Acts 9:11) has, since the middle ages, been shown to pilgrims in various places along the long street and in the course of time has been identified with a small shanty, a Pauline church, a Turkish caravansary, and an Islamic school (Medrese).[8] To this day the "House of Ananias," in which Paul was baptized (Acts 9:18), is pointed out, not far from the East Gate (Bab esh-Sharqi), in the form of a small church, below ground level, and the remains of a temple under the basilica. Converted into a mosque in the middle ages, the place was returned to Christian possession in the seventeenth century (plate 1). The apostle's escape, as described in Acts 9:25, has also been localized. It was first marked by a church built in the southern part of the city wall. This church was converted into a mosque, and it was eventually replaced by a modern structure, which was dedicated only in 1941. For a long time, the grave of the gatekeeper who is supposed to have helped Paul in his escape was still shown outside the wall near the Gate of Saturn (Bab Kaysan); and similarly, somewhat further south in the area of the Christian cemetery, the apostle's place of refuge immediately following his flight.[9] Understandably the place of Paul's conversion has stirred special interest. In the course of time, four sites have been specified. In the sixth and eighth centuries, pilgrims mentioned a church building two miles from the city,[10] perhaps at Der Bisr, where the two monasteries Der Futrus and Der Bawlus are still to be found.[11] Pilgrims of the fourteenth century sought the place only a mile outside Damascus and, later, still closer to the city. Another tradition, known since the time of the crusades, cites as the place of the conversion a building in the village of Kaukab, fifteen kilometers southwest of Damascus on the road to Jerusalem. As recently as 1965, in yet another location (off the road from Damascus to Quneitra), a small round church with an arched court to one side was dedicated to the memory of the decisive experience in the apostle's life.[12]

The search for traces of Paul in the places of his early missionary activity is, on the other hand, again unproductive. That Paul spent the time in Arabia mentioned in Galatians 1:17 in *Petra* is a conjecture unsupported by any archeological evidence at the place itself. In *Antioch*, whose onetime greatness is only reflected by modest remains in present-day Antakya,[13] there is a cave of Peter but—despite the enthusiasm shown for Paul by a John Chrysostom[14]—no noteworthy reminder of Paul, who, along with Barnabas, worked for a whole year in the community and departed from there on his first missionary journey (Acts 11:26; 13:2f.). To be mentioned are only the ruins of a Byzantine church at the site of the present-day Habib Neccar mosque, which is supposed to have been built over Paul's house, and the long-submerged moles in Seleucia, the port of Antioch, which were named after Paul and Barnabas.[15]

In *Perga, Pisidian Antioch, Iconium, Lystra* and *Derbe,* cities that Paul visited on the first missionary journey and in some cases passed through again on the second, no archeological reminders whatever remain.[16] Nor have the amplifications of Acts in *The Acts of Barnabas* or *The Acts of Paul and Thecla* left any visible or tangible deposits. The remoteness of many of these places makes that absence more than understandable. The cities practically vanished from the Christian horizon after the Islamic conquest; they were visited by no early Christian pilgrims; the armies of crusaders could establish no new Christian traditions in them; and some still have not been excavated (in the cases of Lystra and Derbe, even their locations have only quite recently been reestablished with certainty).

But the two islands of Cyprus and Crete, on which an unbroken Christian tradition has endured through the centuries, likewise present few reliable indicators. On *Cyprus,* recollections of other apostolic and early Christian figures predominate. In

Larnaca (ancient Citium), there is a Church of Lazarus but none of Paul; and at the excavations in Salamis, one can visit the prison of St. Catharine and a monastery of Barnabas, but there is no place commemorating Paul. In Paphos, medieval pilgrims were at least shown the prison in which Barnabas and Paul are supposed to have been detained, near the church of St. Solomon, and a column (1.2 meters high) at which Paul is supposed to have been flogged.[17] The hagiographical findings resemble the archeological; the traces that Paul left on the otherwise densely populated hagiographical landscape of the island are equally scarce. In legendary memories of Christian origins, in the cycle of festivals, and in the nomenclature for places and events, Paul falls conspicuously behind other missionaries and bishops of the early period, behind his companions Barnabas and John Mark, and behind Andrew— to say nothing of others. Over against those who lived lifetimes on the island working for the faith, such subordination may be understandable; but even saints introduced from the outside, who never personally set foot on Cyprus, hold stronger places than Paul on the religious map of the island.[18]

On *Crete*, above Kaloi Limenes (Fair Havens), near the city of Lasea (Acts 27:8), a small chapel next to a rather neglected grotto and a rough wooden cross commemorates Paul's brief stay (plate 2).[19] Not far from Aghia Roumeli, at the mouth of Samarias Gorge, in the direction of Loutro (the Phoenix of Acts 27:12), stands a small Byzantine domed church, Agios Pavlos. Somewhat farther on is a barely noticeable spring that is linked to Paul in the older travel reports; he is supposed to have performed baptisms there.[20]

Even in a city in which Paul preached and to whose congregation he wrote, the recollection of Paul clings only to scarce or even lost archeological remains. In *Thessalonica*, a stone slab on which Paul is supposed to have been flogged, and which was preserved in a chapel where the salt-makers held their worship service, has been lost; and even the exact location of the little church has been forgotten.[21] That Paul preached in the crypt of the basilica of St. Demetrius or in Hagios Georgios and that a part of the pulpit from which his sermons were delivered lies in front of the church of St. Panteleimon are folk traditions without any historical value. A cruciform marble stone near the Vlattadon

monastery is supposed to mark the place where Paul knelt and
prayed in the courtyard of a house. In a suburb named after Paul,
a small chapel dedicated to Paul was built in the nineteenth century. Also found there are an ancient spring and a cave surrounded by cedars, both of which bear Paul's name.[22] In *Beroea*,
among the numerous churches, there is not one church of Paul;
but a monument to Paul with three marble steps, restored only in
1960–61, is supposed to commemorate the apostle's preaching.[23]

A glance at *Athens* will conclude our survey of the places of
Pauline activity in Greece. The place where Paul disembarked
after the voyage from Thessalonica is variously identified. Aside
from the Phaleron harbor, the site of the remains of the early
Christian basilica of Glyphada is also mentioned.[24] According
to the account in Acts, the apostle's stay was very brief and
produced no major missionary results. Nevertheless, a Christian
community may have been founded and may have left just as few
marks as the Pauline activity itself. The few churches, memorial
sites, and ritual events that today commemorate Paul in Athens all
stem from modern times,[25] with the exception of a well next
to the early medieval Church of Dionysius at the foot of the
Areopagus. Here, according to a seventeenth-century legend,
Paul is supposed to have been hidden after the people's anger was
leveled against him on account of the conversion of the distinguished Dionysius (Acts 17:34).[26] Other traditions—none of
which, however, are still alive in Athens itself—speak of a cave
rather than the well.[27] The legends characteristically arose in the
time when travelers with scholarly and historical interests began
to inquire about tradition-pregnant places. They attest in their
own way that there were no definite sites in Athens connected
with the veneration of Paul and that the apostle must have gone
into hiding and left the city without great success.

As a conclusion to this brief overview, we may ask what
traces, aside from those in places already mentioned (Crete) or to
be discussed later (Malta), were left by Paul's last journey from
Jerusalem to Rome. In *Caesarea*, where Paul stayed several times,
both in freedom and as a prisoner, no memories remain; nor
do they in *Sidon* and *Myra*. Only in *Syracuse*, in the crypt of
S. Marciano at S. Giovanni, in a side chapel, is there displayed an

altar stone from which Paul is supposed to have preached during his three-day stay in the city (Acts 28:12).[28] More precisely datable is the notice in a liturgical calendar from the twelfth century, which, under March 11, says, "In memory of the arrival of the apostle Paul, who came from Malta to Syracuse to the greatest joy of the Sicilians and, through his preaching and miracles, brought light to the community."[29] But the patron saint of the city of Syracuse is St. Lucia, and a Latin inscription in the nave of the cathedral reads: ECCLESIA SIRACUSANA PRIMA DIVI PETRI FILIA ET PRIMA POST ANTIOCHENAM CHRISTO DEDICATA. Peter is also supposed to have ordained Marcianus, the first bishop of the city.

The ship on which Paul was traveling docked very briefly in *Reggio di Calabria* (Acts 28:13). In the cathedral, a pillar is exhibited at which his ship is supposed to have tied up and which is supposed to have shone when the oil lamp that was providing light for Paul's preaching gave out.[30]

Of Paul's friendly reception by the Christians in *Puteoli*, at the *Forum of Appius* (65 km.) and at *Three Taverns* (49 km. from Rome), each carefully recorded by Luke (Acts 28:13-15), no archeological-historical record can be produced.[31] The same is true for the last two years of Paul's life, which he may have spent in modest quarters under the guard of a soldier in *Rome* (Acts 28:16). Questions about whether and how Paul corresponded with Seneca during this period belong entirely to the realm of speculation.[32] The house in which Paul stayed has been associated with the church of S. Maria in Via Lata.[33] Other traditions name the church of S. Paolo alla Regola or else a medieval house on a street of the same name[34] or even S. Prisca on the Aventine, S. Pudenziana, and S. Prassede.

In contrast, any number of traditions follow Paul's missionary journey to Spain. In *Tarragona*, a chapel built on Roman foundation walls in the inner courtyard of the cathedral is held to mark a site of Paul's preaching. In addition, Paul is supposed to have consecrated the first bishop of the city, Prosperus, and to have converted the two sisters Xanthippe and Polyxene. Understandably, other Spanish cities have not neglected to attribute their founding to Paul—and above all the consecration of their first bishops. That is true of *Tortosa* (Dertosa Julia Augusta) and its bishop Rufus (see Mk. 15:21; Rom. 16:13) and of bishop Crispin of *Éciga* (Astigis) in distant Andalusia.[35]

Since ships put to sea from Ostia bound not only for Spain but also for Gaul, for the port of Marseille or Narbonne, it was inevitable that speculations about a visit of Paul in Gaul should arise. And if not the apostle himself, then at least his disciple Crescens (see 2 Tim. 4:10) is supposed to have come to Γάλλιαν instead of to Γαλατίαν[36] These hypothetical journeys have left no archeological traces.

Such traces appear again only in connection with the death of the apostle in *Rome*. Tradition locates the detention of Paul before his execution in the Mamertine Prison and the execution itself at the third milestone on the Via Ostiensis at the present-day monastery and church of Tre Fontane.[37] But only with the apostle's grave in the basilica of S. Paolo fuori le mura[38] and the place of veneration in the "Triclia" at S. Sebastiano on the Via Appia[39] does one reach the ground of more certain historical testimony—if not to the event itself, at least to the places of early Christian veneration of Paul.

Apart from Rome, palpable archeological traces of an early Christian veneration of Paul have been preserved above all in Philippi, Ephesus, Corinth, and Malta.

Philippi. Philippi was Paul's first mission station on the European continent and one that he probably visited, if only briefly, on three occasions (Acts 16:11–40; 20:1–6).[40] He wrote a letter to this community, to which he was bound by a special relation of trust, just as later did Polycarp, who referred explicitly to Paul (Polycarp *Phil.* 3.2).[41] The ecclesiastical significance of Philippi in later times is evident from three great church buildings that rank among the largest and most lavish from the early Christian era in Greece.[42]

By the eighteenth century, the city had totally collapsed, and today it lies in ruins. Still, memories of Paul have survived in two places. What was originally a cistern from Roman times is traditionally held to be the prison of Paul and Silas. It is located, about halfway up, beside the monumental staircase that connects the forum with the atrium of Basilica A (plate 3). One is still shown places on the walls where the chains that would have held the two prisoners were anchored.[43] The structure, which consists of a vaulted chamber with a central pillar, perhaps making two rooms, was opened up after its accidental discovery by a Greek physician in 1876; unfortunately, the archeological investigation and preservation of the find were not properly conducted, so that today only scant remains of the original, brightly colored frescoes can be discerned (plate 4). These are supposed to have depicted the events that Luke reports in Acts 16:16–34: the healing of the possessed girl, the flogging and imprisonment of Paul and Silas, the baptism of the jailer, and the washing of the prisoners' wounds.[44]

It is unlikely that the cistern ever served as a prison. The divided room can, to be sure, be associated with the inner and outer prison mentioned in Acts 16:24, but a prison of several cells could hardly have been housed in the cistern in its present form. Consequently it has been suggested that the site of the prison lies somewhere else entirely.[45] The fact remains, however, that the congregation of Philippi did localize the events reported by Luke in connection with the arrest and deliverance of the apostle; and this happened no later than the moment when the cistern was transformed into a monument of remembrance for Paul. Precisely when that occurred we cannot say with confidence. The transformation of the cistern into a memorial chamber may have taken place at approximately the same time as the construction of Basilica A. Paul Lemerle dates the addition of the frescoes and a chapel-like extension of the structure above the cistern only in the tenth century.[46] But if one bears in mind that on the east wall there is supposed to have been a representation of a central figure seated on a throne and flanked by two persons, a scene that is also encountered on a Florentine ivory from the end of the fourth century, and that in the red church of Peruštica there are the remains of a fresco from the period around 600 that are likewise supposed to represent a Pauline scene and that resemble the frescoes in the cistern memorial room,[47] it seems at least worth considering an earlier date for the Philippi frescoes as well.

A second indication of veneration of Paul in Philippi came to light only in 1975. South of the Via Egnatia and east of the forum, or of Basilica B, the following mosaic inscription was found in the floor of the so-called Octagon-complex (plate 5):

ΠΟ (ΡΦΥ) ΡΙΟΣ ΕΠΙΣΚΟ
ΠΟΣ ΤΗ(Ν) (Κ)ΕΝΤΗΣΙΝ ΤΗΣ βΑΣΙΛΙΚΗ
Σ ΠΑΥΛΟ(Υ) (ΕΠ)ΟΙΗΣΕΝ ΕΝ ΧΡ(ΙΣΤ) Ω.[48]

Since Bishop Porphyry participated in the synod of Serdica in 343, this inscription must refer to some structure that predated the Octagon—which itself dates from the time of the emperor Arcadius (395–408)—and must belong to the earliest church building known anywhere in Philippi.[49] Basilica A, which lies north of the forum, and even more Basilica B, which belongs to the time of Justinian, are clearly more recent.[50] The Porphyry inscription surpasses in age and certainty of date all other archeological evidences relating to Paul. Other and earlier evidences of Christian life in Philippi are lacking;[51] nor, understandably, has anything been found of the Jewish place of prayer by the river outside the city, where Paul spoke to Lydia and the other women (Acts 16:13).

Ephesus. Paul was certainly in Ephesus twice. At the end of his second missionary journey (summer/fall 51), on the return trip to Jerusalem and Antioch, he made a brief stop in Ephesus, spoke on the sabbath to the Jews in the synagogue, left Aquila and Priscilla behind, and departed with the promise to return if God willed (Acts 18:19–22). A short time later (on the third missionary journey) he was able to make good on his promise and to work for a longer period in the metropolis of the Roman province of Asia.[52] At first, for three months, he taught in the synagogue; then, after the separation of the Christian congregation from the Jews, he taught in the lecture hall of Tyrannus (Acts 19:8–10). The Lucan account (Acts 19:11–40) one-sidedly praises the apostle's miraculous power and his missionary results—all the residents of the province of Asia hear him, many Ephesians burn their magic books, and the riot of the silversmiths on behalf of their goddess Artemis and their own trade breaks down without any personal intervention on Paul's part—and skips over the sufferings and dangers of which Paul speaks in various passages in his letters. Even so, the missionary and theological fruitfulness of the Ephesian period cannot easily be overestimated. Paul found in Ephesus many loyal assistants who carried on his work. The letters to the Ephesians and Colossians, letters thoroughly familiar with Pauline theology and circulated under the apostle's name, originated in Ephesus.[53] A vigorous community developed, to which was addressed the first of the letters to the seven churches in the Apocalypse of John (Rv. 2:1–7). Ignatius too sent one of his letters to the Ephesian community as "a point of passage for those who are being slain for God, fellow-initiates with Paul, who was sanctified, well spoken of, and worthy of praise," who mentioned the Ephesians in each of his letters (Ignatius *Eph.* 12.1f.).[54]

Yet the apostle left in Ephesus very few traces that point unambiguously to him.[55] Only *two* sites may be mentioned: the so-called prison of Paul on the hill of Astyages and the grotto on the northern slope of Bülbül Dagh. Reckoned as Paul's prison is a tower that, on the basis of a local Ephesian tradition, bears the name φυλακὴ τοῦ ἀποστόλου Παύλου, or, for short, φυλακή (plate 6).[56] It is part of a fortification built by Lysimachus for the defense of the city in the second decade of the third century B.C. This consisted of a wall about six miles (ten kilometers) long,[57] which boldly crossed the ridges of Panayir Dagh and Bülbül Dagh before turning back toward the harbor and the city along the slope of the hill of Astyages. The so-called Paul's tower is one of forty-eight towers and sixteen (fifteen) gate towers or sally ports, which are found only along the better preserved and well-surveyed part of the wall between the hill of Astyages and the precipitous slope of Tracheia. It is, like all the towers, rectangular, two-storied, and, together with the tower at the harbor, of four-cell design, with an outside door on the east side and three inside doors. On the south side of the tower was found an inscription that reproduces a lease—necessary for the construction of the wall on the site—contracted with Astyagos (?), the owner of the land.[58]

That the tower could have served as a prison in Paul's time cannot be excluded,[59] even if a change from its actual defensive purpose would not exactly have made good sense. The archeological findings do not make the tradition of Paul's imprisonment here impossible, but of course they cannot substantiate it either.

How might the tradition have arisen? Does it go back to a "pious legend" without any real foundation "according to which, in Ephesus, Paul escaped from prison, with the help of an angel, in order to baptize his two disciples, Eubula and Artemilla, and then was able to return unnoticed to the prison"?[60] The "pious legend" in question here is *The Acts of Paul*, which does in fact give an account of Eubula, the wife of a freedman, who was a disciple of Paul, and Artemilla, the wife of a civic official, who was baptized by Paul in the sea. Paul, who was sentenced to fight the beasts, then returned to the prison while the guards slept. But Paul must have been imprisoned, in this version, in the immediate vicinity of the stadium. When the lion with which Paul was supposed to fight "came to the side door of the stadium [where Paul] was imprisoned, he roared loudly . . . [so that Paul] broke off his prayer in terror."[61] No one who is familiar with *The Acts of Paul* would expect to find his prison on the ridge of a hill far from the stadium.

But the local tradition of a Pauline imprisonment in Ephesus must antedate *The Acts of Paul*. It is much more likely that the *Acts* take up an earlier tradition which had its origin in the Pauline letters themselves. In 1 Corinthians 15:32, Paul says that "as the saying goes, he fought with beasts at Ephesus." Even if this fight with wild animals is intended symbolically and not realistically (2 Tm. 4:17), various remarks regarding persecutions and afflictions in 2 Corinthians (2 Cor. 1:8f.) and Romans (Rom. 16:3f.), together with the apostle's statement in Philippians 1:13 that "throughout the whole praetorian guard and among all the rest it has become obvious that I am in prison for the sake of Christ," make it highly probable that Paul was imprisoned in Ephesus.[62]

Unfortunately, it is not possible to say when the tradition of Paul's imprisonment came to be associated topographically with the tower in the Lysimachan city wall. Previous investigations have been unable to trace the origin of the tradition back beyond the seventeenth century. George Wheler's *A Journey into Greece*, which appeared in London in 1682, contains a map on which "St. Paul's Prison" is registered. From that point on, references and descriptions appear in rapid succession in Thomas Smith, Jacques Spoon, Cornelis de Bruyn, Pitton de Tournefort, Hermann van der Horst, and many others up to Ernst Curtius in an 1874 lecture in Berlin.[63]

The lack of earlier reports cannot be explained by the conquest of the city and its fate under Turkish and Ottoman rule. Except for an interval in the third century, reports of the Ephesian church flow fairly continuously. As a place of pilgrimage, the city was held in the highest regard from the fourth century on. The Third Ecumenical Council convened in the Church of the Virgin Mary in 431, and into the fifteenth century reports on Ephesus from pilgrims and other travelers are attested.[64] In 1106-8, the Russian abbot Daniel came to Ephesus. He mentions the holy dust that streamed from the tomb of John on the anniversary of the saint's death; he visited the relics of the three hundred fathers and of St. Alexander, the cave of the Seven Sleepers, the tomb of Mary Magdalene and that of Timothy; and he saw an image of the Mother of God, as well as the robe that John is supposed to have worn.[65] Ramon Montaner writes, in 1304, of miracles at the grave of John and of the healing power of its exudations. Still later the Turks are supposed to have traded relics of John—splinters of the true cross that John had brought to Ephesus, a garment that Mary made for John, and an autograph copy of John's apocalypse—to Ticinius Zacarius, a Latin prince from Western Asia Minor, for grain.[66] There is, then, no dearth of reports. They are all alike too in the sense that their interest is directed to saints' graves and relics. In relation to Paul, however, nothing of either sort can be produced. Perhaps, then, it is not so strange that the tradition of a Pauline imprisonment should only surface again among travelers of the seventeenth and eighteenth centuries who were led not only by religious but also by archeological and historical interests and who, in visiting Ephesus, did not limit themselves to the basilica of St. John on the Ayasoluk Hill and the region of the Seven Sleepers but also went on into the abandoned parts of the ancient city.

The second place in which a recollection of Paul has survived is a grotto on the northern slope of Bülbül Dagh, in which graffiti concerning Paul are preserved. Unfortunately, the descriptions of the venerated site are inconsistent, even in the most recent publications. In one case, we are supposedly dealing with a passage sixty-five feet (twenty meters) deep which leads to a rectangular room with recesses, on the walls of which "*innumerable* appeals to Paul are etched."[67] In other accounts, it is a matter of a cave converted at an early date to a Christian place of worship, in which, "besides appeals to God, *three* to the blessed Paul ('Paul, help thy servant!')" are scratched on the walls (plate 7).[68]

In addition to the well-known great sanctuaries of the Church of the Virgin Mary, the Church of St. John, and the cave of the Seven Sleepers, several smaller constructions, or rather conversions of pagan structures, which would have been used for purposes of worship in Christian times, have been discovered.[69] There is no need to deal with them in detail here, since as yet no Pauline tradition has been linked to them. A vague connection with the apostle would have been established if a circular building on the street leading to the Magnesian gate, which was transformed into a church by adding a small apse on the east and a narthex on the west, had actually been the grave of the evangelist Luke and not rather a Greek polyandrion, a hero or family tomb.[70] More certain, by contrast, is the grave of Timothy, "the disciple of the master, Paul," as the archdeacon Theodosius expressly notes; Theodosius visited Ephesus between 518 and 530 on his pilgrimage to the Holy Land.[71] The emperor Constantius had the relics of the saint transferred to Constantinople in 356, it is true; but enough remains may have been left behind that visits to and veneration of the grave on Panayir Dagh could have continued.[72] Finally, Paul is recalled by a bronze Byzantine cross from the tenth century, on which are engraved representations of Christ, Mary, angels, and saints. It was found in Ephesus; Paul holds a book in his hands and, in addition to the typically Pauline physiognomy, is identified by the caption Ο ΑΓΙΟΣ ΠΑΥΛΟΣ.[73] It is possible that the four-column monument on the Arcadian Boulevard (named after the Emperor Arcadius), leading from the harbor to the great theater, held a statue of Paul, either on top of a column or simply in one of the many niches in the foundation, but this cannot be proved.[74]

The yield seems scanty, perhaps, considering the long and intensive activity of the apostle in this city. One must remember, however, that the streams of the Pauline and Johannine theological traditions cross in Ephesus. Referring to Paul's word to Timothy,

"You know that all in the province of Asia turned away from us" (2 Tm. 1:15), some exegetes speculate that the Pauline influence was thoroughly displaced by the Johannine tendency.[75] Ignatius of Antioch, Polycarp of Smyrna, and the Pastorals, all of which clearly attest the unbroken authority of Paul in the early second century precisely for the area of Asia Minor,[76] run counter to any overestimate of this displacement hypothesis. But this point does not alter the fact that in popular piety the glamor of John, of the Seven Sleepers, and later of the mother of God eclipsed the remembrance of Paul. That the archeological finds are not clearer and that the lecture hall of Tyrannos, for example, has not as yet been found need occasion no surprise. There is also still no trace of the important Jewish synagogue, which was certainly present.[77]

Corinth. Corinth, since 27 B.C. the capital of the Roman province of Achaia, is, after Ephesus, the city in which Paul worked the longest. He spent many months (Acts 18:11) there in his concern with the Corinthian community, which would continue to cause him much care even after his departure. At first, Paul worked as a tentmaker and lived in the house of Aquila and his wife Priscilla, who, as Christians, had probably already been forced to leave Rome because of Claudius' edict. They later accompanied the apostle to Ephesus (Acts 18:2f.,18).[78] As usual, Paul taught first in the synagogue. When Silas and Timothy arrived with monetary support from Macedonia, Paul was able to devote himself entirely to preaching. After controversies with the Jews, he shifted his activity to the house of a "God-fearer," Titius Justus (Acts 18:5-7). The congregation grew rapidly and, in increasing measure, aroused the animosity of the Jews. Finally, they hauled Paul before the tribunal of Gallio, who was proconsul of Achaia in 50-51.[79] But Gallio declined to become involved in an intra-Jewish dispute over "words and names and your law" (Acts 18:15), with the result that Paul and the congregation remained undisturbed. Their contacts were not broken when he departed. With a whole bundle of letters and with personal visits, Paul had to intervene to protect the congregation from schisms and to answer questions in immediate dispute.[80]

The result of all his pains was an expansive, lively, but easily excited congregation, about which reports do not break off even after the apostle's death.[81] Around 96, the Roman community praises the faithful in Corinth for their faith, their piety, their hospitality, and their knowledge, before disputes again broke out among them.[82] Around 150-60, Hegesippus commends "the church in Corinth," which, he says, "remained in the true doctrine until Primus was the bishop of Corinth. On my journey to Rome, I met the Corinthians and spent several days with them, during which we rejoiced together in the true faith."[83] And even if the so-called Second Letter of Clement does not point to Corinth,[84] Bishop Soter of Rome did send a charitable gift with an accompanying letter to the Corinthians around 166-74.[85] At approximately the same time, they had in Dionysius a highly respected individual at the head of their community.[86] Around the turn of the third century and slightly later, Tertullian and Origen speak positively of the Corinthian congregation.[87] In the following centuries, the city had repeatedly to endure the troubles of war and earthquakes, and it was unable to maintain its economic, political, and ecclesiastical prominence in the long run.[88] But continuity with its apostolic beginnings was never totally lost. What recollections of Paul remained alive in Corinth?

Naturally, the place where Aquila and Priscilla's workshop stood is no longer known.[89] Nor is that of the dwelling of Titius Justus, "which was next door to the synagogue" (Acts 18:7). Further, the site of the great Jewish synagogue can no longer be identified. Neither a stone inscription, [ΣΥΝΑ]ΓΩΓΗ ΕΒΡ[ΑΙΩΝ], nor a marble fragment with a menorah and palm branch from the fifth century, both of which were found in the theater, can be fixed as to place of origin.[90]

In relation to Paul, one can perhaps mention an oblong limestone block, which was used in the repair of the pavement of a small square located at the north end of the street that runs behind the theater (plate 8). The inscription, which is cut off on the left side, contains the following letters, deeply chiseled and probably originally filled in with bronze:

ERASTVS PRO AED

S P STRAVIT

The most plausible reading is: "Erastus pro aedilitate sua pecunia stravit" ("Erastus, in gratitude for his appointment to the aedile-ship, had this pavement laid at his own expense"). That a contribution to the public good should be recorded in an inscription is commonplace, as is the donation of a new surface for a street. What makes the inscription so interesting is that Paul, in his list of greetings in Romans 16:23, mentions a city treasurer (οἰκονόμος τῆς πόλεως) and, in 2 Timothy 4:20, reports that Erastus remained behind in Corinth. Acts 19:22 also mentions an Erastus whom Paul sent ahead with Timothy into Macedonia. If the οἰκονόμος τῆς πόλεως should be identified with the aedile in Corinth or if the city treasurer (= arcarius) should later have risen to the aedileship, it would be entirely possible, chronologically, that the Erastus attested by the inscription is the Erastus mentioned by Paul and that the chance survival of a paving stone unexpectedly calls up the memory of Paul's activity in Corinth.[91] Of course, we can reach no certainty on this point.

Are there also, in addition to such vague connections, places where the recollection of Paul has been consciously and explicitly preserved? Generally, one refers to the bema (plate 9) before which the Jews dragged Paul with the aim of having him condemned by the proconsul, Gallio (Acts 18:12-17). This is identified with a rectangular platform,

> of 49' × 23' (14.90 × 7 m.), which stands on its north front about 7' (2.13 m.) above the level of the agora, while on the south, where the level of the agora is higher, the floors are of approximately equal height. To either side of this platform lie areas of equal size, each of which is bounded by a flight of steps linking the north market to the higher south market. Beyond the steps, again on both sides, there extends a line of Roman shops.[92]

The platform lies approximately in the middle of the market, opposite the place where the Lechaion Road, coming from the harbor, runs through the propylaion to the market. Entry was possible only from the rear, that is, from the south. The platform represents, therefore, a monument that had the form of a podium comparable to the Rostra in the Forum Romanum. It rose more than six and one-half feet (2 m.) above the level of the agora, and its front was smooth, perhaps faced with marble.

The scene is striking and easy to imagine: above, on the platform of the bema, Gallio sits on the judgment seat, surrounded by his attendants; and at his feet, clamoring and gesticulating, are the Jews with Paul in their midst! Unfortunately, the topography of the scene cannot be established beyond question. Certainly βῆμα can designate a rostra-like speakers' platform, but it first of all suggests only a stepped elevation that one can ascend (βαίνειν).[93] The term has no topographical precision. In the history of law too, it is significant that the administration of justice is bound to no particular place but rather to the person of the judge. He does not take up the administration of justice at the place of the bema; instead, the administration of justice occurs wherever he takes his seat. In iconography likewise, no representations are known that locate the function of judgment at a speakers' tribunal. Rather, the judge sits somewhat elevated on the _sella curulis_.[94] It is much more likely that the scene in Acts 18:12–16 took place in one of the judicial basilicas[95] than that it occurred at or in front of the so-called Corinthian bema.[96]

The association of this platform with Paul's experience before Gallio was probably sparked by the fact that the monument later served as the substructure for a small, three-aisled basilica with a triple apse at the east end. Graves in the floor, a beautifully embellished piece of the altar rail, and the few surviving remains of the building make probable a date in the tenth century at the earliest (plate 10).[97] Nevertheless, many want to assume that the place where Paul was accused would have been venerated

> by those who were present at the occasion and by generations of Christians who heard the story told and retold by word of mouth. When finally Christianity triumphed over the old religion, and churches and chapels rose in sundry places to commemorate events in the lives of St. Paul and of the other apostles, what would be more natural than that a church should be erected on the _bema_ itself which was so closely connected with the activities of the renowned missionary?[98]

Whether the tenth-century basilica was dedicated to Paul, whether it had more modest predecessors, or whether enduring memories of the proceedings against Paul at this place led only much later to the building of a church are, at present, simply matters of speculation.[99] Not even the presupposition for these possibilities—"the general tendency of later Christendom to localize references in the Scriptures and to create memorial sites"[100]—can be assumed in the case of Paul; the attestations to Pauline events in monuments from the period of the early church are too weak to support the claim. Only in the present is there a clear-cut connection between Paul and the bema: each year, on June 29, the Archbishop of Corinth conducts a vesper service in the ruins of Old Corinth in remembrance of the accusation of Paul before Gallio.[101] Where Gallio's "judgment seat" (Acts 18:12) was located and when the monument on the south side of the agora was identified with the bema of Acts are, however, questions that remain unanswerable.

Nor has any recollection of Paul been preserved in the archeological remains of the other churches of Old Corinth. A basilica directly against the city wall near the gate leading to Cenchreae, probably in the Craneum quarter mentioned by Pausanias, is held to be an episcopal church.[102] It had three aisles, a narthex, and a triapsal extension on the south that may have served as a burial place.[103] Whether the church was sited "with respect to the Cenchrean Gate through which the apostle Paul entered the city"[104] is more than doubtful; a greatly scaled-down church arose on the same site in the eleventh century, and traces of a third church point to the thirteenth century.[105] A smaller church north of the present-day cemetery of Palaiokorinthos was a memorial of St. Kodratus, who, together with five companions, is supposed to have suffered a martyr's death in Corinth under Decius or Valerian.[106] Additional smaller cultic sites still await careful investigation.[107]

This evidence, meager as it is given the status of Corinth, could be complemented by the churches in the two Corinthian ports of Lechaion and Cenchreae. The church of Lechaion, which was built around 450 in honor of the Corinthian martyr-bishop Leonidas and his companions,[108] ranks by size and by quality of decoration among the most expensive early church buildings in Greece.[109] There is no known Pauline memorial in the church. Unfortunately, there is also no reference to Paul in Cenchreae, the

city that Paul mentions in Romans 16:1 when he commends
"Phoebe, the deaconess of the church in Cenchreae," to the Romans and that also appears in Acts 18:18: "Paul sailed for Syria
together with Priscilla and Aquila. In Cenchreae, he had his head
shaved on account of a vow." Toward the end of the fourth century, a church was built right at the harbor on the foundations of
an Isis shrine that had been reconstructed after the earthquakes of
365 and 375; and this was further taken over and expanded in the
following two centuries.[110]

With regard to other finds, again only a few items have any
bearing on the survival of Pauline traditions in Corinth. Among
the inscriptions in the early Christian cemetery, most of which are
meager and contain only names and dates of the dead, there is one
that belongs to the grave of a certain cattle farmer, Paulos Sitisto-
rios. Whether the name "Paul" has any special significance cannot
be discerned.[111] Of greater interest is a ring found in 1908 on
which a victorious athlete appears with a garland in his right hand.
On either side of the figure the name "PAU LOU" is legible. If one
thinks of the symbol of the athlete in 1 Corinthians 9:24–27, a
connection between the decoration on the ring and the apostle
does not seem impossible.[112]

Anyone who wants to find a more definite remembrance of
Paul must look, as in the case of the bema, to our own time. In
1934 Archbishop Damaskinos laid the cornerstone for the present
cruciform Church of St. Paul in Modern Corinth. The street
across from the cathedral also bears the name of the apostle.[113]

Malta. Paul's stay on the island of Malta was considerably
shorter than in the cities already discussed. After the shipwreck,
he remained on the island for three months before he resumed the
journey to Rome with his escorts (Acts 28:11). Luke says nothing
at all about any conversions or any founding of a church during
this time. And yet Malta is to this day deeply marked by Paul's stay
and strewn with recollections of the apostle. The site of the shipwreck, which tradition has located on the northwest coast, is recalled in the name of St. Paul's Bay and in the bronze statue of Paul
on the tiny isle of Selmunett, which is also called St. Paul's Island.[114] In the small Littoral Church on the bay, the episode of the
snakebite is remembered (Acts 28:3). The church, which was badly

damaged in World War II, is supposed to go back to Byzantine times, to have been destroyed by the Arabs in the ninth century, and to have been rebuilt by Roger I.[115] In the Middle Ages, Maltese soil, *Pauladadum*, was exported to many lands as a cure—through the intercession of St. Paul—for smallpox, fever, and other illnesses. Near the church there is a spring, also adorned with a statue of Paul. A Latin inscription requests that the traveler treat with respect the living water that was given by the shipwrecked Paul to the Maltese.[116]

But it is not only the area around St. Paul's Bay that is stamped with reminders of Paul. In Naxxar, in the San Pawl tat-Targa Church, one thinks of the apostle's preaching; in Rabbat, in a grotto under the Church of Publius, one is reminded of his three-month stay as a prisoner. The adjoining Church of St. Paul memorializes the sermons; and in Mdina, the ancient capital of the island, the cathedral of Paul, which is supposed to be built on the site of the governor's palace, recalls the conversion of Publius and the healing of his father, sick with a fever (Acts 28:7f.). In the present-day capital of Valetta as well, there are two churches of St. Paul: the Anglican cathedral and the St. Paul Shipwreck Collegiate Church.[117]

There are also relics of Paul: in the Church of Publius, a gold arm reliquary that preserves the apostle's right hand and a part of his forearm; in the monastic church of Valetta, another piece of an arm in a silver monstrance and part of the column on which Paul was beheaded; there is even a weeping icon of Paul in a shrine on Saqqajja Square in Mdina.[118] In comparison with other places that Paul visited on his last journey to Rome, Malta has preserved a lively memory of the apostle's winter on the island. Nevertheless, it cannot be claimed that any of the Maltese memorials of Paul mentioned so far certainly goes back to early Christian times.

More worthy of attention is another Church of St. Paul, which lies within view of St. Paul's Bay on a hill overlooking Bur Marrad and is dedicated to San Pawl Milqi (St. Paul Welcomed). This church too is supposed to call to mind the greeting and friendly reception of the apostle by Publius, the "leading citizen of the island" (Acts 28:7),[119] whom Paul, according to Maltese tradition, baptized and appointed bishop of the island. The church is situated on a plot of land on which, from the late second century and certainly from the early first century B.C. until the time of the Arab invasion, stood a Roman *villa rustica* in the midst of an extensive agricultural operation. Excavations in the 1960s uncovered numerous oil presses, wine presses, washing vats, and storage containers; adjoining the agricultural complex to the south and east are potters' workshops and living quarters partly adorned with wall paintings.[120]

In one of these rooms belonging to the Roman villa, three small churches were built in succession. The last of these, which is still standing today, was erected between 1616 and 1622 by Alouf de Vignacourt.[121] It was preceded, probably in the fifteenth century, by a chapel belonging to a wealthy family, with which was connected a distribution to the poor in honor of St. Paul.[122] The oldest church, which consisted of a nave with a rectangular apse, may have been built after the recapture of Malta by Roger I and the revival of Christianity on the island, perhaps around the middle of the twelfth century.[123]

The floor of the Roman villa, which lies under the churches, was covered with uniformly worked travertine tiles, under which was a network of drainage channels that diverted rainwater to various cisterns. One of the cistern openings is located at a prominent point within the church, approximately at the center of the small apse where it meets the nave. The carefully worked and costly marble sheathing of the opening, along with the fact that this cistern, which also remained open in the time of the Arab occupation of the villa, later became the fixed point for the floor plan of the apsidal church, suggests that this room of the Roman complex, together with its water reservoir, was the point to which was attached the tradition of Paul's stay in Publius' house and of his activity in healing the sick, preaching, and making conversions.[124] The hypothesis is supported by finds that go back to the fourth century and confirm the association of this place with a veneration of Paul in the early Christian period.

We can cite, in the first place, a small flagstone, 6 1/2 × 4 5/16 × 2 3/8 inches (16.5 × 11 × 6 cm.), which may have been an architectural element. Carved on its face is a ship which has a high mast, a lateen sail, and a steering oar and sits up on the indications of rocks.[125] On the right side of the block is a graffito that is difficult to interpret but that may also pertain to the ship/sail context.[126] By good fortune, the image on the left side of the stone is clearer. It depicts a bald-headed man with a tapered beard, clothed in a monk-like tunic and leaning on a T-shaped staff (similar to the staff of an Egyptian abbot, to whom the whole image bears resemblance). Furthermore, traces of a ship can be seen.[127] The location of the image and the scenes accompanying it allow the figure to be interpreted as Paul, and it may have been produced in the first half of the seventh century by a monk who had fled before the Arabs. The ship also suggests by its type the seventh or eighth century.[128]

Underneath the Paul figure is a heavily damaged legend, in which an O, an L, and the symbol ₽ can be discerned with reasonable clarity.[129] It is no longer possible to reconstruct any inscription with certainty from the letters and letter fragments. Since Franz Dölger's study, the ₽ has been interpreted almost exclusively as a sign of fortune or victory that finds its use chiefly against the background of circus and athletic contest (*palma feliciter; palma et laurus*).[130] Only Margherita Guarducci insists, on the basis of the symbol's occurrence on Wall g of the so-called Tropaion of Gaius under St. Peter's in Rome, on reading it as PETRUS.[131] But even if a reference to Peter on Malta cannot be excluded, as an inscription in the catacomb of Paul shows,[132] the interpretation of the symbol as a sign of luck and victory such as one finds elsewhere in the Christian world[133] is more likely. As far as date goes, the legend belongs roughly between 320 and 510. It fits particularly well into Pauline iconography and underscores the theme of the athletic contest, which was not foreign to Paul himself (see 1 Cor. 9:24–27).

For the chronological arrangement of these indications of early veneration of Paul, a few additional finds are of significance. On the outer face of a travertine block just beyond the northeast boundary of the church are several Greek letters that could form the name ΠΑΥΛΥΣ. The letters are very unevenly formed. The Latin spelling (*us* instead of *os*) is very uncommon in Greek, but it is adequately attested. Perhaps Π and Α were written earlier than the other, less well executed letters. The full name could not have been carved out before the fourth or after the seventh or eighth century.[134]

Additional finds of Christian provenance, even if without direct Pauline reference, were made in the area east of the church. One of these is a stone with an engraved fish transected by a trident; an additional trident is carved next to the fish. A symbol of similar design in the monastery of Ain Tamba has been thought to have an anti-Arian, trinitarian significance.[135] Another stone, found not far away in the same area, bears a deeply chiseled cross. The original placement or use of the stone can no longer be determined. Finally, two rhombus-shaped floor tiles were found, one supposedly decorated with a Latin cross, the other supposedly with a fish. Since flooring adorned with crosses was forbidden after Theodosius the Great, the tiles are to be dated in the fourth century.[136]

Even if the dating proposed on the basis of the excavations should not prove exact in every case, a recollection of Paul at this site and dating back to the period before the Arab conquest of the island should be well enough established. The proximity of the area to the site of the shipwreck in the region of St. Paul's Bay suggests identification with the estate of Publius. It was large enough, here and in the nearby farmsteads that may also have belonged to Publius (Luke speaks of the χωρία τῷ πρώτῳ τῆς νήσου [Acts 28:7]), to accommodate Paul and the other 275 victims of the shipwreck (see Acts 27:37) for three days.

This connection would lose probability, however, if the shipwreck occurred not in the region of St. Paul's Bay—as assumed to this point—but farther north in the area of Mellieha Bay. This has recently been asserted by Nicolaus Heutger with the argument that only there would Luke's expression διθάλασσος (Acts 27:41) fit the topographical setting. The term does not mean "shoal," "channel," or "sandbank," as translations of embarrassment usually say, but literally "at two seas"—which happens when, next to the bay as the first sea, the flooding of the lower-lying area west of the beach and of the somewhat raised shore road forms a second sea.[137] The excavations at St. Pawl Milqi, which would appear to support St. Paul's Bay rather than Mellieha Bay as the place of the catastrophe, are simply not mentioned by Heutger.

Apart from the finds at St. Pawl Milqi, the only early Christian iconography that even slightly reflects the Maltese events reported in Acts is found outside Malta. There are the Paul scenes on the right half of the ivory diptych in the Museo Bargello in Florence, from the end of the fourth century,[138] and the frescoes with the shipwreck and the viper in the nave of S. Paolo fuori le mura in Rome, most probably from the fifth century to judge by Cavallini's copies.[139] One might also mention the association of the two scenes of Peter sinking and Paul's shipwreck in the mosaics in the triclinium of Leo III. The inscription, however, does not mention Malta specifically but rather the rescue of Paul from three shipwrecks. It is certain that the sinking ship in the Chapel of the Sacraments in the catacomb of San Callisto (A 2) in Rome has no relation to Malta.[140]

For Henri Leclercq it is clear that Paul, despite his theological genius and the extraordinary vitality of his apostolic activity, did not stir people's imagination and devotion to any great degree.[141] Does this judgment hold true, though, when considered in the light of the various ways in which the veneration of a saint could find expression in early Christianity: through the dedication of a church or an altar, through feasts in remembrance of individual moments or deeds in a person's life, through relics and images, through pilgrimages to holy places, through brotherhoods and patron saints as well as through the giving of baptismal names?[142] On the basis of an investigation as narrow in focus as this one, we can expect only a restricted answer. At the same time, the answer will be subjectively colored, since the relation that will obtain between a person's historical significance and the tangible memorials of that person is not something determined according to objective criteria.

With regard to Paul, one could point to the adverse circumstances that were arrayed against an early Christian remembrance of the apostle, and in that light, one could reckon the traditions that actually existed as remarkably sweeping. That other, concurrent traditions were localized in Jerusalem is quite understandable, as is the observation that local saints played a greater role than Paul on Cyprus, in Crete, or in Thessalonica. The fact that important areas of the Pauline mission later became lands without Christianity also had a negative effect. Considered in this light, the memory of Paul, although much reduced in archeological attestations and in local recollections, does not seem so meager.

One could reach a different judgment, however, if one compared the interest in Paul with the affection for others in the early Christian period. In early Christian iconography, for example, Paul clearly trailed Peter, but he also trailed Thecla, his disciple in the apocryphal Acts.[143] In the development of legends and customs, Paul does not by any means compete with the popular veneration given to a St. Martin or a St. Nicholas. But the person and work of the great Apostle to the Gentiles do stand in the bright light of history as compared with the historical darkness surrounding many greatly revered saints. Perhaps this very difference has contributed to the disproportion. Historically fixed personalities provide far less of an opening for folk piety than do unknown holy benefactors who impose no restricting historical facts on the imaginative fantasy of the faithful.[144] Nor were Paul's letters adapted to effective popular retelling. Their portrayal of apostolic sufferings did not lend itself to folkloristic transposition into gripping scenes in the arena such as the accounts in the *Acts of Thecla*.[145] Only a more "intellectual" order such as the Dominicans could turn to Paul in a deeper way and take him as the model of the specifically apostolic task.[146]

These limited observations—which partially neutralize each other—should not be hardened into any final general verdict; that is neither possible nor necessary. For it is not the measure of the veneration of Paul, not the number of past or present memorial sites, that determines his significance for the church but rather the effect of his theology. His word of the cross and his witness to the resurrection must continue to live. That the message is more important than the person of the messenger was the apostle's own conviction. He was ready to step aside, "if only in every way Christ is preached" (Phil. 1:18).

Plate 1. Damascus, church at the "House of Ananias" (photograph, Th. Sternberg).

Plate 2. Crete, Fair Havens, cave and church of Paul (photograph, E. Dassmann).

Plate 3. Philippi, "Paul's Prison," entrance (photograph, D. Korol).

Plate 4. Philippi, "Paul's Prison," inner room (photograph, D. Korol).

Plate 5.
Philippi, Octagon, floor mosaic (photograph, E. Dassmann).

Plate 6.
Ephesus, "Paul's Prison" on the Hill of Astyages (photograph, V. Furnish).

Plate 7.
Ephesus, cave corridor with Pauline inscription on Bülbül Dagh (photograph, L. Hopfgartner).

Plate 8. Corinth, pavement stone with Erastus inscription (photograph, V. Furnish).

Plate 9. Corinth, Bema (photograph, E. Dassmann).

Plate 10. Corinth, Bema church, tenth century, architectural remains (photograph, E. Dassmann).

Notes

THE END OF THE LINE:
PAUL IN THE CANONICAL BOOK OF ACTS

I would like to express my heartfelt thanks to Professor David Rensberger, who responded to my essay at the "Paul and the Legacies of Paul" conference, and to the participants in the conference seminar in which the essay was discussed.

1. There is a massive literature on what is usually termed Luke's "Paulusbild." For surveys of the literature, see Christoph Burchard, "Paulus in der Apostelgeschichte," *Theologische Literaturzeitung* 100 (1975): 881–95; François Bovon, *Luc le théologien: Vingt-cinq ans de recherches (1950–1975)*, Le Monde de la Bible (Neuchatel and Paris, 1978), 370–78; Paul-Gerhard Müller, "Der 'Paulinismus' in der Apostelgeschichte: Ein forschungsgeschichtlicher Überblick," in *Paulus in den neutestamentlichen Spätschriften: Zur Paulusrezeption im Neuen Testament*, ed. Karl Kertelge, Quaestiones Disputatae 89 (Freiburg, Basel, and Vienna, 1981), 157–201; Eckhard Plümacher, "Acta-Forschung 1974–1982 (Fortsetzung und Schluss)," *Theologische Rundschau* 49 (1984): 153–58.

2. I cite the English version of Philip Vielhauer's essay published in *Studies in Luke-Acts: Essays Presented in Honor of Paul Schubert*, ed. Leander E. Keck and J. Louis Martyn (Nashville and New York, 1966), 33–50 (reprinted from *Perkins School of Theology Journal* 17 [Fall 1963]: 5–17); for the German original, see *Evangelische Theologie* 10 (1950/51): 1–15 (reprinted in Vielhauer's *Aufsätze zum Neuen Testament*, Theologische Bucherei 31 [Munich, 1965], 9–27).

    For the German original of Georg Kümmel's essay, see *Zeitschrift für die neutestamentlich Wissenschaft* 63 (1972): 149–65 (reprinted in *Das Lukas-Evangelium: Die redaktions- und kompositionsgeschichtliche Forschung*, ed. Georg Braumann, Wege der Forschung 280 [Darmstadt, 1974], 416–36, and in Kümmel, *Heilsgeschehen und Geschichte*, vol. 2: *Gesammelte Aufsätze 1965–1977*, ed. Erich Grässer and Otto Merk, Marburger theologische Studien 16 [Marburg, 1978], 87–100); the French version is in *Ephemerides theologicae lovanienses* 46 (1970): 265–81, and the English in *Andover Newton Quarterly* 16 (1975): 131–45. See also Edouard Schweizer, "Plädoyer der Verteidigung in Sachen: Moderne Theologie versus Lukas," *Theologische Literaturzeitung* 105 (1980): 241–52; Martin Rese, "Neuere Lukas-Arbeiten: Bemerkungen zur gegenwärtigen Forschungslage," *Theologische Literaturzeitung* 106 (1981): 227.

3. The most optimistic of major recent scholars seems to be Jacob Jervell. See his essay, "Paul in the Acts of the Apostles: Tradition, History,

Theology," in *Les Actes des Apôtres: Traditions, rédaction, théologie*, ed. Jacob Kremer, Bibliotheca ephemeridum theologicarum lovaniensum 48 (Gembloux, 1979), 297–306 (reprinted in Jervell, *The Unknown Paul: Essays on Luke-Acts and Early Christian History* [Minneapolis, 1984], 68–76). Jervell here defends the following thesis:

> The Lukan Paul, the picture of Paul in Acts, is a comple-
> tion, a filling up of the Pauline one, so that in order to get at
> the historical Paul, we cannot do without Acts and Luke.
> . . . We could say regarding the Lukan Paul that that
> which lies in the shadow in Paul's letters Luke has placed in
> the sun in Acts (Jervell, 300).

For my most serious disagreement with Jervell on the theme discussed in this essay, see n. 38 below.

4. See Plümacher, 155 (with bibliography).

5. For a typical example, see Morna D. Hooker and Stephen G. Wilson, eds., *Paul and Paulinism: Essays in Honour of C. K. Barrett* (London, 1982). Apart from the article by Jacques Dupont, there is virtually no reference to Acts in this volume (see the index of passages cited, p. 389); and Dupont's own works on Acts are not cited by anyone but himself (see p. 400). Similarly Gerd Luedemann, in *Paul, Apostle to the Gentiles: Studies in Chronology* (Philadelphia, 1979), begins his section on "The Absolute Priority of Paul's own Witness for a Chronology of Paul" with the observation that, since Vielhauer (and, we would add, Dibelius), "research has generally refrained from using any of Paul's speeches in Acts for the presentation of Paul's theology" (21); see also the first chapter of Robert Jewett's *A Chronology of Paul's Life* (Philadelphia, 1979), which ends with a similar section on the priority of evidence from Paul himself.

6. Note that Vielhauer, at the outset of his article, observes that the "question as to the Paulinism of Acts is at the same time the question as to a *possible* theology of Luke himself" (Vielhauer, 33; emphasis added). See also n. 7 below.

7. Hans Conzelmann, *Die Mitte der Zeit: Studien zur Theologie des Lukas*, Beiträge zur historische Theologie 17 (Tübingen, 1954; 3d ed., 1960); for Conzelmann's sense that he—along with Dibelius—is engaging in something new in contrast to the scholarly tradition of asking only whether Acts is historically trustworthy, see pp. 4–5 of the third edition. His work appeared in English as *The Theology of St. Luke*, trans. Geoffrey Buswell (London, 1960). Martin Dibelius, *Aufsätze zur Apostelgeschichte*, ed. Heinrich Greeven, Forschungen zur Religion und Literatur des Alten und Neuen Testaments N.F. 42 (Göttingen, 1951); English translation: *Studies in the Acts of the Apostles*, ed. Heinrich Greeven, trans. Mary Ling (London, 1956).

8. For Germany, see Walther Eltester, "Lukas und Paulus," in *Eranion: Festschrift für Hildebrecht Hommel*, ed. Jürgen Kroymann (Tübingen, 1961), 1; for the Anglo-Saxon world, see n. 11 below.

9. These commentaries first appeared in 1956 and 1963 respectively. I cite from Ernst Haenchen, *Die Apostelgeschichte*, 7th (posthumous) ed. (Göttingen, 1977), and Hans Conzelmann, *Die Apostelgeschichte*, Handbuch zum Neuen Testament 7, 2d ed. (Tübingen, 1972). For a revised English edition of Haenchen's fifth (1965) edition, see *The Acts of the Apostles: A Commentary*, trans. Bernard Noble and Gerald Shinn (Oxford, 1971). As a sign of the times note that, in 1961, Eltester more or less objected that the third (1959) edition of Haenchen's commentary had restored some of the historical perspective that the first edition, devoted to *Kompositionsforschung*, had lacked (Eltester, 6, n. 10a). For a roughly contemporary appreciation of the abandonment of the quest for Luke's sources and a preference for the recognition of Luke as author and theologian, see also C. K. Barrett, *Luke the Historian in Recent Study* (London, 1961), 51.

10. A historian might well share the complaints voiced by Martin Hengel; see especially his *Zur urchristlichen Geschichtsschreibung* (Stuttgart, 1979); English translation: *Acts and the History of Earliest Christianity*, trans. John Bowden (London, 1979). Such complaints are echoed frequently: see, e.g., Victor E. Vine, "The Purpose and Date of Acts," *Expository Times* 96 (1984/85): 47. Contrary to Plümacher's expectations (Plümacher, 7), they are not limited to the Anglo-Saxon world: see Rese, 227–28.

11. See Kremer, ed., *Les Actes des Apôtres* (note the subtitle given in n. 3 above) and compare that work with the earlier approach to Acts in Fredrick J. Foakes Jackson and Kirsopp Lake, eds., *The Beginnings of Christianity*, Part 1: *The Acts of the Apostles*, 5 vols. (1920–33; reprint: Grand Rapids, Mich., 1966). For the aim of the latter work, see in particular the preface to the first volume.

12. For the presumption that the prologue to Luke applies to both volumes of Luke-Acts, see n. 105 below. On *kathēxes*, see Joseph A. Fitzmyer, *The Gospel According to Luke*, 2 vols., Anchor Bible 28, 28A (Garden City, N.Y., 1981), 1:298–99.

13. See Jacques Dupont, *Études sur les Actes des Apôtres*, Lectio divina 45 (Paris, 1967), 396–97.

14. See Conzelmann, *Apostelgeschichte*, 75; Ernst Haenchen, *Gott und Mensch: Gesammelte Aufsätze* (Tübingen, 1965), 219–20; Stephen G. Wilson, *The Gentiles and the Gentile Mission in Luke-Acts*, Society for New Testament Studies Monograph Series 23 (Cambridge, 1973), 151–52.

15. Luke's dogged refusal to report Galilean appearances of the risen Jesus is most probably to be explained in the same way; see Gerhard Lohfink,

Die Himmelfahrt Jesu: Untersuchungen zu den Himmelfahrts- und Erhö-hungstexten bei Lukas, Studien zum Alten und Neuen Testament 26 (Munich, 1971), 262–65; also Dupont, 397, n. 30.

16. See Acts 2:5, 9–11, 5:16. On the identity of the crowd described in Acts 2, see my "Residents and Exiles, Jerusalemites and Judeans (Acts 7,4; 2,5.14): On Stephen, Pentecost and the Structure of Acts," forthcoming in my *Studies on the Jewish Background of Early Christianity* (Leiden).

17. On this theme in Stephen's speech, see Bo Reicke, *Glaube und Leben der Urgemeinde: Bemerkungen zu Apg. 1–7,* Abhandlungen zur Theologie des Alten und Neuen Testaments 32 (Zurich, 1957), 129–61; W. D. Davies, *The Gospel and the Land: Early Christianity and Jewish Territorial Doctrine* (Berkeley, Los Angeles, and London, 1974), 267–73; and my essay listed in the preceding note. On the point that Luke's interest in the temple ends following Stephen's speech, see Bruno Corsani, "Gerusalemme nell' opera lucana," in *Gerusalemme: Atti della XXVI Settimana Biblica in onore di Carlo Maria Martini* (Brescia, 1982), 25–26.

18. I assume, as is usual, that the crowd in Acts 2 is to be envisioned as totally Jewish. I doubt that the story was originally meant even to fore-shadow a gentile mission; again see my essay cited above.

19. For the term *Zwischenbereich,* see Gerhard Schneider, *Lukas, Theologe der Heilsgeschichte: Aufsätze zum lukanischen Doppelwerk,* Bonner Bib-lische Beiträge 59 (Königstein/Ts. and Bonn, 1985), 233–34. On the Samaritans in particular, see Lk. 17:18 (ἀλλογενὴς) and Jacob Jervell, *Luke and the People of God: A New Look at Luke-Acts* (Minneapolis, 1972), 124; on the lack of clarity regarding the ethnic identity of the Ethiopian, see Haenchen, *Apostelgeschichte,* 303–4, and Wilson, 171–72.

20. That is, the upshot of Acts 15 is that Jewish law is henceforth to be considered a matter only of Jewish custom (*ethos*), not divine mandate, and is therefore not to be required of gentile Christians—any more than Italian Catholics would demand of French Catholics that they speak Italian or eat pasta. On this point, see my "The Futility of Preaching Moses (Acts 15,21)," *Biblica* 67 (1986): 280 (especially n. 26).

21. On the last verse, see Dupont, 217–41. For the usual assumptions that the emphatic nature of Paul's claim of independence in Galatians pre-cludes other visits and that the visit of Gal. 2 is identical with that of Acts 15 (at least), see the next note.

22. For the classic English-language defense of this solution, see Kirsopp Lake, "The Apostolic Conference of Jerusalem," in Foakes Jackson and Lake, eds., *Beginnings of Christianity,* 5:199–204. For some more recent views and literature, see Paul J. Achtemeier, "An Elusive Unity: Paul, Acts, and the Early Church," *Catholic Biblical Quarterly* 48 (1986): 3, n. 3. This is not the place to argue the matter in detail, but I would note that Achtemeier cites John Knox's objection to the equation of the visit of Gal. 2:1–10 with that of Acts 15, viz., "the report in Acts 15 is placed too early in Paul's career" (see Knox's *Chapters in a Life of Paul*

[New York and Nashville, 1950], 67). Knox's theory, however, requires him to suppose that in Gal. 1:21, where Paul says that between his two visits he had been in Syria and Cilicia, Paul omits reference to many other places he had traveled through: Galatia, Asia, Macedonia, and Greece (see Knox, 78–79). Why would Paul do this? Consider, in particular, that the farther away Paul put himself in this part of his narrative, the better it would be for his claim of independence from Jerusalem! Is it not simpler to assume (1) that the fourteen (or eleven; see below, n. 29) years between the visits, spent in "Syria and Cilicia," correspond to the reports in Acts 9:30 and 10:25, (2) that those years were followed by the apostolic conference (as explicitly in Galatians and as I will argue below for Acts), and (3) that the work in Asia and beyond came thereafter?

23. "Cilicia" refers to Paul's stay in Tarsus (Acts 9:30; 11:25; cf. 15:41).

24. The conference would then be a response more to the Hellenists' evangelizing of Gentiles—which is reported in Acts 11 just prior to the report of the famine visit—than to Paul's labors. A similar effort on Luke's part is evident in Acts 28: although Luke attempts to portray Paul as the founder of the Christian community in Rome, the truth nevertheless "leaks" out (28:15); see Haenchen, *Apostelgeschichte*, 113, 688. For the Hellenists as missionaries to the Gentiles, see Martin Hengel, *Between Jesus and Paul: Studies in the Earliest History of Christianity*, trans. John Bowden (London, 1983), 48–64, especially 54–58.

25. See Karl Löning, *Die Salustradition in der Apostelgeschichte*, Neutestamentliche Abhandlungen N.F. 9 (Münster, 1973), 19–21; Stanislas Dockx, *Chronologies néotestamentaires et vie de l'église primitive: Recherches exégétiques* (Paris and Gembloux, 1976), 195; Andreas Lindemann, *Paulus im ältesten Christentum: Das Bild des Apostels und die Rezeption der paulinischen Theologie in der frühchristlichen Literatur bis Marcion*, Beiträge zur historischen Theologie 58 (Tübingen, 1979), 51–52. Dibelius would exclude 8:3, but his footnote offers no justification (Dibelius, 175, n. 1). See also below, n. 27.

26. See n. 52 below.

27. As for 8:3, it is either redactional (sandwiched as it is between two discrete narratives; see n. 25 above) or out of place. Note the extreme vagueness of Luke's statements about Paul's persecution of the church; see on this point, Philippe H. Menoud, *Jésus-Christ et la foi: Recherches néotestamentaires*, Bibliothèque théologique (Neuchâtel and Paris, 1975), 42–43.

28. See Dockx, 189–94; Paul Gaechter, *Petrus und seine Zeit: Neutestamentliche Studien* (Innsbruck, Vienna, and Munich, 1958), 84–93. In my forthcoming volume (in Hebrew) on *Agrippa I: The Last King of Judaea* (Jerusalem), I have suggested a few corrections in details, but they do not affect the argument here. For the date of Pilate's suspension from office (winter or early spring of 37?), see my "Pontius Pilate's

Suspension from Office: Chronology and Sources" (in Hebrew), *Tarbiz*
51 (1981/82): 383–98.

29. For exegesis of Gal. 1:6–2:14, see Luedemann, 44–79; on the question of
"14 plus 3" or "14 including 3," see especially 61–64; Dockx dates Paul's
conversion to the summer of 35 at the latest (Dockx, 194); Luedemann,
to 30 or 33 (Luedemann, 162, 171); Jewett, to October of 34 at the latest
(Jewett, 29–30).

30. I have discussed this matter in greater detail, with bibliography, in the
monograph mentioned in n. 28 above. On the negative associations of
"Herod," see, e.g., Mt. 2 (Herod the Great); Lk. 3:19–20, 9:7–9, 13:31;
Acts 4:27–28 (Herod Antipas); Mk. 6:21–28 (Herodias and her daughter).
But in contrast to the literary evidence, note that the use of "Herod"
for Agrippa I seems now to be evidenced by a coin—which perhaps
makes Acts 12 a little less strange; see Ya'akov Meshorer, *Ancient Jewish
Coinage*, 2 vols. (Dix Hills, N.Y., 1982), 2:57.

31. One such is the case discussed in my article on Pilate's suspension from
office (n. 28 above).

32. Karl Löning is surprisingly misleading when he notes that in Acts
13:38 "wird *erstmals* in der Apg paulinisierend von Rechtfertigung
(δικαιωθῆναι) gesprochen" ("Paulinismus in der Apostelgeschichte," in
Kertelge, ed., *Paulus in den neutestamentlichen Spätschriften*, 226 [em-
phasis added]; see also 231, where Löning's conclusions include the
following: "Als paulinisches Theologoumenon beurteilt Lukas die im
übrigen von allen urchristlichen Autoritäten getragene Lehre von der
Rechtfertigung aus Glauben." Acts 13:38f. is the *only* such occasion!
Similarly Lindemann is none too convincing, although more accurate,
when he emphasizes that "durch 13,38f ist Paulus ein für allemal als
Theologe der Rechtfertigung vorgestellt" (Lindemann, 59). Rather, as
students of Luke-Acts in general (especially since the appearance of
Robert Morgenthaler, *Die lukanische Geschichtsschreibung als Zeug-
nis: Gestalt und Gehalt der Kunst des Lukas*, 2 vols., Abhandlungen zur
Theologie des Alten und Neuen Testaments 14–15 [Zurich, 1949]) and
of Luke's Paul in particular (Acts 9, 22, 26!) must often remember, it is
not Luke's way to say important things only once. On the interpretation of Acts 13:38–39, see below, n. 35, and p. 21.

33. See Acts 7:53, 17:32, 19:28, 22:22, 23:7, 26:24; Dibelius, 66, 138; Bertil
Gärtner, *The Areopagus Speech and Natural Revelation*, trans. Carolyn
H. King, Acta seminarii neotestamentici upsaliensis 21 (Uppsala, 1955),
49–50. See also Löning, who emphasizes that the speakers in Acts "nicht
primär als Theologen, sondern als Figuren der Heilsgeschichte verbal
handelnd in Erscheinung treten" ("Paulinismus," 210).

34. For Paul's miracles in Acts, see 13:6–12, 14:8–18, 16:16–24, 19:12, 20:7–
12, 28:7–10. See also Jervell, *The Unknown Paul*, 77–95; Susan Marie
Praeder, "Miracle Worker and Missionary: Paul in the Acts of the Apostles," *SBL 1983 Seminar Papers*, ed. Kent H. Richards (Chico, Calif.,

1983), 107-29. On miracle stories in Acts in general, see Frans Neirynck, "The Miracle Stories in the Acts of the Apostles: An Introduction," in Kremer, ed., *Les Actes des Apôtres,* 169-213.

35. On the interpretation of these verses in Acts 15, see my "Futility of Preaching Moses," 276-81. The use of the second person plural in 13:38 apparently indicates that the point is not that "works" (as Paul would say) cannot do something, but rather that people could not. This understanding is shared by Jervell, *Luke and the People of God,* 151, n. 55, and is too lightly rejected by Heikki Räisänen, *Paul and the Law,* Wissenschaftliche Untersuchungen zum Neuen Testament 29 (Tübingen, 1983), 215 (Räisänen seems to overlook the fact that Paul is here speaking to non-Christian Jews). It is confirmed by the passages of Acts 15 listed in the text; for their interconnection, see also Löning, "Paulinismus," 226-27.

36. On the negative connotation of "works" and the contrast with "faith" in Paul's epistles, see Roman Heiligenthal, *"ergon,"* in *Exegetisches Wörterbuch zum Neuen Testament,* ed. Horst Balz and Gerhard Schneider, 3 vols. (Stuttgart, 1980-83), 2:126-27.

37. Note that Luke curiously distinguishes Caesarea from Judaea (12:20, 21:10), although Caesarea was in fact the province's capital. Although this may reflect some pattern of common parlance (cf. Josephus *Ant.* 19.351; Acts 15:23: "Antioch and Syria"; and the common "Alexandria and Egypt"), it seems instead to reflect an ethnic understanding of Judaea as "the land of the Jews" (see especially 10:39 and 26:20 where "country of Judaea" stands in contrast to "Gentiles"). See also Martin Hengel, "Der Historiker Lukas und die Geographie Palästinas in der Apostelgeschichte," *Zeitschrift des Deutschen Palästina-Vereins* 99 (1983): 151, 167-68.

38. This is a major point. Jervell argues that Luke's main theme with regard to Paul is "Paul the Jew" and notes that in Acts, Paul is predominantly portrayed as preaching in the synagogues: "Paul's preaching to Gentiles is within the composition of Acts an exception to the rule" (*The Unknown Paul,* 71). This is true, but it misses the point, which is that the book ends differently: with Paul, in God's name, unambivalently rejecting the Jews. See rather Haenchen, *Apostelgeschichte,* 663: "Auf eine Bekehrung der Juden hoffte Lukas nicht mehr. Die Stunde der Bekehrung, die ihnen in Gottes Heilsplan gewährt war, hatten sie nicht genutzt, und nun ist es— nach demselben Heilsplan Gottes—zu spät für sie . . . " So too many others, including Löning, "Paulinismus," 219, n. 44: "Dass die Verstockung eines Teils der Juden ein heilsgeschichtliches Interim zur Rettung der Heiden darstellt, wird bei Lukas als Vorstellung prinzipiell aufgegeben"; also Jürgen Roloff, "Die Paulus-Darstellung des Lukas: Ihre geschichtlichen Voraussetzungen und ihr theologisches Ziel," *Evangelische Theologie* 39 (1979): 526: "Jerusalem hat durch Gottes Setzung aufgehört, Ort des Heils zu sein . . . " Klaus Obermeier, "Die Gestalt des Paulus in der lukanischen Verkündigung: Das Paulusbild der Apostelgeschichte" (diss., Bonn,

1975) summarizes his thesis as one that "den Ubergang der christlichen
Mission von der Juden zu den Heiden, wie er in den radaktionelle Stellen
13,45–49; 18,6; 28,25–28 dem Paul zugeschrieben wird, als die zentrale
Aussage ansieht, von der 'alles' gedeutet werden muss (und kann!) . . . "
(266). On the significance of endings, and the end of Acts in particular, see
especially Joseph B. Tyson, "The Jewish Public in Luke-Acts," *New Testament Studies* 30 (1984): 582.

> Endings not only conclude stories, but they also resolve
> tensions that were developed in the body. They tell how
> the story turned out . . . it is the end of the story that
> is the most impressive. The final words are likely to be a
> distillation of the author's controlling concept. The Jewish
> people has heard but rejected the gospel. Thus the failed
> mission to the Jews is terminated in favour of the mission
> to the Gentiles.

See also below, nn. 76, 80, 89, 92.

39. On the causal relationship between persecution and expansion of the
mission, see B. Dehandshutter, "La persecution des chrétiens dans les
Actes des Apôtres," in Kremer, ed., *Les Actes des Apôtres*, 541–46. In
responding to my paper at the "Paul and the Legacies of Paul" conference, David Rensberger noted that Acts presents the turn to the Gentiles as the fulfillment of prophecy. I would suggest, however, that such
language as "this corresponds to" (15:15) and "well spoke" (28:25) indicates that Luke saw here only the application of apposite verses. As
13:40–41 shows, the fulfillment of scriptural prophecy is not always
inevitable, but instead depends on human behavior.

40. See Gerhard Lohfink, "'Meinen Namen zu tragen . . . (Apg 9,15),"
Biblische Zeitschrift 10 (1966): 108–15; Gerhard Schneider, *Die Apostelgeschichte*, 2 vols., Herders theologischer Kommentar zum Neuen Testament 5 (Freiburg, Basel and Vienna, 1980–82), 2:30. Although I have
found no good Aramaic parallel, it does occur to me that in modern
Hebrew, *lisbol lishmi* means "to suffer on my account"; but it is a difficult
phrase and could easily be mistranslated as "to carry my name." Perhaps
some similar phrase could account for the difficulty here.

41. Roloff welcomes this unanimity as an example of a growing consensus
among scholars regarding Paul's role in Acts (see Roloff, 515). For bibliography, see my article cited in the next note. Here I will note only that
one part of this consensus—that Jesus' mandate refers to witnessing
to Gentiles (and not only to Jews abroad)—was questioned by Karl
Heinrich Rengstorf, "The Election of Mathias," in *Current Issues in New
Testament Interpretation: Essays in Honor of Otto A. Piper*, ed. William
Klassen and Graydon F. Snyder (London, 1962), 186–87.

42. See my "The End of the GĒ (Acts 1:8): Beginning or End of the
Christian Vision?" *Journal of Biblical Literature* 105 (1986): 669–76; also

my forthcoming study "Residents and Exiles," which develops some of the implications of this thesis. Rensberger, in his response to my paper, noted the failure of Acts to report missionizing in Galilee; I would suggest that the summary statement in 9:31 is meant to indicate the fulfillment of the mandate of 1:8.

43. This is a classic sectarian approach; compare, for example, the Pharisees' versions of their breaks with the Hasmoneans (Josephus *Ant.* 13.289–96; *b. Qidd.* 66a; and see my "Josephus and Nicolaus on the Pharisees," *Journal for the Study of Judaism in the Persian, Hellenistic and Roman Period* 14 [1983]: 158–59) and with the Sadducees (*'Abot R. Nat.* A, 5, translation by Judah Goldin, *The Fathers According to Rabbi Nathan*, Yale Judaica Series 10 [New Haven, 1955], 39).

44. Acts 4:1–2, 5–6, 23, 5:17, 21, 27, 7:1, 9:1, 14 (cf. 22:5, 26:10). Löning has shown that it was Luke who introduced the high priests into his material about Paul, to make him an official agent, just as he also tried to turn the killing of Stephen into a trial and execution (*Salustradition*, 117–20). See, in general, Giuseppe Betori, *Persequitati a causa del Nome: Strutture dei racconti di persecuzione in Atti, 1,12–8,4*, Analecta biblica (Rome, 1981), 63–64.

45. On the Sadducean rejection of resurrection, see Jean Le Moyne, *Les Sadducéens*, Études bibliques (Paris, 1972), 167–75, and n. 66 below. For the typically Sadducean affiliation of the high priesthood, see my "Philo's Priestly Descent," in *Nourished with Peace: Studies in Hellenistic Judaism in Memory of Samuel Sandmel*, ed. Frederick E. Greenspahn et al. (Chico, Calif., 1984), 167–69.

46. See Acts 2:47, 3:9–11, 4:21, 5:13, 16, 26; also Augustin George, *Études sur l'oeuvre de Luc*, Sources bibliques (Paris, 1978), 109–10; Betori, 58–61; and my "Non-joining Sympathizers (Acts 5,13–14)," *Biblica* 64 (1983): 550–55.

47. Acts 12:3 (Jews), 4, 11 (people). Haenchen begins his comments on 12:3 by noting, "Bisher hatte die Apg das jüdische Volk als christenfreundlich dargestellt und nur die sadduzäische Führer als Christenfeinde" (*Apostelgeschichte*, 367), but he offers no explanation for the change. For Acts' schematic passage from Jewish acceptance of the gospel to Jewish hostility toward it (but without reference to Acts 12), see Tyson, 574–75.

48. See George, 120, n. 1, and Walter Radl, *Paulus und Jesus im lukanischen Doppelwerk: Untersuchungen zu Parallelmotiven im Lukasevangelium und in der Apostelgeschichte* (Frankfurt, 1975), 321–24. But I am not particularly impressed by the attempt to place the break only in Acts 14 (see the preceding note) and to claim, as Radl does, that "Jude im Sinn von 14,4 ist man nicht mehr durch Abstammung, sondern durch eine Verhaltensweise" (Radl, 322; following Conzelmann, *Mitte*, 135). On the contrary, the hostile behavior is taken to be characteristic of Jews; see Acts 28:24–28.

49. See especially Acts 16:3–4, 18:18, 21, 20:16, 21:18–28, 23:6, 26:5, 28:17.

50. This point was, therefore, one of the pillars on which Vielhauer built his case regarding the non-Pauline character of Luke's Paul (Vielhauer, 37–43).

51. See especially Johannes Weiss, *Über die Absicht und den literarischen Charakter der Apostel-Geschichte* (Marburg, 1897), 26–27, 58–59; Haenchen, *Gott und Mensch*, 224–26, and idem, *Die Bibel und Wir. Gesammelte Aufsätze* 2 (Tübingen, 1968), 368–74. But impressive criticism has been brought against this position; see Eltester, 12; Roloff, 513–15; Löning, *Salustradition*, 186–89; Walter Schmithals, "Die Berichte der Apostelgeschichte über die Bekehrung des Paulus und die 'Tendenz' des Lukas," *Theologia Viatorum* 14 (1977/78): 159–60; Paul W. Walaskay, '*And So We Came to Rome': The Political Perspective of St. Luke*, Society for New Testament Studies Monograph Series 49 (Cambridge, 1983), 100, n. 40; Klaus Haacker, "Das Bekenntnis des Paulus zur Hoffnung Israels nach der Apostelgeschichte des Lukas," *New Testament Studies* 31 (1985): 438–43. Note that the lack of reference to *religio licita* in the seventh edition (1977) of Haenchen's *Apostelgeschichte*, 519, 662–64—as opposed to the corresponding sections of the fourth (1961) edition: 477 and 619–21 (the latter of which summarizes the point of the chapters on Paul's trials!)—may indicate that Haenchen was finally backing down on this question.

52. For the Lucan origin of this pericope, see especially Otto Betz, "Die Vision des Paulus im Tempel von Jerusalem: Apg 22,17–21 als Beitrag zur Deutung des Damaskuserlebnisses," in *Verborum Veritas: Festschrift für Gustav Stählin zum 70. Geburtstag*, ed. Otto Böcher and Klaus Haacker (Wuppertal, 1970), 113–23; also Bovon, 372.

53. The latter is the usual understanding of Paul's response; see, e.g., Betz, 114; Schneider, *Apostelgeschichte*, 2:323.

54. I assume, as is usual, that Luke wrote long after the events described in Acts 28 and could have told more had he so desired; for discussion on this point, see Conzelmann, *Apostelgeschichte*, 160, and Philip Davies, "The Ending of Acts," *Expository Times* 94 (1982/83): 334–35. I have taken the phrase "Q.E.D. of the entire work" from Benjamin W. Bacon, "More Philological Criticism of Acts," *American Journal of Theology* 22 (1918): 10.

55. For bibliography on this theme, see my "The Accusation and the Accusers at Philippi (Acts 16,20–21)," *Biblica* 65 (1984): 357, n. 2; to the references there add Walasky's '*And So We Came to Rome*,' which lists much additional literature.

56. On the possibly positive role of the Empire, see Walasky; on the model for self-defense, see Dibelius, 178–80 (criticized by Haenchen, but see my comments at the end of n. 51 above).

57. See Victor Tcherikover, "Jewish Apologetic Literature Reconsidered," in *Symbolae Raphaeli Taubenschlag dedicatae*, ed. G. Krokówski et al., 3 vols. (Bratislava and Warsaw, 1956–57), 3:169–93.

58. See Eckhard Plümacher, "Die Apostelgeschichte als historische Monographie," in Kremer, ed., *Les Actes des Apôtres*, 457–66, and idem, "Neues

Testament und hellenistische Form: Zur literarischen Gattung der lukanischen Schriften," *Theologia Viatorum* 14 (1977/78): 109–23.

59. On this theme, see, e.g., Jacques Dupont, "Aequitas romana: Notes sur Actes, 25,16," *Recherches de science religieuse* 49 (1961): 354–85; reprinted in his *Études*, 527–52.

60. On this last verse and on this apologetic in general, see Gerhard Delling, "Das letzte Wort der Apostelgeschichte," *Novum Testamentum* 15 (1973): 193–204.

61. See Mk. 15:3; Mt. 27:12; Jn. 18:30, 33–35; and the introduction to Dupont, "Aequitas romana."

62. For this focus of the speech, see Robert F. O'Toole, "Christ's Resurrection in Acts 13,13–52," *Biblica* 60 (1979): 361–72.

63. κηρύσσω τὴν βασιλείαν occurs three times elsewhere in Luke (8:1, 9:2) and Acts (28:31); in each case, it is amplified by τοῦ θεοῦ. Some witnesses have the amplification in 20:25 as well.

64. See n. 38 above and, on the various ways in which the ending of Acts completes Luke-Acts, Jacques Dupont, *Nouvelles études sur les Actes des Apôtres*, Lectio divina 118 (Paris, 1984), 457–511.

65. One is reminded especially of the mother's speech in 4 Mc. 18:7–19; see n. 86 below.

66. See Ulrich Wilckens, *Die Missionsreden der Apostelgeschichte: Form- und traditionsgeschichtliche Untersuchungen*, Wissenschaftliche Monographien zum Alten und Neuen Testament, 3d ed. (Neukirchen-Vluyn, 1974), 61.

67. As Gerhard Lohfink has noted with respect to Acts 1:3 and 28:23, 31, the "Apostelgeschichte wird durch das Thema 'Reich Gottes' geradezu gerahmt" (*Die Sammlung Israels: Eine Untersuchung zur lukanischen Ekklesiologie*, Studien zum Alten und Neuen Testament 39 [Munich, 1975], 79, n. 204; emphasis in original). The same may be said of all of Luke-Acts. On the special prominence of the Nazareth episode in Luke, see nn. 13 and 15 above; also Otto Merk, "Das Reich Gottes in den lukanischen Schriften," in *Jesus und Paulus: Festschrift für Werner Georg Kümmel zum 70. Geburtstag*, ed. E. Earle Ellis and Erich Grässer (Göttingen, 1975), 205.

68. It has often been debated (a) whether Lk. 16:16 includes John the Baptist in the present in which the kingdom of God is available and (b) whether βιάζεται is used favorably or pejoratively. While the second of these questions remains controversial, a consensus seems to have developed on the side of including John in the period of the kingdom of God (*pace* Conzelmann). See I. Howard Marshall, *The Gospel of Luke: A Commentary on the Greek Text*, New International Greek Testament Commentary (Exeter, 1978), 626–30; Michael Bachmann, "Johannes der Täufer bei Lukas: Nachzügler oder Vorläufer?" in *Wort in der Zeit: Neutestamentliche Studien*, ed. Wilfrid Haubeck and Bachmann (Leiden, 1980), 140–50. Even Haenchen eventually agreed: see *Apostelgeschichte*, 6 (Erich Grässer's preface).

69. See Lk. 9:48 and 10:16. In Mk. 9:37 too, however, Jesus is "sent" by God.

70. This worldly understanding of Jesus' kingdom is documented elsewhere as well; see the first two chapters of Oscar Cullmann, *The State in the New Testament* (New York, 1956). Luke's awareness of this perception of Jesus underlies his apologetics with respect to Rome (see n. 55 above). Here I would add only that though it is not at all certain that the chronological problem of Luke 1:5 and 2:1–2 reflects Luke's use of a tradition that linked the birth of Jesus to the revolt at the time of the census of 6 C.E. (as was suggested by Horst Braunert, "Der römische Provinzialzensus und der Schätzungsbericht des Lukas-Evangeliums," *Historia* 6 [1957]: 192–214), it will not do—after all the work of the last few decades on "Jesus and the Zealots"—simply to reject this suggestion out of hand on the basis of a few lines published in 1900 (as is done by George Ogg, "The Quirinius Question To-day," *Expository Times* 79 [1967/68]: 236). For a more balanced discussion of the topic, see Martin Hengel, *Die Zeloten: Untersuchungen zur jüdischen Freiheits-Bewegung in der Zeit von Herodes I. bis 70 n. Chr.*, Arbeiten zur Geschichte des antiken Judentums und des Urchristentums 1, 2d ed. (Leiden and Cologne, 1976), 385–86; and for a review of the literature, see Louis H. Feldman, *Josephus and Modern Scholarship (1937–1980)*, (Berlin and New York, 1984), 651–55.

71. See Joachim Gnilka, *Das Evangelium nach Markus*, 2 vols., Evangelisch-katholischer Kommentar zum Neuen Testament 2.1–2 (Zurich, Einsiedeln, Cologne, and Neukirchen-Vluyn, 1978–79), 2:300.

72. Correspondingly, Luke 23:38 refrains from terming the inscription on Jesus' cross ("king of the Jews") an *aitia* (contrast Mt. 27:37 and Mk. 15:26!); note also Radl, "*aitia*," in Balz and Schneider, eds., *Exegetisches Wörterbuch zum Neuen Testament*, 1:104–5: "sicher bewusst . . . Dass es hier auch schon um politische Apologetik des Christentums gehr, wird besonders deutlich in der Apg."

73. Many critics would rather that he had; see, for example, Lohfink, *Himmelfahrt*, 154; Philip Davies, 334–35; Jacques Dupont, "Die individuelle Eschatologie im Lukasevangelium," in *Orientierung an Jesus: Zur Theologie der Synoptiker, für Joseph Schmid*, ed. Paul Hommann et al. (Freiburg, Basel, and Vienna, 1973), 43, where the matter is put more strongly than in the original French, reprinted in Dupont's *Nouvelles études*, 376–77: "Il ne faut surtout pas en [i.e., from Acts 1:7–8] conclure que l'action missionaire prépare le rétablissement de la royauté davidique" (but how can one conclude from Jesus' failure to correct the apostles that he *disagreed* with them?). For the recognition that Acts 1:7–8 does not reject the national orientation of 1:6, see Haacker, 442, and my "End of the GĒ."

74. On Judas the Galilean and Theudas, see Josephus *Ant.* 18.4–10, 23–25, 20.97–98. See also Haenchen, *Apostelgeschichte*, 246–48, and Heinz

Schreckenberg, "Flavius Josephus und die lukanischen Schriften," in Haubeck and Bachmann, eds., *Wort in der Zeit*, 195–98.

75. See my "End of the GĒ."

76. Once again I must differ with Jervell, who claims that for Luke, "David is the central figure in Scripture and therefore also in history" (*The Unknown Paul*, 128). For Jervell's "is," I would substitute "was" (see n. 3 above). On Acts 15:16, see Jacques Dupont, "'Je rabâtirai la cabane de David qui est tombée' (Ac 15,16 = Am 9,11)," in *Glaube und Eschatologie: Festschrift für Werner Georg Kümmel zum 80. Geburtstag*, ed. Erich Grässer and Otto Merk (Tübingen, 1985), 19–32. Dupont criticizes the view that "a surtout été systématiquement développée par J. Jervell" (21; see also 31, n. 14) and according to which this verse refers only to *Jewish* Christians.

77. See Bruce M. Metzger, *A Textual Commentary on the Greek New Testament* (London and New York, 1971), 452 (on 17:3b), 479 (on 20:21); and, in general, Donald L. Jones, "The Title *Christos* in Acts," *Catholic Biblical Quarterly* 32 (1970): 69–70; Stephen S. Smalley, "The Christology of Acts Again," in *Christ and Spirit in the New Testament*, ed. Barnabas Lindars and Smalley (Cambridge, 1973), 85.

78. Thus, in 28:31, as Hermann J. Hauser notes (*Strukturen der Abschlusserzählung der Apostelgeschichte [Apg 28,16–31]*, Analecta Biblica 86 [Rome, 1979], 117):

> Der neuen Hörerschaft entsprechend wird bei der Nennung des Hoheitstitels 'Christus' nicht mehr von Beweisführung, 'dass Jesus der Christus sei' und Israels messianische Hoffnung erfülle, gesprochen; denn dieser 'Christus' ist Heilsbringer für 'alle' (V.30!), die ihm als Christus und Herrn bekennen; die Grenzen Israels sind gesprengt.

I see no justification, however, for Hauser's view that "Christus" means "Heilsbringer" (he follows Walter Grundmann, *Theologisches Wörterbuch zum Neuen Testament* 9 [1973]: 528, rather than Jones, 70, but Grundmann is not specific regarding 28:31). See further n. 91 below.

79. Although Ferdinand Hahn writes that Luke "die messianische Vorstellung in Zusammenhang seiner Christologie bewusst aufgenommen und breitentfaltet [hat]" ("Christos," in Balz and Schneider, eds., *Exegetisches Wörterbuch zum Neuen Testament*, 3:1156), he emphasizes that what especially characterizes Luke is his use of the title in connection with Jesus' death and resurrection. I would say that Luke was stuck with the term and that he did his best to depoliticize it and, as the story reached its fulfillment, to avoid it.

80. This is the New International Version's translation of this verse; see also the similarly "Judaizing" "our people" in Johannes Munck, *The Acts of the Apostles*, ed. William F. Albright and C. S. Mann, Anchor Bible 31

(Garden City, N.Y., 1967), 240. Munck was one of the pioneers of the tradition that Jervell now represents.

81. On the ambiguous use of *kyrios* in Acts, see Schneider, *Lukas, Theologe der Heilsgeschichte,* 213–26 (with bibliography).

82. On *Kyrios Iesous* in Luke, see the United Bible Societies' Greek New Testament, which rates this reading "D," i.e., "very high degree of doubt"—although some would defend it: e.g., Fitzmyer, 2:1544. In calling it a Lucan phrase, however, Fitzmyer should perhaps have noted that all the other, and assured, instances occur in Acts. Elsewhere in his commentary on Luke, Fitzmyer argues well for the non-messianic "resonance" of *kyrios* (1:203–4). For the occurrences of *Kyrios Iesous* in Acts, see 1:21, 7:59, 8:16, 11:20, 15:11, 16:31, 19:5, 20:24, 35, 21:13; probably also 4:33, 20:21, 28:31.

83. On Luke's predilection for saying something twice when once would do, see the first volume of Morgenthaler's *Die lukanische Geschichtsschrei-bung.* The present passage is listed on p. 29, among other tautologies.

84. For a good recent discussion, see Haacker, 437–51.

85. As John J. Collins notes, "It is apparent that Daniel lacked the enthusiasm for the Maccabean revolt that characterizes the Animal Apocalypse of Enoch . . . Daniel 12 says nothing of a kingdom" (*The Apocalyptic Imagination: An Introduction to the Jewish Matrix of Christianity* [New York, 1984], 90–91). For the close association of resurrection and judgment, and for Dn. 12:1–3 as the background for much of early Jewish thought on the subject, see George W. E. Nickelsburg, Jr., *Resurrection, Immortality, and Eternal Life in Intertestamental Judaism,* Harvard Theological Studies 26 (Cambridge, Mass., 1972).

86. See especially Rv. 11:11 and Tertullian *De resurrectione mortuorum* 29–30. Other references are given by G. A. Cooke, *A Critical and Exegetical Commentary on the Book of Ezekiel,* International Critical Commentary (Edinburgh, 1936), 398. Ez. 37:3 is quoted as part of the argument for eternal life in 4 Mc. 18:17 (see n. 65 above); it would seem to be worthwhile to pursue the question of 4 Maccabees' influence on early Christian understanding of Jesus' death and of martyrdom in general (on which see, with regard to the Odes of Solomon and the Epistle to the Hebrews, [J.] Rendel Harris, "Some Notes on 4 Maccabees," *Expository Times* 32 [1920/ 21]: 183–85).

87. As Haenchen points out (*Apostelgeschichte,* 398), the joyous acceptance of the gospel reported here is meant to symbolize its reception by the gentile world in general.

88. As Haenchen notes (*Apostelgeschichte,* 396), it does not seem that there is any difference here between forgiveness of sins and justification; see also n. 83 above. So too Matthäus Franz-Josef Buss: "Die Rechtfertigung selbst wird hier wesentlich als Sündennachlass verstanden: δικαιόω bedeutet also in vv. 38f. so viel wie 'rein-, freimachen von'" (*Die Missionspredigt des Apostels Paulus im Pisidischen Antiochien: Analyse von Apg*

13,16–41 im Hinblick auf die literarische und thematische Einheit der Paulusrede, Forschung zur Bibel 38 [Stuttgart, 1980], 125).

89. Hence the term *individual eschatology* is used appropriately of Luke's conception by such writers as Dupont (see n. 73 above) and Erich Grässer, "Die Parusieerwartung in der Apostelgeschichte," in Kremer, ed., *Les Actes des Apôtres*, 125. To the criticism of Grässer by Rudolph Schnackenburg ("Die lukanische Eschatologie im Lichte von Aussagen der Apostelgeschichte," in Grässer and Merk, eds., *Glaube und Eschatologie*, 249–65), I would respond that an interest that is attested only by Acts 1:11, 3:19–21, 10:42, and 17:31 (see Schnackenburg, 260)—in other words, an interest not mentioned in the last eleven chapters of Acts—should not be considered lasting or central (on this point, see also n. 38 above). On Acts 17:31, see n. 97 below.

90. The translation is that of the NEB, which begins, however, with "the" rather than "your."

91. On the interconnection of these three σωτήριον-passages in Luke-Acts, see Dupont, *Nouvelles études*, 508–9 (but see the next note). Schneider (*Apostelgeschichte*, 2:419, n. 87) takes the demonstrative in Acts 28:28 ("this salvation") to refer back to ἰάσομαι in the preceding verse, but the linkage of salvation and healing is not obvious in Greek (as it is in German: *heilen, Heil*; see Schneider's translation, 2:410–11). Like Dupont, Hauser correctly and dramatically notes with regard to Acts 28:28 and Luke 3:6 that "[v]om Erschallen der Heraldstimme im Jordangebiet (Lk 3,3) bis zur Verkündigung des Paulus in Rom spannt sich ein Bogen" (Hauser, 137). I would disagree, however, with his assumption that it is "das Herrsein Jesu" that is preached in Acts 28 along with the kingdom of God (see n. 78 above and n. 103 below).

92. This point has been emphasized by George D. Kilpatrick, "The Gentiles and the Strata of Luke," in Böcher and Haacker, eds., *Verborum Veritas*, 87. Against Kilpatrick, Wilson has argued from Acts 13:47 and 26:22–23 that Luke 2:30–32 means that the Gentiles too will be saved and not merely view salvation as an audience (see Wilson, 36–38). As I have noted at several points, however, it is not justified to harmonize Lucan statements from before the turn to the Gentiles with those made after it; again, see n. 38 above. Dupont, *Nouvelles études*, 508–9, takes the fact that the criticism of those who depend on Israelite descent follows the quotation from Isaiah to mean, similarly, that a universal salvation is contemplated here. Luke's John the Baptist does not contrast Jews with Gentiles, however, but rather good and saved Jews with unrepentant and damned Jews.

93. On this point, see Grässer, 124:

> Im übrigen ist die Erwartung des nahen Gottesreiches ersetzt durch die *Verkündigung* seines Wesens . . . Den Platz der Eschatologie nimmt nun das Konzept einer kontinuierlichen

geschichtlichen Verwirklichung des göttlichen Heilsplanes ein. Er ist nach vorne hin offen, was Apg 28fin schlagend belegt dadurch, dass die Parusie hier—kein Thema mehr ist (Grässer's emphasis).

See also n. 89 above. Below I will go even further regarding the nature of this kingdom of God.

94. On this apologetic, see above pp. 12–14. Luke's approach is very similar to that of Josephus; see my "Josephus on the Jewish Contributions and Community," *Scripta Classica Israelica* 7 (1983/84): 30–52, especially 51–52. It is appropriate, therefore, that the argument between those who hold that Luke totally abandoned eschatology and those who maintain that he only put it far off (see n. 89 above) is paralleled in Josephan studies; see Feldman, 483.

95. This would seem to be the point where Luke corresponds most fully to the Paul of the epistles. See Joachim Jeremias, "The Key to Pauline Theology," *Expository Times* 76 (1964/65): 28–30. But whereas Paul drew many additional conclusions from Jesus' resurrection, Luke seems to have remained at the basic level of recognition of the possibility of resurrection. It is this limitation that allows him to portray Paul as such a faithful Pharisee (see especially Acts 23:6–8; also 22:3, 24:14–15, 26:5).

96. On Acts 4:2, see n. 66 above. Robert F. O'Toole concludes that, in Acts 4:1–2, 13:13–52, 17:30–31, and 26:6–8, 22–23, Luke "claims a connection between our own resurrection and Jesus'" and that "Luke viewed our own resurrection as affected by Jesus'" (O'Toole, 371–72). He is equally vague (and claims that Luke is too) in his *Acts 26: The Christological Climax of Paul's Defense (Ac 22:1–26:32)*, Analecta Biblica 78 (Rome, 1978), 122, 159. In my view, Luke's Paul holds simply that the resurrection of Jesus *proves* that people can be resurrected.

97. Note the plural (ξένων δαιμονίων) in 17:18; see Haenchen, *Apostelgeschichte*, 497. Notice also how 17:31—the resurrection and judgment of all is proven by the resurrection of Jesus—is followed by v. 32: "When they heard of the resurrection of the dead . . . " (not "of Jesus").

98. "De didaskalia ist in 28:31 een nadere konkretisiering van het kerygma" (P. A. van Stempvoort, "De Betekenis van λέγων τὰ περὶ τῆς βασιλείας τοῦ θεοῦ in Hand. 1:3," *Nederlands Theologisch Tijdschrift* 9 (1954/55): 351; similarly, see Merk, 205. But both give ecclesiastical interpretations, and Merk depends on Acts 14:22 to retain eschatology, even though Luke speaks of people entering the kingdom of God, not of its coming (Merk, 219–20, n. 66; see also above, n. 89!).

99. Günter Klein, *Die zwölf Apostel: Ursprung und Gehalt einer Idee*, Forschungen zur Religion und Literatur des Alten und Neuen Testaments 77 (Göttingen, 1961); Christoph Burchard, *Der dreizehnte Zeuge: Traditions- und kompositionsgeschichtliche Untersuchungen zu Lukas' Darstellung der Frühzeit des Paulus*, Forschungen zur Religion und Literatur des

Alten und Neuen Testaments 103 (Göttingen, 1970); Eckhard Plümacher, "Apostelgeschichte," *Theologische Realenzyklopädie* 3 (1978): 508, 519; Jacob Jervell, "Paulus in der Apostelgeschichte und die Geschichte des Urchristentums," *New Testament Studies* 32 (1986): 378-84.

100. See, for example, two studies of the call narratives that came to disparate results: Dupont, *Nouvelles études*, 446-56, and Schmithals, 145-65. The former is close to Burchard, the latter to Klein. Dupont's n. 5 lists much additional bibliography. On "early Catholicism" and its implications, see Müller, 163-70, and Hans-Friedrich Weiss, "'Frühkatholizismus' im Neuen Testament?" in *Frühkatholizismus im ökumenischen Gespräch*, ed. Joachim Rogge and Gottfried Schille (Berlin, 1983), 9-26.

101. On these parallels, see Radl, *Paulus und Jesus*; Glenn R. Jacobsen, "Paul in Luke-Acts: The Savior Who is Present," *SBL 1983 Seminar Papers*, 131-46; David P. Moessner, "Paul and the Pattern of the Prophet like Moses in Acts," *SBL 1983 Seminar Papers*, 203-12; Victor C. Pfitzner, "Continuity and Discontinuity: The Lucan View of History in Acts," in *Theologia Crucis: Studies in Honour of Hermann Sasse*, ed. Henry P. Hamann (Adelaide, 1975), 39-43. Note also Barrett's observation: "Luke was interested in what may be called 'religious personalities.' His account of John the Baptist is characteristic. . . . Jesus is such another. So, for that matter, are Peter, Stephen, and Paul, and all of them are concerned in the foundation of the new religious community" (Barrett, 58). In n. 103 below, I will comment on the continuation of Barrett's remarks.

102. On Peter, see Dietfried Gewalt, "Das 'Petrusbild' der lukanischen Schriften als Problem einer ganzheitlichen Exegese," *Linguistica Biblica* 34 (1975): 1-22. Gewalt states that "Petrus ist aber nur ein tragendes Funktionselement" in Luke-Acts (21); the same could be said, I believe, about all of Luke's characters. After Acts 8:40, which left Philip in Caesarea, he is mentioned only once and that in passing (21:8-9); Peter, after disappearing in 12:17, makes only a brief reappearance in Acts 15—which, as I have suggested above, should probably precede Acts 12.

103. I see little justification for the way in which Barrett continues his comments on Luke's interest in "religious personalities" (n. 101 above):

> . . . though Luke never wavers in the conviction that among them all Jesus is unique. He is, however, unique not so much in the outward pattern of His life (though it is always perfectly clear that He is the central figure to whom all the rest are subordinate) as in the fact that after His earthly ministry He was exalted to heaven, there to rule at God's right hand.

I have already protested against similar statements by Hauser (see nn. 78 and 91 above). By the end of Acts there is no talk of Jesus' ruling at all, and Paul is not subordinate to Jesus but rather points to him as one might point to any piece of evidence. Similarly when, in a comment at the beginning of Acts (on 1:6), Lake and H. J. Cadbury write that "Hellenistic Christians, who in the end conquered the Empire, were preachers of the Lord Jesus, as having a present importance for each individual apart from the eschatological Kingdom in which he would ultimately reign," they immediately go on to note that the former is, in Acts, replacing the latter (Foakes Jackson and Lake, eds., *Beginnings of Christianity*, 4:8). See also n. 89 above. As for the point that the transformation begins with John the Baptist, see n. 68 above.

104. This is a Lucan theme that has been much studied recently; see Bovon, 410–15, and Rese, 233–34.

105. With Lk. 1:1–4 compare Mk. 1:1, Mt. 1:1, and Jn. 1:1 (ff.). Luke's failure to refer to Jesus has bothered some—such as Friedrich Pföfflin, who inserted a parenthetical reference to Jesus into Lk. 1:1 in his *Das Neue Testament in der Sprache von heute*, rev. ed. (Heilbronn, 1965), 105. On the emphasis on events (πράγματα) in Luke's prologue, see Eduard Lohse, *Die Einheit des Neuen Testaments: Exegetische Studien zur Theologie des Neuen Testaments* (Göttingen, 1973), 153–55; Günter Klein, *Rekonstruktion und Interpretation: Gesammelte Aufsätze zum Neuen Testament*, Beiträge zur evangelischen Theologie 50 (Munich, 1969), 243. For the assumption that the prologue to Luke is meant for both volumes of Luke-Acts, see Michael Dömer, *Das Heil Gottes: Studien zur Theologie des lukanischen Doppelwerkes*, Bonner biblische Beiträge 51 (Cologne and Bonn, 1978), 9, 14, n. 40. Fitzmyer, who also assumes that the prologue serves both volumes, nevertheless notes, "The prologue has also to be understood in relation to that of Acts, which explicitly names Jesus, unlike the prologue of the first volume" (1:289). He does not elaborate, but his emphasis on Luke's writing as a Christian—taken together with the phrase "explicitly names Jesus"— seems to indicate he means that the prologue of Luke is to be amplified according to that of Acts (compare Pföfflin, above). I would suggest, however, that Luke does not mention Jesus in the prologue to the entire work because Jesus is only one of the figures (however important!) in the story, but does mention Jesus in the opening of Acts because this passage comes in the middle of the story, where Jesus is still the main active character.

PAUL IN THE WRITINGS OF THE APOSTOLIC FATHERS

I am very much indebted to the participants in the seminar of the conference on "Paul and the Legacies of Paul" for which this study was prepared, and especially to Professor Martinus C. de Boer for his most important response to my paper. I have taken his critique into consideration. I am also most grateful to Mrs. Anne Vouga for her help with the English text of my essay.

1. Knowledge of the "Paulusbild" of Acts does not, however, become evident until later in the second century, e.g., in some apocryphal acts and the *Epistula apostolorum*. See my *Paulus im ältesten Christentum: Das Bild des Apostels und die Rezeption der paulinischen Theologie in der frühchristlichen Literatur bis Marcion*, Beiträge zur historischen Theologie 58 (Tübingen, 1979), 68–71 and 109–12; see also the important study of David K. Rensberger, "As the Apostle Teaches: The Development of the Use of Paul's Letters in Second-Century Christianity" (Ph.D. diss., Yale University, 1981), 88–93, 300–304.

2. Although *1 Clement* does not reveal the name of its author, it does identify—correctly, not pseudonymously—its sender (and its addressee).

3. There is no indication that the author of *1 Clement*, Ignatius, or Polycarp was personally acquainted with any of the apostles.

4. On this problem, see my article "Die Gemeinde von 'Kolossä': Erwägungen zum 'Sitz im Leben' eines pseudopaulinischen Briefes," *Wort und Dienst*, N.F. 16 (1981): 111–34, especially 114–16.

5. See Georg Schöllgen, "Monepiskopat und monarchischer Episkopat: Eine Bermerkung zur Terminologie," *Zeitschrift für die neutestamentliche Wissenschaft* 77 (1986): 146–51.

6. So far as I can tell, *1 Clement* contains no indication of primacy for the Roman church, whether claimed in Rome or acknowledged in Corinth (or elsewhere).

7. See Lindemann, *Paulus im ältesten Christentum*, 174–77.

8. Klaus Wengst, ed., *Didache (Apostellehre), Barnabasbrief, Zweiter Klemensbrief, Schrift an Diognet*, Schriften des Urchristentums (Darmstadt, 1984), 115; also 113 on the date of *Barnabas*.

9. See Lindemann, *Paulus im ältesten Christentum*, 272–82; Klaus Wengst, *Tradition und Theologie des Barnabasbriefes*, Arbeiten zur Kirchengeschichte 42 (Berlin, 1971).

10. This dialogue is one of the few secondary "conflict stories" from second-century Christian literature.

11. See Edouard Massaux, *Influence de l'Evangile de saint Matthieu sur la littérature chrétienne avant saint Irénée* (1950; reprint: Louvain, 1986).

12. It is my assumption that there was never a "canon" of Christian writings that did not include Paul's epistles, whether Marcion was the "founder" of the "New Testament" (see Hans von Campenhausen, *Die Enstehung der christlichen Bibel*, Beiträge zur historischen Theologie 39 [Tübingen, 1968], 175) or—as I believe—he was not. See also John Knox, *Marcion and the New Testament: An Essay in the Early History of the Canon* (Chicago, 1942).

13. See the brief discussion of this matter in Lindemann, *Paulus im ältesten Christentum*, 72–73; also Leslie W. Barnard, "Clement of Rome and the Persecution of Domitian," *New Testament Studies* 10 (1963–64): 251–60.

14. For the most part, the translations of passages from the writings of the apostolic fathers are taken from the superb commentary, with texts and

translations, by J. B. Lightfoot, *The Apostolic Fathers*, Part 1: *S. Clement of Rome*, 2 vols. (London, 1890) and Part 2: *St. Ignatius, St. Polycarp*, 3 vols. (London, 1889). The translation of *1 Clement* appears in Part 1, 2:271–305, the translation of Ignatius in Part 2, 2:543–74, and the translation of Polycarp in Part 2, 3:471–76.

15. Karlmann Beyschlag, *Clemens Romanus und der Frühkatholizismus: Untersuchungen zu I Clemens 1–7*, Beiträge zur historischen Theologie 35 (Tübingen, 1966), 280.

16. There is no indication that the "troublemakers" in Corinth who had removed the presbyters from office had appealed to Paul in doing so, e.g., by claiming that Paul himself did not invest presbyters in his churches.

17. The statement does not duplicate any particular logion from the synoptic gospels but is reminiscent of several; see, e.g., Mk. 9:42, 14:21.

18. See *1 Clem.* 62.3: "And we have put you in mind of these things the more gladly because we knew well that we were writing to men who are faithful and highly regarded and have diligently searched into the oracles of the teaching of God."

19. In my view, 2 Corinthians is a composite of several, originally independent letters. Victor P. Furnish, *II Corinthians*, Anchor Bible 32A (Garden City, N.Y., 1984), 41, considers a two-letter hypothesis the most plausible.

20. See Lindemann, *Paulus im ältesten Christentum*, 173–74.

21. The author of 2 Peter considers himself in full agreement with Paul's eschatology; see 2 Pt. 3:15–16.

22. Note the idea of Christ as the *aparchē* and the use of the image of seed (although here cited in the context of the parable of the sower).

23. The catalogue of vices in 30.1 may be illustrative of the situation—although it may, of course, be no more than a traditional listing of immoralities.

24. The idea that justification through faith is valid "from the beginning" is reminiscent, perhaps, of Paul's argumentation in Rom. 4.

25. See n. 17 above.

26. There is virtually no difference from Rom. 13:1–7, despite the fact that there are no verbal correspondences between the two passages.

27. Hans Lietzmann (*Geschichte der alten Kirche*, vol. 1: *Die Anfänge* [Berlin, 1932], 211) claims that in *1 Clement* we do not have even an "abgeklungener Paulinismus" but rather a purely "hellenistisches Proselytenchristentum." See also Rudolf Bultmann, *Theologie des Neuen Testaments* (9th ed. rev.; Tübingen, 1984), 537; Bultmann asks whether the kind of Christianity in *1 Clement* is anything more than "das Selbstbewusstsein, dank des in Christus geschehenen Heilsereignisses Gottes Gnade sicher zu sein."

28. Rom. 3:25 is, of course, a traditional text cited by Paul, but this fact would not have been known to readers at the end of the first century.

29. See William R. Schoedel, *Ignatius of Antioch: A Commentary on the Letters of Ignatius of Antioch*, Hermeneia (Philadelphia, 1985), 7–10; cf. my review of this important commentary in *Theologische Literaturzeitung* 112 (1987): 272–75.

30. See Schoedel, 176.
31. See the discussion in Lindemann, *Paulus im ältesten Christentum*, 199–221.
32. *Eph.* 18.2 reads as follows: "For our God, Jesus the Christ, was carried in the womb by Mary according to God's plan—of the seed of David and of the Holy Spirit—who was born and baptized . . . " (trans. Schoedel, 84). Compare Rom. 1:3–4: "on the human level he was born of David's stock, but on the level of the spirit—the Holy Spirit—he was declared Son of God by a mighty act in that he rose from the dead" (NEB).
33. On Ignatius' christology, see Henning Paulsen, *Studien zur Theologie des Ignatius von Antiochien*, Forschungen zur Kirchen- und Dogmengeschichte 29 (Göttingen, 1978), 175–87.
34. See 1 Tm. 1:4, 4:7; 2 Tm. 4:4.
35. See Hans Conzelmann, *1 Corinthians: A Commentary on the First Epistle to the Corinthians*, trans. James W. Leitch, Hermeneia (Philadelphia, 1975), 264–67.
36. Some comment on the translation of this passage is required. I have used the translation given by Lightfoot. Schoedel translates as follows: "If I do not find (it) in the archives, I do not believe (it to be) in the gospel" (207, and see his comments on 207–8). In my view, the expression ἐν τῷ εὐαγγελίῳ οὐ πιστεύω should be understood in the same way as the similar phrase in Mk. 1:15 (πιστεύετε ἐν τῷ εὐαγγελίῳ): the gospel is the object of belief (or disbelief). See also Henning Paulsen, *Die Briefe des Ignatius von Antiochia und der Brief des Polykarp von Smyrna*, 2d rev. ed. of the exposition by Walter Bauer, Handbuch zum Neuen Testament 18 (Tübingen, 1985), 86.
37. See Rudolf Bultmann, "Ignatius und Paulus," in *Exegetica: Aufsätze zur Erforschung des Neuen Testaments*, ed. Erich Dinkler (Tübingen, 1967), 400–411; Heinrich Rathke, *Ignatius von Antiochien und die Paulusbriefe*, Texte und Untersuchungen 99 (Berlin, 1967), 13–66.
38. See Furnish, 45.
39. See Percy N. Harrison, *Polycarp's Two Epistles to the Philippians* (Cambridge, 1936); Paulsen argues for the unity of the letter in *Die Briefe des Ignatius*, 112–13.
40. See Lindemann, *Paulus im ältesten Christentum*, 23–25. According to Joachim Gnilka (*Der Philipperbrief*, 2d ed. [Freiburg im Breisgau, 1976], 11), *Phil.* 3.2 indicates "dass Polycarp noch um die Existenz mehrerer Philipperbriefe gewusst hat."
41. Of course, we cannot say exactly how many of the Pauline letters were known to Polycarp.
42. See Paulsen, *Die Briefe des Ignatius*, 111: "Diese Übersetzung is recht ungenau und fehlerhaft."
43. Of these, the most important is the suggestion of Adolf Harnack (*Patristische Miscellen*, Texte und Untersuchungen 20.3 [Leipzig, 1899], 92): "qui laudati estis in principio epistulae eius."
44. Here it seems clear that Polycarp knew of only one Pauline letter to Philippi—or is this the knowledge of the Latin translator?

45. Consequently the unfortunate case of Valens, to which Polycarp alludes in 11.1 and 11.4–12.1, is all the more regrettable.
46. For fuller discussion, see Lindemann, *Paulus im ältesten Christentum*, 221–32.
47. " . . . forasmuch as ye know that it is by grace ye are saved, not of works, but by the will of God through Jesus Christ. Wherefore gird up your loins and serve God in fear and truth. . . ."
48. See 1 Tm. 6:10a and especially 1 Tm. 6:7.
49. See Charles M. Nielsen, "Polycarp, Paul and the Scriptures," *Anglican Theological Review* 47 (1965): 199–216. On the probable dependence of *Phil.* 7.1 on 1 Jn. 4:2, 3 and 2 Jn. 7 (cf. 1 Jn. 5:6ff.), see Paulsen, *Die Briefe des Ignatius*, 120.
50. Polycarp, of course, thought these letters to be authentically Pauline. He is not, as has sometimes been suggested, the author of the pastorals.
51. We do not know whether "Clement," Ignatius, and Polycarp were acquainted with any Pauline epistles other than those that they actually quote or to which they actually allude in their writings. There are at least some elements in their theological views, however, that are to be traced back to Paul or to Paul's letters without the possibility of identifying specific quotations or allusions.
52. Rensberger (see n. 1 above) and Ernst Dassmann (*Der Stachel im Fleisch: Paulus in der frühchristlichen Literatur bis Irenaeus* [Münster, 1979]) reach virtually the same conclusion. All the same, it would be interesting to see which aspects of Pauline theology or of Pauline ethical teaching really were unknown (or unimportant) to the "apostolic fathers."

COMMENT: WHICH PAUL?

1. Andreas Lindemann, *Paulus im ältesten Christentum: Das Bild des Apostels und die Rezeption der paulinischen Theologie in der frühchristlichen Literatur bis Marcion*, Beiträge zur historischen Theologie 58 (Tübingen, 1979), 1–6. Lindemann takes as his point of departure the claim of Hans von Campenhausen (*The Formation of the Christian Bible*, trans. J. A. Baker [Philadelphia, 1972]) that Paul was known throughout the second century simply and approvingly as "the apostle" and that his letters played a unique and positive role in the development of ecclesiastical tradition; see Lindemann, 6. Von Campenhausen's views also provided the starting point for my own modest contribution to this discussion in "Images of Paul in the Post-Apostolic Period," *Catholic Biblical Quarterly* 42 (1980): 359–80, an essay completed before Lindemann's major study appeared.
2. See Lindemann, 113, 29, 33 (the quotation appears on 113).
3. Ibid., 35, 401.
4. Ibid., 396.

5. But does not the Roman church seem to claim some kind of "formal authority" with respect to the Corinthian church? Rome has not been asked to intervene but apparently thinks it her right to do so (*1 Clem.* 63) and sends envoys who are to bring back a report (*1 Clem.* 65).

6. It is of more than passing interest that these three common elements of the image of Paul in *1 Clement*, Ignatius, and Polycarp have been significantly downplayed or suppressed in the Acts of the Apostles. (1) The author of Acts refers to Paul as an "apostle" only twice, in passing, in 14:4 and 14:14 (with Barnabas); elsewhere (twenty-six instances) the author reserves the term for the inner circle of twelve disciples (Judas being replaced) who were with Jesus during his earthly ministry and were the privileged witnesses to his resurrection (see Acts 1:2, 21–26; Luke 6:13). (2) The author gives no indication that Paul wrote letters (although that does not necessarily mean that he did not know of them). (3) Paul's martyrdom, although clearly hinted at and anticipated (see the farewell speech in 20:17ff.), is not narrated at the end of Acts, as one might expect it to be.

7. It is noteworthy that *1 Clement* 42 does not (and in fact cannot) cite a letter of Paul in connection with the procedure of "the apostles" in their appointment of bishops and deacons. The author must instead appeal to a passage from the Old Testament "scripture" (42.5) to provide the legitimation for a procedure he knows only from (oral) tradition.

8. J. B. Lightfoot: "Apostles that were highly reputed" (*The Apostolic Fathers*, Part 1: *S. Clement of Rome*, 2 vols. [London, 1890], 2:296); Kirsopp Lake: "Apostles of high reputation" (*The Apostolic Fathers*, 2 vols., Loeb Classical Library [Cambridge, Mass., 1912–13], 1:91). Divine approval may be intended. Compare the use of the verb in *1 Clement* 17.1–2, 18.1, 19.1, 38.2, 44.3, and here in 47.4. See Lightfoot, Part 1, 2:63; Walter Bauer, William F. Arndt, F. Wilbur Gingrich, and Frederick W. Danker, *A Greek-English Lexicon of the New Testament and Other Early Christian Literature*, 2d ed. rev. (Chicago, 1979), s.v. *martyreo*, 2b. See also *1 Clem.* 42.2: In accordance with God's will, the apostles are from Christ as Christ is from God.

9. This seems to me to be confirmed by *1 Clem.* 45, where the motif of endurance (in the face of "envy") also emerges (cf. also 35.3f.), here in connection with Old Testament figures. That is, the theme of endurance reemerges between chapters 42–44 and chapters 46–47, where the work of "our apostles" is mentioned and the Corinthian troublemakers are taken to task for removing the presbyters from their apostolically legitimated office.

10. The troublemakers would presumably have thought of Paul as "their" apostle (along with Peter?), just as the author of *1 Clement* considered him "ours." Did *they* appeal to Paul as an "authority" for their actions?

11. Acts, which does not tell us that Paul wrote letters, has Peter declare at the Apostolic Council that God chose him (Peter) so that "by my mouth

the Gentiles should hear the word of the gospel and believe . . . God
. . . made no distinction between us and them, but cleansed their hearts
by faith . . . we believe that we shall be saved through the grace of the
Lord Jesus just as they will" (Acts 15:7–11). We seem to have here a summary or a distillation of Pauline theology placed on the lips of Peter (cf.
13:38–39, 20:24). See also James 2:14–26 and the discussion of this passage
in Martin Dibelius and Heinrich Greeven, *James: A Commentary on the
Epistle of James*, trans. Michael A. Williams, Hermeneia (Philadelphia,
1976), 174–80. Do the authors of Acts and James know Paul's letters or only
some slogans or catchwords associated with the name of the apostle?

12. See de Boer, 378–79.

13. Cf. Lindemann, 398: "Die Theologie des Paulus wird schlagwortig festge-
halten (insbesondere die Aussagen der Rechtfertigungslehre), tritt aber
sachlich in den Hintergrund, weil das Interesse an den Problemen der
kirchlichen Organisation starker ins Zentrum ruckt." See also p. 12: It is
possible "dass die paulinische Rechtfertigungslehre oder die paulinische
bzw. deuteropaulinische Ekklesiologie bewusst oder unbewusst auch in
solchen Texten rezipiert sind, die eine direkte Beruhrung mit einem der
(deutero)paulinischen Briefe nich erkennen lassen."

14. The approach of his book is also narrowly defined. Lindemann seeks to
answer three questions: (1) Which letters were known to early Christian
authors? (2) How did they make use of these letters in the context of their
own argumentation? (3) Aside from direct literary dependence on Paul's
letters, are "traditionsgeschichtliche" connections discernible? See Lindemann, 12; note also p. 2, n. 4, where "Paulinismus" is understood narrowly
as "der Versuch . . . paulinische Denkelemente zu tradieren."

15. Cf. the perceptive essay of J. L. Martyn, "Paul and his Jewish-Christian
Interpreters," *Union Seminary Quarterly Review* 42 (1988): 1–15.

16. For example, a controlling theological motif in Ignatius is "to get to God";
one could investigate (a) what role the Paul that Ignatius knows (Ephesians, as well as 1 Corinthians and Romans) plays in support of this
conception and (b) to what extent it stands in continuity or discontinuity
with the theology of the historical Paul.

17. Walter Bauer, *Orthodoxy and Heresy in Earliest Christianity*, translation
ed. Robert A. Kraft and Gerhard Krodel (Philadelphia, 1971), 233–34.

APOCRYPHAL AND CANONICAL NARRATIVES ABOUT PAUL

1. See *New Testament Apocrypha*, ed. Edgar Hennecke, rev. Wilhelm
Schneemelcher, translation ed. Robert McL. Wilson, 2 vols. (London,
1963–65), 2:74.

2. *Apoc. Paul.*; the translation is that of George W. MacRae and William R.
Murdock in James M. Robinson, ed., *The Nag Hammadi Library in English* (San Francisco, 1977), 240, 241.

3. *In Ioann. ev.* 98.8.

4. We possess a Greek summary, a series of Latin recensions, and translations in Coptic, Slavonic, and Ethiopic (in four recensions). The Ethiopic *Apocalypse of Mary the Virgin* contains an adapted version of thirty-two of the fifty-one chapters. No adequate textual reconstruction of this apocalypse yet exists. See Hugo Duensing's discussion in *New Testament Apocrypha*, 2:755–59. I have used the English translation in *New Testament Apocrypha*, 2:759–98.

5. *New Testament Apocrypha*, 2:796.

6. For a catalogue of the texts of *The Acts of Paul*, see the listing (by Françoise Morard) in *Les Actes apocryphes des apôtres: Christianisme et monde païen* (Geneva, 1981), 296–97. See also the texts (with critical apparatus) of *The Acts of Paul and Thecla* and *The Martyrdom of Paul* in *Acta apostolorum apocrypha*, ed. Adelbert Lipsius and Maximilian Bonnet, 3 vols. (1891; reprint: Hildesheim, 1959), 1:235–72, 104–17.

7. At least he is in the version of the *Actus Vercellenses* manuscript (see Lipsius and Bonnet, eds., *Acta apostolorum apocrypha*, 1:45–103, for text, and *New Testament Apocrypha*, 2:268–71, for discussion).

8. See Gilbert Dagron, *Vie et miracles de saint Thècle*, Subsidia Hagiographica 62 (Brussels, 1978).

9. For the recensions, see Lipsius and Bonnet, eds., *Acta apostolorum apocrypha*, 1:118–77, and Louis Leloir, *Ecrits apocryphes sur les apôtres: Traduction de l'édition arménienne de Venise*, Corpus Christianorum Series Apocryphorum 3 (Turnhout, 1986), 77–86.

10. Lipsius and Bonnet, eds., *Acta apostolorum apocrypha*, 1:178–222.

11. Pseudo-Cyprian *De rebaptismate* 17; Lactantius *Divinae Institutiones* 4.21.2–4. See the discussion in *New Testament Apocrypha*, 2:92–93.

12. See 1 Cor. 1:22–23: "Jews demand signs and Greeks seek wisdom, but we preach Christ crucified, a stumbling block to Jews and folly to Gentiles."

13. Dieter Georgi, *Die Gegner des Paulus im 2. Korintherbrief*, Wissenschaftliche Monographien zum Alten und Neuen Testament 11 (Neukirchen-Vluyn, 1964).

14. This story is an etiological legend meant to explain the mysterious sinking of Puteoli.

15. Note also that the canonical Acts shares with the later Pauline *praxeis* and with Pauline apocalypses a fascination with Paul's visions. Three times we read about the vision on the road to Damascus (9:4–6, 22:6–11, 26:12–18). Paul receives a vision of the Macedonian beckoning him to travel there (16:9–10). He learns through a vision that he must stay in Corinth (18:9–11). He falls into a trance and is told to leave Jerusalem (22:17–21). He dreams that the Lord tells him he will give witness in Rome (23:11). An angel visits him while he is sailing to Rome and informs him that everyone on board the ship will live through the storm (27:23–26).

16. Charles H. Talbert, *Literary Patterns, Theological Themes, and the Genre of Luke-Acts*, SBL Monograph Series 20 (Missoula, Mont., 1974).

17. Vernon K. Robbins, "Prefaces in Greco-Roman Biography and Luke-Acts," *SBL 1978 Seminar Papers*, ed. Paul J. Achtemeier, 2 vols. (Missoula, Mont., 1978), 2:193–207.

18. C. Perrot, "Les Actes des Apôtres," in *L'annonce de l'évangile*, ed. X. Léon-Dufour and C. Perrot (Paris, 1976), 239–95.

19. E.g., Martin Hengel, *Zur urchristlichen Geschichtsschreibung* (Stuttgart, 1979); W. C. Van Unnik, "Luke's Second Book and the Rules of Hellenistic Historiography," in *Les Actes des Apôtres: traditions, rédaction, théologie*, ed. Jacob Kremer, Bibliotheca ephemeridum theologicarum lovaniensum 48 (Gembloux, 1979), 37–60; and J. P. Classen, "Lukas als Kerkhistorikus," *Noderuits Gereformeerde Teologiese Tydskrif* 21 (1980): 217–24.

20. S. P. and M. J. Schierling, "The Influence of the Ancient Romances on Acts of the Apostles," *Classical Bulletin* 54 (1978): 81–88; Susan Praeder, "Luke-Acts and the Ancient Novel," *SBL 1981 Seminar Papers*, ed. Kent H. Richards (Chico, Calif., 1981); R. J. Karris, "Windows and Mirrors: Literary Criticism and Luke's *Sitz im Leben*," *SBL 1979 Seminar Papers*, ed. Paul J. Achtemeier, 2 vols. (Missoula, Mont., 1979), 1:47–58; and Richard Pervo, "The Literary Genre of the Acts of the Apostles" (Ph.D. diss., Harvard University, 1979).

21. Pierre Gibert, "L'invention d'un genre littéraire," *Lumière et Vie* 30 (1981): 19–33.

22. Helmut Koester, *Introduction to the New Testament*, 2 vols., Hermeneia: Foundations and Facets (Philadelphia, 1982), 2:49–52, 315–23.

23. E. von Dobschütz, "Der Roman in der altchristlichen Literatur," *Deutsche Rundschau* 111 (1902): 87–106; Joseph Flamion, "Les Actes apocryphes de Pierre," *Revue d'histoire ecclésiastique* 9 (1908): 465–90 and 10 (1909): 5–29; E. Plümacher, "Apokryphe Apostelakten," *Paulys Realencyclopädie der classischen Altertumswissenschaft*, Supplementband 15 (1978): 61–62; and, with important qualifications, Jean-Daniel Kaestli, "Les principales orientations de la recherche sur les Actes apocryphes des apôtres," in *Les Actes apocryphes des apôtres*, 49–67.

24. Richard Reitzenstein, *Hellenistische Wundererzählungen* (Leipzig, 1906), and F. Pfister, *Neutestamentliche Apokryphen*, ed. Edgar Hennecke (2d ed.; Tübingen, 1924).

25. Rosa Söder, *Die apokryphen Apostelgeschichten und die romanhafte Literatur der Antike* (Stuttgart, 1932). Against Söder's proposal is the complete absence of this genre in ancient texts.

26. Kaestli, 67.

27. I am convinced, for example, that *The Acts of Andrew* was written as a Christian *Odyssey*, with Andrew as the new Odysseus.

28. See *The Acts of Paul* 11 (the martyrdom); *The Acts of Peter* 37–38; *The Acts of Thomas* 165; *The Acts of Andrew* (reconstructed text of the martyrdom in *New Testament Apocrypha*, 2:416–23). *The Acts of John* does not relate John's death to Jesus'—presumably because, unlike Jesus, John is not

executed. He dies of old age. For comparisons between the deaths of Paul and Jesus in the canonical Acts, see below.

29. François Bovon, "La vie des apôtres: Traditions bibliques et narrations apocryphes," in *Les Actes apocryphes des apôtres*, 141–58, especially 149–52; Hans-Theo Wrege, *Die Gestalt des Evangeliums: Aufbau und Struktur der Synoptiker sowie der Apostelgeschichte*, Beiträge zur evangelischen Theologie 2 (Frankfurt, 1978), 124–60, especially 153–59.

30. *The Acts of Paul* 10 (translation in *New Testament Apocrypha*, 2:381). This passage is quoted in Origen *Comm. in Io.* 20.12.

31. If Schneemelcher's reconstruction of the Myra episode in *The Acts of Paul* is right, a blind man is healed by Jesus "in the form of Paul" (*New Testament Apocrypha*, 2:334).

32. Carl Schmidt argued that the version in *The Acts of Peter* is the earlier, but he did so exclusively on the ground that it fits more smoothly into its literary context Πράξεις Παύλου: *Acta Pauli nach dem Papyrus der Hamburger Staats- und Universitätsbibliothek* [Glüchstadt and Hamburg, 1936], 128ff.). Surely one could argue the opposite, namely that the author of the Petrine Acts adopted a motif from *The Acts of Paul* and provided a better narrative setting for it. See Schneemelcher's discussion in *New Testament Apocrypha*, 2:345–46.

33. See Wilhelm Schneemelcher, "Die Apostelgeschichte des Lukas und die Acta Pauli," *Zeitschrift für die neutestamentliche Wissenschaft* 30 (1964): 236–50; Willy Rordorff, "Tradition and Composition in the *Acts of Thecla*: The State of the Question," *Semeia* 38 (1986): 43–52; and Dennis R. MacDonald, *The Legend and the Apostle: The Battle for Paul in Story and Canon* (Philadelphia, 1983).

34. We are told: Jesus preached that the Kingdom of God is at hand. He "raised the dead, healed diseases, cleansed lepers, healed the blind, made cripples whole, raised up paralytics, cleansed those possessed by demons," multiplied loaves, walked on the sea, and "commanded the winds." He also discoursed with Simon and Philip (*The Acts of Paul* 10; translation: *New Testament Apocrypha* 2:382). Unfortunately our single manuscript for this section (the Hamburg papyrus) breaks off before the end of the speech in which this narrative account of Jesus is contained. We can be virtually certain, however, that it once spoke of Jesus' death, for the narrative begins: "If we endure, we shall have access to the Lord . . . who gave himself for us" (*New Testament Apocrypha*, 2:381–82).

35. For my earlier argument, see MacDonald, 17–33. The story of Frontina is in *The Acts of Paul* 8 (*New Testament Apocrypha*, 2:377–78). Notice that here again, as in the Thecla sequence and the baptized lion story, Paul's closest associate is a woman.

36. On these points, see MacDonald, 23–25, 66–71.

37. Later Pauline *praxeis* for the most part derive from *The Acts of Paul* and demonstrate the persistent hold of his death on pious imaginations. By the fifth century, the martyrdom story from the *Acts* circulated independently;

it has come down to us in Greek, Latin, Coptic, Slavonic, and Ethiopic. We possess a longer *Martyrdom of Paul* (Lipsius and Bonnet, eds., *Acta apostolorum apocrypha*, 1:23–44), inspired by *The Acts of Paul*, which is ascribed to "Bishop Linus" and is extant in seventy-eight Latin manuscripts. There are also a *Passion of Peter and Paul* extant in Greek and Latin (Lipsius and Bonnet, eds., *Acta apostolorum apocrypha*, 1:118–77) and two other short martyrdoms of Paul in Armenian. *The Preaching of Paul* also ends with Paul in Rome and presumably contained an account of his death (see *New Testament Apocrypha*, 2:92–93). In addition there exist two versions of *The Acts of Peter and Paul* (Lipsius and Bonnet, eds., *Acta apostolorum apocrypha*, 1:178–222), a work that likewise emphasizes the death of the apostle and has come down to us in over one hundred manuscripts in Greek, in Latin, and in three different Armenian recensions.

38.   Compare Mk. 5:39–41 with Acts 9:40 and 20:10; Mk 6:20 with Acts 24:24, 26; Mk. 6:56 with Acts 5:15 and 19:12.

39.   According to Bruno Bauer: "Das Original des Petrus und des Paulus der Apostelgeschichte ist der Jesus der synoptischen Evangelien. Der Verfasser der Apostelgeschichte hatte die letzteren . . . vor Augen, als er ihnen die Züge entlehnte, aus denen er das Bild beider Apostel zusammensatzte" (*Die Apostelgeschichte eine Ausgleichung des Paulinismus und des Judenthums innerhalb der christlichen Kirche* [Berlin, 1850], cited in A. J. Mattil, Jr., "The Jesus-Paul Parallels and the Purpose of Luke-Acts: H. H. Evans Reconsidered," *Novum Testamentum* 17 [1975]: 18). See also H. H. Evans, *St. Paul the Author of the Acts of the Apostles and of the Third Gospel* (London, 1884); Henry Cadbury, *The Making of Luke-Acts* (1927; reprint: London, 1958), 231–33; Richard Rackham, *The Acts of the Apostles*, 13th ed. (London, 1947); Michael D. Goulder, *Type and History in Acts* (London, 1964), 34–64 (unfortunately Goulder's entire program is laden with implausible typologies and allegories); Jürgen Roloff, "Die Paulus-Darstellung des Lukas," *Evangelische Theologie* 39 (1979): 510–31, especially 529–31. Gibert claims that Peter and Paul are depicted

> à l'image de leur Maître, dans leur prédication comme dans leurs miracles, dans leur itinéraire et leurs souffrances comme dans leur mort aboutissant, ne fût-ce que symboliquement en ce lieu d'histoire, à une resurrection. Ses premiers lecteurs ne pouvaient s'y tromper: les échos étaient par trop distincts (25–26, see also 29–31).

Hans Windisch is equally emphatic: Paul is "Jesus redivivus" ("Paulus und Jesus," *Theologische Studien und Kritiken* 106 [1934–35]: 465). See also Windisch's larger work, *Paulus und Christus: Ein biblischen-religionsgeschichtlicher Vergleich*, Untersuchungen zum Neuen Testament 234 (Leipzig, 1934). Also important are Mattil's article and Walter Radl, *Paulus und Jesus im lukanischen Doppelwerk: Untersuchungen* zu Parallelmotiven im Lukasevangelium und in der Apostelgeschichte (Frankfurt, 1975), which provides a helpful Forschungsbericht on the Jesus-Paul parallels (44–59). According to Radl, the intention of the parallels is not to make a statement about Paul as an individual but to relate the time and experiences of Jesus to the time and experiences of the early church, of which Paul is a mere symbol (369–95). Susan Praeder provides a cautionary assessment of scholarly opinions concerning these Jesus-Paul parallels in "Jesus-Paul, Peter-Paul, and Jesus-Peter Parallelisms in Luke-Acts: A History of Reader Response," in SBL 1984 Seminar Papers, ed. Kent H. Richards (Chico, Calif., 1984), 23–39.

40. George W. MacRae, "'Whom Heaven Must Receive until the Time': Reflections on the Christology of Acts," Interpretation 27 (1973): 165.

41. In addition to the works of Wrege, Talbert, and Radl, see Norman Petersen, Literary Criticism for New Testament Critics (Philadelphia, 1978), 81–92, and Gundrun Muhlack, Die Parallelen von Lukas-Evangelium und Apostelgeschichte, Theologie und Wirklichkeit 8 (Frankfurt, 1979). According to Muhlack, the parallels between Jesus, Peter, and Paul demonstrate "dass die christliche Gemeinde die Erfüllung des Wirkens Jesu praktiziert" (141).

42. For example, although Gibert sees these parallels between the gospels and Acts and between Jesus and Paul, he argues instead that Acts is the first hagiographon, presenting the apostles Peter and Paul as imitators of Jesus in a way that would become characteristic of later hagiographic legenda. Although I disagree with Gibert's assessment of the praxeis genre, I agree that the canonical Acts did push the representation of the apostles in the direction of later hagiographa.

43. Of course, the prototype of Luke's gospel, Mark, was also open-ended. The reader expects the women in Mark to tell the disciples to meet Jesus in Galilee, but instead, out of fear, they tell no one (16:8).

44. Soon after Paul's conversion, we are told, "the Jews plotted to kill him" and so he had to flee Damascus by basket (9:23–25). He goes to Jerusalem, where the Hellenists "were seeking to kill him" (9:29–30). He was driven out of Antioch of Pisidia (13:50), nearly stoned at Iconium (14:5), actually stoned at Lystra (14:19), beaten and imprisoned at Philippi (16:22–23). He barely avoided lynch mobs in Thessalonica (17:5–10) and in Beroea (17:14) and a riot of silversmiths in Ephesus (19:28–41). Temple mobs do indeed try to kill him (21:31; cf. 22:22, 23:27), and a band of Jews vows not to eat or drink until it kills him (23:12–15).

45. See The Acts of Paul 11 (the martyrdom); translation in New Testament Apocrypha, 2:383–87. The political radicalism of the story is somewhat heightened in the Martyrdom of Paul ascribed to Bishop Linus (Lipsius and Bonnet, eds., Acta apostolorum apocrypha, 1:23–44).

46. There may, however, be an analogous case. In The Legend and the Apostle, 66–71, I suggest that the author of 2 Timothy knew of anti-Roman stories of Paul's martyrdom and wrote the epistle as Paul's last will and testament

to defuse his death of its incendiary political potential. In 2 Timothy we
hear not so much as a whisper of criticism for Rome; there is no reference
to Nero or to soldiers or to the charges against Paul. Paul is a spent old
man resolutely awaiting his inevitable demise.

47. See also Radl, 169–221, 252–65, 325–45.

48. Robert F. O'Toole has demonstrated many other parallels between the
trials of Jesus in Lk. 23 and of Paul in Acts 25–26 ("Luke's Notion of 'Be
Imitators of Me as I Am of Christ' in Acts 25–26," *Biblical Theology Bulletin*
8 [1978]: 155–61); see also Simon Légasse, "L'apologétique à l'égard de
Rome dans le proces de Paul: Actes 21,27–26,32," *Recherches de science
religieuse* 69 (1981): 249–56.

49. Cadbury, 314.

50. See the discussion of this substitution of antagonists in Fredrick J. Foakes
Jackson and Kirsopp Lake, eds., *The Beginnings of Christianity*, Part 1: *The
Acts of the Apostles*, 5 vols. (1920–33; reprint: Grand Rapids, Mich., 1966),
5:193–95, and in Ernst Haenchen, *The Acts of the Apostles: A Commentary*, trans. Bernard Noble and Gerald Shinn (Philadelphia, 1971), 334–85.

51. See also Haenchen, 513–14.

52. For example, if one takes "the thirteenth year" of the Soli inscription to
refer to the thirteenth year of Claudius, which certainly may be debated,
Paul's audience before Sergius Paulus could not have been the first act of
his itinerant mission, as it is in Acts. Luke's reason for presenting this
story so early, argued Gottfried Schille, was to begin Paul's ministry with
his conversion of a Roman proconsul (*Das älteste Paulus-Bild: Beobachtungen zur lukanischen und zur deuteropaulinischen Paulus-Darstellung*
[Berlin, 1979], 36). Schille also suggested, on the basis of 1 Cor. 16:19 and
Rom. 16:3–5, that Aquila and Priscilla were Christians already in Rome
when Claudius expelled the Jews. Luke, reluctant to acknowledge that the
emperor expelled Christians as well as Jews, says in Acts 18:2–3 merely
that they were Jews prior to arriving in Corinth (41–42). Again, Reinhard
Kratz compares Acts 16:11–40 with 1 Thes. 2:2 and 2 Cor. 11:23–25,
and on the basis of parallels in Acts 5:17–25 and 12:6–11 he attempts to
distill tradition from Lucan redaction (*Rettungswunder: Motiv-, traditions-,
formkritische Aufarbeitung einer biblischen Gattung* [Frankfurt, 1979],
474–92). Originally the story involved Paul and Silas imprisoned over-
night in Philippi, where they converted the guard. The next morning the
officials released them on the condition that they leave the city. According
to Kratz, Luke added to the story the earthquake and in particular
vv. 35–40, which emphasize Paul's Roman citizenship, his public vindica-
tion, and even an apology from the magistrates. If Kratz is correct, here
again a traditional tale of Paul's scrapes with political authorities has been
redacted into an *apologia*.

53. Paul W. Walaskay, '*And So We Came to Rome': The Political Perspective of
St. Luke*, Society for New Testament Studies Monograph Series 49 (Cambridge, 1983), 64. Walaskay is opposing those who see in Luke-Acts an

apologia pro ecclesia, i.e., Johannes Weiss, William Ramsey, Henry Cadbury, and Hans Conzelmann. Radl, 336–45, likewise argues that Luke knew of Paul's execution but omitted it in order to make an apology to Rome. This conclusion works against Radl's general assumption that Acts is directed to the church, not to Rome. For example, Radl claims that Paul is a cipher through which the church may come to understand its suffering and mission (see n. 39 above).

54. See also Haenchen, 731–32.

55. See also Bovon: "S'il y a un modèle littéraire, en plus du roman hellénistique qui rend compte du goût des voyages et des plaisirs (ici platoniques) du couple apôtre-femme convertie, c'est l'Evangile, particulièrement l'*Evangile de Jean*, qu'il faut mentionner et non pas les Actes canoniques des apôtres" (150). I would quibble with this statement only in that I would maintain that the canonical Acts itself was generated from the gospel genre.

56. See Gibert, 26–31, who likewise suggests that a legendary tradition existed prior to Acts that identified the sufferings of Jesus with those of his followers.

57. So also O'Toole. C. K. Barrett surely goes too far when he insists that Paul's sufferings in Acts show that he was no *theios anēr* and that Luke does, after all, have a *theologia crucis* ("Theologia Crucis—In Acts?" in *Theologia Crucis-Signum Crucis: Festschrift für Erich Dinkler*, ed. Carl Andresen and Günter Klein [Tübingen, 1979], 73–84).

58. This is true not only of Colossians but also of Ephesians (3:1, 4:1, 6:20), 2 Timothy (1:8–12, 2:8–9), 3 Corinthians (especially 35), and Laodiceans (6–8).

59. So also Bovon, 152 and 158.

COMMENT: WHAT DOES *UNPAULINE* MEAN?

1. Morton Smith, "Pauline Worship as Seen by Pagans," *Harvard Theological Review* 73 (1980): 241–49.

2. Sam K. Williams, *Jesus' Death as Saving Event*, Harvard Dissertations in Religion 2 (Missoula, Mont., 1975); David Seeley, "The Concept of Noble Death in Paul" (Ph.D. diss., Claremont Graduate School, 1985).

3. See John Pobee, *Persecution and Martyrdom in the Theology of Paul*, Journal for the Study of the New Testament Supplement Series 6 (Sheffield, England, 1985).

IRENAEUS' USE OF PAUL IN HIS POLEMIC AGAINST THE GNOSTICS

1. Johannes Werner, *Der Paulinismus des Irenaeus*, Texte und Untersuchungen 6.2 (Leipzig, 1889). See also, for example, J. Hoh, *Die Lehre des Hl. Irenäus über das Neue Testament* (Münster, 1919); John H.

Lawson, *The Biblical Theology of Saint Irenaeus* (London, 1948); J. Ben-
tivegna, "Pauline Elements in the Anthropology of St. Irenaeus," *Studia
Evangelica* 5 [= Texte und Untersuchungen 103] (1968): 229–33; Elio
Peretto, *La lettera ai Romani cc. 1–8 nell' Adversus Haereses d'Ireneo*
(Bari, 1971), which I have not been able to consult; John S. Coolidge,
The Pauline Basis of the Concept of Scriptural Form in Irenaeus, Center
for Hermeneutical Studies in Hellenistic and Modern Culture, Berkeley,
Calif., Protocol of the Eighth Colloquy: 4 November 1973 (Berkeley,
Calif., 1975); François Altermath, *Du corps psychique au corps spirituel:
Interprétation de 1 Cor. 15,35–49 par les auteurs chrétiens des quatre
premiers siècles*, Beiträge zur Geschichte der biblischen Exegese 18 (Tübingen, 1977); and also the brief notes in André Benoit, *Saint Irénée:
Introduction à l'étude de sa théologie* (Paris, 1960); Hans von Campenhausen, *The Formation of the Christian Bible*, trans. J. A. Baker (Philadelphia, 1972); Ernst Dassmann, *Der Stachel im Fleisch: Paulus in der
frühchristlichen Literatur bis Irenaeus* (Münster, 1979); and Andreas Lindemann, *Paulus im ältesten Christentum: Das Bild des Apostels und die
Rezeption der paulinischen Theologie in der frühchristlichen Literatur bis
Marcion*, Beiträge zur historischen Theologie 58 (Tübingen, 1979).

2. On this point, see Werner, 47; Adolf Harnack, *History of Dogma*, trans.
Neil Buchanan, 7 vols. (reprint: New York, 1961), 2:48 n. 2, 51. For a
different view, see Lindemann, 390.

3. For example, see Lawson, 74: "S. Paul gave the great historic witness to the
futility of religion based upon the hope of man earning forgiveness and
righteousness in the sight of God by his own efforts. It is disappointing to
find that S. Irenaeus made so little of this vital element in Romans"; also
Werner, 49.

4. "No one understands, no one seeks for God."

5. *AH* 5.6.1–8.3. This section opens with a quotation of 1 Cor. 2:6, which
raises the question of what Paul means by "the perfect"; it proceeds,
alluding to 1 Cor. 2:15 and 1 Thes. 5:23, to consider the identity of the
pneumatikos and closes off with an allusion to 1 Cor. 2:14.

6. See, in particular, *AH* 3.16.6. Here Irenaeus, like his opponents, develops
the sense of Eph. 1:10 in conjunction with a reading of the christological
hymn of Col. 1:15ff., and the recapitulation in Christ is envisaged primarily in cosmic terms.

7. It is worth noting that Irenaeus takes this interpretation quite seriously.
AH 4.29.1 quotes the text again, in connection with a quite different issue,
but in the course of an argument that makes it plain he is not taking "of
this world" with "God."

8. Cf. Dt. 4:19 and 5:8. The difficulty with this argument, of course, is that
Irenaeus' opponents may have thought exactly the same thing but referred
the creation of the cosmos to these heavenly powers.

9. "But our *conversatio* is in the heavens, whence also we await a savior, the
Lord Jesus, who will transfigure the body of our lowliness to be like
the body of his glory. . . ."

10. See *AH* 5.10.1–11.2 and 5.9.2–4.

11. Thus at *AH* 3.20.3, Irenaeus cites Rom. 7:18 ("I know that no good dwells in my flesh") and 7:24 ("Who will free me from the body of this death?") and, without allusion to any Valentinian reading of the texts in question, simply asserts that Paul's point is that *non a nobis sed a Deo est bonum salutis nostrae.*

12. Even a cursory reading of Elaine H. Pagels, *The Gnostic Paul: Gnostic Exegesis of the Pauline Letters* (Philadelphia, 1975), seems to confirm this suggestion.

13. See *AH* 3.12.9. The references are to the Areopagus speech (Acts 17:22ff., especially vv. 24–28) and to Acts 14:6–13.

14. 1 Cor. 8:6, already referred to, and Rom. 5:17 (*tou henos Iesou Christou*), which Irenaeus cites at *AH* 3.16.9.

15. See *AH* 3.16.9, where Irenaeus cites Rom. 6:3–4, 5:6, 8–10, 8:34, and 8:11 to this effect.

16. Irenaeus clearly takes the christological hymn of Col. 1:15ff. itself to make the very point he is interested in. The description of Christ as the "first-born of all creation . . . in [whom] all things were created" is balanced by the description of him as "first-born from the dead." This can only mean that the Christ is the one Son of God become a human being. Thus in *AH* 4.2.4, the phrase "first-born from the dead" entails the belief that Moses, the prophets, and the Lord himself are *ex una substantia.*

17. Cf. *AH* 4.12.3, where Rom. 10:3–4 is quoted to the same point.

18. See *AH* 4.25.1, where Abraham is described as *princeps et praenuntiator . . . nostrae fidei.*

19. I am inclined to think that the exegesis of Irenaeus' presbyter, which Irenaeus makes his own, is in fact directed against Marcionites primarily if not exclusively.

20. I count thirteen occasions—all save one in Books 3 and 4 of *Adversus haereses*—on which Irenaeus cites one or another expression from Gal. 4:4–6.

21. It should be noted that this expression occurs also at Rom 8:23 and in association with ideas ("first fruits of the Spirit," "redemption of our bodies") that are basic to Irenaeus' theology.

22. To this point Irenaeus also cites Phil. 3:12, where Paul insists that he has not yet received "the prize."

23. See *AH* 3.22.3 and 4.38.2.

24. See, for example, *AH* 4.9.2.

25. On what follows, see also Coolidge's important essay, especially 4 and 12ff.

26. Eph. 4:6 ("One God and Father of us all, who is above all and through all and in all").

27. On this point, see Adelin Rousseau's note in *Irénée de Lyon: Contre les hérésies, Livre III*, ed. Rousseau and Louis Doutreleau, vol. 1: *Introduction, notes justificatives, tables*, Sources chrétiennes 210 (Paris, 1974), 332.

28. Needless to say, this is not the only way in which Irenaeus characterizes that history. He also appeals to the Pauline image of "psychic" first and

"spiritual" second (1 Cor. 15:45–46), which suggests to Irenaeus that the history of humanity with God can be conceived not only as Christ's reversal of Adam's disobedience, but also as a process of maturation or growth. Thus it is Paul who lies at the root of the apparent conflict in Irenaeus' thought between a picture of human history as an affair of fall and restoration and a picture of it as a movement from small beginnings to realized likeness to God.

29. ". . . not that we would be unclothed, but that we would be further clothed, so that what is mortal may be swallowed up by life."

30. See the Greek of the fragment preserved in Theodoret *Eranistes* 3: *en tō nikan kai hypomenein . . . kai anistasthai . . . (Irénée de Lyon: Contre les hérésies, Livre III,* ed. Rousseau and Doutreleau, vol. 2: *Texte et traduction,* Sources chrétiennes 211 [Paris, 1974], 378).

31. And cf. 5.3.1: *per suam infirmitatem cognoscit virtutem Dei.*

32. Again compare Rom. 8:23.

33. See, for example, the well-known passage at *AH* 3.18.7, where it is said of the Christ: *haerere . . . fecit et adunivit . . . hominem Deo;* the possibility of this work of mediation (cf. 1 Tm. 2:5) is seen to depend in part on his being what a human person is.

34. See *AH* 3.16.3 and 4.24.1.

LITERARY ARTIFICE AND THE FIGURE OF PAUL IN THE WRITINGS OF TERTULLIAN

1. See, e.g., Karl H. Schelkle, *Paulus, Lehrer der Väter: Die altkirchliche Auslegung von Römer 1–11,* 2d ed. (Düsseldorf, 1959), passim.

2. Fritz Barth, "Tertullians Auffassung des Apostels Paulus und seines Verhältnisses zu den Uraposteln," *Jährbuch für Protestant Theologie* 8 (1882): 706–56; Eva Aleith, *Das Paulusverständnis in der alten Kirche* (Berlin, 1937), 49–61, see especially 61; Claude Rambaux, "La composition et l'exégèse dans les deux lettres *ad uxorem,* le *de exhortatione castitatis* et le *de monogamia,* ou la construction de la pensée dans les traités de Tertullien sur le remarriage," *Revue des études augustiniennes* 22 (1976): 1–28, 201–17; 23 (1977): 18–62. There have, of course, been more positive evaluations; see, e.g., Gerald L. Bray, *Holiness and the Will of God: Perspectives on the Theology of Tertullian* (Atlanta, 1979), 70–73.

3. Tertullian deliberately rejects the apocryphal *Acts of Paul and Thecla* (*De bapt.* 17.5). See also E. Margaret Howe, "Interpretations of Paul in the *Acts of Paul and Thecla,*" in *Pauline Studies: Essays Presented to Professor F. F. Bruce,* ed. Donald A. Hagner and Murray J. Harris (Exeter, 1980), 33–49.

4. The one exception is a brief allusion to Paul as pharisee in *De res. mort.* 39.2. There is, apparently, no allusion in the entire corpus of Tertullian's works to Paul's own statement in Galatians 1:15 that he was "separated from his mother's womb"; see *Biblia Patristica: Index des citations et*

allusions bibliques dans la littérature patristique, vol. 1: *Des origines à Clément d'Alexandrie et Tertullien* (Paris, 1975), 482.

5. Translated "at work in him" by Ernest Evans, ed., *Tertullian: Adversus Marcionem*, 2 vols., Oxford Early Christian Texts (Oxford, 1972), 2:619; as "instigator" by Peter Holmes in Alexander Roberts and James Donaldson, eds., *The Ante-Nicene Fathers*, vol. 3: *Latin Christianity: Its Founder, Tertullian* (Grand Rapids, Mich., 1973), 466. Holmes refers the term to Eph. 2:2: *spiritus qui nunc operatur in filios diffidentiae* (Vulgate).

6. Tertullian's sense of the growth and development of the apostle should perhaps be placed in the context of his general affirmation of "progress in history." See Jean-Claude Fredouille, *Tertullien et la conversion de la culture antique* (Paris, 1972), 235–300, who finds the notion of progress "une idée chère à Tertullien" (246) and notes that the *vetera-nova* antithesis constitutes "une veritable catégorie de pensée" (297) for him. Fredouille believes that Tertullian's sense of progress in history reflects Stoic influence: "He understood the history of salvation as the disciples of the Porch conceived the progress of individual wisdom and historical development" (293). See also Ludwig Edelstein, *The Idea of Progress in Classical Antiquity* (Baltimore, 1967), especially for the concept of the progress of the individual as well as of society in the writings of Seneca (169–77).

7. Maurice Wiles' attempt to conflate all four underplays the differences among them; see *The Divine Apostle: The Interpretation of St. Paul's Epistles in the Early Church* (Cambridge, 1967), 18–19.

8. There is no evidence that Tertullian has any concern whatsoever with the problem so pressing in modern biblical studies of harmonizing the accounts of Galatians and Acts. I understand his narratives of Paul's visits to Jerusalem to be shaped by a primarily artistic response to the forensic context in each case. I am suggesting that here the figure of Paul as it appears in Tertullian is strongly conditioned by literary artifice.

9. Tertullian appears to read the amazement of the Damascenes recorded in Acts 9:21 into the reaction of the Jews recorded in Galatians 1:23.

10. The interpretation of the passage at this point is undeniably difficult. A. Kroymann finds a textual corruption (see the *apparatus criticus* of his edition of the *Adversus Marcionem* in *Corpus scriptorum ecclesiasticorum latinorum*, vol. 47: *Tertulliani Opera, Pars III* [Vienna, 1906], 575); Wiles, 19, n. 1, evidently agrees. In my view the context requires that we understand the *rudis fides* here of the Galatian Christians, not of Paul, in spite of the similarity of this phrase to that used in *Adv. Marc.* 1.20.2 (*ad huc in gratia rudis*), clearly in description of Paul. Evans' translation reflects the ambiguity of the Latin (2:521), whereas Holmes, 433, understands the phrase to refer to the Galatians. Cf. Barth, 743. Wiles, 19, and Aleith, 53, disregard this issue. The question is apparently not relevant to the narrowly defined aims of E. P. Meijering's commentary, *Tertullian contra Marcion: Gotteslehre in der Polemik Adversus Marcionem I-II* (Leiden, 1977), see 59–60.

11. The striking difference between the portrait of the young neophyte in *Adversus Marcionem* 1 and the picture of the experienced apostle in *Adversus Marcionem* 5 could readily be explained on the view that the fifth book was added later to the third edition of the work (so, e.g., Paul Monceaux, *Histoire littéraire de l'Afrique chrétienne*, vol. 1: *Tertullien et les origines* [Paris, 1901], 198–99, 209). The explanation becomes hazardous, however, in the light of Timothy D. Barnes' defense of a unified composition (*Tertullian: A Historical and Literary Study* [Oxford, 1971], 40 n. 1, and 255–56). It is better to assume that Tertullian was prepared to sacrifice consistency with the earlier portrait in order to give a more controlling position to Acts in which the council of Jerusalem (Acts 15) follows a complete missionary journey (Acts 13–14), thus eliminating the possibility of portraying Paul as a neophyte.

12. In the *De idolatria* (9.6), the fate of Elymas demonstrates that the magic that emulates the divine power has been thrust out by the gospel; in the *De anima* (57.7), Elymas illustrates the attempt of the demonic to counterfeit the truth; in the *De pudicitia* (21.4), the story indicates that apostolic discipline was accompanied by apostolic power, a power lacking in the *episcopus episcoporum* (1.6) whom the treatise addresses.

13. For the context to which this interest in the apostle's growth may belong, see n. 6 above.

14. In *De fuga* (6.6), Tertullian appeals to a further instance of change or development in Paul's life, outside the missionary journeys: in Paul's early career, he followed the command to escape from Damascus by the wall (Acts 9:25; 2 Cor. 11:33); in his last days, he insisted on going to Jerusalem in the face of almost certain death (Acts 21:13).

15. In the late work *De pudicitia* (1.12), Tertullian justifies his own changing commitments as "growth," summoning the figure of Paul as his model and citing 1 Corinthians 13:11 as evidence that the apostle himself was aware of the changes involved in his development, notably his transformation from Jew to Christian.

16. See n. 14 above; note also *De fug.* 12.6.

17. Paul's citizenship was also an issue at Philippi (Acts 16:37–38), but the language in *Scorp.* 15.3 seems to play on Paul's response to the centurion (Acts 22:28) that he was *born* a Roman: "Tunc Paulus civitatis Romanae consequitur nativitatem, cum illic martyrii renascitur generositate." I add here also the few additional references to episodes from the later chapters of Acts concerning Paul's life: (1) the trials before Ananias (Acts 23:1–9) and Agrippa (specifically Acts 26:22), both to demonstrate Paul's belief in the resurrection (*De res. mort.* 39.3–4); (2) Paul's "public" prayer on board ship as reported in Acts 27:35 (*De orat.* 24; see above p. 105); (3) the viper at Malta (Acts 28:1–6), an image of heresy shaken off by divine power (*Scorp.* 1.4).

18. Although, as we shall see, the figure of Paul emerges in various ways in Tertullian's exegesis of the epistles, it would appear that, apart from the sufferings, Tertullian draws relatively few images of Paul from the

epistles—primarily the visions in paradise (2 Cor. 12:1–4) which, he insists, provide no basis for the heretical claim to a special revelation (*De praescr.* 24.5–6), as well as allusions to the apostates Phygelus and Hermogenes (2 Tm. 1:15; see *De pud.* 13.19), to the cloak left at Troas with Carpus (2 Tm. 4:13; see *De orat.* 15.2; *De cor.* 8.3), and to Paul's self-support (1 Cor. 9:12–15; see *Adv. Marc.* 5.7.11).

19. Tertullian also refers (*De res. mort.* 10.4) to the *stigmata Christi* that Paul bore in his body (Gal. 6:17), but without indicating how he understands the *stigmata*.

20. See Barth, 735–41. But note also passages where Paul is cited along with other apostles without any sense of distinction in rank (e.g., *De orat.* 20.2; *De carne Christi* 22.1–3). In citations of scripture Paul is summoned in an order apparently independent of any collegial rank (see, e.g., *De fug.* 9; *Adv. Prax.* 25, 28.2–7).

21. Here, specifically, Paul is given the title *pacificus apostolus*.

22. For the close relation between *disciplina* and *doctrina* in Tertullian, see René Braun, *Deus christianorum: Recherches sur le vocabulaire doctrinal de Tertullien*, 2d ed. (Paris, 1977), 419–25, and the references there to the studies of Marrou and Morel.

23. In Tertullian's usage, the word *doceo* frequently vacillates in meaning between "teach" and "demonstrate" (or "show"). It is unlikely, however, that the connotation of teaching is absent even when the primary sense is "demonstrate."

24. We recognize in these virtues classical, and especially Stoic, ideals; see, e.g., Cicero *De finibus* 3.75 (*gravitas, constantia*); 4.31 (*patientia*); Diogenes Laertius 7.117 (*modestia* [the σοφός as ἄτυφος]). For the personal embodiment of *gravitas* and *constantia*, see Cicero *Orationes Philippicae* 9.10 (Servius Sulpicius); and of *humanitas* and *integritas*, Cicero *Epistulae ad Quintum Fratrem* 1.1.37 (Quintus Cicero). For an excellent recent discussion showing the Stoic-Christian synthesis in Tertullian's view of *patientia* (although more Stoic than Christian), see Jean-Claude Fredouille, ed., *Tertullien: De la patience*, Sources chrétiennes 310 (Paris, 1984), 27–33.

25. On this passage, see J. H. Waszink, ed., *Tertulliani De Anima* (Amsterdam, 1947), 229–36; but also Fredouille, *Tertullien et la conversion de la culture antique*, 162–65, who stresses more decisively than Waszink the classical background of Tertullian's psychology at this point and also provides a useful bibliography.

26. I follow Kroymann's reconstruction of the text here. He understands *apostolus* (rather than *spiritus*) as the noun modified by *ille sanctus* (see his edition of the *Ad uxorem* in *Corpus scriptorum ecclesiasticorum latinorum*, vol. 70: *Tertulliani Opera, Partis II. volumen posterius* [Vienna, 1942], 113, note on line 36), as does Charles Munier, ed., *Tertullien: A son épouse*, Sources chrétiennes 273 (Paris, 1980), who incorporates *apostolus* into his text of Tertullian's work (see 128 and the note on 178).

27. See also *Adv. Marc.* 5.7.2, where Tertullian, in interpreting Paul's words, appeals to Paul's character (*vir tantae constantiae*)—"not to mention the Holy Spirit" (*ne dicam spiritus sanctus*)—to judge the apostle's intent. On Tertullian's appeal to such human factors as "character" in his interpretation of Pauline texts, see Robert D. Sider, *Ancient Rhetoric and the Art of Tertullian* (Oxford, 1971), 91–97.

28. See Robert D. Sider, "Structure and Design in the *De resurrectione mortuorum* of Tertullian," *Vigiliae Christianae* 23 (1969): 177–96.

29. The reference is to 1 Corinthians 15:49, where textual variants witness both to the indicative and to the imperative.

30. See, e.g., *De praescr.* 6.5–6, where Tertullian says, in reference to Paul's anathema of anyone who preaches another gospel (Gal. 1:8), that "the Holy Spirit foresaw" just such an episode.

31. This attitude stands in sharp contrast to that of Origen in his commentary on Romans; see, for example, *Comm. in Rom.* praef. (PG 14:833). At one point, however, Tertullian does admit that the letters of Paul invite more than a surface reading: *De exhort. cast.* 9.1.

32. For a brilliant literary analysis of Tertullian's exegesis here, see Fredouille, *Tertullien et la conversion de la culture antique*, 164–68.

33. See Robert D. Sider, "Tertullian *On the Shows*: An Analysis," *Journal of Theological Studies*, n.s. 29 (1978): 339–65.

34. I acknowledge that neither the frequency with which Tertullian cites Pauline texts nor the more subjectively evaluated degree of vitality the texts enjoy in his argument provides a secure base for reconstructing Tertullian's perception of the "mind" of Paul. When a text is quoted, we can be certain that Tertullian is citing the text as Pauline, and not more generally as "scripture," only if he specifically labels it Pauline. Even when (as often) he does specifically ascribe a text to Paul, one cannot confidently distinguish between what Tertullian likes to quote as Pauline in the interest of his own argument and what he might regard as the genuine core of *Paul's* theological reflection. Even with these qualifications, however, I suggest that it is worthwhile to outline the prominent themes and images as providing clues to, rather than a definitive picture of, Tertullian's conception of the chief foci around which the apostle's thought seemed to move.

35. Emanuele Castorina, ed., *De spectaculis* (Florence, 1961), 276, identifies the spirit here as the divine Spirit, not the human spirit. Ernest Evans, ed., *Tertullian's Tract on the Prayer* (London, 1953), 51, also construes "holy spirit" as the divine Spirit in his comment on the passage from *De oratione* that I cite in the next sentence. It is not my intent, however, to comment here on the considerable scholarship devoted to Tertullian's doctrine of the Spirit. For an imaginative study with a good bibliography, see Claire Ann Bradley Stegman, "The Development of Tertullian's Doctrine of 'Spiritus Sanctus'" (Ph.D. diss., Southern Methodist University, 1979). Stegman argues that Tertullian understands the *spiritus sanctus* to be the "collective" human *spiritus post baptismum* (65). Discussing the *De*

baptismo, she claims: "The key to Tertullian's meaning is his collective concept of humanity. When he is speaking about an individual Christian, he is speaking of that person's human *spiritus* 'reborn' in Christ. When he is speaking in general about the new humanity in Christ, he is speaking of *spiritus sanctus* given to the Church, which as the Body of Christ is for Tertullian the 'new humanity'" (58). It is possible that Stegman over-schematizes Tertullian's usage, but it seems clear that one cannot simply assume that, in Tertullian's works, the term *spiritus sanctus* refers to the third person of the trinity as in classic Christian doctrine.

36. For analogous discussions of the moral significance of the Spirit in Tertullian's earlier works, see *De pat.* 7.7 and *De cultu fem.* 2.1.1.

37. On the importance of "revelation" in Tertullian as in some sense "anti-hellenic," see Braun, 418.

38. On the other hand, even though Tertullian regarded Paul as a preacher of peace, he gives little prominence to Pauline texts on peace.

39. I follow Evans, ed., *Tertullian: Adversus Marcionem,* 1:87, in my interpretation of the phrase *negotium patitur.*

40. An echo, I believe, of the Pauline text in Ephesians 2:13.

41. There is a large body of scholarly literature on the problem of human and divine knowledge in Tertullian. For a sampling of recent scholarship, see Robert D. Sider, "Approaches to Tertullian: A Study of Recent Scholarship," *Second Century* 2 (1982): 247–50.

42. See *De mon.* 3.8, 7.4, 11.4, 14.4; also *Ad ux.* 1.5.4.

43. Tertullian here does not follow the biblical account as we have it. "L'explication doit être cherchée sans doute dans les conditions de transmission du Livre de Job" (Fredouille, ed., *Tertullien: De la patience,* 259).

44. See especially *Adv. Prax.* 4.2–3; see also Eckhard Schendel, *Herrschaft und Unterwerfung Christi: 1 Korinther 15,24–28 in Exegese und Theologie der Väter bis zum Ausgang des 4. Jahrhunderts,* Beiträge zur Geschichte der biblischen Exegese 12 (Tübingen, 1971), 30–73. Schendel's study is concerned only with the exposition of 1 Corinthians 15:24–28 in the fathers; these verses, he argues (30), will play a much larger part in the theologies of Origen and of Marcellus of Ancyra. His work demonstrates, however, the importance of the passage in the *Adversus Praxean.* Of the citations of 1 Corinthians by Tertullian listed in the *Biblia Patristica,* just over 160 are citations of 1 Corinthians 15.

45. This picture of Tertullian's Paul has some similarity to the picture that Bray (see especially 63–65) draws of Tertullian himself, but the "Paul" who has emerged from our study is more historically oriented in his eschatological thought than is Bray's ethically oriented Tertullian.

46. See, for example, the widely differing contexts in which Tertullian appeals to features of the Sermon on the Mount in *Apol.* 45; *De idol.* 2; *De pat.* 11.

47. See Alfred Schindler, "Das Wort 'Gnade' und die Gnadenlehre bei den Kirchenvätern bis zu Augustin," in *Gnadenwahl und Entscheidungsfreiheit in der Theologie der alten Kirche,* ed. Fairy von Lilienfeld and Ekkehard

Mühlenberg, Oikonomia 9 (Erlangen, 1980), 49–50. For a somewhat similar view, see Stegman, 89.

48. In characterizing the eastern and western churches, Ernst Benz similarly distinguishes their respective theological foci in relation to their predominate orientation to one or to the other of these two sets of Pauline epistles; see his "Das Paulus-Verständnis in der morgenländischen und abendländischen Kirche," Zeitschrift für Religions- und Geistesgeschichte 3 (1951): 291. For what it may be worth (see n. 34 above), we can note that Tertullian cites 1 Corinthians far more frequently than he does Romans. The Biblia Patristica identifies approximately 250 references to Romans and approximately 725 to 1 Corinthians in Tertullian's works.

FREE CHOICE AND THE DIVINE WILL
IN GREEK CHRISTIAN COMMENTARIES ON PAUL

1. Theodoret of Cyrus Affect. 5.1-4.
2. Affect. 5.28-32.
3. Martha C. Nussbaum, The Fragility of Goodness: Luck and Ethics in Greek Tragedy and Philosophy (Cambridge, 1986), 2–3 (the citation of Pindar Nemean 8.40-42 appears on p. 1).
4. See David Amand, Fatalisme et liberté dans l'antiquité grecque (Louvain, 1945); Wilhelm Gundel, "Heimarmene," Paulys Realencyclopaedie der classischen Altertumswissenschaft 7 (1912): 2622-45; William Chase Greene, Moira: Fate, Good, and Evil in Greek Thought (Cambridge, Mass., 1944).
5. Nichomachean Ethics 1109b30-1113b2.
6. On fate in Stoicism, see Max Pohlenz, Die Stoa: Geschichte einer geistigen Bewegung, 2 vols. (Göttingen, 1948–49), 1:110ff.; on astrology, see Frederick H. Cramer, Astrology in Roman Law and Politics (Philadelphia, 1954), and Franz Cumont, Astrology and Religion among the Greeks and Romans, trans. J. B. Baker (1912; reprint: New York, 1960); on Carneades, see Amand, 41–70.
7. From the same period come pseudo-Plutarch De fato and, somewhat later, the discussions in Plotinus Enneads 3.1, 2, 3. On works written against fatalism during the second century, see Cramer, 195–208, and Amand, 101–56.
8. Alexander of Aphrodisias De fato 16, trans. R. W. Sharples, Alexander of Aphrodisias on Fate: Text, Translation, and Commentary (London, 1983), 66 (text on 195).
9. Cf. De princ. 3.1.1-5 and Alexander De fato 1-6. See Robert L. Wilken, "Justification by Works," Concordia Theological Monthly 40 (1969); 379–92; Harald Holz, "Über den Begriff des Willens und der Freiheit bei Origines," Neue Zeitschrift für systematische Theologie und Religionsphilosophie 12 (1970): 63–84.
10. Octavius 11.6.

11. 1 *Apol.* 43, trans. Cyril C. Richardson, *Early Christian Fathers* (Philadelphia, 1953), 269 (slightly altered). Prophecy, and hence foreknowledge, was a philosophical problem for others besides Christians. It was considered an argument in favor of determinism in Stoicism (see H. von Arnim, ed., *Stoicorum veterum fragmenta*, 4 vols. (Leipzig, 1903–24; reprint: Dubuque, Iowa, n.d.), 2:943, 944; also Cicero *De divinatione* 2.18). Alexander of Aphrodisias, among others, offers arguments to the contrary (*De fato* 30).

12. *Republic* 617E.

13. *De princ.* 3.1.6-7, trans. G. W. Butterworth, *Origen: On First Principles* (1936; reprint: New York, 1966), 166 (slightly altered).

14. For the purposes of this study, I have focused on problems issuing from the philosophical discussion of freedom and determinism, but it is apparent that in the section on free will in *De princ.* and in the commentary on Romans, Origen is equally concerned to counter Gnostic exegesis of Paul (see, for example, *De princ.* 3.1.23; and the Greek text of *Comm. in Rom.* 5.7 in Jean Scherer, ed., *Le commentaire d'Origène sur Rom. III.5–V.7 d'après les extraits du papyrus no. 88748 du Musée du Caire et les fragments de la Philocalie et du Vaticanus Gr. 762* [Cairo, 1957], 168ff.). On Gnostic interpretation of Paul, see Elaine H. Pagels, *The Gnostic Paul: Gnostic Exegesis of the Pauline Letters* (Philadelphia, 1975).

15. *De princ.* 3.1.1, trans. Butterworth, 157.

16. For the interpretation of Romans in the early church, see Karl H. Schelkle, *Paulus, Lehrer der Väter: Die altkirchliche Auslegung von Römer 1–11* (Düsseldorf, 1956); Peter Gorday, *Principles of Patristic Exegesis: Romans 9–11 in Origen, John Chrysostom, and Augustine*, Studies in the Bible and Early Christianity 4 (New York, 1983); Maurice Wiles, *The Divine Apostle: The Interpretation of St. Paul's Epistles in the Early Church* (Cambridge, 1967); and Ernst Benz, "Das Paulus-Verständnis in der morgenländischen und abendländischen Kirche," *Zeitschrift für Religions- und Geistesgeschichte* 3 (1951): 289–309. For Origen on the question of Pharaoh in particular, see W. J. P. Boyd, "Origen on Pharaoh's Hardened Heart: A Study of Justification and Election in St. Paul and Origen," *Studia Patristica* 7 [= *Texte und Untersuchungen* 92] (1966): 434–42; Marguerite Harl, "La mort salutaire du Pharaon selon Origène," in *Studi in onore di Alberto Pincherle*, 2 vols. (Rome, 1967), 1:260–68.

17. *Comm. in Joannem* 2.191 (on Jn. 1:6). Cf. the fourth-century Latin treatise, *De induratione cordis pharaonis et de aliis quattuor quaestionibus* (PL Supplementum 1:1506–39). This text is discussed in Eugene TeSelle, "Rufinus the Syrian, Caelestius, Pelagius: Explorations in the Prehistory of the Pelagian Controversy," *Augustinian Studies* 3 (1972): 84.

18. *De princ.* 3.1.7.

19. Origen: *Comm. in Rom.* 7.16 (PG 14:1144), in Rufinus' translation. For Theodore, see Karl Staab, *Pauluskommentare aus der griechischen Kirche* (1933; reprint: Münster, 1984), 144ff. Also: Diodore of Tarsus (Staab, 98);

Chrysostom Hom. 16 in Rom. 7 (PG 60:558); Cyril of Alexandria In ep. ad Rom. 9:14–21 (in Philip Edward Pusey, ed., Sancti Patris Nostri Cyrilli Archiepiscopi Alexandrini [Opera], 7 vols. [Oxford, 1868–77; reprint: Brussels, 1965], 5:227).

20. Staab, 144.
21. De anima libri mantissa 23 (text in Sharples, 214).
22. Diodore of Tarsus (Staab, 99); Theodoret of Cyrus Interp. ep. ad Rom. 9:21 (PG 82:157); Severian of Gabala (Staab, 222): Gennadius of Constantinople (Staab, 393).
23. Hom. 16 in Rom. 8 (PG 60:559).
24. Valentin Weber, Kritische Geschichte der Exegese des 9. Kapitels, resp. der Verse 14–23, des Römerbriefes bis auf Chrysostomus und Augustinus einschliesslich (Würzburg, 1889). Eva Aleith's book, Das Paulusverständnis in der alten Kirche (Berlin, 1937), stands in the same tradition, accusing the fathers of not understanding Paul's teaching on justification. On modern interpretation of early Christian commentators on Paul, see Gorday, 24–32.
25. Wiles, 94.
26. Staab, 67.
27. De fato 15, trans. Sharples, 63; elsewhere Alexander says: "To be rational is nothing other than to be a beginning of actions (archēn prakseōn)" (De fato 14, trans. Sharples, 62).
28. Comm. in Rom. 5.2 (Scherer, 138) and 6.1 (Scherer, 178ff.).
29. Staab, 58.
30. Comm. in Rom. 6.1 (Scherer, 178ff.).
31. Galen De usu partium 11.14 (emphasis added). A text and translation of the entire passage can be found in Richard Walzer, Galen on Jews and Christians (London, 1949), 11–13. Cf. 2 Baruch 4:2: "It is not this building that is in your midst now; it is that which will be revealed, with me, that was already prepared from the moment that I decided to create Paradise" (emphasis added; trans. A. F. J. Klijn in James H. Charlesworth, ed., The Old Testament Pseudepigrapha, 2 vols. [Garden City, N.Y., 1983–85], 1:622).
32. Alexander of Aphrodisias De fato 2, trans. Sharples, 42; Chrysippus in von Arnim, 2:1000.
33. Theodoret Interp. ep. ad Rom. 9:14 (PG 82:153); Theodore of Mopsuestia in Staab, 143–44.
34. Albrecht Dihle, The Theory of Will in Classical Antiquity (Berkeley, Los Angeles, and London, 1982), 2. Divine voluntarism is not wholly absent from Platonism. The middle Platonist Albinus wrote:

> [God] is Father by reason of the fact that he is cause of all things and orders the heavenly Mind and the Soul of the World in accordance with himself and with his thoughts; for by his own boulēsis he has filled all things with himself, rousing up the Soul of the World and turning it towards himself,

as being the cause of its Mind. And this latter, being set in order by its Father itself sets in order the whole of Nature within this world (*Didaskalikos* 10; cited in John Dillon, *The Middle Platonists* [Ithaca, N.Y., 1977], 283–84).

Boulēsis, however, means ordering or arranging according to plan, as for example in pseudo-Plutarch:

> The highest, or primary, providence is the *noēsis* or *boulēsis*, beneficent to all things, of the primary God, and in conformity with it all things divine are primordially arranged throughout, each as is best and most excellent (*De fato* 9 [*Moralia* 572F], trans. Phillip H. De Lacy and Benedict Einarson, *Plutarch's Moralia* VII, Loeb Classical Library 405 [Cambridge, Mass., 1959], 343).

Boulēsis is again paired with *noēsis* slightly later in the same section of this work (*De fato* 9 [*Moralia* 573B]). The term is not foreign to Plato: see *Laws* 967A; also *Timaeus* 29E: "he wished (*eboulēthē*) that all things become as similar as possible to himself." Dihle also indicates that voluntarism was more prevalent in the Latin than in the Greek tradition prior to Christianity (pp. 132ff.).

35. Text in J. A. F. Gregg, "The Commentary of Origen upon the Epistle to the Ephesians," *Journal of Theological Studies* 3 (1902): 237.

36. Staab, 304.

37. *Interp. ep. ad Eph.* 1:5 and 1:11 (PG 82:509, 513); see also *Interp. ep. ad Phil.* 2:13 (PG 82:573).

38. *Hom. 1 in Eph.* 2 (PG 62:13); note also *Hom. 1 in Eph.* 4 (PG 62:15), where he says that "according to his good pleasure" means "he desired this, he yearned (*ōdinen*) for it."

39. *In ep. ad Eph.* (at Eph. 1:5), in Henry B. Swete, ed., *Theodori Episcopi Mopsuesteni in Epistolas B. Pauli Commentarii*, 2 vols. (Cambridge, 1880–82), 1:124.

40. Text in Swete, 2:294–95.

41. Swete, 2:295.

42. Richard Norris, *Manhood and Christ* (Oxford, 1963), 218–21, with the citations given in n. 3 on 221.

43. *Comm. in Rom.* 6.6 (Scherer, 214), on Rom. 4:18–22.

44. Staab, 386, 391.

45. Staab, 144. Note also the following: "In all things he manifests clearly that God is not ruled by the order of nature, but that he chooses by grace and favor whomever he considers worthy of choice, who first were worthy of his grace, then are able to contribute on their own, showing their own choice proportioned by grace" (Staab, 144).

46. *Prop. ad Rom.* 13–18 (text and translation in Paula Fredriksen Landes, *Augustine on Romans* [Chico, Calif., 1982], 4–7).

47. Origen says that the task before Paul in the epistle as a whole was to "present the salvation of Israel living according to the law, which was before Christ's advent, but also to present the things that happened after the advent of our Savior" (*Comm. in Rom.* 5.1 [Scherer, 124], on Rom. 3:5–8). On this general topic, see Gorday. Note also Pelagius' approach to Romans. The prologue to his *Expositio in Romanos* presents the epistle as a book about God's relation to the two peoples, Jews and Gentiles, and interprets "law" as referring to ritual law (text in Alexander Souter, *Pelagius's Expositions of Thirteen Epistles of St. Paul*, vol. 2: *Text and Apparatus Criticus*, Texts and Studies 9.2 [Cambridge, 1926], 6–7).

48. Janet Martin Soskice, *Metaphor and Religious Language* (Oxford, 1985), 159.

PAULUS ORIGENIANUS: THE ECONOMIC INTERPRETATION OF PAUL IN ORIGEN AND GREGORY OF NYSSA

I am grateful to Joseph Trigg, David Balas, Richard Norris, Harold Attridge, and Rowan Greer for critical comments incorporated into, or requiring revision of certain parts of, this essay. Eugene TeSelle's comments have been kept in mind throughout.

1. Although scattered comments on, and use of, many of Origen's exegeses of Paul are to be found in works from the Middle Ages to the present, the latest scholarly treatment probably being that of Maurice Wiles in *The Divine Apostle: The Interpretation of St. Paul's Epistles in the Early Church* (Cambridge, 1967), the only study specifically focused on a thorough appreciation of his Paulinism in recent times is Walther Völker, "Paulus bei Origenes," *Theologische Studien und Kritiken* 102 (1930): 258–79. Völker's central point is that Origen combined Paul with Plato in a way that was definitive for the whole later tradition (259), and that he did this by instinctively heading for the passages in Paul's work where the hellenistic influence is strongest (262). Consequently many passages from 1 Corinthians, Ephesians, and Philippians are cited by Origen, in Völker's opinion, to support a combination of ascetic mysticism, allegorical interpretation of scripture, and cosmological Neoplatonism. Further, any sense of an objective salvation-history (271) or of the radical contrast between Judaism and the gospel (262, 265) is completely absent, with the final result that the Pauline view of justification is never clearly seen (274). Völker formulated this view of Paul with two assumptions that are completely inadmissible today: (a) there are a Jewish and a Greek Paul who can be sharply distinguished from one another—but our knowledge of the complex combination of Greek and Jewish elements in pre-Christian Palestine as evidenced, say, in apocalyptic literature rules this view out; and (b) the Jewish Paul is the "real" Paul, and this Paul teaches justification by faith—in fact, primitive

Christianity was a generous pluralism, as was Judaism itself, such that the vaunted specificity of Paul's preaching is not at all clear. Paul seems to have shared much more in common with the church at large than was once thought, especially as his own teaching developed and changed—as, for instance, with regard to the import of the Mosaic law for Gentiles or with regard to the role of Judaism in the eschaton; cf. the work of Hans Hübner and Gerd Luedemann especially on Paul's development from Galatians to Romans. As a matter of method, moreover, Völker did not appeal to the frequency with which Origen used particular Pauline passages or to their location within the structure of an argument. The final charge (275) that Origen was a synergist and teacher of perfection (277-79) is a classification by dogmatic criteria and not a historical judgment.

2. *Biblia Patristica: Index des citations et allusions bibliques dans la littérature patristique*, vol. 3: *Origène* (Paris, 1980). The section covering Origen's use of Pauline texts, excluding the Epistle to the Hebrews, appears on pp. 352-449. There are more citations and allusions from Romans than from any of the other epistles, but that statistic is skewed by the existence of the Romans-commentary; 1 Corinthians is a close second, with 2 Corinthians and Ephesians far behind (3827, 3572, 1264, and 1176 respectively). What matters, aside from sheer frequency (which is not to be ignored), is how one *weighs* these citations and allusions: in what contexts do they appear, across how many works are they scattered, how central do they seem to be to an argument, with what other texts are they combined? These concerns are at least as important as frequency for determining the actual interpretation put on a given text by a commentator or theologian. We still need an adequate hermeneutic of the use of texts in order to understand what writers like Origen make of scripture.

3. The study of the use of Paul by Gnostic groups is still in its infancy. His use by the Valentinians has been extensively studied by Elaine H. Pagels in "The Valentinian Claim to Esoteric Exegesis of Romans as Basis for Anthropological Theory," *Vigiliae Christianae* 26 (1972): 241-58, and *The Gnostic Paul: Gnostic Exegesis of the Pauline Letters* (Philadelphia, 1975). Some good general comments on the Gnostic understanding of Paul are contained in Hans von Campenhausen, *The Formation of the Christian Bible*, trans. J. A. Baker (Philadelphia, 1972), 144-46. As one might expect, differing estimates of the meaning of Gnostic teaching tend to be reflected in differing views of what it is that the Gnostics derive from Paul—or, to state the matter more cautiously, in differing views of what the Gnostics *claim* to derive from Paul.

4. Essential to the discussion of these materials now are Andreas Lindemann, *Paulus im ältesten Christentum: Das Bild des Apostels und die Rezeption der paulinischen Theologie in der frühchristlichen Literatur bis Marcion*, Beiträge zur historischen Theologie 58 (Tübingen, 1979); Ernst Dassmann, *Der Stachel im Fleisch: Paulus in der frühchristlichen Literatur bis Irenaeus* (Münster, 1979); and R. Joseph Hoffman, *Marcion: On the Restitution of*

Christianity: An Essay on the Development of Radical Paulinist Theology in the Second Century, AAR Academy Series 46 (Chico, Calif., 1984). A red thread that runs through all of these studies is the attempt to discern who, in the pluralism of options in the second-century church, really preserved Paul's thought. Dassmann's proposal, that Paul was best preserved by orthodox writers—preeminently Irenaeus—because he was honored as only one voice within the canon and thus his theology was held in tension with other theologies, is probably most reasonable, although it downplays too much the attraction of Paul for individual thinkers who were, ultimately, to be excluded from the orthodox camp.

5. Hoffman, 215.
6. See Hoffman's conclusions (307) and his section (157ff.) on the differentiation of Marcionism and Gnosticism. Despite a sustained attempt on Hoffman's part to make Marcion out as a champion of faith, rather than knowledge, in acquiring salvation, Marcion can still be claimed to belong to the Gnostic sphere of thought where, apropos of this essay, evil is seen to have its origin in divine doing, even if in this case it is the alien, creator God who is responsible.
7. Pagels, "The Valentinian Claim," 242f.: "Our analysis indicates that . . . the Valentinian description of the 'natures' emerges not from a philosophical determinism so much as from a theology of election. More specifically, it indicates that the Valentinians have developed their description of the hylic, psychic and pneumatic 'natures,' as they themselves claim, as an exegetical interpretation of Paul's election-theology."
8. Marguerite Harl, "Les 'mythes' Valentiniens de la création et de l'eschatologie dans le langage d'Origène: Le mot *hypothesis,*" in *The Rediscovery of Gnosticism,* vol. 1: *The School of Valentinus,* ed. Bentley Layton, Studies in the History of Religions 41 (Leiden, 1980), 417–25; also idem, "Origène et la sémantique du langage biblique," *Vigiliae Christianae* 26 (1972): 161–87. The citation appears on p. 185.
9. Kurt Rudolph, *Gnosis: The Nature and History of Gnosticism,* translation ed. Robert McL. Wilson (San Francisco, 1983), 135 and 194f. Rudolph's general definition of Gnosticism is noteworthy: "It is knowledge given by revelation, which has been made available only to the elect who are capable of receiving it. . . . This knowledge freely bestowed can extend from the basic insight into the divine nature of man, his origin and his destiny, up to a complete system. All gnostic teachings are in some form a part of the redeeming knowledge which gathers together the object of knowledge (the divine nature), the means of knowledge (the redeeming gnosis) and the knower himself" (55). Although this formal history-of-religions school definition is perhaps too inclusive, so that Paul himself is made out to be a thoroughgoing Gnostic (301ff.), it rightly emphasizes the Gnostic focus on a saving knowledge of beginnings and endings given from "beyond" to the elect.

10. *Comm. in Rom.* praef. On the question of whether Origen has correctly understood the Valentinian *Dreimenschenklassenlehre*, see Barbara Aland, "Erwählungstheologie und Menschenklassenlehre: Die Theologie des Herakleon als Schlüssel zum Verständnis der christlichen Gnosis?" in *Gnosis and Gnosticism: Papers Read at the Seventh International Conference on Patristic Studies,* ed. Martin Krause, Nag Hammadi Studies 8 (Leiden, 1977), 148–81. In brief, she contends that in framing his response to their teaching as a matter of the freedom of the will in opposition to a strict determinism, Origen has perverted the Valentinian position. Though this point may be true, it is also important to see that Origen argues for real free will only within the context of a position that owes much to the Valentinians.

11. Marguerite Harl, "Pointes antignostiques d'Origène: Le questionnement impie des Écritures," *Studies in Gnosticism and Hellenistic Religions,* ed. R. van den Broek and M. J. Vermaseren (Leiden, 1981), 205–17; also idem, "Origène et les interprétations patristiques grecques de l' 'obscurité' biblique," *Vigiliae Christianae* 36 (1982): 334–71.

12. *Comm. in Rom.* praef. The key phrases are "elocutionibus interdum confusis et minus explicitis utitur" and "ad naturae diversitatem."

13. For example, Patricia Cox, "Origen and the Bestial Soul: A Poetics of Nature," *Vigiliae Christianae* 36 (1982): 115–40.

14. Eric Junod has gathered all of the relevant bibliography in his edition of *Origène: Philocalie 21-27, Sur le libre arbitre,* Sources chrétiennes 226 (Paris, 1976), 107–20.

15. *Comm. in Rom.* 7.16 (PG 14:1145).

16. Junod, 118, n. 1, lists the principal passages.

17. Hal Koch, *Pronoia und Paideusis: Studien über Origenes und sein Verhältnis zum Platonismus* (Berlin, 1932), especially 128–31 for the hardening of Pharaoh's heart. Koch's comment on p. 131 is important: "Es gibt nur Weniges, das für Origenes so charakteristisch ist wie seine Weise, das Problem der Gnostiker hier aufzunehmen und zu einer Lösung zu bringen, und zwar einer solchen Lösung, dass jene Tatsache, welche ihnen die anstössigste von allen schien, nur eine grosse Bestätigung des Grundgedankens in Origenes' Theologie würde." The fault with Koch's treatment, for all its penetration and wisdom, is that it makes Origen too rational in the last analysis, as if everything in his thought could be derived from middle Platonism. In fact, I think, there is more of the mythic structure of Gnosticism in Origen's assumptions than Koch could admit. To argue this case— i.e., that Origen in his interpretation of Paul restates in his own terms a version of the Gnostic view that evil originates in a premundane world and then manifests itself as the fall of souls into corporeality—is to imply that his treatment of free will is *not* of a piece with the later patristic tradition. Relevant here is the now classic argument of Hans Jonas, *Gnosis und spätantiker Geist,* vol. 2, pt. 1: *Von der Mythologie zur mystischen*

Philosophie, 2d ed. (Göttingen, 1966), especially 184–88, that Origen is a Christian Gnostic for whom the Valentinian cosmology is operative but at the same time is *modified* by the biblical view that God is the creator of the world. It must be said, however, that corporeality is not willed by God but is passively acquiesced in and *then* subsumed into the workings of a beneficent providence after the fact. The Valentinians claimed the same scenario.

18. In *De princ.* 1.7.4-5, Rom. 9:14, 2:11, and 8:19–23, appear in close association with 1 Cor. 15:24 and 28. In *De princ.* 2.8.1-4, where Origen discusses the origin of the soul, 1 Cor. 15:44 and Rom. 8:20 stand in close conjunction along with a sprinkling of other texts from 1 Corinthians, Ephesians, and Romans. Much the same is true of *De princ.* 3.5.1-8, where the question of the decay of the cosmos is addressed: Rom. 8:20f., 1 Cor. 15:28, and the christological texts—Phil. 2:7f. and Col. 1:17–19—are interwoven as part of the analysis. The listings in *Biblia Patristica*, vol. 3: *ad loc.*, show the wide extent of their use throughout Origen's work.

19. On Origen's use of Rom. 8:26f., see Wilhelm Gessel, *Die Theologie des Gebetes nach 'De Oratione' von Origenes* (Munich, Paderborn, and Vienna, 1975), 115-27.

20. Cf. *C. Cels.* 5.13, 7.65. On Origen's use of Rom. 8:19–23 in general, see Paul Lebeau, "L'interprétation origénienne de Rm 8.19-22," in *Kyriakon: Festschrift Johannes Quasten*, ed. Patrick Granfield and Joseph A. Jungmann, 2 vols. (Münster, 1970), 1:336–45.

21. Joseph Wilson Trigg, *Origen: The Bible and Philosophy in the Third-century Church* (Atlanta, 1983), 213f. Trigg's general comments on the relation between Pauline theology and the theology of Origen are well taken. There is a problem, however, with the attempt to evaluate Origen's Paulinism by Augustinian standards. Trigg states, "Paul's actual views on predestination were anathema to him" (i.e., Origen), but he then goes on to say: "Origen also relied heavily on Paul's Christological ideas and on his understanding of providence. Origen's idea of redemption rejects predestination without regard to merit but affirms that God orders all events to serve God's purposes" (173). We may assume that, given Origen's view of God as pure moral goodness and his insistence that the cosmos is a rational, i.e., morally meaningful, order, the very notion of "predestination without regard to merit" would never have crossed his mind. The fact is, however, that divine providence is for him *gracious*, i.e., freely given in its working, and thus salvation always requires in an absolute way the divine gratuity.

22. This usage is not in *De princ.* but came later in such passages as *Hom. in Gen.* 2.3 and *Hom. in Ies. Nav.* 25.4.

23. See *De princ.* 3.6.6 and 3.6.8, as well as 3.6 in its entirety, but also frequently in the commentaries on John and Romans.

24. E.g., *De princ.* 3.5.6, where he introduced the notion that the reign of Christ is intended to endure for as long as it takes to teach his enemies what they must know for salvation.

25. See *De princ.* 2.10.1-3, 2.3.6-7, 3.6.1-9, but also *Hom. in Gen.* 9.2 and many places in the Old Testament homilies and the commentary on John. Discussion of the resurrection body is frequent in *Contra Celsum*, as for example in 5.18-19, where Origen defended Paul's preaching of the resurrection of the flesh as an accommodation to the "simple," for whom flesh is synonymous with corporeal and earthly. In fact, the immortality that we will one day put on will be a product of what we have *learned while in the flesh*. In that sense, the flesh will be raised.

26. E.g., in *De princ.* 2.11.7 (Col. 1:16: as we continue to grow, we comprehend spiritual things more and more); 1.7.2 (Col. 1:16: the celestial bodies are part of the cosmos that is contained in him); or 4.4.3 (Col. 1:16–18: all things have been created through the Son as the second member of the trinity). There are a large number of uses of this text throughout Origen's work. See the excellent study of J. A. Lyons, *The Cosmic Christ in Origen and Teilhard de Chardin: A Comparative Study* (Oxford, 1982), especially 97–104, on the Gnostic background of Origen's christology. Lyons argues that Origen's Logos-doctrine is a way of relating God to the world in real terms (hence, the thrust is anti-Gnostic), but also that by teaching the notion of the eternal generation of the Logos, Origen remained tied to Gnostic emanationism. In this regard too, Origen could not escape a certain ambiguity about the divine goodness that eternally contains all things. Christological texts from Colossians, Ephesians, and 1 Corinthians are discussed *passim*.

27. See especially *De princ.* 3.5.6, or *C. Cels.* 4.18 and 6.15, or *Comm. in Matt.* 11.17.

28. Robert M. Berchman, *From Philo to Origen: Middle Platonism in Transition* (Chico, Calif., 1984).

29. Eugene TeSelle, *Christ in Context: Divine Purpose and Human Possibility* (Philadelphia, 1975), 18, has noted the importance of Phil. 2:6 for Origen in explaining how the preexistent Son could take on the form of a slave in the incarnation. For Origen, the preexisting *human* soul of Christ acquires a body for the sake of sinners and at the same time begins to live out a humanity that, although already having an eternal relationship with God, also requires a relation with corporeal humankind.

30. For an elaborate argument to the effect that Origen's exegetical method is itself an *ascesis* for immediate experience of God and the fulfillment of the soul's yearning to be resubmerged in the divine, see Karen Jo Torjesen, *Hermeneutical Procedure and Theological Method in Origen's Exegesis*, Patristische Texte und Studien 28 (Berlin, 1986).

31. The key study is Harl, "Origène et les interprétations."

32. To this extent, then, I would agree with Völker's estimation of Origen and his Paulinism: Origen *did* have a predilection for Pauline passages that appear to be hellenistic-Greek in content. Origen's construal of these passages is, however, much more Pauline in *intent* than Völker allowed.

33. Junod, 118–20.
34. See *Gregory of Nyssa: The Life of Moses*, translation, introduction, and notes by Abraham J. Malherbe and Everett Ferguson (New York, 1978), 70–74, and the notes on 167ff. Origen combined Rom. 2:5f., 1:26 and 28, and 9:16f. in the treatment of free will in *De princ.* 3.1. Gregory's treatment apparently echoes this source.
35. Egidio Pietrella, "L'antiorigenismo di Gregorio di Nissa," *Augustinianum* 26 (1986): 143–76, has carefully analyzed Nyssa's explicit rejection of the preexistence of souls in *De hominis opificio* and in *De anima et resurrectione*. His thesis is that Gregory was in fact rejecting the form that this teaching takes in pagan philosophical texts, and not the doctrine in its Origenian form. Origen's formulation is anti-Gnostic in purpose and is intended as a way of refuting the Gnostic exegesis of certain texts of scripture (160f.), including Rom. 9:9–21. Gregory, of course, operated with an entirely different agenda.
36. This work is sometimes considered spurious; however, its theology is consistently that of Gregory. Consequently, it seems fair to include it here. For an English translation, see Philip Schaff and Henry Wace, eds., *Nicene and Post-Nicene Fathers*, Second Series, vol. 5: *Select Writings and Letters of Gregory, Bishop of Nyssa*, trans. William Moore and Henry Austin Wilson (Grand Rapids, Mich., 1976), 372–81. The passage in question appears on 380f.
37. See *Or. cat.* 8 and 32; also *In sanctum Pascha* in the translation by S. G. Hall in *The Easter Sermons of Gregory of Nyssa: Translation and Commentary*, ed. Andreas Spira and Christoph Klock, Patristic Monograph Series 9 (Cambridge, Mass., 1981), 25. The striking thing about all of Gregory's references to God as the potter is that he nowhere wrestles with the mystery of election; whatever smashing of vases may take place, the action is done solely by human beings.
38. *De an. et res.*; see *Saint Gregory of Nyssa: Ascetical Works*, trans. Virginia Woods Callahan, The Fathers of the Church 58 (Washington, D.C., 1967), 244f.
39. *De hom. opif.* 9, where Gregory continued to work out his whole metaphysics of stability and change with regard to the limits, but also the potential, of creaturely existence. Gregory said explicitly (*Or. cat.* 5) that God created human beings purely for the purpose of enjoying the goodness and glory of existence under the brightness of the divine light. For Gregory, there is no fearful risk, no dark possibility, inherent in the act of creation as there was for Origen.
40. *C. Eun.* 2.10, 3.1, 4.3, 5.4.
41. For instance, *De an. et res.* (*Saint Gregory of Nyssa: Ascetical Works*, 243ff.). There is a vast discussion and bibliography; see *Gregory of Nyssa: The Life of Moses*, 168, n. 102.
42. Louis Bouyer, in *A History of Christian Spirituality*, vol. 1: *The Spirituality of the New Testament and the Fathers*, trans. Mary P. Ryan (New York, 1982),

290, cites Origen *In Jes. Nav. Hom.* 15.5: "This is why we say that God *authorizes and, even more, that He excites the adverse powers* in some way to come out against us, so that we may be victorious over them and that they themselves may be put to death" (emphasis added). Even though Origen's theological explanation of such a statement is orthodox, the very fact that he made the statement at all puts him on the other side of a gulf from Gregory.

43. In one of her earlier essays on the patristic use of scripture ("'From Glory to Glory'; L'interprétation de II Cor. 3,18b par Grégoire de Nysse et la liturgie baptismale," in Granfield and Jungmann, eds., *Kyriakon*, 2:730–35), Marguerite Harl has pointed to the contrast between Origen's understanding of "from glory to glory" as a real participation by the believer in the divine such that he proceeds from one glory (our own as graced by God) to God's glory and Gregory's rather different view; for Gregory, the phrase describes an earthly journey, a road forward, in which there are successive transformations, but not necessarily a deeper appropriation. The difference is subtle, but genuine, and reflects the differing temperaments of the two men. Both understandings merge, according to Harl, in the baptismal liturgy of the fourth century.

44. See the apt remarks of Andrew Louth, *The Origins of the Christian Mystical Tradition: From Plato to Denys* (Oxford, 1983), 80ff., where he formulates this contrast between Origen and Gregory as the difference between a mysticism of light and a mysticism of darkness.

45. This difference of hermeneutic perspective between Origen and Nyssa is difficult to formulate precisely. One must compare what they do with the same text. Monique Alexandre, "La théorie de l'exégèse dans le *De hominis opificio* et l'*In Hexaemeron*," in *Ecriture et culture philosophique dans la pensée de Grégoire de Nysse*, ed. M. Harl (Leiden, 1971), 87–110, has noted (103) that Origen's tendency was to search for the *intelligible reality* contained in the text, whereas Nyssa was more often content to clarify the *sensible phenomena* that God uses to communicate that reality.

46. Maximus Confessor *Cap. theol.* 1.12-13, 2.71ff. There is an English translation in *Maximus Confessor: Selected Writings*, trans. George C. Berthold (New York, Mahwah, and Toronto, 1985), 129–70.

47. Augustine could, I think, strike the Origenian note in wrestling with scripture when, as in interpreting the story of God's connivance with Jacob's deceit of Isaac in order to secure the birthright in Genesis 27, he could say, "Non est mendacium, sed mysterium" (*C. Mendac.* 10.24). Probably this statement reflects some measure of influence on Augustine from the Greek tradition of exegesis.

48. TeSelle, 127ff. See, in particular, his interpretation of Jeremiah 18 and the image of God as the potter (153ff.), a favorite patristic and Pauline image, as we have noted.

49. Peter J. Gorday, *Principles of Patristic Exegesis: Romans 9–11 in Origen, John Chrysostom, and Augustine*, Studies in the Bible and Early Christianity 4

(New York and Toronto, 1983), 34–39; see also the discussion of *oikonomia* in G. L. Prestige, *God in Patristic Thought*, 2d ed. (London, 1952), 57–67.

50. Ian T. Ramsey, *Models for Divine Activity* (London, 1973), 15–27.

51. Ramsey, 26.

THE MAN FROM HEAVEN:
PAUL'S LAST ADAM AND APOLLINARIS' CHRIST

1. In *From Nicaea to Chalcedon* (Philadelphia, 1983), 184–86, Frances Young discusses the problem of "the situation out of which Apollinarius' teaching arose" (184). She emphasizes Apollinaris' debt to the Alexandrian theology expounded by Athanasius without denying the possibility that "opposition to the developing Antiochene christology helped to focus his thinking" (186). Aloys Grillmeier emphasizes Apollinaris' dependence on a traditional Logos-sarx christology (*Christ in Christian Tradition*, trans. J. S. Bowden [London, 1965], 220–33). Richard A. Norris underlines the importance of Apollinaris' opposition to the christology of teachers in Antioch "who thought of the incarnation as a special case of the Logos' indwelling of a human being" (*The Christological Controversy* [Philadelphia, 1980], 21).

2. See Ignatius *Eph*. 20.1; also William R. Schoedel, *Ignatius of Antioch: A Commentary on the Letters of Ignatius of Antioch* (Philadelphia, 1985), *ad loc*. For Irenaeus' use of the notion, see especially *AH* 4.38.

3. The charge is repeated by Grillmeier, 225: "In an unwarranted exegesis of I Corinthians 15.45 (the last Adam was a life-giving spirit) Apollinarius sees in Christ only one life, exclusively controlled by the Godhead." Grillmeier does not explain why the exegesis is "unwarranted."

4. See the discussion in Eugene TeSelle, *Augustine the Theologian* (London, 1970), 158.

5. *Kata meros pistis* 31; text in Hans Lietzmann, *Apollinaris von Laodicea und seine Schule* (Tübingen, 1904), 179.

6. *Anacephalaiosis* 4 (Lietzmann, 244).

7. *Anacephalaiosis* 12-13 (Lietzmann, 243). "Give life" clearly alludes to 1 Cor. 15:45, even though Lietzmann gives 1 Cor. 15:22 as the reference. That Christ's flesh came down from heaven refers, according to Lietzmann, to Jn. 3:13, but I should think a better reference would be to Jn. 6:51.

8. Ibid. 23 (Lietzmann, 244).

9. *De unione* 5 (Lietzmann, 187). The translation is from Norris, 104.

10. *De unione* 2 (Lietzmann, 186); cf. the parallel passage in *Ep. ad Dionysium* 11 (Lietzmann, 261), where this reading of *De unione* 2 is confirmed.

11. See Richard A. Norris' discussion in *Manhood and Christ* (Oxford, 1963), 104-6. What I am suggesting goes one step further by arguing that the "one nature" not only refers to the incarnate Lord but also treats him more as the paradigm of salvation than in terms of the problem of the incarnation or the

question of Christ's person narrowly conceived. The difficulty is to read Apollinaris in his own right without importing into our reading the issues of Cyril's christology and of the Nestorian controversy.

12. See the discussion in Lietzmann, 83–84.

13. The numbers in parentheses here and in what follows refer to Lietzmann's numbering of the fragments. Fragments 13–107 are from the *Apodeixis* and may be found in Lietzmann, 208–32.

14. See Norris, *Manhood and Christ*, 82–87.

15. See fragment 22 (Lietzmann, 209). It may well be that there remains some confusion. Treating the animating soul as an aspect of the body is required in order to make sense of Apollinaris' discussion here, but it may be that he elsewhere reflects the notion that the animating soul is a lower level of the rational soul.

16. See, for example, Gregory of Nyssa *Antirrheticus adversus Apolinarium* in Werner Jaeger, ed., *Gregorii Nysseni Opera*, vol. 3, pt. 1: *Opera dogmatica minora*, ed. F. Mueller (Leiden, 1958), 139, 147–49. Nyssa seems to realize that the preexistence of Christ's humanity and flesh is an implication of Apollinaris' view rather than a point he insists on literally. "For even one of modest intelligence would see the foolishness of the implication even if we had not exposed its shamelessness by our exposition" (Jaeger, 3.1:148). "For he says, 'Behold the preexisting equality of the same Jesus Christ with his Father, his subsequently acquired likeness to human beings. . . . ' He seems to change his mind about what he has said. Let him at least make this one change . . . and we shall stop our refutation" (Jaeger, 3.1:162; fragment 42, trans. Norris, *Christological Controversy*, 109). Gregory Nazianzen seems to have taken the point more seriously: "A pamphlet by Apollinaris has come into my hands, the contents of which surpass all heretical pravity. For he asserts that the flesh which the only-begotten Son assumed in the incarnation for the remodeling of our nature was no new acquisition, but that that carnal nature was in the Son from the beginning" (*Ep.* 202, trans. E. R. Hardy, *Christology of the Later Fathers* [Philadelphia, 1954], 231).

17. See fragment 163, *Ep. ad Dionysium* 7, *Tomus synodalis* (Lietzmann, 255, 259, 262).

18. Cf. Gregory Nazianzen's response to the Apollinarian claim that "we must worship, not a God-bearing man, but a flesh-bearing God" (*Ep.* 102, trans. Hardy, 227–28).

19. *Ep. ad Diocaesareenses* 2 (Lietzmann, 256); cf. *Anacephalaiosis* 30, fragment 150, fragment 151 (Lietzmann, 246, 247, 248).

20. *Anacephalaiosis* 30 (Lietzmann, 246); cf. fragment 22 (Lietzmann, 209).

21. Cf. Robin Scroggs, *The Last Adam: A Study in Pauline Anthropology* (Philadelphia, 1966), 102: "To say that Paul is concerned with the nature of eschatological humanity does not exclude, of course, the assumption that this nature is of an ethically and religiously perfected man; but it does suggest that Paul's main desire is to depict that nature in which such perfection may exist. To translate Paul's Adamic Christology into primarily ethical

categories is both a reduction and a distortion of Paul's intent, however important such a translation may seem to be for contemporary theology." The whole of Scroggs' discussion, especially chapter 5, is helpful; and his view that Paul's aim is less to elaborate a mythology of the two Adams than to express a christology seems to me sound. At the same time, his approach enables him to step round the problems involved in comparing Rom. 5 and 1 Cor. 15 without, I think, fully solving them.

22. Fragment 10 (Lietzmann, 207), trans. Norris, *Christological Controversy*, 108.

23. *Antirrheticus* (Jaeger, 3.1:143). Parenthetical references in the following discussion are to this volume of Jaeger's edition of Gregory's works and to the relevant page numbers.

24. See *Or. cat.* 16-17, trans. Hardy, 292ff.

25. Cf. Gregory Nazianzen: "For that which he has not assumed he has not healed; but that which is united to his Godhead is also saved" (*Ep.* 101, trans. Hardy, 218).

26. See Nyssa's argument in *Or. cat.* 9-25. He begins by trying to show that the Word was not made passible in the incarnation, but despite his attempts to demonstrate this, the objection recurs (10, 15, 16, 17). He finally dismisses the objection without explaining it away. "It should suffice to answer such an objection in this way: Sick people do not prescribe to doctors their manner of treatment" (17, trans. Hardy, 294). Beginning with section 19, he shows how the incarnation befits the character of God.

27. See note 16 above and my suggestion that Nyssa realizes that Apollinaris does not mean to treat Christ's humanity as preexistent in any literal way.

28. One could, for example, read Romans 4 in this fashion. Christ removes the veil from the story of Abraham, and Paul can now read that story in the light of justification by faith. Abraham's friendship with God, Paul learns, explains his obedience and is not its reward. The story, then, yields the timeless truth of God's attitude toward us; and Romans 4 is to be contrasted with Paul's historical treatment of Abraham in Galatians 3.

JOHN CHRYSOSTOM AS AN INTERPRETER
OF PAULINE SOCIAL ETHICS

1. In this regard, see Gerd Theissen's fine book, *Der Schatten des Galiläers* (Munich, 1986), especially chaps. 10 and 18.

2. Still the first work to consult on this point is Wolfgang Schrage, "Die Stellung zur Welt bei Paulus, Epiktet und in der Apokalyptik," *Zeitschrift für Theologie und Kirche* 61 (1964): 125-54 (with additional bibliography).

3. Georg Strecker, *Handlungsorientierter Glaube: Vorstudien zu einer Ethik des Neuen Testaments* (Stuttgart, 1972), 46.

4. This point has often been stressed, especially by Ernst Käsemann; see, e.g., "Amt und Gemeinde im Neuen Testament," in his *Exegetische Versuche und Besinnungen*, vol. 1 (Göttingen, 1960), 109-34, here especially 113f.

5. Ernst Troeltsch had, in his own way, already seen this and stated it in his *Soziallehren der christlichen Kirchen und Gruppen* (Tübingen, 1922; reprint: Aalen, 1965), 50, 72, and often.

6. Strecker, 35.

7. Ernst Käsemann, *An die Römer*, Handbuch zum Neuen Testament, vol. 8a (Tübingen, 1973), 311: "'with appeal to' or, better, 'in the name of'"; on the meaning of οὖν and διά in Rom. 12:1, see also Victor P. Furnish, *Theology and Ethics in Paul* (Nashville and New York, 1968), 101ff.

8. See Käsemann, *Römer*, 313f.

9. See, e.g., Furnish, 224ff. The element of release from a burden, which is contained in this view, is nicely formulated in Ernst Käsemann, "Liebe, die sich der Wahrheit freut," (*Evangelische Theologie* 33 [1973]: 455): "His freedom as the temporal expression of his sovereignty liberates us at the deepest level from concern for ourselves . . . and thereby opens us for our neighbor and the earth. The one who no longer needs to be concerned for self has time, power, and interest for the other. . . . This is just what Christian love signifies: freedom to work for the neighbor and the earth as the sphere of an open life."

10. The notion that genuinely "social-critical" tendencies were preserved almost exclusively among the heretics is actually a *topos* in the literature, and not only on the Marxist side! Anyone who speaks and writes to this effect, however, reveals at best a superficial reading, not only of Chrysostom but also, for example, of Ambrose of Milan and certainly of Basil of Caesarea. What G.E.M. de Ste. Croix calls "the most radical passage" in Pelagius' *De divitiis* (now preserved only in fragments)—"pauci divites pauperum causa sunt multorum"—has, in any case, plenty of analogies among these "orthodox" writers (see de Ste. Croix, "Early Christian Attitudes to Property and Slavery," in *Church, Society and Politics,* ed. D. Baker, Studies in Church History 12 [Oxford, 1975], 34).

11. For the undoubtedly most important representative of this view, see Robert von Pöhlmann, *Geschichte der sozialen Frage und des Sozialismus in der antiken Welt,* 2 vols., 3d ed. (Munich, 1925), 2:476f., 484ff.

12. See especially *Hom. 12 in 1 Tim.* (PG 62:561–64). Arnold Stötzel (*Kirche als "neue Gesellschaft": Die humanisierende Wirkung des Christentums nach Johannes Chrysostomus* [Münster, 1984]) now provides a somewhat contradictory commentary on this. On the one hand, he says that the "etiology of private property" does not indicate for Chrysostom "the way to its abolition but [exposes] primarily and critically the roots of its human origin" (63, n. 146); on the other hand, he states that it is part of the "consequence of this etiology . . . to see in it the abolition of classes and to reestablish the κοινόν."

13. See Rudolf Brändle, *Matth. 25,31–46 im Werk des Johannes Chrysostomus,* Beiträge zur Geschichte der biblischen Exegese 22 (Tübingen, 1979), especially 42ff., 225ff., 326ff.

14. Stötzel, 218; Stötzel lists Brändle's work in his bibliography but, unless I have overlooked something, never comes to terms with it.

15. Chrysostom himself could occasionally describe the content and task of preaching in this way: *Hom. 23 (22) in Ioh.* 1 (PG 59:137f.).

16. Dio Chrysostom, *Or.* 13.33.

17. On the "rule" of Christianity, see *Hom. 25 in 1 Cor.* 3 (PG 61:208); also *Hom. 36 in 1 Cor.* 3 (PG 61:310): "Do you see what is the foundation (κρηπίς) and rule (κανών) of Christianity? As the artisan's (τεχνίτης) work (ἔργον) is to build, so the Christian's is to profit the neighbor in all things (τοὺς πλησίον διὰ πάντων ὠφελεῖν)." On the connection of one's own well-being with the neighbor's, see *Hom. 25 in 1 Cor.* 4 (PG 61:211f.).

18. Rudolf Bultmann, "Das Problem der Ethik bei Paulus," *Zeitschrift für die neutestamentliche Wissenschaft* 23 (1924): 265–81, and in many other works.

19. Albrecht Dihle, "Ethik," *Reallexikon für Antike und Christentum* 6 (1966): 646–796, here 656 and 649. The Stoic emperor, Marcus Aurelius, provides the most salient evidence for this in his *Meditations* (τὰ εἰς ἑαυτόν). It would never have occurred to this man, who so often spoke of the duties of man as ζῶον κοινωνικόν, to think that it might be a question of surrendering or renouncing the value and claim of the individual. And that could have something to do with the fact that, in these "meditations," we completely miss any thoughts of social criticism or even of social reform.

20. One need only compare the discourses of Dio of Prusa—in which such expressions as "the just man [i.e., the philosopher] spends his life, I think, in concern for human beings" (κηδόμενος ἀνθρώπων) and "is eager, so far as possible, to help all people" (βοηθεῖν ἅπασιν; *Or.* 77/78.39, 40) already stand in relative isolation, especially in the diatribes—with the way in which Synesius of Cyrene refers to them in his *Dion, or On My Own Way of Life*. In Synesius, that is, there sounds only the message of the blessing of the "simple life" (compare *Dion* 2.2ff. with, in particular, Dio Chrysostom's celebrated "Euboean Discourse" [*Or.* 7]), while everything "political" is in fact left out of "training in the highest truths" (ἀληθινωτάτη παιδεία; *Dion* 4.2f.).

21. Dihle, 657.

22. This matter is so important, and so controversial in the scholarly literature, that I should like to examine it more closely by way of an excursus. Just as for Chrysostom the exemplary character of the monastery rests not least in its representation of the *societas perfecta*, insofar as in it there is no more private property and no more domination of man over men but only mutual submission and voluntary service (see the texts collected in A. J. Festugière, *Antioche païenne et chrétienne: Libanius, Chrysostome et les moines en Syrie* [Paris, 1959], 330–44, which could easily be multiplied!), so the social question takes a major place in his homilies before his congregations in Antioch and Constantinople. In this connection, Chrysostom recommends from the very beginning the relinquishing of private property and

urges the transfer of everything to the poor, to whom belongs any wealth, whether acquired in a lawful way or received through inheritance (*Hom. 77 in Matt.* 5). He is, of course, fully aware that this relinquishing cannot be enforced, that he is dealing with people "who think they already do much when from their wealth they give only a little in alms." Thus his words should "apply only to the perfect"; the "less perfect," however, are implored to give of their goods to the poor (*Hom. 15 in 1 Cor.* 6).

Nevertheless, "perfection" remains for him the goal to which it is important that everything be compared (*Hom. 21 in Matt.* 4). For him (as for Basil), the monastic ethic and the Christian ethic are at root the same. If one wishes to find in him any basis at all for the distinction between *consilia* and *praecepta*, the only evangelical counsel that could be mentioned beyond the "commandments" binding on all is voluntary celibacy "for the sake of the kingdom of heaven." "Whoever lives in the world," Chrysostom can say, "ought not to have any advantage over the monk except that he" may marry; "in all else however he bears the same obligations as the monk" (*Hom. 7 in Heb.* 11).

"Perfection," and with it the renunciation of property or, positively stated, the community of goods, remains the goal. That is evident, e.g., in a sermon on Ps. 48:17 (*Hom. 2 in Ps. 48:17* [PG 55:512–18]), which dates from the beginning of his preaching activity in Antioch. In accordance with the biblical text to be interpreted ("Be not grieved; when a man grows rich, he increases the splendor of his house"), the primary concern of this sermon is to show that one in fact has no reason to grieve over the wealth of another. Chrysostom thereby shows himself as a man of the people, a man who knows how simple people feel and who expresses it clearly (*Hom. 2 in Ps. 48:17* 1 ad fin., 3 ad fin.; for his criticism of exploitive practices, see also, e.g., *Hom. 61 in Matt.* 8). But the more essential point for us is that in the end, although this was not particularly to be expected from the theme of the whole, Chrysostom lets the cat out of the bag, as it were, and clearly states his view of how the problem of property and wealth is to be solved. His solution centers on the "equality of rights" (ἰσονομία)—thus on a central concept of the Platonic social utopia—and on the "equitable distribution" of earthly goods, just as "nature" (heaven; sun, moon, and stars; air and sea, fire and water; life, growth, aging, and death, etc.) and also "spiritual things" (the table of the Lord, baptism as washing of regeneration and promise of the kingdom of God, righteousness, salvation, and redemption, together with the "inexpressible" eschatological goods that "eye has not seen and ear has not heard" [1 Cor. 2:9]) are common to all.

But that is the goal, not the beginning. And it is a goal for which Chrysostom was ready to work with all the means at his disposal, including accommodation and repetition, those most effective instruments of propaganda that he had learned from Libanius to employ to perfection. Especially impressive to this day is the way he repeatedly makes himself

the advocate and petitioner for the "poor Christ" (see Mt. 25:31–45) in
order, in this way, to arouse and to keep alive among his hearers responsibility for the socially deprived, as also in the previously mentioned sermon
on Ps. 48:17 (see *Hom. 2 in Ps. 48:17 2*).

It could, however, be a beginning—as Chrysostom argues in his interpretation of the pericope about the "rich young man" in his Homilies on
Matthew—if one was to start by getting rid of what is superfluous (*Hom. 63
in Matt. 3*; see also *Hom. 66 in Matt. 3, 4*). It could be a beginning if one
learned at least to distinguish between wealth that is obviously obtained
unjustly and is misused, that is, turned to selfish purposes, and wealth that
is obtained without affront to God, without incurring the blood of the
guiltless, and is employed according to the command of God—a distinction
that already seems necessary to Chrysostom with reference to the biblical
models in Abraham, Jacob, and Job (see *Hom. 34 in 1 Cor. 6*).

In this connection, Chrysostom not infrequently employs formula-
tions that, at least on first glance, are contradictory and misleading. And it
is not at all surprising that he has thereby caused total confusion in the
modern literature! Still, in my view, the whole matter becomes reasonably
clear if one takes his understanding of Christian "perfection" as one's
starting point and, for the rest, duly keeps in mind that Chrysostom
neither wanted to nor could deny that he had, in his youth, received
rhetorical instruction from Libanius. Although he never flaunts his
rhetorical training in his preaching and writing, he remains true to his
origins insofar as he tends to accentuate the ideas that he presents and to
do so, not infrequently, in such a way that he himself fears he will be
misunderstood because people will take his words as no more than hyper-
bole (*De compunct.* 1.2 [PG 47:395]). One must only keep in mind "to
whom" Chrysostom "speaks in any given case . . . and what he wants to
accomplish," in order not to be "misled by rhetorical questions and exag-
gerations" (Ivo auf der Maur, *Mönchtum und Glaubensverkündigung in
den Schriften des hl. Johannes Chrysostomus* [Freiburg, 1959], 13).

A continual source of misunderstandings has been the beginning
of *Homily 34 on 1 Corinthians*. In this sermon, an interpretation of
1 Corinthians 13:8–13, Chrysostom first pursues the sense of the Pauline
text as a "paean of love" and then, as almost always, adds to his homiletical
interpretation a "practical application." Here the bridge is formed by the
thought that we are linked to one another by a thousand ties and that each
needs the other. Thus the poor, he continues, need the rich and vice
versa, as he illustrates with the image of the two cities: the city of the rich
and the city of the poor. But what, in this connection, do *poor* and *rich*
mean? The poor (πένητες) are here equated with workers, artisans, and
people from the common folk (δῆμος). And this means that, at root, this is
not a contrast between wealth and poverty in our sense, but rather between capital and labor (as Theo Sommerlad rightly observes in *Das
Wirtschaftsprogramm der Kirche des Mittelalters* [Leipzig, 1903], 147f.).

One gets the feeling that in Chrysostom's argumentation, there is a distant hint of the train of thought in the "Communist Manifesto" (those in bourgeois society who work gain no profits; those who gain the profits do not work) or even of the opening thesis of the SPD's "Gothaer Programm" of 1875 ("Work is the source of wealth and of all culture"). In spite of that, it is quite clear that Chrysostom did not draw the conclusion that exclusive control over the product of labor belonged to the workers as the sole producers of the wealth of the rich (see Sommerlad, 148).

Still, Chrysostom did try at least twice in public to go to the root of the problem of poverty and thereby to reconcile the divergent interests of capital and labor. The first time was in Antioch, the other in Constantinople. In *Homily 66 on Matthew,* he undertakes an analysis of the economic conditions in Antioch. According to his picture, one-tenth of the residents are wealthy, one-tenth are poor, without possessions of any kind, and the rest occupy a "middle position." The church only has "the income of one of the very rich and one of those of moderate means" (*Hom. 66 in Matt.* 3). From that, according to the official list of the poor, nearly three thousand widows and virgins are supported daily, not counting the prisoners in the prisons, the sick in the hospices, the transients, the cripples, the church beggars, etc. If only ten of the wealthy were willing to spend as much as the church, poverty would be banished from Antioch.

If Chrysostom seems here to present the solution to the social problem in such a way that he assigns particular poor individuals to particular rich individuals and thus wants to call to life something like a community poor-relief system with an honorary and individualistic character (see Sommerlad, 150f., and again, e.g., *Hom. 85 in Matt.* 4), he later moves toward an even more radical social utopia. In his homilies on Acts, delivered in Constantinople, he takes up the idea of community of goods as it was practiced, according to Luke, in the early Jerusalem community. There is no doubt that the bishop and preacher is entirely serious in his proposal, even though he likens it at first simply to an idea hastily thrown out. For at the end he calls for an attempt at the daring venture. If one was actually to do that, it would turn out that this was no mere utopian scheme—as the monasteries have long since proven!

Moreover, Konrad Farner is no doubt quite right when he says that according to the evidence of *Hom. 11 in Acta,* Chrysostom had a more precise conception of a "communist" form of economy than almost any other church father. "First of all, we have to do here with a communism of production," not just a communism of consumption; "second, national economic perspectives (division of labor and cooperation as enhancing productivity) are brought into play; third, sociological perspectives (circumstances with regard to ownership of property as conditioning social and individual morality)" (*Theologie des Kommunismus?* [Frankfurt am Main, 1969], 64). A sharp eye for social reality, along with the still starkly visible need in Constantinople (despite imperial distributions of bread to what the communists call the "Lumpenproletariat"), appears finally to have convinced Chrysostom that no real relief was to be obtained by means of private almsgiving.

For the same reason, he now also speaks more decisively regarding the evaluation of wealth (contra Gilbert Dagron, *Naissance d'une capitale: Constantinople et ses institutions de 330 à 451* [Paris, 1974], 509). That is seen, e.g., in *Homily 12 on 1 Timothy*. In the course of interpreting the text on which this sermon is based (1 Tm. 4:1–10), he addresses the question as to what extent wealth is also a good, as "everything created by God is good" and "nothing is to be rejected if it is received with thanksgiving" (1 Tm. 4:4). His answer is that not only how one comes to have wealth but also, and above all, how one uses it determines this point, namely, that one does not wish to keep for oneself what belongs to the Lord and does not try to keep for oneself the benefit of what is the common property of all; that one recognizes that all our possessions belong to God and thus also to our fellow servants. For "all that belongs to God the Lord is common property" (τὰ γὰρ τοῦ Δεσπότου πάντα κοινά). Considered in Christian fashion, seen in the light of belief in creation, community of goods is the more appropriate form for our life together than private ownership. Indeed, not only would this be the best solution from a Christian point of view, it is also plainly "natural" and uniquely reasonable. For "why is it that no one goes to court over the market place? No one does because it is common to all. Over houses and over money, in contrast, we see endless court proceedings" (*Hom. 12 in 1 Tim.* 4).

23. *Hom. 12 in 1 Tim.* 4 (PG 62:562–64); Aristotle *Pol.* 2.1261b33-38, 1263a11.

24. Ludwig Stein, *Die soziale Frage im Lichte der Philosophie*, cited in Georg Adler, *Geschichte des Sozialismus und Kommunismus von Plato bis zur Gegenwart* (Leipzig, 1899), 176f., who certainly does not himself exclude the possibility that Chrysostom took "the matter more seriously" than was usual among the church fathers.

25. Wolf-Dieter Hauschild, "Christentum und Eigentum: Zum Problem eines altkirchlichen 'Sozialismus,'" *Zeitschrift für evangelische Ethik* 16 (1972): 34–49, quotation on 38.

26. A distant parallel appears only in the reports about Plotinus' plans regarding the founding of a city of philosophers ("Platonopolis"; see Porphyry, *Vita Plot.* 12) or about recollections of the group of like-minded persons as the locus of social-ethical praxis in Hermeticism (*Corp. Herm.* 13.9) and in Neopythagoreanism (Ocellus Lucanus *De univ. nat.* 3.3ff., 6ff.). Apparently no one—except in (commissioned) orations Περὶ βασιλείας—thought about the "state."

27. Joachim Kahl, *Das Elend des Christentums oder Plädoyer für eine Humanität ohne Gott* (Hamburg, 1968), 20, 23; similarly de Ste. Croix, 36.

28. The assessment of these materials has long been in dispute, primarily although by no means exclusively, between Marxist and non-Marxist

interpreters. See, on the one side, R. Müller, "Zur sozialen Utopie im Hellenismus," in *Die Rolle der Volksmassen in der Geschichte der vorkapitalistischen Gesellschaftsformationen*, ed. J. Herrmann and I. Sellnow (Berlin, 1975), 277–86; and, on the other, Hellmut Flashar, *Formen utopischen Denkens bei den Griechen* (Innsbruck, 1974), 14. There is the view that it is rather a question of a literature for entertainment—to be evaluated in much the same way as the "Robinson Crusoe" stories of more recent times—than of social criticism. Against this, it seems, there are two things to be said: (1) to a degree, there had long been a massive critique of slavery, namely in the sophistic enlightenment (see the evidence compiled in Roland Gayer, *Die Stellung der Sklaven in den paulinischen Gemeinden und bei Paulus* [Bern and Frankfurt am Main, 1976], 26ff.; see also Dihle, 667f.) and (2) Aristonicus, the leader of the uprising against Rome in 133 B.C., proclaimed as his *social program* (see Michael Rostovtzeff, *Gesellschafts- und Wirtschaftsgeschichte der Hellenistischen Welt*, 2 vols. [Darmstadt, 1955], 2:635) a social utopia very similar to Iambulus' "city of the sun" (presumably) from the third century B.C. (see the reference in Diodorus Siculus 2.55-60) and called "the crowd of the poor and the slaves which he had gathered and called to freedom" Ἡλιοπολῖται ("citizens of the sun"; Strabo 14.1.38, cited in Gayer, 31).

29. Gayer, 36ff., see the examples on 26ff.
30. Pol. 1.1259b20-1260b8; on this point, see, e.g., Hermann Strasburger, *Zum antiken Gesellschaftsideal* (Heidelberg, 1976), 49–51 (with additional bibliography).
31. See Max Kaser, *Das römische Privatrecht*, 2 vols. (Munich, 1955–59), 2:83ff.
32. Heinz Bellen, *Studien zur Sklavenflucht im römischen Kaiserreich*, Forschungen zur antiken Sklaverei 4 (Wiesbaden, 1971). Dihle is surely right to draw attention to the "great number of well educated slaves of Greek origin who were, among other things, tutors, philosophers, and secretaries, in the homes of Roman aristocrats" as an additional possible factor (668).
33. *Cod. Theod.* 2.25.1; *Cod. Just.* 3.38.11.
34. *Cod. Theod.* 9.12.1 (from 11.5.319).
35. Their function within Roman criminal proceedings was similarly miserable and humiliating (see J. Scheele, "Zur Rolle der Unfreien in den römischen Christenprozessen" [Phil. diss., Tübingen, 1970]).
36. See Gayer, 56ff.
37. Kaser, 2:84 (with additional bibliography).
38. *Weltgeschichtliche Betrachtungen*, ed. R. Stadelmann (Tübingen, 1949), 149.
39. See Henneke Gülzow, *Christentum und Sklaverei in den ersten drei Jahrhunderten* (Bonn, 1969).
40. Thus Peter Stuhlmacher, in his very balanced commentary *Der Brief an Philemon*, Evangelisch-katholischer Kommentar zum Neuen Testament 18 (Zurich, Einsiedeln, Cologne, and Neukirchen-Vluyn, 1981), 58; see also Gayer, 223ff.

41. For him, there is only one form of superordination and subordination grounded in the order of nature rather than in human sin, namely, the "domination" of parents over children. "As your parents gave birth to you," he asserts in support, "you cannot give birth to them." Of slavery, in contrast, it is true that it belongs to the "three kinds of servitude" that "sin introduced." The other two "servitudes" are the subjection of the wife to the husband rather than the originally intended "partnership" and the compulsory rule of the state, which Chrysostom perceives as the most oppressive servitude—a fact that throws significant light on his concept and experience of the state (see especially the fourth and fifth of the *Sermones in Genesim* [PG 54:593–604]; and above all, on this point, Wulf Jaeger, "Sklaverei bei Johannes Chrysostomus" [Theol. diss., Kiel, 1974], which gives an account of this whole matter that is as thorough as it is even-handed). Beyond that, Chrysostom could occasionally demand concretely that, if one otherwise loved his slaves "as himself" (see Lev. 19:18 et passim), he should train them in a craft or give them some other education that would allow them to stand on their own feet and then should set them free (*Hom. 40 in 1 Cor.* 5; from Jaeger [145ff.], we learn that this demand is by no means as isolated in Chrysostom as Stötzel [91] supposes). When, in his excursus on the history of the interpretation and influence of Paul's letter to Philemon, Stuhlmacher (58ff.) sees a line of "anti-emancipation" interpretation that begins with Chrysostom, he bases this on a complete isolation of the homilies on Philemon from Chrysostom's work as a whole and on an interpretation of these homilies—largely determined by this isolation—that is too one-dimensional. To avoid misinterpretation, one must proceed methodically as sketched above (in n. 22) with regard to the problematic of property and ownership.

42. See Jaeger, 212f., quotation on 212.

43. Wolfgang Schrage, "Barmen II und das Neue Testament," in *Zum politischen Auftrag der christlichen Gemeinde*, ed. A. Burgsmüller (Gütersloh, 1974), 127–71, quotation on 165.

44. See A. M. Ritter, *Charisma im Verständnis des Joannes Chrysostomos und seiner Zeit* (Göttingen, 1972), 90ff.; for a different view, see Stötzel, who wrongly asserts that Chrysostom goes so far as "to dispute that asceticism is a Christian form of life" (23; see also 173, 200 [Chrysostom "wanted no monasteries"!], and often).

45. In this regard, see my essay "Die altchristliche und die byzantinische Utopie," which is to appear in the *Akten des Salzburger Symposiums zur antiken Rechts- und Sozialphilosophie (22–24 Oct. 1986)*. There, in conclusion, I state (with reference, in particular, to the chapter "Kritik und Rechtfertigung der Utopie"—no less important now than when it was written—in Paul Tillich, *Die politische Bedeutung der Utopie im Leben der Völker* [Berlin, 1951]; reprinted in Tillich's *Gesammelte Werke*, vol. 6: *Der Widerstreit von Raum und Zeit* [Stuttgart, 1963], 157–210): "If . . . Christian theology can, and indeed must, learn something from the history

of utopia, then it is primarily this: that, because of the evident ambiguity of the utopian consciousness, it is today urgently required that we renounce any attempt at raising it to the religious level (not least because of the danger of totalitarianism latent in it). But if the utopian consciousness, with its tendency toward concrete reality as related to the future (in the interplay of short-term and long-term goals), is clearly distinguished from the Christian hope, then it can contribute to the effectiveness and, no less important, to the communicability of Christian action. It holds a potential that can be mobilized responsibly because it can serve the purposes of criticism and judgment."

COMMENT: CHRYSOSTOM AND PAULINE SOCIAL ETHICS

1. In addition to the references in Ritter's n. 11, see Aimé Puech, *Saint John Chrysostom, 344–407*, trans. Mildred Partridge, 2d ed. (London, 1917), 63.

2. *Hom. 7 in Acta.*

3. *Hom. 63 in Matt.* 2 (the rich young man); *Hom. 64 in Matt.* 1, 5.

4. *Hom. 78 in Matt.* 2; see also *Vidua eligatur* 15, *Hom. 3 de poen.* 2, *Hom. 50 in Matt.* 5, *Hom. 6 in 2 Tim.* 3.

5. *Hom. 79 in Matt.* 1-2.

6. *Hom. 89 in Matt.* 4; see also *Ad illuminandos catechesis 2* 4.

7. *De laud. S. Pauli 3.*

8. *Hom. 85 in Matt.* 3-4 (on poor relief); *Hom. 11 in Acta* 3 (on Acts 4:23ff.); *Hom. 12 in 1 Tim.* 4.

9. *Hom. Philem.* argumentum.

10. *Hom. 19 in 1 Cor.* 5; *Hom. Philem.* argumentum.

11. *Hom. 19 in 1 Cor.* 5.

12. *Hom. 10 in Col.* 2; *Hom. 16 in 1 Tim.* 2 (on 1 Tm. 6:2); *Hom. 16 in 1 Tim.* 1 (on 1 Tm. 6:1).

13. *Hom. 9 in 1 Tim.* Chrysostom asks, in writing about the household code in Colossians, "Why doesn't Paul give these commands everywhere, not just in Ephesians, Timothy and Titus?" He tries "situational" answers: because these sorts of disruptions were known only in these particular cities to which Paul wrote or because Christians in those places were correct in other respects and needed advice only on these points (*Hom. 10 in Col.* 1 [on Col. 3:18–25]).

14. *Hom. 31 in Rom.* 1-2 (on Rom. 16:6). Chrysostom reads the text of Rom. 16:7 to refer to Junia, a woman, and notes that she is worthy to be called an apostle.

15. *Quales ducendae sint uxores* 7; see also *Hom. 20 in Eph., De virginitate* 66.

16. *De sacerd.* 3.9.

17. *Hom. 34 in 1 Cor.* 6; *Hom. 22 in Eph.* 2 (on Eph. 6:9). For discussion, see Anatole Moulard, *Jean Chrysostome: Sa vie, son oeuvre* (Paris, 1984), 176.

18. *Serm. 2 in Gen. 2; Hom. 12 in Col. 5.*
19. Rather, Chrysostom uses it, e.g., to urge servant girls not to participate in night wedding ceremonies—thus they can show that they too exemplify the virtues of the freeborn (*Hom. 12 in 1 Cor.* 11-12). He can also apply the verse to devout women of the past and to contemporary women who adopt the ascetic life—but not to contemporary matrons (*Hom. 5 in 1 Thess.*).
20. *Hom. 12 in 1 Tim. 4.*
21. *Hom. 40 in 1 Cor. 6.*
22. *Hom. 22 in Eph. 2* (on Eph. 6:9); *Hom. 40 in 1 Cor. 6.*
23. E.g., *Hom. 26 in 1 Cor. 3, Hom. 17 in Gen. 6, Serm. 2 in Gen. 2, Hom. 23 in Rom. 1.*
24. *Summa Theologica I. 92.*
25. *Hom. 20 in Eph.* (on Eph. 5:33); *Hom. 37 in 1 Cor. 1; Hom. 16 in Gen. 1.*
26. *Hom. 11 in Acta 3* (on Acts 4:23ff.). According to Chrysostom, God gave us hands and feet so that we could take care of our own needs (*Hom. 40 in 1 Cor. 6*).
27. *Hom. 68 in Matt. 3; Adv. Oppug. 2.11.*

AUGUSTINE AND THE PAULINE
THEME OF HOPE

1. H.-G. Link, "Hoffnung," *Historisches Wörterbuch der Philosophie* 3 (1974): 1157–66, especially 1160; also Karl M. Woschitz, *Elpis-Hoffnung: Geschichte, Philosophie, Exegese, Theologie eines Schlüsselbegriffs* (Vienna, 1979), 10–15.
2. *Apol.* 39.1; cf. *Ad nat.* I.7.29f.
3. See Paul Zemp, *Die Grundlagen des heilsgeschichtlichen Denkens bei Gregor von Nyssa*, Münchener Theologische Studien 2.38 (Munich, 1970), 92–96; Jean Daniélou, *L'être et le temps chez Grégoire de Nysse* (Leiden, 1970), 222f.
4. See Raniero Cantalamessa, *Ostern in der Alten Kirche*, trans. Annemarie Spoerri, Traditio Christiana 4 (Bern, 1981), sections 13, 24, 31, 58, 93, and Eusebius, *Vita Constantini* 3.65.2; Balthasar Fischer, *Die Psalmen als Stimme der Kirche* (Trier, 1982); and, for a pre-Augustinian exposition of Romans, see especially Origen's *Comm. in Rom.* and Francesca Cocchini, ed., *Origene: Commento alla lettera ai Romani*, vol. 1: *Libri I–VII* (Casale Monferrato, 1985).
5. See especially *Conf.* 9.10.23 (citing Phil. 3:13), 11.29.39, 13.13.13-14.15 (with most of the biblical texts Augustine had come to cherish); also (already) *De mag.* 1.2 (with Ps. 4:5f.).
6. It cannot be stressed enough that, at his conversion in the fall of 386 and still less in his retirement at Cassiciacum, Augustine did not need to convert to the Christian faith. At that time, it was rather a matter of

integrating his childhood faith with all that he was and had so as to be able fully to affirm it. See also Alfred Schindler, "Augustin," *Theologische Realenzyklopädie* 4 (1979): 648–98, especially 660ff.

7. See especially the fundamental program of *Sol.* 1.2.7: "Deum et animam scire cupio," and 2.1.1: "Deus semper idem, noverim me, noverim te. Oratum est"; also *Epp.* 3 and 4; *Conf.* 7.10.16.

8. On the Cassiciacum dialogues, see the introductions by Régis Jolivet and Pierre de Labriolle in *Bibliothèque augustinienne,* vol. 4: *Dialogues philosophiques* 1, ed. Jolivet (Paris, 1945), and vol. 5: *Dialogues philosophiques* 2, ed. de Labriolle (Paris, 1948) respectively; *Nuova biblioteca agostiniana,* vol. 3: *Dialoghi,* pt. 1 (Rome, 1970); Peter Brown, *Augustine of Hippo* (London, 1967), 115–27.

9. See *Sol.* 2.7.14, where Augustine refers to the novelty of the *genus litterarium,* and *Ep.* 3.1.

10. See *Sol.* 1.3.8: "Sed ego quid sciam quaero, non quid credam. Omne autem quod scimus, recte fortasse etiam credere dicimur; at non omne quod credimus, etiam scire"; also *C. Acad.* 3.20.43.

11. See *C. Acad.* 2.2.5: "Respexi tantum, confiteor, quasi de itinere in illam religionem, quae pueris nobis insita est et medullitus implicata: verum autem ipsa me ad se nescientem rapiebat."

12. See *Sol.* 1.4.9f. on the *scire Deum;* 1.6.12 on the intellectual and moral presuppositions of the knowledge of God; *De ord.* 2.11.30 on the definition of *ratio;* also *Bibliothèque augustinienne* 5:15f.

13. See *Sol.* 1.6.12 and 1.8.15–10.16; see also Ragnar Holte, *Béatitude et sagesse: Saint Augustin et le problème de la fin de l'homme dans la philosophie ancienne* (Paris, 1962), 312, with reference to *C. Acad.* 3.19.42.

14. *Sol.* 1.6.12–7.14. See also Olivier du Roy, *L'intelligence de la foi en la Trinité selon saint Augustin* (Paris, 1966), 143–47; *Nuova biblioteca agostiniana* 3, pt. 1:336f.; Isabelle Bochet, *Saint Augustin et le désir de Dieu* (Paris, 1982), 235–39 (textual analysis without regard to the philosophical sources).

15. *Sol.* 1.6.12: "Ergo animae tribus quibusdam rebus opus est, ut oculos habeat quibus iam bene uti possit, ut aspiciat, ut videat." *Sol.* 1.7.14: distinction between *visio in hac vita* and *post hanc vitam.*

16. See especially *Sol.* 1.7.14: "tamen quia etiam corporis sensus utuntur opere proprio, si nihil quidem valent ad fallendum, non tamen nihil ad non ambigendum, potest adhuc dici fides ea qua his resistitur."

17. *Sol.* 1.7.14: "tamen, quia multas molestias corporis sustinet, sperandum est ei post mortem omnia ista incommoda non futura." On the meaning of *praesumere,* see *De beata vita* 4.35: "Haec est nullo ambigente beata vita, quae vita perfecta est, ad quam nos festinantes posse perduci, solida fide, alacri spe, flagrante caritate praesumendum est."

18. *Sol.* 1.7.14: "Sed cum post hanc vitam tota se in Deum collegerit, caritas restat qua ibi teneatur."

19. Ibid. 1.7.14: "et nisi ingenti amore oculum infixerit, nec ab aspiciendo uspiam declinaverit, manere in illa beatissima visione non poterit."

20. Ibid. 1.7.14: "Fides quare sit necessaria, cum iam videat?"
21. Ibid. 1.7.14: "Spes nihilominus, quia iam tenet" and "neque quidquam sperandum ei restat, cum totum secura possideat."
22. On the interpretation of 1 Cor. 13:13, see Hans Conzelmann, *Der erste Brief an die Korinther* (Göttingen, 1969), 270–73. Conzelmann not only presents the triad of faith, hope, and love as Pauline but also stresses that according to the whole context, only love can endure. See especially p. 271, with the reference to Jewish anticipations of the triad, as in 4 Mc. 17:2–4. So also Ceslas Spicq, *Agapè dans le Nouveau Testament*, 3 vols. (Paris, 1959), 2:365–78.
23. Compare especially *Sol.* 1.7.14: "Caritati vero non solum nihil detrahetur," with 1 Cor. 13:8: "caritas numquam excidit."
24. See *De beata vita* 4.35 (cited in n. 17), with the whole context, in which Monica refers to the hymn of Ambrose (*sacerdotis nostri*) *Deus creator omnium; Sol.* 1.1.3: "Deus cui nos fides excitat, spes erigit, caritas iungit, Deus per quem vincimus inimicum, te deprecor," with the commentary by du Roy, 200; *Sol.* 1.13.23; *De lib. arb.* 2.20.54 (perhaps after 391): "porrectam nobis desuper dexteram Dei, id est Dominum nostrum Iesum Christum, fide firma teneamus, et exspectemus certa spe, et caritate ardenti desideremus"; *De mus.* 6.17.59 (a treatise begun in 386 but completed only much later): "et colunt eam [Trinitatem] credendo, sperando, diligendo."
25. It is noteworthy that Ambrose (*De Isaac* 4.26), in a context that is philosophical although inspired by Origen, speaks of the love that is greater and more fruitful than faith and hope.
26. See Plotinus, *Enneads* 1.2 and 5.9.10; also du Roy, 145ff., especially 145, n. 4, where, however, Ciceronian influences are also noted.
27. Compare *Sol.* 1.6.13: "Ipsa autem visio, intellectus est ille qui in anima est, qui conficitur ex intelligente et eo quod intelligitur," with *Enneads* 5.3.8; see also du Roy, 145.
28. *Sol.* 1.4.9: "Nunc illud responde: si ea quae de Deo dixerunt Plato et Plotinus vera sunt, satisne tibi est ita Deum scire, ut illi sciebant?"
29. Holte, 316, also p. 60, where reference is made to *Enneads* 1.3.1, a passage in which Plotinus lets *pistis* precede *gnosis*.
30. *Enneads* 4.7.15 and 6.9.10. See Heinrich Lausberg, *Handbuch der literarischen Rhetorik*, 2 vols. (Munich, 1960), sections 348–430.
31. See especially *Sol.* 1.4.9, on the *scientia* of Plato and Plotinus, as well as *Sol.* 1.13.23: "His quodammodo ipsa lux sanitas est, nec doctore indigent, sed sola fortasse admonitione. His credere, sperare, amare satis est"; also Karl-Heinrich Lütcke, "*Auctoritas*" *bei Augustin* (Stuttgart, 1968), especially 90–94, as also 76ff.
32. See *C. Acad.* 3.20.43; *De ord.* 2.9.27; also Lütcke, 119–48, especially 119ff.
33. For what follows, see Christine Mohrmann, *Études sur le latin des chrétiens*, vol. 1: *Le Latin des chrétiens*, 2d ed. (Rome, 1961), 195–203, with the texts in which Augustine discusses the nuances of the three expressions,

credere Deo, credere Deum, credere in Deum. According to this account, credere Deo signifies, in particular, the acceptance of divine authority as source of truth (198). Here, however, it is a matter of Augustine's later usage. For the earlier texts, see Magnus Löhrer, Der Glaubensbegriff des hl. Augustinus in seinen ersten Schriften bis zu den Confessiones (Einsiedeln, 1955), 117–33.

34. See Sol. 1.15.30: "Constanter Deo crede, eique te totum committe quantum potes . . . Domini te servum esse profitere"; 2.1.1: "Credamus Deum adfuturum"; 2.20.34: "si auctor sit cui fides habenda est, non recordaturus, sed crediturus es" (with regard to a recollection of one's infancy); also Sol. 2.6.9: "Deus cui nos commisimus, sine dubitatione fert opem, et de his angustiis, modo credamus, et eum rogemus devotissime" (context: deliverance from error).

35. See Lütcke, 119–28; and De ord. 2.9.27.

36. Sol. 1.14.26; also Holte, 314; Mohrmann, 201.

37. Sol. 1.10.17. See Plato, Phaedrus, 66b–67c; Symposium, 193d; also François van Menxell, Elpis, Espoir, Espérance (Frankfurt, 1983), 102–15.

38. Enneads 1.6.7, 9 (especially: "when you perceive yourself having become thus, then you are yourself sight; you acquire confidence [tharsēsas] in yourself").

39. Sol. 1.1.5; also du Roy, 205f.

40. See Sol. 1.7.14 (cited in n. 17); note the connection of sperare and certus esse in Sol. 1.10.17; see also De lib. arb. 2.20.54 (cited in n. 24).

41. See Sol. 2.20.36 (cited below, n. 57).

42. See Plotinus Enneads 1.6.7, 9; but note Conzelmann, 261, and the literature cited in his n. 25.

43. Sol. 1.7.14 (cited in nn. 18 and 23); and on Plotinus see Cornelia J. de Vogel, Greek Philosophy, 3 vols. (Leiden, 1964), 3:547.

44. On what follows, see Willy Theiler, Die Vorbereitung des Neuplatonismus (1934; reprint: Berlin, 1964), 147–52; Édouard des Places, "Jamblich und die Chaldäischen Orakel," in Die Philosophie des Neuplatonismus, ed. Clemens Zintzen (Darmstadt, 1977), 294–303 (originally published in 1964); Angelo R. Sodano, ed., Giamblico: I Misteri Egiziani (Milan, 1984), 341ff., n. 108.

45. Compare Sol. 1.6.13 with Porphyry Ad Marcellam 24, in Vogel, 3:546f.

46. See Iamblichus De mysteriis 5.239 (context: on prayer), and Sodano, 342, who, following des Places, supposes a Chaldean influence here; Proclus In Timaeum 1.208.24, 1.212.19-24; In Alcibiadem 356.31; also Édouard des Places, "La prière des philosophes grecs," Gregorianum 41 (1960): 253–72, especially 270ff.; and Édouard des Places, ed., Oracles Chaldaiques (Paris, 1971), 28, 78ff., 132f.

47. A Christian influence is possible in the view of Vogel, 3:547.

48. See Suzanne Poque, "L'expression de l'anabase plotinienne dans la prédication de saint Augustin et ses sources," Recherches augustiniennes 10 (1975): 187–215, especially 214f.

49. See *Conf.* 7.21.27, 8.5.11, 8.6.14, 8.12.28ff.

50. *C. Acad.* 2.2.5; see *Sol.* 1.1.3: 1 Cor. 15:24 and Gal. 4:9. On this and other texts: Pierre Courcelle, *Recherches sur les Confessions de saint Augustin*, 2d ed. (Paris, 1968), especially 199, n. 1, and 308; du Roy, 202f.; and the biblical indices in *Nuova biblioteca agostiniana* 3, pt. 1:563 and 3, pt. 2:800f.

51. *Sol.* 2.20.36. On the biblical sense of *quaerentibus nobis*, see *C. Acad.* 2.3.9 citing Mt. 7:7; also *De mus.* 6.1.1: " . . . si ut spero, et supplex deprecor, Deus et Dominus noster propositum meum voluntatemque gubernaverit . . . "

52. See *Retr.* 1.4.2f. with an explicit reference to Porphyry's well-known dictum; also the notes in *Bibliothèque augustinienne*, vol. 12: *Les revisions*, ed. Gustave Bardy (Paris, 1950), 290ff. (references to *Ad Marcellam* 8, 32, 34 and to fragments of *De regressu animae*: 292, n. 3).

53. See the chronological overview in *Nuova biblioteca agostiniana*, vols. 25–28: *Esposizioni sui Salmi* (Rome, 1967–77), 25:xlivff. According to this dating, Augustine gave the *enarrationes* on Pss. 43, 45–49, 60, 62, 65, 73, 79, 91f., 109 during Lent in 412. In addition, he preached on a series of other Psalms during the same year.

54. I have used the edition in *Corpus Christianorum, Series Latina*, vol. 39, ed. Eligius Dekkers and Iohannes Fraipont (Turnholt, 1956), 1278–90.

55. *En. in Ps. 91* 1, 2; also cited are Rom. 3:4; 1 Cor. 4:7 (twice); 2 Cor. 9:7; and Eph. 2:10.

56. See Brown, 151f. The writings of 394–95 are in view here: *Epistulae ad Romanos inchoata expositio; Expositio epistulae ad Galatas; Expositio quarundam propositionum ex epistula ad Romanos*. To these may be added *De div. quaest.* qq. 66–75 (from approximately the same time); *Ad. Simpl.* 1 (in 396) (see *Retr.* 2.1). The sermons on individual Pauline pericopes, on the other hand, come for the most part from a later period. See *Nuova biblioteca agostiniana*, vol. 29: *Discorsi* (Rome, 1979), cxxif.

57. See, above all, *Ad. Simpl.* 1; also *De praed. sanct.* 4.8.

58. On the relation of Augustine's exegesis of Paul and that of Pelagius, see Alexander Souter, *Pelagius's Expositions of Thirteen Epistles of St. Paul*, 3 vols., Texts and Studies 9 (Cambridge, 1922–31), and now Flavio G. Nuvolone, "Pélage et pélagianisme," *Dictionnaire de spiritualité*, 12 (1983): 2895f.

59. Augustine's first genuinely anti-Pelagian work, *De peccatorum meritis et remissione et de baptismo parvulorum*, comes from the year 412. See *Nuova biblioteca agostiniana*, vol. 17: *Natura e grazia*, pt. 1 (Rome, 1981), 3–6.

60. On the *schola Christi*, see *En. in Ps. 79* 1; also Brown, 244–58.

61. See *Conf.* 9.4.8-12: reading of the Psalms and reflection on Ps. 4; 9.7.15: singing of hymns and Psalms in Milan; 9.12.31: praying the Psalms at the burial of Monica. In the early writings there are, apart from the *De lib. arb.* and the *De mus.*, only two citations from the Psalms: *De quant. an.* 33.75 (387–88): Ps. 50:12; *De mag.* 1.2 (389): Ps. 4:5f. (with *sperate in Domino*).

62. Augustine's intimate knowledge of the Psalms is evident, above all, in the *Confessiones;* see Georg N. Knauer, *Psalmenzitate in Augustins Konfessionen* (Göttingen, 1955). For the dating of his annotations and sermons on the Psalms, see the chronological table in *Nuova biblioteca agostiniana* 25:xlivff. In particular, he had already written expositions of the first thirty-two Psalms before his consecration as bishop; see also Knauer, 27f., and especially Marie-Josèphe Rondeau, *Les commentaires patristiques du psautier,* 2 vols. (Rome, 1982–85), 1:167–75.

63. See Rondeau, 2:365–88.

64. See Jerome *Liber psalmorum iuxta Septuaginta interpretes* (at Ps. 91:15): *et bene patientes erunt.*

65. See *En. in Ps. 45* 11; *En. in Ps. 49* 22; *En. in Ps. 60* 4, 10; *En. in Ps. 62* 6; *En. in Ps. 65* 1, 24; *En. in Ps. 92* 1; *En. in Ps. 109* 8, 12, 14.

66. See especially *De ver. rel.* (390) and *De nat. bon.* (after 404); also *Retr.* 1.13.1 and 2.9.

67. See F. van der Meer, *Augustinus der Seelsorger* (Cologne, 1951), 202–9.

68. See especially *Serm.* 105 (410–11) and *Serm.* 296 (410–11); also Brown, 287–98.

69. See *Serm.* 50.11 (before 400) on overcoming pride; and on patient endurance, see *Serm.* 213.5 (before 410): "In passione quid egit; docuit quid toleremus"; *En. in Ps. 61* 2: "In this life, we cannot be without temptation, but Christ has already overcome our temptation"; *En. 2 in Ps. 32* s.1.5ff. (403): "always to thank God and to love his righteousness"; *En. 2 in Ps. 21* 4 (395 or 407); *Serm.* 23A(= Mai 16) 2ff. (412–16).

70. See *Conf.* 7.7.11-8.12, 8.5.10-12, 8.8.19-12.30.

71. See Yves Congar in *Bibliothèque augustinienne,* vol. 28: *Traités anti-Donatistes 1,* ed. Congar (Paris, 1963), 85f.

72. See *In Ioann. ev.* 6.2 (with Rom. 8:26), 27.11, 28.11; *C. ep. Parm.* 3.5.27; *En. in Ps. 9* 9-12 (392–94): "to hope in God and his righteousness"; *En. in Ps. 136* (412–15): "concerning the Christian attitude toward Babylon."

73. See *Ep.* 55, especially 2 and 3; also A. Roth, "Pascha und Hinübergang durch Glaube, Hoffnung, Liebe," in *Mélanges Christine Mohrmann* (Utrecht, 1973), 96–107; Ovila Brabant, *Le Christ, centre et source de la vie morale chez saint Augustin* (Gembloux, 1971), 9–76.

74. See *De cat. rud.* 7.11 (ca. 400): "Narratione finita spes resurrectionis intimanda est, et pro capacitate ac viribus audientis, proque ipsius temporis modulo, adversus vanas irrisiones infidelium de corporis resurrectione tractandum . . . "; also *De cat. rud.* 25.47; *Serm.* 261.1 (397–418); *Serm.* 229H(= Morin Guelf. 12) 3 (412); and Ladislaus Ballay, *Der Hoffnungsbegriff bei Augustinus* (Munich, 1964), 171–83.

75. *Ep.* 130.8.16: "quoniam qui sperat aeternam vitam, quae retro sunt obliviscitur et in anteriora se extendit"; and *Ep.* 130.6.12-7.14.

76. See *En. in Ps. 91* 1: "quia fides rerum est quae non videntur; erit autem species cum visae fuerint; et spes rei est quae non tenetur; quae adveniente ipsa re, non erit iam spes, quia tenebimus, non sperabimus"; also

Sol. 1.7.14: "Fides quare sit necessaria, cum iam videat? spes nihilominus, quia iam tenet." Under the influence of Rom. 8:24, the *non videre* is also applied to hope. On the other hand, behind the *non videre* of faith stands not only the antithesis *fides-species* of 2 Cor. 5:7, but also the "invisible things hoped for" of Heb. 11:1. On the closeness of hope and faith in Paul, see the specific references in Rudolf Bultmann, "ἐλπίς," *Theologisches Wörterbuch zum Neuen Testament* 2 (1935): 527ff.

77. See *En. in Ps. 91* 1: " . . . ut gaudeamus cum viderimus, et fidei nostrae succedat species lucis eius, ubi iam non nobis dicetur: Crede quod non vides, sed, gaude quia vides" and *En. in Ps. 91* 2: "et si laborat in praesenti, extenditur spe futuri, et serenatur omne nubilum tristitiae; sicut dicit apostolus: Spe gaudentes. Ipsum autem gaudium in tranquillitate spei nostrae, sabbatum nostrum est." See also *En. in Ps. 91* 14; *Serm.* 21.1 (with Ps. 63:11).

78. See *En. in Ps. 91* 1: "Spes etiam nostra incommutabilis est, et figatur in illo, et non nutet et fluctuet, non agitetur; sicut ipse Deus in quo figitur, non potest agitari."

79. See *En. in Ps. 91* 1 (with Rom. 8:24f.); also *Serm.* 37.11.

80. See *En. in Ps. 91* 1, particularly: "Ubique sit gratus, nusquam ingratus: et Patri consolanti et blandienti gratus sit, et Patri emendanti et flagellanti et disciplinam danti gratus sit."

81. *En. in Ps. 91* 1.

82. See *En. in Ps. 60* 4: "Habemus enim duas vitas; sed unam in qua sumus, alteram quam speramus. In qua sumus, nota nobis est; quam speramus, ignota nobis est"; further, *En. in Ps. 120* 6: "The resurrection of Christ has already occurred; ours is yet to be" (with the interpretation of Exod. 33:20, 23 and of what the apostle "urged most strongly" in Rom. 10:9); *Ep.* 130.2.5 (after 411): "Porro si nulla tentatio, iam nulla oratio: non enim ibi adhuc erit promissi boni exspectatio, sed redditi contemplatio; unde: Placebo, inquit Domino in regione vivorum [Ps. 114:8], ubi tunc erimus, non in deserto mortuorum, ubi nunc sumus" (Col. 3:3 follows).

83. See Brabant; and Basil Studer, "Soteriologie in der Schrift und Patristik," *Handbuch der Dogmengeschichte*, vol. 3, fascicle 2a (Freiburg, 1978), 158f.

84. See *En. in Ps. 91* 8; *En. in Ps. 65* 24.

85. See *En. in Ps. 91* 10.

86. *En. in Ps. 60* 4; see also *En. in Ps. 65* 1 (Lent, 412); *En. in Ps. 101* s.2.14 (395); *En. in Ps. 26* s.2.4 (411–12 or 415).

87. *En. in Ps. 60* 4: "Ergo factus est ipse spes nostra, qui dedit nobis Spiritum sanctum et ambulamus modo ad spem; non enim ambularemus, nisi speraremus" (prior to this passage, Rom. 5:3ff. is cited; following it, Rom. 8:24f.).

88. *En. in Ps. 91* 1; also *En. in Ps. 62* 6: "Quomodo animae nostrae promittitur beatitudo, sic et carni nostrae promittitur resurrectio. Resurrectio carnis talis nobis promittitur; audite et discite, et tenete quae sit spes christianorum, quare sumus christiani"; *Serm.* 108.1.1 (no date): "Ad

hanc exspectationem et propter hanc spem christiani facti sumus . . .
Ab amore saeculi huius vocati sumus, ut aliud saeculum speremus et
diligamus" (interpretation of Lk. 12:35f. and Ps. 33:12–15); *Serm.* 198.2:
"One becomes a Christian through faith, hope, and love." Note also *En.
in Ps. 131* 19f. (21 December 412), where human beings are represented
as creatures of hope.

89. See *Ep.* 55.2.3 (with Gal. 5:6; Rom. 8:24; Rom. 6:4, 6; Eph. 2:6; Col. 3:1f.,
3:3; 1 Cor. 15:53; Rom. 8:33, 8:10f.; Col. 1:18; and see n. 73 above); also
En. in Ps. 60 4 (citations in nn. 82 and 87 above); *Serm.* 206C(= Mai 95) 7
(393–395 or after 409): "huius diei sempiterni spem semper in corde
gestate."

90. See *De doct. chr.* 1.39.43 (with the whole context); in addition, *Ep.*
263.3f. (a letter of consolation): Christians have hope for eternal life,
pagans do not (with reference to 1 Thes. 4:13); *Ep.* 208.7: hope in the
monastic life.

91. See *Ep.* 238.2.13 (date?): "Quod enim fecit in multis sanctis in adop-
tionem filiorum vocatis cohaeredibus Christi una fides et una spes et una
caritas, ut esset eis una anima et cor unum in Deum"; *Serm.* 88.12.21 (ca.
400); *De. Gen. ad litt.* 12.28.56.

92. On holding fast in persecution, see *cath. fr.* 20.56; and on the church as
a community of hope, *En. in Ps. 50* 22 (411–13): "Interpretatur enim
Sion speculatio, et Ierusalem visio pacis. Agnoscitis ergo vos in Sion et
in Ierusalem, si certi exspectatis spem futuram, et si pacem habetis cum
Deo." Also: *Serm.* 188.3.4 (25 December, year uncertain); *Ep.* 187.8.28
(417).

93. See *De civ. Dei* 1 praef. and *De civ. Dei* 15.18: "In spe igitur vivit homo
filius resurrectionis [i.e., of the son of Seth]; in spe vivit, quamdiu peregrinatur hic civitas Dei, quae gignitur ex fide resurrectionis Christi."

94. See *Serm.* 193.1; *Serm.* 188.3.4; *Serm.* 198.2 (New Year).

95. See *Ep.* 55.2.3-4.5.

96. See *Serm.* 223I(= Wilmart Add. [15]) (date?): "Ergo humilitate nostra hu-
militatem Domini nostri Iesu Christi in memoriam revocemus. Humiliter
vigilemus, humiliter oremus, piissima fide, firmissima spe, ferventissima
caritate, cogitantes qualem nostra claritas habitura sit diem, si nostra hu-
militas noctem vertit in diem." Further: *Serm.* 223E(= Wilmart 5) 1 (date?);
Serm. 229.2 (405–11).

97. *Serm.* 260C(= Mai 95) 7: "Praeterita itaque obliviscentes, et in ea quae
ante sunt extendentes, secundum intentionem sequentes ad palmam
supernae vocationis (See Phil. 3:13f.), fratres et filii carissimi, etiam cum
sacramentorum signacula posueritis, huius diei sempiterni spem semper
in corde gestate; vestesque nitidas . . . ita mutate, ut illud quod indi-
cant non mutetis, fidei luce et veritatis effulgens; . . . ut in illo die non
nudi inveniamini; et a gloria fidei in gloriam speciei sine ulla difficultate
transeatis."

98. See *Serm.* 105.3.3-5.7.

99. See *Serm.* 90.8 (date disputed); *Serm.* 71.10.16 (418–20); *De trin.* 13.20.26 (with Rom. 1:17 and Gal. 5:6), 15.18.32 (with Gal. 5:6 and Jas. 2:19); *Ench.* 29.112.

100. *De fid. et op.* (412f.). See the reference in *Ench.* 18.67f. to the *apostolica manifestissima et apertissima testimonia*, which stand out in this writing.

101. See *Serm.* 53.10.11 (413–415), citing Gal. 5:6; *In Ioann. ep.* 8.12f.; *In Ioann. ev.* 83.3; *Ep.* 130.8.16f.: prayer as an expression of faith and hope.

102. *Serm.* 108.2 (date?); see also *De civ. Dei* 19.4: the necessity of hope emphasized in a discussion of the moral virtues.

103. *En. 2 in Ps. 31* 5 (412–15); also *De doct. chr.* 1.40.44; *De trin.* 8.4.6; *Ench.* 32.121.

104. See 2 Cor. 3:12 (and the whole context); 2 Cor. 7:4.

105. See the thorough discussion of dating in Josef Barbel, ed., *Enchiridion de fide, spe et caritate/Handbüchlein über Glaube, Hoffnung und Liebe,* Testimonia 1 (Düsseldorf, 1960), 6f. On Laurentius, see Barbel, 5; also André Mandouze, *Prosopographie chrétienne du Bas-Empire,* vol. 1: *Prosopographie de l'Afrique chrétienne (303–533)* (Paris, 1982), 629.

106. Adolf von Harnack, *Lehrbuch der Dogmengeschichte,* 3 vols. (4th ed., 1909; reprint: Darmstadt, 1960), 3:220–36; Reinhold Seeberg, *Lehrbuch der Dogmengeschichte,* vol. 2: *Die Dogmenbildung in der alten Kirche* (3d ed., 1920; reprint: Darmstadt, 1953), 550–67.

107. See *Ench.* 1.2: "Quaerisne aliquid dici brevius, qui petis a me, ut breviter magna dicantur? An hoc ipsum tibi fortasse desideras breviter aperiri atque in sermonem brevem colligi, quonam modo sit colendus deus?"; also *Retr.* 2.63 (90).

108. See *Ench.* 1.5-6: "Quae disputatio tam multorum est voluminum, ut etiam infinita videatur. Tu autem enchiridion a nobis postulas, id est, quod manu possit adstringi, non quod armaria possit onerare." Augustine considers it particularly difficult also to defend Christian teaching against dissenters in a small handbook. Later, he will devote a separate writing, *De haeresibus,* to the task.

109. See *Ench.* 33.122: "Sed sit aliquando huius voluminis finis, quod ipse videris utrum enchiridion vel appellare debeas, vel habere."

110. See, above all, *Retr.* 1.3.2 and its critique of *De ordine;* also Henri I. Marrou, *Saint Augustin et la fin de la culture antique,* 4th ed. (Paris, 1958), 345–52.

111. See Suzanne Poque, *Le langage symbolique dans la prédication d'Augustin d'Hippone* (Paris, 1984), 239f.

112. See *Ench.* 1.8: "nonnulli in arte grammatica verbi huius utuntur exemplo ad ostendendam impropriam dictionem . . . "; 4.14: "illa dialecticorum regula deficit, qua dicunt nulli rei duo simul inesse contraria"; 11.40: "valde prolixae disputationis est"; 5.17: definition of *error;* 15:59: "Cum ista quaeruntur, et ea sicut potest, quisque coniectat, non inutiliter exercentur ingenia, si adhibeatur disceptatio moderata, et absit error opinantium se scire quod nesciunt. Quid enim opus est, ut haec atque huiusmodi

affirmentur vel negentur vel definiantur cum discrimine, quando sine crimine nesciuntur?"

113. See Ench. 5.1, 7.20, 13.44 (with grammatical exegesis); see also the entries in the index of Bibliothèque augustinienne, vol. 9: Exposés généraux de la foi, ed. J. Rivière (Paris, 1947), 444.

114. See Ench. 1.2 (cited in n. 107); in other passages—Ench. 33.122 and Retr. 2.63(90)—he speaks of this work as a liber; see Barbel, 5f. It is worth noting that there was, in antiquity, only one theory of "speech." The rules for tractates that treat a quaestio infinita, as well as for commentaries, are derived from those for the three kinds of speech. On this matter, see Lausberg, and Manfred Fuhrmann, Die antike Rhetorik (Munich, 1984).

115. Ench. 1.1-2.8 and 33.122.

116. See Ench. 1.1: "Dici non potest, dilectissime fili Laurenti, quantum tua eruditione delecter, quam te cupiam esse sapientem . . . " (with 1 Cor. 1:20; Wis. 6:26; Rom. 16:19).

117. See Ench. 1.2: "Hominis autem sapientia pietas est." An explanation of pietas, with references to theosebeia and eusebeia, follows. The section concludes with the question: "quonam modo sit colendus deus?" On the concept of pietas, see De trin. 12.14.22; 14.1.1. In both of these passages from De trin., this concept is developed together with that of sapientia. In addition, the first passage says, "Et quis cultus eius, nisi amor eius, quo nunc desideramus eum videre, credimusque et speramus nos esse visuros; et quantum proficimus 'videmus nunc per speculum in aenigmate, tunc autem' in manifestatione?" (1 Cor. 13:12).

118. See Ench. 1.3: "Hic si respondero fide, spe, caritate colendum deum, profecto dicturus es, brevius hoc dictum esse quam velles." See also De trin. 12.14.22 (cited in n. 117).

119. See Ench. 1.4. The postulata of Laurentius concern the distinction between orthodoxy (quid sequendum maxime) and heresy (quid fugiendum), the relation of ratio and fides in religio; the question of what should be held fast at the beginning and what at the end; the summa totius definitionis; the foundation of the Catholic faith. Ratio is concerned with vel a sensibus corporis inchoata vel ab intelligentia mentis inventa; of faith, on the other hand, he says that it rests on those witnesses who, with the help of God, composed scripture on the basis of their own experience or of prophecy.

120. Ench. 1.5. Note how the goal of the ascent is described as a blessed vision of ineffabilis pulchritudo; see also Ench. 7.21: "per fidem veram ad aeternam beatitudinem tendimus."

121. Ench. 1.5 (with 1 Cor. 3:11). See n. 108 above.

122. See Ench. 1.4 (see n. 119 above).

123. See Lausberg, section 272; note also Ench. 1.5 and 2.7: "Nam ecce tibi est symbolum et dominica oratio! Quid brevius auditur aut legitur? quid facilius memoriae commendatur?"

124. See C. Acad. 3.19.42; De util. cred. 12.27; De trin. 12.14.22, 14.1.1ff.: on the relation of sapientia to cultus dei and to scientia. In the last of these

texts, 1 Cor. 12:8 is explicitly cited. 1 Cor. 12:8ff. also, however, stands in the background of *Ench.* 1.5.

125. See also *Ench.* 33.122: "Ego tamen cum spernenda tua in Christo studia non putarem, bona de te credens in adiutorio nostri redemptoris ac sperans teque in eius membris plurimum diligens, librum ad te, sicut valui, utinam tam commodum, quam prolixum, de fide, spe et caritate conscripsi."

126. See *Ench.* 2.7.

127. *Ench.* 2.8: reference to the grammarians who, with regard to Lucan *Bellum civile* 2.15 and Vergil *Aeneid* 4.419, say, "sperare dixit pro timere."

128. *Ench.* 2.8, especially: "Spes autem non nisi bonarum rerum est, nec nisi futurarum, et ad eum pertinentium, qui earum spem gerere perhibetur. Quae cum ita sint, propter has causas distinguenda erat fides ab spe, sicut vocabulo, ita rationali differentia."

129. See *De bapt.* 5.10.12 (400–401); *Serm.* 105.8.11 (410–11); *Serm.* 27.5 (418); *De nupt. et conc.* 1.18.20 (419–21); *Ep.* 130.2.5: "non enim ibi adhuc erit promissi boni exspectatio, sed redditi contemplatio" (with the whole context). For the Latin classical period, see, above all, Cicero, *Tusculanae Disputationes* 4.80, where *spes* as *exspectatio boni* is distinguished from *metus* as *exspectatio mali*; also Woschitz, 186–218.

130. See *Ench.* 2.8, especially: "nam quod attinet ad non videre, sive quae creduntur, sive quae sperantur, fidei speique commune est" and "Proinde nec amor sine spe est, nec sine amore spes, nec utrumque sine fide."

131. See *Ench.* 2.8. For his appreciation of this method, see C. *Cresc.* 1.13.16-14.18, where Augustine defends the use of dialectic, of *peritia disputandi.*

132. *Ench.* 30.114-16.

133. See *Ench.* 30.114, especially: "Sed de his omnibus, quae fideliter sunt credenda, ea tantum ad spem pertinent, quae oratione dominica continentur. . . . Ideo nonnisi a domino deo petere debemus, quidquid speramus nos vel bene operaturos, vel pro bonis operibus adepturos."

134. *Ench.* 30.115f.

135. See *Ench.* 30.115: "Proinde apud evangelistam Matthaeum septem petitiones continere dominica videtur oratio, quarum tribus aeterna poscuntur, reliquis quattuor temporalia, quae tamen propter aeterna consequenda sunt necessaria," as well as 30.116: "Evangelista vero Lucas in oratione dominica petitiones non septem, sed quinque complexus est; nec ab isto utique discrepavit, sed quomodo istae septem sint intelligendae, ipsa sua brevitate commonuit."

136. See *Ench.* 30.115: " . . . et hic inchoata, quantumcumque proficimus, augentur in nobis; perfecta vero, quod in alia vita sperandum est, semper possidebuntur."

137. See *Ench.* 31.118f. On this matter, see above all August Luneau, *L'histoire du salut chez les Pères de l'Église: La doctrine des âges du monde* (Paris, 1964), 357–83.

138. Luneau, 357ff. (with the texts) and 360f. (assessment).

139. Luneau, 359f. (with the texts) and 361 (assessment).

140. On Augustine's doctrine of grace, see, e.g., the introductions in *Bibliothèque augustinienne*, vols. 21–24.

141. See *De pecc. mer.* 1.18.23 (412 A.D.): *salus in spe; De spir. et litt.* 29.51 (412): "Ita multa multitudo dulcedinis eius, hoc est, lex fidei, caritas conscripta in cordibus atque diffusa perficitur sperantibus in eum, ut anima sanata non timore poenae, sed amore iustitiae operetur bonum"; *De spir. et litt.* 36.64; *De nat. et gr.* 48.56 (413–15); *De perf. iust. hom.* (415–16); *C. duas ep. Pel.* 3.3.4f. (421).

142. See *De pecc. mer.* 1.3.3ff., 2.32.52; further, the texts in the index of *Nuova Biblioteca Agostiniana* 17, pt. 2:669f. Also *De civ. Dei* 10.25: "adhaerere autem Deo tunc perfectum erit, cum totum, quod liberandum est, fuerit liberatur. Nunc vero fit illud quod sequitur: Ponere in Deo spem suam" (with the whole anti-Porphyrian context and the exegesis of Ps. 72).

143. See *De spir. et litt.* 29.51 (cited in n. 141), 32.56; *Serm.* 53.10.11 (413 A.D.): "Adest ergo spes, et est comes fidei. Deinde et caritas, qua desideramus, qua pertingere conamur . . . Si enim credis, et non amas, non te moves ad bonum opus: et si moves, ut servus moves, non ut filius: timendo poenam, non amando iustitiam" (with the whole context); also Basil Studer, "Le Christ, notre justice, selon saint Augustin," *Recherches augustiniennes* 15 (1980): 99–143, especially 121f.

144. This theme belongs to the later anti-pelagian polemic. See *Ench.* 11.36, 11.40 (virgin birth as a sign of grace); *De corr. et gr.* 11.30; *De praed. sanct.* 15.30f. Yet it reveals itself even earlier: see *De pecc. mer.* 2.17.27, and above all the texts that present grace as *gratia Christi: De nat. et gr.* 20.22f., 40.47, 54.67 (with the often cited passage: "Gratia Dei per Iesum Christum Dominum nostrum" [Rom. 7:24]).

145. See *Ench.* 9.30ff.: necessity of the grace of Christ; 13.42-14.49: on baptism; 17.66: baptism does not remove the *mala* themselves from children, "ut intelligamus totum quod salutaribus agitur sacramentis magis ad spem venturorum bonorum, quam ad retentionem vel adeptionem praesentium pertinere"; 24.97-27.103: freedom and predestination, with an interpretation of 1 Tm. 2:4.

146. See *Ench.* 31.117.

147. *Ench.* 31.118: "Sed cum in altissimis ignorantiae tenebris nulla resistente ratione secundum carnem vivitur, haec sunt prima hominis." See Luneau, 363–67 (commenting on *De div. quaest.* q. 66.3), on "l'âge de l'inconscience dans le péché."

148. *Ench.* 31.118: "Deinde cum per legem cognitio fuerit facta peccati, si nondum divinus adiuvat spiritus, secundum legem volens vivere vincitur, et sciens peccato peccatoque subditus servit . . . " See Luneau, 367ff. (commenting on *Prop. ad Rom.* 13-18), on "l'âge de la prise de conscience de notre déchéance" (370).

149. *Ench.* 31.118: " . . . concupiscitur adversus carnem fortiore robore caritatis, ut . . . ex fide iustus vivat . . . in quantum non cedit malae

concupiscentiae vincente delectatione iustitiae. Haec sunt tertia bonae spei hominis in quibus, si pia perseverantia quisque proficiat. . . . " See Luneau, 369-74, (commenting on *Prop. ad Rom.* 13-18), on "l'âge de la victoire libératrice de l'amour."

150. *Ench.* 31.118: "postrema pax restat, quae post hanc vitam in requie spiritus, deinde in resurrectione etiam carnis implebitur." See Luneau, 374ff. (commenting on *Prop. ad Rom.* 13-18), on "l'âge de la résurrection des corps."

151. *Ench.* 31.118: "Harum quattuor differentiarum prima est ante legem, secunda sub lege, tertia sub gratia, quarta in pace plena et perfecta." It presents no great difficulties that Augustine assumes even for the first two periods a *gratia mediatoris*, "quamvis pro temporis dispensata velata et occulta." On the other hand, it seems less fitting when, in the next section (31.119), he speaks of a *gratia regenerationis*, in the sense of a forgiveness of sins, for all four ages. Perhaps, in the case of the fourth age, he is thinking only of its beginning, when the enslavement to guilt contracted at birth is finally overcome. In any case, it is obvious that he subordinates all four ages to Jesus Christ. See Luneau, 377f. (citing *De gr. Chr. et de pecc. orig.* 2.24.28; *De ver. rel.* 10.19; *Retr.* 1.12.3), on "Jésus-Christ, unité des quatre âges."

152. See the texts cited in Luneau, 369-74, especially *De div. quaest.* q. 66.6. On the expression *tertia bonae spei hominis*, see *Ench.* 30.114: " . . . nascitur spes bona fidelium, cui caritas sancta comitatur"; also *Ench.* 32.121, citing 1 Tm. 1:5, where, according to Augustine, *spes* is reflected by *bona conscientia* (see the citations in n. 103 above). These parallels seem to preclude the possibility that *bona* is a classical reminiscence. See also 2 Thes. 2:16.

153. The fourth step corresponds, of course, with the fourth age.

154. In *Sol.* 1.6.12-7.14, Augustine still does not speak of works of the Holy Spirit. On the other hand, see *De div. quaest.* q. 66.6 (with Rom. 8:9f.); also Luneau, 372; and *Ep.* 187.8.26f.: on the presence of the Holy Spirit in the soul.

155. See *Ench.* 31.118: "Si autem respexerit Deus, ut ad implenda quae mandat ipse adiuvare credatur," and *De pecc. mer.* 2.6.7; see also *Bibliothèque augustinienne*, vol. 23: *Premières polémiques contre Julien*, ed. F. J. Thonnard, E. Bleuzen, and A. C. de Veer (Paris, 1974), 806ff.

156. See *Ench.* 31.118 (cited in n. 149). Here Augustine obviously assumes the stronger conception of evil concupiscence that he adopted around 420 and according to which the Christian needs a special grace in order to be able to resist *concupiscentia.* See *Bibliothèque augustinienne* 23:770-78, on the history of interpretation of Rom. 7. On the expression *vincente delectatione iustitiae*, see *Ench.* 22.81: "Contra quae [mala ignorantiae et infirmitatis] quidem pugnare nos convenit; sed profecto vincimur, nisi divinitus adiuvemur, ut non solum videamus, quid faciendum sit, sed etiam accedente sanitate delectatio iustitiae vincat in nobis earum rerum delectationes. . . . " See *Bibliothèque augustinienne* 23:778-82, with *C. duas ep. Pel.* 1.9.15 (420), and *Serm.* 159.3.3.

157. See *Ench.* 31.118 (cited in n. 149). The theme of *perseverantia* was fully developed by Augustine only in 429 in *De dono perseverantiae*. But it reveals itself already in those texts in which he assumes a continuing influence of divine grace. See *Bibliothèque augustinienne*, vol. 10: *Mélanges doctrinaux*, ed. G. Bardy, J. A. Beckaert, and J. Boutet (Paris, 1952), 39f. On the idea of progress, see C. *duas ep. Pel.* 3.7.17ff., especially 19: " . . . ut perveniat [ad plenitudinem iustitiae] bene procedit, sicut possumus dicere perfectum esse viatorem, cuius bene promovetur accessio, quamvis non perficiatur intentio nisi fuerit facta perventio." Also *Bibliothèque augustinienne* 23:806ff.

158. See *Ench.* 31.118 (cited in n. 150). On the importance of *spes resurrectionis*, see above, n. 142.

159. See *Ench.* 31.117: "Tamquam si speret vitam aeternam . . . et non amet iustitiam, sine qua nemo ad illam pervenit. Ipsa est autem fides Christi, quam commendat apostolus, quae per dilectionem operatur, et quod in dilectione nondum habet, petit ut accipiat . . . "

160. *Ench.* 32.121 (with 1 Tm. 1:5): "Omnis itaque praecepti finis est caritas, id est, ad caritatem refertur omne praeceptum. Quod vero ita fit vel timore poenae, vel aliqua intentione carnali, ut non referatur ad illam caritatem, quam diffundit spiritus sanctus in cordibus nostris, nondum fit, quemadmodum fieri oportet, quamvis fieri videatur"; also *En. 2 in Ps. 31* 5.

161. See *Ench.* 2.8 (cited in n. 127).

162. Augustine is very fond of Phil. 3:13f. See *Conf.* 9.10.23; *Serm.* 105.5.7 (410–11); *Ep.* 130.8.16; *De spir. et litt.* 36.64; *De perf. iust. hom.* 8.19; *In Ioann. ep.* 4.6; *Serm.* 169.15.18 (416): on Phil. 3:3–16; *C. duas ep. Pel.* 3.7.22. He no longer cites the passage in the last writings: see the index in *Bibliothèque augustinienne*, vol. 24: *Aux moines d'Adrumète et de Provence*, ed. Jean Chéné and Jacques Pintard (Paris, 1962), 847–48. But he still refers to the context: see *De gr. et lib. arb.* 1.1; *De praed. sanct.* 1.1. Above all, he maintains the concern: see *De praed. sanct.* 11.21: it is better to entrust oneself to the will of God than to one's own will, and especially *De dono pers.* 22.62: "Absit autem a vobis, ideo desperare de vobis, quoniam spem vestram in ipso (Patre) habere iubemini, non in vobis" (citing Jer. 17:5; Ps. 117:8; Ps. 2:11ff.).

COMMENT: AUGUSTINE'S PAULINE LEGACIES

1. *De gest. Pel.* 12.28.

2. Henri Marrou, *The Resurrection and Saint Augustine's Theology of Human Values*, trans. Mother Maria Consolata (Villanova, 1966); also in French (with Anne-Marie La Bonnardière): "Le dogme de la résurrection des corps et la théologie des valeurs humaines selon l'enseignement de saint Augustin," *Revue des études augustiniennes* 12 (1966): 111–36.

3. Paula Fredriksen Landes, *Augustine on Romans* (Chico, Calif., 1982), and Paula Fredriksen, "Paul and Augustine: Conversion Narratives, Orthodox Traditions, and the Retrospective Self," *Journal of Theological Studies*, n.s. 37 (1986): 3–34.

4. Note Studer's comments on the place of Romans in *En. in Ps.* 91.

5. Fredriksen, 24.

6. Marrou, 23–25.

BEYOND THE BODY/SOUL DICHOTOMY: AUGUSTINE'S ANSWER TO MANI, PLOTINUS, AND JULIAN

1. Julian's arguments appear *apud* Augustine in the second book of *De nuptiis et concupiscentia*. For an incisive examination of the role scientific medicine plays in Julian's polemic, see Elizabeth A. Clark, "Vitiated Seeds and Holy Vessels: Augustine's Manichean Past," in her *Ascetic Piety and Women's Faith: Essays on Late Ancient Christianity* (Lewiston, N.Y., and Queenston, Ontario, 1986), 291–349; also Peter Brown, "Sexuality and Society in the Fifth Century, A.D.: Augustine and Julian of Eclanum," in *Tria Corda: Scritti in onore di Arnaldo Momigliano*, ed. E. Gabba (Como, 1983), 49–70. See now also a later version of the present essay, revised in light of the conference seminar, "Beyond the Body/Soul Dichotomy: Augustine on Paul against the Manichees and Pelagians," *Recherches augustiniennes* 33 (1988): 87–114; and the recent study by Peter Brown, *The Body and Society: Men, Women, and Sexual Renunciation in Early Christianity* (New York, 1988), especially 33–57 (Paul) and 387–427 (Augustine).

2. See, e.g., *De duab. an.* 10.13-15; *De ver. rel.* 14.27; *C. Fort.* 15, 20; *De lib. arb.* 1.1.1.

3. *C. Iul.* 2.4.8, 5.15.54.

4. Ibid. 5.15.52.

5. *De pecc. mer.* 2.25.39; see also *C. duas ep. Pel.* 1.13.26f.

6. *C. Iul.* 5.15.55.

7. *De praed. sanct.* 1.3.7, 4.8; *De don. pers.* 20.52.

8. "The Pelagians should not think that I agreed with them when I said" (*Retr.* 1.10[9].2, re: *De Gen. c. Man.*); "The Pelagians may think that my statement was made to their advantage" (*Retr.* 1.15[14].2, re: *De duab. an.*); "Wherefore do not let the Pelagians exult as if I had been pleading their case" (*Retr.* 1.9[8].3, re: *De lib. arb.*).

9. See n. 2 above.

10. E.g., *C. Fort.* 7, 17, 18, 20, 21; see also Possidius *Vita Augustini* 6.

11. His allegorizing exegetical work, the *De Gen. c. Man.*, was written before the dispute, in 388–89.

12. *Prop. ad Rom.* 13-18.

13. *De div. quaest.* qq.66-68. *Ad Simpl.* 1.1 implicitly treats man in stages one and two, *ante legem* and *sub lege*; 1.2 how man passes from *sub lege* to *sub gratia*.

For an overview of Augustine's interpretations of Romans: Karl H. Schelkle, *Paulus, Lehrer der Väter: Die altkirchliche Auslegung von Römer 1–11* (Düsseldorf, 1956). For analysis of the theology and exegesis of these particular commentaries: Alexander Souter, *The Earliest Latin Commentaries on the Epistles of St. Paul* (Oxford, 1927); more recently, William S. Babcock, "Augustine's Interpretation of Romans (A.D. 394–396)," *Augustinian Studies* 10 (1979): 55–74. For the works of this period generally: Magnus Löhrer, *Der Glaubensbegriff des hl. Augustinus in seinem ersten Schriften bis zu den Confessiones* (Einsiedeln, 1955); Eugene TeSelle, *Augustine the Theologian* (London, 1970), 132–82; Alberto Pincherle, *La formazione teologica di Sant' Agostino* (Rome, 1947). For the personal and historical context of these writings: F. E. Cranz, "The Development of Augustine's Ideas on Society before the Donatist Controversy," in *Augustine: A Collection of Critical Essays*, ed. R. A. Markus (Garden City, N.Y., 1972), 336–403; Peter Brown, *Augustine of Hippo: A Biography* (Berkeley and Los Angeles, 1967), 132–81. Auguste Luneau, *L'histoire du salut chez les Pères de l'Eglise: La doctrine des âges du monde* (Paris, 1964), provides a good introduction to Augustine's scheme of the four ages.

14. *De div. quaest.* q.66.3.
15. *Prop. ad Rom.* 13-18; see also *Prop. ad Rom.* 46; *De div. quaest.* q.66.3, 6.
16. *De div. quaest.* q.66.6.
17. E.g., *Prop. ad Rom.* 36.
18. Ibid. 13-18, 53.
19. Ibid. 13-18; *De div. quaest.* q.66.7.
20. Cf. *Prop. ad Rom.* 61: *nostrum enim est credere.*
21. *Prop. ad Rom.* 36; *De div. quaest.* q.66.1-2.
22. " . . . which moves some people to think that the apostle Paul has done away with the freedom of the will" (*Prop. ad Rom.* 60).
23. *Prop. ad Rom.* 55, 61; *De div. quaest.* q.68.5.
24. *Prop. ad Rom.* 62; cf. *Exp. ep. ad Rom. inch.* 9: . . . *vocantem deum non spreverunt.* By implication, some *could* choose to spurn God's call; see also *De div. quaest.* q.68.4-5.
25. *Retr.* 1.9(8).1; "the work as a whole gives a stratigraphic record of the course of Augustine's thought between 388 and 395 or 396" (TeSelle, 135).
26. E.g., *Prop. ad Rom.* 13-18, 44, 60, 62; see also *De div. quaest.* q.68.5.
27. TeSelle, 156.
28. John H. S. Burleigh, ed., *Augustine: Earlier Writings* (Philadelphia, 1953), 106.
29. *De lib. arb.* 2.16.41.
30. *De lib. arb.* 3.7.23, 18.52.
31. Ibid. 3.20.57, 23.70, 22.64.
32. Ibid. 3.20.56, 3.24.72-25.76.
33. *Ep.* 37.3 (Augustine's letter acknowledging Simplicianus' request).
34. *Ad Simpl.* 1.2.5; cf. *Prop. ad Rom.* 60, 62; *De div. quaest.* q.68.4.
35. *Ad Simpl.* 1.2.10; cf. *Exp. ep. ad Rom. inch.* 9.

36. Prop. ad Rom. 55: vocatio secundum propositum dei.

37. Ad Simpl. 1.2.13; see also Löhrer, 259–61.

38. Ad Simpl. 1.2.20. This is the first time Augustine uses the term tradux peccati; it does not yet have the value that he will give it in his anti-Pelagian writings. For the evolution of this and other related terms, see especially Athanase Sage, "Péché originel: Naissance d'un dogme," Revue des études augustiniennes 13 (1967): 211–48; Eugene TeSelle, "Rufinus the Syrian, Caelestius, Pelagius: Explorations in the Prehistory of the Pelagian Controversy," Augustinian Studies 3 (1972): 61–95; Alfred Vanneste, "Saint Paul et la doctrine augustinienne du péché originel," Studiorum Paulinorum Congressus Internationalis Catholicus, 2 vols., Analecta Biblica 17-18 (Rome, 1963), 2:513–22.

39. Cf. De lib. arb. 3.19.53, where Augustine had said just the opposite. On the novelty of Augustine's conclusion in the Ad Simpl., see Julius Gross, Geschichte des Erbsündendogmas, vol. 1: Entstehungsgeschichte des Erbsündendogmas (Munich, 1960), 271.

40. Augustine had considered the relation of delight and love to human motivation before: e.g., De mor. 1.21.39-22.40; De fid. et sym. 9.19; Serm. 159 3.3; Exp. ep. ad Gal. 49, commenting on Gal. 5:22–23. God saves man by sending the Holy Spirit who infuses caritas, thereby reorienting man's affections so that he will love righteousness and fulfill the law out of love, not fear (Prop. ad Rom. 44, 48; De div. quaest. q.66). Increasingly, however, Augustine emphasized the compulsive, uncontrolled aspect of human affections, in which habit and custom play such a large role. In the De lib. arb., he had granted that although no man can control when an object will affect him once he perceives it (quo viso tangatur nulla potestas est; 3.25.74), man could at least decide how to respond to the affective object. In the Ad Simpl., however, Augustine emphasizes the lack of effectiveness such a decision has: man can no longer exercise control over his own response to these objects.

41. E.g., De ordine 1.8.24; also De util. cred. 12.27; De lib. arb. 1.1.2.

42. On the campaign against swearing: De serm. Dom. 1.17.51; Brown, Augustine, 150; against astrologers: Exp. ep. ad Gal. 35; on taming the laetitiae: Epp. 22 and 29; F. van der Meer, Augustine the Bishop, trans. Brian Battershaw and G. R. Lamb (London and New York, 1961), 498–526.

43. On the harshness of God's instruction (disciplina): Exp. ep. ad Rom. inch. 1, 10, 18, 19; on the benefits of fear, etc.: also De lib. arb. 3.19.53, 23.70, 25.76; Ad Simpl. 1.1.2, 2.18. See also TeSelle, Augustine, 133; Brown, Augustine, 33.

44. C. duas ep. Pel. 4.7. For a reconstruction of Augustine's use of Ambrosiaster during this later controversy, see Bernard Leeming, "Augustine, Ambrosiaster and the massa perditionis," Gregorianum 11 (1930): 58–91.

45. Vanneste, 514, n. 1; Stanislas Lyonnet, "Augustin et Rom. 5,12 avant la controverse pélagienne," Nouvelle revue théologique 89 (1967): 842–49; also idem, "Rom V,12 chez saint Augustin: Note sur l'élaboration de la doctrine

augustinienne du péché originel," in *L'homme devant Dieu: Mélanges offerts au Père Henri de Lubac*, vol. 1: *Exegèse et patristique* (Paris, 1963), 324–39. Cf. Gustav Bardy in *Bibliothèque augustinienne*, vol. 10: *Mélanges doctrinaux*, ed. Bardy, J. A. Beckaert, and J. Boutet (Paris, 1952), 758f.; TeSelle, *Augustine*, 158.

46. "Nam et ego quod iussisti non negligo et de Tyconii septem regulis vel clavibus, sicut saepe iam scripsi, cognoscere quid tibi videatur exspecto" (*Ep.* 41.2, dated 396). Given Augustine's excitement, I assume that he saw in Tyconius more than a restatement of the position he himself had already spelled out in the commentaries of 394.

47. *Liber reg.*, pp. 25–26 (pagination refers to Texts and Studies, vol. 3, no. 1: *The Rules of Tyconius*, ed. F. C. Burkitt [Cambridge, 1894]).

48. *Liber reg.*, p. 22. See William S. Babcock, "Augustine and Tyconius: A Study in the Latin Appropriation of Paul," *Studia Patristica* 17 (1982): 1209–15.

49. *Liber reg.*, p. 19; Babcock, "Augustine and Tyconius," 1213f.

50. Though, of course, he provides that too; TeSelle, *Augustine*, 182.

51. *Liber reg.*, p. 19.

52. Ibid., p. 25. The larger context of Tyconius' remark is divine foreknowledge, which Augustine, as we have seen, specifically repudiates as the grounds for election.

53. *Ad Simpl.* 1.2.22.

54. van der Meer, 577: "the optimistic convert of the year 388 was thus soon transformed *by his study of the Epistle to the Romans* into a man broodingly contemplating the spectacle of sin and grace" (emphasis added). Romans was the occasion, but not the cause, of this transformation; and other careful readers, such as Origen, were not so transformed.

55. For Pelagius' commentaries, see Souter, 205–30; on this "generation of S. Paul" in the West, see Brown, *Augustine*, 151.

56. *C. Acad.* 2.2.6, written the summer immediately following his conversion in 386.

57. See, even earlier (c. 392?), *En. 2 in Ps.* 32 1-2 on Paul's conversion as depicted in Acts 9.

58. Cranz, 361; see now Paula Fredriksen, "Paul and Augustine: Conversion Narratives, Orthodox Traditions, and the Retrospective Self," *Journal of Theological Studies*, n.s. 37 (1986): 3–34, especially 23f.

59. *Conf.* 1.13.20-22, 2.4.9; cf. his ruminations on the theater in 3.2.2.

60. Of course one need not be celibate to join the church, and Augustine knew this (*Conf.* 8.1.2), but the fashion of celibacy was very strong among the elites of both pagan and Christian society; see Brown, *Augustine*, 106. On both popular and elite expressions of this fashion and its roots in classical culture, see E. R. Dodds, *Pagan and Christian in an Age of Anxiety* (Cambridge, 1965), 1–36.

61. *De lib. arb.* 1.13.29.

62. *Conf.* 10.30.41.

63. Plotinus' anthropology recapitulates in microcosm the problems he con-
fronts when attempting to account for the One's relation to the physical
universe itself. See, e.g., *Enneads* 1.8, 2.4, 3.6. Plotinus maintained both
that human life was the way it was because matter, itself deficient in being,
communicated its deficiency to the soul through the body and that soul
lived in the body as a result of a pre-incarnate fall. Why, then, does disem-
bodied soul fall? See Augustine's critique of Platonism's inconsistencies on
this point in *De civ. Dei* 14.5. On the dichotomy between *self* and *body*:
Dodds, 24–29; on pagan Neoplatonism's views on the body/soul problem:
R. T. Wallis, *Neoplatonism* (New York, 1972), especially pp. 61–82, and the
essays by A. H. Armstrong in *The Cambridge History of Later Greek and
Early Medieval Philosophy*, ed. Armstrong (Cambridge, 1970), 222–35;
for Augustine's views: R. A. Markus' essays in the same work, especially
pp. 354–61.

64. In addition to the works on Neoplatonism cited in the preceding note, see
Hans Jonas, *The Gnostic Religion: The Message of the Alien God and the
Beginnings of Christianity*, 2d ed. rev. (Boston, 1963), 3–47; also idem,
"The Soul in Gnosticism and Plotinus," in *Le néoplatonisme: Colloque
international sur le néoplatonisme* (Paris, 1971), 45–53.

65. "Higher" in a spatial as well as an ontological sense. In the architecture of
the cosmos, the earth stood at the center of the heavenly spheres, where
the heaviest matter had sunk; the more perfect entities were increasingly
distant, in realms of increasing stability, as one went "up" past the seven
planetary spheres to the realm of the fixed stars. See Jonas, *Gnostic Religion*, 43; and on the religious significance of the physical picture of the
cosmos that later antiquity inherited from Aristotle and the hellenistic
philosophers, see Dodds, 43.

66. On Augustine's rejection of Julian's invocation of this model of virtue, see
Clark, 310; also Markus in Armstrong, ed., *The Cambridge History*, 380–94.

67. The Cassiciacum dialogues are most marked by this; see, e.g., *C. Acad.* 1.3.9;
Solil. 1.14.24; and Augustine's critical review of his earlier statements in *Retr.*
1.1-4. On the influence exerted by Neoplatonic dualism on Augustine's
early thought, see Pincherle's *Formazione*; Brown, *Augustine*, 88–127. On
the congeniality of the classical tradition's view of human perfectibility and
moral autonomy to the sensibilities—and level of education—of Pelagius'
aristocratic Roman audience, see Brown, *Augustine*, 367; also Peter Brown,
"The Patrons of Pelagius," in his *Religion and Society in the Age of St.
Augustine* (London, 1972), 208–26.

68. See Brown, "Sexuality and Society," 54ff.

69. E.g., Tertullian *De anima* 28.5-6; Cyprian *Ep.* 64.5. Augustine invoked this
tradition especially in his anti-Donatist essay *De baptismo*, written c. 400.

70. On the ways in which the Origenist controversy affected this debate, see
TeSelle, "Rufinus the Syrian"; also Henry Chadwick, *Early Christian
Thought and the Classical Tradition* (New York, 1966), 114ff.

71. Markus (Armstrong, ed., *The Cambridge History*, 392) notes that this statement in *De Trin.* is one of only three "singled out by Augustine for criticism" in the *Retr.* (2.15.2).

72. He brings both issues together in Book 10 of *De Gen. ad litt.*

73. "una anima primi hominis facta, de cuius propagine omnes hominum animae crearentur" (*De Gen. ad litt.* 10.3.4); " . . . non videmus quid aliud possit intellegi nisi unumquemque parvulum non esse nisi Adam et corpore et anima" (*De Gen. ad litt.* 10.11.19).

74. Ibid. 10.25.42-26.44.

75. The second sentence cited in n. 73 continues, "et ideo illi Christi gratiam necessarium." In other words, to be saved one must be in Christ; to be in Christ one must be baptized; therefore, the unbaptized are not saved because they are not in Christ. But this would be unjust if they were condemned without having sin; therefore, since they are damned, they must in fact have sin. Too young to have committed sins of their own, infants must have the sin of another—namely, Adam—for which reason they are baptized *in remissione peccatorum*. Julian argued that such reasoning proved the opposite: such a God would be a caricature of justice. See, e.g., *De pecc. mer.* 1.16.21, 3.4.7; *De grat. Chr. et de pecc. orig.* 2.40.45; the comments in Vanneste, 316.

76. See n. 73 above. Elsewhere Augustine remarks, "The entire nature of man is certainly spirit, soul, *and body*, therefore, whoever would alienate the body from man's nature, is unwise" (*De an. et orig.* 4.2.3, trans. Peter Holmes in Philip Schaff, ed., *Nicene and Post-Nicene Fathers*, First Series, vol. 5: *Saint Augustin: Anti-Pelagian Writings* [Grand Rapids, Mich., 1956], 355, emphasis added).

77. *De Gen. ad litt.* 3.21.33, on the divine injunction to be fruitful and multiply, in relation to which Augustine also concludes that Adam and Eve were created with the natural (i.e., physical) bodies necessary for sexual intercourse; the subsequent immortality of the body would have been achieved had they been obedient (6.26.37).

78. That God had always intended humans to procreate was proved by his creation of Eve (*De Gen. ad litt.* 9.3.5-11.19).

79. Ibid. 9.10.16-18.

80. A point Augustine reiterates constantly: e.g., *De nupt. et conc.* 2.27.45 (with reference to Rom. 5:12); *De grat. Chr. et de pecc. orig.* 2.36.41; *De pecc. mer.* 1.16.21; *De Gen. ad litt.* 11.31.40-41.

81. *De Gen. ad litt.* 11.32.42; cf. 9.10.16-18.

82. *De praed. sanct.* 1.3.7, 4.8; *De don. pers.* 20.52.

83. *De praed. sanct.* 1.4.8; because the Pelagians missed Paul's "autobiographical" reference in Rom. 7, they misread the entire work (*C. duas ep. Pel.* 1.8.13-11.24; note 10.22, where Augustine refers to his own earlier, "erroneous" understanding of this passage).

84. *C. duas ep. Pel.* 1.11.24, on concupiscence; *In Ioann. ev.* 123.5, on Paul's and Peter's fear of death.

85. Augustine had first formulated this understanding of "spirit" and "flesh" during his intensive study of Paul in the mid 390s; see *Prop. ad Rom.* 13-18, 46; *De div. quaest.* q.66.6, where he distinguishes between *caro* and *qualitas carnalis*; cf. *De Gen. ad litt.* 10.12.20, where he explains that by "flesh" Paul intends not "body," but those impulses arising from both body and soul that separate man from God: "Thus, the cause of carnal concupiscence is not in the soul alone, much less in the body alone. It comes from both."

86. For precisely this reason, Augustine attributes the origin of Christ's soul not to Adam but to the origin of Adam's soul, namely God (*De Gen. ad litt.* 10.18.33-20.36).

87. See Brown's astute remarks (*Augustine*, 266-69 and 411f.). Augustine was renouncing something he assumed would continue to exist; however, by 426, the year in which he finished this book, the days of classical education in the West were numbered.

88. *C. Fort.* 21, here Fortunatus supports his contention that "apart from our bodies evil things dwell in the whole world" (trans. Albert H. Newman in Philip Schaff, ed., *Nicene and Post-Nicene Fathers*, First Series, vol. 4: *St. Augustin: The Writings against the Manichaeans and against the Donatists*, 120) with numerous references to Paul, against Augustine's narrowly androcentric argument; cf. Henri Marrou, *St. Augustine and his Influence through the Ages*, trans. Patrick Hepburne-Scott (New York, 1957), 72f., on the "disappointing" narrowness of Augustine's interpretation of Rom. 8:8-24. For Augustine, the *creatura* that groaned for redemption was man himself (*Prop. ad Rom.* 53).

89. See Thomas E. Clark, "St. Augustine and Cosmic Redemption," *Theological Studies* 19 (1958): 133-64.

COMMENT: AUGUSTINE, PAUL, AND
THE QUESTION OF MORAL EVIL

1. These nicely balanced adverbs, *exegetically* and *autobiographically*, come, of course, from Fredriksen.

2. *Conf.* 3.4.7 (Cicero) and 7.9.13 (*libri Platonicorum*).

3. For Augustine's account of his movement from Cicero to the Manichees, see ibid. 3.4.7-6.11.

4. The supreme study of this period in Augustine's life and thought remains Peter Brown, *Augustine of Hippo: A Biography* (Berkeley and Los Angeles, 1967), 79-157.

5. Brown, 151.

6. Eric Osborn, "La Bible inspiratrice d'une morale chrétienne d'après Clément of d'Alexandrie," in *Le monde grec ancien et la Bible*, ed. Claude Mondésert (Paris, 1984), 127-44. For the statistics, see p. 127.

7. For a discussion of the relevant works by these three, see Alexander Souter, *The Earliest Latin Commentaries on the Epistles of St. Paul* (Oxford, 1927).

8. See my "Augustine's Interpretation of Romans (A.D. 394–396)," *Augustinian Studies* 10 (1979): 55–74, for a major part of the story.
9. *Retr.* 2.1.1 (commenting on *Ad Simpl.* 1), trans. John H. S. Burleigh, *Augustine: Earlier Writings* (Philadelphia, 1953), 370.
10. *De doct. chr.* 3.33.46.
11. *Ad Simpl.* 1.2.5, tacitly rejecting the view Augustine had himself worked out in *Prop. ad Rom.* 60.
12. The (very brief) summary of the *regula tertia* in André Mandouze, *Prosopographie chrétienne du Bas-Empire*, vol. 1: *Prosopographie de l'Afrique chrétienne (303–533)* (Paris, 1982), 1124–25, is far better than most. For a longer discussion, see my article, "Augustine's Interpretation," 67–74.
13. *Ep.* 41.2: " . . . et de Tyconii septem regulis vel clavibus, sicut saepe iam scripsi, cognoscere quid tibi videatur exspecto."
14. *Exp. ep. ad Gal.* 7-8.
15. *Ad Simpl.* 1.2.22, trans. Burleigh, 406.
16. *De lib. arb.* 1.2.4, trans. Burleigh, 115. In *Conf.* 7.3.4-5, Augustine puts essentially the same question in much the same terms (and with obvious verbal reminiscences of *De lib. arb.* 1.1.1-2.4) as part of the perplexity that ultimately left him disenchanted with the Manichees. In this respect, it would seem, his route into Manicheism and his route out were one and the same.
17. *De lib. arb.* 1.3.8-4.9.
18. In ibid. 1.4.10, Augustine defines "culpable cupidity," or lust, as "love of things which one may lose against one's will" (trans. Burleigh, 118). Later in the treatise, these "things" are identified with temporal as opposed to eternal goods (e.g., 1.15.31).
19. Ibid. 1.11.21, trans. Burleigh, 125.
20. Ibid. 1.11.23, trans. Burleigh, 126.
21. Ibid. 1.12.24.
22. Ibid. 1.13.29, 12.26, trans. Burleigh, 129, 127.
23. See *Retr.* 1.9.(8).3-4.
24. *Conf.* 10.4.5.
25. The Paul, that is, of *Ad Simpl.* 1.2.
26. See ibid. 1.2.16-17, 22.
27. Pelagius, following Origen (whose commentary on Romans he appears to have known only in Rufinus' Latin translation), treats Rom. 9:14–19 as a series of opposing scriptural witnesses (*ex adverso testimonia*) to which Paul briefly responds in order to show that they are being misused and that his own position is quite different. For Augustine, of course, these verses are central to the dynamic of Paul's own theology of grace. See Pelagius *Exp. in Rom.* at Rom. 9:14 (text in Alexander Souter, *Pelagius's Exposition of Thirteen Epistles of Paul*, vol. 2: *Text and Apparatus Criticus* [Cambridge, 1926], 75).
28. See *Ad Simpl.* 1.2.22 *ad fin.*
29. Augustine speaks of God's *occulta aequitas* in *Ad Simpl.* 1.2.16.

30. *De lib. arb.* 1.11.22-23.
31. See Malcolm E. Alflatt, "The Development of the Idea of Involuntary Sin in St. Augustine," *Revue des études augustiniennes* 20 (1974): 113–34. Alflatt perhaps overdramatizes the role of Augustine's debate with Fortunatus, the Manichean priest, in 392; but the debate is undoubtedly central to the development he traces.
32. Augustine is already exploring this position in *De lib. arb.* 2.20.54-3.1.3 and 3.17.47-25.76. He treats the matter autobiographically in the famous episode of the theft of pears in Book II of the *Confessions.* He elaborates the view that the first evil will is uncaused most fully—and for the last time— in *De civitate Dei* 12.1-9 (the angels) and 14.10-13 (human beings), after having approached the question again, with regard to the angels, in *De Genesi ad litteram* 11.16-26. The push back to the first instance is already evident in *C. Fort.* 22, where Augustine states, precisely in response to citations from Romans and Galatians: "Liberum voluntatis arbitrium in illo homine fuisse dico, qui primus formatus est. . . . Postquam autem ipse libera voluntate peccavit, nos in necessitatem praecipitati sumus, qui ab eius stirpe descendimus."
33. *De lib. arb.* 1.13.29, trans. Burleigh, 129.

THE PAULINE CORPUS
AND THE EARLY CHRISTIAN BOOK

1. See especially the widely influential study of Colin H. Roberts, "The Codex," *Proceedings of the British Academy* 40 (1954): 169–204, which has now been revised, updated, and enlarged in Roberts and Theodore C. Skeat, *The Birth of the Codex* (London, 1983); also Eric G. Turner, *The Typology of the Early Codex* (Philadelphia, 1977).
2. The evidence is fully set out by Roberts and Skeat, 35–44. For data regarding individual mss., see Roger A. Pack, *The Greek and Latin Literary Texts from Graeco-Roman Egypt* (Ann Arbor, 1952; 2d ed., 1965); Joseph van Haelst, *Catalogue des papyrus littéraires juifs et chrétiens* (Paris, 1976); Kurt Aland, ed., *Biblische Papyri: Altes Testament, Neues Testament, Varia, Apokryphen,* Repertorium der griechischen christlichen Papyri 1 (Berlin, 1976); K. Treu, "Christliche Papyri 1940-1967," *Archiv für Papyrusforschung und Verwandte Gebiete* 19 (1969): 169–206, as well as the continuations, especially "Christliche Papyri VI," *Archiv für Papyrusforschung und Verwandte Gebiete* 27 (1980): 251–58, supplementing information in van Haelst and Aland. Also useful are the tables provided by Turner, 102–85.
3. This was already recognized by Frederic G. Kenyon, *Books and Readers in Ancient Greece and Rome* (Oxford, 1932), especially 94–99, but was established chiefly by Roberts, "The Codex." See also, however, the earlier studies by C. C. McCown, "Codex and Roll in the New Testament," *Harvard Theological Review* 34 (1941): 219–50, and "The Earliest Christian Books," *Biblical Archeologist* 6 (1943): 21–31.

4. See Roberts and Skeat, 40–42, listing fifteen Christian texts that they assign to the second century, of which all are codices save two. Only one of these two is a true roll (P. Oxy. iii, 405, carrying Irenaeus' *Adversus haereses*), whereas the other (P. Mich. 130, *The Shepherd of Hermas*) is an opisthograph. There is inevitably some disagreement among paleographers about the dating of mss., but the general picture is altered very little by the questionable cases, which, if anything, would show a still greater preponderance of the codex among the earliest Christian mss.

5. An instructive chart showing the relative percentages of rolls and codices for Greek literary texts over the first five centuries is provided by Roberts and Skeat, 37.

6. For a more detailed survey of the alleged advantages of the codex over the roll, see Roberts and Skeat, 45–53; and also the comments of Theodore C. Skeat in "Early Christian Book Production: Papyri and Manuscripts," in *Cambridge History of the Bible*, vol. 2: *The West from the Fathers to the Reformation*, ed. G. W. H. Lampe (Cambridge, 1969), especially 67–70, and of Colin H. Roberts in "Books in the Graeco-Roman World and in the New Testament," in *Cambridge History of the Bible*, vol. 1: *From the Beginnings to Jerome*, ed. P. R. Ackroyd and C. F. Evans (Cambridge, 1970), especially 58.

7. Theodore C. Skeat, "The Length of the Standard Papyrus Roll and the Cost Advantage of the Codex," *Zeitschrift für Papyrologie und Epigraphik* 45 (1982): 169–75, calculates a saving of 26 percent.

8. On the question of the inconvenience of rolls, see the comments of Eric G. Turner, *Greek Papyri: An Introduction* (Oxford, 1968), 7–8.

9. Martial *Epigrams* 2.1; 14.184, 186, 188, 190, 192. For discussion, see Roberts and Skeat, 24–29.

10. Turner, *Typology of the Early Codex*, 75–77, discusses pagination and concludes that it was not integral to the invention or common transcription of the codex.

11. For all aspects of codex construction and size, Turner's treatment in *Typology of the Early Codex* is the most detailed and useful. See especially 43–71.

12. It is indicative that the earliest Christian codices normally contained only a single document.

13. Roberts, "The Codex," 187; cf. Roberts and Skeat, 53.

14. Roberts, "The Codex," 187–91; and see also his earlier studies, "The Ancient Book and the Ending of St. Mark," *Journal of Theological Studies* 40 (1939): 253–57, and "The Christian Book and the Greek Papyri," *Journal of Theological Studies* 50 (1949): 155–68.

15. Roberts, "The Codex," 188, 189. Peter Katz, "The Early Christians' Use of Codices Instead of Rolls," *Journal of Theological Studies* 46 (1945): 63–65, claimed that Christians adopted the codex in order to differentiate, in outward appearance, Christian writings from Jewish ones, which were always written in rolls. But it is not obvious why such a differentiation would have been desirable or necessary.

16. On this now see Birger A. Pearson, "Earliest Christianity in Egypt: Some Observations," in *The Roots of Egyptian Christianity*, ed. Pearson and James E. Goehring (Philadelphia, 1986), 132–56, especially 137–45 on "The Mark Legend," with reference to the pertinent literature. Pearson comments that the historicity of the tradition associating Mark with early Egyptian Christianity, "though unprovable, should not be ruled out" (144). Nevertheless, it is not a tradition in which confidence can be vested.

17. In the Egyptian papyrus evidence, the Gospel of Mark is represented in only one manuscript prior to the fourth century, viz. p^{45}, where it appears with the other gospels and Acts. This situation has recently been acknowledged by Colin H. Roberts, *Manuscript, Society, and Belief in Early Christian Egypt* (London, 1979), 59, 61, who as a result has ceased to think that the founding of the Alexandrian church was connected with the appearance of the Gospel of Mark in Egypt (59, n. 5). See also Roberts and Skeat, 56–57.

18. Turner, *Typology of the Early Codex*, 35–42, has successfully called into question the standing assumption that the earliest codices were made of parchment, and has given good reasons for thinking that papyrus was the first material used in codices.

19. For this see Saul Lieberman, *Hellenism in Jewish Palestine*, 2d ed. (New York, 1962), Appendix III: "Jewish and Christian Codices," 203–8, commenting that the use of the codex was the most suitable way for the rabbis to indicate "that they were writing the Oral Law for private, or unofficial use, and not for publication" (205).

20. Roberts and Skeat, 57–61, quotation on 59. Roberts and Skeat appeal in this connection to the phenomena of the *nomina sacra*, which comprise another paleographical peculiarity of early Christian manuscripts (on which see especially Roberts, *Manuscript, Society, and Belief*, 26–48). They consider the evidence for a common origin of codex and *nomina sacra* to be "*prima facie* strong." It is suggestive, but yields no clear or compelling conclusion (Roberts, *Manuscript, Society, and Belief*, 47, pleads *non liquet*). A common origin, if it could be shown, would point, in their opinion, to either Jerusalem or Antioch since these were the "only two early Christian churches having sufficient authority to devise such innovations and impose them on Christendom generally" at such an early time (58). They favor Antioch, since the influence of the Jerusalem church was early eclipsed by the Jewish revolt.

21. Roberts and Skeat, 60.

22. Helmut Koester, *Synoptische Überlieferung bei den apostolischen Vätern*, Texte und Untersuchungen 65 (Berlin, 1957).

23. For a concise survey of the major theories, see Harry Y. Gamble, *The New Testament Canon: Its Making and Meaning* (Philadelphia, 1985), 36–41.

24. The evidence has been conveniently gathered up and carefully discussed by Hermann J. Frede, "Die Ordnung der Paulusbriefe und der Platz des

Kolosserbriefs im Corpus Paulinum," in *Vetus Latina: Die Reste der alt-lateinischen Bibel*, vol. 24, pt. 2: *Epistulae ad Philippenses et ad Colossenses*, ed. Frede (Freiburg, 1966–71), 290–303. But see also Jack Finegan, "The Original Form of the Pauline Collection," *Harvard Theological Review* 49 (1956): 85–104; Charles H. Buck, "The Early Order of the Pauline Corpus," *Journal of Biblical Literature* 68 (1949): 351–57; and Nils A. Dahl, "Welche Ordnung der Paulusbriefe wird vom muratorischen Kanon vorausgesetzt?" *Zeitschrift für die neutestamentliche Wissenschaft* 52 (1961): 39–53.

25. Our chief witness to the content and order of Marcion's *Apostolikon* is Tertullian *Adv. Marc.* 5. Here Tertullian considers Philemon after Philippians, and thus presumably as the last letter in Marcion's collection (*Adv. Marc.* 5.21–22). But according to Epiphanius (*Pan.* 42.9.4, 11.8, 12) Philemon followed Colossians and stood before Philippians. On this point see further below, n. 37.

26. P^{46} also contains Hebrews, but it is not in the least likely that Hebrews belonged to the original contents of the edition otherwise reflected in this manuscript, in spite of Charles P. Anderson, "The Epistle to the Hebrews and the Pauline Letter Collection," *Harvard Theological Review* 59 (1966): 429–38. On Hebrews' relation to the Pauline corpus, see William H. P. Hatch, "The Position of Hebrews in the Canon of the New Testament," *Harvard Theological Review* 29 (1936): 133–51.

27. For this theory and its witnesses, see Theodor Zahn, *Geschichte des neutestamentliche Kanons*, 2 vols. (Erlangen, 1892), 1:73–75; Krister Stendahl, "The Apocalypse of John and the Epistles of Paul in the Muratorian Fragment," in *Current Issues in New Testament Interpretation*, ed. W. Klassen and G. F. Snyder (New York, 1962), 239–45; Nils A. Dahl, "The Particularity of the Pauline Epistles as a Problem in the Ancient Church," in *Neotestamentica et Patristica*, Novum Testamentum Supplements 6 (Leiden, 1962), 261–71.

28. The evidence is assembled by Frede, 294–95, who designates this as the "W" (Western) order. Frede assumes, however, that the Pastorals were included with this edition, which is unlikely.

29. Thus Frede, 292; Nils A. Dahl, "The Origin of the Earliest Prologues to the Pauline Letters," *Semeia* 12 (1978): 233–77 (especially 253, 263).

30. Dahl, "The Particularity of the Pauline Epistles."

31. This is apparent especially in the case of Romans; see Harry Y. Gamble, *The Textual History of the Letter to the Romans*, Studies and Documents 42 (Grand Rapids, Mich., 1977), 115–124.

32. Apart from Romans, only 1 Corinthians among the authentic letters offers evidence of generalizing emendation (1:2b). Ephesians poses a somewhat different case as an inauthentic letter, but whether the omission of the address in 1:1 is original or secondary, it symptomizes a comparable interest in relieving the Pauline letter of particularity.

33. It is important to notice that what is commonly called the "Marcionite order" of the letters is not exclusively associated with Marcion in the

evidence. The sequence Galatians-Corinthians-Romans is attested for the old Syriac by the Catalogus Sinaiticus and by the commentary of Ephrem, on which see respectively Agnes S. Lewis, comp., *Catalogue of the Syriac Mss. in the Convent of S. Catharine on Mount Sinai*, Studia Sinaitica 1 (London, 1894), 13–14, and Theodor Zahn, "Das Neue Testament Theodors von Mopsuestia und der ursprüngliche Kanon der Syrer," *Neue kirchliche Zeitschrift* 11 (1900): 788–806, especially 798–99. The evidence is assembled by Frede, 295–97. Cf. Josef Kerschensteiner, *Der altsyrische Paulustext* (Louvain, 1970), 172–76, who expresses some reservations.

34. This was already seen by Adolf von Harnack, *Marcion: Das Evangelium vom fremden Gott*, 2d ed. rev. (Leipzig, 1924), 168–69, and John Knox, *Marcion and the New Testament* (Chicago, 1942), 60–70, and idem, *Philemon Among the Letters of Paul*, rev. ed. (New York, 1959), 78–82.

35. That Marcion merely took up, and used as a basis for his own revisions, a preexisting edition of the Pauline letters is also strongly suggested by the large number of readings that Marcion had in common with the Old Latin "I-type" text. See J. J. Clabeaux, "The Pauline Corpus Which Marcion Used: The Text of the Letters of Paul in the Early Second Century" (Ph.D. diss., Harvard University, 1983).

36. Additional and strongly confirmatory evidence of this is offered by the so-called Marcionite prologues to the Pauline epistles, and especially if they are not indeed Marcionite in origin, as argued particularly by Hermann J. Frede, *Altlateinische Paulus-Handschriften* (Freiburg, 1964), 165–78, and in greater detail by Dahl, "The Origin of the Earliest Prologues to the Pauline Letters." Formal analysis of the prologues (Dahl, 246–51) shows that only six of those now available are original and that a seventh (for Laodiceans/Ephesians) must have been replaced. This means that in the original set of prologues, ten letters of Paul were reckoned as "letters to seven churches." In fact, the prologues concern themselves with the churches far more than with the letters.

37. Thus Knox, *Marcion and the New Testament*, 43–45; idem, *Philemon Among the Letters of Paul*, 83–86. This would agree with the characterization of Marcion's collection by Epiphanius (see above, n. 25). In any event, the prologue to Philemon is clearly secondary, and this indicates that Philemon must have been taken along with Colossians by the author of the prologues.

38. It must be emphasized that the seven-churches edition taken up by Marcion was not identical with the presumably original seven-churches edition, at least in the arrangement of the letters, but was a secondary variation of it. The order of the letters attested for Marcion is not at all likely to have been his innovation, contrary to the common view. The order as a whole is more readily understood as an effort to present the letters chronologically than as a consequence of dogmatic considerations. See

Frede, *Altlateinische Paulus-Handschriften*, 165–66, and idem, "Die Ordnung der Paulusbriefe," 295. The relatively early placement of Romans in a chronological arrangement was enabled by the presence of chaps. 15–16 in the text of Romans that belonged to that edition. Thus we may think of an original seven-churches edition arranged strictly by decreasing length (letters to the same community being counted together), which was modified (i.e., partially reordered) according to chronological ideas. It was this modified edition that was appropriated by Marcion.

39. This observation was coined by Edgar J. Goodspeed in connection with his own theory of the origin and primitive character of the Pauline corpus; see *New Solutions of New Testament Problems* (Chicago, 1927), 1–64.

40. On the manufacture of papyrus, see the careful study of Naphtali Lewis, *Papyrus in Classical Antiquity* (Oxford, 1974), 34–69. Even codices were constructed, as a rule, not from individual sheets of papyrus but from cut-up rolls (Turner, *Typology of the Early Codex*, 43–51).

41. *Naturalis Historia* 13.77 (*numquam plures scapo quam vicenae*), with the comments of Lewis, 54–55.

42. On the sizes of sheets, see Turner, *Typology of the Early Codex*, 48, but also his further remarks in "The Terms Recto and Verso: The Anatomy of the Papyrus Roll," *Actes du XVe Congrès international de papyrologie*, 4 vols. (Brussels, 1978–79), 1:60–61. Pliny's statements about the widths of sheets (*Naturalis Historia* 13.78) correspond rather well to what can be observed in extant rolls of the period.

43. Skeat, "The Length of the Standard Papyrus Roll," 169–70.

44. Frederic G. Kenyon, *Books and Readers in Ancient Greece and Rome*, 2d ed. (Oxford, 1951), 54. There is broad agreement on this point among papyrologists.

45. Kenyon (2d ed.), 53, remarks that "the length of a finished roll of literature might vary, but convenience and custom proposed limits." In fact, in certain types of literature, the capacity of the normal roll (*volumen*) must have dictated the author's divisions of his work. See Theodor Birt, *Das antike Buchwesen in seinem Verhältniss zur Literatur* (Berlin, 1882), 141–50.

46. The figures are adapted from Skeat, "The Length of the Standard Papyrus Roll," 173, who employs them to calculate costs of transcription.

47. Left out of account are initial and final margins, as well as attached uninscribed sheets at the beginning and end for the protection of the roll (the *protokollon* and *eschatokollion*), on which see Turner, "Recto and Verso," 20–24.

48. Of a (presumed) manufactured roll of 80 feet, Skeat, "The Length of the Standard Papyrus Roll," 170, comments by understatement that it would be "much too long to be handled in one piece."

49. It is remarkable how little consideration has been given to the possibility that the collected letters of Paul were initially made available in a codex. I am able to cite only Finegan, 88, and Günter Zuntz, *The Text of the*

Epistles: A Disquisition upon the Corpus Paulinum (London, 1953), 15, both of whom simply take it as a supposition and do not argue the case.

50. The question of the place of origin of a seven-churches edition of Paul's letters, and thus presumably the locale of its transcription in a codex, cannot be answered with any confidence, but Antioch is a strong possibility. See Frede, *Altlateinische Paulus-Handschriften*, 167, 178; idem, "Die Ordnung der Paulusbriefe," 296; and Clabeaux, 245–47. In that case, the *nomina sacra* (above, n. 20), should they be drawn into connection with the Christian adoption of the codex, would not tell against the hypothesis that the codex was initially employed to transcribe the Pauline corpus.

51. Against this it might have been objected until recently that Paul's letters were early co-opted by heterodox groups (Marcion and the Gnostics) and thus commanded little general esteem during the second century until Paul was "reclaimed" and "domesticated" within emerging orthodoxy. See, e.g., Wilhelm Schneemelcher, "Paulus in der griechischen Kirche des 2. Jahrhunderts," *Zeitschrift für Kirchengeschichte* 75 (1964): 1–20, and Walter Bauer, *Orthodoxy and Heresy in Early Christianity*, translation ed. Robert A. Kraft and Gerhard Krodel (Philadelphia, 1971), 212–28. But several recent studies have made this claim untenable: Andreas Lindemann, *Paulus im ältesten Christentum: Das Bild des Apostels und die Rezeption der paulinischen Theologie in der frühchristlichen Literatur bis Marcion*, Beiträge zur historischen Theologie 58 (Tübingen, 1979); David K. Rensberger, "As the Apostle Teaches: The Development of the Use of Paul's Letters in Second-Century Christianity" (Ph.D. diss., Yale University, 1981); Ernst Dassmann, *Der Stachel im Fleisch: Paulus in der frühchristlichen Literatur bis Irenaeus* (Münster, 1979).

52. Roberts and Skeat, 62.

53. Zahn, *Geschichte*, 1:150–92; Adolf von Harnack, *The Origin of the New Testament*, trans. J. R. Wilkinson (New York, 1925), 68–83.

54. For these dimensions of the history of gospel literature in the early church, see Koester, *Synoptische Überlieferung*; idem, "Apocryphal and Canonical Gospels," *Harvard Theological Review* 73 (1980): 105–30; Oscar Cullmann, "The Plurality of the Gospels as a Theological Problem in Antiquity," *The Early Church*, ed. A.J.B. Higgins (London, 1956), 39–54; Helmut Merkel, *Die Widersprüche zwischen den Evangelien: Ihre polemische und apologetische Behandlung in der alten Kirche bis zu Augustin* (Tübingen, 1971); and idem, *Die Pluralität der Evangelien als theologisches und exegetisches Problem in der alten Kirche* (Bern, 1978).

55. The only sure exception is $p^{64, 67}$, which contained both Matthew and Luke. Somewhat later is p^{75}, which offered both Luke and John.

56. Hans von Campenhausen, *The Formation of the Christian Bible*, trans. J. A. Baker (Philadelphia, 1972), 174.

ARCHEOLOGICAL TRACES OF
EARLY CHRISTIAN VENERATION OF PAUL

1. See, e.g., Wolfgang E. Pax, *Auf den Spuren des Paulus* (Olten, 1977); Henry V. Morton, *In the Steps of St. Paul* (London, 1936); Stewart Perowne, *The Journeys of St. Paul* (London, 1973; German translation: Freiburg, 1975); Edward Schillebeeckx, *Paulus: Der Völkerapostel* (Freiburg, 1982); Norbert Hugédé, *Saint Paul et la Grèce* (Paris, 1982); R. Breitenbach, *In Sachen Gottes unterwegs: Erlebnisse auf den Spuren des Paulus* (Würzburg, 1985).

2. Otto F. A. Meinardus: *St. Paul in Greece*, 3d ed. (Athens, 1977; German translation: *Paulus in Griechenland* [Athens, 1978]); *St. Paul in Ephesus and the Cities of Galatia and Cyprus* (New Rochelle, N.Y., 1979); *St. Paul's Last Journey* (New Rochelle, N.Y., 1979); *Die Reisen des Apostels Paulus* (Hamburg and Regensburg, 1981). Further articles will be cited at the appropriate places.

3. *Apoc. Paul.* 1f., German translation in E. Hennecke and W. Schneemelcher, *Neutestamentliche Apokryphen*, vol. 2: *Apostolisches Apokalypsen und Verwandtes*, 3d ed. (Tübingen, 1964), 540. See also Ernst Dassmann, "Paulus in der 'Visio sancti Pauli,'" in *Jenseitsvorstellungen in Antike und Christentum: Gedenkschrift A. Stuiber*, Jahrbuch für Antike und Christentum Ergänzungsband 9 (Münster, 1982), 120f.

4. Meinardus, *Reisen*, 13.

5. Ludwig Schneller, *Tarsus und Damaskus: Bilder aus dem Leben des Apostels Paulus* (Cologne, 1913), 11. By the same author, we have the small volumes *Antiochia, Cypern, Galatien* (Cologne, 1914); *Von Syrien bis Macedonien* (Cologne, 1916); *Athen und Korinth* (Cologne, 1917).

6. Theophylactus Simocatta *Historiae* 8.13.16 (ed. Charles de Boor [Leipzig, 1887], 311); P. Goubert, "Édifices byzantins de la fin du VIe siècle," *Orientalia Christiana Periodica* 21 (1955): 107; Ernst Dassmann, *Paulus in frühchristlicher Frömmigkeit und Kunst* (Opladen, 1982), 20.

7. Donatus Baldi, *Enchiridion locorum sanctorum* (Jerusalem, 1935), 747f. (emphasis added). P. Bargil Pixner, O.S.B., of Jerusalem, is to be thanked for the reference.

8. Otto F. A. Meinardus, "The Site of the Apostle Paul's Conversion at Kaukab," *Biblical Archaeologist* 44 (1981): 57–59; L. Jalabert, "Damas," *Dictionnaire d'archéologie chrétienne et de liturgie* 4 (1920): 133f.

9. Meinardus, "Kaukab," 58; idem, *Reisen*, 23–25; Jalabert, 134–35.

10. *Antonini Placentini Itinerarium* 46 (CSEL 39:190).

11. Herbert Donner, ed., *Pilgerfahrt ins Heilige Land* (Stuttgart, 1979), 312.

12. Meinardus, "Kaukab," 59; idem, *Reisen*, 19f.; Jalabert, 129–33.

13. Victor Schultze, *Altchristliche Städte und Landschaften*, vol. 3: *Antiocheia* (Gütersloh, 1930), 372f.

14. Ernst Dassmann, "Zum Paulusverständnis in der östlichen Kirche," *Jahrbuch für Antike und Christentum* 29 (1986): 33, n. 3. A remark of

Chrysostom's (*Hom. 30 in Rom.* 4; PG 60:666) may suggest that there were in his time numerous memorial sites: "For if we feel exalted the moment we, after so long a time, enter a place where Paul stayed, where he lay in chains, or where he sat and taught, and if the places summon forth in us the memory of him, what godly stimulation must that host then have felt when the remembrance of these things was still fresh?"

15. "St. Paul's house and a table," which were shown at the time of John Chrysostom (see PG 60:666), mentioned also by Glanville Downey, *A History of Antioch in Syria* (Princeton, 1961), 284, n. 47; for the moles, see Meinardus, *Reisen*, 32, 35.

16. Meinardus, *Reisen*, 49–73; idem, *St. Paul in Ephesus*, 19–49. Breitenbach, 42, mentions a small Church of Paul in Konya.

17. Meinardus, *Reisen*, 39, 42, 47; idem, *St. Paul in Ephesus*, 7–18; Claude Tresmontant, *Paulus in Selbstzeugnissen und Bilddokumenten*, Rowohlts Monographien 23 (Hamburg, 1959), 84.

18. Hippolyte Delehaye, "Saints de Chypre," *Analecta Bollandiana* 26 (1907): 264–74.

19. Meinardus, *Reisen*, 195; idem, *Last Journey*, 71.

20. Meinardus, *Reisen*, 210; for further material, see Otto F. A. Meinardus, "Cretan Traditions about St. Paul's Mission to the Island," *Ostkirchliche Studien* 22 (1973): 172–83.

21. Raymond Janin, *Les églises et les monastères des grands centres byzantins* (Paris, 1975), 405, 416; Dassmann, *Frömmigkeit*, 7f. According to Archbishop Simeon of Thessalonica, who died in 1429, it lay at the Acheiropoietos Basilica; see Iōannēs M. Phountoulē, *Marturiai tou Thessalonikēs Sumeōn peri tōn naōn tēs Thessalonikēs*, Epistēmonikē Epetēris Theologikēs Skholēs (Thessaloniki, 1976), 175f.

22. Meinardus, *Reisen*, 96f.; idem, *Paulus in Griechenland*, 30–40; Hugédé, 70–78.

23. Meinardus, *Reisen*, 99; idem, *Paulus in Griechenland*, 40–44; Hugédé, 94–96.

24. Meinardus, *Reisen*, 106f.; Hugédé, 110.

25. An enumeration of these appears in Hugédé, 154–57.

26. E. Vanderpool, "The Apostle Paul in Athens," *Archaeology* 3 (1950): 34–37; Pax, 113; Winifried Elliger, *Paulus in Griechenland*, Stuttgarter Bibel-Studien 92–93 (Stuttgart, 1978), 179; Meinardus, *Reisen*, 117f.; idem, *Paulus in Griechenland*, 45–69.

27. Meinardus, *Reisen*, 117.

28. Ibid., 221; Meinardus, *Last Journey*, 96f.

29. Meinardus, *Reisen*, 222.

30. Ibid., 223.

31. R. Calvino, "Cristiani a Puteoli nell'anno 61: Riflessioni sull'importanza della notizia concisa degli 'Atti' (28,13b–14a) e riposta all'interrogativo sulle testimonianze monumentali coeva," *Rivista di Archeologia Cristiana* 56 (1980): 323–30; S. Garofalo, "I Romani di San Paolo," in *Studi*

Paolini, ed. Paolo Brezzi (Rome, 1969), 56f.; Meinardus, *Reisen,* 229; A. Maiuri, "La Campania al tempo dell'approdo di San Paolo," *Studi Romani* 9 (1961): 135–47; M. Adinolfi, "San Paolo a Pozzuoli (Atti 28,13b–14a)," *Revista Biblica* 8 (1960): 206–24.

32. A. Kurfess, "Der apokryphe Briefwechsel zwischen Seneca und Paulus," in Hennecke and Schneemelcher, *Apocryphen,* 2:84–89.

33. A signpost in front of the church cites Acts 28:16; cf. Meinardus, *Reisen,* 240. In the crypt, a drawing depicts Peter, Paul, Luke, and Martial; see *Roma e dintorni,* Guida d'Italia del Touring Club Italiano 16, 6th ed. (Milan, 1962), 167.

34. *Roma e dintorni,* 249.

35. Meinardus, *Reisen,* 255–58; idem, "Paul's Missionary Journey to Spain: Tradition and Folklore," *Biblical Archaeologist* 41 (1978): 61–63; idem, *Last Journey,* 125–33; V. J. Serra, *San Pablo en España: Commemoración del XIX Centenaria du sa venida* (Tarragona, 1963); A. C. Vega, "La venida de San Pablo a España y los Varones Apostólicos," *Boletin de la Real Academia de la Historia* 114 (1964): 7–78.

36. Eusebius *Ecclesiastical History* 3.4.8; Élie Griffe, *La Gaule chrétienne a l'époque Romaine,* vol. 1: *Des origines chrétiennes a la fin du IVe siècle,* 2d ed. (Paris, 1964), 16–18.

37. Meinardus, *Reisen,* 261–64; idem, *Last Journey,* 134–44. His renown is due to the monastery in the early Middle Ages, but above all to Anastasius. Cf. F. Antonelli, "I primi monasteri di monaci orientali in Roma," *Rivista di Archeologia Cristiana* 5 (1928): 109–14.

38. Englebert Kirschbaum, *Die Gräber der Apostelfürsten,* 3d ed., with an additional chapter by Ernst Dassmann (Frankfurt am Main, 1974), 172–203; B. M. Apollonj Ghetti, "Le basiliche cimiteriali degli apostoli Pietro e Paolo a Roma," in *Saecularia Petri et Pauli,* ed. Apollonj Ghetti, Studi di antichità cristiana 28 (Vatican City, 1969), 22–34.

39. Kirschbaum, 205–10; Daniel W. O'Connor, *Peter in Rome: The Literary, Liturgical and Archeological Evidence* (New York, 1969), 135–38, with bibliography, 214–26.

40. Günther Bornkamm, *Paulus* (Stuttgart, 1969), 70, 78–80, 106, 111; Gerd Lüdemann, *Paulus, der Heidenapostel,* vol. 1: *Studien zur Chronologie,* Forschungen zur Religion und Literatur des Alten und Neuen Testaments 123 (Göttingen, 1980), 272f.; Dassmann, *Frömmigkeit,* 8–10.

41. Philipp Vielhauer, *Geschichte der urchristlichen Literatur: Einleitung in das Neue Testament, die Apokryphen und die Apostolischen Väter* (Berlin, 1975), 156–70, 522–66; Ernst Dassmann, *Der Stachel im Fleisch: Paulus in der frühchristlichen Literatur bis Irenaeus* (Münster, 1979), 153f.

42. Elliger, 70–77.

43. Meinardus, *Reisen,* 88; idem, *Paulus in Griechenland,* 22.

44. Paul Lemerle, *Philippes et la Macédoine orientale à l'époque chrétienne et byzantine: Recherches d'histoire et d'archéologie,* vol. 1: *Texte* (Paris, 1945), 36, 59f., 285f., 296f.; Elliger, 70f.

45. William A. McDonald, "Archaeology and St. Paul's Journeys in Greek Lands," *Biblical Archaeologist* 3 (1940): 21, assumes, referring to Vitruvius, that the city prison was "on the site of one of the buildings whose lower courses still border the forum."

46. Lemerle, 1:296f.

47. Viktor N. Lazarev, *Storia della pittura bizantina*, Biblioteca di storia dell'arte 7 (Turin, 1967), 87; A. Frolow, "L'Église rouge de Peruštica," *Bulletin of the Byzantine Institute* 1 (1946): 35–37, pl. XIII.

48. Stylianos M. Pelekanidis, "Anaskapsē Philippōn," *Praktika tēs en Athēnais Archaeologikēs Hetairias 1975* (1977): 101 and pl. 93; also *Praktika 1978* (1980): 70–72 and pl. 60; and idem, "Kultprobleme im Apostel-Paulus-Oktogon von Philippi im Zusammenhang mit einem älteren Heroenkult," *Atti del IX Congresso internazionale di archeologia cristiana*, vol. 2: *Communicazioni su scoperte inedite*, Studi di Antichità cristiana 32 (Rome, 1978), 393.

49. J. D. Mansi, *Sacrorum Conciliorum nova et amplissima collectio*, 3:48, lists *Porphyrius a Macedonia de Philippis* seventy-fourth among the bishops attending the council; on the dating, see Elliger, 74f.

50. Lemerle, 1:283, 406, 467–83.

51. McDonald, 21, mentions—although without any authority—a Greek inscription from the year 262–63 with the notice: "Aurelius Capito, junior presbyter of the universal church, set up this monument to his own parents and his own wife, Bebia Paula, and to his dearest son Elpidius." Another basilica from the middle—or, at the latest, the second half—of the fourth century was found 1.5 km. from Philippi in the village of Kranides; see Elliger, 76, n. 84.

52. On the chronology of Paul's journeys, critically analyzed with respect to the data in Acts, see Lüdemann, 1:205f., 272f.

53. Bornkamm, 94–102; Wolfgang Metzger, *Die letzte Reise des Apostels Paulus: Beobachtungen und Erwägungen zu seinem Itinerar nach den Pastoralbriefen*, Arbeiten zur Theologie 59 (Stuttgart, 1976), 33–36; Pax, 150; Floyd V. Filson, "Ephesus and the New Testament," *Biblical Archaeologist* 8 (1945): 78f.

54. Dassmann, *Stachel*, 129–31.

55. This is the shared judgment of Erich Lessing and Wolfgang Oberleitner, *Ephesos: Weltstadt der Antike* (Vienna, 1978), 245.

56. W. Michaelis, "Das Gefängnis des Paulus in Ephesus," *Byzantinisch-neugriechische Jahrbücher* 6 (1927–28): 2.

57. Ibid., 4, speaks of 12 km.; Josef Keil, *Ephesos: Ein Führer durch die Ruinenstätte und ihre Geschichte*, 5th ed. (Vienna, 1964), 21, of more than 9 km.

58. Michaelis, 5–7; Winifried Elliger, *Ephesos: Geschichte einer antiken Weltstadt* (Stuttgart, 1985), 50f.

59. Contra Merrill M. Parvis, "Archaeology and St. Paul's Journeys in Greek Lands, Part IV: Ephesus," *Biblical Archaeologist* 8 (1945): 69.

60. Thus Lessing and Oberleitner, 94f.; see also Otto Benndorf in *Forschungen in Ephesus 1* (Vienna, 1906), 62; Paul Feine, *Einleitung in das Neue Testament*, 3d ed. (Leipzig, 1923), 106f.

61. *Acts of Paul 7*, trans. Hennecke and Schneemelcher, 2:255f.

62. Bornkamm, 96f.; Elliger, *Ephesos*, 143–45; Meinardus, *Ephesus*, 79–81; George S. Duncan, *St. Paul's Ephesian Ministry* (London, 1929), 66–71, 108–11.

63. Michaelis, 15–18; Meinardus, *Ephesus*, 83; Jan N. Bakhuizen van den Brink, *De oudchristelijke Monumenten van Ephesus* (The Hague, 1923).

64. Victor Schultze, *Altchristliche Städte und Landschaften*, vol. 2, pt. 2: *Kleinasien* (Gütersloh, 1926), 108; Bernhard Kötting, *Peregrinatio religiosa: Wallfahrten in der Antike und das Pilgerwesen in der alten Kirche*, Forschungen zur Volkskunde 33–35, 2d ed. (Münster, 1980), 177–80; Keil, 25.

65. Meinardus, *Ephesus*, 109; Kötting, 180.

66. Meinardus, *Ephesus*, 109; on the rule of the crusaders in Asia Minor, see Hans E. Mayer, *Geschichte der Kreuzzüge* (Stuttgart, 1965), 257.

67. Wilhelm Alzinger, "Nachträge: Ephesos B," *Paulys Realencyclopädie der classischen Altertumswissenschaft*, Supplementband 12 (1970): 1685.

68. Lessing and Oberleitner, 245; Breitenbach, 72; H. Engelmann, D. Knibbe, and R. Merkebach, eds., *Die Inschriften von Ephesos IV*, Inschriften griechischer Städte aus Kleinasien 14 (Bonn, 1980), 156, §§1,3, and 158, §17.

69. See Alzinger, 1685; Keil, 82f., 104, 137, 142. Pax, 150, mentions a chapel in memory of Paul at the place of veneration of Mary on the top of the hill Aya Kapalu east of Ephesus; it is not otherwise mentioned in the literature.

70. Keil, 137; Parvis, 70; Michaelis, 10f.; L. Bürchner, "Ephesos," *Paulys Realencyclopädie der classischen Altertumswissenschaft* 5 (1905): 2819; Henri Leclercq, "Ephèse," *Dictionnaire d'archéologie chrétienne et de liturgie* 5 (1922): 131–33.

71. *De situ terrae sanctae* 26 (*Corpus scriptorum ecclesiasticorum latinorum*, vol. 39: *Itinera Hierosolymitana saeculi III–VIII*, ed. Paulus Geyer [Vienna, 1898], 148); see also Kötting, 178; Donner, 190–98.

72. On the veneration of Timothy in Ephesus, see Richard A. Lipsius, *Die Apokryphen Apostelgeschichten und Apostellegenden*, 2 vols. (Braunschweig, 1884), vol. 2, pt. 2: 372–400; Schultze, vol. 2, pt. 2:103; Meinardus, *Ephesus*, 118f.; Hippolyte Delehaye, *Les origines du culte des martyrs*, 2d ed. rev. (Brussels, 1933), 55, 62, 145f.; Josef Keil, "Zum Martyrium des hl. Timotheus in Ephesus," *Jahreshefte des österreichischen archäologischen Instituts in Wien* 29 (1934): 82–92.

73. Now in Vienna, Kunsthistorisches Museum, Antiquities collection no. 3072; see Erich Lessing, *Paulus: in 114 Farbbildern* (Freiburg, 1980), 270.

74. Keil, "Martyrium," 71f., 83f.

75. Ulrich B. Müller, *Zur frühchristlichen Theologiegeschichte: Judenchristentum und Paulinismus in Kleinasien an der Wende vom ersten zum*

zweiten Jahrhundert n. Chr. (Gütersloh, 1976), 10–12; Walter Bauer, *Rechtgläubigkeit und Ketzerei im ältesten Christentum,* Beiträge zur historischen Theologie 10, 2d ed. (Tübingen, 1964), 87–90; Helmut Köster and James M. Robinson, *Entwicklungslinien durch die Welt des frühen Christentums* (Tübingen, 1971), 143–46.

76. Dassmann, *Stachel,* 172.

77. Lessing and Oberleitner, 246.

78. See Suetonius *Vita Claudii* 25.11; also Bornkamm, 85f. Lüdemann, 1:155–202, provides an entirely revised arrangement of the information in Acts and the Pauline letters.

79. Gallio is known through a Delphic inscription that, because it can be dated, provides the basis for an absolute Pauline chronology; see Hans Conzelmann, *Geschichte des Urchristentums,* Grundrisse zum Neuen Testament 5 (Göttingen, 1969), 20; Alfred Wikenhauser, *Einleitung in das Neue Testament,* 3d ed. (Basel, 1959), 256; Lüdemann, 1:181–83.

80. Bornkamm, 91–94; Otto Kuss, *Paulus: Die Rolle des Apostels in der theologischen Entwicklung der Urkirche* (Regensburg, 1971), 138–62. Characteristically, an apocryphal exchange of letters between the Corinthians and Paul arose alongside the canonical one and found its way into *The Acts of Paul;* see Hennecke and Schneemelcher, 2:224f., 234f., 240, 258–60.

81. Adolf von Harnack, *Die Mission und Ausbreitung des Christentums in den ersten drei Jahrhunderten,* 4th ed. (Leipzig, 1924; reprint: Wiesbaden, 1965), 789f.

82. *1 Clem.* 1.2.

83. In Eusebius *Ecclesiastical History* 4.22.2.

84. Dassmann, *Stachel,* 231–35.

85. Eusebius *Ecclesiastical History* 4.23.9f.; see also Berthold Altaner and Alfred Stuiber, *Patrologie,* 8th ed. (Freiburg, 1978), 109.

86. Eusebius *Ecclesiastical History* 4.23.1–13.

87. Tertullian *De praescriptione haereticorum* 36.2 and *De virginibus velandis* 8.4; Origen *Contra Celsum* 3.30.

88. For the history of the city of Corinth, see Elliger, *Paulus,* 200–225; Jerome Murphy-O'Connor, "The Corinth that Saint Paul Saw," *Biblical Archaeologist* 47 (1984): 147–59, with further bibliography; also Murphy-O'Connor's *St. Paul's Corinth: Texts and Archaeology,* Good News Studies 6 (Wilmington, Del., 1983).

89. Meinardus, *Paulus in Griechenland,* 81, conjectures that it was outside the marketplace on the road to Lechaion; see Murphy-O'Connor, *St. Paul's Corinth,* 167–70.

90. Meinardus, *Paulus in Griechenland,* 83; Henri Leclercq, "Corinthe," *Dictionnaire d'archéologie chrétienne et de liturgie* 3 (1948): 2959f., and "Inscriptions latines chrétiennes," *Dictionnaire d'archéologie chrétienne et de liturgie* 7 (1926): 794.

91. Meinardus, *Paulus in Griechenland*, 87f.; Elliger, *Paulus*, 227–30; Hugédé, 199.

92. Erich Dinkler, "Das Bema zu Korinth: Archäologische, lexicographische, rechtsgeschichtliche und ikonographische Bemerkungen zu Apostelgeschichte 18:12–17," *Marburger Jahrbuch für Kunstwissenschaft* 13 (1941): 12 (reprinted in *Signum Crucis* [Tübingen, 1967], 118–33); Oscar Broneer, "Corinth: Center of St. Paul's Missionary Work in Greece," *Biblical Archaeologist* 14 (1951): 91f.

93. Dinkler, 13.

94. Ibid., 21f.; further material in *Signum Crucis*, 129f.

95. Meinardus, *Paulus in Griechenland*, 91, suggests: "possibly in the northern basilica, which lay parallel to the Lechaion road."

96. Alternatively: Elliger, *Paulus*, 226f.

97. Ibid., 27; Meinardus, *Paulus in Griechenland*, 89f.; William A. McDonald, "Archaeology and St. Paul's Journeys in Greek Lands, Part III: Corinth," *Biblical Archaeologist* 5 (1942): 44f.; Ferdinand-Joseph de Waele, *Corinthe et saint Paul*, Les hauts lieux de l'histoire 15 (Paris, 1961), 95f.

98. Oscar Broneer, "Studies in the Topography of Corinth at the Time of St. Paul," *Archaiologikē ephēmeris* (1937): 128.

99. Elliger, *Paulus*, 227; McDonald, "Archaeology III," 45; Broneer, "Studies," 128.

100. Dinkler, 21f.

101. Meinardus, *Paulus in Griechenland*, 91f.

102. Waele, 92.

103. Ferdinand-Joseph de Waele, "Korinthos," *Paulys Realencyclopädie der classischen Altertumswissenschaft*, Supplementband 6 (1935): 198; Elliger, *Paulus*, 251; D. Pallas, *Les monuments paléochrétiens de Grèce découverts de 1959 à 1973*, Sussidi allo studio delle antichità cristiane 5 (Vatican City, 1977), 153–56.

104. Waele, "Korinthos," 198.

105. Ibid.

106. Pallas, 156–63; Elliger, *Paulus*, 251, refers to this under the name Quadratus.

107. Waele, "Korinthos," 189f., identifies them on a map without returning to them in the text.

108. Delehaye, *Les origines*, 227; Meinardus, *Paulus in Griechenland*, 79–81.

109. Elliger, *Paulus*, 251; Pallas, 165–71.

110. Robert Scranton, Joseph W. Shaw, and Leila Ibrahim, *Kenchreai, Eastern Port of Corinth: Results of Investigations by The University of Chicago and Indiana University for the American School of Classical Studies at Athens*, vol. 1: *Topography and Architecture* (Leiden, 1978), 75–78; Pallas, 171f.

111. Waele, *Corinthe*, 101f., 174.

112. Leclercq, "Corinthe," 2964f.; A. J. Reinach, "Le Congrès archéologique du Caire 1909," *Revue archéologique* (1909): 442.

113. Meinardus, *Paulus in Griechenland*, 92.

114. Quentin Hughes and P. de Mendelssohn, *Malta*, 2d ed. (Munich, 1978), 348; Meinardus, *Reisen*, 211; idem, *Last Journey*, 85–95.

115. Meinardus, *Reisen*, 212; Michelangelo Cagiano de Azevedo, *Testimonianze archeologiche della tradizione paolina a Malta*, Studi Semitici 18 (Rome, 1966), 35, n. 61.

116. Meinardus, *Reisen*, 212f., 216f.

117. Ibid., 213, 215f., 217.

118. Ibid., 214, 216, 218.

119. Michelangelo Cagiano de Azevedo, "Elementi di antica vita christiana a Malta negli scavi della Missione Archeologica Italina," *Akten des VII Internationalen Kongresses für Christliche Archäologie*, 2 vols., Studi di antichità cristiana 27 (Vatican City, 1969), 1:402f.; also idem, *Testimonianze*, 9, with further literature, n. 1. A pedestal inscription from the time of Hadrian in the museum of Mdina refers to the designation of office of Publius: (MUNIC)IPI MEL(ITENSIUM) PRIMUS OMNIUM; Cagiano de Azevedo, *Testimonianze*, 64 and 69, with the bibliography cited in n. 1.

120. Cagiano de Azevedo, *Testimonianze*, 10f.

121. Michelangelo Cagiano de Azevedo, "Gli scavi della compagna 1964," in *Missione Archeologica Italiana a Malta: Rapporto preliminare della Campagna 1964* (Rome, 1965), 184; idem, *Testimonianze*, 52.

122. Gian Paolo Marchi, "Ricerche storiche negli archivi di Malta," in *Missione Archeologica Italiana a Malta: Rapporto preliminare della Campagna 1964* (Rome, 1965), 31; Cagiano de Azevedo, *Testimonianze*, 18, 52f.

123. Cagiano de Azevedo, *Testimonianze*, 54.

124. Ibid., 12, 16f.

125. Ibid., 21, pl. VII, and 22f., pl. IX.

126. Ibid., pl. X.

127. Ibid., 23f., pl. VIII.

128. Ibid., 32–35.

129. Ibid., 36f., pl. IX.

130. Franz J. Dölger, "Eine christliche Grabinschrift vom Jahre 363 mit exorzistischen Zeichen als Zeilensicherung," *Antike und Christentum* 1 (1929): 299–315, especially 310f.; Theodor Klauser, "Neues zum Monogramm ☧," *Antike und Christentum* 6 (1950): 325–27; E. Coche de la Ferté, "Palma et laurus," *Jahrbücher der Berliner Museen* 3 (1962): 134ff.

131. Margherita Guarducci, *I graffiti sotto la Confessione di S. Pietro in Vaticano*, 3 vols. (Vatican City, 1958), 1:411ff.; Cagiano de Azevedo, *Testimonianze*, 37f.

132. Erich Becker, *Malta sotteranea: Studien zur altchristlichen und jüdischen Sepulkralkunst*, Zur Kunstgeschichte des Auslandes 101 (Strassburg, 1913), 140f.

133. Jean Daniélou, *Les symbols chrétiens primitifs* (Paris, 1961), 9ff.

134. Cagiano de Azevedo, *Testimonianze*, 42–47, pl. XIV.
135. Ibid., 47–49, pl. XV; W. Seston, "Le monastère de Ain Tamba et les origines de l'architecture monastique dans l'Afrique du Nord," *Mélanges d'archéologie et d'histoire de l'École française de Rome* 51 (1934): 82ff.
136. Cagiano de Azevedo, *Testimonianze*, 49–50, pls. XVII, XVIII.
137. Nicolaus Heutger, "'Paulus auf Malta' im Lichte der maltesischen Topographie," *Biblische Zeitschrift*, N.F. 28 (1984): 86–88.
138. Wolfgang F. Volbach, *Elfenbeinarbeiten der Spätantike und des frühen Mittelalters*, Kataloge vor- und frühgeschichtlicher Altertümer 7, 3d ed. (Mainz, 1976), 78 (no. 108; pl. 58); Cagiano de Azevedo, *Testimonianze*, 69f.; Dassmann, *Frömmigkeit*, 30.
139. Stephan Waetzold, *Die Kopien des 17. Jahrhunderts nach Mosaiken und Wandmalereien in Rom*, Römische Forschungen der Bibliotheca Hertziana 18 (Vienna, 1964), 58f.; J. Withe, "Cavallini and the Frescoes in San Paolo," *Journal of the Warburg Institute* 19 (1956): 84ff.; Cagiano de Azevedo, *Testimonianze*, 70f. and pls. XXX, XXXI.
140. On the mosaics in the triclinium of Leo III, see Becker, 141, n. 2; for the ship in the Chapel of the Sacraments, see Joseph Wilpert, *Die Malereien der Katakomben Roms* (Freiburg, 1903), 419–21, pl. 39,2.
141. Henri Leclercq, "Paul (Saint)," *Dictionnaire d'archéologie chrétienne et de liturgie* 13 (1937): 2679.
142. Hippolyte Delehaye, "Loca sanctorum," *Analecta Bollandiana* 48 (1930): 23.
143. Dassmann, *Frömmigkeit*, 25–29.
144. Ibid., 47 (B. Kötting's comment).
145. Ibid., 48 (H. Lausberg's comment).
146. Ibid., 24; Heribert C. Scheeben, *Albertus Magnus*, 3d ed. (Cologne, 1980), 25,55,62.

Bibliography

Full bibliographical data for all works cited in the text are supplied in the notes. The following bibliography lists only a selection of those books and articles that touch most directly on the topic of the volume as a whole. It concentrates on, but is not limited to, secondary studies rather than editions of primary texts or collections of sources; and it includes some important older works (even if now outdated), as well as more recent scholarship.

BOOKS AND DISSERTATIONS

Les Actes apocryphes des apôtres: Christianisme et monde païen. Geneva, 1981.

Les Actes des Apôtres: Traditions, rédaction, théologie. Edited by Jacob Kremer. Bibliotheca ephemeridum theologicarum lovaniensum 48. Gembloux, 1979.

Aleith, Eva. *Das Paulusverständnis in der alten Kirche.* Berlin, 1937.

Altermath, François. *Du corps psychique au corps spirituel: Interprétation de 1 Cor. 15,35–49 par les auteurs chrétiens des quatre premiers siècles.* Beiträge zur Geschichte der biblischen Exegese 18. Tübingen, 1977.

Burchard, Christoph. *Der dreizehnte Zeuge: Traditions- und kompositionsgeschichtliche Untersuchungen zu Lukas' Darstellung der Frühzeit des Paulus.* Forschungen zur Religion und Literatur des Alten und Neuen Testaments 103. Göttingen, 1970.

Clabeaux, J. J. "The Pauline Corpus Which Marcion Used: The Text of the Letters of Paul in the Early Second Century." Ph.D. diss., Harvard University, 1983.

Coolidge, John S. *The Pauline Basis of the Concept of Scriptural Form in Irenaeus.* Center for Hermeneutical Studies in Hellenistic and Modern Culture, Berkeley, Calif., Protocol of the Eighth Colloquy, 4 November 1973. Berkeley, Calif., 1975.

Dassmann, Ernst. *Paulus in frühchristlicher Frömmigkeit und Kunst.* Opladen, 1982.

————. *Der Stachel im Fleisch: Paulus in der frühchristlichen Literatur bis Irenaeus.* Münster, 1979.

Elliger, Winfried. *Paulus in Griechenland.* Stuttgarter Bibel-Studien 92–93. Stuttgart, 1978.

Gorday, Peter. *Principles of Patristic Exegesis: Romans 9–11 in Origen, John Chrysostom, and Augustine.* Studies in the Bible and Early Christianity 4. New York, 1983.

Hoffman, R. Joseph. *Marcion: On the Restitution of Christianity: An Essay on the Development of Radical Paulinist Theology in the Second Century.* AAR Academy Series 46. Chico, Calif., 1984.

Landes, Paula Fredriksen. *Augustine on Romans.* Chico, Calif., 1982.

Lindemann, Andreas. *Paulus im ältesten Christentum: Das Bild des Apostels und die Rezeption der paulinischen Theologie in der frühchristlichen Literatur bis Marcion.* Beiträge zur historischen Theologie 58. Tübingen, 1979.

Luneau, August. *L'histoire du salut chez les Pères de l'Eglise: La doctrine des âges du monde.* Paris, 1964.

MacDonald, Dennis R. *The Legend and the Apostle: The Battle for Paul in Story and Canon.* Philadelphia, 1983.

Pagels, Elaine H. *The Gnostic Paul: Gnostic Exegesis of the Pauline Letters.* Philadelphia, 1975.

Paulus in den neutestamentlichen Spätschriften: Zur Paulusrezeption im Neuen Testament. Edited by Karl Kertelge. Quaestiones Disputatae 89. Freiburg, Basel, and Vienna, 1981.

Radl, Walter, *Paulus und Jesus im lukanischen Doppelwerk: Untersuchungen zu Parallelmotiven im Lukasevangelium und in der Apostelgeschichte.* Frankfurt, 1975.

Rathke, Heinrich. *Ignatius von Antiochien und die Paulusbriefe.* Texte und Untersuchungen 99. Berlin, 1967.

Rensberger, David K. "As the Apostle Teaches: The Development of the Use of Paul's Letters in Second-Century Christianity." Ph.D. diss., Yale University, 1981.

Schelkle, Karl H. *Paulus, Lehrer der Väter: Die altkirchliche Auslegung von Römer 1–11.* 2d ed. Düsseldorf, 1959.

Schendel, Eckhard. *Herrschaft und Unterwerfung Christi: 1 Korinther 15,24– 28 in Exegese und Theologie der Väter bis zum Ausgang des 4. Jahrhunderts.* Beiträge zur Geschichte der biblischen Exegese 12. Tübingen, 1971.

Schille, Gottfried. *Das älteste Paulus-Bild: Beobachtungen zur lukanischen und zur deuteropaulinischen Paulus-Darstellung.* Berlin, 1979.

Souter, Alexander. *The Earliest Latin Commentaries on the Epistles of St. Paul.* Oxford, 1927.

Staab, Karl. *Pauluskommentare aus der griechischen Kirche.* 1933. Reprint. Münster, 1984.

Werner, Johannes. *Der Paulinismus des Irenaeus.* Texte und Untersuchungen 6.2. Leipzig, 1889.

Wiles, Maurice. *The Divine Apostle: The Interpretation of St. Paul's Epistles in the Early Church.* Cambridge, 1967.

ARTICLES

Babcock, William S. "Augustine's Interpretation of Romans (A.D. 394–396)." *Augustinian Studies* 10 (1979): 55–74.

———. "Augustine and Tyconius: A Study in the Latin Appropriation of Paul." *Studia Patristica* 17 (1982): 1209–15.

Barth, Fritz. "Tertullians Auffassung des Apostels Paulus und seines Verhält-nisses zu den Uraposteln." *Jährbuch für Protestant Theologie* 8 (1882): 706–56.

Bentivegna, J. "Pauline Elements in the Anthropology of St. Irenaeus." *Studia Evangelica* 5 [= Texte und Untersuchungen 103] (1968): 229–33.

Benz, Ernst. "Das Paulus-Verständnis in der morgenländischen und abendlän-dischen Kirche." *Zeitschrift für Religions- und Geistesgeschichte* 3 (1951): 289–309.

Boyd, W. J. P. "Origen on Pharaoh's Hardened Heart: A Study of Justification and Election in St. Paul and Origen." *Studia Patristica* 7 [= Texte und Undersuchungen 92] (1966): 434–42.

Burchard, Christoph. "Paulus in der Apostelgeschichte." *Theologische Liter-aturzeitung* 100 (1975): 881–95.

Dassmann, Ernst. "Paulus in der 'Visio sancti Pauli.'" In *Jenseitsvorstellungen in Antike und Christentum: Gedenkschrift A. Stuiber*. Jahrbuch für Antike und Christentum Ergänzungsband 9. Münster, 1982.

———. "Zum Paulusverständnis in der östlichen Kirche." *Jahrbuch für Antike und Christentum* 29 (1986): 27–39.

de Boer, Martinus C. "Images of Paul in the Post-Apostolic Period." *Catholic Biblical Quarterly* 42 (1980): 359–80.

Fredriksen, Paula. "Beyond the Body/Soul Dichotomy: Augustine on Paul against the Manichees and Pelagians." *Recherches augustiniennes* 33 (1988): 87–114.

———. "Paul and Augustine: Conversion Narratives, Orthodox Traditions, and the Retrospective Self." *Journal of Theological Studies*, n.s. 37 (1986): 3–34.

Harl, Marguerite. "'From Glory to Glory': L'interprétation de II Cor. 3,18b par Grégoire de Nysse et la liturgie baptismale." In *Kyriakon: Festschrift Johan-nes Quasten*, edited by Patrick Granfield and Joseph A. Jungmann. 2 vols. Münster, 1970.

———. "La mort salutaire du Pharaon selon Origène." In *Studi in onore di Alberto Pincherle*. 2 vols. Rome, 1967.

Howe, E. Margaret. "Interpretations of Paul in the *Acts of Paul and Thecla*." In *Pauline Studies: Essays Presented to Professor F. F. Bruce*, edited by Donald A. Hagner and Murray J. Harris. Exeter, 1980.

Jervell, Jacob. "Paulus in der Apostelgeschichte und die Geschichte des Urchris-tentums." *New Testament Studies* 32 (1986): 378–92.

Lebeau, Paul. "L'interprétation origénienne de Rm 8.19–22." In *Kyriakon: Festschrift Johannes Quasten*, edited by Patrick Granfield and Joseph A. Jungmann. 2 vols. Münster, 1970.

Pagels, Elaine H. "The Valentinian Claim to Esoteric Exegesis of Romans as Basis for Anthropological Theory." *Vigiliae Christianae* 26 (1972): 241–58.

Roloff, Jürgen. "Die Paulus-Darstellung des Lukas: Ihre geschichtlichen Voraussetzungen und ihr theologisches Zeil." *Evangelische Theologie* 39 (1979):
510–31.

Schneemelcher, Wilhelm. "Die Apostelgeschichte des Lukas und die *Acta
Pauli.*" *Zeitschrift für die neutestamentliche Wissenschaft* 30 (1964): 236–50.

————. "Paulus in der griechischen Kirche des 2. Jahrhunderts." *Zeitschrift für
Kirchengeschichte* 75 (1964): 1–20.

Vanneste, Alfred. "Saint Paul et la doctrine augustinienne du péché originel." In
Studiorum Paulinorum Congressus Internationalis Catholicus. 2 vols. Analecta
Biblica 17–18. Rome, 1963.

Völker, Walther. "Paulus bei Origenes." *Theologische Studien und Kritiken* 102
(1930): 258–79.

Index of Biblical References

Index of Modern Authors

421